From Mission to Microchip

The publisher gratefully acknowledges the generous support of the Valerie Barth and Peter Booth Wiley Endowment Fund in History of the University of California Press Foundation.

From Mission to Microchip

A HISTORY OF THE CALIFORNIA
LABOR MOVEMENT

Fred B. Glass

UNIVERSITY OF CALIFORNIA PRESS

University of California Press, one of the most distinguished university presses in the United States, enriches lives around the world by advancing scholarship in the humanities, social sciences, and natural sciences. Its activities are supported by the UC Press Foundation and by philanthropic contributions from individuals and institutions. For more information, visit www.ucpress.edu.

University of California Press
Oakland, California

Library of Congress Cataloging-in-Publication Data

Names: Glass, Fred, author.
   Title: From mission to microchip : a history of the California labor movement / Fred B. Glass.
   Other titles: History of the California labor movement
   Description: Oakland, California : University of California Press, [2016] | Includes bibliographical references and index.
   Identifiers: LCCN 2015048154 (print) | LCCN 2015049982 (ebook)
   ISBN 9780520288409 (hardcover : alk. paper)
   ISBN 9780520288416 (pbk. : alk. paper)
   ISBN 9780520963344 (epub)
   Subjects: LCSH: Labor movement—California—History. | Labor—California—History. | Labor unions—California—History.
   Classification: LCC HD8083.C2 .G53 2016 (print) | LCC HD8083.C2 (ebook) | DDC
   331.8809794—dc23
   LC record available at *http://lccn.loc.gov/2015048154*

Library of Congress Cataloging-in-Publication Data

Manufactured in the United States of America

25   24   23   22   21   20   19   18   17   16
10   9   8   7   6   5   4   3   2   1

The paper used in this publication meets the minimum requirements of ANSI/NISO Z39.48–1992 (R 2002) (*Permanence of Paper*).

For Maureen, Ally, and Joe

The most important word in the language of the working class is "solidarity."

— HARRY BRIDGES

CONTENTS

ILLUSTRATIONS

PREFACE: WHY CALIFORNIA LABOR HISTORY?

Admittedly, a state labor history is an artificial construct. The boundaries of "California" were drawn in the mid-nineteenth century, based on a brief war with an outgunned Mexico that had only just gotten free of Spanish colonialism. Why should that vanished world exert any influence over the shape of a history about working people striving for their share of the American Dream, written in the twenty-first century? As we all know, international forces, even more than national ones, increasingly define that struggle. States might be considered irrelevant to the dominant economic engines of our time.

And yet no time seems more fitting than now to consider the particular contours of California labor history. In the wake of recent events, it's clear that for labor politics, states are where the action is. In states that have elected conservative legislatures, the first order of business has been to roll back worker rights and laws—often in place for decades—that enabled working people to call themselves "middle class" by virtue of their ability to organize collectively on their own behalf.

In Wisconsin, public employee unions no longer have the right to bargain the terms of their members' employment. And the Badger State, like former automobile worker union stronghold Michigan, now has a "right-to-work" law forbidding unions to collect dues from workers who opt out, yet whose jobs are protected through contracts negotiated by those unions.

In California, however, unions led a successful campaign in the 2012 elections to defeat a similar policy placed on the state ballot by antiunion forces. And despite the reputation of the Golden State as an antitax stronghold, the labor movement also steered to victory a measure to increase income taxes on the wealthiest Californians in order to fund schools and services starved for decades. The two campaigns reverberated with one another; class themes

FIGURE 1. Union members and community supporters in Watsonville helped stop an anti-union ballot measure, Proposition 32, and pass a tax on the wealthy, Proposition 30, in the 2012 statewide election. Francisco Rodriguez, photo.

emerged as the electorate voted to defend worker rights and demand that the wealthy pay a fairer share of taxes.

When we ask, What's the difference between California and these other states? we begin to see why now might be a good time for a state labor history. California has been famous for its "exceptionalism" since the Gold Rush: fine weather, the vast riches in its extractive industries, its literal edginess at the far western end of the pioneer trail on the Pacific Rim, and the recurrent eruptions of various gold rushes that seem to suggest Horatio Alger perpetually makes his home here. But what seems exceptional often turns out to be a variation on tendencies shared with the rest of the country.

In 1978, it seemed exceptional when the state's voters overwhelmingly passed Proposition 13, which rolled back property tax rates and set a two-thirds supermajority bar for legislative passage of any tax. The action reversed decades of the New Deal consensus that the role of government is to provide services for the common good, and replaced it with an experiment in low taxes, small government, and the joint demonization of public employees (providers of services) and people of color in poverty (recipients of services).

But within two years, the elevation of native son Ronald Reagan to the presidency showed that California was just the wedge state for a national program tilting the playing field away from "the most good for the most

FIGURE 2. California's unions have embraced immigrant workers on a scale and with tactics largely unseen elsewhere. David Bacon, photo.

people" to big business and the rich. California may be ahead of the curve, but probably only a bit farther down the same track.

So it may be with the state's labor movement. An historian only attempts to predict the future on the basis of the past with caution. But here is a safe bet. The demographic trend by which immigrant workers have fueled California's population increases will continue, in California and increasingly in other states. The high proportion of immigrants who come to this land to work ensures that a sizeable number will bring along familiarity with, and often sympathies for, the goals of organized labor. In some cases, that will include personal histories of union involvement.

Recent working-class immigrants, once they've become citizens, have tended to vote in lower numbers than people who have been here longer. But one major difference between California's unions and those in other states has been the embrace of immigrant workers on a scale, and with tactics, unseen elsewhere. Labor's voter education and mobilization programs aimed at infrequent voters have come on the heels of organizing outreach to concentrations of immigrant workers in service and manufacturing jobs.

Unless older white workers begin reproducing at a more rapid rate— an unlikely development—younger workers of color, including a high proportion of immigrants, are the future face of the workforce and the electorate. Because the labor movement has understood this fact and designed its efforts around it, California's unionization rate remains at 16 percent while the national average is 11 percent.

More than any other state, California incessantly recomposes its working class with waves of immigration. True in 1850, it remains true today. Employers who wish to defeat labor know that expanding and exploiting potential divisions in the working class always provide their best opportunity for success; and a diverse, heterogeneous working class has historically made such an outcome not just possible but the usual run of events. On the other side of the coin, conscious efforts by labor to overcome working-class divisions and to demonstrate the common interests of all workers to one another can supply—and often has—the necessary antidote, preserving or even expanding worker rights and share of the economic pie.

California labor history has plenty of both types of stories. It is my hope that learning about the defeats will give the reader lessons to mull over, and the victories a renewed understanding of why "the union makes us strong."

ACKNOWLEDGMENTS

As with any project that takes twenty-five years to complete, many people helped me. The ones I remember are noted below. My apologies to the ones I have forgotten.

I owe deep gratitude to the California Federation of Teachers for its generous support in the earlier stages of this project, and for employing me with a job that has excellent vacation benefits, enabling me to finish the book. The CFT Labor in the Schools committee has been a continuous source of inspiration in this work over the years, only slightly more concentrated in that way than my day-to-day work with the members, officers and staff of the CFT.

I thank the University of California Institute for Labor and Employment for a grant that allowed the book to begin to take shape. Thank you to June McMahon and Kent Wong for assistance in applying for the grant.

Members of the *Golden Lands, Working Hands* Scholars Committee read the manuscript at various points and provided invaluable feedback. These were David Brody, Dan Cornford, Juan Gomez-Quinones, Yuji Ichioka, Sherry Katz, Glenna Matthews, Shirley Ann Moore, Mary Tyler, and Charles Wollenberg.

Friends and colleagues who read the manuscript and discussed it with me include Jeremy Brecher, Norm Diamond, Sue Englander, Kelly Mayhew, and Gene Vrana. Joe Berry read over early articles that became the seeds of the book. Devra Weber and Harvey Schwartz helpfully reviewed areas in which they are expert.

People who were involved in events I wrote about and read the parts they lived through and participated in include Gloria Busman, Bill Callahan, Freddie Chavez, Joan Goddard, Linda Gregory, Dolores Huerta, Ken Jacobs,

Shaw San Liu, Marty Morgenstern, David Novogrodsky, Peter Olney, Tom Rankin, Susan Sachen, and Margaret Shelleda.

My student assistants Carey Dall, Kim Woo, and Greg Gruzinski helped me with research so long ago they probably don't even remember it, but I do.

Year after year my students in LBCS 88, California Labor History at City College of San Francisco, read versions of the book as it emerged and gave me real life focus groups to improve it.

I am grateful to the archivists, librarians and photo curators who assisted me at the Labor Archives and Research Center at San Francisco State University; the Anne Rand Research Library, International Longshore and Warehouse Union; UC Berkeley Bancroft Library; San Francisco History Center, San Francisco Public Library; USC Regional History Collection; the African American Museum and Library in Oakland; the University of Michigan Library (Special Collections Library); Walter P. Reuther Library at Wayne State University; the Huntington Library, San Marino, California; and the UCLA Department of Special Collections. Special shout outs to Marcia Eymann, Catherine Powell, Gene Vrana, and Robin Walker. I was also ably served by Patricia Akre, Peter Blodgett, Lynn Bonfield, Erin Chase, Meghan Courtney, Susan Goldstein, Julie Herrada, Sean Heyliger, Michael Lange, Crystal Miles, Christina Moretta, Octavio Olvera, Susan Sherwood, and Dace Taube.

David Bacon, Cathy Cade, Jaclyn Higgs, Dennis Kelly, Francisco Rodriguez and Jos Sances generously provided images they made. Lincoln Cushing, Eric Mann and Kerry Newkirk took the time to find me photos. Michelle Katz and Richard Steven Street gave perfect advice on photo rights, and Jono Shaffer on how to secure one essential image.

Claire Cunliffe rescued the bibliography from my failure to put the periods and commas in the right places.

I am thankful for the expert professional assistance offered by the University of California Press personnel at every step of the publishing process—Bradley Depew, Kate Hoffman, Niels Hooper—and their eagle-eyed copyeditor Kathleen MacDougall and indexer Margie Towery.

My wife, Maureen Katz, gave me the space to write, heard about all the adventures, put up with the ridiculous time frame, and served as my day-to-day sounding board. The book would not have been possible without her love and support, and the forbearance of my children, Ally and Joe, whose generation's task it is to put the book's lessons to the test.

PART I

———————

Before the Beginning

Where in California Is Its Labor History?

IN AN AUDITORIUM in Disney's California Adventure Park, a film titled *Golden Dreams* screened a dozen times each day in the early 2000s. Hollywood star Whoopi Goldberg played Queen Calafia, a character lifted from a five-hundred-year-old Spanish romance. In that story, Calafia ruled over Amazons on an island west of the Indies named "California." This is the origin of the Golden State's name.

Calafia is our host through reenactments of well-known moments in California history. She shows us the first contact between Spanish *conquistadores* and the native population; the Gold Rush; building the railroads; the heyday of Hollywood; spread of suburbs and the "good life" of the 1950s; and the psychedelic era of the late 1960s, with hippies dancing in San Francisco's Golden Gate Park.

In addition to these standard snapshots in the state's family album, we also view images added in recent years, including the mistreatment of Asian immigrants by the white majority in the nineteenth and early twentieth centuries and the migration of African Americans from the South to work in shipyards during World War II. The film makes an earnest effort to showcase the many ethnic strands of California history.

And yet something important is missing from *Golden Dreams.* Chinese laborers hang over cliffs in baskets in the Sierra Nevada to blast a passage through the rock for the Central Pacific Railroad. But we don't see railroad workers striking for pay equal to that of white workers, as thousands did in the spring of 1868. Black shipyard workers suffer discrimination. But we don't catch them demonstrating to gain full membership in the segregated union that controlled hiring, as occurred later.

What the film lacks is a sense of collective struggle by working people on their own behalf, without which most workers would have made little progress toward their goal—the California variation of the American Dream.

True, we catch a glimpse of an actor playing Cesar Chavez calling Mexican American farm laborers out of the fields. Yet, when the workers respond to Chavez's entreaty, as they did so many times in the 1960s and 1970s, *Golden Dreams* fails to reveal that he is asking them to join a union, the United Farm Workers, the only farmworkers union that ever lasted more than a few years, which was Chavez's singular historical achievement.

It isn't as if the filmmakers didn't have any labor history in California to draw on. The state is home to more than two thousand union locals, ranging in size from a handful of workers to tens of thousands. At the peak of unionization in the 1950s, more than 40 percent of the nonfarm workforce belonged to unions. To a great degree, it was the successful struggles of unions, organized through the volunteer activism of their members in the mid-twentieth century, that lifted the working-class majority up into the middle class of home ownership and disposable income, in California as in the rest of the nation. Today, when the rate of union membership has fallen to its lowest point in nearly a century, over two million Californians still carry union cards.

But California labor history doesn't begin and end with union membership. Forming and maintaining unions is one part of a broader story, repeated countless times—in the coastal seaports, the Central Valley farms, the southern oilfields, and the Sierra foothills, in financial high rises and bungalow classrooms—of workers' journeys from isolation and powerlessness to community, strength, and hope. Their toolbox contains unions, to be sure, but also lawsuits, legislation, election campaigns, community murals, songs, demonstrations, and a mountain of dedication by ordinary people to shared ideas of fairness and social justice.

If Disney's filmmakers had considered California history from the point of view of working people, perhaps its narrator would have been Anna Smith, the widow of a disabled Civil War veteran and a single mother, who migrated to the state in 1875. She spoke at demonstrations called by the Workingmen's Party of California in the late 1870s, and led several hundred workers—who had elected her their "general"—on a march intending to join the protest by Coxey's Army in Washington, D.C. against the horrendous economic depression of the early 1890s.

With the benefit of Smith's perspective, maybe the film would have presented events that not only had an impact on California workers' lives but also involved workers organizing themselves to make history. We might have seen a reenactment of the 1934 San Francisco General Strike, where a struggle by dockworkers and sailors against terrible wages and unfair and oppressive hiring practices escalated due to violent employer resistance. Hundreds of unarmed workers were injured in clashes with police and hired thugs using, boasted one manager of the strikebreakers, the latest antiworker weapons. Two workers were killed. In response, after a dramatic silent funeral procession on the city's main boulevard, more than one hundred thousand workers, acting in solidarity, joined a four-day walkout from their jobs.

When the dust settled, the maritime workers achieved union recognition, a fair contract, and a hiring hall that shared the available work equally. But the effects of these events reached beyond the city and the state. The San Francisco General Strike contributed to sentiments in the U.S. Congress that led to passage of the National Labor Relations Act a year later, which set up the legal machinery for modern labor-management relations. In its wake, hundreds of thousands joined California unions, and millions more did so across the country. For many people, especially immigrants, the unions they joined in the 1930s provided their first access to participation in democratic institutions, economic security, and home ownership.

After World War II, California changed in important ways. So did the ways workers approached solving their problems. In place of direct workplace action, workers more often concentrated on political and legislative activities. We might easily imagine Anna Smith's view of the statewide election of 1958, which pitted a coalition of labor federations and civil rights groups against the gubernatorial ambition of a wealthy newspaper owner from Oakland, William Knowland, who bankrolled an antiunion "right-to-work" initiative on the same ballot.

The candidate favored by labor, Edmund "Pat" Brown, promised, if elected, to sign a bill outlawing employment discrimination based on race. (At the time it was legal for bosses to hire, fire, or promote someone based on skin color.) According to Alex Alexander, a Los Angeles laborer who worked on Brown's election campaign, once enacted, "the Fair Employment Practices Act made an enormous difference in the daily lives of people of color."

Golden Dreams might have looked for inspiration in its own backyard. High-profile struggles to unionize by Hollywood studio film workers before and after World War II—including Disney cartoonists—led to hearings in 1947 by the House Un-American Activities Committee. At these public events, created for maximum publicity effect by foes of unions and worker

We lined the waterfront with determined, marching pickets.

The mayor of San Francisco called the militia out against the men who were asking for a

Against us the employers poured hundreds of thousands of dollars into tear gas, bullets, lies.

chance to earn a decent wage, for recognition of their unions.

We had to stand up to beatings, threats and death.

In San Francisco, two of our men were shot in the back. In Seattle, Portland, San Pedro, our men faced the same bitter struggle.

FIGURE 3. Artist Giacomo Patri's depiction of the 1934 West Coast maritime strike, from a 1945 union pamphlet for new members. Labor Archives and Research Center, San Francisco State University [Marine Cooks and Stewards].

rights such as J. Parnell Thomas, the first shots were fired on the domestic front of the Cold War. Focusing on movie stars, screenwriters, and directors but extending their reach to technical and craft workers as well, anticommunist politicians used the hearings to divide workers, destroy progressive unions, and intimidate anyone who questioned their methods or authority. Hundreds of people (many of them union members) who refused to cooperate, or named by others as Communists, were placed on a blacklist, preventing them from working in the industry, launching what became known as "McCarthyism."

Instead of psychedelia, Anna Smith's perspective on the 1960s might have shown antiwar students becoming public sector union activists, bringing their compensation up to private sector standards. More recent depictions could have shown Central American and Southeast Asian immigrants organizing unions and worker centers to fight wage theft and enforce labor laws.

The import of these events is indisputable. Where, then, do we find this labor history of the Golden State? Not in *Golden Dreams*. Its racial sensitivity was intended, in all fairness, not to explain the past but to roll out the welcome mat for the theme park's diverse millions of visitors. This wasn't history for participants in a democracy, but a guide for paying customers.

A better question might be, Why are these significant events, and the accomplishments of people like Anna Smith, missing from other films, from television programs, from textbooks, and from the awareness and memory of most people in California?

In exploring such questions in the following pages, the reader will enter into a largely submerged history. The lives and activities of working people have been neglected in the shadows cast by "great men"—politicians, military leaders, the very wealthy—whose actions in the glare of media attention seem to bestow on them a sense of inevitability and destiny.

Over the past few decades, new avenues of thought have been opened up by historians interested in other kinds of history: stories of women, of immigrants from non-European nations, of people of color. These studies have broadened our understanding of historical experience, but also fragmented what had once been a more unified view of our past. Critics of the new histories believe that in the transition to history with many voices and many experiences we are losing something crucial to a democratic society: a common knowledge of our past, a shared heritage we all value and use as a point of reference in our discussions and debates today.

These critics have a point. But it makes little sense to try to turn back the clock to a type of history that can no longer satisfy everyone in our increasingly diverse society. *From Mission to Microchip,* like other labor histories, has a different perspective on how to achieve the important goal of a shared understanding of history. It proposes that the majority of the population has always been and will continue to be working people. Most women, most immigrants, most people of color, and most white people are workers, whatever else they might be. This means, once we begin to look at things from this point of view, that most history is *labor history.*

2

On a Mission

HOW WORK DESTROYED NATIVE CALIFORNIA

A MISSION CULTURE

If you have spent much time in California, eventually you notice the tug of the mission period on the state's culture. For one thing, the missions themselves still attract tourists in the summer and busloads of fourth graders throughout the rest of the year. The visitors come to examine the reconstructed churches and outbuildings, walk through the cemeteries, and tour the modest museum exhibits. You can purchase mission souvenirs—"Collect plaster models of all twenty-one missions for $50!" advises a typical display—along with books and religious articles in the gift shop.

Beyond their cultural impact, the physical design of missions continues to exert an impressive architectural influence. A substantial number of public buildings built before 1950, especially in southern California, reflect the Spanish Revival or Mediterranean style. To this day a popular model of tract home continues to sprout row after row of little missions across the landscape.

Partly because of this visibility, the mission era also occupies a fuzzy spot at the back of public consciousness, in a borderland between historical knowledge and cultural dreams. Most Californians are somewhat aware that before the United States took in California as the thirty-first state, it belonged to Mexico and before that to the Spanish empire. They understand that the mission era involves Indians, colonization, the Catholic Church, and fine horsemanship by people speaking Spanish—even if the precise relationships among these elements aren't completely clear.

Earlier generations knew this picture through many movie remakes of *Zorro,* also a popular television series in the 1950s. But the real credit for forging the link between Californians and fond memories of something that never exactly existed belongs to a writer who intended no such consequence.

New England author Helen Hunt Jackson knew something about the situation of California's Native Americans, having served as a special agent of the federal government investigating their conditions. Her 1883 "Report on the Condition and Needs of the Mission Indians of California" eventually helped sway Congress to pass the Act for the Relief of Mission Indians in the State of California, which set aside reservation lands for a few thousand Indians; this didn't happen, however, until after Jackson's death.

To expose the wrongs committed against the California Indians to a wider public, the crusading Jackson wrote her novel *Ramona* (1884), hoping it would become popular enough to generate pressure on Congress to act. Her story of doomed lovers—a beautiful adopted daughter of a *ranchero* (ranch owner) and Alessandro, the quintessential noble savage—crushed by the American takeover of Indian lands, indeed sold well, captured the public imagination, and drew attention to the Indian cause. The book led, among other consequences, to the beginning of the restoration of the missions, most of which by the 1880s had crumbled into disrepair.

Despite Jackson's fervor, *Ramona*'s principal effect was to firmly establish the nostalgic but inaccurate image of the mission era as a golden age for California and the Indians, before the terrible fall from grace that occurred after the American conquest. That's why today, scores of printings later, you can find *Ramona* for sale in every mission gift store.

One thing you won't find highlighted in any of the mission museums, two centuries after the mission heyday, is a simple comparison: in 1769, when the first mission was established in Alta California, there were about 300,000 California Indians. By the time the missions were declared by the Mexican government to be "secularized" (separated from their state-sponsored religious function) in 1833, there remained less than half of that number. Along the coast, the Indian population had fallen from over 70,000 to less than 20,000. What had happened to half of the California Indians in sixty-five years—the span of one lifetime?

To answer this question we need to consider the differences between the ways that California Indians lived before and after the arrival of the Spanish in their lands, and especially differences in the ways that they worked.

More than likely, the first humans settling in what became California did so for reasons similar to what motivated the rest of us later on: a great climate, bountiful natural resources, and the promise of a better life than the one they were leaving behind. Most likely the first people arrived from Asia. Traveling by a land bridge between what is now Siberia and Alaska, or by water, they arrived in North America toward the end of the last Ice Age, some fifteen to twenty thousand years ago, gradually making their way southward along the western coast between six and ten thousand BCE.

The early Native Americans of California understood their economic relationship with nature as a harmonious give and take. Due to the good fortune of geography, California Indians spent an average of only ten or fifteen hours a week hunting, fishing, gathering, and producing what they needed to eat and wear. California's superb natural resources—a readily accessible high-protein diet of fresh fish, acorns, small game, and a cornucopia of edible plants, insects, and roots—made a subsistence economy easy. Starvation was virtually unknown. Unlike other Native American groups in the rest of North America, the original Californians had no need for agriculture, and only a few tribes in southern California tilled the fields.

With no written language, their oral tradition was rich, passing down through hundreds of generations their knowledge of nature and the spiritual traditions of their ancestors. The Indians were attuned to the rhythm of the seasons, as they needed to be in order to know when to harvest nuts, berries, and fruits, or where and when to meet the salmon runs or migratory herds of elk.

That spiritual philosophy was clear at the time of the Spanish conquest. As one old woman from the Wintun tribe said to an ethnographer in 1930,

> When we Indians kill meat we eat it all up. When we dig roots we make little holes. When we build houses we make little holes. When we burn grass for grasshoppers we don't ruin things. We shake down acorns and pine nuts. We don't chop down trees. We only use dead wood.

Hard work was not unknown to them. When the season demanded it—as with salmon runs, acorn harvest, or the yearly moment of contact with animal migration—they worked hard. But then they rested and played. And why not? *The purpose of work was to provide for life.*

The population grew during the passage of generations and spread out. With about a third of a million natives, the area of California was one of the most densely populated regions of the pre-Columbian world—even though that amount of people would represent less than 1 percent of the population in California today.

More than fifty Native American tribes—speaking hundreds of languages and dialects—led lives adapted to what the land provided in their areas. The Chumash, living around present-day Santa Barbara, were expert fishermen as were the Miwok on San Francisco Bay.

Many tribes, like the Yokuts in the San Joaquin Valley and Miwoks in the northern Sierras, relied on acorns as a staple food. They would gather the acorns in the fall from the various big oak tree species. A large tree could yield hundreds of pounds each year. Mixing rituals thanking the Great Spirit with several distinct work processes (gathering, drying, basket-making, grinding the nuts into meal, leaching out the bitter tannins, cooking) the Indians transformed the inedible acorns into cereal and cakes.

All the tribes practiced basket making. Baskets served as backpacks, drinking and cooking tools, water storage containers, and carriers of natural and handmade goods across the lengthy and intricate trade routes between tribal areas. But each tribe used different roots, stems, and grasses for their materials, and decorated them in unique ways.

The Ohlone who occupied the Santa Clara Valley, in addition to these forms of hunting, gathering, and handicraft production, regularly burnt the grasslands to increase the yield of acorns and seeds. Most tribes occupied regions that supplied them with two or more staple foods, for variety but also in case one failed. In short, the California native peoples were efficient managers of their environment.

The pre-Columbian California Indians had no conception of linear history, so far as we know; nor, given their way of life, did they need one. They viewed time as cyclical. The concept of work by a clock was unknown to them. Building a canoe, according to one old Chumash man, did not take place on a fixed schedule:

> With their tools the Indians were united in spirit. They had plenty of time to take in their canoe workmanship. The old-time people had good eyes, and they would just look at a thing and see if it was right. No one hurried them up—it was not like the Whites. The Indians wanted to build good canoes and they did not care how long it would take.

All of these time-honed practices would change once the Spanish came. They introduced new ways of working into the Native American communities. Under the mission system, the Spanish reorganized the Indians from tribes whose lives included work, into a *workforce*. This new way of working quickly disrupted and eventually destroyed the traditional subsistence economies and cultures that had flourished for thousands of years.

ON A MISSION

At dawn the Indians rose to the sound of bells. Mission bells called them to pray. When it was time to eat, bells let them know. Bells insisted on the hours of work. To sleep at night, there were bells. And when the Indians died, the ringing of bells followed them to their unmarked graves.

The Spanish missionaries, arriving in what they called "Alta California" in the late eighteenth century, brought conceptions of time with them that differed sharply from that of the land's first inhabitants. Their goal, in setting up twenty-one missions near to the coast from San Diego to Santa Rosa, a day's horse ride apart, was to secure the farthest flung outposts of their empire against a perceived threat of takeover from rival European powers. For the Franciscan missionaries, the Native Americans, like nature itself, existed to serve the goals of God and Empire. The Spanish originally envisioned pagan Indians becoming Christians within ten years. They would enroll the Indians in the church, teach them in the missions the civilizing virtue of work in various occupations, and then release them into nearby *pueblos* (villages).

At that point, the Indians would become *gente de razón* (people of reason) worthy of participation in the affairs of Spanish colonial society. It was assumed that the Native Americans—viewed as simple and childlike creatures—would embrace their place in the Spanish empire.

Understandably, many Indians were not quite so eager to participate in the Spanish plan as its principal architects, such as Padre Junipero Serra, imagined. While some were recruited through theatrical church ceremonies conducted in the villages by the Franciscans, the converts, in the early years of the missions, were often forcibly captured by Spanish soldiers. Once inside the mission, the Native Americans were not allowed to leave.

Typically, the Spanish did not consider this to be the same as imprisonment, since it was a temporary arrangement, and for the good of the Indians.

A California history textbook from 1962, like many of its era uncritically accepting the Spanish viewpoint, told its readers, "The Franciscans were humane men whose attitude toward their Indian charges was that of a father to his children. Any punishment of the Indians was for the discipline of their souls, because the padres felt that they could not always reason with these simple savages." But as a visiting French fur trapper observed, "The greater part of the Indians were brought from their native mountains against their own inclinations, and by compulsion, and then baptized; which act was as little voluntary on their part, as the former had been. After these preliminaries, they had been put to work, as converted Indians."

Nearly all the work in the missions was performed by the Indians. Failing to attract sufficient numbers of Spanish colonists to the primitive conditions of Alta California, the padres soon turned to the natives to build the missions and carry out the work needed to maintain them.

The first workers were Baja California Indians, who had learned agricultural and construction skills in the missions and pueblos south of the new territories. Without these pioneering but nameless to history Baja field hands, the padres might have failed to establish the missions.

Pablo Tac, a rare surviving Mission Indian voice, recorded how the padre of Mission San Luis Rey ordered Indians "to carry stone from the sea . . . for the foundations, to make bricks, roof tiles, to cut beams, reeds and what was necessary" to raise the church.

Once established, the missions became the hub of the economic life of the Spanish colony. At the center of the hub was Native Californian labor. The padres brought in Spanish and Mexican craftsmen to train the Indians in various crafts. Just how many trades is suggested by Scotsman Hugo Reid, who married a Gabrieleno Indian and recorded his wife's catalog of work in the mission.

There were baqueros, soap-makers, tanners, shoemakers, carpenters, blacksmiths, bakers, cooks, general servants, pages, fishermen, agriculturalists, horticulturalists, brick and tile makers, musicians, singers, tallow-melters, vignerons, carters, cart-makers, shepherds, poultry keepers, pigeon tenders, weavers, spinners, saddle makers, store and key keepers, deer hunters, deer and sheep skin dress makers, people of all work, and in fact everything but coopers, who were foreign; all the balance, masons, plasterers, &c., were natives.

In recalling one activity at a mission—sweeping—Fernando Librado, a Chumash Indian who worked as a cook at Rancho Purisma, conjured up a composite portrait of the many other types of work that the sweeping was connected with.

> Before the missions were abandoned they were places of life and activity. At Mission San Buenaventura, for example, there were the sweepers. It was the obligation for old men to bring brooms every Saturday. Some of these brooms were for the nuns, some for the department where they had twelve metates [grinding slabs for making flour] going all the time, some for the kitchen, the church, the padres' rooms, the wine cellar, and for the loom room. The loom room required four brooms alone.

From these and similar accounts emerge a picture of people who made crucial contributions to a number of early California industries without being able to enjoy a reasonable share of what they produced. Food, shelter, religious and vocational instruction, and clothing (and not even much of that) was what the Indians received in exchange for their work—not wages. The mission economy was precapitalist, at least so far as the Native Californians were concerned.

Getting the Indians to adjust to working in these ways required strict regimentation and harsh discipline. In contrast to their earlier lives outside the mission, the "neophyte" (the term for Native Americans as they were being trained) lived in an atmosphere of repression and intolerance, and the work they performed was forced labor.

Unlike some slaves in the southern United States at the same time, Native Americans did not work twelve- or fourteen-hour days in the missions: at thirty to forty hours per week, they were not literally worked to death. Nor were they owned by the padres. But the regulation of the day by the padres into a rigid schedule announced by Church bells and reinforced by punishments for breaking the rules, ran completely counter to the traditions of the Native Americans. For Chumash who did not care how long it took to build a good boat, so long as it was good when it was done, it made little sense to live or work this way.

Consequently punishments for ignoring routine or rebelling were frequent, and often severe. According to Julio Cesar, a Luiseño Indian who years later recalled his life as a neophyte,

> When I was a boy the treatment given to the Indians at the mission was not good at all. They did not pay us anything, but merely gave us food and a breechclout and blanket, the last renewed every year, besides flogging for any fault, however slight. We were at the mercy of the administrator, who ordered us to be flogged whenever and however he took notion.

FIGURE 4. Native Californians tilling the fields outside the mission at Carmel. Jos Sances, screen print ceramic tile from scratchboard drawing.

Indian men and women in the mission, if they weren't married, were kept in segregated housing. Some observers noted that the Indians were forced to live more like monks and nuns than like a Catholic peasantry of Europe; others commented how foolish it was to treat the native population so badly if the desired goal was to convert them into useful members of society. A Russian otter hunter held prisoner by the Spanish in one of the southern California missions recounted the gruesome torture and murder of runaway Indians forced to return:

> They were all bound with rawhide ropes and some were bleeding from wounds and some children were tied to their mothers. Some of the runaway men were tied on sticks and beaten with straps. One chief was taken out to the open field and a young calf that had just died was skinned and the chief

was sewed into the skin while it was yet warm. He was kept tied to a stake all day, but he died soon and they kept his corpse tied up.

No wonder the neophytes came up with various forms of resistance, especially a refusal to work as enthusiastically as the padres wished. Many simply left the missions and didn't return unless forced to. Theft of goods and livestock was frequent. Occasionally Indians assassinated the Franciscan padres. The most dramatic type of resistance was armed revolt, which broke out from time to time almost from the first days of the missions and ranged from individual attacks on soldiers or padres to battles involving hundreds of Indians. (One chronicler maintained that the missions' familiar red tile roofs originated with an early rebellion at Mission Santa Ynez. Thereafter the Franciscans decided to replace the buildings' thatched roofs with red baked tiles so that the Indians could no longer burn them down with flaming arrows.)

The missionaries were disappointed in their failure to motivate the Indians to work full-heartedly for God and Spain. Ignorant of the complexities of the Native Californians' lives before the appearance of the Spanish, Fermin de Lasuen, the Franciscan leader in Alta California after Junipero Serra's death complained, "Here then, we have the greatest problem of the missionary: how to transform a savage race such as these into a society that is human, Christian, civil and industrious. This can be accomplished only by denaturalizing them."

CREATION OF A SURPLUS

Despite these problems for the Spanish, Native American labor founded many of California's industries. The Indians generated surplus agricultural products and the textile, leather, wood, and metal goods with which the missions supplied the adjacent *presidios* (military stockades) and traded with nearby pueblos (towns) and foreign ships in the growing global trade networks for otherwise unavailable items. But while the mission storerooms held grains, vegetables, dairy products, and fruit and wine, especially in the early days of the missions the neophytes were fed a monotonous diet based on oatmeal or cornmeal mush called *atole*. While not universal, and varying from mission to mission, hunger—and even starvation—was often cited by runaways as one main reason for escaping. Another was the frequent beatings and lashings.

Malnutrition, coupled with punishments for infractions of rules they only barely understood, weakened the Native Americans' resistance to disease. In their traditional villages, the nomadic Indians would simply burn down their always-temporary homes and move nearby to establish new ones to deal with flea infestations or epidemics. In the missions, the Indian men and women, forced to live in permanent buildings, suffered from crowding and unsanitary conditions without recourse, which in turn facilitated the spread of European diseases such as measles, syphilis, and tuberculosis, against which the Native Americans had no natural immunities.

These factors—forced labor, diet, living conditions, disease—contributed to a very high death rate and equally low birth rate. Over half the Indian children born inside the missions died before they turned five. In other words, mission life was the equivalent of a death sentence for the California Native American population, which, by 1834, had been reduced to less than half of its size at the founding of the first mission in 1769. Lamented Padre Jose Viader of Mission Santa Clara in 1830, "There are many deaths and few births. Sickness is always with us, and I fear it is the end of the Indian race."

Work itself was not the immediate cause of the horrible population decline of the Native Americans. It would, however, be accurate to blame the coerced labor *system* of the missions, since the Indians were brought to the missions primarily to work.

During the thousands of years before the Spanish came, the work of the Indians simply provided for living. From the Spanish point of view, it was the other way around: the Indians lived to work for them. The precipitous loss of half the Native Californians within a single lifetime followed their transformation from free subsistence hunter-gatherers into a class of coerced laborers, forced to create a surplus for their Spanish masters.

THE MEXICAN PERIOD

Alongside their missions and presidios the Spanish colonists set up pueblos in Monterey, San Jose, and Los Angeles, following a model of colonialism that had served the mother country well for two hundred and fifty years in South America. The religious institution put into place cultural support for a local economy that could extract a surplus for the empire from the native population. The military stockade defended the mission from the common instances of violent refusal by the natives to participate in their own "betterment."

The pueblo was meant to be the future in an expanding society of settlers who worked the land and merchants who traded the goods. In Alta California, it was also supposed to be a mechanism to absorb the labor of the newly Christianized Indians after their spiritual and vocational education in the missions had been completed. There was a tension, from the beginning, between the Franciscans who needed "their" Indians in the missions to accept food, lodging, and religion in exchange for work, and the rancheros, who offered the Indians goods and sometimes wages for their labor.

The rancheros won this struggle. Secularization of the missions helped to transform Indian work decisively toward wage labor, although the process took decades, based on loss of their traditional lands and lack of rights under the Spanish, Mexican, and especially American governments. Once Mexico achieved independence from the Spanish crown, the process of granting tracts of land to soldiers and other colonists as a reward for their services accelerated. There were just twenty existing secular land grants in 1823. By the mid-1840s the Mexican governors had distributed nearly 800, including some to Europeans and Americans. These were large holdings, averaging ten thousand acres. John Sutter was given fifty thousand acres near what was to become Sacramento. General Mariano Vallejo, after whom the northern California town is named, received almost a hundred thousand acres near present-day Petaluma. Formerly, of course, these were Indian lands.

With all that land, the settlers—also called "Californios" —would set aside part of their holdings for cultivation. The rancheros had to grow such daily necessities as beans, corn, squash, and melons. Occasionally they could prevail on the Franciscans to give them seeds and cuttings to begin vineyards and gardens with pear, apple, orange, olive, and plum trees. In most instances the Franciscans preferred to keep these exclusively for their own use and trade. But with the major portion of their ranch land the Californios could do but one thing on such a large scale: raise herds of cattle for the hide and tallow trade based in New England.

Richard Henry Dana's *Two Years Before the Mast,* his narrative of voyaging on a small trading ship from Boston to California, was written during the peak years of rancho cattle raising. The brig he sailed on brought goods from Boston to exchange for hides and tallow (rendered fat), with which his ship returned to supply the leather industries, especially shoemaking, near his home.

When the missions were secularized in 1833, fifteen thousand Mission Indians were confronted by three options. They could stay where they were. The Mexican government had decreed that the Indians should be given half the mission lands in the form of thirty-three-acre parcels, and the padres were told to tally up the mission's land, cattle, produce, and handicraft goods to prepare for sale to the settlers and division among the Indians. As the power of the Franciscans dwindled, the settlers ended up with much of the lands surrounding the missions, including that intended for the Indians, often purchased for practically nothing. In Mission Santa Clara, just seven of the former thousand neophytes received an allotment of land.

A few thousand Indians stayed in or near the missions, despite the broken promise. Some had been born and raised there, didn't speak a tribal language, and didn't know the native traditions. Under the circumstances, it seemed best to continue to live with what they knew, serving the padres.

The rest could travel past the settlements to the interior of Alta California, where they might try to live as they had before the Spanish came; or go to work on the ranchos and in the small but growing pueblos. The nearby ancestral homes of the Indians were gone or going, owned by Spanish, Mexican, European, or American rancheros. Here, hundreds of thousands of cattle and other livestock had trampled what had once been the diversely fertile lands of native territories. Much of the formerly abundant game had been chased farther inland. On the north coast, the Russians were in the process of killing off the otters, seals, and sea lions. By 1842, with no more fur-bearing sea mammals to kill, they would leave, selling their land and buildings to John Sutter.

The remaining ten thousand Mission Indians chose to make the journey to live with inland tribes. Although they mostly spoke other languages and had different traditions, it felt better than giving up their cultural identity entirely.

Before the Mexican-American War (1846–1848) brought Alta California into the United States (along with Texas and the Southwest), a mere few thousand non-Indians lived in the territory with the declining but still much more numerous Indian population. If there was work to be done, there was little doubt as to who would do it.

The growing ranchos of the Californios acted as a magnet for the former Mission Indians, as well as for a number of Native Californians drifting from their slowly disintegrating traditional cultures. At the missions the Indian men had been taught to work in the workshops, the orchards, and with cattle and horses, and they offered these skills to the rancheros. The Native California women had learned domestic skills, as the padres sought to replicate the European division of labor between the sexes.

In the pueblos and on the ranchos, California Indians became the predominant labor force, as they had been in the missions, alongside a smaller number of Mexicans. Far from an idyllic life for the Indian laborers, the agrarian economy of the Californios offered mostly hard labor. For every skilled *vaquero* (cowboy) position, there were ten menial and mostly seasonal jobs on the rancho. The slaughter of cattle, separating the carcasses from their hides and fat, and then preparing these for trade, were tedious and filthy processes by hand. The racist epithet "greaser" was originally applied to the Mexican and California Indian workers who scraped the hides before stretching and drying them. The Indians rendered the tallow and hauled the hides from the pueblos and ranchos to the sea, where the American ships waited to load them.

They also knew how to cultivate the crops. According to a white employee of John Sutter at his New Helvetia ranch, the wheat harvest was conducted by Indian labor with the crudest of tools.

> Imagine three [or] four hundred wild Indians in a grain field, armed, some with sickles, some with butcher knives, some with pieces of hoop iron roughly fashioned into shapes like sickles, but many having only their hands in which to gather up by small handfuls the dry and brittle grain; and as their hands became sore, they resorted to dry willow sticks, which were split to sever the straw.

Pay varied from subsistence to less. In some cases the Indian workers received small amounts of money. In most ranches the compensation for work was room, board, and clothing—no different than in the missions. Once outside the missions, Indians became acquainted with white man's alcohol, accepting it, in many instances, as their wages.

The Indians' relationships with the rancheros ran the gamut from free but poorly compensated labor to slavery. A traveler observed that on Sutter's ranch, he kept

> 600 or 800 Indians in a complete state of Slavery and I had the mortification of seeing them dine I may give a short description 10 or 15 troughs 3 or 4 feet long ware brought out of the cook room and seated in the Broiling sun all the laborers grate and small ran to the troughs like so many pigs and feed themselves with their hands as long as the troughs contain even a moisture.

In the south, the laboring Indian population of the Los Angeles pueblo grew following secularization. Close to two hundred farms and ranchos needed their labor by the late 1830s. While not as brutal as on Sutter's farm, their lives were circumscribed by hard work, seasonal employment, lack of legal rights, and above all, landlessness, all within living memory of a time when things had been very different.

Unpleasant histories, like painful events in an individual's memory, are often pushed beneath the surface of consciousness. The ways that Californians remembered and reinvented "Mission Days" had to do with the commercial needs of tourism and real estate interests. These businesses found in the myth of a golden era before statehood— consisting of beautiful señoritas, handsome overseers of cattle ranches, and peaceful, contented Indians—an ideal image for attracting people and business to the state. Examining the harsh realities of coerced labor, disease, and death for the first Californians, by contrast, attracted no one except the occasional reformer. Histories of conflict are remembered chiefly through the accounts of the victors. This is all the more true when the vanquished had no written culture, and when their numbers were reduced so greatly that few were left to tell their side of the tale.

PART II

Early Days

3

———

Striking Gold

FROM THE GOLD RUSH emerged not only gold. Sifting through its events, we find the glimmering origins of California's industrial economy, its transportation systems, its premier urban center, and the first signs of organized labor—workers learning to represent themselves and their interests collectively to the rest of society.

Prior to the Gold Rush there was no labor movement, for there was no working class, no capitalist class, and no relationship binding them one to another, in a manner central to the state's economy. There was, in fact, no state, and comparatively little economy. The land was at the farthest reaches of the American frontier. In such a place before modern social classes had taken root, an ambitious individual could make rapid improvements in his life.

James Marshall was a carpenter and millwright in the employ of John Sutter, overseeing construction of a sawmill on the south fork of the American River, a day's ride by horse from present-day Sacramento, in January 1848. Marshall, like most of the few thousand United States citizens in California, was an immigrant. He had come to California from Missouri to seek his destiny on the frontier. He served in the U.S. Army during the Mexican-American War (1846–1848) that relieved Mexico of Alta California and the American Southwest. Afterward he went to work for Sutter.

As Marshall's work crew was nearing completion of the sawmill, he inspected a newly dug millrace (a channel of water to flush away waste) and caught sight of shining yellow flecks at its bottom. Highly agitated, he rode to Sutter's residence, where his boss, after some rudimentary research, confirmed the finding: gold.

Sutter owned fifty thousand acres of Mexican land grant, on which he built his "Sutter's fort" and ranch, New Helvetia. He employed dozens of

Mormons to run a number of mills and workshops. He did particularly well in his large grain fields by paying hundreds of Indians almost nothing to work on the harvest.

The discovery of gold by Marshall caused his crew of workers to desert the nearly finished sawmill. Soon the rest of New Helvetia's industries fell silent, as Sutter's former workers—despite his efforts to persuade them to stay with double wages—quickly turned themselves into gold miners.

Teamsters delivering goods to nearby Coloma spread the word. Initially none of the six hundred inhabitants of San Francisco believed the story, due to previously discredited rumors of gold elsewhere. Once merchant Sam Brannan appeared in town waving a fistful of gold, however, the Gold Rush was on. Within four months the *Californian* newspaper, based in San Francisco, complained it had to shut down, because

> The whole country, from San Francisco to Los Angeles, and from the sea shore to the base of the Sierra Nevada, resounds with the sordid cry of "gold, GOLD, *GOLD!*" while the field is left half planted, the house half built, and everything neglected but the manufacture of shovels and pickaxes.

By mid-summer, four thousand new miners were standing in icy waters and mud while the sun baked their heads, swirling pans and rocking various sifting devices to filter gold from sand. Perhaps half were California Indians, but only a handful of them were independent miners. Most of the Native Californians arrived as employees of rancheros. Sutter, giving in to the inevitable, brought one hundred of his Indian laborers to the gold fields, where they received the same subsistence payment for their work as they had on his ranch. When Sutter failed to amass a golden fortune, he blamed his problems on the continual drunkenness of his workforce.

Just four years later, a hundred thousand miners competed for the yellow mineral across a swath of land in the mother lode country three hundred miles long by fifty miles wide. In the earliest days of the Gold Rush most miners worked alone or in small groups. The cost of entry to the "placer" (a deposit of minerals) diggings was the price of getting there plus a pick, shovel, and pan. The veins of gold in the earth were so plentiful, and so close to the surface in some places, that such primitive means were sufficient. The first miners averaged twenty dollars a day at a time when a skilled craftsman in the eastern United States made three dollars, and miners in Pennsylvania made a dollar or less for their day's labor.

The discovery of enormous gold deposits seemed to fulfill an expectation or prophecy harking back to time immemorial. The popular sixteenth-century Spanish novel by Garcia Ordonez de Montalvo that invented the fictional island of California had proposed that the only metal there was gold. Fiction aside, everyone knew the Spanish had, over several centuries, wrested a slow but enormous fortune in gold from South American mines (and, of less interest to the Forty-niners, from the coerced labor of the Indians). This was different. As the *New York Herald* put it, "The El Dorado of the old Spaniards is discovered at last."

From that moment to the present day, everything about California has been "golden." The Golden State beckons to the rest of the world as the place to come make a fortune. Adventurers crossing the oceans were dubbed "Argonauts," after the Greeks who sailed with Jason in his quest for the golden fleece. This peculiarly golden sensibility permanently affected the ways people worked and how workers saw themselves in the state. The Gold Rush became the template for all California history. The cultural currency stamped in this foundry has insistently reappeared, in various forms, down through the years.

THE DIGGINGS

Many of the Forty-niners hailed from other countries. It could take six months to travel from the East Coast of the United States to California. There were but three options: a grueling overland journey by wagon train; a lengthy ocean voyage around Cape Horn; or a shorter boat ride to the Isthmus of Panama, making the dangerous land crossing through the jungle to the Pacific, and then another boat trip to San Francisco. Latin Americans could make the trip more quickly.

Most American Argonauts were not poor when they set out on their journey west. The price of travel made sure doctors, merchants, master craftsmen, and better-off farmers and lawyers were well represented among the Forty-niners. It took at least three hundred dollars, more than the average yearly income for most mid-nineteenth-century American workers and farmers. A disproportionately high percentage of the American workers in the early diggings were sailors because they didn't need to pay for passage. They simply abandoned ship in San Francisco, leaving vessels to rot in the harbor, their hulls full of unloaded goods.

A number of the immigrants from Baja California and points south, on the other hand, were miners already—skilled, but poor—from the metallic ore regions of Mexico, Chile, and Peru. Although many of the earliest Chinese travelers were merchants, nonetheless a high percentage of poor Chinese peasants came to *Gam Saan,* the Golden Mountain.

Once in the mother lode, though, everyone was a miner. Work was the great leveler, and difficult physical labor the daily reality for all in the gold camps. One historian described the work as "most nearly akin to ditch digging." A miner wrote home, "You can scarcely form any conception of what a dirty business this gold digging is and of the mode of life which a miner is compelled to lead. We all live more like brutes than humans."

Few of the Americans had ever mined before. Even if the gold lurked just beneath the surfaces of riverbeds and their banks, some methods proved more effective for extracting the yellow metal than others. The Argonauts rapidly viewed the more skilled foreign workers as dangerous competitors. As soon as California became the thirty-first state in 1850, the white miners persuaded the new state legislature—itself mostly miners—to pass a Foreign Miners' tax, which charged noncitizens twenty dollars per month. Since by this time the average daily "wage" had declined to ten dollars per day, the tax represented two full day's earnings, or, with a six-day week of work, a twelfth of the month's take. The tax persuaded thousands of non-natives to pack up for home.

Other forms of persuasion removed competitors from the field. White Oregonians, involved in wars of extermination with Native American tribes north of the California border, brought their prejudices with them, along with their guns. Half the miners in 1848, the Indians were nearly gone within a few years. The white miners, virtually all of whom were armed, sometimes settled differences of opinion among themselves with guns, as well. Most of the organized violence in the gold country, however, was aimed by whites at the miners of other races and from other countries.

The work itself presented hazards. In the early days, a slippery riverbank or crumbling cliff, misplaced shovel, or swing of the pick could lead to injury. You could be thrown from your horse or donkey. But the perils of simple placer mining, not much different from any outdoor work on the frontier, were trivial compared with the dangers of the industrial mining that followed.

By the mid-1850s, as surface gold sources became scarcer, workers incorporated more advanced forms of technology to get at the metal embedded deeper in the earth. Hydraulic mining used pressurized water to separate gold from dirt and rock. It required capital for pumps, hoses, and flumes (elevated water channels), and transformed gold mining from individuals prospecting with simple tools to groups of workers toiling for wages. Hydraulic mining had a tragic environmental impact, changing river courses and washing away entire mountain sides, to the horror of townspeople and farming communities downstream.

Ultimately the most effective form of industrial mining was quartz or hardrock mining, which also employed the most workers by the 1860s in both gold and silver mines. In areas like Grass Valley and Nevada County, corporations that owned quartz mines hired miners by the hundreds. Quartz methods involved mining, milling, and smelting: tunneling into the earth and bringing ore to the surface; grinding or crushing the ore with increasingly heavy and powerful stamping mills; and separating the gold from quartz and other minerals through amalgamation, using heat, acids, and mercury—also called "quicksilver"—to chemically remove the gold.

A rare photo taken underground in the late 1860s provides clues to conditions facing hardrock miners in the early industrial era, when the rush for gold and silver was over and its extraction had settled down into steady production through capital-intensive methods. Thick wooden beams hold up a fifteen-foot ceiling over the heads of six miners. Standing by their ore carts, the men are getting into or emerging from three hoist shafts, simple wood and metal elevators. They are dressed warmly (the photo was probably taken during winter) and wear felt hats, no doubt to keep dust and grit out of their eyes, since the hats would serve no other protective purpose. No hard hats, goggles, or gloves can be seen. Quartz mining in 1868 is clearly uncomfortable, dirty, and dangerous work.

Also not seen in this image is the ironically nicknamed "honey bucket," by means of which human waste was hauled from the mines, since there were no toilets or washrooms underground. Sanitation problems competed with chemical hazards from the amalgamation process and alcoholism as invisible occupational dangers in hardrock mining. What one can see, in the faces of these men, is their toughness. But no matter how tough he was, an individual couldn't win against a badly placed stick of dynamite or working too long with mercury without proper ventilation. Workers learned they needed each other for safety and for the power to change these conditions.

FIGURE 5. Hardrock miners and ore carts in the Savage Silver Mining Works, Washoe, Nevada, 1868. Timothy O'Sullivan, photo. Courtesy of the Bancroft Library, University of California, Berkeley.

In 1850, 75 percent of the working men in the state were miners. By 1860, while the population of California had tripled, miners had declined to just over a third of the workforce. The daily take for a miner had plunged to a few dollars a day, due to competition and depleted gold. By the early1870s, when more money was being made in Nevada silver mining than California gold, fewer than one-quarter of the miners owned their own homes. As John Hittel observed in the *New York Daily Tribune*, on December 27, 1858, "In 1851 labor pocketed all the profits of the mines; in 1858 capital pockets most of it."

Not many people had gotten rich, even in the early years, from mining gold. The few who became wealthy did so "mining the miners" by one means or another. The real money came from supplying the miners with food, clothing, and equipment; employing them; and in the profits from constructing a huge boomtown in San Francisco from scratch. The Gold Rush swept away the agrarian Spanish economy on a tide of American enterprise, throwing dispossessed Indians and disappointed miners into an emerging capitalist labor market. As gold mining settled into something resembling one industry among others, overseen by a state government, the possibilities of the early days for instant riches receded. The new society would, like the rest of the United States, have a large working class, a small capitalist class, and various middle classes in between.

4

"All That Is Solid Melts into Air"

GOLD RUSH SAN FRANCISCO

AN ALMOST HALLUCINOGENIC LANDSCAPE and social atmosphere reflected the tremendous changes taking place in San Francisco as, for a few years, California produced close to half the world's gold. During that time Yerba Buena grew from a tiny frontier outpost in 1848, with six hundred people clustered near a decaying mission, into San Francisco, the feverishly expanding capital of the western United States, containing 50,000 people by 1853 and 150,000 in 1870.

People from all over the world mingled in the streets. Their interactions were aided by extravagant use of the great social lubricant, alcohol. Gambling, drinking, and prostitution—and shortly, more respectable forms of entertainment—filled the time outside work.

At first most work in the new city supported the Gold Rush and supplied the miners. Early manufacturing focused on mining equipment. But mining technologies were also steadily redirected to the industries necessary to raise up a large city. Manufacturing expanded alongside occupations supporting the passage of freight and people by sea as well as construction of the streets, residential and commercial buildings, wharves, factories, and mills, all serving the daily needs of a rapidly growing population.

Starting from nearly nothing, a certain amount of creativity was called for. Derelict ships, abandoned by gold-seekers in the bay, were hauled ashore or transformed in the water to serve as stores, prisons, saloons, churches, brothels, warehouses, and hotels. The ones dragged onto land stood alongside tents and prefabricated wooden and iron dwellings, shipped from the East Coast and Europe.

Nothing was permanent. Buildings were built and fires burnt them down several times in the early 1850s. New ones rose again in their place, phoenix-like. The iron prefabs, briefly fashionable, lost their allure when many people died inside them during the great fires that swept the city in 1851. Believing the manufacturers' advertisements that the iron buildings were fireproof, their occupants were broiled alive after doors and windows fused shut from the heat. The firestorms then incinerated the structures themselves.

Not even the land could be taken for granted. It shook ferociously on occasion, but more often changed shape through human intervention. A hill one day became flat land the next. Where last month had been water, now was land, with people walking unconcernedly on top of transported sand and dirt streets, lined by freshly transplanted buildings, as if just yesterday there hadn't been ocean tides instead of crowds in that spot.

San Francisco seemed a living illustration of the famous phrase of Karl Marx and Friedrich Engels in their pamphlet, *The Communist Manifesto*, published the same year as James Marshall's discovery of gold on Sutter's land. In describing the impact of capital on traditional trades and commerce, and the cultures surrounding these economic activities, the Europeans wrote, "All that is solid melts into air." They might have been describing the new city, or perhaps the Forty-niners' dreams of gold.

In the early 1860s, Mark Twain captured in his column in the *Daily Call* newspaper the collective sense of disorientation at such uncertainty and rapid change.

> If you have got a house, keep your eye on it, these times, for there is no know-ing what moment it will go tramping around town. We meet these dissatis-fied shanties every day marching boldly through the public streets on stilts and rollers, or standing thoughtfully in front of gin shops, or halting in quiet alleys and peering round corners, with a human curiosity, out of one eye, or one window if you please, upon the dizzy whirl and roar of commerce in the thoroughfare beyond.

Twain's surreal image relies on eliminating workers from his description of house moving. Humorously portraying the fierce pace of urban transforma-tion, his literary device nonetheless reflects a common practice of writers and historians: rendering work and workers invisible. Other writers, with less self-consciousness about their craft, also missed the workers, and more, in their descriptions of the glittering surface of Gold Rush San Francisco.

A visitor from Paris, Albert Benard de Russailh, was charmed by the car-nival appearance around the waterfront. Taking in the commotion on Commercial Street, near the docks, he reported

Shops right out on the pavement, and counters before every door filled with all kinds of food-stuff, from across the bay, make it a regular market place. Wagons in unending lines drive along this street from morning till evening, taking provisions for the mines to steamers that run to Sacramento, Stockton, Marysville, Trinidad, and Humboldt, and bringing back the cargoes of ships that have just come from Europe. Nearly the entire length of the street is occupied by stores, all heaped high with goods. Everywhere flags are floating, and make the city look as if an eternal fair were going on.

Besides workers (store clerks behind the counters, teamsters driving the wagons, porters loading the goods), what the Parisian failed to see in his delight at the commercial bustle was the lack of infrastructure in this American Potemkin village. There were no fire hydrants in the early 1850s, because no water system beneath the streets yet existed. Drinking water was shipped to the peninsula from outside to augment insufficient wells. It wasn't until the fourth major fire that the city even scraped together volunteer fire companies.

There were no sewers and no waste disposal system beyond dumping chamber pots into the streets and larger amounts of garbage into the bay. Due to the vast quantities of alcohol consumed by the Forty-niners, empty bottles and broken glass were everywhere. The first brewery had risen in 1850, quickly followed by dozens more. Hundreds of stores sold liquor by 1853. Letters home from San Francisco in these years complained about the sickening smells, especially at low tide. Lack of effective trash removal fattened the rats and nurtured their fleas, which feasted on vermin and human alike.

Bathhouses, let alone bathtubs, toilets, and sinks, were fewer by far than needed to keep the population clean. Personal hygiene, public health, and delicate sensibilities suffered together. Hundreds, perhaps thousands, perished during the cholera epidemics of 1850–1852.

None of these obstacles prevented the Forty-niners from building the first metropolis on the West Coast. In fact, solving these very problems of city-building created employment and new industries flourished.

MARITIME LABOR

In 1853, a thousand vessels delivered more than three-quarters of a million tons of cargo onto the newly built wooden wharves that extended far into San Francisco Bay from the city's waterfront. As soon as the goods reached

California, hundreds of tons a day during peak season were rerouted north through the delta to Sacramento, to Marysville, and other departure points for the diggings. When vessels pulled in from their sea voyages, or the smaller boats from the inland delta trade routes north of the bay, dockworkers swarmed atop the wharves, loading and unloading, while boatmen rowed back and forth from ships with too deep a draft to dock.

Necessary for the survival and growth of the port city, sea trade proved extremely profitable for some merchants and shipowners and provided a living for sailors, dockworkers, shipwrights, and the boatmen who ferried passengers and freight to the deepwater ships. But to function properly, the maritime economy needed ships to come and go from the harbor.

The problem was that many of the boats pulling into San Francisco Bay were not leaving. The whaling industry, a major American enterprise in the Pacific, suffered through the Gold Rush. One captain reported in 1849 that "after the season on the Off Shore I went to San Francisco to recruit, intending to go into the Bays for elephant oil, but the excitement there in relation to the discovery of gold, made it impossible to prevent the crew from running away."

A sailor on another vessel revealed ships' officers, too, could succumb to the sudden desire to become a miner: "Our captain has concluded to go to the mines instead of proceeding on a whaling voyage. He intends to take all hands with him, and will give us two-thirds of the gold we procure."

Sailors, at the time, unlike workers on land, had no legal right to quit their jobs. To leave a ship was called desertion, and made the sailor subject to criminal prosecution. In fact, the first labor legislation passed in California, in 1847, imposed a sentence of six months at hard labor for abandoning ship. Such was the power of the gold lust, however, that sailors and captains alike ignored legal consequences as they fled to the Sierras. And why not? Alongside them on the trail to the diggings could also be found the very people charged with enforcing the law.

Under these circumstances, recruitment of the maritime workforce took a strange turn. In November 1853 the *Daily Alta* newspaper used the word "shanghaiing" for the first time to describe how unsuspecting men were kidnapped off the streets and out of waterfront boardinghouses to become sailors in the worker-starved maritime trades. At a time when housing supply raced, ineffectively, to keep up with demand, the boardinghouses gave the sailors a roof over their heads on land.

Beside room and board, the landlords offered the men large quantities of cheap alcohol, and advances on their wages when they ran out of cash. But these services were provided by their operators at a steep price. Usually the men would end up owing the owners money. Then the boardinghouse operators would literally sell the sailors—sometimes drugged and unconscious—to ship captains, who would pay off the owners.

This system, with innovations, was to grow along with San Francisco. It served the needs of shipowners, government officials, and businessmen alike to keep goods flowing through the city's economy. And the rights of maritime workers took a distant second place to that need.

Once on board things were even worse. Americans on the East Coast had already learned of the wretched conditions at sea prior to the Gold Rush, thanks to Richard Henry Dana's *Two Years Before the Mast*. Work aboard a brig or clipper ship in the mid- nineteenth-century offered an escape from boredom or troubles on land, but part of the adventure was encountering danger, which took two forms: natural and man-made.

Captain C. M. Scammon sketched a picture of what faced the crew of the brig *Boston* while on an 1857 whaling voyage to the lagoons of Baja California.

> On the third day the gale abated and the brig and her consort made their way to the head of the unexplored waters. Whales were found in great numbers, and the next day two large cows were captured. Next morning, however, a boat was staved by a dash of a whale's flukes. The boat was smashed in fragments and the crew was thrown in all directions. One man had a broken leg, another a fractured arm, and three more were more or less injured.

While hazards in the natural work environment were a constant, if unpredictable, force, sailors' conditions in the sail era also included bad food, low pay, long hours of work, and virtually unlimited power by officers over crew. In this era, as detailed by Dana, Herman Melville, and lesser-known authors, physical violence was commonly inflicted on the men for the slightest infractions of many rules. Until well into the twentieth century, maritime employment practices—on sea and on land—featured an unfortunate combination of poorly compensated wage labor and legally sanctioned coercion.

CONSTRUCTION TRADES

By the end of 1849, hundreds of ships lay abandoned in the waters of Yerba Buena cove in an area roughly one hundred city blocks square, which is precisely what the cove became once San Francisco's workingmen, within a few years, had dumped it full of landfill.

The city's business and financial center literally rose from the bay. Half of what became the downtown area was hauled from nearby hills and sand dunes covering much of the peninsula. Rearranging the landscape and seafront continued for many years. As the business district expanded, uneven terrain presented an obstacle to movement of materials, machinery, and merchandise between the foundries and factories south of Market Street and the commercial centers and residential areas of the city. In the earliest years hills were reduced by hand, with pick and shovel, wheelbarrow and mule. Soon, however, manual labor—mostly supplied by Irish immigrants—was augmented with new construction technologies, like blasting powder, which could level a small hill or fill in a ravine with one or two explosions.

There were also digging machines called "steam paddies" (after "Paddy," a derogatory slang term for the Irish) shipped from the East Coast. As soon as the steam paddies leveled the land, crews of laborers moved in, grading streets and laying out lots. Hundreds of men were employed moving houses and buildings over the evolving topography of the city. These skilled workers could raise or lower a multistory brick building, or transport a wood frame house across the city to its newly graded resting place.

Whatever earthmoving method was used, the results were similar: long lines of wagons heavily loaded with earth, rock, and sand, steered by teamsters, sweating and swearing at their mules and pedestrians, to the ever-receding shoreline. Another mechanical improvement—rails laid down on the streets—carried boxcars to move the hills to the bay.

Extending the wharves from the shoreline required many kinds of work. Pile drivers would take the enormous wooden poles, or "piles," prepared by carpenters in sawmills, and slam them into the bay bottom. Once these were set up in stable rows marching out into the water, hefty beams could be lashed to them. Then the men would cover the tops with sturdy planks, which in turn would support the traffic of ship's passengers and construction of warehouses and stores for maritime commerce. The most spectacular of these was built for the Pacific Mail Steamship Company for its deepwater vessels. The aptly named "Long Wharf" reached more than two-fifths of a mile into the bay.

Obstacles to the growing wooden pathways over the water had to be removed, too. Lodged in the mud beneath the tides or riding on top of them, the ships abandoned by gold-crazed crews slowly disappeared, but the process took years. Some were retrofitted by shipwrights, caulkers, and chandlers, and sent back to sea. Most were dismantled. As late as 1859 several "ship-breakers" still made their living by taking apart the derelict vessels. Working with hired crews of Chinese laborers drawn from a small fishing village on the southeastern shore of the city, they removed and sold the reusable parts, burning what remained.

All of this construction (and deconstruction) activity created magical results. In 1851 the Frenchman Albert Benard de Russailh could remark,

> The brilliance of the lights on Commercial Street and the life we saw every-where astonished me. I had expected something quite different. Like so many other emigrants, I had thought to find on my arrival here the beginnings of a town, a cluster of tents and rude shacks, where I should scarcely obtain shelter from bad weather. But I was greatly surprised to see, instead, large and fine streets, well laid-out, and wooden and brick houses, all in regular order.

Beside hundreds of wooden structures of various sizes, over six hundred brick and stone buildings filled the main section of the city, three miles square, lined with two hundred and fifty streets, dozens of which were "paved" with wooden planks, and, by 1855, a few with asphalt.

Most residential construction was for modest three- and four-room wooden houses, suitable for workers and their families. But larger and grander commercial and public buildings went up at a furious rate as well. All of this meant a great deal of work for carpenters, plumbers, masons, bricklay-ers, stonecutters, painters, plasterers, and general laborers, along with teamsters moving stone, bricks, lumber, and nails, piled high on horse-drawn wagons, to construction sites. So did rebuilding the city after its many fires.

Not only private capital funded construction. The U.S. government rec-ognized the enormous revenues to be gained from customs duties on imports. By 1853 San Francisco already ranked fourth among the nation's ports in trade tonnage. The federal government paid for building a large, elegant three-story structure to hold the customs house and post office at a cost of nearly a million dollars—the most expensive structure yet raised in the city.

Scarcity of skilled labor in the early years of the city enabled wages for construction workers to shoot erratically at moments to astronomical heights. Merchants and builders were forced to pay top dollar to men willing to give up the opportunity to try their fortunes with a pick and pan. Laborers at construction jobs could make ten to fifteen dollars a day for a while.

As wages declined in the gold fields (by 1853 miners were averaging five dollars per day), the price of labor in the city tended to fall as well. But the cost of living continuously overshadowed wages. When bread went for a few pennies a loaf elsewhere, in San Francisco it sold for a dollar. Construction materials, too, went for exorbitant rates: bricks, like eggs, could also cost a dollar apiece. This inspired the genesis of several brickyards south of Market Street, along with foundries, a stone quarry, and lumber mills.

One way around the high cost of construction labor was to import it. A banker paying to build an office building at the corner of Montgomery and California streets in 1851 purchased granite cut in China. But when the stone blocks appeared, they could not be assembled: the instructions had come in Chinese. The banker sent across the sea for Chinese stonemasons. Working from sunrise to sunset, each day they received a dollar, a half pound of rice, a quarter pound of fish, and an hour lunch break. Here began a California employment tradition: import foreign labor to undercut local labor costs.

METAL TRADES: BACKBONE OF INDUSTRY

Assisting the birth of San Francisco manufacturing in the first half of the 1850s were a dozen foundries, ironworks, and machine shops, gradually employing two hundred workers. The metal trades produced the ore-crushing stamping mills and other iron machinery and parts needed for the mines, and repaired and maintained steamships after their long voyages to the city. A measure of the skill and versatility of these craftsmen is that they managed to produce the first small locomotive in California by 1855 at the Vulcan Iron Works. Blacksmiths, iron molders, and boilermakers found employment in Happy Valley, which grew into the city's principal industrial area in the flatlands alongside the bay.

East Coast foundries and machine shops tended to specialize, catering to niche markets, thanks to the well-developed urban centers and transportation networks in which most of them were located. In California, flexible production and constant innovation predominated, due to geographic isolation and the enormous hunger of the new metropolis for manufactured metal products.

This industry grew to more than forty enterprises by the mid-1860s, its skilled workforce producing wire and cable, drills, agricultural equipment, and steam engines. The first standard-gauge locomotive built on the West Coast,

"The California," came out of the Union Iron Works in 1865. That firm alone, founded in 1849, employed 500 workers in eight crafts by the 1870s, and boasted that it produced 90 percent of the machinery used in Nevada's Comstock Lode silver mines. Another Happy Valley-based business, the California Wireworks Company, perfected the use of wire to pull ore from below the earth, in carts on rails, to the surface. The company reengineered the technology a few years later to launch San Francisco's cable car system in 1873.

At the heart of mid-nineteenth-century industrial technology were the enormous steam engines and boilers that propelled everything from pumps and compressors in the mines to the machines in factories and mills. While some new industrial enterprises purchased off-the-shelf machines from the East, more sent business to the foundries and metal shops south of Market Street. The first sugar refinery was built in San Francisco in 1856, using Union Iron Works–made engines; the first woolen mill in 1858 likewise purchased local machinery. As each new industrial sector established a foothold, it enlarged the local production of machinery and parts. Within its first decade the state's manufacturing output grew at a yearly rate of 500 percent, and ranked eighteenth in the country by 1860. By then more than a thousand workers toiled in the metal trades of San Francisco.

FIRST STIRRINGS OF THE LABOR MOVEMENT

In early San Francisco, workers faced serious problems every day. Their workplaces were dangerous. Maimed workers with missing body parts were common sights on the streets. As one observer noted,

> The path of the ironworker is literally strewn with danger, for as he walks along, the innocent-looking fragment, no longer glowing, may be a piece of hot iron of which the touch, if he stepped upon it, is enough to cripple him; one splash of the molten stream may blind him; if he were to stumble as he walks along the edge of that sandy platform where the iron is bubbling and rushing into the moulds he would never get up again.

Workers labored long hours, in some industries ten-hour days, in others twelve or more. A workweek typically lasted six and sometimes seven days. No laws protected worker health and safety, or made sure that children went to school instead of a factory or the streets. Little was understood about the relationship between diseases and occupations. Workers were often left homeless and destitute when fires swept through the city. Petty crime flourished. Law enforcement was unequal to its task. Employment in the construction trades was seasonal (as it remains today).

The onset of cold weather in the gold country during the 1850s drove miners down into San Francisco each year. In the winter of 1852, the *Alta California* newspaper reported that "there has never been so deplorable an exhibition of mendicancy in our streets as may be witnessed daily at this time . . . hundreds of destitute men and scores of women and children besieging the pockets of society in public and private, indoors and out."

At least when it rained for a week, workers knew what to blame for their enforced idleness. But business cycles sometimes exercised a greater impact on employment. In the 1850s four economic downturns idled workers for long periods. Isolated by thousands of miles and months of travel from the rest of the country, the San Francisco economy wobbled greatly from one year to the next, vulnerable to chance: if a ship arrived a month late, merchants could be ruined and workers thrown out of work.

In seeking remedies to these problems, most workers relied on individual solutions. Out of work, they scrambled from place to place, job to job. Injured, they patched themselves up as well as they could. If they had a bit of money saved, they could start up a business. If all else failed, they might return to where they came from. Many workers looked for help in bottles of locally made beverages.

But for some San Francisco workers, individual solutions weren't enough. Taking a broader view, groups of workers decided to improve matters through collective action.

In November 1849, San Francisco carpenters earned $12 a day (in New York carpenters made less than $2) but still couldn't keep up with enormously inflationary prices for food and rent in the rapidly growing city. On November 10, when their employer refused to raise their pay to $16, a group of these workers declared the first recorded strike in California history. A week on strike brought a compromise: a dollar a day raise, from $12 to $13, to be followed by another dollar increase after three weeks.

The following year, newspaper printers founded the first union local on the West Coast, the San Francisco Typographical Society. Printers set newspaper type by hand, transferring lead letters and numerals from trays onto the printing presses. The society asked newspaper owners to change printers' compensation from a daily wage to a piece rate. The newspaper owners agreed, for a couple years, to the new method of payment.

FIGURE 6. Newspaper printers, like these shown in Anton Refregier's New Deal murals in San Francisco's Rincon Annex Post Office lobby, formed the first union in California. Fred Glass, photo.

In August, wagon drivers in San Francisco established a political association and elected one of their members, James Grant, to a seat on the city council. In 1853, pressured by steadily growing numbers of workers' organizations, the California State legislature passed the first protective labor law, limiting legal hours of work to ten in a day.

Historian Lucille Eaves, writing more than a half century later, puzzled over these actions: "There are evidences of such early trade-union activity in San Francisco that one is tempted to believe that the craftsmen met each other on the way to California and agreed to unite." Alternative answers to Eaves's whimsical conspiracy theory are not hard to find. Scarcity of labor, a violent culture, and traditions of working-class organizing carried from elsewhere by the immigrant population help us to understand how collective worker activities occurred from the outset.

Even with the steady influx of newcomers, labor power was one of the scarcest commodities, especially considering the amount of work to be done. San Francisco workers could make high wages because *everything* cost a lot of money. The price charged by labor was dictated by the comparison in everyone's minds with the take of a gold miner in a day, and the willingness of workers to leave for the diggings and participate in what Forty-niner Dame Shirley described as "Nature's great lottery scheme."

San Francisco wasn't the only place in California where these actions were taking place. Strikes erupted in Sacramento, Marysville, and Stockton. Workers in the entire region perceived the strength of their position, and could focus their desire to share in the profits of a promising—if unpredictable—time with group action.

It was probably to the advantage of workers, on occasion, that the frontier society lacked effective legal structures. There was little centralized authority, and everyone was armed. Western labor relations took root within a broader violent culture. The lawlessness of San Francisco reached the point in 1856 that several thousand citizens organized themselves into pick-handle brigades to patrol the streets and clean up marauding gangs.

It would be odd, under these circumstances, if some workers were *not* using force to achieve their ends. The *Alta California* in August 1853 reported an attack by a group of strikers on other workers. It was moved to state that "This is not the first time that violence has been used and threatened by the strikers, and it is high time that something be done to preserve a little better order for the future."

The *Alta* might have been recalling events during the cold wet winter of 1849–1850. The newspaper's unsympathetic reporter wrote that

> thousands were returning sick and impoverished from the mines. . . . As this influx of labor caused a great diminution of wages, the prices of provisions remaining the same, discontent and indignation prevailed among the lower orders, and nightly meetings took place, attended by crowds of the rabble, ripe for pillage or riot, but luckily without a leader. . . . These nocturnal assemblies had in them something appalling, being composed of between three hundred and one thousand cut-throats, armed with bowie knives and

fire-arms, and often intoxicated. . . . Both master and men felt themselves subject to an inquisition and control making them fearful of entering into any contracts together.

In the days before modern collective bargaining laws, spontaneous acts of collective violence could seem a useful path of action to workers without recourse to other means of solving their problems.

California workers benefited more, in the long run, from political experiences imported by Forty-niners from the East Coast and other countries. The Irish—the largest group of Europeans—brought their traditions of anticolonial organizing to America. German artisans, though fewer in number, carried their experience of craft organizations and socialist politics in their flight from the failed European revolutions of 1848. English workers came with Chartist ideas of republicanism. Such streams of political thought—along with currents of homegrown American revolutionary traditions—fed the formation of unions and short-lived but influential workingmen's parties in the eastern states in the 1820s and 1830s.

The early workers' organizations supported free universal public education and extending suffrage to white working men (in the earliest days of the republic, nonproperty owners couldn't vote). The parties called for the abolition of prison labor and the end of imprisonment for debt. They were sympathetic to unions, whose members wanted dependable, secure employment with higher wages and shorter hours of work.

The unions helped journeymen workers develop the weapons they needed to improve their circumstances, including strikes, boycotts, and solidarity with workers in other crafts. The early workingmen's parties and unions had mostly disappeared by the 1840s, but not before many of their egalitarian ideas had been absorbed into planks of Andrew Jackson's Democratic Party platforms.

We might ask why printers built the first union in California. The answer is that members of this occupation were literate, had deep roots in guild traditions, and were already doing similar things around the country. The enthusiasm for public education in the early republic created a readership for newspapers, books, and printed materials of all kinds. The spread of literacy meant growing markets for the printed word and jobs for printers. But the industrial revolution, urban competition, and advances in printing technology put steady pressure on the craft of printing. Printing had been based on hand-run printing presses, and on guilds, in which masters taught apprentices and journeymen and all shared age-old cultural traditions and expectations.

By the time it got to California, printing was an occupation in transition. The small shop, typical of the early nineteenth century, featured a relaxed pace of work and close relations between a few journeymen and masters. The new arrangements were different: larger workplaces, with greater numbers of workers, steam-driven presses, and foremen overseeing work. It took more capital to start a business. Fewer journeymen could become masters. Guilds broke up; masters joined employers' groups, and journeymen formed unions. As early as 1817 the printers' society in New York declared that "the interests of journeymen are separate and in some respects opposite to those of employers."

In 1850, printers representing union locals from all over the country met in Philadelphia to plan a course of action. Two years later, in May 1852, they founded the first national labor organization, the National Typographical Union. The San Francisco Typographical Society reorganized itself in December 1854 as the Eureka Typographical Society, Number 21; it received the first local charter on the West Coast issued by a national union.

The first to act, printers were soon joined in organizing by San Francisco workers of many occupations, including unions of sailors, musicians, cigar makers, dockworkers, painters, and others. From practically the beginning of the Gold Rush, collective actions by workers contradicted the common image that popularly represents mid-nineteenth-century California: the lone miner, pan in hand, wresting a fortune in precious metal from the land through the sweat of his brow. He existed, briefly, but was never typical, and soon gone. James Marshall, the carpenter and millwright credited with discovering gold, died a penniless alcoholic.

In the 1850s the first workers' institutions began to take root in the conditions faced by California workers in their places of employment and elsewhere in the frontier society. However, due to the state's volatile new economy and the strongly held belief in individual initiative shared by mid-nineteenth-century workers, these early organizations were mostly ephemeral. Only the printers' and longshoremen's unions managed to last out the decade.

But workers had begun to choose collective weapons from a simple but effective arsenal to resolve conflicts with their bosses: taking direct action, forming organizations, mustering electoral efforts, and pressing legislators to pass protective laws.

5

Work, Leisure, and the Struggle for the Eight-Hour Day

WHEN HE WAS BEGINNING to research his major work, *A History of the Labor Movement in California,* early in the twentieth century, Ira Cross was startled to discover that current labor activists could not name the leaders on whose shoulders they stood. The pioneer organizers had been forgotten, just a few decades after their struggles to establish, preserve, and extend the rights of California workers.

An explanation for this social amnesia can be found in the attitude of one early leader, Frank Roney. Cross approached Roney in 1908, when the aging Irish immigrant was working in the Mare Island naval shipyards in Vallejo. Roney, an iron molder, was then sixty-seven. The work of pouring hot liquid metal into molds was hard enough for a younger man. But he couldn't retire because he had no money. He had served as president of union locals, as a vice president of his national union and the Workingmen's Party of California, and assisted in setting up unions in other crafts as well as founding and leading central labor organizations.

Modest to a fault, Roney didn't think his life and work was of much interest to anyone. It took a decade and a half for Cross to convince Roney to write his memoirs, and it only happened because of Cross's tireless insistence and steady help.

In the era before the eight-hour day, few workers had the time to record their experiences, even had they been interested in doing so. Roney kept a diary for just two years, in the mid-1870s, soon after arriving in San Francisco. One of the things he did was to note the hours he worked each day. From his journal we find that iron molders worked at least ten hours a day, six days a week; when *could* he write?

Keeping a journal that survived the passage of time made Roney almost unique. While a growing number of workers in the nineteenth century were literate, not many had the habit of writing. And if they could find the time to write, why write about work?

In their few hours of leisure during the week, or perhaps during periods of unemployment, San Francisco workers might choose to participate in various cheap amusements. A ride on a railroad train from San Francisco to San Jose provided mid-nineteenth-century thrill seekers with a diversion like no other, at once an expedient means of travel and a moment of awe at the wonders of modern technology. Even hauling a locomotive to its tracks could prove entertaining. When the first standard-gauge engine produced at the Union Iron Works, The California, was ready to roll, in August 1865, it weighed twenty-nine tons.

> Twenty strong drayhorses dragged her through the city streets some eight or ten blocks to the railroad. It was not an easy journey. Many times the heavy engine sank to the axles in the soft pavement and hydraulic jacks were called upon to lift her out and on her way. The delighted crowd, which included most of the small boys in town followed, shouting bits of unappreciated advice to the perspiring teamsters.

Or there was Woodward's Gardens, an amusement park that opened in 1866. The gardens sprawled over four acres in the Mission district, featuring the largest zoo on the West Coast, exotic plants, an art museum, a saltwater aquarium, a theater with shows and plays, and a small lake. Even Roney, suffering stretches of unemployment, could afford the twenty-five cents admission one Sunday in 1875.

But this was an unusual diversion for him. As with the working-class activists who preceded him, time that he didn't spend working—or looking for work—or sleeping, went to organizing. And despite Roney's reluctance to take credit, these efforts made some important differences in the lives of workers and their families, even if progress proved slow, uneven, and didn't always last.

ECONOMIC PROSPERITY

The 1860s were generally prosperous years in California. The population of the Golden State increased to more than half a million people. San Francisco's population grew to 150,000, and the number of jobs to 68,000, during the decade.

Over a thousand homes and stores were built in the city in 1864, the year that Mark Twain's house went "tramping around town." Horse-drawn street-car lines spun a web of transportation across the peninsula. Ferry service brought commuters to work over the bay from Oakland, and families could take the boats the other direction on Sundays to enjoy the East Bay's open spaces and recreational opportunities. Railroads began to connect the towns and cities scattered across the state.

California's isolation from the rest of the country contributed to the flourishing economy. It was cheaper and more profitable to produce many goods locally rather than import them by ship. In the first half of the decade the preoccupation of eastern manufacturers with the Civil War encouraged San Francisco businessmen and bankers to increase investments in mills, factories, and other commercial enterprises, some on a fairly large scale. San Francisco became the ninth largest manufacturing center in the country by 1870.

The development of industrial mining in the Sierras and in neighboring Nevada placed a great demand on San Francisco's machine shops and iron industry south of Market Street. As production for mining expanded their capacity, the metal industries supported the growth of other California businesses. There were ten lumber mills in the state in 1850. A decade later, nearly three hundred mills processed vast stretches of redwood and Douglas fir forests. As wheat farming gradually replaced cattle raising on the old Spanish and Mexican land grant tracts—now mostly owned by American farmers and speculators—more than a hundred capital-intensive mills ground grain into flour, employing an eighth of the steam engines produced in the state in 1870.

San Francisco's foundries were known for their flexibility and innovation. The same shop in the south-of-Market industrial zone could produce machinery and parts used in agriculture, sugar milling, railroads, and shipping, as well as in the mines. Frank Roney's diary entries while working at the Union Iron Works for one month note the casting jobs he worked on: flywheels, pipes, brakes, wheel hubs, a slide, a walking beam for a pumping engine, a spur wheel, cylinders (one of which weighed fourteen tons), hand iron, and various plungers. The great metal works built in Benicia by the Pacific Mail Steamship Company to repair its fleet's engines, employing hundreds of skilled craftsmen and laborers at its peak, closed in 1861, because Happy Valley forges and machine shops could take care of the company's needs more efficiently.

The Pioneer Woolen Mills at Black Point was one of many new textile and clothing-related businesses employing hundreds of workers by the mid-1860s, including women. Less than 10 percent of the white population of California in 1850, by 1870 white women were over one-third of the San Francisco population; most needed to work.

Although records of women's work were very poorly kept, we know that as women slowly settled in the city they worked in a restricted range of occupations. These included domestic services—keeping house, washing, cooking, sewing, and tending for children of the well-to-do—and commercial industries offering similar types of work in restaurants, laundries, hospitals, and clothing manufacturing.

Their traditional nurturing social role gave women access to another important workplace. The framers of the 1849 California constitution based their ideas about public education on the "common schools" concept that supported education in the eastern states through local taxes and sale or rental of public lands. Public school advocates argued that in a self-governing republic, the state must provide free education to all children so that when they grew up they could participate knowledgeably in public affairs. But it had taken many local battles across the country to turn these ideas into reality for the children of workers and farmers.

In California public schools proved difficult to maintain outside larger cities until the Gold Rush subsided, although by 1854 more than four thousand children were enrolled in forty-seven common schools for at least one-quarter of the year.

By 1860, San Francisco employed seventy-two teachers for six thousand registered students. Of these teachers, fifty-seven were women, working in seventeen schools, including two segregated schools for African American and Chinese children.

One early educator was Kate Kennedy. Kennedy emigrated from Ireland to New York with a brother and sister following the potato famine of the mid-1840s. She sewed clothes in the "sweating" system, in which subcontractors took work from master tailors, and paid women and children to bring materials home to work on. She and her sister saved enough money to fund their education as teachers and to bring the rest of their family across the ocean. Kennedy and five sisters moved to San Francisco in 1856 and joined

FIGURE 7. Early public education activist and Irish immigrant Kate Kennedy fought for equal pay for equal work. San Francisco History Center, San Francisco Public Library.

the teaching workforce. Kennedy also became a forceful advocate for equal rights for women and equal pay for female teachers.

By all accounts a remarkable teacher, Kennedy was promoted to principal of North Cosmopolitan Grammar School in 1867. She discovered that male principals were paid more than she was. Irish-American politicians helped her write and pass a state law guaranteeing "equal pay for equal work." However, to get around the law, school administrators simply kept elementary wages lower, where they congregated women; in secondary schools, pay scales were higher, and they only hired men.

Kennedy found herself, in public education, in a box just like the one that women confronted in the broader world of work: what economists call "discriminatory labor market segmentation," meaning some jobs for women and others for men.

Even so, she didn't do badly. Educated, white, and upwardly mobile (within limits) she owned her own home and some modest real estate holdings when she died. Her trajectory was the model shared by many San Francisco working people: work hard, improve yourself, rise in the world. And like Kate Kennedy, who joined and participated actively in a number of labor organizations, many saw collective action as necessary to their successes as individuals.

UNION REVIVAL

San Francisco unions—largely dormant in the late 1850s—revived together with the economy. Prosperous business conditions and rising prices encouraged workers to organize for their share. Workers in the maritime trades formed unions. So did building and construction tradesmen. The trend included cigar makers, hairdressers, teamsters, and hat finishers. In 1861 coopers (barrel makers) founded a Mechanics' League to fight against convict labor—prison inmates used by capitalists, with the permission of the state, for little or no wages. San Francisco printers welcomed new locals in Sacramento and Stockton, and another that existed briefly in tiny Los Angeles in 1860.

According to the *San Francisco Evening Bulletin,* in fall 1863, "Striking for higher wages is now the rage among the working people of San Francisco." A walkout by the Journeymen Painters Union resulted in the first closed shop agreements (in order to work for an employer, the worker must join the union first).

In 1863 a prolonged strike of tailors for higher pay led to the formation of the first central labor body in the state, the San Francisco Trades' Union. Fifteen unions from diverse trades joined to coordinate activities of common interest to their members. The outstanding leader of the San Francisco Trades' Union was Alexander Kenaday.

The son of Irish immigrants, Kenaday was born in Virginia in 1824. His parents moved to Saint Louis, where Kenaday learned the printing trade. Like Mark Twain, he worked on a Mississippi River steamboat for a time. He joined the U.S. Army during the Mexican War, earning sergeant's stripes. He had returned East at the end of the war when news reached him of the discovery of gold. Retracing his steps to California, he prospected without success until he decided a printer in San Francisco might make a better living than a miner. Working for various newspapers, he helped to organize the Typographical Society, and later served as its president.

Under the leadership of Kenaday, the Trades' Union facilitated "the giving of moral and material aid in times of distress" to its unions, generating support for workers during strikes. Doing what came naturally for a printer,

Kenaday published the first monthly labor newspaper on the West Coast, the *Journal of Trades and Workingmen*. It lasted just five issues.

The Trades' Union provided assistance in one of the major labor struggles of 1864. Seeking a minimum wage of four dollars for a ten-hour day, iron molders struck several employers. The molders, facing a loss of craft control over the work process in foundries as companies grew into corporations and industrialization added new technologies, had established a national union in 1860. The local molders followed the progress of the national organization, and knew their problems in San Francisco weren't unique. Soon they were joined on the picket lines by the Journeymen Boilermakers' Protective Union. The two unions' members stayed out of work for several months. They widely publicized their actions to the public, and promised a violent retaliation to anyone who attempted to take their jobs.

What set this strike apart from others were two things. The Happy Valley foundry employers formed an association—just the second on the West Coast—to combat their workers. They vowed that the first company to break ranks and give in "to the workmen's demands" would have to pay $1,000 to the association. The association also attempted to import strikebreakers from the East Coast, paying their way to San Francisco and promising better wages than they could make at home.

Learning of the employers' plan, the ironworkers and boilermakers, along with the Trades' Union, came up with an effective counterstrategy. They sent representatives to the Isthmus of Panama. There they met the strikebreakers and, informing them about the strike and the issues involved, convinced them to join the union. When the union representatives and their new recruits arrived back in San Francisco, the employers gave in. The iron molders and boilermakers went back to work with the new wage scale in place. However, over time, the employers found a way to undermine the victory: strike leaders were gradually fired, one by one.

STRUGGLE FOR THE EIGHT-HOUR DAY

The most important effort expended by Kenaday and the Trades' Union was in building a movement, beginning in 1865, for an eight-hour-day law for all California workers. Employers tended to view limits on work hours as interference with their right to employ workers as they chose. A growing number of workers felt otherwise, agreeing with Knights of Labor leader Uriah

Stephens, who described long workdays as "an artificial and man-made condition, not God's arrangement and order."

A state ten-hour law had passed in 1853, but was only loosely enforced. Most trades with active unions had achieved a ten-hour day by the mid-1860s, but within a six-day workweek. In dry goods stores (which sold nonperishable products), salespeople formed a Clerks' Association. It successfully waged a struggle for "early closing"—which at that time meant 8 P.M. In 1863 bakers struck successfully for a twelve-hour, six-day week. This may not sound like much of a victory—until we learn that previous to the strike they worked fourteen hours, seven days a week!

Thus, when Kenaday, through the Trades' Union, issued a call "which of itself should unite every class of laboring men ... the passage of a law constituting eight hours a legal day's work," his words resonated. After a series of meetings in December 1865, Kenaday was armed with a resolution and instructions to convince San Francisco's delegation to the state legislature to pass such a measure. At his own expense, he spent the next few months lobbying and organizing.

Many impatient workers didn't wait for a law. In December, the union of ship caulkers (workers who sealed ships watertight) struck and became the first granted the new hours. Other maritime unions quickly achieved the same goal in the early part of 1866, some by walking off the job, others through simpler negotiations with their employers.

In February, the state assembly passed a version of the eight-hour bill and sent it to the state senate. Kenaday presented a twenty-two-foot-long petition with 11,000 signatures supporting the eight-hour day to the senate. But after vocal opposition from the iron trades' employers association, the bill was narrowly defeated. Kenaday later sent the petition on to the California delegation to the U.S. Congress, when it was considering an eight-hour bill for federal workers. That law passed in June 1868.

The San Francisco Trades' Union lasted only a few years—it was dead by mid-1866—but the interest in coordinated action continued. In 1866 and 1867, union by union, and sometimes in groups, activists created "eight-hour leagues" and presented employers with demands for eight-hour work days, and with a date by which the employer had to comply. By June of 1867, the *Morning Call* newspaper acknowledged that "despite the existence of Eight-Hour Laws in other communities, the fact exists that the eight-hour system is more in vogue in this city than in any other part of the world, although there are no laws to enforce it."

A mass parade and demonstration in San Francisco bolstered the movement that same month. The marching order of the unions was determined by who had achieved their eight-hour day first. Reflecting the strength of the most well-organized workers, the procession was dominated by skilled tradesmen from the construction, ship-building, and metal industries. One newspaper observed that "there was nothing incendiary in the nature of their speeches; no threats were indulged in, nor any efforts made to intimidate those who disagreed with them, but they evidenced a determination to achieve success by proper and legitimate means."

Despite the show of strength, only a few thousand workers were employed under eight-hour contracts, out of 60,000 in the city. Employers formed a ten-hour league society in response to the workers' movement. Ship employers, starting with the Pacific Mail Steamship Company, fired employees who had been working eight hours and advertised back east for replacement workers. A compromise was reached when the fired workers were allowed to return at eight hours per day but with a slight cut in pay.

At the end of the year unions created the Mechanics State Council. (The term "mechanic" referred to skilled craft workers in any trade—not, as we mostly use it today, to mean someone who works on engines.) It was formed to promote the eight-hour movement throughout California. Within months General A. M. Winn, a retired carpenter and state militia officer, helped the state council to enroll twenty-three unions with a membership of eleven thousand workers. Fifty leagues affiliated with the council, including activists in Sacramento, Oakland, Vallejo, San Jose, and Los Angeles. Carpenter unions, perhaps because of their connection with Winn, were prominent in the movement.

Momentum grew until the San Francisco Board of Supervisors passed a law establishing the eight-hour day in all city and county employment. Finally in February 1868 an eight-hour-day law for all California workers was passed by the state assembly and state senate, and signed by the governor. A huge torchlight procession in San Francisco celebrated passage of the law, the second statewide eight-hour law in the country (after Illinois the previous year). Far from perfect—the law lacked effective enforcement mechanisms— it nonetheless marked a high-water point for the struggle for a shorter workday.

It meant that perhaps a few hours, wrested from the long workweek, might allow "the mechanic and citizen to pass his leisure under the control of mechanics."

Despite the sustained struggle for passage of an eight-hour-day law, and its achievement in a handful of trades where workers were well organized, its promise went unfulfilled in many industries due to the determined resistance of employers.

One spectacular instance of a strike for a shorter workday, and of its brutally efficient suppression by business owners, occurred beneath the surface of one of the most famous engineering feats in California history: carving a passage for the Central Pacific Railroad eastward across the Sierra Nevada.

Railroad building was the great industrial project of the American nineteenth century. It employed more people, expended more capital, pushed greater development of technology, and did more to unify the sprawling geography of the country than any other industry of its time. Its impact on local economic life and culture cannot be overstated. The massive machinery, its thunderous noise and commanding appearance, and its unparalleled speed, dominated every space, urban and rural, it entered. The railroad conquered the frontier, captured the imagination of the country and came to stand for the very idea of "progress" as a visual symbol and multifaceted reality.

It also made a great deal of money for a few men, who quickly became so rich that they changed the balance of power in the democratic republic. The railroad barons—a branch of the broader nineteenth-century ruling-class group dubbed the "robber barons"—used their enormous wealth to live lives of unbelievable luxury, and also to control state legislatures and, ultimately, the U.S. Congress. In California the picture was no different.

More than a century after the deaths of Leland Stanford, Charles Crocker, Collis Huntington, and Mark Hopkins, their continuing presence in the state remains impressive. Their names are still memorialized on cities, streets, banks, hotels, libraries, parks, beaches, schools, and universities. They had failed at gold mining, succeeded in retail businesses supplying miners, and converted their modest storekeeping fortunes into the seed money for the Central Pacific. Yet, how accurate is it to describe them, as standard histories do, as "the men who built the railroad" across the Sierras?

The actual work of building the railroad from Sacramento to Promontory Point, Utah, fell to more than ten thousand laborers and another couple of thousand skilled craftsmen and supervisors. We might expand the definition of that work to include the miners who dug the iron ore and the foundry workers and mill craftsmen who forged the rails and produced the spikes. It could reasonably encompass the lumber workers who felled the trees, and the carpenters and sawyers who fashioned the railroad ties from the timber; the teamsters who hauled these products to and from the docks of the West Coast, the longshoremen who wrestled the loads on and off of ships, and the sailors who transported the logs and ties in the coastwise trade. But certainly, the men who literally built the railroad were the ones employed by the Big Four—Crocker and his three business associates, Stanford, Huntington, and Hopkins—to grade the roads, pack the embankments, dig and blast the passages through Sierra rock, build the winter snow sheds, and lay down the ties and the rails and hammer them together.

CROCKER'S LABOR PROBLEM

At the outset, Crocker, delegated by the other three capitalists to oversee the work in the field, had a labor problem. Fewer than half the workers whose passage to the railhead he paid stuck around to receive their first paycheck from him. Most, like the crews and captains of ships during the first years of the Gold Rush, left immediately for the diggings, this time across the state border in Nevada, where the Comstock Lode silver rush was in full swing. These enterprising individuals were nearly all white.

With such turnover, the Central Pacific was making slow progress—just fifty miles in its first two years. The railroad's directors experienced great anxiety over the snail-like pace, because the United States government compensated them by the mile. They were all too aware that the Union Pacific, working its way westward with steady infusions of Irish immigrant laborers, was making tracks at a much faster rate across the flat prairies of the Midwest. When Central Pacific workers threatened to strike for higher wages, the Big Four considered their options. The local labor supply failed to keep up with their needs. Child labor, like twelve-year-old Robert Gifford from nearby Dutch Flats, could perform some tasks. He worked for three months leading a horse team and dump cart. But this was no solution for the heavy labor, which comprised most of the work.

Before the close of the Civil War the Central Pacific's owners proposed bringing thousands of Confederate prisoners, under military guard, to the tracks. When the war ended, they talked about importing Mexican peasants but discarded that idea in favor of another pushed by Crocker.

FIGURE 8. Chinese laborers at work on the Central Pacific Railroad Secret Town trestle in the Sierra Nevada. Carleton Watkins, photo. The Oakland Tribune Collection, the Oakland Museum of California, Gift of the Alameda Newspaper Group.

CHINESE WORKERS

Supposedly inspired by the efficient work of his own personal servant, Ah Ling, Crocker brought in fifty Chinese workers as an experiment. They proved industrious beyond his expectations. By the end of 1865 three thousand Chinese were employed by the Central Pacific; soon, close to ten thousand. Crocker described their behavior approvingly: "More prudent and economical, they are content with less wages." He actually paid them the same wages as white laborers—thirty dollars per month—but the white men received room and board, and the Chinese set up their own camps and fed themselves. While some white workers grumbled about working alongside Chinese, most gained from the company's decision, moving up to fill foremen, teamster, and blasting positions that paid more than the laborer jobs performed by the Chinese.

Crocker told his partners that there was "no danger of strikes among them." So happy was Crocker with his new workforce that he foolishly refused to try out the new steam-driven drill sent up the mountain by his partners to help bore the main shaft through the rock, the Summit Tunnel, nearly a mile long. He preferred to rely on the steadfast handiwork of his "pets," as he liked to call them, which took thirteen months, including two of the most severe winters on record. The Sierra passage was the last major railroad tunnel in the country to be cut by hand.

It came at a high cost. The company estimated it at $23 million, a fantastic sum in the 1860s. But the workers might have reckoned the price differently, had anyone asked. A local newspaper ran a story on Christmas Day 1866, detailing the deaths of a half-dozen laborers in a snow slide, one of many such incidents. The following winter, as reported two decades later by one of Crocker's chief foremen to Congress, "The snow slides carried away our camps, and we lost a good many men in those slides; many of them we did not find until the next season when the snow melted."

Even during the rest of the year, the engineering miracle of traversing the Sierras placed a tragic burden on the workforce that accomplished it. Blasting through the mountainsides with the unstable industrial explosives of the period, many lost their lives. Avalanches killed others. One particularly harrowing type of work involved lowering workers over the sides of sheer rock cliffs in woven baskets to drill slots, stuff the holes with dynamite, and light the fuse. Coworkers had to pull them to the top before they were blown up along with the granite. Not all made it back.

In June 1867, several thousand Chinese workers had had enough. They went on strike near Cisco, proclaiming "Eight hours a day good for white men, all the same good for Chinamen." They wanted forty dollars a month, up from thirty. The Central Pacific, perhaps unwilling to imagine its "pets" might think for themselves, told the newspapers that the strike must have been the result of agitation by Union Pacific representatives. The company wanted to maintain the public impression that it treated its workers well and that only external meddling might have induced the workers to take such drastic action. When the laborers refused a Central Pacific offer to raise their wages to thirty-five dollars, the company surrounded their camps with armed guards, choking off food supplies. After a week, the workers were forced to return to their jobs with no improvements in hours or pay. Nonetheless, an interesting event had occurred: the largest job action yet seen in California and by a group of workers believed to be strike-proof.

The successful resolution of the struggle for the eight-hour day in California, as elsewhere in the country, was not yet ready to happen in the 1860s and 1870s. For but a moment, historically speaking, working people could savor that possibility. A few extra minutes in a day to call one's own, away from the economic necessity of the job and the biological imperative of sleep, would have to wait for decades until it was inscribed in federal law. Until then, leisure remained mostly the playground of the rich and, to a lesser degree, the middle classes, with the working class on the outside looking in.

6

Sandlots and Silver Kings

THE WORKINGMEN'S PARTY OF CALIFORNIA

THE COMPLETION OF THE TRANSCONTINENTAL railroad in 1869 brought the Pacific Ocean within reach of travelers on the East Coast in a mere eight days. For those with the money, riding in the Pullman Palace car offered plush velvet seats, wooden scrollwork, ornate brass fixtures, pile carpets with lush floral designs, and superior springs beneath the forty-foot-long coaches to smooth the ride. A supreme example of the aesthetics of the Gilded Age, the Pullman car also provided rattle-free windows through which to view the spectacular vistas of the journey—and through which passengers, in this pre-environmentally educated age, discharged their firearms when they came across animals within range. The trains moved steadily at twenty-two miles per hour across the countryside.

For the less affluent, the regular passenger coaches featured more spartan accommodations. The cars were heated by a wood stove and served by a small toilet. There the frills ended. The cushionless wooden benches soon lost their charm, especially since the cars' undercarriages lacked adequate springs. Straw pillows and a board lain across the seats, rented to the passengers, created their "beds." The trains sometimes stopped, and sometimes didn't, at eateries (bribing the conductors could help), and unlike in the Pullmans, these cars had no food service. After a week of this, passengers were more than ready to disembark.

The two-tiered train service across the United States reflected a growing class divide during the Industrial Revolution. After the Civil War, the widespread development of industrial manufacturing fueled a steady movement off the land in rural America to the cities, and the conversion of small farmers, skilled craftsmen, and urban artisans into workers in large-scale industries, where, after brief training, they tended machines.

This wasn't entirely a one-way process. A small number of master crafts-men were able to accumulate capital and move up to join the elite of indus-trial capitalists growing fabulously wealthy from these changes. But many more artisans, farmers, and village dwellers mourned the loss of their tradi-tional ways of work and life.

Part of their unhappiness had to do with the demands of the industrial marketplace to standardize work processes and products. However, artisans also viewed the problem politically: as industrial capital accumulated in the hands of the few, it concentrated power there as well and eroded the demo-cratic promise of the American Revolution for working people.

Other changes complicated the political and economic picture further. Freed slaves entered into competition for wages in the workforce. New arriv-als from other shores—to the East Coast from southern European countries and into California from Ireland and China—also fed the reserve army of labor, presenting challenges to worker unity and to traditional notions of what it meant to be "American."

The transcontinental railroad arrived in California together with these developments. Its disruptive effects soon came to symbolize the shift of wealth and power taking place in the country, and unleashed a period of turmoil and transformation for the state's young working class and its labor movement.

THE END OF ECONOMIC ISOLATION

After Leland Stanford drove the golden spike into the dirt of Promontory, Utah, joining East and West, some Chinese workers were able to continue with the Central Pacific Railroad, building spurs off the main line, or laying tracks across other portions of the state. At the same time, however, the com-pany discharged thousands of laborers. Many moved into the central valleys, becoming part of an already growing army of Chinese migrant farm labor.

More former railroad workers went to San Francisco. There they joined thousands of workers flowing across the country westward. California's population jumped by nearly sixty thousand at the end of the 1860s. The increase had gotten underway even before completion of the railroad, thanks to heavy promotional efforts back east in working-class communities by California businessmen. Forming the Immigrant Aid Association, and the California Labor and Employment Exchange, the businessmen painted glowing pictures of plenty by the Pacific for their impoverished audiences.

They sent similar messages to immigrant workers' former European homes. The employers' goals were simple: to lower wages and undermine the eight-hour day by flooding the state with increased numbers of workers. With the help of unforeseen economic changes, they succeeded beyond their dreams.

Drought diminished the yield of California agriculture for several years. Together with the influx of Chinese railroad workers, this pushed white migrant farm laborers to the cities. The amount of cargo shipped by sea dropped steeply, throwing maritime workers into unemployment. The gold mines, beginning in the mid-1860s, went into permanent decline, causing the metal trades industries specializing in mining technologies to contract and aging miners to return to San Francisco.

Due to the railroad, California businesses were no longer isolated from the national economy. Manufactured goods flowed into the state. Businesses accustomed to geographic protection lost control of their local markets, which had extended beyond the Bay Area and California. The products of San Francisco—the regional economic powerhouse—cost more, due to higher labor costs and smaller markets. Once the railroad linked eastern manufacturers more directly with western territories, the Happy Valley metal industries, along with clothing manufacturers and others, found themselves at a competitive disadvantage.

For example, the workers and management of the Union Iron Works were proud of the craftsmanship and high quality of the seventeen locomotives the firm had produced between 1865 and 1873. When The California rolled down to Palo Alto on its first run, "she had cost less than an eastern engine plus the freight," noted one writer (that is, including the cost of sending it by ship). Once the rails ran coast to coast, there was no comparison. Three thousand men worked in three specialized Paterson, New Jersey locomotive works in 1873. Those shops poured more than *eleven hundred* locomotives onto the rails of America between 1871 and 1873.

The prosperous economy of the 1860s evaporated swiftly. Already in 1870, one in five San Francisco workers found themselves without jobs. These numbers soon grew worse.

LOSING THE EIGHT-HOUR DAY

Over the next few years, San Francisco workers fought a rearguard battle to hold onto the eight-hour day. As the number of would-be workers in the city expanded, the local economy shrank. For union activists who could remember the effects in the 1850s of economic depression on their organizations, the results would not have been surprising. Even the strongest unions—the printers and iron molders—suffered defeats and demoralization.

In fall 1869, employers presented printers across the state with a demand for a one-third reduction in wages. Their bosses pointed out that "the recent opening of the overland railroad brings the offices of this city into direct competition with those of the east, where work can be done at much lower wages." The printers refused and walked out, but returned to work when their employers began to import strikebreakers from the East. The reduced wage scale went into effect not only in San Francisco but in Sacramento, Stockton, and elsewhere.

San Francisco iron molders fared no better. In 1867 they had affiliated with the national iron molders union. Molders in several workplaces, with the backing of the newly chartered Molders Local 164, established the eight-hour day and a $4.50 per day wage scale. But the molders lost two strikes against wage cuts in 1869, with the second strike dragging on in the face of replacement workers for a year. The losses ended with the temporary dissolution of Local 164.

When Frank Roney went to work in Happy Valley foundries in 1875, there were 1,700 men working in mostly nonunion conditions in the metal industries, a thousand in just three shops. At the largest, the Union Iron Works, Roney found wages had sunk to $3.50 per day. His first three days on the job he worked forty hours, or thirteen-hour days, without overtime pay. Roney later claimed that iron molding made him want to drink.

SILVER AND CAPITAL

Despite the serious problems facing working people, much of the public's attention focused elsewhere. A national depression, hitting its worst moments in 1873–74, had yet to roll into San Francisco. The talk on Montgomery Street was all of the Comstock Lode, in Virginia City. The silver mines provoked a minor scale reenactment of the Gold Rush. Like the Gold Rush, the Comstock Lode helped a handful of men rise from the proverbial rags to riches. Unlike the Gold Rush, there was no egalitarian moment, when everyone sweated alongside one another, swishing pans by hand in the diggings. This time large amounts of capital were needed from the outset to fund the quartz mining methods and hire industrial workers, who quickly organized themselves into a union that negotiated wages of four dollars a day.

The Comstock Lode also greatly expanded the San Francisco banking industry and the formation of joint stock companies, which stimulated a speculative financial bubble. Huge investments in the mines, beginning in 1859, were made through the San Francisco stock exchange. Some companies were legitimate, returning sizeable profits for its investors. In others, unscrupulous financiers swindled millions of dollars from worthless stock in the land beneath Virginia City.

A handful of men made large fortunes through their positions atop the Comstock mining companies and its web of financial interests. The silver kings, as they were called, joined with the Big Four railroad owners to employ the most skilled building craftsmen to raise enormous mansions on Nob Hill. No costs were spared. Their ornate homes featured some of the finest furnishings pillaged from European cultural history. Charles Crocker's 12,500 square foot house boasted a seventy-six foot tower and a theater. Mark Hopkins's garish wooden castle included an oak-paneled dining room with seats for sixty. Silver mining engineer and capitalist George Hearst had a mansion built a block away from Crocker's. His son, William Randolph, later to become owner of the nation's most extensive media empire, drew inspiration for his San Simeon castle from memories of the neighborhood of his youth.

Silver kings and railroad barons mostly socialized with members of their own class. But they invested in a joint product of their industries that provided the curious traveler with a peek into their universe: the Silver Palace car. A western alternative to the luxurious Pullman car, the Silver Palace car didn't have the superior springs of a Pullman car, but its handcrafted interior, rich in detail, provided its clientele with a momentary sojourn in the world of the very wealthy.

A visible symbol of the Gilded Age, like the mansions of the Nob Hill elite, the Silver Palace car illustrated the two sides of the period: the wealth of the new rich in America, which could afford to purchase everything it wanted or imagined it wanted, covered in precious metal, or "gilded." But gilded also implies the work of gilding, highly skilled handcrafted labor that creates works of art out of everyday objects: door knobs, street lamps, advertising signs, the interiors of railroad cars. Except for employment, the relationship between the wealthy and the workers who did their work was distant and grew even more so as the 1870s advanced.

FIGURE 9. Irish immigrant Frank Roney: iron molder, Workingmen's Party leader, trade union and central labor body organizer. Courtesy of the Bancroft Library, University of California, Berkeley.

DEPRESSION, RACE, AND IMMIGRATION

The national economic depression arrived in California in 1875, the same year as Frank Roney and another working-class immigrant, Anna Ferry Smith. The Comstock speculative bubble burst and a number of California banks failed, including the largest, Bank of California. Between 1875 and 1877, employment in San Francisco's foundries, iron works, and boiler factories declined from over 1,700 to 1,200.

It was Frank Roney's luck to roll into San Francisco along with hard times. An Irish revolutionary who had apprenticed as an iron molder before emigrating to New York in 1868, by the time Roney reached San Francisco with his wife and small child he had already served as president of the molders' local in Omaha, Nebraska. His diary entries recorded firsthand the impact of the nation's first major industrial depression on one worker's efforts to find employment in his craft. He spent more time looking for work than employed. He noted the efforts of a friend to hock a ring, and his family's unhappiness at renting and then losing some furniture due to inability to pay for it. His wife had a second child, and he worried, with good reason, about his ability to provide for his growing family.

Roney was not alone. San Francisco had become home, since the Gold Rush, to a large immigrant Irish population. Emerging from the Irish countryside, they were mostly—unlike Roney—uneducated and possessed few skills useful in rapidly industrializing American cities. They were considered by white people on the Eastern Seaboard to be social, economic, and cultural inferiors. The men found work in heavy manual labor, the women in domestic services and, to a lesser extent, in mills and factories. These were the lowest rungs of the economy, and ethnic prejudices largely kept them there. The dominant Yankee elites were Protestant; the Irish were Catholic. The newcomers spoke with a distinctive accent, leaving them open to easy identification and ethnic discrimination.

During the Civil War, as free blacks moved north, the Irish, described by newspaper commentaries as "white niggers," found themselves competing with freed slaves for the available unskilled and semi-skilled jobs. Irish workers in New York rioted against their black neighbors—and in the city's wealthier sections—to protest the Draft Law of 1863. The law made service in the armed forces mandatory, but allowed well-to-do men to buy their way out for $300. Most Irish didn't make that much money in a year, and they weren't especially interested in fighting a war that would create competitors in the job market. The Draft Riots were put down with considerable force, increasing the resentment of Irish workers over their social status.

No surprise, then, that those who could afford it set out for California. By 1870 one in three San Franciscans was of Irish origin. As a group, the Irish did relatively well in San Francisco. Given a strong economy and facing less ethnic prejudice than they did back east, Irish immigrants experienced a general upward mobility. Kate Kennedy's successes in her teaching career and in achieving home ownership were not so different from a significant number of her former countrymen.

But while some scrambled up the social ladder as high as silver king John Mackay, the majority remained concentrated in unskilled and semiskilled work. Clustered in jobs within a few industries, such as boot and shoe manufacture and cigar making, the Irish were particularly hard hit with the economic downturn. To make matters worse, they found themselves directly pitted against the next largest immigrant group for dwindling jobs.

The Chinese had faced discrimination and job market segmentation practically from the earliest days of the Gold Rush. While they came, like everyone else, seeking greater opportunity for economic advancement, the Chinese—already numbering 25,000 in California in 1852—were also fleeing the breakdown of their country's political system. In the 1840s drought and famine swept the land. Bandits roved the countryside. Civil wars flared in numerous provinces. The Taiping Rebellion in southeast China lasted a dozen years, with millions dead and displaced.

Most of the Chinese who journeyed to *Gam Saan* (Golden Mountain) in California were unskilled or semiskilled contract laborers. An American or Chinese company would pay for their transport in return for a number of years of work. Out of their earnings the ticket price would be deducted. (Despite charges that the Chinese immigrant workers were "coolies"—the term designates a slave trade in poor Chinese prevalent in other parts of the world—few if any Chinese workers in California came over by that method. The term literally meant "bitter strength.")

The trip took eight or nine weeks across the Pacific, often under horrendous conditions. Shipwrecks were common, but greater problems were poor sanitation and overcrowding, and on occasion deliberate cruelty by the crew. Perhaps the most extreme voyage was that of the *Libertad* in 1854, which pulled into San Francisco with one-fifth of its five hundred passengers dead.

Initially the majority of Chinese passed through San Francisco and immediately went to the Sierras to mine gold. As the Chinese grew into the most numerous minority in the diggings, laws like the Foreign Miners' Act of 1850 became merely part of a wide range of racist, exclusionary actions taken against them in the state. The law was repealed and reinstated a number of times, and finally declared unconstitutional in 1870.

By then better than one in eight workers in San Francisco were Chinese. Cloistered in the crowded Chinatown, their unfamiliar cultural behaviors became the basis for speculation and prejudice. Urban folklore magnified the practices of some into the traits of an entire people. A popular song of the mid-1850s imagined the meals of "John Chinaman":

> I thought of rats and puppies, John
> You'd eaten your last fill;
> But on such slimy pot-pies, John,
> I'm told you dinner still.

Newspaper cartoons of Chinese crudely and commonly caricatured them as subhuman. Hemmed by discrimination into a few occupations, the Chinese workers faced a belief that these were the only types of work they could actually do. Forced by circumstances to be thrifty and more careful in their work than others—as in the gold fields, where Chinese miners frequently took diggings abandoned by whites and eked out the metal that remained—they accepted lower wages, then faced blame for reducing wage scales and taking jobs away from white workers.

A washerwoman's lament circulating in the 1870s included these lines in rough Irish dialect:

> For I kin wash an' iron a shirt,
> An' I kin scrub a flure;
> An' I kin starch a collar as stiff
> As any Chineseman, I'm sure;
> But these dhirty, pigtailed haythens,
> An' ther prices they are paid
> Have brought me to the state you see—
> They've entirely ruint the thrade.

Such prejudices were curious, given the parallels between Chinese and Irish immigrant histories: flight from persecution or famine in their home countries; bad treatment when they arrived in the United States; suffering ridicule for their curious languages or accents, clothing, and cultural customs; and taking unskilled jobs. Despite these similarities there was one crucial difference: the Irish were white and the Chinese were not. In American culture of the nineteenth century, this difference cannot be overstated. Racism and economics had been at the center of the recently fought Civil War. Despite the emancipation of the slaves, the relationship between these issues had not been resolved. What happened to the California Indians after statehood was one illustration of how exploitation of people of color was conveniently perceived as part of the "natural order of things."

The Irish had been on the bottom of the economic ladder but thought their prospects for improvement on the West Coast were good. When the Great Depression of the 1870s punctured their dreams, the Chinese, already the object of prejudice, became scapegoats.

XENOPHOBIA

As early as 1869 Chinese workers were hired as strikebreakers by San Francisco shoe manufacturers Buckingham, Hecht and Company when white workers at the company put down their tools. By the mid-1870s Chinese workers comprised slightly over half of the boot and shoe industry, and a larger majority of cigar makers. Yet unions in these industries refused to include Chinese workers. Instead they created "white workers labels" to distinguish their goods from those produced by Chinese labor. The Knights of Saint Crispin, a union representing shoemakers, in 1870 had two locals in San Francisco, one for men and one for women. It called for and enforced boycotts against Chinese-produced goods. (A "boycott" means refusing to patronize a business or its products. The term came from the landlord's name in a famous rent strike in Ireland, although the practice predated the word.)

As unemployment grew to 25 percent in the city, working people suffered proportionately. Rates of robbery, suicide, murder, divorce, and alcoholism skyrocketed in workers' communities. A homeless population grew along the docks. The ranks of workers willing to strike for the eight-hour day dwindled. There were too many hungry men—Chinese and white alike—willing to replace them for ten hours or more. Unions fell apart. Conditions of work deteriorated, and wages fell. For white workers who had struggled throughout the 1850s and 1860s to form unions and win relatively decent standards of wages, hours of work, and political rights, the increasing numbers of Chinese workers seemed to provide a simple, sufficient answer to the question, Why is this happening to me?

In 1876, the U.S. Congress established a Joint Special Committee to Investigate Chinese Immigration. It held hearings in San Francisco, interviewing workers and business owners. One of those who testified was Anna Ferry Smith, who described herself as "a general working woman." Smith, like Frank Roney, had arrived in San Francisco in 1875.

Born in New York in 1833, Smith went to work while still a child in domestic service. Moving slowly west, she worked in a succession of jobs and industries: in a shoe factory, as a janitor in girls' schools, as a nurse for the Union Army during the Civil War, as a washerwoman, and ironing in laundries. She married a disabled war veteran, who was fired from his job with the Pennsylvania Railroad because of his disability. He died in Missouri. Anna with his child went to Denver.

Although she never received any formal education, part of her compensation while employed as a janitor was permission to attend classes. Apparently she did so and became an enthusiastic reader.

In California, at first she cooked and kept house on ranches. At last she arrived in San Francisco, putting a roof over her head as a seamstress, broken up by periods of unemployment. Her young son worked more than she did.

Smith was reported in a San Francisco newspaper as "well informed on matters connected with the labor question." Her testimony on Chinese immigration before the congressional committee backed up that opinion; the transcripts show her to be intelligent, articulate, and able to hold her own in exchanges with U.S. senators. When one senator tried to get her to say that Chinese workers were the cause of the wretched condition of working women in San Francisco, she responded with a question of her own. She politely inquired as to " why the condition of the working people in the East, where there are no Chinamen, is worse than it is here?"

Smith's views contrasted with those of others in her adopted city. Edward Cortage, a worker in a broom factory, told the congressional committee that in the past he had been able to make twenty or twenty-one dollars per week. He acknowledged his boss was generally kind, and tried to help him out because Cortage was a married man with four children. But while Cortage was "in favor of anybody making a living that possibly can," now he was making less than fifteen dollars per week, and "I put in 14 hours a day, including traveling backward and forward from Oakland. If the Chinaman has a mind to work for my firm he gets employment and I have to compete with him. He offers to work for about one third less the price I am working for now."

THE JULY DAYS

In July 1877 railroad workers across the United States went on strike, protesting wage reductions below the level possible to feed a family. The nationwide strike was a desperate move by working-class communities to resist the destruction of their standard of living at the hands of the railroad owners, *some of whom made more money each hour than their workers earned in a year.* In many cities large-scale battles erupted between strikers and police. The communities mostly sided with the strikers, despite large city newspapers portraying the workers as crazed subhuman thugs. Workers in St. Louis, led by the socialist Workingmen's Party of the United States, organized a general strike, taking over and peacefully running the city for a week.

The Central Pacific Railroad reduced wages at first, too. But when word arrived over the telegraph wires of the huge strikes back east, the railroad shrewdly beat a quick retreat and restored pay to its previous level. Nonetheless, in San Francisco, members of the Workingmen's Party of the United States held a rally in support of the nation's railroad strikers.

FIGURE 10. San Francisco anti-Chinese demonstration, 1880, from Frank Leslie's Illustrated Newspaper. San Francisco History Center, San Francisco Public Library.

Thousands of people gathered in a large vacant lot in front of the unfinished city hall to express solidarity with their eastern brothers.

Open air speeches were a major form of entertainment in the late nineteenth century. Public speaking was a highly developed art, and no wonder: without electronic mass media, or even amplification of voices, speakers had to be eloquent—and loud—to hold their audience's attention. It was a common experience for city dwellers at that time to come upon a crowd gathered on a street corner, listening to a speaker and arguing among themselves about the merits of the speech.

The Workingmen's Party speakers called for an end to government subsidies of the railroads and for an eight-hour day for all workers. But at the end of the rally, the crowd was joined by members of an "anti-coolie" club. The anti-Chinese agitators found ready listeners when they blamed the Chinese for high levels of unemployment among white workers. Despite efforts of the Workingmen's Party to stop them, a portion of the crowd marched to Chinatown and burnt down two dozen Chinese laundries, a few other Chinese-owned businesses, and a church.

For three nights the riots continued. Chinese were murdered by whites. Battles were fought between armed crowds and the forces of order. A lumberyard near the docks and warehouse of the Pacific Mail Steamship Company—blamed by the rioters for bringing Chinese into the country—was set ablaze. One Chinese laundry worker, Ah Wah, told the *San Francisco Chronicle*:

> I was employed in Si Sow's laundry. . . . There were eight of us Chinamen. We then attempted to escape by the front door and were fired upon with pistols by the crowd in the street. There were about fifteen white men there and more than ten shots were fired. I did not see the deceased at the time. [One of the Chinese workers was found dead in the wreckage the next day.] The rest of us ran away and hid in the bushes. We heard the white men breaking open boxes. The proprietor's chest, in which he kept his money, was in the house. In about half an hour after we escaped we saw the house on fire.

The mobs claimed non-Chinese victims, too. Most of the rioting occurred south of Market Street, home to various working-class ethnic neighborhoods. Fires spread from Chinese businesses and residences to those of their neighbors. When firefighters arrived, the mobs cut their hoses. Bystanders were accidentally shot. Finally the rioters were driven from the streets by a massive display of force by police, national guard, and hastily mobilized quasi-official vigilante groups.

Within a few days California Governor William Irwin declared the danger had passed and dissolved the vigilante groups. He interpreted for the public whom to blame for the civil disturbances, denouncing "hoodlums," "thieves," and "Communists." Practically no one, including individuals in newspaper reports and early historians of the events, identified the rioters as working people. Yet it is hard to imagine, with unemployment at one-quarter of the workforce, that a considerable number of the participants weren't workers venting anger at their condition.

THE WORKINGMEN'S PARTY OF CALIFORNIA

Ten weeks later appeared a new organization, the Workingmen's Party of California (WPC). It is probable that at least some of its activists came from the ranks of the rioters, and certainly a great many of its supporters were unemployed. A large percentage were Irish immigrants. It was dedicated to the belief that the democratic traditions of the American Revolution had been subverted by great wealth amassed in the hands of the robber barons, who respected no laws, particularly laws that protected common people. Despite its name, it was open to small businesspeople as well as workers. In that respect the party's ideas resembled those of other late nineteenth-century workers' movements, which tended to define Americans as either useful "producers" or parasitical "exploiters."

Leaders of the Workingmen such as Denis Kearney, a drayman (wagon driver), blamed the Big Four Central Pacific owners, the silver mine kings, and land speculators for corrupting the state's political process. He contrasted their lavish mansions atop Nob Hill with the densely populated firetrap apartments occupied by working people on the other side of Market Street.

WPC leaders told white workers they were being squeezed on two sides: by the very wealthy and by their tool, Chinese workers, who took the available jobs. Thus the racism practiced by the Workingmen's Party of California was rooted in economic fear. Like all racism, however, it went beyond rational calculation and slid quickly into the shadows of the irrational.

Not all members of the WPC blamed the Chinese for their troubles. Frank Roney argued that the measures being proposed against the Chinese were "brutal and such as no self-respecting people would dream of imposing on any race within their midst." Despite his experiences with unemployment, he didn't consider the Chinese the source of his personal misery. He felt that the Chinese workers, if left alone, would gradually improve their economic position like other immigrant groups and cease to undercut the wages of other workers.

But more San Franciscans were swayed by another Irish immigrant. Denis Kearney had arrived in the city in 1868. Within a few years he had saved enough money to buy a small drayage firm. He became a naturalized citizen in 1876. A convincing, if crude, orator, Kearney articulated the resentments of white workers at the decaying economic conditions facing them, even though he had become an employer. He also reflected the fears of small business and property owners that only a thin, weak barrier separated them from financial ruin.

Kearney coined the WPC's slogan, "The Chinese must go!" He was jailed a number of times for his inflammatory sandlot speeches. In fall of 1877 he led a meeting of several thousand on Nob Hill, across the street from Mark Hopkins's mansion. He delighted the crowd by promising to lead them "to the City Hall, clean out the police force, hang the Prosecuting Attorney, burn every book that has a particle of law in it, and then enact new laws for the workingmen." He also said, "If I give an order to hang Crocker, it will be done."

The WPC expanded with breathtaking speed, organizing neighborhood by neighborhood, block by block. Soon it thoroughly displaced the Democratic Party as the political choice of working people. Its platform, devised in January 1878, stood for an eight-hour work day, public works to employ the unemployed, a tax system that would prevent the vast accumulation of wealth by greedy capitalists, compulsory public education "for rich and poor alike," and restrictions on Chinese labor. Ultimately the party would only realize the last of these goals.

Anna Ferry Smith became involved in the Workingmen's Party (which, despite its name, did contain at least a few women activists). A newspaper reported that she delivered "folksy" sandlot speeches, bringing one to a conclusion by suggesting it was time for everyone to eat: "she wanted something to keep her jaws going and give her tongue a rest." Unlike the fiery Kearney, she mostly concentrated her efforts on practical matters such as helping unemployed women find shelter, by taking over abandoned or empty buildings.

Although Smith demonstrated more sensitivity to the plight of Chinese workers than many in the Workingmen's Party, she was not immune to anti-Chinese ideas. She informed one sandlot crowd that 250 Chinese were occupying a public building leased for fifty dollars a month to a shoe manufacturer. In a more subtle way than Kearney might have done it, her implication was that the crowd should go and take care of the matter itself.

Spreading to cities and towns throughout California, the Workingmen's Party elected a third of the delegates to the California constitutional convention of 1878 and swept to power (briefly) in many municipalities besides San Francisco. Beneath the surface of the party's apparent unity, however, emerged a battle between followers of Roney and Kearney. Roney's partisans were more trade union-oriented and wanted to focus the party on its egalitarian economic demands. Kearney and his followers placed greater emphasis on the exclusion of the Chinese from California. Charging Kearney's faction with corruption and "selling out to corporations," his opponents elected Roney chairman.

The two groups held separate state conventions in San Francisco. They were reunited only after large numbers of Kearney's followers invaded the other groups' meetings and intimidated them into adopting the Kearney positions. When the WPC elected delegates to the California state constitutional convention, these men proved unable to win over the other delegates to their positions on any issue except Chinese exclusion and the formation of a state Railroad Commission to oversee the activities of the Central Pacific. Although the new state constitution did not look much like the Workingmen's Party platform, Kearney declared victory and urged Californians to vote for it. Frank Roney, by now outside the party, opposed it. It was adopted by the public in a statewide vote the following year.

The WPC's success in passing racist exclusion laws did not result in any real gains for workers. This simplistic solution did not challenge the power of the railroad monopoly and landowners over working people's lives. It failed to address the great changes created by the industrial revolution. By focusing its attention on the divisive side issue of Chinese exclusion, an opportunity to build alliances among all groups of working people was lost.

Chinese workers were often willing to serve as strikebreakers, if that was the only work they could get. But they were also open to collective action, as they demonstrated in the Sierras in 1867, and again in March 1876, when hundreds struck two San Francisco shoe manufacturers. Most of them wanted what most white workers wanted: to pursue the American Dream of economic advancement. Unfortunately, racial prejudices and economic fears blinded white workers to the possibility of unity.

As Smith pointed out in her testimony to the congressional committee, Chinese workers were here because the United States and other western powers had demanded China open its borders to trade with the world. The beneficiaries of that trade were merchants and industrial capitalists, who developed new markets for their goods. What workers got out of the deal was increased competition among themselves for jobs.

Railroad magnate Crocker was not alone in seeking to curb the power of white workers and their unions by hiring Chinese laborers. When the first California miners' union went on strike in 1869 in Grass Valley over the risk to miners' safety posed by new explosives, the mine owners threatened to replace them with Chinese workers. However, when Chinese railroad workers went on strike in 1867, Crocker investigated replacing *them* with black workers before realizing it would be simpler and cheaper to starve them out. These complex issues in the background of the Chinese question would not be taken care of by banning Chinese immigration.

The WPC declined almost as quickly as it arose. By 1881 it had virtually disappeared. But its work had been accomplished, at least on the terms it wanted. In 1882 the U.S. Congress passed the Chinese Exclusion Act, forbidding further immigration to Chinese workers. The party spawned successor groups in California labor that lasted well into the twentieth century. And it left behind a legacy of hatred against Asian Americans and an anti-immigrant climate that has never completely left the political atmosphere of the state.

Was there an alternative to the approach taken by the Workingmen's Party and Denis Kearney? Undoubtedly. The more tolerant attitude and deeper economic understanding of individuals like Frank Roney and Anna Ferry Smith represented the possibility of workers uniting with one another in their common interests. White workers in the eastern and southern United States faced with free black labor during Reconstruction confronted a similar choice.

In 1879, the same statewide ballot that featured the proposed new state constitution contained a referendum on the desirability of complete Chinese exclusion. Although it was later thrown out by the courts, the vote total is revealing: 150,000 for, just 900 against. In the face of such a climate of opinion the voices of tolerance had little chance.

7

Building Paradise

THE MAKING OF THE LOS ANGELES WORKING CLASS

LOS ANGELES AT MID-CENTURY was a violent little frontier city, much like Hollywood images of the lawless western town before the good sheriff arrived. The reality in Los Angeles was even uglier, meaner, and messier than the movies portrayed. In the early stages of its transition from a pueblo near Mission San Gabriel to the largest city on the West Coast, Los Angeles boasted the highest homicide rate in the West, with a murder a day among a population of a few thousand.

So commonplace were the town's violent deaths that local newspaper reporters couldn't work up a sweat over such stories:

> The week has been comparatively quiet; four persons have been killed, it is true, but it has been considered a poor week for killing; a head or two has been split open, and an occasional case of cutting has occurred, but these are minor matters and create but little feeling.

Much of the violence occurred around "Nigger Alley," a malevolent neighborhood north of the old central plaza, occupying the same land as today's Chinatown. It was filled with failed miners, dispossessed Indians, and lawless riffraff—gamblers, murderers for hire, petty criminals—washed up from the western territories onto the country's farthest shore.

One October evening in 1871, a Chinese man shot a white police officer in Chinatown. Upon hearing about the shooting incident, a mob of several hundred white men gathered, and—assisted by the police—swarmed into the Chinese quarter, indiscriminately attacking and lynching the immigrant population. More than twenty Chinese died, and over forty thousand dollars worth of property was destroyed or stolen. Even jaded Los Angeles public opinion was disturbed. One hundred rioters were eventually indicted by a grand jury investigation, and the federal government paid indemnities to the families of the victims. But only six men were sentenced to jail, and they were soon set free.

LOS ANGELES WORKINGMEN'S PARTY

Seven years later the Workingmen's Party of California (WPC) swept briefly to power in Los Angeles. Relatively few Chinese lived in Los Angeles County, just 3 percent of the population in 1880. Unlike in San Francisco, they were not in competition for jobs with white workers. There was little manufacturing in Los Angeles, and the Chinese occupied niches in the economy outside the interest of white labor. The party platform, as in the rest of the state, did feature anti-Chinese sentiments. But it would have proven difficult to base the Los Angeles WPC simply on the "cheap labor" economic arguments of its northern counterpart.

For these reasons, in 1878, the Los Angeles Workingmen's Party leaders stressed the peaceful nature of its platform, and emphasized popular reform ideas such as universal suffrage, free public education, and government ownership of the railroads and telegraph. Its members purchased and ran the oldest daily newspaper in the city, and elected a majority to the city council.

The party's relative moderation and antimonopolist themes attracted allies among small businessmen and farmers, whose votes provided the margin of victory in the sparsely populated city. Paying lip service to anti-Chinese immigration ideas, the party mainly served as a vehicle for politicians who, not workers themselves, recognized that the energy behind the movement could propel them into public office. Once elected, most rapidly abandoned the more progressive, proworker sentiments that had elevated them to power.

Not that a great deal of power rested in these politicians' hands. The largest city in southern California, in 1880 Los Angeles claimed only 11,000 inhabitants. Its small population was but one factor that slowed development of workers' political consciousness and unionism. Before the meteoric rise and fall of the Workingmen's Party, only two organizations affiliated with the cause of labor had surfaced in Los Angeles. The Typographical Union first appeared in 1859 as Local 44 and lasted one year, reestablishing itself in 1875 as the International Typographical Union (ITU) Local 174. A branch of the Mechanics' Eight-Hour League achieved a toehold in 1868, reducing hours for fewer than one hundred workers.

CONSERVATIVE CULTURE

In the following years, retirees and convalescents attracted to the mild climate contributed to a conservative political atmosphere. Following completion of the Southern Pacific's railroad link from San Francisco in 1876, a "boom-town" get-rich-quick mentality based in land speculation encouraged individual advancement, not collective action.

The Southern Pacific Railroad, the biggest real estate promoter of the West, sold the wonders of climate, health, and prosperity to the rest of the country with millions of pieces of colorful and often fanciful literature and traveling exhibitions. This advertising campaign lasted for decades, consolidating in the minds of envious non-Californians an ever-evolving golden dream full of images like the classic one: row upon row of orange trees bursting with their fruit, while in the background snow-topped mountains hinted that, yes, southern California had winter, too, but it didn't get in anyone's way.

The "booster" mentality of the city's landowners, real estate agents, tourism industry, and railroads soon dominated the public atmosphere. Workers who could scrape together a few dollars laid them willingly into the hands of the boosters in hopes of making a fortune.

In the mid-1880s, the publication of Helen Hunt Jackson's *Ramona* irritated the city's boosters, who felt the crusading novel damaged the reputation of southern California. Within a few years, their attitude sharply reversed as the recently hatched Chamber of Commerce grasped *Ramona*'s potential to organize the travel plans of eastern tourists and empty the bank accounts of immigrants into the waiting arms of Los Angeles realtors. Making lemonade from lemons, the boosters put together Ramona tours, Mission Days festivals, and recast the city's Mexicano population as a colorful reminder of the city's Spanish heritage.

Capitalizing on the good fortune of its actual geography and reinvented history, Los Angeles began to shape itself as the city of other people's dreams. Mundane details remained: as the town's population expanded, so did its need for all types of labor. Soon enough, immigrants from the rest of the

United States, answering the call of tourist and real estate promotion, far outnumbered homegrown workers in the local labor market.

During the last quarter of the nineteenth century a white American working class emerged for the first time in Los Angeles, one hundred years after the Spanish founded the pueblo. Its growth accelerated after the completion of the Southern Pacific rail link in 1876 and, especially, in 1886, when a second railroad line, the Santa Fe, arrived from the southeast and sparked a fare war between the corporations. Equally encouraging to the flood of immigrants was the steep decline of the old pastoral economy, which allowed the breakup of the huge ranchos into smaller inexpensive lots for purchase and settlement.

The new working-class majority coexisted uneasily with the earlier inhabitants—Indians, Chinese, and Mexicans—viewing them as remnants of the Wild West: colorful and useful so long as they knew their place, which was mostly menial labor in jobs whites rejected for themselves. When they ventured outside their assigned seats in society they became objects of suspicion and prejudice.

In the 1850s and 1860s the majority of laborers were former Mission Indians. A few thousand worked and often lived on the huge ranches, in the fields and orchards spreading out from the town, and as day laborers. No laws protected their rights. In fact, in much the same way as the first state law addressing the employment of sailors (1847) spelled out penalties for workers, not for employers who brutalized them, the rights of Indian workers were limited by legislation.

During the mission period, at least the Spanish and Mexican laws provided certain protections for Native Californians, even if ignored when considered inconvenient by the padres and soldiers. Under the rule of the United States, the laws changed for the worse.

California's Act for the Government and Protection of Indians (1850) combined with local restrictive ordinances to insure a steady supply of cheap labor for employers. It stated that an Indian without means of subsistence could be declared a vagrant, a condition that might be addressed by a public auction for his or her services. Another provision of the law allowed Indian minors to be "apprenticed" to white masters—a form of virtual slavery.

Repealed in 1863, nonetheless the law had created the conditions for the accelerated decline of the native southern California population. And long after the legal end of the act, the employment of Indians in Los Angeles continued to reflect its spirit.

Large landowners used the Los Angeles county jail as their employment bureau for casual Indian labor. According to one observer,

> Los Angeles had its slave mart as well as New Orleans and Constantinople— only the slave at Los Angeles was sold fifty two times a year as long as he lived, which generally did not exceed one, two or three years under the new dispensation. They would be sold for a week, and bought up by the vineyard men and others at prices ranging from one to three dollars, one-third of which was to be paid to the peon at the end of the week, which debt due for well-performed labor would invariably be paid in *aguardiente,* and the Indian would be happy until the following Monday morning having passed through another Saturday night and Sunday's saturnalia of debauchery and bestiality.

At the end of the weekend, or at some point of inebriation during it, the Indian worker would be thrown in jail. On Monday morning he would be auctioned and released into the care of the employer.

Hundreds of Indian workers were still around in the late 1870s, performing the chores of seasonal farm labor, although most had been dispersed to the ranches outside Los Angeles and smaller towns in the surrounding valleys. Within a few years, the remaining California Indians, including those who had taken up arms, were removed to reservations. By then, the growth of intensive agriculture, along with the decline of the Indian population, created a shortage of farm labor. Prevailing ideas about the Yellow Peril caused debates within farming circles about the morality of employing Chinese labor. But while they debated, most farm owners continued to hire.

Chinese laborers released from employment with the transcontinental railroad after 1869 didn't end up solely in San Francisco or the northern central valleys of California. In the 1870s tiny Chinatowns sprang up in the small but growing urban centers of southern California. In 1875 Chinese work gangs blasted the tunnel through mountain into the San Fernando Valley for the Southern Pacific. The Chinese labored on farms, filling the void left as the Indian population shrank, but also in domestic industries, in laundries, and as servants. They worked in small-scale vegetable and fruit cultivation, helped to pioneer crops like celery and citrus, and fished alongside the coastal cities. From just a couple hundred in 1870, the Los Angeles

Chinese population steadily increased to more than a thousand a decade later, peaking at over four thousand in 1890 before the long-term effects of the Exclusion Act of 1882 drove their numbers back down again.

Confronting the prejudices of the white society—which occasionally erupted into mob violence—and separated by language and culture from their surroundings, the Chinese immigrants kept to themselves when not working. Their neighborhood in Los Angeles, as in other California towns, was segregated. Usually it could be found next to, or overlapping with, the living area of the other major non-Anglo population—those who spoke Spanish.

The Californios—formerly the proud owners of Alta California—had arrived at their day of reckoning. A handful managed to hold onto their privileged status as landed ranchers or merchants, continuing to intermarry with the growing Anglo elites. But between 1850 and 1880, most lost the titles to their vast properties. Some returned to Mexico. Many gradually fell into the labor market, alongside their former rancho employees and a slow trickle of northward immigration from Mexico. Erstwhile landowners descended from "Californio" to "Mexican" in the eyes of the whites, becoming subject to the prejudice they had escaped before due to their economic advantages.

The loss of the few thousand Californios' extensive lands occurred by various means. One random factor forcing the exchange of land ownership between descendants of Mexico and Europe was the weather. Its mild reputation proved false in the early 1860s. Two years of heavy rains and flooding were followed by three drought years. By 1865 two-thirds of the state's livestock were dead, and so was the southern California cattle industry. Many rancheros never recovered from these losses.

The overall historical trend for the Californios, however, was anything but random. The terms of the Treaty of Guadalupe Hidalgo granted ownership to rancheros who had documented title to the land, and also bestowed upon them American citizenship—which was more than Native Californians and Chinese could boast. But just what constituted "clear title" was often impossible to prove, given the casual paperwork of the Spanish and Mexican land grants. Forced into court by Anglo speculators and under continuous pressure by squatters, citizenship meant the ability to rack up legal fees, fall into debt, borrow money at murderous interest rates, mortgage the land, and then lose it when payment came due.

More numerous than the Californios were the people who had worked on their lands. Each of the larger ranchos employed anywhere from dozens to hundreds of workers. Dispossession of the lands and the end of the cattle era forced the skilled laborers and artisans of the pastoral economy into a radical shift in employment. Vaqueros, saddle makers, sheepshearers, harness makers, smiths: as their occupations evaporated, some resisted the drop into menial unskilled labor status, opting for seasonal employment at their trades or migrating elsewhere.

But for most there was no other choice but to go to work for Anglo employers in the emerging capitalist economy. Much as the Chinese had replaced Native Californian farmworkers, the new Mexican working class, in the last two decades of the nineteenth century, began to fill the vacuum in farm labor as Chinese employment dwindled in the wake of the Exclusion Act. As if anticipating the trends around the corner, on the final leg of the San Francisco to Los Angeles railroad construction, from the San Fernando Valley in 1876, Spanish-speaking Indians and Mexican laborers took the place of Chinese workers on the road gangs.

By the 1880s, the Spanish-speaking inhabitants of Los Angeles found themselves segregated in two barrios near the old downtown pueblo area. The narrowing geographical horizons of the Mexicans' residential ghetto paralleled their restriction in employment to the lowest rungs of the economic ladder. The men were forced increasingly into unskilled employment as construction laborers, ditch diggers, and agricultural and food processing workers. Growing numbers of households were headed by women, who worked as seamstresses, domestics, or prostitutes, or took in boarders.

The barrio was relegated to second-class status, stigmatized by whites as "Sonoratown." But it also helped to preserve the Mexican cultural heritage. Spanish-language newspapers and organizations sponsored holiday pageantry and celebrations of Mexican nationalism. This was seen as necessary by the community's leaders as the percentage of Spanish-surnamed people fell from one-fifth of Los Angeles in 1880 to less than 10 percent within eight years.

THE NEW WORKING-CLASS MAJORITY

It was only partly accurate for one commentator to characterize the new arrivals as "middle aged, middle class, and middle west." True, large numbers of small farmers and shopkeepers, many already retired, came seeking land and sun. From 11,000 in 1880, Los Angeles grew to 80,000 in just seven years.

Once settled in the southern California paradise, some opened small businesses or planted orange trees. Often the newcomers learned how to grow fruit by working in nearby vineyards and orchards. Many improved their bank accounts by some combination of selling produce from their little plots of land and the sale of their wage labor.

The promise of individual upward mobility made it very difficult for most white workers in southern California to imagine organizing on the basis of shared needs. Add a shifting mix of ethnic cultures, prevailing racist attitudes, the sprawling geography without an effective transportation system, and enormous changes in the economy, and it would have come as no surprise if few workers sought collective action. Yet some did.

The land frenzy stimulated a building boom, attracting skilled construction tradesmen from the East, who rode out on emigrant trains alongside the Iowan family farmers. In the boom years of 1886–87, new "cities" were created by real estate speculators who purchased and rapidly subdivided old rancho lands into small plots. Here was plenty of work: laying out the streets, putting in streetcar tracks and water lines, and building homes and commercial buildings.

When the skilled workers arrived in southern California, they found the same workplace pressures and many of the social dilemmas as elsewhere in Gilded Age United States. Carpenter Arthur Vinette put it this way: "An American city had begun to crowd out the historic adobe as well as the rough board shanties. Mechanics flocked in from all parts of the country, wages were lowered, and a pernicious system of piece-work was undermining the carpenters' trade."

As a result, despite the opportunities—real and imagined—for upward mobility in and around Los Angeles, many workers chose to organize. From a mere 107 carpenters listed in the Los Angeles directory in 1875, the recently formed Carpenters Local 56 boasted that it had enrolled 800 members by 1886. Twenty-three house and sign painters from the old directory had been joined by hundreds of immigrants to create not just a single organization but two: a craft union, Local 29 of the Painters and Decorators, affiliated with the national painters' union, and Painters' Assembly 3167 of the Knights of Labor. Bricklayers, hod carriers, sheetmetal workers, plumbers, and granite cutters all crossed the country to construct the new southern California civilization, and all formed unions there throughout the 1880s.

No matter that most of the speculative new land developments weren't completed for years, some languishing, partly built, for decades. Enough of

FIGURE 11. Arthur Vinette founded the United Brotherhood of Carpenters and Joiners Local 56 in Los Angeles in 1884 and helped organize the city's first central labor council. Courtesy of the Bancroft Library, University of California, Berkeley.

them filled with cheap homes on cheap land in places like Alhambra, Glendale, Azusa, and Monrovia to convince workers who couldn't afford to purchase the American Dream elsewhere to keep coming.

CHOICES FOR LABOR

The major Los Angeles trade union was the United Brotherhood of Carpenters and Joiners Local 56. Its founder, Arthur Vinette, raised by his Canadian father to be a ship's carpenter, came to Los Angeles via New York and Colorado in the early 1880s. He discovered conditions for carpenters deteriorating in the midst of the building boom. Disregarding his complete lack of previous union experience, Vinette decided the remedy was to organize Local 56. Thanks to the voracious need for skilled carpenters, along with Vinette's persistence, it soon became the largest union in southern California. At its peak in 1887 nearly a thousand members paid dues to the organization.

Demonstrating a strong sense of solidarity and commitment to workers outside their own craft, the members of Local 56 established an employment bureau—the forerunner of the modern hiring hall—for all construction trade workers in the area. Their assistance was critical in settling a plasterers' strike, called because the employer had failed to pay his workers. Local 56 also set the pace for workers' political action, successfully lobbying the Los Angeles City Council to establish the office of Building Inspector, which the leaders and members of the union felt was necessary to curb corruption and insure industry building standards.

Unlike later craft unions, the Carpenters' local admitted some employers to membership. Allowing contractors to belong to the union reflected the fluid nature of employment in the construction industry. Loose membership requirements demonstrated the recognition that carpenters might become contractors, and vice versa, on any given job.

Printing and construction trade unions grew during the mild boom of the early 1880s, and thrived through the economic expansion of 1886 and 1887. For a time the building trades unions were able to enforce a nine-hour day in construction. The example of their successes encouraged other workers to organize.

Retail clerks, hotel and restaurant employees, machinists, and workers in other industries, taking advantage of the general prosperity, formed unions and engaged in various collective actions. The retail clerks and butchers gained shorter hours. Bakers, forming Journeymen Bakers' Union Local 45 in 1886, managed to reduce their workweek to seventy-five hours, eliminating Sunday work in every bakery but one in the city. The White Cooks', Waiters' and Employees' Protective Union, Branch 3, was organized in a renewed wave of anti-Chinese fervor with the assistance of the San Francisco local. It was probably the first Los Angeles union to admit women—thus making it simultaneously more and less inclusive than most other unions.

A few craft unions, led by the printers and carpenters, pulled together the first central labor council in southern California, the Trades Council, in 1884. It grew to fifteen unions by 1887. At the same time, reflecting an ambivalence felt by activist workers about the proper direction for labor's future, a half-dozen local Knights of Labor assemblies emerged in Los Angeles, too, comprising a few hundred members. These assemblies in turn formed a regional governing body, District Assembly 140.

However, neither the Trades Council nor the District Assembly of the Knights amounted to much more than a rough draft of a coordinating body. The Los Angeles labor movement was too numerically weak and unstable to support broader governing structures. With twenty-one unions and three thousand members clustered in just a few industries, union density probably reached about 10 percent of the workforce at the height of the boom. But unionism, centering in the construction, railroad, and printing trades, was not well represented in the broader economy.

Leading Los Angeles union activists like printer Frank Colver and carpenter Arthur Vinette belonged to the Noble Order of the Knights of Labor as well as to their craft unions. The two types of worker organization represented overlapping but differing philosophies. Craft (or trade) unionists believed that the most effective form of worker power could be generated on the job. By bringing together all carpenters at a job site under one collective bargaining agreement, the union would provide stability of employment for its members and for employers: "a fair day's work for a fair day's wage." Its main weapon was the closed shop, backed up by the threat of a strike. Understanding that workers shared interests across craft lines, the craft unions also formed city and state central labor organizations and, by 1886, a national federation, the American Federation of Labor (AFL). The goals of the AFL were limited to what was obtainable through peaceful means of reform, leaving the capitalist system intact.

Many workers, however, lacked a union in their industry. In 1886 just 3 percent of the national nonagricultural workforce was represented by craft unions. For the overwhelming majority of workers, the Knights represented the only alternative. Members of the Knights could organize two types of "assembly." One type, based in a single craft or industry, might function like a craft union, negotiating wages and working conditions with local employers. While acceptable to the Knights, this form of assembly wasn't the preferred one.

"Mixed" assemblies, which included workers and "producers" of all kinds, also welcomed unskilled workers, African American workers, and women, few of whom were to be found in the craft unions. San Francisco teacher Kate Kennedy joined the Knights, decades before the existence of teacher unions. She was probably a member of the Women's Labor League, Assembly 5855. At its zenith in 1886, over three-quarters of a million "producers" belonged to the Knights, more than double the number of AFL members. The only people officially excluded by the Knights were gamblers, lawyers, stockbrokers, liquor dealers, and bankers—although, especially in California, Chinese were also not admitted.

But what attracted more workers to the Knights than to the AFL was its broader vision of society. The Knights desired the establishment of a "cooperative commonwealth" that would do away with the vast disparities of wealth and power typical of the Gilded Age. While engaged in countless struggles for higher wages and better working conditions, its members looked beyond "wage slavery" to a world in which cooperation, not competition, guided the economy and cultural life toward a more equal distribution of wealth.

The hard-nosed, practical approach of the craft unions appealed to workers' need to make a living in the here and now, while the Knights' idealism provided a home for people who wished for something more. The Knights' outlook particularly attracted politicized workers who viewed the promise of the American revolution—democracy and opportunity for all—in danger at the hands of a new parasitic class, symbolized by the ostentatious living and growing power of the robber barons.

Ultimately the AFL proved more adaptable for workplace organizing. The Knights declined and virtually disappeared by the late 1890s, unable to resolve internal differences and the victim of a government and business backlash. Many sympathizers with the Knights' vision of a just society transferred their allegiances to left-wing political movements that flourished with the approaching century. One was Nationalism, a philosophy founded by Edward Bellamy, the author of a utopian novel, *Looking Backward,* which imagined a state-run, socialist society one hundred years in the future. Nationalist clubs sprang up all over the country, including in Los Angeles. For a time the southern California Nationalist organizer was Anna Smith, the sharp-edged former Workingmen's Party of California sandlot speaker from San Francisco.

Los Angeles's economic boom collapsed in 1888. Members fell away from their unions—AFL and Knights alike—as unemployment decimated the workforce. Thousands of new Los Angelenos packed up and left town, seeking work elsewhere. Closed shops became open again, wages fell, and hours of work rose to preboom levels in most industries. The surge of organizing relapsed into southern California's customary efforts to achieve the American Dream one worker at a time.

8

_____

Newspapers, Railroads, and the Los Angeles Labor Movement

AGAINST A BACKDROP OF ECONOMIC DEPRESSION and organizational weakness workers fought two major battles that defined the early outlines of Los Angeles unionism: a printers' strike and boycott of the *Los Angeles Times,* which helped build a new union solidarity in the city; and the Pullman strike of 1894, the first time a national struggle involved the local labor movement.

These events shaped Los Angeles labor as a radical force in a conservative town, with small platoons of organized workers facing a consolidating citadel of open shop politics, each side determined to defend its opposing vision of economic opportunity.

NEWSPAPERS

As in San Francisco a quarter century before, printers formed the first permanent union in Los Angeles, Local 174 of the International Typographical Union (ITU), in 1875. Local 174's membership—a few dozen in the mid-1870s—multiplied sevenfold by 1886, allowing the union to maintain its position as one of the leading labor organizations in Los Angeles.

Key to Local 174's success was Frank Colver, who crossed the country by train from Ohio, landing in Los Angeles in 1883 at the age of fifty. He had gone to college for two years in his hometown of New York, before apprenticing in the printing trades. He joined the ITU in the mid-1850s, and split his time working as a printer and teacher. Colver co-owned a newspaper at one point and also served as local ITU president two times, once in Kansas and again in Ohio.

Colver joined Local 174 soon after arriving in Los Angeles and took a leadership role in the union's first-ever strike, in August 1883 against the *Los Angeles Times.* The union called the strike when the newspaper's new boss, Harrison Gray Otis, fired a union member in retaliation for the local's support of a printers' strike in San Francisco. Otis persuaded the Los Angeles chief of police to direct his officers to accompany scabs to work, a move that caused "sober observers," as one historian put it, to see the tactic as a transparent ploy "to overdramatize" the strike and gain public sympathy.

Otis overestimated his ability to hold onto his strike replacements. As the strike wore on, the scab printers became socially unpopular, and drifted, one by one, from the *Times.* Local 174 gained declarations of support and financial assistance from other craft unions and from Knights of Labor assemblies. In October Otis had to hire back his former employees, including installing a union foreman. Colver assisted in the negotiations, and his fellow printers were so pleased with his efforts they elected him treasurer of the local.

In the wake of the victory, Local 174 prospered, organizing a union of pressmen and achieving the nine-hour day and higher wages for all its members. Local 174 got local newspapers to stop using "boilerplate," previously prepared type on plates of steel, which filled unused space in the newspaper but reduced employment of union members. It seized upon the departure of Otis's co-owner, who founded a rival newspaper, *The Tribune,* to make another advance: a closed shop (all employees must belong to the union) in the major printing offices in town, including the *Times.*

Facing his partner-turned-competitor, and with a huge new print job awarded to the *Times* by the county's registrar of voters, Otis couldn't afford to antagonize his employees, and submitted. But he didn't forget this affront to his authority and bided his time for payback.

RAILROADS

In the early 1880s, Los Angeles engineers, firemen, and conductors organized local branches of railroad brotherhoods. In the beginning these were not unions, but "beneficial associations" disinterested in strikes, boycotts, and the closed shop. Affiliated with national organizations, they took little part in local labor affairs. Their national connections helped them survive when locally based Los Angeles unions fell apart following the collapse of the building boom. At the same time, the centralization of railroad corporate power forced the brotherhoods to think and act more like unions.

The Brotherhood of Railway Conductors was formed by unhappy workers on the Santa Fe Railroad in southern California. When the boom of 1886–87 faded away, rail travel fell off. The conductors—like growing numbers of engineers, brakemen, and switchers—understood they needed the strike weapon at their disposal. Breaking away from a more conservative Order of Railway Conductors, they established their national headquarters in Los Angeles in 1889. After two years the order got the message, rewriting its constitution to allow strikes. The new conductors' organization declared victory and returned to the fold.

Recognizing the need for closer relationships with workers in other industries, the brotherhoods sought cooperation with the Los Angeles Council of Labor, although they stopped short of formal membership. The council had been set up in 1890 to replace the defunct Trades Council by the printers when they went on strike against the *Los Angeles Times* and realized they needed broad-based support. The railroad brotherhoods were warmly received when they pledged to endorse two causes dear to the council: boycotts of both the *Times* and Chinese-run businesses.

From a distance of more than a century, we might note an irony in the brotherhoods' antagonism to the Chinese. For better than two decades, the majority of the workers laying down the roadbeds and tracks of California's trains were Chinese. The conductors, engineers, firemen, and brakemen were in continuous visual contact with the laborers, and their own work literally rested on the achievements of the Chinese workers. This insight, however, was not able to overcome the racist exclusion mentality of the nineteenth-century labor movement.

THE *LOS ANGELES TIMES* STRIKE AND BOYCOTT

Emblazoned across the masthead of the newspaper owned by Harrison Gray Otis was the motto, "True Industrial Freedom." By this Otis meant "freedom from unions." Since making his concessions to Local 174, Otis had consolidated his leading position in the business community. Under his guidance, business leaders set up the Los Angeles Chamber of Commerce in 1888. While its main function remained supporting the boosterism that all viewed as the key to the prosperity of Los Angeles, the chamber also coordinated antiunion efforts. In these matters Otis took great interest and displayed keen creativity.

By 1890 he felt ready to launch a new offensive against *Los Angeles Times* workers. At that time printing type was set by hand, by typographers, or "typos." Otis demanded that they accept a pay cut of thirty-five to fifty cents per one thousand "ems." (An em was a standard unit of type, the size of the letter "m.") This amounted to a 20 percent reduction in wages. When the printers refused to accept the pay cut and voted to strike, Otis got the other three daily newspapers in town to lock out their typos at the same time.

Two of the papers surrendered when picket lines appeared, taking back the union members. The third paper capitulated a few weeks later. But Otis didn't want a settlement; he wanted to break the union. He imported strike-breaking printers from Kansas City at considerable expense. Otis paid his new workers union scale—a rate he had told the union he couldn't afford. Both sides made preparations for a long siege.

The union printers voted to assess all members working more than three days a week 10 percent of their wages to support the strikers. The typos also gained financial assistance from their national organization, the ITU, which sent out a union staffer to help. The printers pulled a number of other unions together to establish the Los Angeles Council of Labor, and began, with the council's help, to organize a citywide boycott of the *Times*. San Francisco union organizer Michael McGlynn rode a train south to help run the boycott.

While most union members honored the boycott, this represented but a small fraction of the newspaper-reading population of Los Angeles. Only mildly successful in cutting the paper's circulation, the boycott brought Otis to the negotiating table when the unions spread their activities to a Los Angeles department store.

SECONDARY BOYCOTT

The People's Store was a major *Times* advertiser. The unions pressured the store to withdraw its advertising from Otis. Supporters operated picket lines proclaiming a "secondary boycott" during all store hours, turning sympathizers away from patronizing the place. (A secondary boycott tries to halt commerce with another business that has trade with the original offending business.) From time to time, individuals went in to fill up shopping carts with goods. At the checkout counter they would ask the clerk, "Does this store advertise in the *Times?*" At that point they would exit, leaving the full shopping cart to be unloaded back on the shelves.

The store owner, his profits eroded by the secondary boycott, was persuaded to try sitting Otis down to talk with the printers. Otis could not afford to ignore one of his main sources of advertising income. He compromised, allowing a few union printers back to work—but as individuals, without a union contract. He also promised to eventually hire more union men. The printers agreed to end the strike and boycott, believing it would only be a matter of time before they could reorganize the *Times* completely.

As it turned out, they were wrong. The *Times* stayed an open shop for decades, long past Otis's death in 1917. When Otis broke his promise to hire more union members, the printers tried to resurrect the boycott. But they had been outmaneuvered. Otis had carefully signed long-term contracts with his biggest advertisers. The union's secondary boycott weapon was rendered useless.

The *Los Angeles Times* was one antilabor tool wielded by Otis. The other was the Merchants and Manufacturers Association (M&MA). Founded in 1896, within a few years the M&MA dedicated itself to the principle of keeping Los Angeles an open shop town. Otis was its leading member.

The M&MA enforced its rule over businesses in Los Angeles with a simple mechanism. No member of the association was allowed to tolerate a closed shop. If they did, the other M&MA members would refuse to do business with them. Thus, the M&MA's effectiveness was based partly in ideological antiunionism and partly on economic fear of a business boycott. Its success was a source of great happiness for Otis. For many years the association was the real economic ruler of Los Angeles.

LABOR'S RADICAL RESPONSE

But the activities of Otis and his M&MA, while generally successful in maintaining Los Angeles as an open shop town, had an unintended effect, making the local labor movement far more radical than it otherwise might have been. From the 1890s on, unions and socialists worked together more closely than anywhere else in California. In 1897 A. M. Green of the retail clerks union was elected president of the Los Angeles Council of Labor. At the same time Green served as chairman of the executive board of the Social Democracy

Party, a forerunner to the Socialist Party. Fred Wheeler, a carpenter, became president of the labor council while a leader of the Los Angeles Socialist Party. Eventually Wheeler was elected to the Los Angeles City Council (1913–1917) as a Socialist.

Not all unionists in Los Angeles in the first decade of the twentieth century were Socialists, nor did most workers even vote Socialist much of the time. But the brutality of the police in carrying out the philosophy of the Merchants and Manufacturers' Association, the often dreadful working conditions in many industries, and the antiunion laws and injunctions handed down by legislators and judges controlled by the M&MA, all gave workers good reason to consider supporting anticapitalist political alternatives such as the Socialist Party. The beginnings of socialist sympathies for Los Angeles unionists emerged out of their hard experiences with the Merchants and Manufacturers, Otis, the *Los Angeles Times,* and with one other early epic battle: the Pullman strike of 1894.

THE AMERICAN RAILWAY UNION IN CALIFORNIA

When Eugene Debs left his well-paid position as national secretary of the Brotherhood of Locomotive Firemen in 1892 he was angry. He had just witnessed the breaking of a switchmen's strike in Buffalo, New York by federal troops, while the other railroad brotherhoods stood by and offered no assistance. Debs, who had urged his fellow railroad workers against strikes during the Uprising of 1877, was now convinced that railroad workers needed a single powerful national industrial union. With a few other railroad workers, Debs launched the American Railway Union (ARU) in 1893, dedicated to the idea that all workers in the industry belonged in the same union.

Later that year in Los Angeles, Local 80 of the ARU was founded with 138 workers' signatures on its charter. Membership was kept secret, as the railroad corporations were not fond of unions. But the railroad workers were even less fond of the companies they worked for. Encouraged by a visit from Debs in spring 1894—and with workers upset by chronically late paychecks—Local 80 boasted a thousand members within six months of its origin. Strong ARU locals sprang up in Oakland and Sacramento, too. What was behind this surge of union membership?

Less than one hundred thousand railroad workers belonged to the elite craft brotherhoods, leaving most railroad workers outside their protection—

although, as Debs discovered, even that protection often didn't extend beyond craft boundaries. Debs especially wanted to include the tens of thousands of unskilled workers that the railroad brotherhoods had always disdained; but the new union also welcomed skilled craft workers who agreed with its philosophy. Eligibility requirements were loose. Practically anyone working in any job associated with a railroad could become a member. ARU dues and fees were set lower than the brotherhoods' to encourage all to join.

Almost all. Over Debs' objections, the founding convention of the ARU voted by a narrow margin to restrict membership to whites. While typical of the prejudices of white workers in the period, the decision disappointed Debs. If anything, the closeness of the vote was cause for surprise.

The ARU's idea of industrial unionism fell on fertile ground. Within weeks of its formation in 1893 the national office of the American Railway Union was swamped with applications. After just a few months of existence, the administrative problem of simply processing so many new members was made worse by a welcome complication: the ARU organized and led a successful strike of workers on the Great Northern Railroad, forcing the company to back down on wage cuts. Now the new memberships were coming in at a rate of two thousand per day. In less than a year the national ARU grew from an idea to nearly one hundred and fifty thousand men—almost as large as the entire AFL. Industrial unionism was taking hold.

THE MODEL TOWN OF PULLMAN

Across the country in Illinois, events were unfolding which were soon to shape an enormous struggle in California. Six thousand workers and their families lived in the company town of Pullman, near Chicago. George Pullman was proud of his town, home to the men who produced the luxurious sleeping cars—Pullmans—attached, for passengers who could afford it, to overnight trains. His town was considered a "model" town because it had been so carefully planned and laid out. Unfortunately, the planning was by a corporation—the Pullman Palace Car Company—intent not on its citizens' free development in a democracy but on maximizing its own profits.

The citizens of Pullman had to purchase all their food, clothing, and other necessities from company-owned stores. They rented neat, clean Pullman-owned apartments—at prices 25 percent higher than in surrounding towns. Pullman appointed all public officials and had a system of spies to ensure a proper Pullman spirit in public discussion. Pullman purchased water from the city of Chicago for four cents per gallon—and charged the workers ten cents. As one worker put it, "We are born in a Pullman house, fed from the Pullman shop, taught in the Pullman school, catechized in the Pullman church, and when we die we shall be buried in the Pullman cemetery and go to the Pullman hell."

Pullman took the occasion offered by the 1893 depression to cut wages by 25 to 40 percent, despite the company's continuing profitability. He overlooked a similar opportunity to cut prices in his stores, or rents for his houses.

Pullman workers were eligible to join the ARU. They didn't need much urging. In the spring of 1894 they organized nineteen branches of the ARU, with four thousand members. When a committee was sent to meet with Pullman to ask for a restoration of the wage cuts, he dismissed it and the next day fired three of the spokesmen. The robber baron also refused to place the dispute before an arbitrator (a neutral individual empowered to hear both sides and resolve the issue). Four thousand workers walked off the job in protest, and Pullman closed the plant, believing he could starve his employees back to work.

THE AMERICAN RAILWAY UNION
MAKES A FATEFUL DECISION

One month later the first national convention of the ARU was held in Chicago. Pullman workers called on the delegates to boycott the Pullman Palace cars. If their brother railroad workers would refuse to handle any trains that included Pullman's sleeping cars, Pullman would be forced by the railroads to negotiate with his workers. Or so the reasoning went.

Debs was not enthusiastic about placing the ARU, less than a year old, in the position of taking on all the railroads in the country at once. The union had inadequate financial resources for a battle of that magnitude, he argued. At his request, the Pullman workers went back to meet once more with their boss, who again refused arbitration. The fateful decision was made: beginning June 26, no ARU member would handle a Pullman car. The convention also voted to assess every ARU member ten cents per week to support the Pullman workers' strike fund.

The railroad companies, unimpressed, responded by deliberately ordering workers to put together trains including Pullman cars. Anyone refusing was discharged. Debs ordered workers out on strike wherever anyone was fired. The result exceeded even Debs' expectations. Within days trains in twenty-six states had come to a stop.

In California Debs brought the Southern Pacific and Santa Fe workers out on strike after the companies fired boycotting trainmen. Public support for the striking ARU members was initially high, despite some newspaper coverage—echoing the railroads' assertions—that portrayed the strikers as violent and obstructing the U.S. mails (which was sent across country by train at that time).

In fact, the ARU had offered to keep the mail flowing, so long as Pullmans were uncoupled from the trains. Notwithstanding the press distortions—particularly by the *Los Angeles Times*—most people understood it was the companies' decision to insist on running the Pullmans that was holding up their mail. One prostriker newspaper even scoffed that the lack of train service "was done in the interests of Pullman, so that by inconveniencing the public in a most distressing way sympathy may be withheld from the strikers." Otis's paper predictably editorialized that "This is not a dispute between a railroad company and its employees, but between the great masses of law-abiding citizens on the one hand and a small faction of lawless men on the other."

The level of public support for the ARU was also impressive given the hardship on farmers, dependent on timely shipping of their produce to market. The outpouring of sympathy for strikers was a measure of the depth of public hatred of the railroad corporations felt by most Californians at that time. With the exception of Chicago, where the Pullman strike began, no area of the country was more involved or public passion more inflamed than in California.

Among the least beloved of railroad personalities was Collis Huntington, the southern California member of the original Big Four Central Pacific owners. In the early days of the strike, perhaps recalling Charles Crocker's brainstorm during the Chinese workers' strike of 1867, he wrote to his nephew that one way to reassert labor peace would be to import large numbers of African Americans to replace white union members in Southern Pacific employment: "I think we should almost immediately commence getting some colored people from the South for our yard men all over our lines, doing it in a quiet way, putting a few here and a few there until the change is made."

Eventually the resources of the young American Railway Union proved, as Debs had feared, unequal to the fight against the combined power of the railroads. Owners were increasingly joined together in antilabor associations to maximize profits and coordinate actions such as wage cuts, layoffs, and blacklists industry-wide. The most important of these groups was the General Managers Association (GMA), representing twenty-four railroad companies. The GMA created the strategy for the railroads in dealing with the challenge of the Pullman strike and the ARU.

In California the web of corporate interests surrounding the railroads was mostly controlled by the owners and managers of the huge holding company, Southern Pacific, of which the original Central Pacific Railroad was now but a small part. Since 1886, the Santa Fe Railroad had also run trains across country to Los Angeles. The two railroads set aside their customary rivalry to deal with the threat to both.

Following the advice of the GMA, they prevailed upon the Los Angeles district attorney to request permission from U.S. attorney general Richard Olney to prosecute the strikers for conspiracy. Olney, a former railroad lawyer and GMA member, was pleased to grant permission. The companies then persuaded a friendly judge in Los Angeles to do two things. On June 29, he summoned a grand jury to determine whether the striking workers were guilty of conspiracy for obstructing mails and interstate commerce. And the following day he issued an injunction which directed workers to end the strike or resign.

Olney authorized sending federal troops to Los Angeles, despite the nearly complete lack of violence among the highly disciplined strikers. According to one of the soldiers, they were not enthusiastic at their assignment, "this idea of shooting down American citizens simply because they are on a strike for what they consider to be their rights. . . . All of the boys are against it from first to last, and many are in sympathy with the strikers." The heavily armed troops were deployed to escort strikebreakers, run trains, and intimidate strikers.

One of the only recorded instances of violence in Los Angeles occurred when newspaper boys, refusing to distribute the *Los Angeles Times* because of its antistriker perspective, roughed up another carrier. They were arrested and given a suspended sentence. That evening union printers from the *Herald* bought the boys dinner and, two days later, helped them organize Newsboys' Union Local 1.

A more serious incident in Sacramento helped turn public opinion against the ARU and bring the strike in California to an end. The early days of the Pullman boycott and strike in Sacramento, as in Oakland, were marked with an almost festive feeling. Huge crowds of workers and their families took over the train yards in both cities and stood off contingents of state militia. These were volunteer units filled, often, with friends and family of the strikers. Oakland, the western terminus of the transcontinental railroad, was a railroad town. It was also a union town. Fully aware of the strength of Oakland's labor movement, a city council member addressing a meeting of strikers and supporters told the crowd, "Your cause is a just one and you will win."

The ARU and its supporters were highly organized. Mrs. Thomas Roberts, spouse of an Oakland ARU leader, quickly assembled a Strikers' Sympathetic League—all women—which raised funds, produced favorable publicity, and distributed rosettes made by Eugene Debs's wife as a badge of solidarity for local women to pin to their clothing.

In Sacramento a tense confrontation between a few thousand strikers and a thousand militia men on July 4 ended, bloodlessly, with the retreat of the militia. The impressive solidarity of the workers and community was, for the moment, holding fast, and it was contagious. The *San Francisco Chronicle* reported:

> After the troops fell back from the depot this afternoon two companies were ordered to take a Gatling gun and move to the American River bridge for the purpose of guarding it from possible distruction [*sic*]. As the men had already walked a considerable distance, they were glad to avail themselves of an electric car which ran as far as Twenty Eighth street. Orders were given to hitch the gun to the rear end of the car. The conductor objected, but without avail.
>
> For the first ten blocks the streets are paved with asphalt and the gun ran without a jolt, but the motorman, who was interested in the strikers' cause, bided his time, and when the car approached Eleventh street, where the smooth pavement ends and cobblestones commence, he threw the lever to the top notch and the car sprang forward at full speed. The result was that the gun was so badly damaged that it will have to go to a machine shop for repairs.

One week later the first train left the station since the strike started. A couple miles outside the city it plunged off a trestle. Four soldiers and the engineer died, victims of sabotage: someone, presumably strikers, had pulled

FIGURE 12. American Railway Union leader and five-time Socialist Party candidate for president Eugene Debs speaks to Los Angeles crowd. Wilshire family papers, Library Special Collections, Charles E. Young Research Library, UCLA.

bolts out of the rails. Troops responded in kind. Strikers were shot in Sacramento, and in Oakland, bayoneted. Within days the strike was over.

Debs and several other national leaders of the ARU had been arrested and charged with conspiracy during the last days of the strike. His conviction, reduced to the single charge of contempt, put him in jail for a few months. Thus it was a shock when a half-dozen local ARU leaders in Los Angeles were found guilty of conspiracy, fined, and sentenced to eighteen months in prison—courtesy of the same judge who had issued the injunction against the strikers.

ARU locals, disintegrating around the country, stayed together long enough in Los Angeles to coordinate fundraising on behalf of the jailed union officers, who had appealed the decision to the Supreme Court. The rest of the Los Angeles labor movement contributed generously, and turned out in large numbers to hear Debs at a fundraiser in the spring of 1895. Although the appeal failed, the Los Angeles ARU eventually gained its leaders' release through a presidential pardon.

LESSONS OF THE PULLMAN STRIKE

Despite their defeat, Los Angeles union members came out of the Pullman strike with some important lessons. Although the events were similar in many respects to the 1877 railroad strikes, there were significant differences. The 1877 rebellion was a more or less spontaneous combination of local strikes and working-class community uprisings, loosely connected by a still-primitive telegraph communication system and the even looser national political structure of the Workingmen's Party of the United States.

Seventeen years later the newly formed ARU *organized* a national boycott of Pullman cars, leading to the lockout and subsequent coordinated strikes of up to a quarter million railroad workers. At the center—the strike's organizational backbone—stood the ARU, however reluctantly.

Few workers believed that the strike had represented a "conspiracy" by the ARU. Rather, it had become painfully clear that if a conspiracy existed, it was among the railroads and various branches of government, which combined powers to force the strikers to their knees. Many workers, having believed in the neutrality of the government in conflicts between labor and capital, were disillusioned. They saw that the money and organization of the employers far outweighed democratic principle in the actions of Attorney General Olney, who authorized the conspiracy arrests and trials, and President Grover Cleveland, who ordered federal troops to aid the railroads.

They also saw that the Sherman Anti-Trust Act of 1890, meant to protect citizens against excessive corporate power, could be twisted by judges into its opposite. Thus the legal tool of the "injunction"—which gave judges power to issue orders to "cease and desist"—was used to curtail union activities because they were deemed harmful to the corporations.

As a result of the Pullman strike, Los Angeles unions emerged from their isolation from the rest of the country's labor movement. In the face of nationally organized employers assisted by national structures of government, the assistance of nationally based unions and union federations seemed necessary and inevitable. Before the strike was over, the Los Angeles Council of Labor voted to affiliate with the national AFL.

The unique experience of Los Angeles unionists, involved with the Council of Labor, often put them at odds with their national parent body. Nowhere was this more true than in politics. The national AFL, led by Samuel Gompers, a former cigar-maker, asserted the need for labor to stay out of party politics. Gompers, in a famous formulation, urged AFL members to "reward our friends and punish our enemies," without regard to party affiliation. But in Los Angeles, the severe conditions imposed by the Merchants and Manufacturers Association on the ability of workers to organize led unionists to eventually conclude that only political affiliation could help them.

9

Land, Machines, and Farm Labor

LAND OWNERSHIP AND LARGE-SCALE AGRICULTURE

In the late nineteenth century California developed into one of the great food-producing states. Already in 1870, agricultural income surpassed gold mining. Land ownership patterns inherited from the prestatehood period meant that huge farms with thousands of acres made up a higher percentage of cultivated land than in any other part of the United States outside the south. The large estates and California's climate created perfect conditions for a new type of gold rush: the bonanza wheat farms. Growing wheat on the vast tracts of former Spanish and Mexican land grants made the same kind of sense for their new American owners as raising cattle had for the Californios.

From the late 1850s, wheat production steadily increased until it peaked around 1890, when California ranked second in the nation. Author Edwin Markham recalled, "Ten thousand acres was the average of the great farms, and many reached up to fifty thousand acres. The floor of the great central valley became an emerald sheen in winter, a golden sea in spring, and a tawny vastness after the time of the harvest."

At the same time that large holdings dominated planting and production, land speculators trafficked in smaller portions of the old rancho properties. Newcomers bought the fertile but undeveloped lands in convenient parcels for a few dollars per acre. Those who could not afford to buy farmland rented until they could make enough money to purchase it.

Alongside the huge wheat farms, smaller fruit and vegetable farms gradually made inroads into the agricultural economy. Fruit, in fact, occupied the largest sector under cultivation by the end of the 1880s, with more than twenty-five million trees in orchards by 1900. The boosters dubbed California "the fruit basket of the nation," and their advertisements were true. Before 1900 grapes (for winemaking) and cherries, plums, peaches, pears, and apricots had made their entrance as major crops. In the new century citrus orchards soon took the leading spot in acreage.

Three decades earlier, immigrant journalist Charles Nordhoff had foretold the reasons for the extraordinary productiveness of his adopted state's fruit farms. Calling southern California "the Italy of this continent," he boasted that "we have in our favor a climate which experience has now proved to be peculiarly adapted to these trees; the soil which they require; a region so healthful and pleasant that life in it is a pleasure; and our trees, so far, seem secure from any serious disease."

Behind the fine words, an industrial model of agriculture was taking root. For limited periods during the year the highly profitable wheat farms required large numbers of migrant laborers, or as they later came to be known, "bindlestiffs" ("bindle" for the bundle of clothes, bedding, and gear they carried on their backs; "stiff" as slang for worker). While the rest of the state sank into the Great Depression of the 1870s, wheat remained one of the few industries providing steady—if low paying—seasonal employment. But when the work ended, the migrants were expected to hit the road again.

Outside observers and some farmers themselves viewed the development of large-scale industrial agriculture in California with alarm. At a time when the majority of Americans still lived on farms, these critics wondered how the ideals of the republic and Jeffersonian democracy could survive if free yeoman farmers were no longer the backbone of the nation, and instead were replaced by a system featuring a shuffling mass of transient workers, moving from one vast farm to the next, owned by the relative few. Social critic Henry George condemned the enormous California wheat farms and the ruthless, corrupt, and lucrative land speculation that made them possible.

Influenced by George's analysis of the evils of monopoly landownership, Frank Norris in his novel *The Octopus* denounced the Southern Pacific Railroad, the state's largest owner of real estate. *The Octopus* also contained a more direct and detailed description of the changing face of California agriculture than had yet appeared in fiction. Norris's novel devoted long passages to the lives of farm laborers and to the complex work processes they performed.

A prolonged movement rippled from team to team, disengaging in its passage a multitude of sounds—the click of buckles, the creak of straining leather, the subdued clash of machinery, the cracking of whips, the deep breathing of nearly four hundred horses, the abrupt commands and cries of the drivers, and, last of all, the prolonged, soothing murmur of the thick brown earth turning steadily from the multitude of advancing shears.... From time to time the gang in which Vanamee worked halted on the signal from foreman or overseer.... For the moment, one of the ploughs was out of order, a bolt had slipped, a lever refused to work, or a machine had become immobilised in heavy ground, or a horse had lamed himself. Once, even, toward noon, an entire plough was taken out of the line, so out of gear that a messenger had to be sent to the division forge to summon the machinist.

On the biggest farms, the need for planting and harvesting enormous stretches of earth resulted in a high degree of mechanization. Combines (so-called because they "combined" different tools and types of work into a continuous, mechanical process) were pulled by horses during the first decades and powered by steam later on. They were expensive but made more money for their owners than they cost.

Mechanization reduced the time and amount of human labor needed to produce each bushel of wheat. On the ranch of Hugh Glenn (after whom Glenn County was named) his use of combines in 1882 resulted in a reduction of per acre costs from $3 to $1.75 and eliminated many members of the traditional threshing crew. Overall, however, combines probably didn't reduce the number of workers employed in California agriculture. That's because machinery made possible expansion of the number of acres under cultivation. In turn, the need for human beings to perform the work of driving, threshing, plowing, binding, and other types of farm labor continued to increase as well.

The combines also enlarged another harvest: the bloody crop of injuries and deaths of the farmworkers who ran them. The farm laborer's day was not an easy one under any circumstances. They had reason to complain of the physically hard work and, like any outdoor worker, sweated in the summer and froze in the winter. But it got worse. A wheat thresher around 1880 succinctly summarized some of the problems: "Oh, we were always scratching. We ate burned beef. We drank filthy water. Our bunkhouses were crowded. Sometimes we lived with the chickens and the cows. We were always dirty. We never had any money. We stank to hell."

A daunting array of more serious hazards faced the wheat farm laborer. Working with animals and machinery, often from dawn to dusk, farm laborers suffered diseases originating with poor sanitation, cuts and bruises prone to infection, heat-related illnesses, and injury and death as body parts were pierced or severed by the exposed sharp parts of the combines. Far too common were incidents such as the one that took the life of Dominic Deveney, who on a Colusa County farm in 1876 "was struck by a derrick fork and thrown into the separator feet foremost. Both legs were torn off and Deveney died the following day."

Although spontaneous acts of collective resistance by farm laborers dated back to the mission era, few nineteenth-century workers actively or consciously organized against these conditions. The occasional strike did occur. But with no union tradition in the fields to guide them, farm laborers tended instead to vote with their feet: workers simply left employers when the pay was too low, food or living quarters intolerable, or dangers too great to bear.

An exception, near the beginning of the industrial era, occurred one night near Livermore in 1869. After a demonstration of a combine's capabilities earlier that day, farmhands fearful for their future employment possibilities burned the machine and the wheat it had threshed. Another moment of retaliation left combine-using Hugh Glenn dead at the hands of one of his employees, who had disagreed with the wheat farmer's practice of taking 10 percent off his workers' paychecks for the "service" of giving them cash instead of making them ride seventy miles to Sacramento to his bank.

Neither murder nor isolated acts of industrial sabotage could stem advancing farm technologies, make the work safer, or improve pay. And the economic depression raging in the cities in the 1870s ensured that the pool of labor in the countryside remained large enough to supply the wheat farmers' needs and keep down the price the workers could demand for their services.

THE ROLE OF THE FARM LABORER

Expanding rapidly, California agriculture had a voracious appetite for two types of labor: the relatively small workforce of permanent "hands," and a large army—the bigger the better, as far as the growers were concerned—of temporary, seasonal workers.

The year-round employees were mostly white, although cooks, between 1870 and 1910, were often Chinese, and Mexican American workers, particularly in southern California, were employed year-round too. Some had lived

FIGURE 13. Family members and friends, year-round workers at the Maulhardt ranch in Ventura County. Personal collection of author.

in the area with their families for decades, knew the land and sometimes the people who had bought their own land from them.

The year-round farmhands maintained machinery, took care of animals, and often were treated like "one of the family" of their employer, eating in the kitchen and socializing with their boss and his family. Depending on the size of the farm or ranch, the permanent farmhands might live in the farmhouse or in a place of their own. On the twelve-hundred-acre Pleasanton Hop Company ranch, it took thirty permanent workers to tend the vines and keep the equipment in working order.

On the large farms and ranches, migrant workers arrived at the moments of high demand in agriculture—the planting and harvesting. Depending on the crop, they stayed for weeks or months while the crop matured. More than a thousand migrant workers swelled the Pleasanton Hop Company's employment rolls each August to bring in the crop. With sugar beets, the fields also needed blocking and thinning throughout the spring.

The migrant laborers confronted a wide, usually dismal, variety of living arrangements. They might find themselves in rough bunkhouses away from the farmhouse and eat in a separate facility or outdoors. On the larger beet farms, like that belonging to Claus Spreckels in Salinas, the living and eating buildings were segregated by race. These might be made of wood or canvas tents. Especially where nonwhite farmworkers predominated, ethnic labor contractors often provided housing and board to their countrymen. Sometimes seasonal workers were put up with the animals in the barn. Other ranches might offer nothing more than a place for the bindleman to roll out his blanket outdoors.

White migrant laborers usually traveled alone, or with two or three buddies who tramped the roads in search of work together. Tramp life was often a lonely one, marked by a sense of isolation and alienation from the more prosperous people with whom they came into contact, which was virtually anybody who wasn't a migrant farm laborer.

Due to labor contracting systems set up by the immigrant Chinese community, and later by Japanese contractors, migrant workers of color did not often travel individually across the farm districts of California. But they felt a double exclusion from society, on the margins of the majority white culture and distant as well from the dynamic commercial urban world of San Francisco and other growing cities of the Golden State.

A song written by one migrant laborer captured their outsider status:

> They'll work you eight hours and eight hour more.
> You'll sleep in a bunkhouse without any door.
> They'll feed you on mutton, sow-belly and sheep.
> And dock you for half of the time that you sleep.
> Twenty-four hours through sunshine and rain.
> Or your blankets you'll roll on the San Joaquin plains.

The gulf between the lives of seasonal and permanent farmworkers was visible away from work in their leisure pursuits, the places they lived, what they aspired to. A white year-round farmhand might eventually find a way to own a farm himself. Better paid than the migrants, and with room and board taken care of, the hand could carefully put away money. Time away from work could be spent reading, going to revival shows, dancing, courting, or playing a musical instrument. Following the introduction of hand-held cameras in 1900, a number became "shutterbugs," unintentionally creating visual records of rural working-class life when nearly no one else was doing so. After a decade or two, if no disasters befell them to eat up their precious savings, or if they managed not to drink or gamble it away, it was possible to move up: to purchase some land of their own to farm, or perhaps move to a city to own a home or open a business.

While never a majority of the farm labor workforce in California, Chinese immigrants, for a time, predominated in several important crops and provided the bulk of workers in some counties. Growers praised them for their sober and industrious habits, much as Charles Crocker had for their work on the Central Pacific Railroad, and for doing work that white men preferred not to at wages whites refused to accept. Between 1860 and 1890 Chinese farmworkers assisted in the beginning of many specialty crops, enabling important sectors of California agriculture to get started. They also contributed the hard labor for numerous heavy rural construction projects, and became famous for their tolerable cooking in an occupation better known for its hazard to palate and health alike.

In Sonoma one hundred Chinese were working for pioneering winemaker Agoston Haraszthy as early as 1857, and their role in the development of that county's wine industry cannot be overestimated. They cleared the land and put hundreds of thousands of grape vines into the ground for their employer. They pruned the plants, picked the grapes, dug wine cellars, constructed press houses, and worked the vats. Haraszthy kept careful notes on their speed at these tasks, and their work rates and wages became the industry standards. Hired by other wine grape growers in the area as well, by 1869 the Chinese had planted most of the area's 3.2 million vines, in the process helping Sonoma to rival Los Angeles as the state's premier wine growing center.

Sixty miles east, Chinese work gangs in the Sacramento delta drained the swamps and built the levees that allowed agriculture to arise from water and marshes. To say the words "drain the swamps" gives no inkling of the enormous labors involved nor the dangers in doing so in the nineteenth century. In 1869 land speculator George Roberts contracted with "China bosses" (Chinese labor suppliers) to hire hundreds of laborers—many just released from constructing the transcontinental railroad—and put them to work on Twitchell Island, 3,600 acres of peat bog, tangled vegetation, and dense forest.

As with the building of the pyramids thousands of years earlier, the massive levees rose slowly, block by block. At least the Chinese laborers had wheelbarrows, which they rolled up plank ramps constructed as they built the levees higher and higher, adding floodgates and other water control mechanisms.

It was filthy, backbreaking work, much of it spent waist-deep in muck. And it was deadly. No one kept count of how many workers died on Twitchell

Island, or elsewhere across the delta as Chinese labor pushed back the waters so that farmland might be created out of swamp. The mosquitoes swarmed so thickly that supposedly they could put out a candle's flame. Malaria and dysentery claimed their victims, as did drowning and a great variety of other work accidents.

After levees ringed the island, the workers moved to the interior to prepare the land for farming. First they cleared the ground of its dense stands of tules. The most efficient way of doing this was burning, but the highly flammable peat below the surface often caught fire along with the plants, leaving unquenchable smoldering fires until the rainy season. To solve the problem of tule roots running beneath the surface, the Chinese workers invented "tule busters," plows equipped with sharp knives, which they had to pull through the peat several times before the land was arable. Within three years, the formerly inhospitable island sprouted wheat and vegetables on more than a thousand acres.

For the next quarter century, Chinese farm laborers exhibited the same qualities of perseverance and ingenuity in crop after crop across the state. As the Native American population died off and the remainder was pushed into reservations, the Chinese worked alongside their dwindling numbers and replaced them as the largest nonwhite farm labor group. Admired by growers for their hard work and comparatively low wages, they came to be viewed as essential to California's farms. The minister in charge of the Methodist church in San Francisco's Chinatown argued in 1877, "If we had not the Chinese, our famous fruit ranches would be turned back into pasture grounds."

The successes and prominence of the Chinese in agricultural labor represented a two-edged sword. Favored by the growers, in hard economic times they attracted the angry attention of racists and unemployed white workers seeking an explanation for their troubles. Why were the "Celestials" able to find work when none was available for white men? By the late 1870s the Chinese exclusion movement reached the fields and villages. Until the beginning of the twentieth century, Chinese workers suffered from a systemic racism that, in its legal form, produced a series of laws choking off immigration. On the streets of the urban centers, and flaring periodically in the countryside, a violent white mob culture rivaled that in the Jim Crow southern United States of the period, replete with lynchings, the forced removal of entire Chinatown populations, and other types of organized mayhem.

The Chinese population in California slowly declined from its peak of around one hundred thousand after the early 1880s. This meant trouble for

FIGURE 14. Chinese immigrant workers, released from railroad employment, found their way to farms and ranches in the central and coastal valleys. Personal collection of author.

growers. Defenders of employing Chinese labor such as John Bidwell faced arson and boycotts of his commodities. After several of his buildings had been torched, he was forced to release his remaining Chinese workers in 1886. But the central problem of large-scale California agriculture now reasserted itself: who would do the seasonal work of planting and harvesting the crops?

Under severe political pressure, growers attempted to replace the Chinese with various schemes, few of which proved successful. These included importing African American laborers from the rural southern United States, workers from southern European countries, and, closer at hand, children from schools near their farms and ranches. A few farmers even began to hire Native Americans once more. But the pay was too low, the conditions too hard, and the numbers of the Chinese too great to replace them by such piecemeal methods.

The future solution sought by the growers to California's farm labor problem was right across the border. But the time had not yet arrived for Mexican farm labor. There were but eight thousand Mexican-born residents of California in 1900, and perhaps that many more of Mexican ancestry. This was nowhere near a large enough population to offset the loss of the Chinese, although it worked for some southern California farms. Oddly, the effect of the anti-Chinese movement was to replace one Asian immigrant farm labor group with another.

THE JAPANESE FARM LABORER

In the early 1890s Japanese laborers began to arrive in large numbers in California. Most were under twenty-five years old when they landed in San Francisco, and saw their stay as temporary. The great adventure for a young Japanese male in the early twentieth century was to come to America and make enough money to return and buy land in Japan. They came, like the Chinese before them, from a rural culture in flux and turmoil. Some had been field hands in Japan, roving the countryside with labor contractors. So while the American experience was exotic, the industrial landscape wasn't completely unfamiliar to them.

Japanese farmworkers seemed like the answer to California growers' prayers. They were well organized. Contractors, who were often educated and spoke English, took care of negotiating wage rates and securing room and board for their workers. They astonished the white farmers with the productivity of their crews. Their labor quickly came to dominate certain crops and various geographic areas across the state.

The role of the contractors, or *keiyaku-nin,* was key to the Japanese laborers' success. They were ruthlessly competitive and able to draw on strong bonds of ethnic solidarity in their workforce in an often hostile American rural culture. They also carefully watched and learned from the China bosses, who in the 1890s, as the numbers of their countrymen declined, occasionally took advantage of labor shortages by staging walkouts in order to boost their share of the harvest.

By 1896 more than eight thousand Japanese worked in the farm labor contracting system. They underbid Chinese and white labor, and seemed to turn up ready to work just as the first signs of trouble arose between other crews and their employers. As the new century dawned, Japan Towns—also called "Little Tokyos"—were popping up across California, often nearby or replacing the Chinatowns that had preceded them. In Los Angeles alone there were ninety-two Japanese boardinghouses in 1907.

On the weekends, or in between work, the Japanese laborers traveled from their camps on the ranches and farms to relax in the Japan Towns. They had good reason. Conditions in the contractors' bunkhouses and farm labor camps ranged from rudimentary to abusive. The contractors either prepared food cheaply or provided it for the workers to cook themselves. But they ran their establishments like little ethnic company towns, selling the men other necessities at inflated prices. Isolated from American culture, many workers didn't know the difference. Various fees cut into their pay. Sometimes contractors ran off with the entire payroll for a large job, leaving the workers stranded and penniless.

In contrast to the migrant camps in the fields, the Little Tokyos were more comfortable and offered a sense of community, with amenities like bath houses, pool halls, red light districts, and gambling houses, along with restaurants, laundries, and banks. Gambling especially was a widespread recreational choice for these young workingmen far from home.

As the Chinese work force shrank, the Japanese moved in, occasionally sparking interethnic conflict. Newspapers reported arguments and fistfights between Japanese and Chinese farmworkers and delighted in recounting battles between the two groups. But communication between the older and newer immigrants wasn't always so poor. In the spring of 1891, a shortage of workers in the Vacaville fruit orchards encouraged the Japanese to demand a fifteen cent per hour raise, and the Chinese workers went out on strike alongside them. (The strike proved unsuccessful when the growers imported white strikebreakers from Sacramento.)

At its peak in 1909, Japanese farm labor furnished the bulk of agricultural workers on the large farms in the state, and dominated the field in berries, grapes, vegetable cutting, asparagus, and sugar beets. The 30,000 Japanese workers represented over 40 percent of the total farm labor force.

Few, however, worked on the giant wheat farms, where decades of tradition and a declining market share created local cultures of racist exclusion.

From the outset, the Japanese workers, led by their contractors, demonstrated militancy, and a keen understanding of the timing and tactics necessary to control the farm labor supply. Most of the time these actions did not represent class consciousness or a desire to join with other workers in the service of a broader social vision, such as the Knights of Labor had espoused in their late-nineteenth-century "cooperative commonwealth." The Japanese immigrant farmworkers organized, withheld their labor at strategic moments, demanded written contracts, formed unions, and bargained collectively with their employers. But they generally did so within a practical picture of what worked in order to gain power over their situation. The goal was to make more money and then either to return to Japan with it or to lease or buy land and take advantage of economic opportunities in the United States.

Within this arrangement, the contractors wore many hats. Leaders of their expatriate communities, they functioned as travel hosts, labor brokers, commissioned salesmen, real estate agents, owners of company stores, and when the occasion demanded it, union leaders.

10

The Oxnard Sugar Beet Workers Strike

All honor to the martyrdom of Luis Vasquez!—the first man to
lay down his life for his mates in the town of Oxnard.

JOHN MURRAY

FOR A FEW MONTHS IN 1903 in the little town of Oxnard, California,
about halfway between Los Angeles and Santa Barbara in Ventura County,
a sugar beet workers' strike captured the attention of the newspapers. On
March 24, the day following headlines of "Union Riots in Oxnard," Los
Angeles Labor Council activist John Murray took a train to the farm town
sixty miles north of his home. He verified from his conversations with eye-
witnesses that something resembling a Wild West shootout had indeed taken
place. But contrary to the newspapers' coverage, Murray found that union
members had been the victims, not the perpetrators, of attacks caused by the
owners of the large sugar beet farms and carried out by hired thugs.

To understand the distance between the news and the truth in these
events, it helps to recall the example of *Los Angeles Times* publisher Harrison
Gray Otis, and remember who owned the newspapers, and how and why they
slanted their stories about workers and the labor movement. But first it might
be useful to know something about sugar.

THE ECONOMIC HISTORY OF SUGAR

Sugar is one of the most common household items. It's cheap. No well-
equipped kitchen lacks a five- or ten-pound bag of it. Each American con-
sumes, on average, a hundred pounds of sugar per year. But its harmless
appearance, inexpensive price, and sweet taste hide a history only hinted at
by the nickname applied to it in the seventeenth century: white gold. For
several centuries, sugar was one essential corner of a triangular world trade
system that also featured slavery and rum.

European slave traders brought rum—distilled molasses, itself a byproduct of sugar production—to Africa. In the eighteenth century, slave merchants could purchase an African adult for about 120 gallons of rum, and a child for 80 gallons. Hundreds of thousands of slaves were brought to sugarcane plantations in the New World, where they produced sugar for Europe's ravenous sweet tooth, and more molasses, which was distilled into rum, to be traded for more slaves.

Inspired by the French and American revolutions, the half-million sugar plantation slaves of St. Domingue (later Haiti) overthrew their French colonial masters in 1791 with an armed revolt, and abolished slavery early in the nineteenth century, establishing the first free black republic in the world. Slowly the rest of the European sugar producers moved from a slave-based workforce to wage labor. It wasn't until 1888 that the last link between slaves and sugar production was broken when Brazil outlawed slavery.

The unchanging dark secret hidden within the clean white crystals is that sugar has always been the product of extensive amounts of cheap labor. Mindful of what happened to their French competitors in Haiti, the British rulers of Guyana in the West Indies, after abolition of slavery in 1838, imported three thousand contract laborers per year from India to ensure a steady supply of workers and, not coincidentally, to divide the workforce between Africans and Indians and thereby make it more difficult for them to organize resistance to the plantation owners. Large numbers of unorganized workers and low wages made and kept sugar cheap and profitable.

SUGAR IN CALIFORNIA

Three-quarters of world sugar production originates in cane fields. Yet in the United States today, nearly as much sugar is grown and processed from beets as from cane. This was also true a century ago.

In California, sugar beets were not cultivated in quite the same quantities as orchard fruits and occupied fewer acres than wheat. But in the 1890s sugar beets came to dominate agricultural production across large regions of Ventura County in the south and Salinas Valley to the north. Beets, requiring a more temperate climate than sugar cane, thrived in the soil of the cool coastal valleys.

Sugar beets had been a significant California crop since 1870, when a refinery arose in Alvarado, near today's Union City. A few years later, travel writer and California booster Charles Nordhoff, paid by the Central Pacific Railroad to write *California for Travellers and Settlers,* enumerated the reasons why it made more sense to raise beets than wheat. Beet farming was more efficient. Unlike the grain, beets didn't wear out the land. Livestock near the Sacramento sugar works he visited were fattened on beet pulp (mixed with hay and molasses) left over from refining.

Best of all, beets were lucrative. "As population increases in California, I see no reason to doubt that beet sugar-making will become one of the most profitable and one of the most important industries in the state." True to Nordhoff's prediction, by 1900, of the thirty-five beet sugar factories in the United States, the two largest and newest refineries were to be found in California.

Claus Spreckels was known as the "sugar king" due to his control over most of the sugar production in the western United States. Encouraged by passage of higher import tariffs on European sugar by Congress in 1897, the king quickly expanded his empire. That year Spreckels bought up thousands of acres in the Salinas Valley on behalf of his Western Beet Sugar Company. He paid for building the largest beet sugar refinery in the world, Factory Number 1, which opened in 1899 near Salinas, in the company town of Spreckels. Factory Number 1 soon processed one-quarter of all beets in California.

To feed the factory, growers in the Pajaro and Salinas valleys cultivated tens of thousands of acres of sugar beets. Some owned their land. But Spreckels also leased his land in ten- and twenty-acre parcels to tenant farmers, who, guaranteed an annual buyer for their crop, obligingly planted beets.

Their success was made possible by the labor provided by Japanese contractors like Sakuko Kimura. Based in Watsonville, Kimura saw the trend toward sugar beet production in the surrounding farmlands. Alongside his general labor contracting business, he began to specialize in sugar beet labor. China bosses had been contracting their workers for $1.25 per ton of sugar beets; Kimura undercut them by bidding seventy-five cents per ton, although he raised his price to one dollar as soon as he secured the work.

A couple hundred miles south, the Oxnard brothers, who already owned one sugar processing plant in Chino, put up capital for construction of another in Ventura County. It began production the year before Spreckels's Factory Number 1. It soon employed hundreds of workers, importing skilled engineers and mechanics from Germany's advanced sugar beet mills, and scooping up laborers from the surrounding rural landscape. Nearly the entire population of Port Hueneme relocated. A number of families put their modest homes on wheels and moved them closer to the factory, glad to be making twenty cents an hour for steady, if often dangerous, work indoors.

In gratitude for their prosperity and good fortune, farmers and merchants near the factory named the little town forming around it "Oxnard," a designation already in use before incorporation in June 1903. As in Salinas, farmers in the area rapidly converted their land to beet growing. Within a few years, the Oxnards' American Beet Sugar Company was nearly as productive as the operation owned by Spreckels, purchasing two hundred thousand tons of beets from Oxnard growers by 1903 and sending one-sixth of California's sugar into the market.

CULTURE AND WORK

Oxnard, like Salinas, was part company town, part crossroads trade and distribution center for the surrounding farms and their products. With their main industry consolidating, the owners and managers of the town's businesses soon had comfortable houses and enjoyed a modest set of "proper" social activities on the west side of Oxnard. A private club served the needs of the middle-class merchants and professionals in their evening hours, providing reading and smoking rooms and facilities for parties and dining.

Working-class cultural options amounted to the stuff of the frontier—not as wild and lawless as Los Angeles in 1870, but not exactly genteel, either, chiefly consisting of gambling, drinking, shooting pool, dancing, and other affordable diversions that helped workers to forget the work they did for too little money and too much time. Japanese and Mexican laborers brought to Oxnard to tend the beet fields and other crops lived outside town or rented rooms on the east side, where their numbers quickly outgrew the bustling but modestly sized Chinatown and Sonoratown. They slept in crowded boardinghouses near their recreational facilities and the storefronts of labor contractors from their own countries who, for a fee, found them work. The massive brick sugar beet factory, with its two giant smokestacks towering above the town, was never long out of sight or mind.

Work in the beet fields was not for the frail, faint hearted, or very many white men. The work demanded intensive labor stooped closely over the ground. The plants grew quickly, and once their shoots had been sent through the soil, they needed to be blocked, thinned and hoed, all by hand. Blocking involved pulling out sections of plants from the field, leaving a foot or so between clumps of the largest ones. Thinning required removing most of the clump. Soon afterward, workers had to cut away weeds with short handled hoes, and repeat the process. These labors occurred over two months in spring, much of it performed by workers on their knees.

Harvesting was even more physically demanding, and with a sharp beet knife, wielded by the worker for long hours, using the same motions countless times in a day, hazardous. The sugar beet had to be stabbed through the ground, lifted out, separated from the rest of the plant, and piled alongside the rows for the loaders to stack in wagons.

Sugar beet work did not appeal to many white bindlestiffs. An effort in early 1899 to recruit local white laborers for beet thinning ended quickly and unsuccessfully. Instead, Oxnard farmers had to rely on contractors to supply seasonal immigrant workers for the more labor-intensive moments of cultivation. The first years of beet production around Salinas and Oxnard coincided with large-scale Japanese immigration.

As a result, Japanese labor contractors in Oxnard did well for themselves from 1899 to 1901. Sakuko Kimura found his prospects there superior to Watsonville, and moved his business south. Other *keiyaku-nin,* like Kosaburo "Joe" Baba and San Francisco-based Y. Yamaguchi, made a good living as the go-betweens for their countrymen and the Oxnard sugar beet industry's need for efficient seasonal labor. The contractors' storefronts were busy with the comings and goings of workers—around a thousand of them—dispatched to the fields and collecting their pay.

THE FORMATION OF THE WESTERN AGRICULTURAL CONTRACTING COMPANY

Their prosperity wasn't popular with everyone. Early in 1902 the largest beet growers, officials of the American Beet Sugar Company, presidents of the town's banks, and other leading citizens formed the Western Agricultural Contracting Company (WACC) in an effort to force the ethnic contractors out of business. The previous year had seen a wave of job actions by Japanese farm labor crews in other agricultural districts around the state. An economic boom in the urban centers had emptied farm districts of white laborers eager to find nonagricultural work, creating an opening for the Japanese contractors to drive up wages. The formation of WACC represented a preemptive move by Oxnard business leaders against what they saw as too much control by Japanese contractors over the price of labor in the fields, and who were eager to keep "their" casual labor force that way in Ventura County.

WACC opened an employer-controlled hiring hall. It advertised to beet growers, and sent its recruiters around the state to hire and bring back workers. It built camps to house more than six hundred Japanese and Mexican beet thinners. Its workers ended up harvesting half the beet crop in 1902. In December, its president declared WACC's intent to eliminate the remaining ethnic contractors entirely and consolidate control over sugar beet labor.

They almost succeeded. But the WACC overreached. In January 1903, it lowered the rate paid per acre for beet thinning and required its workers to pay fees to itself and to subcontractors for the privilege of employment in the fields. Angered, several dozen Japanese field hands, including students recruited from San Francisco, accused growers of lying to them about the rates, demanded a return to the terms under which they had been recruited, and said they would be willing to strike if their terms were not met. WACC refused to negotiate. The response of the Japanese workers, led by *keiyaku-nin* Kosaburo Baba and Y. Yamaguchi, was to form a union.

THE JAPANESE-MEXICAN LABOR ALLIANCE

Exactly what kind of a union the Japanese-Mexican Labor Alliance (JMLA) was has been the subject of scholarly dispute over the years. Certainly the reasons given by Yamaguchi for organizing, in a letter published by the *Oxnard Courier*, sound like those of any labor leader of the period:

> Many of us have families, were born in the country, and are lawfully seeking to protect the only property that we have—our labor. It is just as necessary

for the welfare of the valley that we get a decent living wage, as it is that the machines in the great sugar factory be properly oiled—if the machine stops, the wealth of the valley stops, and likewise if the laborers are not given a decent wage, they too must stop work and the whole people of this country suffer with them.

But the relationship between the labor contractors and the men they represented differed from typical unions. The contractors' role as leaders in the Japanese immigrant worker community, and as liaison with the surrounding American culture, meant that they had to call upon a range of tactics to deliver workers to the employers and employment to their men. Unions were on one extreme end of this range, and not necessarily the favored choice.

The Japanese contractors were also different because of how dependent the workers were on them for jobs, bonds that were reinforced by the immigrants' isolation in American culture through the language barrier and unfamiliarity with customs. This could and did lead in some instances to severe forms of exploitation of the workers by their countrymen. But the contractors' interests and the welfare of the workers they represented certainly overlapped. On occasion, this led to concerted militant action.

Sugar beet workers, with contractors taking a lead role in the meeting, founded their union on February 11, 1903. The workers wanted four things to happen. They wanted the Western Agriculture Contracting Company to pay the rates it had promised them. They wanted the fees rescinded. They demanded that they be paid in money, not company scrip, which was redeemable only at certain stores that charged them inflated prices. And they wanted WACC to withdraw from the contracting business in favor of the Mexican and Japanese contractors who had been displaced.

Colonel J. A. Driffill, a friend of Robert Oxnard and former official at the Oxnards' Chino refinery, was appointed spokesman for the employers' group, including the growers and American Beet Sugar Company. He told Yamaguchi,

> I have heard that you have a scale of prices which is detrimental to the interests of the farmers, and the interest of the farmers are our interests, because if you raise the price of labor to the farmers and they cannot raise beets at a profit, we will have to take steps to drive you out of the country and secure help from the outside—even if we have to spend $100,000 in doing so.

With neither side prepared to back down, the stage was set for a confrontation.

Kosaburo Baba was elected president, and Yamaguchi secretary of the Japanese-Mexican Labor Alliance. Yamaguchi, a capable organizer, pulled together meetings and parades and brought hundreds of workers into the fledgling organization. So effective was he that Oxnard sheriff Edmund McMartin thought it necessary to "quiet troubled spirits" by throwing him in jail, charged with inciting a riot. But he was tried and acquitted two days later.

Despite the impressive growth of the union, it could not have succeeded if it were limited to Japanese workers, comprising three-quarters of the farm labor force. Another 20 percent were Mexican, or claimed Mexican ancestry, and some Chinese still worked the beet fields, although probably no more than 5 percent of the total. The WACC had hired a Mexican contractor to bring in laborers from his community, and a few hundred were employed in WACC-run fields.

Enter two men from Los Angeles. Fred Wheeler was in his mid-thirties in 1903, a carpenter, seasoned union organizer, and Socialist activist. Soon after arriving in Los Angeles from Florida in 1892, he had been elected president of his Carpenters Union local, and served two terms as president of the Los Angeles Labor Council in the late 1890s. At the time of the Oxnard strike, Wheeler was working as state organizer for the new California State Labor Federation, affiliated with the American Federation of Labor. He was one major reason why Los Angeles labor was experiencing a spurt of growth.

Accompanied by John Murray, another Socialist active in Los Angeles's labor council, Wheeler took the train sixty miles north to Oxnard and helped the Japanese union leaders meet with Mexican labor contractors in the area, resulting in the formation of the Japanese-Mexican Labor Alliance. The JMLA elected J. M. Lizarras secretary of its Mexican section and sent him to organize in Sonoratown. A contractor himself, he was able to deliver his own workers to the JMLA. But as a member of the local Mexicano community, he could tap his social connections with other contractors, many of whom, like Lizarras, were prominent civic leaders. Soon several hundred Mexican workers swelled the ranks of the union.

On February 28, sugar beet workers began to leave the fields on strike. Holding trilingual meetings every evening, Yamaguchi and Lizarras discussed the union's issues with field hands in Japanese and Spanish, with English pro-

FIGURE 15. Japanese and Mexican sugar beet workers formed the first union in California's fields in Oxnard in 1903. Bill Rodgers, photo. Personal collection of author.

viding a bridge when necessary. The union's insignia—a pair of clasped hands across a red rising sun—appeared on buttons and signs everywhere. Within a week an estimated 90 percent of the workforce, or twelve hundred laborers, had stopped working for the WACC. On March 6, a Saturday, the workers marched en masse through Oxnard. The *Oxnard Courier*'s account: "Dusky skinned Japanese and Mexicans march through the streets headed by one or two former minor contractors and beet laborers four abreast and several hundred strong. They are a silent grim band of fellows, most of them young and belonging to the lower class of Japanese and Mexicans."

The *Courier* agreed with the *Ventura Daily Democrat* that the workers were incapable of understanding the bigger economic picture, and agitators and anarchists were primarily responsible for stirring up violent sentiments. It was expected that the strike would soon collapse.

ORGANIZING THE STRIKE

While the mostly white merchant community in Oxnard was inclined to oppose unionization and job actions by the farm labor population, they faced a problem as the strike wore on: striking workers had no money to spend in their stores. The shopkeepers had been angered by the WACC's plan to pay the sugar beet workers in scrip, which was no good in most stores. The arrogance of WACC unintentionally built sympathy for the workers among the town merchants.

Community support was but one weapon at the disposal of the JMLA. The workers knew their labor was increasingly necessary as the thinning season advanced. Encouraged by this leverage, the union quickly matured, becoming a highly organized and disciplined operation. It distributed food and medical assistance to its members' families, coordinated legal defense of arrested leaders and activists, and ran all aspects of a strike that resembled a military campaign in its complexity.

JMLA leaders stayed on top of all these matters. The union leadership efficiently kept picket lines running, and provided security patrols for its members against attacks by armed scabs. The JMLA also staged continuous demonstrations of solidarity, and informed the community of the workers' perspective through meetings and letters to the local newspapers.

The growers, under increasing pressure as the seasonal clock ticked, agreed to meet with the union in a public meeting on March 21. J. M. Lizarras and Fred Wheeler spoke on behalf of the strikers, and Colonel Driffill represented the employers, before a hall full of beet workers and contractors, with an uneasy minority of farmers and American Beet Sugar Company officials seated amongst them. Despite a lengthy discussion, no agreements were reached.

The following day, Lizarras and Yamaguchi were arrested while speaking at a street gathering, and the growers announced formation of a company union, run by Japanese contractors. Few if any JMLA members joined.

Meanwhile the WACC attempted to recruit more workers from Los Angeles and San Francisco. The company paid their railroad fare to Oxnard. But like the San Francisco iron molders who, during their 1864 strike, learned of their employers' long-distance scab recruitment and shipped organizers to meet and reason with them, the JMLA sent groups of strikers up the tracks. They boarded the train along the way, and as one newspaper reported, "by the time these men reached Oxnard they were on the side of the union."

SHOOTOUT IN OXNARD

In late 1903 the Edison Company released *The Great Train Robbery,* a melodramatic movie set in the Wild West, featuring a band of masked cutthroats on horseback who rob the passengers on a train. After fleeing with their loot, they are chased by a posse and, in a hail of bullets, meet their just reward.

The Great Train Robbery and other early so-called Western films portrayed a type of frontier life that was rough, violent, and—to the extent that it existed—largely gone by the time working-class audiences experienced it vicariously in the saloons and storefronts exhibiting these entertainments in the opening years of the twentieth century. But the potential for such explosions of violence hadn't entirely disappeared, especially in small western towns that combined large, temporary populations of migrant workers (many of whom carried sidearms) with employers who failed to understand the need to treat their workers with basic human dignity—towns such as Oxnard on March 23, 1903.

On this morning, sugar beet grower Henry Fraho expected a wagon full of scab workers and supplies sent by WACC to arrive at his farm in nearby Port Hueneme. Fraho had publicly signaled his intention to hire strikebreakers two days previously. Hearing of the wagon rolling out from WACC's boardinghouse in Chinatown, a crowd of JMLA men quickly gathered around it. During the scuffle that followed, someone ran out of the WACC building with a shotgun. JMLA member Perfecto Olgas wrestled it away from him. Another armed WACC employee emerged from the WACC building, shot Olgas in the neck, and continued to fire at JMLA members, who produced their own weapons and fired back. Others from both sides—including beet farmer Charles Arnold, who had been deputized the day before—joined in the battle, getting off more than fifty shots.

Before order was restored by the Ventura County sheriff, five men had been wounded. Despite the carnage, union leaders kept relatively cool heads. As John Murray reported, "They pursued and captured the fleeing Arnold and, after disarming him, handed him over to the police. Sheriff McMartin himself told me that if it were not for the protection afforded by the union leaders, Arnold would have been hung on the spot."

Within days JMLA member Luis Vasquez died of his gunshot wounds. Murray described what happened next.

> Nearly a thousand men escorted the body to its grave. Japanese and Mexicans, side by side, dumb through lack of a common speech, yet eloquent in expressions of fraternity, marched with uncovered heads through the streets of Oxnard. On the hearse was a strange symbol to Western eyes, a huge lotus flower—an offering from the Japanese union.

Fearful that the outrage and anger among JMLA members would result in bodily harm to them, few workers answered the WACC's calls to work in the fields. When negotiations continued to stall, Lizarras threatened to transport JMLA members outside the area to find work. Around the same time, the Japanese consul in San Francisco, alarmed at the potential for further violence, called to remove his striking countrymen from the region in order to calm things down.

WACC had reached the end of the line. Expenses were mounting for the employers, who were paying a small army of armed men to protect their farms and factory. With thinning season upon them, the sugar beet farmers had to get workers back into the fields. WACC agreed to withdraw its contracts from all but one farm. Since the farm, the Patterson Ranch, was owned by the American Beet Sugar Company, that seemed a reasonable compromise to the JMLA. The strike ended with farmers agreeing to employ their workers through the Japanese and Mexican contractors associated with the JMLA. They also agreed to restore wage rates to the level in place before WACC lowered them. Over the next several months the JMLA's contractor-leaders were able to enforce these negotiated terms, and labor peace reigned in Oxnard.

FROM THE JAWS OF VICTORY

Soon after the JMLA's victory over the WACC in Oxnard, the union renamed itself the Sugar Beet and Farm Laborers' Union (SBFLU). Heartened by the support it had received from Wheeler, Murray, and the Los Angeles Labor Council, J. M. Lizarras wrote to AFL president Sam Gompers, applying for membership in the national labor federation.

No doubt aware of the AFL's exclusionist policies and Gompers's racist attitudes, Lizarras and the other Oxnard union leaders nonetheless had good reason to hope their application for the SBFLU would be accepted. Under Wheeler and Murray's prodding, the AFL-affiliated Los Angeles Labor Council had passed a resolution in late March in support of the Oxnard struggle, and for organizing farmworkers without regard to "race or national distinction." The resolution balanced the high principle of labor solidarity with the practical necessity of organizing all workers so that some groups could not be recruited as scabs against others.

Despite the sound logic of the council's official position, the AFL was not ready for such a sea change. Gompers's response indicated his willingness to grant a charter to the SBFLU on one non-negotiable condition: "Your union will under no circumstance accept membership of any Chinese or Japanese." Lizarras, writing back on behalf of the SBFLU leadership—and explicitly for the Mexican section—rejected Gompers's proposal:

In the past we have counseled, fought and lived on very short rations with our Japanese brothers, and toiled with them in the fields, and they have been uniformly kind and considerate. We would be false to them and to ourselves and to the cause of unionism if we accepted privileges for ourselves which are not accorded to them.

The dispute reverberated for a few months during local and national AFL meetings and in the labor press. But Gompers's mainstream AFL point of view easily prevailed over Wheeler and Murray's apostate Socialist perspective. The leader of the Sailors Union of the Pacific, Andrew Furuseth, no doubt spoke for the majority when he said, "We are in favor of Japanese being organized and Chinese being organized, but we want them organized in Japan or China, not in the United States."

The Oxnard sugar beet workers' union did not long survive this exchange. It was difficult enough to maintain a union of any kind in California agriculture, let alone one created by two groups that did not speak one another's language, consisting of seasonal laborers, many of whom might be hundreds of miles away when the next crop ripened. The harsh unfairness of the WACC had united the sugar beet workers of Oxnard, and the social skills of the Japanese and Mexican contractors allowed the hot anger of the field hands to forge a collective capable of sustained action.

When the WACC dissolved, much of what held the migrant labor union together evaporated along with it. The union also lost an important leader when Y. Yamaguchi left Oxnard for Japan in mid-April to attend to his ailing father. As new migrant farm laborers, unaware of what had occurred, floated into Oxnard over the summer, and many of those who had taught themselves about power during the strike drifted away to work elsewhere in California's fields, the critical elements necessary to keep the union going no longer existed.

SUCCESS, FOR A MOMENT

We don't know exactly what finally happened to the JMLA/SBFLU, or to most of its principal actors in this historical drama. When labor peace returned to the sugar beet fields of Oxnard, its everyday events no longer qualified as "news." And the lives of the workers receded into the shadows in which they usually dwell, so far as the commercial mass media are concerned.

Precisely when the union stopped meeting, and whether there were any efforts to renew it or not, and whether any of the officers and activists of the JMLA went on to union activism elsewhere, must have proven less exciting stories from the point of view of selling newspapers, for they remained unreported.

But we do know this. People who were "impossible" to organize organized themselves. The common interests of working people became more important, for a time, than the differences that customarily divide them. For the first time, two groups of workers, speaking different languages, from different countries, came together to show that farmworkers could form a union in California's fields, go on strike, and force, albeit temporarily, a successful conclusion to their battle with their employers. Entirely sweet their victory may not have been. But like sugar, for a moment it tasted good.

PART III

From Pride of Craft to Industrial Unionism

11

Building San Francisco

SAN FRANCISCO IN TRANSITION

San Francisco at the beginning of the twentieth century was the largest city on the West Coast. A third of a million people lived within the boundaries of the hilly peninsula framed by ocean and bay on three sides. Most of the land had been built on, the stretches of sand dune, marsh, and pasture that had greeted the Forty-niners fifty years earlier now filling in.

Each day countless drivers rumbled through the crowded business district, tugging at the reins of coaches and wagons pulled by teams of horses, moving goods to and from the waterfront and between warehouses and stores and homes. Passenger vehicles, invisibly clamped to moving cables beneath the city's streets, whirred past storefronts and pedestrians. A San Francisco fixture for a quarter century, the cable cars carried their passengers up the steep hills that challenged the muscles of even the sturdiest horses.

But now the cables were facing growing competition. Drivers guided newfangled electric streetcars over Market Street's cobblestones, powered by overhead trolleys attached to a maze of wires. The electric streetcar lines boasted nearly half the cars in the city by 1902. Most were owned by the United Railroads (URR) corporation.

The streetcar system was appreciated by the public, because the extension of track throughout San Francisco made it easier for workers to live outside the industrial districts in more comfortable neighborhoods, and helped housewives, students, and retail customers to get around. The private company that owned URR was another matter, seen as too powerful, and occasionally the subject of public ownership conversion discussions.

Streetcar drivers and conductors faced the challenge of navigating their enormous vehicles safely through traffic while remaining polite and informative with their human cargo. We can glimpse what the occupants experienced at rush hour through these verses, popular in San Francisco around 1900:

> Never full! Pack 'em in!
> Move up, fat man, squeeze in, thin.
> Trunks, valises, boxes, bundles,
> Fill up gaps as on she tumbles.
> Market baskets without number
> Owners easy nod in slumber.
> Thirty seated, forty standing,
> A dozen more on either landing. . . .
> Toes are trod on, hats are smashed,
> Dresses soiled, hoop-skirts crashed.
> Thieves are busy, bent on plunder,
> Still we rattle on like thunder.
> Packed together, unwashed bodies,
> Bathed in fumes of whiskey toddies;
> Tobacco, garlic, cheese and beer,
> Perfume the heated atmosphere.

In an era of widespread public drunkenness, the task of driving often competed with maintaining order on the car. Officially the job of the conductor, peacekeeping sometimes drew drivers into the fray. Small-scale worker protests over safety, hours of employment, and wages frequently interrupted service. On occasion—for instance, for a week in April 1902—anger boiled over into full-blown strikes. Through actions such as these the drivers built their carmen's union—the Amalgamated Association of Street and Electric Railway Employees of America Local 205—into a strong advocate for its two thousand members.

Most of the streetcar lines terminated at the foot of Market Street, before the sandstone clock tower that soared 235 feet above the busy Ferry Building fronting the bay. On either side of the structure, graceful clipper ships rode at anchor along the endless wharves. Here, on the edge of the wide Embarcadero, sails and men rested between West Coast voyages and longer journeys across the seas. Squat steam schooners looked even uglier when seen side by side with the elegant sailing ships. But their numbers were increasing while the day of the windjammer was fading.

The bustling port, one of the world's largest in terms of cargo tonnage and length of its waterfront, employed fifteen thousand workers daily to bring in its vessels, offload the passengers and goods from finger piers poking into the bay, and transport them elsewhere in the city. One in twenty adult San Francisco males worked for the waterfront in 1910. This doesn't include the various services that provided food, clothing, shelter, cleaning, and other types of maintenance in a maritime hub city.

One service that had flourished on the docks since the Gold Rush was detested by the very people it supposedly helped. "Crimps" were individuals who supplied sailors to ship captains and found the newly arrived maritime worker a place to lodge until the next time he shipped out. All too often, the boardinghouse ran an efficient mechanism to "help" the sailor run up debts through large quantities of alcohol served with (or without) his meals in the lower floor saloon. The crimps were parasitic go-betweens, serving captain and boardinghouse owner well, and keeping the sailor locked into a system outside his control. They thrived in a nasty underground economy that employed hundreds of thugs and crooks who, during labor conflict, moonlighted as scabs.

Scores of boardinghouses were jammed along the Embarcadero among bars, restaurants, and cheap hotels. Many rested on wooden piles over the waters of the bay, leaving room for small boats to maneuver beneath. The worst of the boardinghouses were equipped with well-designed trap doors imperceptibly traced on the saloon floor. Here the crimp practiced the notorious art of "shanghaiing." The unsuspecting sailor, offered or sold a drink, would not know it contained knockout drugs. After falling unconscious, he would be dropped through the trap door to a small boat riding on the waters beneath the boardinghouse and then rowed to a waiting ship. He would be well outside the Golden Gate before he awakened.

Small wonder that the Sailors Union of the Pacific (SUP), based on the San Francisco waterfront since its founding in 1891 but operating in all major West Coast ports, made continuous efforts to set up its own hiring halls to give sailors an alternative to the crimping system. The union also waged legislative battles to make the involuntary servitude of maritime workers at sea illegal. More powerful business forces and their political allies had prevented these changes from taking place in the late nineteenth century. But as the SUP gained strength, it drew public attention to such abuses, and began to make friends among politicians interested in addressing such problems.

Although unionism was gaining favor among transportation and maritime workers, the building trades' wages, working conditions, and power were the envy of all. Carpenters Local 22 headed a federation of construction worker unions so influential that one contemporary writer, examining its position in San Francisco economic and political life, claimed that in this city "unionism holds undisputed sway."

This observation remained far from true, even in the labor movement's building trades' stronghold. But in the first fifteen years of the twentieth century these workers did manage to achieve a level of control over their work lives—the pace of the work, its methods, its compensation—rare since the onset of the industrial age.

Proud of their accomplishments, construction workers could (and often still do) take friends and family over to a building and say, "I built this." In 1900, San Francisco's buildings were something to be especially proud of. The rows of Victorian houses in the city's residential neighborhoods and the commercial and public buildings lining Market Street and other major thoroughfares were well made and pleasing to the eye.

Yet, the carpenters and their union leaders were under pressure to exchange their traditional skills and the time it took to craft that ornamental beauty for a more hurried, standardized industrial style of production. In place of the all-around mechanic who could do virtually every job on the construction site well, contractors pushed to reduce jobs into repetitious tasks like floor laying or window hanging. Construction trades unionists found themselves in a rearguard action to preserve a work culture that was doomed but worth fighting for.

In short, San Francisco in 1900 was a city in transition. Behind the ornate façade of the Gilded Age bubbled a deepening class struggle, brewing faster than the suds in the city's South of Market beer factories.

INSTITUTIONAL POWER

From its beginnings, isolated from the rest of the country, San Francisco offered favorable advantages to workers. Labor was scarce. Workers found they could talk with one another, organize a union, and gain a better deal from their employer. Although people came from all over the planet to seek their fortune, once mining receded in importance in the broader economy, the overwhelming majority of workers came from just a few European countries and, unlike workers in the eastern United States divided by language and custom, they could talk with one another about their shared economic needs.

Out of these circumstances quickly emerged institutions of working-class power: unions, eight-hour leagues, central labor bodies, and political parties. While most came and went with changes in the economic winds, their chronic renewal and presence over a half century created a culture of worker militancy and solidarity that survived the demise of individual organizations.

Then, inside one decade, San Francisco workers created four permanent labor coalitions: the San Francisco Labor Council (1892), the San Francisco Building Trades Council (1896), and the California State Federation of Labor and the State Building and Construction Trades Council (both in 1901). Each organization immediately played major roles in improving workers' lives, and all continue to do so more than a century later. What allowed this array of institutional power to finally emerge?

There had been lean years for unions in the 1890s. Economic depression and a repressive political atmosphere in the wake of the Haymarket affair of 1886 led many workers across the nation to consider individual solutions to their problems more prudent than the risk of collective action. Nonetheless, Frank Roney and other San Francisco immigrant labor leaders helped to keep the flame of unionism alive. Roney founded and led the Federated Trades Council, a forerunner to the San Francisco Labor Council. In his own industry, he helped forge the Iron Trades Council, which promptly struck the Union Iron Works, San Francisco's premier shipyard, in support of a protest by boilermakers against the hiring of nonunion men. This display of solidarity failed when the largest metal trades firms formed an employers association and provided financial support to the Union Iron Works, which was then able to import strikebreakers from the East Coast.

A more successful local outcome emerged from the assault by a new national brewery employers' association on the union shop. In San Francisco, close to a thousand workers labored in beer manufacturing. Most of these workers were German immigrants who had imported their craft skills with them. They carried a left-wing prejudice against unions, viewing such organizations as obstacles on the road to socialism, when workers would own the means of production. Unions (they reasoned), by offering workers better conditions under the existing capitalist system, would slow down and perhaps entirely block the development of socialist ideas among working people.

One immigrant who disagreed with this perspective was Alfred Fuhrman. At fifteen he left Solingen, Germany and became a sailor, making his home in San Francisco in 1880. He helped organize the Coast Seaman's Union in 1885, a predecessor to the Sailors' Union of the Pacific. He was serving as a delegate to the Federated Trades Council when his fellow immigrants in the breweries asked him to aid them. His organizing skills, combined with the example of other unions' successes and the dire conditions of the brewery workers, resulted in the formation of the Brewers and Maltsters Union of the West Coast, which soon became Local 16 of a new national brewery workers' union.

According to Fuhrman's later recollection, the beer workers badly needed organizing. They worked sixteen to eighteen hours a day and were forced to live in the breweries, where they were provided with food and drink but had to pay for the privilege out of their wages of fifteen dollars per week.

> The men were compelled to turn out at 4 o'clock in the morning, the usual time being from 4 to 5. When I first addressed the men at Turn Verein Hall, about two-thirds of the men were drunk, and the balance were asleep. I found that owing to the fact that these men were compelled to work early in the morning without having any breakfast, and naturally, being compelled to work at the beer business, they drank beer, and it happened many times that the men were drunk in the forenoon; that they were, in fact, drunk before they had eaten breakfast.

Fuhrman organized a strike for union recognition, and gained an agreement granting a ten-hour day and a six-day week (for the same wages the workers had received previously for working many more hours), a union shop, freedom for the brewery workers to live where they pleased, neutral dispute resolution, and ... free beer. When the national brewery employers association attempted to roll back the union shop, Local 16, under Fuhrman's leadership, struck first one brewery, and then four more. It called for a boycott of the offending companies' beer. So many of San Francisco's workers observed the boycott that the city's saloons stopped ordering those brands, and eventually the companies gave in and agreed to call off their antiunion campaign.

The outcome of such battles often hinged on the relative ability of the workers and employers to mobilize support. The boilermakers at Union Iron Works lost because the employers were better organized than the new Iron Trades Council; the brewery workers won because they could draw on the support of both their national union, which provided strike benefits and publicity for their cause, and the Federated Trades Council, which spread the word about the beer boycott to its affiliated unions and their members.

In the construction industry employer cooperation mostly didn't exist. Contractors underbid one another for jobs, amassed insufficient capital to support growth into large corporations, and in general fought one another as much as they did the organizations formed by their workers. This was one key to the success of the Building Trades Council (BTC). But the other was the hard work of union leaders, who had learned to set aside ideological differences—Socialists, anarchists, Populists, Knights of Labor proponents, and AFL pure and simple unionists—in order to build their institution of working-class power.

By the late 1890s, an economic upturn gave a boost to union organizing throughout the country. It's easier to organize when jobs are plentiful. Workers will more easily risk their livelihood if they are confident of being able to find another paycheck. But even before the recession lifted workers were rebuilding their organizations.

In 1895 carpenters laid the foundation for the Building Trades Council. Enrolling a couple thousand workers, representing about five out of every six carpenters, three locals jointly issued a union card to each member in good standing, and notified the contractors that from then on, they should expect to observe the eight-hour day, with time and a half for overtime, and the union shop on every job site. No employer, the unions emphasized, should hire a carpenter without a card. Enforcement took the form of the carpenters walking off jobs that failed to live up to these expectations.

Painters began an organizing drive later that year, inspired by the carpenters' success. Having signed up seven hundred members, they were growing, but not yet in as good a position as the carpenters, and the master painters had a strong employers association on their side. Nonetheless, the painters copied the working-card idea from the carpenters and, hoping to receive reciprocal treatment, voted to walk off any job struck by the carpenters. They also urged other construction crafts to join in creating a council.

In February carpenters and painters came together with unions from several other construction trades to form the Building Trades Council. The new organization boasted four thousand members at the start. After a two-week strike by painters in March achieved a wage increase, eight-hour day, and union shop in only a few workplaces, delegates to the council rethought its strategy.

They voted to replace the separate craft union cards with a single BTC working card. This innovation meant that each union needed to pay attention to the conditions of the other workers, not just its own, and not just when other workers asked for help; it built cross-union solidarity into union membership in any craft. It also placed a great deal of leverage in the hands of council leaders, consolidating their ability to call out all workers on a job site when any were being treated unfairly.

The BTC working card became its main organizing tool. With the power to stop a job in its tracks, the council expanded until it included every construction union in San Francisco. The working-card system was not welcomed enthusiastically by all employers. Strikes called by "walking delegates" showed the contractors the logic of the situation.

Within three years practically every construction job site was a union shop. Within five, the three dozen BTC unions had increased their dues-paying membership to fifteen thousand. By 1905 council secretary Olaf Tveitmoe reported that "there was nothing more to organize" in San Francisco's building industry—an exaggeration, but not by much.

So strong was the BTC that unlike most labor organizations it disdained collective bargaining. BTC official Olaf Tveitmoe expressed a view—closer to that of the Industrial Workers of the World's than a traditional AFL position—that contracts were like "shackles by which the workers have locked their own hands and through which they have repeatedly signed away the only right they have—the right to quit work when and where they please." In place of the often lengthy contract negotiations between representatives of workers and bosses at a table, the BTC had a remarkably simple approach to adjusting wages, hours, and working conditions: it announced that as of a certain upcoming date, a twenty-five cent raise would be in effect. And for more than two decades, that's how it happened.

THE RANK AND FILE CARPENTER: GEORGE FARRIS

What that institutional power meant for the daily lives of individual members of the BTC may be gleaned from the diary of carpenter George Farris. As with the journal of Frank Roney, the survival of Farris's reflections is a rarity for manual workers in this era.

Farris spent his childhood in Iowa. He was raised in the Methodist church. Moving to California at the age of fourteen in 1867, he worked as a farm laborer in Yolo County. He enjoyed traveling by boat and train in the area. On one visit in 1879 to Woodland, Farris heard Denis Kearney speak, "along with a circus and theatrical troupe." Farris was not very interested in politics to begin with, and Kearney's violent style of rhetoric put him off: "We did not stop long to hear Kearney as his language did not suit our fastidious tastes but went to the theatre to see *Pinafore*."

After more than a decade during which he developed various skills, including carpentry, on a number of farms near Sacramento, Farris moved to San Francisco in the early 1880s. He soon joined Carpenters Local 22, and remained a member at least until 1910 when his diaries stop.

Farris attended union meetings, but also those of the Good Templar lodge. He made enough money at his trade to dabble in the stock market, favoring mining stocks. He had musical talent, playing the zither in his leisure hours. He dated women, but remained unmarried.

His entries of 1902 let us know that he was inconvenienced by a paycheck that was two weeks late, that he attended a carpenters' picnic, and that he did not drink alcohol. He took pride in his craft, and his diaries are full of references such as this one: "The wind last night blew down a two story building on Sacramento Street that was nearly ready for the lathers. Our building stood the wind all right."

Not a union activist, nonetheless he stopped by the union hall to sharpen his tools on its "electric grinder" and to pick up a white straw hat to wear in the 1902 Labor Day parade. According to Farris, "The parade was splendid; the papers said it was the largest ever seen in San Francisco; it took two hours and 40 minutes to pass a given point." He also reported on the issues discussed in Local 22 meetings he attended, including vote totals and attendance, which often ranged over a thousand members.

Farris, although suffering bouts of unemployment typical for the seasonal work of carpentry, could afford small investments and to indulge his love of theater. He continued to travel to the countryside surrounding the Bay Area for recreation. He owned a nice gold watch but lived in a residence hotel. He frequently mentioned minor injuries on the job. And occasionally his loneliness as a bachelor surfaces: "The store windows are filling up with Christmas presents—I am afraid I will not get many."

Farris's diary illustrates the advances for craft workers since Roney's 1875 journal entries. The precarious status of a skilled iron molder—his union barely holding on to its existence during an economic depression—contrasts with the general confidence expressed by Farris that he will continue to make a decent living and be able to afford modest amusements in his leisure time, thanks to his Local 22 membership, BTC working card, and the eight-hour day they represented.

THE BUILDING TRADES COUNCIL LEADER:
P. H. MCCARTHY

The man responsible for running the organizations that supported Farris and his fellow BTC members was, like many San Francisco union leaders, an immigrant. Patrick Henry McCarthy was orphaned in County Limerick, Ireland, at the age of eight in 1871. Working a few years later as a carpenter's apprentice on a Catholic church, he felt that the priest's order to work overtime was unfair and led the crew in a short strike. The young worker had found his niche.

Joining Carpenters Local 22 on his arrival in 1886, McCarthy soon led the union. He was a large man with an impressive moustache. His dominating personality helped him organize workers and argue with business and civic leaders with equal success. Elected head of the Building Trades Council in 1898, McCarthy demanded loyalty from his lieutenants and absolute obedience to the council's work card rule. While he fully understood the power of construction trades unity, his sense of solidarity did not extend to the rest of the labor movement—except when he wanted it to.

For years McCarthy ordered the BTC to hold Labor Day parades separate from the labor council's and fought bitterly with renegade carpenter union locals that wanted, against McCarthy's wishes, to maintain memberships in both central labor bodies. (George Farris' diary refers often to the heated discussion of these disputes at Local 22 meetings.) But when he ran for mayor, and needed the support of a united labor movement, dual membership seemed a good idea.

A pragmatic man, he advocated fiercely for his members' interests but drew the line whenever he felt the workers' demands would compromise the ability of the contractors to make a profit. He believed his ability to deliver the goods for the holders of the BTC working card depended on the health of the construction industry, and part of his effectiveness was in knowing just how hard he could push the employers.

BUILDING TRADES COUNCIL TACTICS AND POWER

The event that consolidated the BTC's control over construction employment for nearly a quarter of a century occurred in 1900. Carpenters and machinists working in planing mills south of Market Street had struck several times for the eight-hour day in the previous decade but could not over-

FIGURE 16. Irish immigrant, San Francisco Building Trades Council leader, and mayor Patrick Henry McCarthy. Labor Archives and Research Center, San Francisco State University.

come the mill owners' determined resistance. Despite the highly competitive nature of wood finishing, the owners of two dozen small mills agreed to stand together, maintaining that their margin of profit was so slim that they could not afford an eight-hour day when their rural competition ran nine and ten hours. Organized in the Planing Mill Owners Association (PMOA) they thought their doors, windows, molding, and other products were so essential that the contractors would back them in holding the line against the union.

In February 1900 McCarthy announced that the members of the mill-men's union, beginning in August, would enjoy the eight-hour day. The mill owners disagreed, and by the deadline, they had locked their workers out of all but two of the area's planing mills. In response, the BTC extracted a pledge from dozens of contractors not to use materials from the mills that had locked out its members. BTC officials and members also went from one construction site to the next collecting the mills' products; wagonfuls were returned to their origins.

To keep construction moving, the BTC granted exemptions to the few eight-hour mills: they could operate around the clock, including holidays. The nine-hour PMOA mills offered high wages to mill men willing to scab. The strike ground on in a virtual stalemate until late September, when a creative solution broke the logjam. With the BTC's support, the millmen's union built a small shop to compete with the locked-out mills.

When it proved successful, the BTC quickly raised funds from its affiliates, as well as the national carpenters' union, and by December built a new state-of-the-art mill south of Market Street. The second biggest wood finishing shop in the state, Progressive Planing Mill Number One employed one hundred workers. Facing its competition, and potential bankruptcy, several PMOA mills reopened on an eight-hour basis.

Eventually, the mill employers association agreed to arbitrate. The decision found middle ground on a number of issues. It allowed mill men who had scabbed to return to work alongside the locked-out union members and excluded foremen from the eight-hour day. It stated that BTC members on construction sites would handle only the products of mills that employed eight-hour union labor—a win-win, since it guaranteed purchasers for the PMOA's products. It extended the deadline with a phased-in implementation of the eight-hour day. But on the central issue there was no compromise; by September 1901, all planing mills were eight-hour mills.

Thus the Building Trades Council achieved, through a convincing campaign, its dominance over the industry, including closed shop status on virtually every building site. Each worker needed a BTC-issued union card to work. Each contractor needed to hire union workers and use only union-made materials to build. These simple rules were efficiently enforced: deviations were punished either by a hearing before the BTC executive board, which would hand down decisions like a court, including fines (donated to charity) or suspensions for contractors or, more directly, brief but effective work stoppages.

The BTC's strength, and its generally careful use of that power, ensured mostly harmonious relations with the contractors and continuous work for its members. Over two decades, only a couple BTC-sanctioned strikes lasted longer than a week. From time to time, however, it was forced to demonstrate why agreement with its principles made sound business sense. When McCarthy found that a contractor running a job building a large downtown bank had decided to cast a fancy conference room ceiling in an outside workshop, instead of employing plasterers on site to do it, he pulled all the plasterers off the job and called a meeting with the employer. The contractor threatened to import outside plasterers. The next thing the contractor knew, every worker from every trade on the job—hundreds of card-carrying BTC members—took an unscheduled holiday. The following day BTC plasterers began work on the ceiling on site.

Viewed as arrogance or dictatorship by the business community, at times the BTC's institutional power could degenerate to that. But in most circumstances McCarthy and the Building Trades Council were at pains to make sure they didn't kill the goose that laid the golden egg. From 1896 to the post–World War I era, the system generally worked to the advantage not only of San Francisco's unionized building trades workforce—people like George Farris—but on behalf of the businessmen who made their living from construction as well.

Organizing San Francisco

THE CITY FRONT STRIKE

The night before the great San Francisco earthquake of 1906, sailors and longshoremen drank, talked, and dreamt of the sea in the bars and boardinghouses along the Embarcadero. Their employers, and workers who could afford it, applauded Enrico Caruso's vocal efforts at the Opera House. A short walk away tired immigrants packed themselves into storefront theaters for silent moving pictures, near the growing Italian community in North Beach, or sauntered down to the Barbary Coast for the consumption of less genteel amusements. None imagined the natural calamity that would, within hours, overtake them. But five years previous, a few keen social observers might have predicted a man-made cataclysm gathering beneath the city's surface.

Below Market Street—"south of the slot," as Jack London put it in his short story of that name—teemed the city's Irish, German, and Scandinavian workers in their shabby neighborhoods, one sulphur match away from fiery oblivion in their densely populated tenements. Scattered among the working-class residences and industrial shops, hundreds of establishments served liquor and beer, most of which arrived via horse and wagon driven by teamsters. The drivers had formed a union in August 1900. Through a master agreement with the drayage employers association, the union kept its members' working hours down to a mere twelve per day, with overtime pay for more.

If that deal doesn't sound so special, bear in mind it was attractive enough to sign up twelve hundred members in less than two months. For good reason: before the contract was inked, building materials teamsters received $1.75 for working fourteen or more hours, and many were forced to live in

FIGURE 17. International Brotherhood of Teamsters leader Mike Casey (center, pouring) and friends at union picnic. Labor Archives and Research Center, San Francisco State University.

flea-ridden boardinghouses run by the big contractors as a condition of employment.

The draymens' association of owners realized that a standard, citywide contract would help to regulate the cutthroat competition in their transportation business. Following some brief job actions, the employers signed, and harmony smiled on their industry. But the following year they locked out teamsters who had refused—in accordance with the terms of their contract—to work alongside nonunion drivers. The owners of the drayage companies, who had begun to accept the stability of the union shop, reversed field at the command of a newly formed, secretive but well-funded Employers Association determined to rid San Francisco of its growing union blight. The association, led anonymously by large business interests, planned to pick off the swelling unions one by one before they grew too strong.

In response to the lockout of this relatively small group, Teamster leader Mike Casey—an Irish immigrant, like much of his membership—called out the entire union. Tall, muscular, a blue-eyed father of six, Casey was forty years old but looked older from a lifetime of moving horses and freight. He knew that a defeat in one corner of the new union's jurisdiction would quickly ignite a wholesale rebellion by the other draymen. His action shut down building sites and factories dependent on teamsters' deliveries around the Bay Area.

The team drivers were not alone on strike. Metal tradesmen in fourteen unions had "hit the bricks" in spring to keep their nine-hour day. Machinists and their allies in the other metal trades—boilermakers, blacksmiths, molders, and apprentices—shuttered shipyards, foundries, and other businesses in the southeast industrial districts.

A thousand restaurant workers seeking a ten-hour day, six-day week, and union shop were also parading in front of their employers' businesses; another couple hundred bakery workers had struck in sympathy. The teamsters found plenty of support among the city's workers wherever they went.

This included building trades craftsmen. The rank and file members of the construction trades, no stranger to conflict with employers, felt an instinctive bond with striking workers, and understood what it meant to their ability to feed and clothe their families when they decided to walk off the job. The officers of the BTC, however, followed P. H. McCarthy's lead in disdaining any official gestures of support for unskilled workers attempting to organize.

When the Employers Association proved disinterested in mediation between the draymen and the teamsters, Casey took his case to the San Francisco Labor Council. The council leaders wanted to clearly demonstrate their solidarity of purpose to the employers association. At the same time, they were anxious to avoid a confrontation, head to head, of the city's recently energized labor movement with the most powerful employers in the business community. They were also concerned that middle-class public empathy stay with the city's labor movement—a difficult proposition, given the growing numbers of workers on strike.

The council proposed direct negotiations between the Draymen's Association and the teamsters. This was intended to make clear to the public that the interference of the Employers Association had caused an unnecessary conflict.

The Employers Association refused to consider the council's proposal, and rejected another idea that council officers meet with representatives of the employers' group. Casey, his patience at an end, asked for approval of a sympathy strike by unions in the recently organized City Front Federation of waterfront unions, amounting to a more or less general strike of economic activity relating to shipping.

There was much debate among union leaders over what kind of impact this would have on other trades, and especially the employment of the council's members in retail businesses, as well as on the overall economy of the city. At a long meeting on July 29, the council's unions authorized a strike of the port by fourteen waterfront labor organizations.

As these deliberations were occurring, thousands of members of the waterfront unions awaited word in gatherings around town. The scene at the San Francisco Athletic Club, host to two thousand teamsters, was typical. After midnight, Casey appeared and told his members the council's decision. As reported the next day,

> A scene of the wildest enthusiasm ensued. Cheer after cheer was given. Since the inception of the strike the teamsters have been compelled to fight the merchants and bosses single-handed, and it was generally admitted that the strikers would be ignominiously defeated unless other unions rendered immediate assistance. Thus the men had come to look on the City Front Federation, embracing the strongest combination of united labor on the Pacific Coast, as their most desirable ally.

The man chosen to coordinate the strike action was Sailors Union of the Pacific leader Andrew Furuseth. Born in Norway in 1854, Furuseth became fluent in several languages as a result of his voyages from the age of nineteen. He went to sea at a time when most vessels were sailing ships, and most West Coast sailors were, like him, northern European immigrants. He left a British ship and made San Francisco his home port in 1880.

Furuseth detested the slave-like working conditions at sea and the degraded position of sailors in society. In Furuseth the AFL philosophy of craft unionism was raised to the level of religion. "It is skill," he said once, "that puts the mechanic nearest the gods."

A simmering rage at that contrast between skills and social standing turned Furuseth into a founding member of the Coast Seamen's Union, which became the Sailors' Union of the Pacific. The craggy-faced seaman's oratorical talents soon became legendary. By the turn of the century he was a respected labor leader in San Francisco and a moral authority whose eloquent voice on behalf of sailors was beginning to be heard in the legislative corridors of Washington, D.C. As the City Front strike began he warned, "Every man is determined and the sooner the association appreciates this the better it will be for them and the business interests of this city and vicinity. All the talk has been done. This is action."

Over 15,000 workers were on strike by early August. The port was tightly shut down, with scores of ships riding at anchor in the bay and unable to deliver their goods. Half the city's business ground to a stop. For a week the situation remained peaceful. At first Mayor James Phelan resisted employer demands that he authorize police and deputize thugs to ride shotgun with scab drivers. Phelan told the Chamber of Commerce, "I must say that up to date the workingmen of San Francisco have acted with moderation and with prudence which becomes citizens of a free country whose privileges they understand and appreciate."

During the Teamsters' strike in July more than half the city's police had already been assigned to fulltime strikebreaker protection. Now the mayor, under enormous pressure from the city's businesses, turned a deaf ear to the argument by unionists that the police should at least remain neutral and instead increased their numbers during the City Front strike escalation. Rank and file workers, along with their leaders, became infuriated with His Honor.

Daily physical battles soon raged between strikers and the police and special "deputies" drawn from the ranks of crimps and vacationing University of California football players. The streets along the waterfront and south of Market erupted into fistfights and gun battles at the appearance of wagons driven by scabs or strikebreakers walking to and from the docks. Furuseth pleaded with the strikers to remain nonviolent in the face of provocations by the strikebreakers: "Turn yourself into martyrs, suffer any indignity, but don't permit them to draw you into any violence."

Despite Furuseth's plea, the mayhem, and the strike, alternately sputtered and exploded for ten weeks. Several combatants were killed, and hundreds injured. Maneuvering for position, the unions opened a restaurant to feed strikers, raised funds from workers across the country, and in time-honored San Francisco labor tradition, sent members on trains to meet scabs and convince them to join the union cause.

Neither Furuseth's powers of persuasion nor the strikers massed along the Embarcadero were able to crack the Employers Association's determination to break the power of San Francisco's workers. On the other hand, the employers couldn't dissolve the spirit of the strikers nor help normal business to resume. And that's where things stuck until October 2, when California governor Henry Gage arranged a truce.

Both sides claimed victory. But the unions, thwarting the central goal of the Employers Association, endured. Their survival had been made possible by intense union organizing in the workplace and the solidarity and bravery of thousands of workers. Their resulting economic strength taught the Employers Association that they could not lightly take on the task of making San Francisco over as an open shop town.

UNION LABOR PARTY

A few weeks before the conclusion of the City Front strike, several dozen unions sponsored the founding convention of the Union Labor Party (ULP). Seeking to benefit from widespread working-class anger developed during the strike, the ULP delegates nominated Eugene Schmitz, president of the Musicians Union, for mayor of San Francisco. A month after the strike's end, San Francisco voters elected him.

Although for years the American Federation of Labor–affiliated unions of the city had maintained a nonpartisan political position, the events of the waterfront strike had converted them to a new view of politics. In the words of Furuseth, "I found that we had a class government already, and inasmuch as we are going to have a class government, I most emphatically prefer a working class government."

Whether the Union Labor Party in office was a working-class government remains subject to debate. From its beginnings the party represented a mismatch between its voters' expectations and what its leaders actually intended to accomplish. The City Front strike and labor turmoil in other industries created a moment of ripe worker consciousness. The mayoral election of November 1901, in which the Democratic and Republican parties fielded candidates against the ULP's Schmitz, took place along sharply divided class lines. The plurality of 42 percent by which Schmitz won came largely from the city's working-class precincts, despite the refusal of both the labor council and BTC to endorse Schmitz. The issue that proved key was Schmitz's promise to keep police out of labor disputes.

The party's standard-bearer was not a typical labor leader, but he was a perfect San Francisco mayoral candidate. Eugene Schmitz served as president of the Musicians Union. He had also run small businesses and was the leader of a popular dance orchestra. Part Irish, like most of the union leadership, he also claimed German and Scottish blood. He was handsome, a family man, Catholic, a homeowner, and willing—all too willing, as it turned out—to compromise.

At first it seemed that the ULP would represent workers' interests. In April 1902 Schmitz turned down the request of United Railroad boss Patrick Calhoun to arm scab drivers during a carmen's strike and also declined to place police on the cars. As a result, the carmen were able to return to work after a week with a slight increase in pay.

Schmitz's action showed employers they could not count on mayoral interference in labor affairs. Consequently draymen and teamsters signed a new contract restoring the union shop in the hauling industry. By 1903 the once-feared Employers Association dissolved.

But Schmitz listened more closely to his lawyer, friend, and advisor Abe Ruef than to his labor constituency. Ruef had written the ULP platform, which he characterized as "true to every principle of labor, yet conservative." He was half right. Ruef didn't care about labor principles; beneath his educated and cultured manner, he cared mostly about power and money. Soon the party's elected leaders, with Ruef's assistance, were accepting bribes from the city's business elite to create municipal policy.

The actions of the ULP leadership had nothing to do with a broad labor vision. The problem wasn't that no vision existed. The Socialist Party had begun to sink roots in the working class in San Francisco, just as it was doing elsewhere in the country. Within a decade scores of American cities elected Socialist mayors who helped implement major improvements in the lives of workers and their families, such as extension of electrical service, sewage lines, and garbage collection to areas of the cities that had never seen such things before. Socialist officeholders boosted the bargaining position of unions confronting employers shaped by late nineteenth-century Social Darwinist values, employers who—conveniently—believed that the capitalist economy was an individualist meritocracy, overseen by a divine partnership between God and Adam Smith that rewarded the most deserving men.

Socialists argued, in contrast, that while individual working men and women might occasionally rise above their humble births, the overwhelming majority of workers could only advance through collective action, in the workplace through their unions and in the political arena by voting Socialist.

Schmitz and Ruef had no interest in such a perspective. During the first few years of the ULP regime in San Francisco, their perspective pragmatically revolved around how to accumulate wealth for themselves, prompting ex-mayor James Phelan to tell a group of businessmen in 1904 that

Once upon a time there was an election, the result of which affrighted the conservative businessmen ... who were greatly alarmed, lest it be anarchistic, until the banner of the administration was unfurled, and then what seemed at first to be the red flag of anarchy turned out to be the red flag of the auctioneer.

On the surface the ULP remained a labor party, and threw just enough bones in the direction of workers to keep the pretense believable; for instance, Schmitz continued to hold police out of labor disputes. But behind the scenes corruption became commonplace in city hall. The muckraking Progressive editor of the *San Francisco Bulletin* newspaper, Fremont Older, began to print stories about financial arrangements overseen by Ruef involving the renewal of liquor licenses in "French restaurants," which featured food on the lower floors and brothels above.

Unfortunately for Older and his allies in the city's business elite who hoped to see even a weak labor government disappear, their campaign ran into two problems. First, the initial investigations failed to produce convincing evidence of the corruption that was taking place behind closed doors. Second, an ill-timed effort by a new antiunion organization to reestablish the open shop in San Francisco gave the Schmitz administration the perfect issue to divert attention from the financial scandals, and make it seem as if the ULP was the staunch defender of workers' interests.

By attacking Schmitz and the ULP at the same time as it was carrying on its antiunion campaign, the business-backed Citizens' Alliance blundered into a winning strategy for the ULP in the 1905 election; the alliance made it appear as if a vote for Schmitz's opponent—a Democratic/Republican fusion candidate—would be a vote for the open shop. P. H. McCarthy, who had faced Citizens' Alliance interference in a number of workplaces, brought the Building Trades Council into alignment with the ULP for the first time. The night before the election, McCarthy headed a union parade and told the crowd that any worker who didn't vote for Schmitz was a scab.

Buoyed by the building trades' official support, and able to cloak itself as champion of workers' rights, the day after the election the ULP found itself in full command of city government, sweeping all eighteen seats on the board of supervisors while reelecting Schmitz by a comfortable majority.

It also didn't hurt the ULP cause that the city used voting machines for the first time. Fearing losing their vote for the popular Schmitz, many voters pulled the lever for the straight ULP ticket rather than sort through the various moves necessary to vote across party lines for supervisor.

The flagrant corruption of the new board, and the carelessness with which board members flaunted the favors they received, produced a backlash. Fremont Older, former mayor James Phelan, and sugar baron Rudolph Spreckels combined forces to launch an investigation into the regime. Older contributed an expanded program of muckraking articles, Phelan the connections with federal government law enforcement agencies, and Spreckels a generous amount of money to hire detectives.

There was plenty of dirt under the rug. Even Ruef was appalled at the greed of the minor union officials and prolabor small businessmen elected to the board of supervisors in 1905.

The more important story, though not yet known at that moment, involved large amounts of money passing from United Railroad executives, including URR president Patrick Calhoun, and from operators of the city's utilities, to Ruef in efforts to bend city policy. The URR, for instance, wanted to convert its last cable car lines to overhead electrical trolleys. An "attorney's fee" of two hundred thousand dollars—paid to Ruef by Calhoun and other top executives of the URR, and spread around the pockets of the new supervisors—soon brought about the desired transformation.

EARTHQUAKE AND REBUILDING THE CITY

Just after five o'clock in the morning on April 18, 1906, the city shook for forty-eight seconds in the grip of a massive earthquake. San Francisco's new seven-million-dollar city hall became an instant wreck. In the business corridor along Market Street and to the west, some of the well-constructed modern stone and brick office buildings stood firm alongside others that were reduced to rubble. The middle-class Western Addition and stable working-class Mission neighborhoods south of 20th Street remained largely intact.

But south of Market, the wooden frame boardinghouse rooms and apartments of San Francisco's working families collapsed like houses of cards. Within the splintered ruins flames from overturned oil stoves and ruptured gas mains quickly spread across the area. Joining together, the individual fires became a roaring storm. Firefighters watched helplessly, their water mains severed by the quake, as the conflagration leaped across Market Street and consumed a third of the city in two days.

About three thousand people died, half the population became homeless, and more than a billion dollars in property were lost. South of Market's working-class slums and industrial establishments were incinerated down to the ground. Democratic in its effects, the fires also reduced most of the mansions on Nob Hill to ash.

Mayor Schmitz for once acted swiftly and decisively, regrouping city government and requesting federal assistance while stopping the distribution of alcoholic drinks. Within days, hundreds of plumbers were at work fixing water pipes and sewers. The United Railroad restored service to the Market Street electric car line in a couple of weeks. Cable cars ran by August. Union carpenters built nearly six thousand "earthquake shacks," working with industrial efficiency in eleven parks around the city, to house the homeless, by fall 1906. In all, more than twenty thousand new buildings in three years rose over the cold embers of the fire.

Luckily, the city's economic lifeline, the waterfront, was largely untouched by the disaster, allowing assistance from the rest of the country to pour in and rapid restoration of trade as the city rebuilt. By 1910, much of old Victorian San Francisco, its buildings grimed with decades of industrial and residential coal smoke, was gone, and in its place stood a cleaner modern metropolis running on electricity and gas.

One important reason for the city's ability to reconstitute itself was the high level of organization of the Building Trades Council. Craftsmen hurried from all parts of the country to the massive construction zone and were issued union cards, swelling the BTC's ranks by nearly 50 percent. There was more than enough work to go around.

For a brief period, everyone pulled together to restore the city in a mood of "earthquake love." The labor council and the BTC suspended many work rules, and the BTC enforced a wage freeze. But the honeymoon was short lived. Landlords took advantage of the scarcity of housing to raise rents by an average of triple pre-earthquake prices. Building materials cost more, and mechanics had to purchase new clothing and tools to replace the ones that had been lost.

When some unions, rebuffed by employers, resorted to strikes for higher pay, antilabor spokespeople accused the unions of gouging during the emergency. General Frederick Funston, who oversaw martial law in the earthquake and fire's aftermath, gladdened the hearts of capitalists by proposing that union workers in construction should be replaced by prisoners (it didn't actually happen). But modest rises in wages—BTC members earned an average of four dollars a day—only helped workers keep up with prices.

In the wake of the earthquake and fire, rebuilding the city naturally took center stage. Public attention to the graft prosecution was short circuited by the emergency, just as the investigation was finally bearing fruit. The grand jury indicted Schmitz and Ruef in late 1906 for extortion. In March 1907 nearly all of the supervisors were indicted, granted immunity in exchange for testifying, and forced to resign. Their testimony led to the indictments of corporate executives responsible for the bribery of Schmitz, Ruef, and the supervisors. Schmitz was convicted and removed from office in June. The trials continued. But the context for the investigation had irrevocably changed, and not just because of the need to rebuild the city.

When it appeared to San Francisco's wealthy class that the targets of graft investigation were corrupt labor-leaning politicians, it had applauded and supported the prosecution. With the shoe on the other foot, and such pillars of the business community as Patrick Calhoun under investigation, former fans of the prosecution among elite San Francisco society turned against it. Eventually, Ruef alone served significant prison time.

Carmen, Women, and Their Unions

If the rich men are all sticking together, what is the duty of the people who earn wages? Is it not their duty to stick together as close, if not closer, than the rich men?

FATHER PETER YORKE

THE 1907 CARMEN'S STRIKE

Patrick Calhoun and the United Railroad corporation purchased the Market Street Railroad in 1902. Along with cars, tracks, and employees they inherited an extensive system of labor espionage: paid secret agents among the carmen, spies who followed the men around after work, and a blacklist circulated to all streetcar companies in America. The company made use of recent advances in photographic technology, like the handheld 35-millimeter cameras on the market since 1900, to surreptitiously record suspected union members' movements and, after steaming open letters addressed to union officers, photograph them.

Calhoun's support for these tactics reflected the prevailing philosophy of railroad executives in his day. The same year Calhoun acquired the United Railroad in San Francisco, George Baer, president of the Reading Railroad in Pennsylvania, promised that "The rights of the laboring man will be protected, and cared for, not by the labor agitator but by the Christian men to whom God has given control of the property interests in this country."

Perhaps unaware of the religious commitment of railroad bosses to their welfare, San Francisco carmen struck in 1902 for reinstatement of three dozen drivers fired because of their union activities and for reduction of hours from eleven and a half to ten per day. When Mayor Eugene Schmitz refused to grant gun permits to Calhoun's scabs and likewise turned down Calhoun's request for police to ride shotgun on the streetcars, the railway boss was forced to rehire the union drivers and reduce the hours of work. The

FIGURE 18. San Francisco musician's union leader and mayor Eugene Schmitz (bearded, on streetcar) refused to order police to break strikes by the Amalgamated Association of Street and Electric Railway Employees Local 205. San Francisco History Center, San Francisco Public Library.

defeat locked in his desire for revenge against Local 205 of the carmen's union and the Schmitz administration.

In 1906, with Schmitz and the Union Labor Party (ULP) in full control of city government, Calhoun agreed to submit unresolved differences with the carmen's union to an arbitrator. The arbitrator's decision settled negotiations peacefully, granting wage increases to the Carmen and three other United Railroad unions that had been out on strike. But the carmen remained unsatisfied: while workers at the other unions had been granted the eight-hour day, the arbitrator had ruled that the ten-hour day would remain in effect for them.

In 1907, with the removal of the ULP from office, Calhoun felt no need to restrain himself from satisfying his wish to crush the carmen's union. And he proved as adept at this as he did in escaping punishment for the massive bribery of Ruef and the supervisors. His long-awaited opportunity came on May 4, 1907 (the day after he was questioned by the grand jury for bribery of the Schmitz administration), when the Local 205 membership voted to strike for the eight-hour day.

The men's anger was understandable. Calhoun had rejected the union's request to renegotiate its contract in the wake of the earthquake, which had brought about many changes to the drivers' working conditions and eroded the purchasing power of their wages. His refusal was particularly infuriating compared with the situation in Oakland, where management of the Oakland Traction and Key Route companies voluntarily increased wages while thanking the men for their work in a difficult situation.

The vote to strike occurred over the objections of union president Richard Cornelius and against the advice of other labor leaders and friends of labor in the community such as Mike Casey, Andrew Furuseth, and Father Peter Yorke. Yorke, a Catholic priest with a working-class constituency in St. Patrick's Church on Mission Street, had become a visible supporter of the labor movement during the 1901 City Front strike.

But in 1907 Yorke foresaw that the postearthquake political climate and the ULP's disgrace would leave the carmen dangerously exposed in a labor dispute. He agreed with Local 205 president Cornelius, a forty-two-year old English immigrant, who told his members he thought they were "all acting like crazy fools" before they voted to strike.

The carmen apparently believed that Calhoun's indictment would turn public opinion in their favor. At the outset of the work stoppage, the labor movement united solidly behind Local 205. Unions voted to fine members who rode streetcars during the conflict. Schmitz, still on the job at the start of the strike, turned down the United Railroad's ritual request for gun permits or police protection for strikebreakers.

But the business community viewed Calhoun as a hero for drawing a line in the sand with the union. Sympathizers saw his indictment as an expansion of the unfair tilt against business interests by the ULP, spearheaded by Progressive do-gooders more interested in their prosecution than the overall welfare of the community. Calhoun's war with Local 205 earned him unconditional support from his class. Andrew Furuseth charged that Calhoun had deliberately provoked the strike to gain sympathy while under indictment.

In an increasingly complex political situation, three power blocs maneuvered for position behind the scenes of the graft investigation and in the open conflict between labor and capital.

The prosecution and its advocates viewed the investigation as a prime example of how Progressive Era "good government" ideals could elevate society above the swamp of labor-capital conflict and urban machine politics. These ideals crossed class lines, although Spreckels, Older, Phelan, and their supporters tended to represent a coalition of middle class and ruling class. The investigation left room for ambitious politicians to fill the power vacuum left by the discredited Schmitz administration.

Traditional business interests understood the investigation as an opportunity to rid themselves of a prolabor administration. They supported the prosecution so long as it targeted unionists and opposed its extension to the capitalists who had bribed the ULP officeholders.

The labor movement was split between two positions. After the mass resignation of the ULP supervisors, McCarthy and the Building Trades Council (BTC) reconstituted the party in pursuit of McCarthy's desire to become mayor. McCarthy's campaign proposed lifting immunity from the ULP supervisors so they could be prosecuted, he said, along with the businessmen who had bribed them. While fair sounding, the practical effect of his idea would have been to end the prosecution, because without immunity the former supervisors would have refused to testify.

San Francisco Labor Council leaders, including Furuseth, Casey, and Cornelius, wanted the businessmen to be swiftly convicted. Stretched by the growing number of strikes in spring and summer 1907, union leaders feared their ability to wage them successfully all at once—although Socialist leaders in the council were beginning to talk about a general strike. Despite their anger at the ULP's corruption, Cornelius and the others felt immunity for the former supervisors was necessary to convict the corporate leaders—especially Calhoun—who had bribed them.

Unfortunately, the resignation of the supervisors had resulted in the leaders of the graft investigation appointing a new city government that decided the police had no right to search Calhoun's scabs, effectively giving them the green light to carry guns.

On May 4 Calhoun hired four hundred hard-boiled men from James Farley, who ran an East Coast firm specializing in strikebreaking. Calhoun lodged them, well-stocked with food and ammunition, behind barricades in streetcar barns throughout the city. Thus began what has been called the "most violent streetcar strike" in American history. On May 7, "Bloody Tuesday," the company sent several streetcars out of the barns into crowds of hundreds of strikers and sympathizers. Two men were killed (one striker, one scab) and twenty injured and wounded. The police chief, along with the labor movement, condemned Calhoun for arming the strikebreakers and provoking the strikers.

The carnage didn't end there. Although many of the scab carmen were experienced drivers, the hills of San Francisco posed difficult challenges.

Combined with the threat of rocks and bullets at any moment and the occasional tree mysteriously felled across the tracks under cover of darkness, conditions for the scabs didn't encourage safe and healthy rides through the city. For the first few weeks, large numbers of riders stayed away, as accidents and violent incidents continued to take a toll on strikers, scabs, and hapless members of the public.

Nonetheless, with each passing week, more cars entered service. Feelings about the strike split along class lines. Union workers and their families boycotted the streetcars; increasingly, others didn't. Much of the ridership, perhaps a majority, was middle class. Middle-class neighborhoods depended to a greater degree on the streetcar lines for their residents to get to and from work. In the south of Market and Mission working-class districts, distances between home, work, shopping, and leisure were smaller, often within walking range.

In the second week of June, the BTC and the labor council voted to create a joint strike support committee and assess their members a per capita tax to financially help the strikers for the duration of the conflict. In all, the BTC, the San Francisco Labor Council, and Local 205, through its international union, brought in over $300,000 in contributions for the strikers. Rallies were held, guerilla actions flared against the strikebreakers, and pledges were made to stand firm as long as necessary. Father Yorke told his congregation that the Good Lord supported the strikers and their fight was justified because "Where there is no justice, there cannot be peace."

But it wasn't enough. Public opinion gradually swung over to Calhoun as long months passed and the URR proved able to resuscitate service. Labor unity dissolved due to infighting around the city elections and the graft prosecution. Despite his vigorous support for the carmen's strike, McCarthy couldn't keep most of the unions in the labor council in his column for the election, due to his position against the supervisors' immunity and the widespread belief he had made a secret deal with Calhoun. In late summer unions in the labor council, including the carmen's, began to work for McCarthy's election opponent. Soon the Building Trades Council announced they were withdrawing from the joint strike committee.

Although the entire labor movement understood that a defeat of the carmen would be disastrous, by August all the cars were running again. In September, after one final spasm of violent battles between strike supporters and scab carmen, the labor council lifted the boycott. While the strike didn't officially end until March 1908, it was dead months before then. So were more than thirty people, with a thousand more injured in accidents and wounded in street battles. And finally, so was the carmen's union, which turned in its charter in December 1908. It would not be resurrected for more than two decades.

McCarthy lost the election in November. Calhoun, who escaped the graft prosecution through a hung jury, demonstrated that a determined, deep-pocketed corporation could, through organized violence, careful planning, and a police force with a mandate to look the other way, humble a militant union. It did not help the carmen that their labor support was divided, and unlike teamsters in the 1901 City Front strike, they did not have the ability in their industry to bring the San Francisco economy to a halt.

Public outrage that Calhoun had eluded justice brought an electoral coda to the carmen's strike of 1907. McCarthy succeeded in welding together united labor support and finally became mayor in 1909. One year after the carmen's union folded, he backed the passage of bonds to establish a municipally owned railway. The first cars began running in 1912 to compete with the United Railroad and ultimately replace it. Many of the former Local 205 members, who had been blacklisted for years after their defeat, went to work for the Municipal Railway. One was Richard Cornelius—but not for long. The former president of Local 205, the Amalgamated Association of Street and Electric Railway Employees of America, Cornelius contracted tuberculosis and died in 1914 at 49, leaving a wife and two young daughters behind.

WOMEN IN THE SAN FRANCISCO LABOR MOVEMENT

Newspaper coverage of the early days of the carmen's strike noted the role of women on both sides of the conflict. On Bloody Tuesday an elderly woman lay down on the tracks to stop a scab-run streetcar. With the men and boys, women pelted United Railroad cars with rocks and bricks. Women in the earthquake camp on California Street threw "missiles" at scabs and stood on the tracks, babies in their arms, refusing to allow the streetcars to pass.

Who were these women battling alongside the strikers? For starters, with more than 1,500 men on strike, many would have been family members of the strikers, together with friends and neighbors. Beyond such personal connections, women had been increasing their presence in the workforce for years and had begun to participate in the labor movement at many levels since the 1880s, and especially after 1900. Newspaper stories identified some of the carmen's female supporters in the streets as "telephone girls"; five hundred female operators happened to be on strike at the same time against the Pacific Telephone and Telegraph (PT&T) company and no doubt could relate to the carmen's struggle.

The biggest and most stable unions with large numbers of women were the Steam Laundry Workers Local 26 and the Cooks' and Waiters' Alliance Local 30. Although the majority in the laundry workers' union were women, men predominated in leadership, as they did in the cooks' and waiters' union. This changed in early 1906 when the women in Local 30, with a vote supported by the men, formed their own union, Waitresses Local 48, comprising 250 members. Within a few years it doubled in size, successfully riding out the earthquake.

Louise LaRue was a founding officer of the union. Like most of her members she needed work to survive. A widow, LaRue had time outside work that would have been difficult for married waitresses to find to devote to union office. Local 48 successfully fought for the reduction of hours of work, more sanitary working conditions, and increased wages. It held picnics and dances to raise money for its members' sickness and death benefit fund.

Its contracts also protected the boundaries of the work performed by its members, excluding janitorial and kitchen tasks from their duties. When Maud Younger showed up for her first day in a unionized San Francisco restaurant shortly after the earthquake, she was expecting the same work she had experienced in unorganized New York eateries. She asked the head waitress whether she should wash the floors or tables. Younger was told, "Women don't wash floors in San Francisco." As in many AFL unions at the time, a strong sense of craft skill and pride in doing one's job well helped the women to weave a collective culture and solidarity.

Often, though, solidarity among working women went only so far in a male-dominated universe. Younger contributed five dollars to the telephone operators' strike fund, as did many Local 48 members. The operators organized a union in spring 1907 and walked out of the Pacific Telephone and Telegraph Company offices the day before the carmen's union struck in May. The women augmented traditional demands for higher wages and union recognition—and protesting the firing of union activists—with a call to end sexual harassment by male supervisors. They also wanted what today would be understood as "ergonomic" improvements: some operators had to use stools because there weren't enough chairs, which hurt their backs; and they requested rearrangement of their work space to shrink painful stretches on the switchboard down to a reasonable reach.

Aware of discontent, managers attempted to address the problems with gestures such as setting out food for their "girls" at lunch. Union president Alice Lynch was scornful: "Lunch! Do you call a scrap of bologna sausage lunch? Or a spoonful of beans? Or a cup of cheap tea?" Another obstacle to the success of this managerial goodwill program was that the company had previously eliminated the operators' break time, thereby preventing them from actually eating the food.

Company officials finally pushed the women out the door when supervisors brought them, twenty at a time, into a room on payday and presented them with union resignation forms together with their paychecks. Almost every woman refused to sign the forms. At their next union meeting the vote to strike was unanimous. The *Chronicle* reported, "The spirit of revolt was rampant in the closely packed gathering of femininity, and one might as well have tried to stem a hurricane."

The labor council only reluctantly supported the job action, one of several concurrently draining its resources. Higher on their priority list were the carmen's strike, a general strike in the Bay Area metal trades, and a walkout by 1,500 laundry workers. Council leaders worried—and for good reason—that the fledgling union had overreached in taking on PT&T, a powerful opponent even without its corporate parent, Western States Bell. Believing it would fail, the council torpedoed a motion for a boycott.

The telephone operators didn't have a connection to a national union. Worse, their coworkers—skilled male telephone workers, linemen, and cable splicers represented by the International Brotherhood of Electrical Workers, and capable of curtailing many of the company's functions—waited two months before voting a sympathy strike.

Public empathy buoyed the hopes of the operators in their unequal struggle. Women from other unions, as well as men, swelled the picket lines. In a parallel with the carmen's strike, two top PT&T executives were indicted by the graft investigation for bribery. The operators' strike publicity asked, reasonably, how a corporation that had spent $80,000 on bribes couldn't afford a raise for its poorly paid women workers.

But with bigger fish to fry, the labor council and BTC devoted inadequate attention to the operators. When the two councils in August announced they had reached an agreement with the company that included small wage increases, the restoration of fifteen-minute breaks, and hiring strikers back without prejudice, the women voted to return to work.

Unfortunately the company seemed to have missed the last part, and the councils didn't get the agreement in writing. The operators were only allowed to reapply for their jobs as individuals, and in the process most of the union leaders were weeded out. The union was broken and didn't stage a comeback for a decade, victim of a two-sided attack by a strong adversary and half-hearted supporters.

Despite the operators' defeat, women continued to organize. Several factors contributed to the greater percentage of women in unions in San Francisco (around 10 percent) compared to the rest of the country (3 percent) at this time. The high degree of unionism in the city, supported by a prolabor municipal government, created a favorable social climate. Most Irish, and Irish-American women, especially, expected that they would work at least part of their lives, and they felt a working-class identity that often included a readiness to embrace unionism. These first- and second-generation immigrant women hailed from northern Europe and, like the overwhelming majority of San Francisco women, spoke English.

Not just white, they were, in fact, *aggressively* white, aligning themselves with the anti-Asian tendencies of the white labor movement. Many women trade unionists, including LaRue, were active in the Asiatic Exclusion League and similar organizations. Some became union members in industries—like laundries but also shoemaking and garment production—that needed low-wage workers after passage of the Chinese Exclusion Act of 1882 resulted in declining Chinese participation. Here the women absorbed and perpetuated xenophobic and racist attitudes, joined at the hip with union sympathies.

Female union leaders were politicized in more constructive ways as well. They recognized that advancement for women workers depended on political efforts alongside workplace organizing, and campaigned for Union Labor Party candidates in the 1907 and 1909 municipal elections.

They also joined with middle-class women in suffrage politics. California's male voters rejected a ballot measure in 1896 to give women the vote. LaRue and other union leaders like Maud Younger (in the waitresses' union) and Minna O'Donnell (typographical workers' union) spent a lot of time and energy strengthening support for woman suffrage among union men, and worked in alliance with middle-class women to build the suffrage movement in the broader society.

Younger herself was a one-woman bridge between the two social blocs in the suffrage movement. Born into a prominent San Francisco professional family, she led a privileged life until after she turned thirty in 1901. At that point she experienced a conversion in New York and plunged into "settlement" work—helping poor and working-class families. She soon decided that organizing workers to help empower themselves in unions made more sense. When she moved back to the Bay Area, she joined Waitresses Local 48, became active in the labor and suffrage movements, and worked tirelessly to forge closer bonds between the two.

Relationships between working women and their middle-class suffrage movement partners, however, were far from smooth. Extending back decades, various issues often divided women along class lines. With unconscious condescension, wealthy and educated women sought to "uplift" their working-class sisters with moral crusades. The temperance movement and campaigns to curb the sale and use of alcohol found a bedrock of support in upper middle-class women reformers. Working-class women tended to view restaurants that served liquor through a pragmatic lens, as places of employment within a limited range of economic opportunities, rather than the devil's playground. They opposed temperance as meddling in other people's business, not to mention threatening their jobs.

Not surprisingly, female worker activists—even the most enthusiastic suffragists—tended to think unions represented the best hope for improving the lot of working women; their middle-class counterparts, while sometimes supportive of labor, believed the ballot offered a more comprehensive solution for all women.

At a time when more women were entering the workforce, cultural questions about "proper" feminine behavior arose when new commercial leisure opportunities—like going to the movies—attracted the money that women themselves had earned. That money, and what could be done with it, meant something different to the women who earned it with the sweat of their brow than to the women who received it from their husbands.

In 1907, storefront theaters showing motion pictures were spreading rapidly across urban landscapes, including in San Francisco. Silent movies offered cheap entertainment for immigrant workers, who didn't have to worry about the language barrier to enjoy themselves. Upper-middle-class moralists—usually the same ones who supported temperance movements—fretted that "respectable" women wouldn't go to such places. But working women, seeking independence and economical ways to spend their leisure time, flocked to the nickelodeons.

If middle-class morality frowned on movie attendance as "improper public behavior," what might it mean for women workers to walk picket lines and hurl rocks at scabs? The generally antilabor *San Francisco Chronicle* presented lavish photographic coverage of well-dressed women, some accompanied by children, pointedly ignoring the streetcar boycott and braving the wrath of the strikers to climb on board streetcars in May, 1907. The *Chronicle* also reported women in middle-class neighborhoods cheering and presenting scabs with bouquets and kisses. "You can just imagine how we felt about it," Louise LaRue told a national meeting of women trade unionists.

Some of the San Francisco women who chose to violate the boycott and ride the streetcars belonged to the Equal Suffrage League. Waitress union activists, including Maud Younger and Louise LaRue, were also involved in the league. The Local 48 membership voted, like other unions, to boycott Calhoun's cars for the duration of the strike and to assess themselves ten cents per week, and an additional twenty-five cents in August, to donate to the carmen's strike fund.

The actions of their middle-class sisters in the suffrage movement deeply offended Local 48 leaders, who demanded to know why league women couldn't support the strike. According to LaRue, the answer was unsatisfactory: "It was not the right time" for the strike to occur. As a result, said LaRue, "We had to pull out" of the league.

The union suffragists did not abandon the battle for the vote. Refusing to return to the Equal Suffrage League, they nonetheless kept the dispute out of the public eye so that suffrage opponents might not take advantage of it and worked through other channels—primarily in the labor movement—toward the same end. Younger and LaRue even brought an Equal Suffrage League leader to a meeting of the California State Federation of Labor, where the three women argued successfully for a resolution on behalf of placing a suffrage measure on the state ballot.

In August 1908 Younger wrote "Why Wage-Earning Women Should Vote," an article for the San Francisco Labor Council's newspaper. Simultaneously arguing for unions and suffrage, she pointed out for the publication's mostly male readership that "the union cannot do everything" and that "If food is unpure, trust prices exorbitant, dwelling houses unsanitary, public schools bad, public hospitals poor, police protection inadequate," it doesn't matter to the rich, who can afford to purchase whatever services they need. But such necessities of life, and the ability to improve public services, would be within the reach of working women only through the right to vote.

The following month Younger, LaRue, and Minna O'Donnell founded the Wage Earners' Suffrage League (WESL), dedicated to "better conditions for working women and . . . to promote the suffrage idea." Their league lobbied in Sacramento on behalf of women's right to vote from the distinct point of view of working women. In February 1911 the WESL, building on feminist coalition work that had moved the Progressive forces in the Republican Party to adopt a prosuffrage platform for the first time, testified in committee hearings. Soon afterward the legislature agreed to send the voters Amendment 8 to the state constitution for a vote. That year the league was also instrumental in the successful effort to pass a statewide eight-hour-day law for women.

However, the agitation that Younger, LaRue, O'Donnell, and other WESL activists undertook among working people in northern California constituted the heart of its unique and historic contribution to the suffrage cause. The league occupied an office in the Labor Temple building and its leaders had access to the unions that paid dues to the San Francisco Labor Council.

In the months prior to the October 1911 statewide election, the WESL took full advantage of that connection, meeting with dozens of unions in the Bay Area and labor councils in San Jose and Stockton. The league established branches in Richmond, San Jose, and as far away as Los Angeles. Its message, honed through years of practice, was warmly received by men who had never attended a prosuffrage event. LaRue told them, "We are your own women who are asking you to do this for us. Every member of our league is a union woman." More than seventy unions passed resolutions supporting Amendment 8.

The WESL leaders participated in broader public events, such as a rally at the state fair in Sacramento attended by three thousand. Its activists supported the Union Labor Party's campaign to reelect P. H. McCarthy and, together with Berkeley's Socialist mayor, J. Stitt Wilson, appeared with McCarthy at a packed meeting in San Francisco's Mission district.

Perhaps the league's grandest moment came during the Labor Day parade, when it cosponsored an elaborate float with Local 48. Younger sat in front, reins of the six horses in hand. Behind her, women workers posed, representing a half-dozen trades while "Minerva," Roman goddess of wisdom and most prominent figure in the state seal of California, presented them with a ballot. The sides of the float featured signs exhorting viewers to vote for

FIGURE 19. Women union leaders left the Equal Suffrage League to form the Wage Earners' Suffrage League, establishing branches as far away as Los Angeles, when the ESL refused to support the Carmen strike and boycott. The Huntington Library, San Marino, California.

Amendment 8. AFL president Sam Gompers urged passage of the ballot measure during his speech later that day in Shellmound Park in the East Bay.

On Election Day, Amendment 8 passed statewide by a mere three thousand votes. In San Francisco, the measure was actually defeated in each assembly district. But while the WESL hadn't managed to push a majority of the city's male electorate to support suffrage, the pro-Amendment 8 percentages in the working-class precincts were higher than in any other part of the city. In comparison with the 1896 vote, the greatest increase in favor of suffrage was registered in the working-class districts—a result for which the WESL could legitimately claim credit and a total representing far more than the statewide margin of difference.

The following year, in June of 1912, thirty-nine-year-old Frances Nacke Noel left her husband and ten-year-old son in Los Angeles and took the train to San Francisco. She was not unhappy with her marriage or her family. She had discussed the opportunity with her husband, and he had given his blessing to the proposal made by the San Francisco labor movement to bring her north.

Noel, a Los Angeles Labor Council delegate, had previously campaigned against child labor and had founded the Los Angeles branch of the Wage Earners' Suffrage League. She had been approached to deal with a problem following passage of Amendment 8. Despite the enthusiasm of women trade unionists with their historic victory, suffrage had not translated automatically into voter registration of women in working-class districts.

This worried not only the women, but the men of the San Francisco Labor Council, which allocated five hundred dollars to set up an office and hire a woman organizer for the successor to the Wage Earners' Suffrage League, called the Humane Legislation League (HLL). Putting her talents at the disposal of the HLL, Noel and her sister activists leafleted workplaces, spoke at meetings, and went door to door with registration literature.

Noel and the HLL were unsuccessful in meeting one goal, which was to raise the proportion of working-class women voters as high as their middle-class counterparts'. In particular, workers' wives not employed outside the home didn't flock to register, most likely because it was harder for the organizers to find them. But by the time Noel left San Francisco later that year, more women had registered in working-class districts, in terms of absolute numbers, than in any other part of town, including the middle- and upper-class neighborhoods.

I4

Otistown

FAVORING THE OPEN SHOP

The Merchants and Manufacturers' Association (M&MA) had always maintained that it wasn't opposed to unions. Unions were fine. What the M&MA didn't like were strikes, boycotts, collective bargaining, picket lines, and any legal restrictions on the power of bosses over workers. Of course, if workers were deprived of the use of these tools, it would be difficult for them to function as a union. So although the M&MA was usually careful to insist that it had no objections to "reasonable" unions, the only union it might have tolerated would have been unrecognizable to a unionist.

In 1903 the National Association of Manufacturers changed its purpose from promoting probusiness public feeling to an explicitly antiunion philosophy. It created local antilabor organizations around the country, which it called "Citizens' Alliances," mostly consisting of business owners and conservative public officials. The Merchants and Manufacturers Association in Los Angeles eagerly embraced the new group. The M&MA's Felix Zeehandelaar agreed to serve as secretary for the local Citizens Alliance, and Harrison Gray Otis stepped up to the plate as chairman of its board. Henry Huntington—nephew of Collis, and owner of the Pacific Electric Railway—pitched in with a financial contribution and his hearty endorsement.

Also in 1903, the giant United States Steel Corporation formed the National Erectors' Association to fight union efforts of ironworkers, the men who assembled the skeletons of a new element in the urban scene, skyscrapers. The association soon became one of the most powerful of the employer groups. It also stopped at nothing, including criminal tactics, to achieve its open shop goal, and by 1906 had gained its objective everywhere in the country except Chicago and San Francisco.

Civil liberties attorney Clarence Darrow, who later declared that U.S. labor laws weren't "worth a pinch of snuff," wrote a pamphlet, "The Open Shop," in 1909 outlining the characteristics of the open shop philosophy and its implications for a democratic society. Twenty thousand copies were distributed in Los Angeles in 1910. Some of the less violent antiunion devices the M&MA and Citizens' Alliance used to fulfill their dream of an open shop paradise included firing union members; circulating "blacklists" among employers of known union activists so no one would hire them; establishing employment agencies for professional strikebreakers; responding to a unionization effort by locking workers out (refusing to let employees come to work); hiring labor spies, who pretended to be union sympathizers; and simply declaring that a union shop no longer was one.

The M&MA pledged financial assistance to companies with "labor troubles" and—interestingly, given its opposition to union boycotts—boycotted businesses that allowed unions. It fueled the dark side of southern California boosterism by recruiting workers from other parts of the country with lavish promises of nonexistent jobs in order to swell the local labor pool, drive down wages, and dampen organizing.

With their money, power, and high level of organization in "the scabbiest town on earth," the open shop conspirators elected politicians to do their bidding. They influenced city policies and the hiring of sympathetic individuals to key positions in government departments. The M&MA's crowning achievement in 1910 was passage of a city ordinance that sharply reduced free speech and freedom of assembly for workers. Written by M&MA attorney Earl Rogers in response to a lengthy metal workers strike, it banned all picketing within L.A. city limits.

To understand the real meaning of the "open shop," however, we have to step down from the Olympian world of Otis, Zeehandelaar, and Huntington and examine its effects on the way workers lived in the first decade of the twentieth century in Los Angeles.

CONDITIONS FOR WORKERS IN L.A.

Ironworkers needed strong bodies and steady nerves. They made the least money of all the building trades' workers, yet worked the most dangerous jobs. Skilled craft workers often looked down on them, because ironworkers didn't have to pass through the lengthy apprenticeship of a carpenter, electrician, or bricklayer. The members of Carpenters Local 158 were making four dollars per day with a five and a half day week by 1907 in Los Angeles. On these wages they could support a family.

Ironworkers at the same construction site made only two dollars per day, working nine hours and six full days. But as commercial buildings began to rise to greater heights, ironworkers gained a grudging respect from their coworkers. For it was their job to tie together beams and girders in thin air to make the steel skeleton of the skyscraper. They had to be tough, fearless, and maintain a necessary disregard for the danger they faced daily, perched high above the ground.

These men were not inclined to sit quietly while the National Erectors' Association tried to smash their union. When the association hired gangs of thugs to break strikes with violence against picketers, ironworkers did not turn the other cheek. When an employer fired and blacklisted union members, it was not uncommon for his construction site to be the target of dynamite, planted at night, destroying some or all of the work in progress.

John McNamara and Frank Ryan, elected to national leadership of the International Association of Bridge and Structural Iron Workers in 1905, understood this situation as class war, plain and simple. They encouraged members to fight back with all means at their disposal. Since there were no national laws regulating labor-capital conflict, the vacuum was filled with violence. Between 1905 and 1910 dozens of construction sites across the country were wrecked by dynamite. Remarkably, no one was killed in any of the explosions. No one claimed credit, and no one was caught planting dynamite, either.

Working conditions in other industries might not have been as extreme as in commercial building construction but could be just as frustrating for employees on the receiving end of low wages and unlimited employer authority. As streetcar lines expanded throughout the city, stitching together islands of development left over from the boom of the 1880s, Henry Huntington's immense fortune helped him to consolidate control over the tracks through his Pacific Electric Railway.

He offered mostly Mexican laborers $1.50 a day to dig up the streets and lay down the rails. They lived in crowded *colonias* in the northeast Sonoratown area, where the rent they could afford allowed them to coexist with the stench of nearby packinghouses. Side by side in small, hand-built houses, they raised food in tiny gardens and attempted to chase away the neighborhood odors with their traditional cooking.

In 1903 their labor extended Huntington's reach from downtown to the ocean. Although the Pacific Electric Railway ended at undeveloped sand and marshes by the water, a plan was already in place to create a replica of Venice, Italy, where Angelenos could live and play in a *faux* Renaissance setting. Within two years the real estate developers' vision had become reality, sort of. Anticipating by a decade and a half massive Hollywood sets built for epic films like D. W. Griffith's *Intolerance,* which stood for years afterward as tourist attractions, the new Venice reproduced parts of the old with stucco and wood, complete with a smaller but still impressive Grand Canal and a web of lesser waterways. Arched bridges over the canals and colonnades along the main avenues provided a scenic backdrop to hundreds—eventually thousands—of new housing units.

Given their wages, it was unlikely that many of the laborers who had laid the tracks could live in Venice, California, although they might be able to spend the money for streetcar fare to visit its canals and boardwalk amusements. African Americans were also welcome—they were the predominant group among building janitors in Venice.

Unlike the occupants of Sonoratown, African Americans were not restricted to a couple of segregated Los Angeles ghettos. Just over two thousand blacks called Los Angeles home in 1900. They faced less discrimination at this time than Mexicans and Mexican Americans, who outnumbered them four to one and faced a steep legacy of anti-Mexican prejudice. Because of the sprawling city's cheap land prices, a steady job put ownership of a modest home within the reach of more than a third of the black households scattered across a half-dozen neighborhoods.

A significant number possessed relatively high education levels and middle-class expectations, even if the occupational reality for most black Angelenos remained decidedly working class. Women could work as domestics and in retail services, and over 50 percent of all black male employment was to be found in a handful of occupations: general laborers (mostly in construction and the railroads), porters, janitors, waiters, and servants. Otis's *Times* praised the hard work and upwardly mobile aspirations of the city's small black community.

Two reasons motivated Otis in his uncharacteristic generosity. As a Republican who served in the Civil War for the North, Otis genuinely—if paternalistically—believed in "advancement for the Negro race." But as the ruthless overseer of antilabor forces, he understood that if one group of workers could be set against another during times of industrial conflict, so much the better.

UNION ORGANIZING CAMPAIGNS

A rapidly growing economy and a population that leaped from one hundred thousand to a third of a million within a decade demanded new buildings, new services, and more workers to provide them. Despite the prevailing official optimism about life in sunny southern California, many recently arrived working people found themselves living and toiling in unexpectedly difficult circumstances. When union organizers went looking for workers to sign up, it wasn't hard to find them, even within the city's repressive open shop atmosphere.

The Los Angeles Council of Labor authorized two dedicated and capable leaders, Fred Wheeler and Lemuel Biddle, to devote their time and energy to help workers who wanted a union. The California State Labor Federation, formed in 1901, hired Wheeler as its state organizer in 1903 and secured financial assistance from the national American Federation of Labor to help pay for Wheeler and Biddle's work. Biddle served as AFL district organizer from 1901 to 1907. These two organizers were personally responsible for increasing the number of unions affiliated with the council from 26 to 64 in a few years—and that represented just part of the movement's growth. Between 1900 and 1904 Los Angeles union membership more than quadrupled.

Born in Philadelphia and trained as a machinist and shoemaker, Lem Biddle passed through many other jobs, several unions, and a number of states before arriving in Los Angeles in 1888 at the age of forty-two. Biddle had been blacklisted by the railroad companies for his role in the Pullman strike in 1894. So he was no stranger to organizing when he accepted the challenge of assisting Mexican railway workers form a union.

In April 1903, at the same time as Wheeler was attending to the sugar beet workers strike sixty miles north in Oxnard, Biddle was asked to help workers on the Main Street line of *el traque*. Main Street was a center of commerce and industry. But the track workers, who made fifteen cents an hour, had little opportunity to either shop or work in the businesses on either side of the ditches they were digging.

FIGURE 20. Mexican workers building the Pacific Electric Railway in 1903 made fifteen cents an hour. The Huntington Library, San Marino, California.

Biddle quickly enrolled several hundred in a newly chartered AFL federal union local. (Federal unions were offered by the AFL to groups of workers without a natural fit within an already existing national union. They were also designed as a way of giving minority workers a union when the appropriate local refused to take them in.) With a workers' committee, Biddle approached a Pacific Electric Railway manager, who initially agreed to increase wages to twenty cents an hour for day work, thirty cents at night, and forty cents on Sundays.

Huntington reversed the decision, and several hundred workers walked off the job. Within a week, their numbers had grown to fourteen hundred. They received financial support from the Socialist Party and the labor council, and other workers joined them in solidarity on the picket lines. But Huntington was ready.

Recalling the letter from his uncle Collis during the Pullman strike, in which the old man urged recruitment and transportation of black scabs from the southern United States, Huntington imported an enormous number of African American workers—by some accounts, nearly doubling the size of Los Angeles's black community at one stroke—who accepted twenty-two and a half cents an hour to work for the Pacific Electric Railway. They were joined in strikebreaking by a smaller number of unemployed Japanese workers, and even a few Mexicans who ignored community pressures and crossed the picket lines.

The wives and girlfriends of the strikers didn't give up. On one occasion a few dozen of them confronted the scabs, going so far as to attempt to wrestle their tools away. They were chased off by police.

Despite the solidarity of the local labor movement and militant actions such as the women's, the strike could not be sustained. Unlike the situation Wheeler found in Oxnard, Biddle could build on no ongoing relationship between the groups of workers. The Mexican track laborers replicated the results of the Anglo streetcar drivers and conductors, who had attempted union campaigns for the previous three years running, but failed to crack Huntington's open shop citadel. The carmen were at a disadvantage; Huntington had persuaded the obedient city to place policemen in every streetcar and had infiltrated the union with hired detectives.

During the time of M&MA dominance over industrial relations, such defeats were predictable and occurred far more often than worker victories. But the first few years of the twentieth century offered more of an opening, thanks to an economy that needed workers and experienced militant workers willing to risk their jobs—and sometimes more—to organize a union.

As a result, a startling number of successful organizing drives occurred around the city. Waiters and waitresses, building tradesmen, garment workers, candy makers, teamsters, and laundry workers found their way to collective action and unions. In all, more than 122 new locals were chartered between 1900 and 1904. The city's union membership jumped from just over two thousand to nearly ten thousand.

This was small potatoes compared to San Francisco, the heart of the closed shop in California, and one of the strongest union towns in America. But soon after the earthquake, San Francisco labor was forced to face a problem created by its own successes. Union leaders were warned by powerful businessmen that the competition from open shop Los Angeles would eventually either drive San Francisco owners into bankruptcy or force them to reduce wages in the northern city. These representatives of business issued a challenge to San Francisco labor: organize Los Angeles and level the California labor market playing field, or be prepared for the consequences.

P. H. McCarthy and other northern California labor leaders took the warning seriously. They raised money and dispatched organizers to southern California, sparking a resurgence of organizing at the end of the decade. These activities brought Los Angeles labor to a new peak of membership and militancy. By 1910, the growing Los Angeles labor movement boasted 12,000 members. Several large strikes were in progress by midyear. Hundreds of angry union activists were willing to test the new antipicketing ordinance, filling the county jails. A full collision loomed between workers intent on expanding their share of the pie and Otis's open shop forces.

THE TRIALS OF JOB HARRIMAN

When Frances Nacke Noel arrived in Los Angeles in 1899, an immigrant from Germany by way of New York and Colorado, she stayed with Job Harriman and his wife, Theo, in their Highland Park home. Like Noel, Harriman was a staunch Socialist. He introduced her to similar-minded political circles, and over the years their paths crossed often.

There were few Socialist activists Harriman didn't know in Los Angeles. A transplanted Indiana farm boy, he came to southern California after giving up the pulpit to become a lawyer. He was also seeking a better climate to combat recurrent tuberculosis. In Los Angeles Harriman immediately became involved with struggles for social justice.

Thanks to his impressive speaking ability and strong organizational sense, in 1900 he was asked to run for vice president of the United States with the fledgling Social Democratic Party, soon to become the Socialist Party, USA. He was thirty-nine years old. Eugene Debs was the party's presidential candidate. Their ticket drew 100,000 votes and helped bring national recognition to the emerging party.

Throughout the first decade of the twentieth century, Harriman functioned both as a Socialist activist and labor lawyer. He became the attorney for Los Angeles's labor council, winning a large circle of friends and admirers among the labor movement. He viewed his work on behalf of the victims of Otis and the Merchants and Manufacturers as part of the struggle for socialism.

His vision of a peaceful path to democratic socialism clashed with that of the party's revolutionary wing. The revolutionaries, like Oakland-based author Jack London, wanted to end the capitalist system by any means, including violent insurrection if necessary. Harriman stood for labor-socialist "fusion": the belief that workers' best hope for achieving their goals in the workplace was their union, their best bet in politics was to vote for Socialist candidates, and the two goals would best be served through mutual support.

In Los Angeles Harriman's view came to predominate, thanks to the uncompromising antilabor attitude of the city's business elite, which pushed

FIGURE 21. Frances Nacke Noel (with sign) narrowly missed winning a Los Angeles City Council seat on the Socialist ticket, and organized for women's rights and against child labor. The Huntington Library, San Marino, California.

Socialists and unionists toward each another. An important moment in the evolution of labor-socialist fusion occurred in 1907.

At the request of Otis, a close friend and business associate of the corrupt Mexican dictator Porfirio Diaz, police arrested several leaders of the opposition to Diaz, exiled in Los Angeles. The incarceration and trial of Ricardo Flores Magon, one of the founders of the Partido Liberal Mexicano (PLM), touched off a protest movement that quickly spread beyond the Mexican American community. Defense of Magon and his associates, arrested on

FIGURE 22. Ricardo (left) and Enrique Flores Magon spent time in Los Angeles County jail for their work organizing the Partido Liberal Mexicano. *Los Angeles Times* Photographic Archive, Library Special Collections, Charles E. Young Research Library, UCLA.

trumped-up charges of "violating neutrality laws," united the Los Angeles labor movement and political left. PLM activists rubbed shoulders in demonstrations and legal defense committees with anarchists, Socialists, and AFL unionists.

Magon asked Harriman to lead his legal team, and the labor attorney was happy to do so. Preparing the case from his office in the Higgins Building at Second and Main in downtown Los Angeles, Harriman defended the PLM leaders ably; eventually the case against them was dropped. But Magon's enemies weren't through with him. In October 1908 he was extradited to Arizona, convicted on other charges, and sent to prison for eighteen months.

Harriman remained certain of his labor-socialist fusion perspective. But events prevented him from focusing on electoral politics, calling on his skills in the courtroom instead. The rising tide of struggle of Los Angeles workers against the open shop was met with a Merchants and Manufacturers Association–led counterattack. The centerpiece of the union assault was a Metal Trades Council strike for the eight-hour day, involving eight unions representing 1,500 workers against the largest iron works, shipbuilding companies, and tool manufacturers in town, extending to Long Beach. A tenhour day, low pay, and yellow dog contracts (contracts that stipulated the worker would not join a union) had been the industry standard for years. The workers also had to contend with company spies, whose reports resulted in the firing of any worker determined to be a union member.

San Francisco metal trades unions sent organizers in early 1910 to prepare the ground. They organized hundreds of metal trades workers into unions—too many to fire. By mid-May, after the employers rejected a proposal for four dollars for an eight-hour day and time and a half for overtime, the workers walked out. The Bay Area's major labor councils and building trades councils, along with the California AFL and state Building Trades Council, formed a General Campaign Strike Committee and assessed their entire memberships twenty-five cents per week, which brought in nine thousand dollars per week to disburse in strike benefits for the Los Angeles workers.

The M&MA urged landlords to grant the smaller companies shuttered by the strike a reduced rent for the duration of the conflict. It collected a large war chest. Job Harriman described the struggle to the national AFL convention later that year; he informed the delegates that Henry Huntington had personally given one hundred thousand dollars to the bosses' collective fund.

Parallel to the metal trades strike burned a fierce conflict in the only fully unionized industry in Los Angeles. Through effective use of the boycott in working-class communities over the years, brewery workers had won union shops in a half-dozen companies. But when they attempted in 1910 to raise the lowest-paid workers' wages, the companies refused. The workers struck four companies, and the other two firms locked out their employees. They joined leather workers and employees of the major gas works on the sidewalks.

The employers persuaded Mayor George Alexander in mid-June to proclaim that strikers who blocked the streets would be arrested. The following week the police chief began to carry out the threat, and one week later cooperative judges issued injunctions preventing picketers from appearing near the larger struck companies.

This was not enough for the M&MA. On July 1, its attorneys proposed a new law to the city council. It outlawed picketing, loitering, the display of signs and banners, loud noises, and unusual verbal proclamations on the streets of Los Angeles. It also provided for steep fines and imprisonment of violators of the ordinance.

The city council invited both sides to speak. Harriman, appearing with officers of the metal trades' and brewery workers' unions, protested that the law would violate basic freedoms of speech and assembly. The council ignored these arguments and unanimously passed the ordinance. Mayor Alexander dutifully signed it. The jails soon filled with hundreds of strikers, keeping Harriman occupied defending them in court.

If the intent of the law was to demoralize the strikers, it had the opposite effect. Northern California unions sent down more organizers and raised more money, and prevailed on the national AFL to do the same. Only a handful of the jailed picketers were ever convicted. Despite months out of work, the strikers' ranks remained solid. A boycott on local beer exacted a deep financial toll on the breweries. In the first sign of a crack in the owners' united front, one of the brewing companies signed a contract with its workers.

By the end of September, the new seven-story Labor Temple on Maple Street, which had opened in February, was a beehive of activity. On its premises, in addition to the offices of the Los Angeles Labor Council and a number of affiliated unions, were the headquarters of the Socialist Party. The party had grown by more than a thousand members since moving in the same day the M&MA presented its antipicketing ordinance to the city council. The building also housed offices of organizers sent from San Francisco for more than a dozen unions; the local office of the northern California-based General Campaign Strike Committee; and the recently formed Union Labor Political Club, which pledged to endorse candidates who agreed with a labor platform.

On September 30 the breweries, acting against M&MA directives, reached agreement with their unions. Measured by the unprecedented level of union organizing and membership growth, increasingly united labor political action, and public support for major strikes in the face of hostile employer groups and their allies in city government, the Los Angeles labor movement had seemingly arrived at a new position of strength.

15

Almost Mayor

BOMBS, BALLOTS, AND FUSION POLITICS

THE CASE OF THE MCNAMARA BROTHERS

At 1:07 in the morning on October 1, 1910, a series of enormous explosions ripped through the *Los Angeles Times* building on the corner of First and Broadway streets in downtown L.A. Firefighters arriving at the scene with their horse-drawn equipment could only watch helplessly as the fire raged out of control. Twenty newspaper workers putting out the morning edition were killed. The three-story fortress-like building was left a smoking ruin.

Using another printing plant nearby owned by the *Times,* a small edition of the morning paper actually made it to the newsstands. Its headline screamed, "Unionist Bombs Wreck the *Times.*" Public opinion immediately divided between those who believed labor had the most likely motive to destroy the building of its most powerful enemy, and those who thought the disaster was either an accident or that Otis himself had a hand in it.

For weeks stories had circulated that gas leaks were sickening workers in the *Times* building. The sole labor representative in municipal government, Ben Robinson of the Typographical Union, who served on the Board of Fire Commissioners, had asked for an investigation of the leaks, but his request had been ignored. Otis had not renovated his structure for years; instead he had decided to fund a new plant nearby, and all his available capital had been diverted to that project.

Many public officials were ready to forget due process and the presumption of innocence until proven guilty, including California governor James Gillett, who said, "Whether guilty or not, the labor unionists will have to be blamed for the crime, until shown they are not guilty, as everything points to a desire to wipe out property and lives of those who have been fighting organized labor for years."

The opposite view was expressed by AFL president Sam Gompers, who stated, "The greatest enemies of our movement could not administer a blow so hurtful to our cause."

One quick impact of the bombing was stepped-up picket line arrests and a chill on civil liberties for workers. Another effect came immediately; the breweries reneged on their one-day-old contracts with their workers. As inflamed accusations were hurled through the employer-controlled newspapers, several metal trades and brewery strike leaders were arrested. Without any evidence pointing to them, though, they were soon released.

As the year's end neared with no new information regarding the identity of the bombers, a growing certainty took hold among working people that labor had had nothing to do with the bombing; this was but another baseless charge coming from Otis and the M&MA. Even when another bomb went off on Christmas Eve at the Llewelyn Iron Works, one of the companies struck by metal trades workers, the labor movement and most workers didn't change their minds.

Instead, a determination to finally overcome labor's open shop enemies infused energy into union organizing drives. At the same time, having experienced the result of a municipal government controlled by their enemies, unions made preparations for increased participation in municipal elections in 1911.

In April, detective William Burns arrested John McNamara, his brother James, and ironworker Ortie McManigal on suspicion of the *L.A. Times* bombing. McManigal soon confessed his part in the bombings. Burns, hated by unionists for his work providing labor spies to employers, was hailed as a hero by Otis. The labor movement had a different idea about Burns and his agents, seeing in the arrests a repetition of events in 1907 in Idaho, when Big Bill Haywood and other miners' union leaders were accused of assassinating the state's antilabor governor. That case ended in vindication for the labor leaders when their defense attorney demonstrated conclusively they had been framed.

Job Harriman was already working on a case defending three metal trades union leaders under suspicion of planting dynamite at another downtown Los Angeles building site (the three were later found innocent). He signed on as the lead attorney for the McNamara brothers, but took a back seat on the legal team when Sam Gompers persuaded Clarence Darrow to come to Los Angeles and oversee the case.

Darrow had built a deserved reputation as a defender of the downtrodden and friend of labor. He had represented Eugene Debs in 1894 following the Pullman strike, and he was the lead lawyer for the Idaho bombing case. Beside his labor cases, he took on scores of murder trial defenses, in which he argued so effectively against the death penalty that in only one case did his guilty client die at the hands of the state.

At first Darrow was reluctant to move from Chicago to Los Angeles for what he believed would be a lengthy and difficult trial. He was in poor health and thought his expenses would far outrun what he would be paid. But Gompers told the attorney he was the best man for the job. The AFL president, certain of the McNamaras' innocence, insisted he would personally make sure Darrow got paid properly. Soon Darrow moved into offices across the hall from Harriman in the Higgins Building.

Darrow's appearance was one reason Harriman stepped back from the lead role in the McNamaras' defense. There was another. In late April, Harriman announced he was running for mayor. He received the endorsements of the Socialist Party and the Union Labor Political Club, surrogate for the labor council.

From this moment on, the McNamara case, Harriman's run for mayor, and the Los Angeles union organizing campaign were tightly linked. Although not a Socialist himself, John McNamara endorsed Harriman's campaign, saying "There is but one way for the working class to get justice: elect its own representatives to office."

FUSION POLITICS

Indeed, by the time Harriman ran for mayor in 1911, socialism and the Los Angeles labor movement were so closely allied that it seemed the natural connection for thousands of workers, and Harriman was their hero and spokesman—and not the only one. When Fred Wheeler announced his intent to run for city council alongside Harriman on a full Socialist Party slate, he had just served the last of several terms as president of the Los Angeles Labor Council. He left that office in the hands of a fellow Socialist (and strike leader in the Metal Trades Council), machinist E. H. Misner.

Another member of the Socialist electoral slate was an African American, George Washington Whitley. Born in Missouri in the last year of the Civil

War, one of twelve children, he arrived in Los Angeles in 1903. He set up and ran small businesses whenever he could scrape together the money but experienced long stretches of wage labor between entrepreneurial efforts. He also displayed considerable skills as a political operative. Hired as the state organizer in 1906 for the Afro American League, a Republican-leaning political club for black Californians (and a predecessor to the NAACP), he expanded its membership from fifteen hundred to ten thousand and set up twenty local chapters in addition to the eight he inherited.

Alongside his work with the league, Whitley ran an employment agency in the black community and helped provide strikebreakers during at least one industrial dispute in the early years of the century. By 1910 he had changed his thinking about sending black workers to scab on white workers. In an article in the labor council's newspaper, *The Citizen,* Whitley told the journalist interviewing him,

> When the brewery workers went out I was asked for one hundred men to go to work in the breweries. I told the agents of the companies, who came to me, that under no circumstances would we again be used as strikebreakers.... We now know that we must organize industrially and politically along with our white brothers.

So convinced did Whitley become of his new perspective that he worked with unions to form the Mutual Organization League, for the purpose of organizing black workers. The labor council affiliated the league and offered it a home in the Labor Temple.

Other groups traditionally marginalized from politics were becoming involved with the Socialist Party. Around the same time in early 1911 as Whitley and his comrades formed a Negro branch, special locals of young people, foreign language groups, Christian Socialists, and women swelled the ranks of the party.

For working-class women, the expectation of a statewide vote on suffrage by fall lent a new edge to their political activism. In June Frances Noel, with labor council assistance, formed the Los Angeles Wage Earners Suffrage League (LAWESL), modeled on San Francisco's. Like that organization, the LAWESL brought together women from various unions and "ladies' auxiliaries." And like Maud Younger, Noel acted as a link between working-class and middle-class women's organizations to strengthen the movement for women's enfranchisement.

Noel was in her late thirties. Married to another Socialist and mother of a young son, she had been active in the Los Angeles Socialist Party for nearly a decade. She worked part-time at the labor council, wrote and spoke out for years on the necessity to eradicate child labor, and participated enthusiastically in innovative efforts to convince working-class men of the importance of suffrage. She argued with men on sidewalks outside bars about politics and evaded the antipicketing law, which prohibited outdoor political gatherings, by organizing picnics for suffrage.

Job Harriman clubs erupted in neighborhoods throughout Los Angeles County, which presently found itself host to fifty thousand registered Socialist voters. The national party leadership, recognizing the importance of the moment, sent organizers. By the end of summer, Harriman for Mayor rallies were taking place every few days, drawing large crowds and an excited feeling that fundamental change in the citadel of the open shop was possible.

Harriman's fusion perspective made sense to growing numbers of workers, union leaders, and their sympathizers in the general populace who were tired of the high-handed, antidemocratic, and often corrupt ways of the city elite. He promised to undo the antipicketing ordinance "half an hour" after he was elected and to investigate real estate deals tied to the Owens Valley aqueduct project, from which Otis and his friends had profited enormously. Before the aqueduct was officially begun, and the decision made to conclude it at the outer edge of the San Fernando Valley, Otis's syndicate had purchased two-thirds of the valley's land, much of it considered worthless before the arrival of cheap water.

Harriman also pledged to lower costs for city services by taking them out of the hands of capital and putting them under government control, and to embark on a program of building community centers, public pools and baths, and increased support for public schools. These ideas resonated with ordinary people who had come to southern California expecting to improve their lives but whose dreams had fallen short.

Even Sam Gompers dropped his longstanding opposition to endorsing Socialists for political office, and told Los Angeles union members to vote for Harriman. He renamed Labor Day 1911 "McNamara Brothers Day. " True to his word to Darrow, he urged workers across the nation to contribute money to the McNamara defense, and the funds came pouring in from his call and from the strong efforts of labor councils and building trades councils across California.

FIGURE 23. American Federation of Labor president Samuel Gompers (center) declared Labor Day 1911 "McNamara Brothers Day" in his belief that James (left) and John McNamara were innocent of bombing the Los Angeles Times. AFL-CIO Archive, Special Collections, University of Maryland Libraries.

On Labor Day, 25,000 singing and chanting supporters marched in front of the Los Angeles County Jail, calling for the release of the McNamara brothers and the election of Harriman and the rest of his ticket. It was the largest political demonstration that had ever taken place in Los Angeles. Thousands more listened to Harriman's speech that night in Luna Park in Venice, as he laid out plans to establish a city-run weekly newspaper to compete with Otis's *Times*.

Inside the McNamaras' cells, the prisoners were no doubt heartened by the parade in their honor, and the solidarity shown in countless small contributions by workers and larger ones by their unions. The trial began on October 11. Jury selection dragged on for weeks. It looked like the trial might last a long time. The national AFL convention, meeting in late November, asked every delegate to donate a day's wages to the McNamara defense.

Otis, meanwhile, had been doing everything he could to tie Harriman's campaign to the McNamara case, too. He editorialized that this election was "the forces of law and order against Socialism; peace and prosperity against misery and chaos; the Stars and Stripes against the red flag."

Otis didn't need Harriman's speeches, or any new reasons, to hate Harriman and the Socialists, who stood for everything he detested. But his hatred turned to fear on Halloween, the night of the primary election. Los Angeles had open primaries (all the candidates from all the parties ran in the same race). Against a field of four other contenders, including Mayor George Alexander, Harriman picked up almost as many votes as his two nearest rivals combined, although not quite the 50 percent needed to win outright. Suddenly, going into the runoff election against Alexander a month later, the Socialist candidate was the favorite. Fred Wheeler polled more primary votes for city council than any other candidate, and eight of the nine seats had Socialists running ahead.

In November 1911, Los Angeles workers were on the brink of transforming their city. Fifteen thousand workers belonged to unions—more than ever before. Their candidates for public office threatened to replace the antiunion men who had recently passed an antipicketing law. The Harriman campaign was staging seventy-five events each week, bolstered by union officers from San Francisco and Socialist organizers sent from as far away as the East Coast. Los Angeles metal trades workers split their time between their own strike activities and volunteering with the Harriman effort. Campaign leaders had reason to believe that passage of the California woman suffrage measure on October 10 would also work to the benefit of the Socialists.

Although five of the six daily newspapers vied with one another to support Alexander—publishing articles attempting to link Harriman to violent unionism and a huge decline of property values should he win, along with scary stories about Socialists in office elsewhere in the country—the public mostly wasn't buying it.

Until December 1, four days before the election. On that day James McNamara confessed that he had blown up the *Los Angeles Times* building, pleading guilty to murder; his brother John pled guilty to conspiracy in the bombing of the Llewellyn Iron Works. Harriman was stunned. Concentrating on the political campaign, he had had little contact with the prisoners or Clarence Darrow for weeks. From the moment he heard the news he knew his long quest for worker political power through labor-socialist fusion had ended.

What had happened? Detective William Burns had been investigating the bombings of Erector Association building sites in summer 1910. One of his

FIGURE 24. McNamara brothers' defense attorneys Job Harriman (left) and Clarence Darrow (standing), with Ortie McManigal's wife, Emma, and children. Courtesy of University of Southern California, on behalf of the USC Libraries Special Collections.

informants, Herbert Hockin, an organizer for the International Association of Bridge and Structural Iron Workers, had turned spy for the industry. Hockin told Burns the ironworkers were behind the sabotage of Burns's clients' worksites. In exchange for Burns's promise not to reveal some unsavory aspects of his past, Hockin joined the plotters. He recruited McManigal as a leading dynamiter and set up a number of bombings.

As a result, Burns knew something that Darrow had anxiously suspected from the beginning: the McNamaras were guilty. Sharing information with Mayor Alexander, the M&MA, and a few other insiders, the detective patiently gathered evidence and developed strategy before laying down his hand.

There were good reasons for his careful attention to detail. Dozens of newspaper correspondents from across the nation and Europe had planted themselves in hotels near the courtroom for months. Their readers were mesmerized by the drama. Behind the scenes, politicians, men of wealth, powerful cultural figures, and others sought to influence the proceedings. With the eyes of the world on the event, and Los Angeles's open shop hanging in the balance, Burns wanted no missteps on the way to hanging the McNamaras.

The election on December 5 was anticlimactic. Harriman lost 85,492 to 51,423. The entire Socialist slate was dragged down with him. The conviction of the McNamara brothers that same day was also a foregone conclusion. Darrow had bargained the confession and its timing—just before the election—in exchange for the lives of his clients, conscious that this would mean Harriman's defeat. When Harriman confronted him, Darrow admitted he couldn't bring himself to tell Harriman before the public announcement because he knew the consequence for his fellow attorney. But he also understood that if he chose any other path, the McNamaras would be executed.

Instead, the brothers went to San Quentin, the labor movement in Los Angeles was plunged back into the open shop for twenty years, and Job Harriman, after one more run for mayor, left behind urban politics for a utopian socialist colony. As for Clarence Darrow, defender of the damned, his days as a labor attorney were over. He was reviled by the same unionists who had placed their hopes in his skilled hands. They could not understand why Darrow had not advised his clients to wait five more days before confessing.

AFTERMATH

When Frances Noel returned to her family in Los Angeles from San Francisco, where she had been organizing women workers to register to vote, her pace didn't slow down. In 1913, running on the Socialist Party ticket, she narrowly lost election to the city council. Her defeat did not curb her enthusiasm for political involvement. Indeed, she was heartened by the election of Fred Wheeler, the first Socialist to serve on the city council. Noel accepted an appointment to an advisory committee created by the council that investigated the living and industrial conditions of low-wage workers. Two years later, she supported the successful campaign of Echo Park journalist Estelle Lawton Lindsay, also a Socialist, and first woman to hold a city council seat.

The strength of the Socialist movement had consequences in state politics. Pushed from below, the Progressive administration of Governor Hiram Johnson passed proworker legislation, including a workers compensation law, limits on the hours of women's and child labor, repeal of a law restricting sailors' ability to quit their jobs, and creation of the Industrial Accident Commission to oversee workplace safety standards.

But the city council victories were the end of the line for Job Harriman's fusion politics in Los Angeles. Wheeler kept his spot on the council, except for one two-year term, until his retirement in 1925, and stayed an advocate for workers throughout his political career. By that time the Socialist Party had gone into irreversible decline.

Job Harriman drew the conclusion that the capitalist class remained too powerful to defeat at the ballot box and retreated from his optimistic view, held for a quarter century, that socialism could be built through electoral politics. Instead, he led hundreds of idealistic leftists to Llano del Rio, an extraordinary but short-lived experiment in democratic communal living in the desert to the northeast in Antelope Valley. Under tremendous political pressure even in the middle of nowhere, Llano collapsed and removed itself to Louisiana. Harriman made the journey but, needing a drier climate for his health, returned to Los Angeles before he died, the same year Wheeler retired from the city council.

Prompted by the McNamara case, a group of business leaders and government officials petitioned President Taft late in 1911 to investigate the conditions that bred industrial violence. Established by Congress in 1912, the Commission on Industrial Relations held hearings and took thousands of pages of testimony delivered by workers and capitalists alike, from Mother Mary Jones to John D. Rockefeller.

The nine commissioners were unable to agree on conclusions, and issued three separate reports in 1915 summarizing their findings. However, the commission clearly exposed to public eye the ruthlessness and brutality of large employers in dealing with worker unrest. The findings of the commission underscored the view that when workers were prevented from organizing and subject to workplace and social repression without recourse, eruptions of violence and lawlessness were to be expected.

Reflecting years later on the events in Los Angeles, Eugene Debs argued that

> [i]f you want to judge McNamara you must first serve a month as a structural ironworker on a skyscraper, risking your life every minute to feed your wife and babies, then being discharged and blacklisted for joining a union. Every floor in every skyscraper represents a workingman killed in its erection.

16

Open Shop

CALIFORNIA WORKERS IN THE JAZZ AGE

THE MCNAMARAS' CONFESSION and Harriman's loss were devastating, not just to the cause of labor-socialist fusion in Los Angeles but to workers across the country. San Francisco labor's financial and logistical support for organizing came to an abrupt end. Southern California unionists retreated onto a few fortified islands in an open shop sea, and mostly stayed there until the 1930s. Even in San Francisco, the once powerful stronghold of the labor movement suffered a series of defeats. In the rest of the United States, the Los Angeles debacle served as a warning: Socialism doesn't work, violent class struggle leads to defeat, accept the open shop.

World War I replaced the sense of worker internationalism fostered by socialism with the nationalism of war fever, providing conservative business interests with a convenient patriotic weapon to wield against the more radical, antiwar wing of the labor movement. Following the war, a recession and ramped-up "Red Scare" forced worker militancy into retreat. The Immigration Act of 1924 drastically curtailed the inflow of workers from other countries, reinforced xenophobia, and deepened divisions among workers. At the same time, the roaring stock market, rise of Hollywood, and an oil boom dangled the possibilities of instant riches in the faces of dazzled Californians.

A more modest but pragmatic vision of ascending to middle-class economic security was proposed by the "Fordist" consumer ethos of the 1920s (Henry Ford's belief that fair wages would create a working class with enough disposable income to consume the goods it produced). It promised working people homeownership, an automobile, and up-to-date appliances like refrigerators and vacuum cleaners—in short, a stake in the capitalist system. The new popular music, jazz, poured out of yet another triumph of technology, the radio, and its exuberant energy lent its name—the Jazz Age—to the era. The great majority of workers turned their attention to individual solutions for their economic and workplace problems, to commercial entertainment, and to other paths away from collective action.

The new prosperity did not reach all or even most working people. In the middle of the decade Calvin Coolidge said, "The man who builds a factory builds a temple. The man who works there worships there." If the president had spoken with itinerant workers, San Francisco building tradesmen, oil workers in the Central Valley, or technicians in Hollywood, he would have learned that not everyone shared his opinion.

THE INDUSTRIAL WORKERS OF THE WORLD

The Industrial Workers of the World (IWW) founded locals in California's rural areas beginning in 1909, advocating for the creation of "one big union" of all workers, regardless of occupation, skill, race, sex, or national origin. Its solution for workers' problems was syndicalism, a democratic worker-run society based in workplace industrial councils. It proposed that when the time was ripe, a massive general strike would lead to revolution and the abolition of capitalism. Until then workers should prepare themselves to run society through the school of direct action.

The IWW—or "Wobblies," as they were also known—saw AFL unions as timid and tied to a narrow view of unionism and social change. Eugene Debs and the Socialist Party helped to found the IWW in 1905; three years later they parted ways, due to the IWW perspective that ballot-box socialism wasn't achievable.

Although its national membership probably never topped one hundred thousand, the IWW led large and important strikes in Lawrence, Massachusetts, and Paterson, New Jersey, and developed a substantial following across the West among miners, lumbermen, railroad workers, agricultural laborers, maritime workers, and others—especially migrant workers—who felt marginalized by or disenchanted with mainstream society. Its popularity and notoriety in California was growing in the early 1910s, following spirited civil disobedience campaigns for the right to deliver speeches on the streets of Fresno, San Diego, and other cities and towns.

The 1912 San Diego free speech battle, in particular, rippled through that southern California city's laws and culture. In a city controlled by a tight-knit

FIGURE 25. A nameless IWW supporter during the San Diego Free Speech Fight of 1912 practices his soapboxing. Joseph A. Labadie Collection, University of Michigan Library (Special Collections Library).

booster business clique led by sugar magnate John D. Spreckels, any challenge to authority was met with a swift response. Wobbly organizing among street-car workers, posing the threat to unite Anglo and Mexican workers, eventuated in the most restrictive city ordinance curtailing free speech in the country. The ban on soapboxing brought together AFL, Wobbly, Socialist Party, and liberal supporters in the California Free Speech League to resist. The IWW filled the downtown Stingaree working-class district with thousands of members, who came from across the western United States to suffer police beatings, hosings, imprisonment, and vigilante attacks, for the cause.

Wobbly campaigns featured a mix of bread and butter reform issues and more audacious demands. The IWW loudly advocated industrial sabotage against abusive employers, and marshaled humor and music in support of its members' brave insistence on workers' rights, often in the face of violent reprisals. It offered, through meeting halls in the poorest parts of the cities, an alternative to the Salvation Army (which Wobblies derisively called "the starvation army") for food and a place to sleep. An added bonus was well-stocked bookshelves, including literature, politics, and IWW publications. "Job delegates," or volunteer organizers, worked alongside the men they recruited in the fields, factories, and countryside, earning their respect and allegiance to the cause. The IWW's little red membership card served as a ticket to ride free on trains with sympathetic conductors and brakemen.

Its audience came largely from the mass of itinerant workers, the state's poorly paid casual labor force, without which agriculture and other seasonal industries could not function. Too often only law enforcement and employment sharks paid any attention to these traveling workers. Known variously as hoboes, bums, tramps, and bindlestiffs, their numbers were impossible to nail down precisely. Careful contemporary observers such as University of California Berkeley labor economist Carleton Parker estimated it to be 150,000. He believed that 5,000 "have been at some time connected with the IWW." Itinerant laborers followed the work, and during the winter months flowed into the larger cities to swell the population of unemployed and underemployed.

According to one account, the most famous movie star of the silent era, Charlie Chaplin, based his screen persona on a tramp he met over lunch one afternoon in San Francisco. The social type Chaplin's character represented was familiar and emotionally appealing; the tramp was everywhere casual labor was needed, and it was needed in a lot of places.

FARMER DURST'S RANCH

It was the custom of California growers to enlarge the labor pool whenever possible to create competition and drive down the wages they paid to temporary migrant workers. So what Ralph Durst did was nothing out of the ordinary. Needing about 1,500 workers to harvest his hops, he advertised for 2,800 all over California and in Nevada and southern Oregon. His flyers promised "the going wage" for hop-picking, a job for "all white pickers who make application before August 1st," and a bonus for workers who stayed for three or four weeks, or to the end of the harvest.

The 3,000 workers who appeared at California's largest hop ranch in Wheatland were single men, groups of bindlestiffs, and entire families. They were native-born and immigrants speaking more than two dozen languages. About a third were women. Few preparations were made to house them or take care of their sanitary needs.

Instead, they were expected to pitch tents or sleep under the sky in a field near the ranch. There were just nine toilets, which soon overflowed. Garbage was disposed of in piles on the ground. The two wells were pumped dry before sunrise each day and quickly became contaminated. In place of drinking water, Durst's cousin sold "lemonade" made from water and citric acid; one worker said that it "almost cut the insides out of us." These conditions led to widespread dysentery in the camp within a week, as well as cases of malaria and typhoid.

The workers found that Durst was paying ninety cents per one hundred pounds of hops picked, which was ten cents less than the "going wage;" the "bonus" simply restored the rate to the normal dollar per hundred pounds.

The temperature averaged over one hundred degrees. The men driving the lunch wagons that circulated in the fields refused to give away any water unless the workers bought food. One picker reported that "There were a great many children in the field who cried for water and it was very pitiful to see them suffer for want of it. Many times I gave my water away to little children."

Scores of Wobblies were among the workforce, including a group of thirty camping together. Within a week, after Durst refused to do anything about the conditions of the camp—and struck IWW organizer Richard "Blackie" Ford across the face—they organized a mass meeting on Sunday afternoon under the broiling sun. Ford held up a baby during his speech calling for a strike and told the crowd, "It's for the life of the kids we're doing this." The group was singing the popular Joe Hill song "Mister Block" when the sheriff and a posse of deputies drove up in a few automobiles.

To "sober the crowd," a deputy fired a shot in the air. This was a mistake. Many migrant workers were armed. More than twenty shots were fired by both sides. Two pickers, the Yuba County district attorney, and a deputy sheriff died of gunshot wounds. The workers and their families poured out of the camp, most leaving before dark. The next morning the National Guard arrived in force. They arrested more than one hundred workers. Ford and another Wobbly, a slightly mentally retarded man, Herman Suhr, were eventually discovered on the run, convicted of murder in early 1914 (although both had counseled nonviolence to the crowd), and sentenced to life in prison.

Wheatland produced two results. Across the state, IWW members were arrested and thrown in jail, along with any migrant workers disliked for any reason by local authorities. The newspapers cooperated fully with the largely illegal police sweeps, creating an atmosphere of fear by printing endless articles about supposed IWW violence and mayhem. The IWW itself provided some of the ammunition for the news media with its calls for industrial sabotage and class warfare. Dozens of Wobblies languished in jail throughout California.

Hiram Johnson's Progressive state reform government responded to the events at Durst's ranch by forming a Commission on Immigration and Housing to investigate conditions for migrant labor. Together with the federal Commission on Industrial Relations, the state commission's attention led to reports, public concern, and well-intended albeit largely inadequate efforts to clean up agricultural labor camps. It also contributed to a consensus that the IWW represented a disturbing social symptom of outrage and resistance to the often intolerable conditions facing California's casual labor force which, if left alone, would only grow worse.

BLACK GOLD RUSH

Several months before the tragic events in Wheatland, and three hundred miles south, a new motion picture, *Opportunity,* premiered in the San Joaquin Valley town of Taft. A fast-expanding town in 1913, Taft rested atop of one of the biggest oil fields in the country. Which was why in January a Hollywood film crew accompanied movie star Fatty Arbuckle to Taft, where they recruited residents to play bit parts and used the Standard Oil production facilities as background for their story: a young man wins the hand of his true love by rising from oil worker to superintendent of the company and mayor of the town.

Filling the local theater, members of the audience at the first screening were delighted to recognize hometown sites and friends and neighbors' faces. They were charitable in assessing the filmmakers' lack of knowledge of oil production, which resulted in several technical errors in the story, visible to people knowledgeable about the industry. Company supervisors and officials mingled with oil workers and their families in the auditorium, cheering the appearance of each familiar face.

Major oil fields had been discovered in California before 1900. Since then thousands of wells had been brought into production around the state. By the time of the Lakeview gusher of 1911 in the Midway-Sunset oil fields, a few miles from Taft, California had risen to first among oil-producing states. A new California gold rush was starting up, if in slow motion. Some men were making lots of money. Gradually the industry was spreading along the central coast, into south Los Angeles, and in the Central Valley. But twelve-hour shifts for $3.50 in most of the companies left oil workers feeling left out of the "Black Gold" Rush.

Exactly four years after the first screening of *Opportunity,* the AFL issued a federal union charter to Oil Field Workers Local 6 in Taft. It turned out it wasn't so easy as the movie made it seem for an individual to rise from worker to boss. Instead, the employees of Standard, Shell, and other companies decided the most likely way to improve their circumstances was to organize for a five-dollar-per-day minimum, eight-hour shifts, and union recognition.

Within a few months another half-dozen oil workers' locals popped up in the Central Valley—in Maricopa, Bakersfield, McKittrick, Coalinga, Lost Hills, and Fellows. Thanks to the strong leadership of Coalinga local organizer and Scottish immigrant Walter Yarrow, and a Washington administration enforcing labor-capital harmony to unify the war effort, federal mediators brokered a deal for the eight-hour day and four dollars pay. It prevented strikes and kept the corporations' union-busting efforts under wraps—at least, until the war was over.

The Central Valley locals soon became a major force in the formation of a new international union, the Oil Field, Gas Well and Refinery Workers of America, founded in June 1918. Of its first twenty locals, eleven were chartered in California.

More locals were organized in southern California following the discovery of enormous underground seas of oil southeast of Los Angeles, beneath Huntington Beach, Long Beach, and Santa Fe Springs by 1921. Now the Black Gold Rush was on for real. Lucky homeowners who discovered thick dark liquid bubbling up in their backyards appeared regularly in newspapers and newsreels. Real estate agents bought up the land, subdivided it, and subdivided it again, selling lots like chances to win the lottery. Sleepy communities in transition from farm country to suburbs sprouted oil derricks.

Like the effect of the 1850s Gold Rush on San Francisco's early metal and machine industries, the oil wells begat refineries and mills and machine tool shops serving the petroleum gods. Across mile after greasy mile between downtown Los Angeles and the San Pedro harbor and points south, industrial operations and working-class residential neighborhoods blended together. By the mid-1920s California was producing one-fifth of the world's oil.

The greed and speculation, the heated growth of industry and wealth, the dreams and disappointments of workers, the battles between labor and capital: all were observed first hand and captured in a sprawling novel by Upton Sinclair, appropriately titled *Oil!* The Socialist author of *The Jungle* lived in

Pasadena. His wife owned a plot of land in what turned out to be an oil field (Signal Hill). He accompanied her to meetings of the neighbors as they struggled to figure out how to proceed. His book began in these meetings. Eventually Sinclair scored big on the Black Gold Rush but through the back door: *Oil!* became a runaway national bestseller, going through seven printings in less than a year.

RED SCARE

The rapid growth of their union gave oil workers hope that it could survive a renewed open shop offensive following World War I. The end of hostilities in Europe signaled a revival of class conflict in the United States, orchestrated by corporations and conservative politicians against the advances made by workers over the previous few years. United States attorney general A. Mitchell Palmer authorized high-profile raids on radical organizations and individuals. Hundreds of politically active immigrants were detained as "subversives" and deported, often with little or no due process. Vigilante groups worked hand in glove with law enforcement agencies in a xenophobic frenzy.

The campaign actually began during the war, when antiwar advocates were labeled "traitors." Socialist leader Eugene Debs was sentenced to ten years in the Atlanta federal penitentiary for making a public speech against the war in violation of the Sedition Act, passed in 1918 as an amendment to the Espionage Act of 1917. (In 1920, still in prison, he ran his fifth Socialist campaign for U.S. president, drawing nearly a million votes.) Both acts were repealed in 1921, and Debs received a pardon.

Debs was an internationally known figure; his release was meant to convey that the United States was still a democracy. The nonfamous were not so fortunate. The campaign against the IWW that began after Wheatland intensified during the war. The entire California leadership of the IWW was imprisoned for much of the 1920s under a state law, the Criminal Syndicalism Act, passed in 1919.

The Russian Revolution, in October 1917, provided a new tool in the antiunion arsenal. Chambers of Commerce across the country made sure all employers knew that calling union activists "Bolsheviks" (the revolutionary faction of Russian Communists) would have a calming effect on labor unrest. Known as "red-baiting," due to the color of the Communist flag, the tactic played a major role in the open shop drive, dovetailing with the identification of union activities as "unpatriotic." On the other hand, the employers attempted to convince workers and the public that the open shop represented the pinnacle of patriotism by renaming the concept the "American Plan."

AFL leaders such as Sam Gompers were not unhappy that their rivals in the IWW were experiencing difficulties. But the conservative assault soon focused on the mainstream labor movement. Any advocacy for workers— whether union organizing drives or attempts in union shops to increase pay or improve working conditions—was interpreted for the public as "unpatriotic" by employers. The biggest strike wave in United States history unfolded in 1919, as workers attempted to hold onto their unions and the wages and conditions they had achieved during the war. A massive effort by the AFL to organize the steel industry ended in a failed strike, blacklisting of union leaders, and the open shop.

The Sailors' Union of the Pacific (SUP) joined in a national walkout with its parent organization, the International Seamen's Union, at the end of which the SUP was reduced to a quarter of its size. The founding of the California State Federation of Teachers in 1919 by six locals led to a dozen more within two years. But most of these were soon gone or intimidated into inactivity, due to the firing of key leaders and repeated accusations that by organizing unions public school teachers were undermining American democracy.

THE 1921 OIL WORKERS STRIKE

Within this unpromising context oil workers in the Central Valley voted to strike. They were faced with a pay cut of a dollar per day (amounting to a 25 percent decrease for many) and withdrawal by the oil companies of their recognition of the union as bargaining agent for the workers. The workers worried that if they lost their union, the eight-hour day would be the next target. The oil companies organized themselves for battle in the Oil Producers Association of California. They rejected an appeal from the union for federal mediation, instead issuing a brief statement of their philosophy: "More business in government, less government in business."

On September 11, 1921, eight thousand members of the Oil Field, Gas Well and Refinery Workers of America shut down the fields throughout the San Joaquin Valley.

Spirits were high and the job action well organized. The men and their families held parades in the towns. The union drew on World War I veterans in its ranks to create roving "law and order" patrols. They made sure the picket lines weren't smashed by company-hired goons. They also ran IWW organizers out of the fields, hoping to maintain a patriotic public image for the AFL union. The oil producers association did their best to prove the opposite. When the union attempted to gain federal government intervention, one of its complaints was that the companies had depicted it as "worse than Russian Soviets."

On the third day of the strike the producers association tried to send in a few hundred strikebreakers hired through the Jerome agency in San Francisco on a specially chartered Southern Pacific train. It arrived that night at the station near Maricopa, but the union was not sleeping. Two thousand strikers and supporters from other unions met the train. Led by the union's law and order patrols, the strikers relieved the would-be scabs of "bagloads of weapons" and sent the train back to San Francisco under union escort.

The strike created new leaders such as Harvey Fremming of Fellows, who later went on to become president of the Oil Workers International. Fremming drove over the western mountain range and secured the support of refinery and field workers along the coast. He and Yarrow, and the Coulter brothers, John and James, oversaw the operations of a strike on a grand scale: thousands of men, in dozens of locations, across hundreds of square miles. The local business communities, dependent for their living on the workers, sided with the strikers. Merchants in Taft contributed four thousand dollars to the strike fund. In all, during the strike the union raised more than half a million dollars from the labor movement and community allies, paying out ten dollars per week to single men and fifteen dollars to families.

But the reactionary political atmosphere, an antiunion federal administration that refused to intervene, and the now unfettered postwar power of the oil producers association proved stronger than the resolve of the strikers and their community support. Soon the companies began eviction proceedings for strikers' families in company-owned housing, aided by conservative law enforcement officials in the small towns dotting the valley.

Oil union locals in other parts of the country had already given way to the Red Scare and employers' assault; the Oil Workers International was nearly penniless and in no position to offer much help. Meanwhile, the deep pockets of the oil corporations, led by the giant Standard Oil, allowed the association to wait out their foes. By November 3 the strike was lost, and so were the contracts held by most of the locals.

The outcome of the strike broke the union's power if not its spirit for more than ten years. Hundreds of blacklisted workers migrated to the huge developing oil fields in and around Los Angeles. The group included most of the valley's union leaders, who continued their activities on the coast. Long Beach Local 128, chartered in early 1922, took many of them in.

It recruited James Coulter of Bakersfield's Local 19 to serve as the Local 128 secretary. Coulter and his brother John had originally come to the valley from Tennessee. Superb organizers, they built Long Beach into the biggest local in the country and the savior of the threadbare Oil Workers International during the difficult decade that followed. It held the only continuous oil field collective bargaining agreements in California for many years.

The demise of the union in the Central Valley was immediately felt in skyrocketing rates of injuries and deaths on the job. In the early 1920s a California oil worker died every five days. Local 128 was able to tap its connections in the labor movement to persuade the state Industrial Accident Commission to issue and enforce Petroleum Industry Safety Orders in 1924 that reduced the fatalities by half, largely through training and commonsense measures (e.g., safety railings in front of moving machinery) resisted previously by the companies as too costly.

The Oil Workers International survived, if barely, thanks to the Long Beach local and the Coulters, preserving an industrial union model that, in better times, might regenerate.

FALL OF THE BUILDING TRADES COUNCIL

The decisive influence exerted over construction in San Francisco by the Building Trades Council (BTC) lasted twenty years. But when the United States declared war in the fall of 1917 and joined the Allied powers, the construction sector of the local economy was in a prolonged slump. P. H. McCarthy, president of the powerful Carpenters Local 22 and former mayor of San Francisco, held sway over a shrinking empire. With fewer craftsmen employed, the reduced dues monies paid by his members failed to cover the expenses of union staff, causing layoffs.

His trusted inner circle of construction union officials was showing gaps, too. Some had gone into business or politics, others had died or moved away. He had replaced dynamic men who had strong roots in their locals with faceless "yes" men on the council. Olaf Tveitmoe, the editor of the BTC's lively publication, *Organized Labor,* suffered a debilitating stroke, and the paper went into decline. Almost unnoticed, the council lost its control over the building materials supply chain, so crucial to its ability to enforce discipline on contractors.

Other events exerted an impact on the balance of power between the BTC and San Francisco employers. In July 1916, during a bitter longshoremen's strike, the city staged a "Preparedness Day" parade to promote United States entry into the war in Europe. The event was supported by the Chamber of Commerce and boycotted by the city's unions, AFL and IWW alike. The union leadership believed the war was going to be fought by working people while the rich stayed safely at home, making money on their war investments. Shortly after the parade began a bomb went off, killing ten onlookers and wounding forty more.

Socialist Party activists Tom Mooney and Warren Billings were arrested, along with three others, including Mooney's wife, as accomplices. Mooney was a member of Iron Molders Local 164, and a controversial figure in the labor movement due to his pugnacious left-wing politics and personality. He had worked on Eugene Debs's presidential campaign in 1908, riding for a time on Debs's famous Red Special train. He had been arrested but not convicted on previous dynamiting charges.

The event and trial were reminiscent of the McNamara brothers' trial for the *Los Angeles Times* bombing. The difference was that Mooney and Billings were innocent. The trial was conducted in an overheated lynch mob atmosphere, fanned by irresponsible journalism and a prosecuting attorney, Charles Fickert, interested in the trial more as a stepping-stone to higher office than in justice. Ignoring obvious conflicts in witnesses' testimony and numerous proofs of perjury, the judge sentenced Mooney and Billings to death, later commuted to life in prison.

The jurors, within a few years, realized their error and petitioned the governor, unsuccessfully, for a pardon. (In a similar outbreak of remorse, eight of the jurors who convicted Herman Suhr of the Wheatland murders petitioned in 1925 for his pardon, referring to the "inflamed" state of public feeling about the IWW at the time for their decision.) The Mooney-Billings case and the campaign to free them became a worldwide labor cause for the next two decades.

In San Francisco, the deadly incident and its legal aftermath shifted middle-class opinion against labor, providing an opportunity for employers to restart their deferred campaign for the open shop.

The largest businesses in the city formed the San Francisco Industrial Association, a local coordinating center for the "American Plan." When it convinced contractors to break their alliance with the Building Trades Council, the once mighty BTC could no longer protect its members. Two lost strikes and humiliating terms of surrender led to the open shop in construction and to McCarthy's resignation in 1922. The BTC broke into factions divided by jurisdictional disputes and political differences.

The employers now replaced all the industry structures once dominated by the BTC. The Builders Exchange, an employer-controlled outfit, took care of hiring. The exchange set up its own apprenticeship programs. Contractors had to apply for permits to purchase building materials, and could only qualify for the permit if they maintained an open shop and paid the Builders Exchange's wage schedule. Building supplies were produced in nonunion facilities.

The effect on building craftsmen in San Francisco was huge. Besides a decline in real wages, they faced the arbitrary and often degrading authority of bosses unconstrained by any counterbalancing power in the workplace. Recalled carpenter Joseph O'Sullivan, "If you wanted to take a piss out on a job, you had to go in a corner like a cat. . . . We had no conditions."

O'Sullivan, an Irish immigrant, played a role in the final effort of the decade by San Francisco carpenters to recapture their lost "conditions." In 1926 the national carpenters union sent organizers and funding to support an eight-month war with the Industrial Association. Five thousand carpenters walked off the job on April 1. From the start it was brutal, the most violent conflict seen since the 1907 streetcar strike. Unlike in the heyday of the BTC, the carpenters were on their own. Their pivotal position in construction shut down many job sites until the Industrial Association brought in strikebreakers from the Jerome agency.

Then each site became contested territory. Police escorted strikebreakers through picket lines. The union formed "wrecking crews," groups of strong young carpenters who would physically intimidate strikebreakers. The twenty-four-year-old O'Sullivan formed a "crew" with his brothers and friends.

> No other trades would join us. Just the carpenters. When we shut a job down, nobody worked—they got out fast. We just used our hands but we worked the scabs over, threw their tools into forms, broke levels. Maybe it was the right thing to do, maybe it was wrong. But that's the way they wanted it, and that's the way it got done.

The carpenters' strike fund, organizing assistance, and violence weren't enough. The strength of the BTC had been based in the council's union card, carried by all crafts. When one group went out, the employer knew that all would follow. This was no longer the case. Without cooperation from the other unions or the ability to control the supply of building materials, the strike was doomed. After a year it was over and O'Sullivan, like many other strikers, was blacklisted and had to travel across the bay to Vallejo to get work. The "American Plan" ruled San Francisco construction until the mid-1930s.

HOLLYWOOD'S LABOR PAINS

If the open shop in San Francisco was a new indignity for construction workers, in Los Angeles it simply remained business as usual. This was a key reason for the birth and growth of the film industry in Hollywood.

Charlie Chaplin began working in the motion picture industry in 1913, the same year that Henry Ford introduced the moving assembly line into his first automobile plant. Over the next few years the movie business would come to resemble Ford's factories in many ways. Film producers rationalized production processes along the lines suggested by Frederick Taylor, who directed an army of stopwatch-wielding efficiency specialists on behalf of American business. Taylor subjected workers to close examination, resulting in the "scientific management" of their time on the job for maximum profit.

The first motion picture studios were not opened in Hollywood until 1911. From the inception of the movies in the mid-1890s production had originated on the East Coast. But poor weather during the long winter months idled the outdoor movie sets and brought exploratory expeditions to Los Angeles beginning in 1906. The advance scouts of the industry were pleased with southern California's climate and the diversity of the surroundings—urban, rural, and natural—within easy driving distance all year round. But just as important was the economic factor. As film financier Benjamin Hampton put it, "the cost of the lumber was low and the wages of the carpenters and other mechanics was 25 to 50 per cent less than in New York."

In 1914 the first craftsmen were dispatched by the Los Angeles Building Trades Council to work in the studios. These were mainly drawn from the electricians' (International Brotherhood of Electrical Workers) and carpenters' unions. Members of the International Alliance of Theatrical Stage

Employees (IA), organized in Stagehands Local 33, could likewise be found working in motion pictures when times were slow in the city's live theater. Unlike the AFL craft unions, which organized workers according to the craft they practiced, the IA sought to bring all workers into one union, both in its original theater jurisdiction, and now in the movies.

By 1915 film production employed more than 15,000 people, centered in Hollywood but sprawling throughout Los Angeles County. Under open shop conditions, most studio workers had little job security. As on the larger farms in the California countryside, the studio workforce was divided between a small permanent "inside" studio staff and a much larger pool of temporary or casual "outside" labor. When working, the hours were typically long; ten- or even twelve-hour shifts without breaks were common. There was no overtime or vacation pay, no sick leave or pension. The casual laborers would show up at the studio gate in the early morning, and if they were offered work they would work. If there was no work they would move on to the next studio and try their luck there.

Such conditions attracted AFL organizer Jim Gray in 1916. The IA brought in organizers the following year. Studio bosses, aware of the union activity, set up the Motion Picture Producers Association (MPPA), uniting seventeen employers to standardize wages and maintain open shop labor policies.

Collisions between the open shop bosses and their workers were inevitable, especially after each side began to organize. Unfortunately for the studio workforce, jurisdictional disputes (disagreements over who had the right to represent the workers) between the AFL building trades unions and the IA made the task of organizing more difficult. Also, women, who labored for lower wages than men who did the same work in film labs, costume and editing departments, and the studio's front offices, were ignored by all the unions. This left close to one-eighth of the studio workforce outside any organizing efforts.

The MPPA and its successor, the Association of Motion Picture Producers, formed in 1924, played the IA and building trades unions against one another until 1926. During these years, strikes by the IA were undermined by strikebreakers from the electricians and carpenters, and vice versa.

At one point it seemed as if there might be a breakthrough. The national AFL, through a series of meetings between 1919 and 1921, had gotten the two groups to agree to represent different crafts instead of competing, and just in time. In July 1921 eleven studios locked out a thousand workers who refused to accept pay cuts and the re-imposition of the ten-hour day. Expecting the usual squabbling between unions, the employers were stunned to find a united front parading with signs before their gates. For two weeks production slowed at all companies and shut down completely in several studios.

But within a couple weeks, the Merchants and Manufacturers Association recruited strikebreakers for the MPPA. The *Los Angeles Times* reported "un-American" comments at union meetings. The IA abruptly voted to return to work, and the strike collapsed. Competition for representation rights resumed for several more years, and the bulk of studio workers remained poorly compensated for irregular work.

In 1925 the studios set up a hiring hall and called it the Mutual Alliance of Studio Employees. It was a company union—an organization that resembled a union in certain respects but was controlled by the employers. Over the unions' protests, it began to supply several studios with workers belonging to neither the IA nor the building trades unions. This move pushed the warring labor groups into serious discussions with each other. By September 1926 they had reached agreement. Now they turned once more to the studios and demanded union recognition, a closed shop, wage increases, overtime, a standard eight-hour day, and six days off with pay each year.

The unions were in a stronger position than they had mustered in 1921. In the interim, the IA had organized film projectionists in several major cities around the country. If the studios did not agree to their proposals, the unions would shut down movie theaters showing films by the struck studios. Just before the strike deadline of December 1, the two sides found a compromise. They called it the Studio Basic Agreement (SBA).

The SBA was a memorandum of understanding, not a contract. It did not include a closed shop, but it did include union recognition and set up committees to handle collective bargaining over wages, hours, and working conditions, and deal with grievances. It wasn't everything the unions wanted, but it was a breach in the walls of the open shop. The employers were even less happy about it. They knew, however, that they needed a guarantee of labor peace if they were to convince the banks to lend them the money they needed to convert to sound production.

In an attempt to repair the crack, the producers founded the Academy of Motion Picture Arts and Sciences in May 1927. Its five divisions (producers, directors, actors, writers, and technicians) were meant to simultaneously bring everyone together in industrial harmony, even as—with membership by invitation only—it represented an effort to divide the industry's workers between the best and the rest. Its philosophy of cooperation between employees and employers, the award ceremony that celebrated it, and the timing of its founding, were viewed with suspicion by the active members of the IA and building trades.

Over time the Academy Awards took on a life of its own. As Hollywood unions, beginning with the Studio Basic Agreement, grew larger and more secure over the years, the academy's original impulse was ignored and then forgotten.

PART IV

Divisions in the Growing House of Labor

17

Radical Responses to the Great Depression

Unemployment is the result of the capitalist system, where a few
own the factories and we millions must slave for them or die of
starvation. When they can make profits out of us, they buy our
labor power; when they cannot, we starve.

FROM A COMMUNIST LEAFLET, OAKLAND, 1930

THE GREAT DEPRESSION LASTED for a dozen years, threw tens of millions
of people into hard times, and transformed the country in fundamental ways.
Its early years produced mass misery and despair but also social movements that
channeled desperation into collective action. In the fall of 1933 the Cannery and
Agricultural Workers Industrial Union, led by Communists, helped farm laborers conduct the biggest strike in Central Valley history, and anarchist organizer
Rose Pesotta assisted immigrant Russian Jews and Mexicans to unionize Los
Angeles garment sweatshops. The following year, a few months after the San
Francisco General Strike, Socialist novelist Upton Sinclair scared the daylights
out of ruling elites when working-class voters almost elected him governor on a
platform of "production for use." Pushed by events, organizations, people, and
political ideas like these, the federal government improved and strengthened a
"New Deal" to fix the economy and put people back to work.

The severity and duration of the Great Depression was partly due to the
magnitude of the stock market crash of 1929. When Franklin Delano
Roosevelt took office in January 1933, thousands of banks stood closed across
the country, a consequence of the breakdown of the financial system after the
crash. In the unregulated financial markets of the pre-Depression years,
investors bought stocks in a speculative frenzy "on margin" (paying a small
fraction of the actual price, with the rest of the payment only due when the
stocks were sold). When increasing numbers of people began to sell their
overleveraged stocks, the money wasn't there to redeem them.

This was but one example of an unprecedented overextension of credit at all
levels of the economy, from capital investments to consumer spending. Such

fiscal irresponsibility prompted FDR to observe, "We have always known that heedless self interest was bad morals; we know now it is bad economics."

With the crash, a crisis of confidence gripped capital lenders and investors. Employers quickly began to lay off workers. Within a few months, unemployment rose more than 800 percent, from a half million to more than four million.

The stock market disaster occurred during what was already a sharp economic downturn brought on by overproduction and inadequate consumer demand. Henry Ford's stated intention may have been to pay his workers enough so that they could consume the goods they produced. But the open shop philosophy of most large employers prevented this purchasing power from taking root in the working class. Once the more affluent classes had bought their radios, vacuum cleaners, and automobiles, corporate sales projections overestimated the actual amount of disposable cash in the pockets of workers, leaving vast piles of consumer products in warehouses and slowing or shutting factories.

These events resulted in prolonged economic devastation for millions of people through no fault of their own. By Roosevelt's inauguration, one-quarter of the country's workforce was unemployed. Certain geographic areas, and some sectors of the economy, fared worse. In Los Angeles, 50 percent of building trades workers were jobless by 1932. The following year, overall unemployment in the city hit 30 percent. Foreclosures ravaged homeowners in the working-class suburb of South Gate; the rate of ownership fell from 89 percent to 55 percent between 1929 and 1935. African American unemployment in the city of sunshine reached 50 percent by 1934.

An even higher percentage of people were suffering, including family members who depended on now-jobless breadwinners. Roosevelt famously referred to "a third of a nation ill housed, ill clad, and ill nourished." For the unemployed worker, the worst years of the Depression meant lowered living standards and deep uncertainty about what tomorrow might bring. Harry Bridges, living in San Francisco, recalled, "I was married to Agnes then, and we were losing our house. Couldn't afford to keep it anymore. After that we moved down to a little flat on Harrison Street, and when that got too expensive—twenty five bucks a month—we moved next door for fifteen."

Student Ersey O'Brien and his unemployed mother would go before school two or three times a week to scavenge food at the outskirts of the downtown Los Angeles central produce market. Survival was more important than fussiness.

I'd take my little wagon, we'd go to market and pick up spoiled fruit that they had discarded, cut the bad part off.... You got a wagon full of fruit or potatoes, maybe a little spoiled and you couldn't sell it in the market, but it was still good.

Things were no better in the San Joaquin Valley. Jessie De La Cruz, a child of farmworkers, lived in 1933 in an abandoned granary outside Weedpatch while her family worked tying vines near Bakersfield. Due to hunger and lack of money, she was reduced to foraging with her brother for mustard greens and wild mushrooms, "and that was not only my family but all the families around us." Poisoned by the mushrooms, she almost died.

"Dust Bowl" migrants (or "Okies") from the American Southwest left their drought-stricken farms and attempted to settle in the fertile California agricultural valleys. Tens of thousands discovered that the land was already all owned, the available work was poorly paid, and local authorities were unable or unwilling to offer assistance to desperate families.

As the Depression grew worse in the early 1930s, Americans wondered why their government was failing to act to help them and why factories with perfectly good machinery sat silent and shuttered when workers needed jobs.

POLITICAL RESPONSES

Relief programs were largely in the hands of state and local governments, but there was little public money set aside for the poor and unemployed, especially in the quantities needed in hard times. Los Angeles County provided $16.20 per month for the unemployed breadwinner with a family—about one-tenth of a living wage for a family of four. The state set up an Unemployed Commission in 1931 to coordinate local relief efforts, but with greatly reduced revenues due to the Depression, state resources were soon exhausted.

Although government and private industry seemed disinterested in the problems of working people, there were other institutions ready to do what they could. Radical political organizations offered to help workers directly challenge and change the oppressive conditions they faced in the Great Depression. Communists and Socialists found growing audiences among working people. The Socialists (through elections) and Communists (through revolution) differed on how to achieve a worker-based political and economic system, and also on how exactly such a system would run. But they did agree about some things.

Both proposed that the economic system of capitalism had outlived its day and should be replaced with a system run by and for working people. The problem, they said, is that in a system managed for profit, with economic cycles of "boom and bust," the only people protected during an economic depression were the rich, a small fraction of the population. Working people actually produced the wealth of the country. Without them, no work could take place, no factories or offices function; indeed, society itself would stop without the daily contributions of working people. The profits made by big business and corporations, argued the radicals, were essentially stolen from the pockets of workers. Capitalists were parasites. Working people would be better off running the economy and the country themselves.

The radical groups didn't stop with talk. They organized in workplaces and communities eager for action. Socialist presidential candidate Norman Thomas polled almost 900,000 votes in 1932 (63,000 in California). Members of his party led the garment workers unions based in New York. Communists helped put together unemployed councils to demonstrate and lobby for jobs and assistance in finding housing and food. In 1930 Communist-led demonstrations drew a million people nationwide on March 6 to protest unemployment and call on an unresponsive national government for jobs.

Still in high school, Dorothy Ray (later Healey) was smart, energetic, and deeply concerned about poverty and injustice. Within a few years she would be organizing farmworkers in California's central valleys. In 1930 she joined with other young Communist activists on street corner protests against unemployment in Berkeley and Oakland. She later described what she was attempting to do:

> Starting with that first big unemployed protest in 1930, we understood that you had to have a daily plan of building a demonstration, and that holding a demonstration could only be part of a larger strategy. You started with small demonstrations in relief offices, or in various neighborhoods around the city, and then built up to a big central demonstration. That's the way to turn out a mass following, so that you're not just bringing out your own militants each time. We didn't organize a demonstration just to express our own outrage at one or another injustice, or, worse, as an occasion for self-display. We brought new people to demonstrations as a way of increasing their knowledge of the power of collective endeavor.... And we could see that organization gave them a power that they hadn't ever had before, and that perfecting that organization was our greatest, indeed our only, hope for success.

The Communist Party grew steadily throughout the 1930s, from 25,000 in 1932 to a hundred thousand by 1940. California had the second highest number of members, behind New York. The party's influence extended far beyond its membership because it was organized, offered plausible explanations for the problems people faced, and proposed actions that encouraged the hope that things could change.

THE NEW DEAL

People who might not have listened sympathetically to anticapitalist arguments a few years previously were starting to pay attention now—and Roosevelt knew it. Events in 1934 in California and elsewhere indicated that if the government did not move quickly to create a means for resolving widening disputes between labor and capital, class warfare might break out on a national scale. The mass action and violence leading up to the San Francisco General Strike had equivalents in Toledo, Ohio, in Minneapolis, Minnesota, and in a great arc across the eastern and southern United States, when more than a third of a million workers joined a bitter strike in the textile industry.

The New Deal was not a plan that emerged, full-grown, from Roosevelt's head. It represented an experimental and evolving government response to the economic crisis and to growing numbers of workers organizing outside social norms and official channels of law. Roosevelt was no radical. He was a pragmatic and flexible leader who adjusted his course to best meet conditions. New Deal legislation expanded the rights of workers and the entitlements of American citizenship. It provided socially useful jobs to millions when the market economy failed to do so, through programs like the Works Progress Administration. It modestly extended the promise of democracy from political life into the economy. It borrowed sparingly and cautiously from socialist ideas. But it was also designed to contain growing collective discontent within the legal boundaries of the capitalist system.

Roosevelt's first task was to stabilize the nation's finances. In 1933 the Glass-Steagall and the Securities acts established federal regulation and enforcement powers over banking and stock exchanges, and began to restore confidence in the country's banks and financial markets. Both acts represented a shift in public opinion and business philosophy from a semimystical belief in the free market to the recognition that the public interest required government oversight and regulation.

At the same time as Roosevelt and his majority in Congress were putting in place rules for business they began to address the causes of labor unrest. A first effort was the 1933 National Industrial Recovery Act (NIRA), overseen by the National Recovery Administration. The act attempted to regulate business practices with codes of fair competition and voluntary cooperation by industry in setting hours of work, wages, and prices of goods and services. The NIRA also, through its section 7(a), set up a labor board. It said,

> Employees shall have the right to organize and bargain collectively through representatives of their own choosing, and shall be free from the interference, restraint or coercion of employers of labor, or their agents, in the designation of such representatives or in self-organization or in other activities for the purpose of collective bargaining or other mutual aid or protection.

Section 7(a) allowed for various forms of worker representation, without favoring one over another. Unions, workplace councils, and other worker groups could bargain with employers or employer associations. So could company unions.

Many employers rushed to create company unions, such as the Mutual Alliance of Studio Employees in Hollywood and the "Blue Book union" on the docks in San Francisco, reflecting a strategy by employers to keep real unions out of the workplace. Such "unions" typically negotiated without any benefits for workers, and their leaders were often handpicked by the companies.

The NIRA left numerous details about resolving workplace disputes vague, including enforcement. Despite such problems, the NIRA, as a broad statement of workers' collective rights, helped to unleash organizing energy that had simmered, without an effective outlet, for more than a decade. Longshoremen flooded into the International Longshoremen's Association (ILA) in San Francisco and Los Angeles and demanded union recognition. Garment workers joined the International Ladies' Garment Workers' Union (ILGWU) in Los Angeles. Farm laborers, although uncertain whether the act applied to them, organized unions and went on strike in the central valleys. And these new worker movements provided writer Upton Sinclair with the opportunity to bring a modified version of Socialist politics for serious consideration before the California electorate.

The latest in a long line of California boom crops, cotton was seen by Central Valley newspapers as "white gold," like sugar before it. Its growers profited from the plight of farmers in the southern United States, who were plagued by boll weevils, bad weather, and exhausted land. At the end of the 1920s more than two hundred thousand acres along the west side of the San Joaquin Valley grew the wiry green plants with the fluffy white bolls, utilizing modern mechanized techniques of planting. Following the state's historical pattern, large farms of hundreds, and sometimes thousands, of acres dominated the cotton industry. At least 35,000 laborers, more than a third of whom were migrants, were needed during the long harvest, which lasted from September through January.

In 1926 cotton pickers in the San Joaquin Valley made $1.25 per one hundred pounds. The workers were predominantly Mexican and Mexican American, although growers also employed a sprinkling of Okies and African Americans. Rosaura Valdez was twenty-four years old, with two small children, in 1933, laboring in the fields of the Peterson ranch with her husband, hefting one hundred pound sacks.

> I'd have a twelve-foot sack, about this wide. I'd tie the sack around my waist and the sack would go between my legs and I'd go on the cotton row, picking cotton and just putting it in there.... So when we finally got it filled real good then we would pick up the sack, toss it up on our shoulders, and then I would walk, put it up there on the scale and have it weighed, put it back on my shoulder, climb up a ladder up on a wagon and empty that sack in.

That year, due to the Depression, wages in cotton had sunk to forty to sixty cents per hundred pounds. Conditions were dire for many migrant families.

Family and cultural ties going back to shared regional origins helped the Central Valley Mexican population survive. Most workers based themselves for as much of the year as they could in one location. By the 1920s, large numbers of San Joaquin cotton workers lived in and near Los Angeles, or south in the Imperial Valley. They often traveled in families and groups of families, recreating their communities in the farm labor camps, then returning to barrios and homes. Years of following the same patterns of travel for work established ongoing relationships between workers and employers and among the workers. Cotton maintained community due to its long harvest season.

Mutual aid societies provided structure for Mexican communities. Several supported a brief strike of a thousand cantaloupe workers who organized themselves into La Union de Trabajadores del Valle Imperial (Imperial Valley Workers Union) in May 1928. In 1930, near Brawley, five thousand lettuce workers, including Filipinos, struck the fields with the assistance of a mutual aid society. A few organizers from a Communist union, the Agricultural Workers Industrial League (AWIL), showed up, armed with a mimeograph machine. Their assistance prolonged and broadened the strike but proved unequal to the resources of the growers and their local government allies. The AWIL's intervention ended in prosecutions for "criminal syndicalism" (a deliberately vague law that allowed authorities to interpret many union tactics as illegal) and prison sentences for the Communists, including one Filipino activist, and repatriation for several Mexican workers.

These acts of resistance were significant responses to the deterioration of conditions for California farm laborers as the Depression deepened. But the main event came in 1933.

THE GREAT COTTON STRIKE OF 1933

After passage of the NIRA, farmworkers believed (falsely) that the law applied to them and felt emboldened to form unions and strike. Dozens of strikes, beginning in the spring, slowed or stopped large swaths of agricultural production in various crops. Most were led by the Cannery and Agricultural Workers Industrial Union (CAWIU), which had emerged out of the AWIL in 1931. The union had few weapons except the fiery dedication of its mostly young organizers, solidarity and community networks among the workers, and the thin but critical organizational backbone of the Communist Party.

Caroline Decker was a twenty-one-year-old daughter of eastern European Jewish immigrants. She served as a CAWIU organizer, and later told an interviewer, "You had me and Pat Chambers and three or four people down there. A communist here. A radical worker there. No money. No knowledge of how to do these things. Just all good will and idealism." The union's staff, however, learned quickly.

Through the spring and summer a number of strikes resulted in wage increases, but the growers drew the line at union recognition—especially of a "subversive" organization like the CAWIU. In August the union held its founding convention to solidify nineteen small Central Valley locals. Its members set down their "radical" principles: industrial unionism (field and cannery workers together); the right of agricultural workers to organize, strike, and picket; the right of members to vote on contracts; and no employer discrimination based on sex, race, color or belief. The union's program specified seventy-five cents per hour for skilled labor, an eight-hour day, overtime pay, sanitary working conditions and housing, the abolition of piecework and contract labor, equal pay for women, childcare, unemployment insurance, and an end to child labor.

On October 4 the CAWIU called a strike in the cotton fields for a dollar per hundred pounds and union recognition. Eighteen thousand workers, spread over an expanse one hundred miles long and forty miles wide of the fertile San Joaquin Valley, left the fields—the largest agricultural job action in California's history. More than three-quarters of the strikers were Mexican and Mexican American, and their ranks provided the bulk of the strike's leadership, although fifty-five-year-old Dust Bowl migrant "Big Bill" Hammett, supported by his five sons, quickly emerged as a strike leader as well.

Growers formed armed vigilante groups and blocked food shipments to the strikers on the roads, including relief supplies sent by the federal government. When they evicted workers and their families from the labor camps, the strikers set up encampments on the lands of sympathetic farmers. The biggest was established at Corcoran, where the union made its strike headquarters among 3,500 people. The camp was organized like a small town on four acres, with "streets" of tents surrounded by a barbed wire fence for protection from attack. A central space was reserved for nightly meetings and entertainment by a traveling Mexican troupe, the Circo Azteca.

From its strongholds the union moved car caravans along the narrow country roads to head off strikebreakers and pull workers from the fields. The growers sent contingents of armed men, including hastily sworn in deputies, to break up strikers' meetings and picket lines. They left the Corcoran camp alone, after a couple of carloads of thugs, sent to make trouble, assessed the farm worker patrols arrayed around the perimeter and thought better of it.

Six days into the strike, on October 10, Pat Chambers was speaking in front of the CAWIU office to a crowd of strikers in Pixley. Ten carloads of growers with guns pulled up. As Chambers and the union members retreated into the union hall, the growers opened fire on the unarmed group. Within minutes two strikers and a representative of the Mexican consulate lay dead, and eight more workers were wounded.

FIGURE 26. Strikers' caravan in the San Joaquin Valley during the Great Cotton Strike of 1933. Courtesy of the Bancroft Library, University of California, Berkeley.

The same day, seventy miles south, in Arvin, thirty armed growers stood between 250 strikers and scabs working in the Frick ranch. After several hours of a heated standoff, striker Pedro Subia was shot and killed, and several others wounded. Law enforcement officials in due course arrested eleven growers and seventeen strikers, including Pat Chambers, for disturbing the peace. No one was convicted for the shootings.

The murders unified strike sentiment. Several thousand people marched in Fresno to honor the dead strikers, an event captured for posterity by members of the Workers Film and Photo League on motion picture film. The grower violence drew the attention of the federal government. The director of California's National Recovery Administration (NRA) told Governor Rolph that the New Deal's recovery programs were jeopardized by such employer lawlessness and that state government needed to provide protection "not only to propertied interests but to working men as well." The situation was judged so extreme that the NRA—although farm labor disputes were officially outside its authority under the NIRA—forced Rolph, who had maintained a hands-off attitude, to form a commission to investigate the strike and recommend a settlement.

Federal officials also pressured Rolph to provide milk and food to the strikers. Corcoran strikers accepted the supplies following government promises that strikers receiving the food would not be deported. The strikers then voted, somewhat reluctantly, to end the strike after the commission recommended wages of seventy-five cents per hour, without union recognition, as the terms of settlement. Even so, as the strikers' camps began to close down and most of the strikers drifted back to southern California, about one-fifth of the workers refused to go back to work under those terms.

The cotton strike lasted more than three weeks. Its impact was felt not only in higher wages for the workers but also in the formation of the Associated Farmers the following year, a growers' organization opposed to farm worker unionism. The CAWIU continued to organize until 1935, when much of its leadership was found guilty in a high-profile trial in Sacramento of criminal syndicalism. Several Mexican CAWIU leaders, including John Diaz and Francisco Medina, were deported. Pat Chambers and Caroline Decker served time in prison. Chambers became the unwilling model for one of the main characters in John Steinbeck's fictional portrayal of farm labor strife, *In Dubious Battle*. In real life, after prison, he worked quietly as a union carpenter.

ORGANIZING THE SWEATSHOPS

The cotton strike occurred at the same time as another strike, by garment workers, in Los Angeles. The International Ladies' Garment Workers' Union (ILGWU), founded in 1900, expanded from its base in New York and Chicago to California in the 1910s. The union represented a stabilizing force in a fiercely competitive industry. The owners of countless workshops, large and small, believed the only way to survive in their volatile economic sector was to keep wages as low as possible. This was the industry that gave us the term "sweatshop."

The union attempted to show the employers that through an industry-wide master contract that paid a living wage, economic competition could be restricted to efficient organization of production, distribution, and sales of the product, clothing. But this was a lesson that the owners needed to learn time and again, starting with two massive New York strikes in 1909 and 1910. One of their best instructors was Rose Pesotta.

Rachelle Peisoty was born in the Ukraine to Jewish parents in 1896. Her name was changed to Pesotta in 1913 by an immigration official in Ellis Island when she arrived in the United States with her grandmother. Soon after going to work in a New York garment factory she became active in Local 25 of the ILGWU, a lively organization bubbling with left-wing politics among its Jewish and Italian immigrant members.

After hearing Emma Goldman speak at a meeting Pesotta became an anarchist. Sympathetic to the IWW, she nonetheless organized on behalf of her sister and brother workers through the AFL union she belonged to. She helped to establish an education department in Local 25 and became an imaginative, energetic, and fearless organizer with a deep commitment to rank and file worker empowerment. In the 1920s she received formal training, attending labor colleges in Bryn Mawr and Brookwood. She became active in the campaign to defend Nicola Sacco and Bartolomeo Vanzetti, two anarchists tried and ultimately executed for murder, whom most labor activists believed to have been framed. Late in the decade, recognizing her skills, the ILG international executive board hired her.

In 1933 the union was in the midst of a NIRA-inspired organizing drive and enormous growth in the eastern United States. Responding to a call for assistance and hoping to extend the NRA garment codes to California, the union sent Pesotta to Los Angeles.

A local of Jewish immigrant male cloak and suit makers had survived the antiradical witch hunt of the 1920s and a failed strike in October 1930. That job action was crushed when an explosion tore through the Los Angeles Garment Center Building, twenty years after the McNamara brothers' bombing of the *Los Angeles Times* building.

The Merchants and Manufacturers Association, with the *Times,* accused the cloak and suit makers (ILGWU Local 65) of marking the anniversary in this violent fashion. It turned out the explosion had resulted from a gas leak—a weird echo of the past, because it was what the labor movement suspected had occurred in 1910 but in fact had not. Although the local lost the strike, it continued to meet, recruit members, and bide its time despite an industry blacklist for its members.

The small but relatively stable Local 65 provided a base of support for Pesotta. Part of her assignment was to help Local 65 gain a citywide contract. She was also determined to build a strong organization among women dressmakers. Complicating her efforts, Communists were competing with the ILGWU for allegiance of the city's garment workers, both within existing ILG locals and through an ultramilitant independent union, the Needle Trades Workers Industrial Union (NTWIU).

Ultimately the treatment of the workers by the employers gave Pesotta what she needed to build her campaign. Several thousand dressmakers—predominantly Latina but with significant Italian and Yiddish-speaking Russian-Jewish minorities—worked in often terrible conditions in the downtown manufacturing district for about two hundred companies. The employers ignored minimum wage laws and avoided, by various strategies, paying for the full amount of time women spent in the workplace.

In her autobiography, *Bread Upon the Waters,* Pesotta recounted the description given her by dressmaker Maria Flores of her job in a sweatshop, which included many hours of uncompensated time. "I come in the morning, punch my card, work an hour, punch the card again. I wait for two hours, get another bundle, punch card, finish bundle, punch card again. Then I wait some more—the whole day that way." Pesotta also described the "open door system."

> Women hunting jobs were given the "freedom of the building." Doors leading to staircases were left unlocked, so that they could take the elevator to the top floor, ask at each shop if there was work, walk down to the next floor, and repeat the performance until, if lucky, they found a few days' employment for the price offered. . . . As soon as the order was filled, they would be laid off. . . . Garment factory owners regarded their employees as casual workers, in the same class as migrants who harvested fruit and vegetable crops.

Pesotta found that even women lucky enough to find full-time work were surviving only because they were enrolled at the same time in meager government or private charitable assistance programs. Although many of the white male leaders of the Los Angeles ILGWU didn't think the Latinas were organizable, Pesotta thought differently. Within weeks of her arrival, after visiting workplaces and homes of the workers, she wrote to ILGWU president David Dubinsky, "It is the experience of many old residents here that no Mexicans came willingly to join the union. But now they all come, smiling and happy to help and their 'Solidarity Forever' blends very well with ours."

Like cotton workers, these women shared the recent heritage of the Mexican Revolution. While their relationship to the politics of the revolution varied, they understood collective resistance to oppression. Many had eagerly followed recent events in the garment industry in the eastern United States, and knew, if incompletely, of the NRA. They readily responded to Pesotta's attention, like these employees of the Clare Dress Company.

"We want a strike," said Carmela, a tiny creature with flashing black eyes. "We want to picket our shop." "Have you ever been on strike before?" I asked. "No, but if others can go out and win, like the Philadelphia and New York dressmakers, why can't we?" "They say the NRA is back of us—what is the NRA anyway?" another wanted to know.

In mid-September, Pesotta helped the dressmakers charter Local 96 of the ILGWU. Moving quickly, the new members signed up their coworkers "by the dozens." Pesotta and her assistant, Bill Busick (who had served as campaign manager for Socialist Norman Thomas's run for U.S. president the year before) rented a vacant three-story building at 1108 South Los Angeles Street, convinced a local Spanish-speaking radio station to run a program on the union's organizing drive two evenings a week, produced a four-page bilingual newsletter twice a week, and distributed thousands of leaflets.

Pesotta contributed something less tangible but just as important to the organizing effort: she listened closely to the women workers, and learned. An immigrant woman worker herself, she could relate to their history, as she wrote:

> From the beginning of the twentieth century, Mexican tillers of the soil and their families had been encouraged to come into the Golden State in steadily increasing numbers to gather the seasonal crops and then to depart. . . . Poorly paid and hard driven, many of these agricultural workers, seeking to leave their thankless labors, naturally gravitated to the principal California cities, where compatriots had preceded them. Thus hundreds of Mexican women and girls, traditionally skillful with the needle and eager to get away from family domination, had found their way into the garment industry in Los Angeles.

Pesotta understood their fear of deportation and promised legal action on behalf of any worker who received threats from her boss that he would report her to the authorities if she signed a union card. Her rapport and reassurances brought new members surging into Local 96.

On September 25 the cloak makers called a ninety-minute work stoppage to hold a mass meeting and strike discussion. Two days later, dressmakers did the same. The meetings took place at a large auditorium on Grand Street. The unions voted to strike, essentially for the same things: union recognition, a thirty-five hour workweek, employer agreement to abide by the NRA wage codes, an hour lunch break, various labor-management conflict resolution procedures, and crucially, that no worker would have to punch a time card except on actually leaving or entering the factory.

By early October it was clear that the employers, pressured by the Merchants and Manufacturers Association, would not negotiate seriously with Dressmakers Local 96. Activists were being fired daily for transparently anti-union reasons. Pesotta couldn't afford to let either the bosses or the NTWIU know exactly when the strike would occur. Instead, night after night, scores of workers came into the union headquarters, setting up the strike structure: training shop-based picket captains, creating committees, setting up a kitchen to feed thousands of people, printing and distributing striker identification cards, gathering support from other unions and community groups, and finally printing ten thousand bilingual strike flyers that called on all garment workers—union members, nonmembers, unemployed, skilled and unskilled, men and women—to leave the shops and join the picket lines.

Without officially issuing a strike call, Pesotta marshaled her forces. The two hundred member "organization committee" met in the hall the evening of October 11. The activists were told to report the next morning at 5 A.M. to receive flyers to distribute. When they arrived, they found the flyers were headlined, "Dressmakers' general strike declared today!" They took their bundles to their shops and the strike began. Instead of reporting to work, more than three thousand workers walked to the union hall and registered for their strike cards. Another thousand simply refused to work. Nearly the entire Los Angeles garment industry was shut down.

From the start the job action's innovative tactics received favorable publicity. The picket lines featured well-dressed women, many with family members and friends. Singing union songs in Spanish, English, and Yiddish, the strikers entertained shoppers and won their support. When the radio station owner was intimidated into withdrawing the prounion show, the union bought time on a Tijuana station, out of reach of the employers association but with a strong enough signal to cover Los Angeles. On Halloween, three hundred children, dressed in costumes, were entertained at the festively decorated union hall; after lunch they paraded two by two to the garment center, drawing reporters and amused crowds. *La Opinion* editorialized on behalf of the union.

Five days into the strike the cloak makers were granted recognition and a union shop by the employers and returned to work. They continued to support the dressmakers financially and by volunteering in the union headquarters. Pesotta and the dressmakers publicly celebrated the cloak makers' victory, but a key part of the pressure on the manufacturers was removed when they left the picket lines.

As a result of this and other factors (especially the brutality of the Los Angeles police Red Squad arrests of strikers and protection of scabs) the dressmakers' strike was not a solid success, although important in a number of ways. The strike ended on November 6, with an agreement arbitrated through a neutral board. (One of its members was former Los Angeles Labor Council activist and Socialist city council candidate Frances Noel.) Pesotta was dissatisfied with the settlement, which on paper included such union demands as a thirty-five-hour week and raising wages, bringing them into line with the NRA codes for dress manufacturing. But like the codes, it lacked enforcement mechanisms.

Despite these disappointments, the conclusion of the strike proved to doubters that Latinas were willing to organize and strike, and convinced the women to continue fighting. Pesotta helped the new local hold elections and establish an executive board. Seven of the nineteen new leaders were Latinas. Within two years the dressmakers achieved a union shop in much of the city's dress industry, elevating wages and establishing better conditions for thousands of workers.

ENDING POVERTY IN CALIFORNIA

Encouraged by signs that large sections of the working class were beginning to stir, Upton Sinclair thought the New Deal might address some of the problems he saw around him in the Golden State; but he did not think it would cure the Depression entirely nor was he inclined to wait patiently for this to happen. Instead, the longtime Socialist pamphleteer and best-selling author of *The Jungle* and *Oil!* decided the time had come to run for governor—as a Democrat. In the biggest news for the California electoral left since Harriman's run at the mayor's office of Los Angeles in 1911, Sinclair won the Democratic nomination with more votes than anyone had ever received in a California primary. He seemed poised to win the election.

His plan, which he called "End Poverty in California," or EPIC, was breathtakingly simple: to put the state's unemployed (29 percent in 1933) to work by bringing them together in "cooperative colonies" in the empty factories and vacant fields dotting the economic landscape. They would trade the results of their labors with each other directly, without the intervention of money. The resultant "production for use" would replace production for profit and jumpstart a new economy. Before passage of the Social Security Act, Sinclair called for a pension for every needy person over sixty, widows with children, and the disabled.

Sinclair wrote and published a booklet to popularize his ideas, *I, Governor of California, and How I Ended Poverty: A True Story of the Future.* His followers pulled together an impressive organization based around circulation and discussion of the pamphlet, which sold more than a quarter million copies. They launched hundreds of EPIC clubs and ran a slate of candidates for the California legislature.

The heart of Sinclair's support was the huge span of industrial suburbs sprawling from downtown Los Angeles south to San Pedro and Long Beach, and working-class neighborhoods in the major cities. EPIC also benefited from the political journey of African Americans, now reaching a decisive moment thanks to the Depression. Historically Republican since Lincoln's time, blacks were switching allegiances in the 1930s as their party failed to come up with adequate responses to the economic crisis, which for them was magnified by racism restricting workforce participation to the bottom levels of employment. Sinclair's plan made good sense to Augustus Hawkins, the first African American elected to the California state assembly, who ran as an EPIC candidate.

Unfortunately for Sinclair, EPIC also made sense to the organizations of the employing class—the same kind of sense they had made of Job Harriman's campaign two decades earlier. They funded what Sinclair called "the Lie Factory," a ferocious assault on Sinclair's ideas, character, and candidacy. The owners of the newspaper, radio, and motion picture industries in California closed ranks to wage a furious media war, masterminded by a Los Angeles advertising firm. The campaign for incumbent governor Frank Merriam virtually ignored its own candidate, running an all-negative onslaught targeting Sinclair. One low tactic among many others: short films, pretending to be documentary newsreels of "man in the street" reactions to Sinclair and his ideas, were shown in every movie theater in the state. Produced by the movie studio bosses, they were completely scripted and acted, including scenes of hoboes flooding into California in expectation of the good life after a Sinclair victory.

Beaten, the EPIC campaign nonetheless contributed important steps forward for California politics. It built a progressive prolabor wing in the Democratic Party and elected dozens of its candidates to the legislature, including future governor Culbert Olson. The ambitious scale of EPIC's ideas helped Roosevelt's policy advisors to think big (although the president refused to endorse Sinclair himself). It also provided a vision of industrial democracy that reverberated with workers waiting for an organization that could help them realize that idea.

18

The San Francisco General Strike

ON MAY 9, 1934, SAN FRANCISCO LONGSHOREMEN got tired of waiting. They had waited patiently for negotiations to produce an acceptable agreement. They had postponed striking when President Roosevelt asked them to, even though they had voted for a coast-wide walkout by an overwhelming 6,616 to 699. They had waited for a government-appointed mediation board to come up with a reasonable resolution to their differences with the waterfront employers.

Since they had been waiting for fifteen years, they figured they could wait a few months longer. But when all their other options failed, twelve thousand longshoremen from every major port along the West Coast walked off their jobs.

This was the beginning of an eighty-three-day struggle. By the time it was over forty thousand maritime workers had joined in a remarkable display of solidarity and courage. Several workers had been killed and hundreds injured. Close to a thousand workers, supporters, and innocent bystanders had been arrested. But shipping had been brought to a complete standstill along the California, Oregon, and Washington coasts. Most astonishingly, San Francisco workers staged a four-day general strike, shutting down the entire city, to protest employer and government-sponsored violence against working people. As a result industrial unionism took root in California and the entire West Coast.

THE SHAPE-UP AND THE FINK HALL

That's the way any of them bosses looked at the men, like animals— to be used in any way it was possible to attain their end. They didn't care if they killed you or not. You were just so much scum.

SAN PEDRO LONGSHOREMAN AL LANGLEY

Dock work was hard work. Loading cargoes on and off ships with the long-shoreman's hook meant long hours of difficult physical labor. But the men who performed this work in the harbors of San Francisco and San Pedro didn't mind the physical hardship as much as the way the work was organized.

In 1919, after losing two strikes in three years, the oldest industrial union in San Francisco, the Riggers and Stevedores, affiliated with the International Longshoremen's Association (ILA), was destroyed. For the next fifteen years longshoremen were hired on the West Coast docks by two methods universally hated by the workers, called the "shape-up" (San Francisco) and the "fink hall" (other ports).

Early each morning San Francisco longshoremen would gather or "shape up" at the docks by the edge of the bay. "Gang bosses" would appear and hire men from among the crowd. Sometimes it would be afternoon before hiring began. Sometimes there was no hiring for days. If he were lucky enough to be hired, a longshoreman might work for twenty-four or thirty-six hours in a row at a killer pace. The practice of using "short gangs" (four or six men when eight were needed) made a bad situation worse. The accident rate was extraordinarily high. But there was always someone willing to take the place of a man that got hurt.

With many men and few jobs, workers devised individual strategies to ensure work. "They had all kinds of little systems," recalled San Pedro long-shoreman Frank Sunstedt. "For example, the old timers would wear matches stuck in their hat bands. Three matches was a code. Maybe it meant a duck to the boss, or a chicken, or a turkey, or a bottle of wine or whiskey." The gang boss might accept bribes of cash, alcoholic beverages, or painting his house over the weekend, in exchange for choosing a man to work. At the Dollar Steamship Company it was the accepted custom for a worker to "kick back" 10 percent of his wages to the gang boss. Since in 1933 a San Francisco long-shoreman earned seventy-five cents per hour—when he worked at all—there wasn't very much to kick back.

In most West Coast ports outside San Francisco work could be found through the "fink halls," as they were called by the workers, run by the employers. These hiring halls were little more than indoor shape-ups. In some ports the employer association would post job listings from several companies. In other cities individual employers might run their own fink halls. But getting work depended on the same personal contacts and bribery schemes as in the San Francisco shape-up.

An organization called the "Longshoremen's Association of San Francisco and the Bay Area" issued little blue books to longshoremen. To get work on the docks, you had to belong to the "blue book union." (The books were blue to distinguish them from the red books issued by the old ILA Riggers and Stevedores union.) The trouble was, the so-called Longshoremen's Association wasn't a union at all. Created by gang bosses during the 1919 strike and run by the employers, it existed to prevent the formation of a real union.

Harry Bridges attended one meeting. He reflected, "It became obvious to me that it was a company controlled union and a racket." Bridges, born in Australia in 1901 to a Catholic family, went to sea at fifteen and was shipwrecked twice. His exposure to sailors' conditions and a general strike in Australia during World War I began his union education.

In 1920 he left an Australian ship in San Francisco, joined the Sailors Union of the Pacific (SUP), and sailed in the coastal trade. Angered at the SUP leadership after the crippling loss of a 1921 strike, he briefly joined the IWW affiliate for maritime workers, the Marine Transport Workers Industrial Union. He was soon disappointed in the Wobblies' leadership as well. But their syndicalist vision of workers' control of society and direct action to resolve industrial conflict stayed with him. This perspective fed his contempt for the blue book union after he came ashore and began working on the docks.

About one thousand San Francisco longshoremen, or one-quarter of the workforce, carried blue books. The rest—Bridges among them—refused to do so, and either worked when there was so much cargo on hand the bosses had no choice except to hire them or left the waterfront for other employment.

Representatives of the blue book union kept track of men who agitated for a real union and maintained a blacklist to assist employers in remembering troublemakers. Bridges later recalled, "I was so well-known to the delegate of the blue book union that soon it was impossible for me to get employment for more than a day or so on a job before the blue book delegate would catch up with me and have me fired."

Occasionally a longshoreman would be foolish enough to go to the blue book union for help. "Foghorn Charlie" demanded that the American Hawaiian Steamship Company pay him, according to the company's own rules, for working through his dinner hour. After a blue book representative spoke to the company, Charlie was paid. But the next time he was standing in the shape up, "nobody saw Charlie. They saw the fella behind him, and the fella on the right of him, and the fella on the left of him, but they didn't see him. They all went to work, and he was left standing there."

By mid-1933, when the National Industrial Recovery Act (NIRA) became law, longshoremen were ready to rebuild their union. Almost without any effort by the ILA, thousands of West Coast dockworkers joined, encouraged that section 7(a) of the new law seemed to say unions were OK.

In San Francisco, a handful of waterfront Communists, a few ex-Wobblies, and fed-up rank and file longshoremen—including Bridges—had been producing an occasional mimeographed newsletter. The *Waterfront Worker* enjoyed a wide readership among the frustrated dockworkers because the ideas in its pages resonated with their experience. It urged longshoremen to create a militant industrial union that would not only stand up for them but act in solidarity with other maritime workers too.

The publication also insisted on democratic unionism, arguing that rank and file workers should debate policy and vote on all major decisions. The *Waterfront Worker* helped focus the attention of the ILA's new rank and file members on a few key demands: sharing the available work equitably through a union-controlled hiring hall, a dollar an hour wage, coast-wide bargaining, and a six-hour day and thirty-hour work week.

SAILING IN TROUBLED SEAS

In 1933 the seamen still had their union, the Sailors Union of the Pacific. But the SUP was not as far along as the ILA in recovering its strength. The disastrous 1921 strike that had so angered Bridges, called by the SUP's parent organization, the International Seamen's Union, left the SUP in tatters, reduced from 9,000 members to less than 1,500. At that time the longshoremen, weakened by their defeats in 1916 and 1919, were unable to offer much assistance. In fact, many longshoremen, remembering that the seamen had scabbed during their strikes, turned around and did the same.

As a result West Coast sailors worked fourteen- to sixteen-hour days, ate wretched food, and lived at sea in a space they compared to prison. They endured a steady erosion of working conditions, pay, and craft skills. The number of crew members per ship was reduced, causing greater workloads for those remaining. And sailors, too, were dispatched to work out of employer-run "fink halls."

Through the 1920s, sailors and longshoremen bided their time. Few occasions allowed serious opportunities to resist the open shop. The most important, a 1923 strike, ended with the virtual destruction of the IWW in the maritime trades. Many former Wobblies joined a new, Communist-backed union, the Marine Workers Industrial Union (MWIU), when it was founded several years later. The MWIU, while never exceeding a few thousand members nationally, exerted influence on maritime workers beyond its membership, especially on the West Coast. Like the IWW before it, the MWIU kept alive the idea of industrial unionism until a more opportune moment. That moment arrived in 1934.

REMAKING THE INTERNATIONAL LONGSHOREMEN'S ASSOCIATION

West Coast longshoremen met in San Francisco toward the end of February. Elected by their coworkers in every port, their purpose was to breathe new life into the ILA. While friction was evident between the militant membership and their more cautious leaders, the delegates agreed enough to send a bargaining proposal to the waterfront employers. Influenced by the *Waterfront Worker,* the longshoremen demanded a union-controlled hiring hall in every port to replace the shape-up and the fink hall; a six-hour day and thirty-hour week, so that longshoremen could share available work; coast-wide bargaining, ensuring that the shipowners couldn't penalize militant longshoremen in one port by switching their cargo deliveries to another one; and a dollar an hour wage.

The owners refused to consider their proposal. The countdown to a strike began.

In April the San Francisco ILA membership suspended its president, Lee Holman, for dragging his feet in preparations for the strike. Holman had asked national ILA president Joe Ryan to cancel all union meetings on the coast in hopes of stopping the strike. Instead, the members dumped Holman. In his place they created a new leadership structure: a fifty-member strike committee, chaired by Harry Bridges. On May 9 the longshoremen in San Francisco, and in every port on the coast, walked off their jobs. The war-like tone for the strike was set that first day when one hundred police officers on motorcycles and horses rode into a crowd of two hundred picketers, indiscriminately clubbing and arresting the men.

By the middle of May the ranks of the striking longshoremen were swelled by the addition of all the seafaring unions, each of which, inspired by the longshoremen's action, struck for its own demands. But for the first time in decades, it wasn't a case of "every union for itself." Quickly the unions formed joint strike committees in each port, and the longshoremen and the sailors agreed that no one would go back to work unless every union was granted its demands. In another key demonstration of solidarity, the Teamsters unions—first in San Francisco, then in Oakland, Los Angeles, and Seattle—voted to boycott the waterfront: drivers refused to transport goods to or from the struck companies on the docks.

THE DEATH OF DICK PARKER

The companies did not stand still while this was happening. Organized into the Industrial Association in San Francisco, the Merchants and Manufacturers Association in Los Angeles, and similar organizations elsewhere, they hired strikebreakers, bought the latest antiriot weapons and donated them to police departments, and supplied the newspapers with a steady stream of antiunion articles. They made plans to open the ports themselves if the local or state governments failed to do so.

Soon the employers began to achieve results from their hard work. In San Pedro a group of 300 striking maritime workers surrounded a stockade housing 400 strikebreakers. Twenty-year-old Dick Parker, who had joined the ILA the day before, was shot by the police through the heart and died. Veteran longshoreman Tom Knudsen was also shot, dying a few months later. Seaman Bob McElroy had been standing a few feet from Parker when he was shot. He said, "There was no provocation, no commotion, no threats, no nothing—just a gun going off and Parker going down."

Young Parker's death, rather than intimidating the strikers at the L.A. harbor, helped to unify and strengthen them. From a few hundred picketers at the docks in the beginning of the strike, their numbers grew to nearly two thousand each day. More than five thousand attended a funeral and march for Parker.

But this was just the beginning of the employers' assault and the strikers' response. In San Francisco a thousand or more strikers would gather daily on

FIGURE 27. Harry Bridges (hatless, left of International Longshoremen's Association sign) leads striking maritime workers on Embarcadero march, May 1934. Courtesy of the Anne Rand Memorial Library, International Longshore and Warehouse Union.

the Embarcadero, the street running the length of the docks, and march quietly behind the American flag and union banners. On May 28 hundreds of police suddenly and without warning attacked the marchers with clubs, tear gas, and finally bullets, shooting one striker in the back.

One of the police captains presiding over the attack justified his actions on the grounds that the strikers were "led by Communists." His lieutenant vowed that "If the strikers come back for more, you'll find some of them in the morgue after the next time." Both of these men were later dismissed from the force in disgrace for corruption. But for the time being their comments were widely and approvingly reprinted in the newspapers.

On May 30, a few hundred high school and college students gathered to demonstrate against war and fascism near the ILA hall. Called by the Communist Youth group to mark Memorial Day, the demonstration had been denied a permit by city officials. According to Mike Quin's classic account, *The Big Strike,* as soon as one of the conference organizers stepped on a soapbox to announce the rally had to be cancelled, the police moved in with clubs and beat the kids to the ground. Sixty-five young people were sent to the hospital with fractured skulls.

A couple of days later five thousand workers and students marched to protest the police violence of the previous week and express their solidarity with the demands of the strikers.

RYAN'S AGREEMENTS

National ILA president Joe Ryan flew out from New York and quickly signed an agreement with the employers. The expensively dressed Ryan, a close friend of business leaders and government officials in the East Coast, didn't have a clue about the desires of West Coast longshoremen. They had been developing a perspective of solidarity with the other maritime unions, best summed up in the old Wobbly slogan, "An injury to one is an injury to all." They had also created a democratic coast-wide union structure with rank and file representatives elected from all the docks.

Ryan didn't care about workers in other unions, and even less for union democracy. Accustomed to running his New York local and the national ILA as he pleased—often enforcing his will with gangs of hired criminals—Ryan viewed rank and file participation in union policies as "communistic." (Twenty years later Ryan went to prison for using the union treasury as his personal bank account.)

On the basis of Ryan's "agreement," newspaper headlines cheered the "end of the strike." Ryan received the congratulations of the leaders of the Industrial Association and San Francisco mayor Angelo Rossi. Unfortunately Ryan hadn't bothered to consult with the rank and file longshoremen. When he came to a mass meeting of 3,000 San Francisco ILA members the follow-ing day, his "agreement," which included virtually none of the strikers' demands, was unanimously rejected. Deciding that he had been the victim of "Reds" in the leadership of the San Francisco union local, Ryan traveled north to Portland, where his proposal met the same fate.

Undeterred, representatives of the federal government joined with municipal authorities and the employers in more useless talks with Ryan. He was accom-panied by other top ILA officials, longtime San Francisco Teamster leader Mike Casey, and Dave Beck, a regional Teamster representative. The negotiations were ridiculous because Ryan had no authority to negotiate for the ILA rank and file, and the employers refused to allow rank and file representatives into bargaining sessions. The bosses were also uninterested in allowing the union membership to vote on their agreement. In mid-June, mass meetings of rank and file long-shoremen overwhelmingly rejected another agreement signed by Ryan. This one called for a hiring hall jointly controlled by the union and employers, and made no provision for settlement with the other striking unions.

Meanwhile, Harry Bridges was rising fast as a leader, due to his fearless-ness, grasp of strategy, and a brilliantly direct speaking style. He was elected to chair the coast-wide Joint Marine Strike Committee of all ten unions. He later explained to a government-appointed mediation board the reasons why the longshoremen rejected Ryan's agreement. "If we do not control the halls the unions can and will be destroyed by discrimination and blacklist-ing, and the men who took part in this strike would be driven out of the industry. We can't permit a fink hall." Emphasizing the solidarity of the dif-ferent groups of workers, he added, "We don't intend to repeat our former mistake of one group settling without the other. The maritime workers will go back to work only when all of their controversies are settled."

Ryan's peevish last words, before he returned to the East Coast: "Bridges does not want this strike settled. My firm belief is that he is acting for the communists."

"I HAVE NO FEELING IN THE MATTER"

Ships were tied up in the harbors. Huge stacks of merchandise lay piled on ships and in dock warehouses. Employers were losing millions of dollars every day. Leaders of the Industrial Association decided they would move the goods themselves. Well, not exactly *themselves,* but with the help of an army of strikebreakers they had hired.

They knew they could count on the cooperation of the police. Thanks to the generosity of the Industrial Association, the police were well stocked with the latest antiriot gear. A rivalry developed between salesmen represent-ing two tear gas manufacturers. To scientifically determine which product was best, the police obligingly allowed the salesmen to come along to the picket lines to try their wares on real live longshoremen.

One particularly enthusiastic salesman, Joseph Roush, was rewarded by the police for his services; they named him a "special officer" of the department. Roush described to his boss in a letter the reason why: "I might mention that during one of the riots, I shot a long-range projectile into the group, a shell hitting one man and causing a fracture of the skull, from which he has since died. As he was a Communist, I have had no feeling in the matter and I am sorry that I did not get more." (The twenty-six-year-old longshoreman Roush hit, James Engle, was not a Communist nor did he die. He recovered from his injury and continued on strike.)

LEARNING FROM HISTORY

Among the thousand strikebreakers hired when the strike began were a few hundred black longshoremen. Henry Schmidt, a white rank and file activist who later became an elected union officer, drew a crucial lesson from the 1916 and 1919 strikes: if blacks were excluded from the union, they couldn't be blamed for scabbing. The ILA no longer had an officially racist position by 1934, but memories on the docks were long; only a few blacks had signed up in the recent ILA resurgence. Schmidt went with a black ILA member to the pier where most of the regular black longshoremen worked. Together the two unionists asked them to join the union and the strike. Schmidt later recalled, "On the same afternoon or the next day these Negro brothers came to the union headquarters. I can still see them coming up the stairs and entering the premises." The black longshoremen said, "Well, we're here. Do you want us?"

Two of the men were asked to serve on the local ILA strike committee. By the end of the maritime strike the San Francisco ILA had signed up a hundred black longshoremen. The West Coast longshore union soon became one of the strongest defenders of civil rights in the entire American labor movement and one of the most racially integrated (except in Portland).

The San Francisco newspapers were more reliable friends of the Industrial Association. Throughout the eighty-three-day strike the four dailies alternated between misleading reports that the strike was "over" and lurid descriptions of a desperate city teetering on the edge of revolution. In late June, the *San Francisco Chronicle* published an article on "American Legion Week." It began, "San Francisco trains its guns on communism this week." The head of the San Francisco Chamber of Commerce pronounced that the strike "is not a conflict between employer and employee—between capital and labor—it is a conflict which is rapidly spreading between American principles and un-American radicalism. . . . There can be no hope for industrial peace until communistic agitators are removed as the official spokesmen of labor."

The inflammatory media, employer determination to break the unions, the strikebreakers they had hired and armed, and a corrupt police department all combined to create a situation in which violence was inescapable.

BLOODY THURSDAY: DEATH LIGHTS THE FUSE

On Tuesday, July 3, the Industrial Association "opened the port." A small group of trucks moved out of Pier 38 in the early afternoon protected by seven hundred police massed on foot, on horseback, and in patrol cars, and delivered merchandise to a nearby warehouse. It was a symbolic action, meant to prove that the employers, not the strikers, were in charge of the port. But the strikers weren't into symbolism. Against the police force armed to the teeth, the strikers flung themselves. For four hours, along portions of the Embarcadero and spilling over into downtown San Francisco, thousands of workers fought desperately for themselves, for their families, and for the chance to make a decent living.

Mike Quin described the carnage: "Bricks flew and clubs battered skulls. The police opened fire with revolvers and riot guns. Clouds of tear gas swept the picket lines and sent the men choking in retreat. Mounted police were dragged from their saddles and beaten to the pavement."

The newspapers reported that twenty-five men had been brought to the hospital, including nine policemen. But this number was misleading. Many more wounded strikers had been taken by comrades to homes, because injured workers were being arrested as soon as they came into the hospital.

The Industrial Association declared the port "open" and announced that in observance of Independence Day no cargo would be moved on the next day, July 4. But July 5, promptly at 8 A.M., the trucks rolled again as police launched tear gas grenades into the line of four thousand pickets. In an instant the fighting resumed more fiercely than two days before. An eyewitness reported:

> Struggling knots of longshoremen, closely pressed by officers mounted and on foot, swarmed everywhere. The air was filled with blinding gas. The howl

of the sirens. The low boom of the gas guns. The crack of pistol-fire. The whine of the bullets. The shouts and curses of sweating men. Everywhere was a rhythmical waving of arms—like trees in the wind—swinging clubs, swinging fists, hurling rocks, hurling bombs. As the police moved from one group to the next, men lay bloody, unconscious, or in convulsions—in the gutters, on the sidewalks, in the streets. Around on Madison Street, a plain-clothesman dismounted from a radio car, waved his shotgun nervously at the shouting pickets who scattered. I saw nothing thrown at him. Suddenly he fired up and down the street and two men fell in a pool of gore—one evidently dead, the other, half attempting to rise, but weakening fast.

That night heavily armed National Guard troops were deployed onto the docks, where they stayed for several weeks. One might think that the strikers would have given up in the face of such a display of force. But the events of that day, seemingly a defeat, were instead the turning point of the great maritime strike of 1934.

LABOR BURIES ITS OWN

Two men died July 5 on the street near the ILA hall. One was Howard Sperry, a longshoreman, ILA member, and World War I veteran. The other was Nick Bordoise, a Marine Cooks' union member and a Communist. He had been recovering from an operation when the strike broke out and left his bed to volunteer in the kitchen set up to prepare meals for the strikers. The morning after their deaths strikers made a sidewalk memorial on the spot where Sperry died. A square of flowers surrounded large words drawn in chalk. On two sides was written "Police murder." In the center it read "Two ILA men killed" and, below that, "shot in the back."

On July 9, beginning near the waterfront at the ILA hall on Steuart Street where services were held for Sperry, a huge funeral parade moved up Market Street. Conservative estimates placed the number of marchers at 25,000. No police were present; the marchers had asked to provide security for the event themselves, and the mayor, perhaps shocked at Bloody Thursday's horrible outcome, agreed. The coffins were placed on trucks, with more trucks carrying flowers behind those. Harry Bridges rode in one open car with Tom Mooney's mother, and Bordoise's widow with Sam Darcy in another. Darcy was a Communist Party leader and an editor of *Waterfront Worker*. A union band played a slow Beethoven funeral march. The flow of people, silent except

FIGURE 28. Longshoremen Howard Sperry and Charles Olsen, shot by unknown police assailant, on Bloody Thursday, July 5, 1934. Labor Archives and Research Center, San Francisco State University [People's World Collection].

for the music and the sound of shuffling feet, moved forward beneath the hot summer sun, row upon solemn row, for two miles. Mike Quin reported that there was

> not one smile in the endless blocks of marching men. Crowds on the sidewalk, for the most part, stood with heads erect and hats removed. Others watched the procession with fear and alarm. Here and there well-dressed businessmen from Montgomery Street stood amazed and impressed, but with their hats still on their heads. Sharp voices shot out of the line of march: "Take off your hat!" The tone of voice was extraordinary. The reaction was immediate. With quick, nervous gestures, the businessmen obeyed.

Paul Eliel, a leader of the Industrial Association, knew with a sense of dread as the march ended that a general strike could not be avoided. The discipline of the marchers, the level of organization, and the grim determination of the strikers and their supporters all pointed to one conclusion: that the deaths of Sperry and Bordoise would not be for nothing.

Within days, sixty-three San Francisco unions voted to strike, as did numerous others in Alameda County, across the bay. One of these, the Amalgamated Streetcar Workers, not only resolved to walk out. Catching the mood, it suggested that the streetcar system be taken over by its employees and run "as a mass transportation system for working people."

THE ROLE OF THE LABOR COUNCIL LEADERS

The relatively conservative officials of the San Francisco Labor Council confronted a dilemma. Opposed to a general strike, they knew they would have to put the question to a vote of all the member unions of the council.

There had only been a handful of general strikes in U.S. history, the last in Seattle in 1919. A general strike occurs when all workers in a city or region simultaneously stop work. Usually this is done to protest a government or employer action or policy felt to be against the common interest of workers. An extraordinary event, it takes a rare combination of circumstances to bring it about: a high degree of cooperation in a labor movement, widespread anger among working people, union leaders willing to stick their necks out and call for it to happen, and a spark or symbolic incident that crystallizes people's willingness to act. All of these elements were in place in San Francisco in July 1934.

Council president Ed Vandeleur warned union representatives that a general strike was against AFL rules and unions' charters could be revoked if they voted to join one. At a mass meeting on July 14, five representatives from each union in the council heard Mike Casey, militant hero of the 1901 waterfront strike, argue against a general strike, despite his own Teamster local's previous vote to support it. But the vote was overwhelmingly in favor of a general strike, to begin the following Monday. Most of the council officers finally voted for the resolution, because they understood if they opposed it they would simply be ignored by their own members. They then appointed themselves to head the General Strike Committee.

In fact, the San Francisco General Strike was already getting underway. Several unions, including the Teamsters, had stopped work. Store shelves had been stripped by anxious consumers. Gas stations were closed and streetcars had mostly ceased running. By the official deadline of Monday, July 16, few workers remained on the job. Workshops and factories were quiet. Large picket lines on highways outside the city turned deliveries away. Just nineteen restaurants in the downtown area and medical facilities throughout the city were allowed to stay open. The city was shut down.

The mayor declared a state of emergency and granted himself dictatorial powers. The police department swore in five hundred new policemen. The head of the National Recovery Administration, Hugh Johnson, a former U.S. Army general, made a speech at the University of California, Berkeley campus, in which he declared that the "subversive element" in unions "must be run out like rats."

For the four days of the general strike, headlines insisted that the city was running out of food and gas, and that strikers allowed only themselves to receive food; that the strike was "bred in Moscow"; and Communists were fomenting an insurrection, using the strikers as their pawns. One paper reported the frightening news that an army of Communists was marching on San Francisco. That none of these reports were true did not worry the publishers, who considered it their civic duty to support the Industrial Association.

The National Guard and police, operating in cooperation with the Industrial Association, staged a series of raids on suspected radical gathering places. When the Marine Workers Industrial Union hall was raided by police dressed up as "unionists," the papers dutifully reported that "Unionists Smash Radical Hangouts in Purging Move." The San Francisco raids stimulated a mini-Red Scare, with imitators in cities across California, especially in the Central Valley.

The police and mayor vowed they were cleaning alien communists out of San Francisco. Besides wrecking several offices, police arrested hundreds of people on a variety of charges. Of these twelve turned out to be deportable aliens; three were Communists. The rest were released after varying stays behind bars.

Each day of the general strike the labor council's strike committee allowed more places of business to open and services to be restored. On the fourth day, by a close vote and over the angry objections of the maritime unions, the strike committee called off the general strike.

BURNING THE FINK BOOKS

The maritime strike continued. But the inconclusive end of the 1934 general strike convinced most longshoremen and many seamen that with their biggest weapon used up, the time had come to compromise. Within a week West Coast longshoremen voted to submit all strike issues, including the hiring hall, to arbitration: a neutral, federally appointed National Longshoremen's Board would reach a decision, which workers and employers had to obey.

At a tempestuous Sailors Union of the Pacific meeting in San Francisco Harry Bridges attempted to explain to the angry sailors what had happened. He had personally opposed the decision of the longshoremen to return to work. He had pleaded with them to honor their vow to stay on strike until all the maritime unions had achieved their goals. But, as he told the sailors, the longshoremen were exhausted. The best thing to do now, said Bridges, was for all the maritime unions to return to work together, still united, and see what happened with arbitration.

The sailors knew that without the longshoremen they had no choice but to return to work. Old Andrew Furuseth, however, had the last word. As a final gesture of defiance against the waterfront employers, he proposed a symbolic action: "We are going to build a fire. Alongside that fire we will have a can of petroleum and each man who has got a fink hall book will come along there and he will dip it into that petroleum and throw it on the fire."

The day before returning to work a huge crowd of SUP members, with Furuseth looking on, made a bonfire on the docks and burnt their "fink books."

A NEW DAY

Bill Rutter recalled that on the first day after the strike, his gang of longshoremen decided they would only take fifteen sacks of barley per sling load, instead of the usual twenty. They informed the bosses of their decision, much as construction trade workers had done in San Francisco a quarter century before them. When twenty sacks came down anyway, "The guys all went and got their coats and were standing there waiting to pull out." The bosses changed their minds; fifteen was OK with them, after all. Incidents such as this were repeated the length of the coast until work rules were understood to be a matter of discussion, not dictation.

The new sense of solidarity extended beyond work rules. On docks and ships, the workers refused to labor alongside men who had scabbed during the strike. The employers, reluctant to fire the loyal strikebreakers, nevertheless had to give in when confronted with "quickie" strikes and picket lines put up by the maritime workers that were honored, in turn, by teamsters and other workers.

An enlarged sense of comradeship grew from the strike. The San Francisco ILA—an officially racist union until but recently—put a gang boss on "trial" for "slandering colored brothers." When maritime workers responded to employer provocations two years later with another coast-wide strike, fifteen black longshoremen served on the local strike committee. Within a few years a third of the local membership was African American.

On October 12, the federal arbitrators unveiled their decision. The longshoremen were granted nearly everything they wanted: a thirty-hour week, six-hour day, coast-wide bargaining, and ninety-five cents per hour (they had asked for one dollar). On the critical issue of the hiring hall, the arbitrators imposed a hall jointly administered and funded; but they gave control over naming the job dispatcher to the union. Since the dispatcher determined who worked where, the union in effect ran the hiring hall.

The sailors had to wait until early 1935 to receive their decision, and they didn't like what they got. The arbitration board ruled that hiring would remain in the hands of the shipowners. But for months the sailors had already enforced hiring of union men on West Coast shipping by a simple act: whenever a nonunion sailor was brought on board they stopped work until he was escorted off again. Now they weren't about to let a government pronouncement prevent them from maintaining a union shop.

The shipowners were furious, but there was little they could do against the united sailors. It was as if the eighty-three-day strike had been a school in industrial warfare for the seamen. They were disciplined and effective. Besides breaking down the resistance of the owners, the sailors' direct action tactics also finished off the old SUP officers. Furuseth, ailing for years, died in 1938, but he and the men around him had been left behind by the events of 1934. In their place rose a new generation of young leaders headed by Harry Lundeberg, who understood the power of instantaneous rank and file action and felt free to utilize it whenever and wherever necessary.

LIVING AS HUMAN BEINGS

Although their gains had to be defended time and again over the years, maritime workers had changed the fundamental nature of their relationship with the bosses. Their union contracts, backed by their own direct action, now set up a solid barrier to the exploitation of the past.

Years later a longshoreman's wife compared how things were before 1934—"the insecurity, my children in made-over clothes, thin and pale, my husband weary and beaten after sweating the docks day after day with maybe a day's work now and then, myself in a constant state of worry and nervous tension"—with afterward, when they "have been living as human beings, my husband has lost that haggard, beaten look, my spirits are high, my children properly fed and clothed, merry-eyed and round-cheeked."

On July 5, 1935, Bloody Thursday was commemorated by West Coast maritime workers with an unofficial holiday. Year after year, nothing moved on July 5. Finally, weary employers agreed to write Bloody Thursday into coast-wide collective bargaining agreements as an official holiday. It remains in place today for longshoremen as a reminder of Howard Sperry, Nick Bordoise, and the ultimate sacrifice workers can make for each other and future generations.

19

The CIO

CIVIL WAR AND CIVIL RIGHTS

What was needed, especially in the crisis of the depression, was industrial organization in which all workers, skilled and unskilled, would be represented by one union.

BERT CORONA, CIO ORGANIZER

THE NATIONAL LABOR RELATIONS ACT

In May 1935 the U.S. Supreme Court declared the NIRA unconstitutional, due to its failure to define "fair competition." The labor movement was not sorry to see it go, because of the act's support for company unions and lack of enforcement authority.

But rules to resolve worker-employer conflict were still badly needed. On July 5, 1935—exactly one year after Bloody Thursday—President Roosevelt signed the National Labor Relations Act (NLRA), or Wagner Act. It authorized the creation of a National Labor Relations Board (NLRB) to protect workers' self-organization activities. The board was empowered to oversee union representation elections in workplaces, make decisions in workplace disputes, and enforce them with penalties. A key provision outlawed company unions.

The board would function like the U.S. court system but would focus specifically on resolving differences between workers and employers. The act guaranteed workers the legal right to create and join unions of their choosing, and to picket, boycott, strike, and bargain collectively in pursuit of their economic goals.

Called "labor's Magna Carta" by its author, the NLRA was not without problems. Intended to level the playing field between workers and bosses, it contained flaws not immediately apparent. Left outside its protections were public employees, agricultural laborers, and domestic workers. Over time, court decisions and unabated employer opposition undermined the original intent of the act, tilting the field decisively back to capital. But for a dozen years, until after World War II, it empowered and emboldened workers to act collectively in their common interests.

THE CONGRESS OF INDUSTRIAL ORGANIZATIONS: LABOR ON THE MARCH

When John L. Lewis, president of the United Mine Workers, punched Carpenters leader Bill Hutcheson during the 1935 AFL convention, he demonstrated that the divorce between two groups of unions and the philosophies they represented would not be an easy one. The unions that Lewis led believed workers in the modern mass production enterprises at the heart of the U.S. economy could not be effectively organized on a craft basis by different unions, but only through industrial unionism, uniting all workers in a workplace under the same contract.

Within a few years, inspired by this vision—and protected by New Deal labor law—millions of workers enrolled in the Committee for Industrial Organization, later called Congress of Industrial Organizations (CIO). The CIO rekindled the flame of industrial unionism kept alive through the years by the Knights of Labor, IWW, and Communist unions like the Cannery and Agricultural Workers Industrial Union (CAWIU), and helped create a much more militant wing of the AFL.

Furniture workers in south Los Angeles, miners and lumberjacks in the Sierras, dockworkers along the Pacific Coast, public employees in the Bay Area, and oil workers in the San Joaquin Valley joined autoworkers and steelworkers across the nation in a progressive labor alliance. The ethnic immigrant and racial makeup of the industrial workforce, combined with the inclusive orientation of the CIO, created a union movement broadly supportive of struggles for social justice.

Among the better-known labor officials who founded the CIO, including Lewis, and David Dubinsky and Sidney Hillman of the garment workers' unions, was Harvey Fremming of the oil workers. Fremming was the sole Californian among the national CIO leaders; but it was his dinner conversation with Lewis after the 1935 AFL convention that sparked the CIO's inception.

Alongside visionary leaders, critical to the CIO's success were the large numbers of workers pushed by the Great Depression to understand the need for fundamental social change and who believed that through their collective efforts a better day was possible. For every Harry Bridges, appointed West Coast director of the CIO by John L. Lewis in 1937, there were thousands of rank and file workers willing to walk off the job or take time from their personal lives to help build their unions. Soon after General Motors opened a new automobile assembly plant on what had been forty acres of bean fields in South Gate in southeast Los Angeles County in 1936, three dozen workers—out of three thousand—showed up at the first United Auto Workers (UAW) meeting. Within four months these volunteer organizers had recruited almost the entire workforce to UAW Local 216.

The CIO produced growth in the crucial middle layers of the unions: the "grasstops," those local officers and staff drawn from the ranks who might not have had a chance in the old AFL due to its male and often conservative culture. Typical of the new breed of secondary leadership were immigrants Luisa Moreno and Rose Pesotta. Hired by CIO unions as organizers, both rose to become vice presidents of their national unions. Pioneers, they inspired a generation of women workers.

The CIO was an idea whose time had come. Economic policy advisors in the Roosevelt administration supported industrial unionism for pragmatic economic reasons. Mass production industries had absorbed millions of immigrants in low-paid jobs. Until they were better compensated, their families would be unable to take their place in the consumer economy. New Deal administrators wanted workers to even out the equation, "mass production equals mass consumption." If the CIO succeeded in organizing and representing these workers, it had the potential to massively bolster sales of consumer goods and thus contribute to lifting the country out of the Depression.

AMERICAN FEDERATION OF LABOR VERSUS THE CIO

Not everyone was thrilled by the CIO. National AFL president William Green and the more conservative leaders of the AFL craft unions felt threatened by this new labor grouping. They suspended CIO unions in 1936 and ordered AFL state federations and labor councils to expel all delegates from CIO-affiliated unions in March 1937.

This didn't happen overnight. Feelings of friendship and solidarity among regional union leaders and activists, forged over many years of common struggle, could not just be set aside. The California State Federation of Labor and local labor councils met the national AFL's decision to eject the CIO unions with mixed and often strongly negative reactions.

However, the California State Federation of Labor (CSFL), originally supportive of the CIO in a 1936 convention vote, reversed its position following Green's edict. CSFL president Ed Vandeleur immediately began attacking CIO leaders as "Reds," initiating a pattern that would last twenty years. The expelled unions, representing sixty thousand workers, formed the California CIO Council in August 1938. Slim Connelly, an editorial writer and leader of the Los Angeles Newspaper Guild, was elected president.

Even before then, central labor body authority over member unions had been deteriorating, and smoldering jurisdictional conflicts were breaking out into the open across the state. In spring 1937, the Alameda County Central Labor Council supported a strike of International Longshoremen's Association (ILA) members in two East Bay warehouses. Leaders of Teamsters Local 70, one of the oldest locals in the council, refused orders from its national union—which viewed warehouses as its jurisdiction—to send their members across the ILA picket lines. National Teamsters leaders Dave Beck and Dan Tobin removed Local 70 president Cliff Lester and the other defiant local leaders from their elected positions and put the local into trusteeship.

When Alameda's labor council declined to seat newly appointed Local 70 trustees as council delegates, the AFL revoked the charter of the pro-unity council and established a new one without CIO unions. By summer the CIO set up a rival Alameda Industrial Union Council, and the West Coast ILA voted to leave the AFL and join the CIO, founding the International Longshoremen's and Warehousemen's Union (ILWU).

Thirty miles north, the Contra Costa Central Labor Council included recently organized CIO unions active in nearby mills and factories. It too refused to unseat CIO local delegates, and the AFL installed another new council here.

In Los Angeles and Oakland, Labor Day became the occasion for public displays of mutual antipathy, not solidarity, when AFL labor councils refused to march with the upstart federation's unions, forcing the cities to issue separate morning and afternoon parade permits.

Worse than holiday disputes were the battles between AFL and CIO unions over representing workers in collective bargaining. Across the state, the opposed unions settled their differences through contested representation elections or, on occasion, with fists and baseball bats in the streets. Sharp conflicts erupted over local and state politics, leading to splits in the working-class vote.

One exception to this pattern was to be found in the Kern County Labor Council in Bakersfield. Here, a progressive council leadership committed to a united front for labor only expelled three CIO affiliates when forced to by the AFL and did so with "no bitterness, with handshaking all around, and with pledges of cooperation." CIO banners hung without interruption on the walls of the council hall, and these unions' delegates never stopped coming to labor council meetings.

The CIO, which changed its name to the Congress of Industrial Organizations in 1938, continued to organize, and its rapid growth forced AFL unions to organize, too. The divided California labor movement doubled its membership between 1930 and 1940. The AFL claimed half a million members, and the two-year-old CIO had more than 150,000.

THE MARCH INLAND

One key to the CIO's organizing successes in California was the prestige and strength of the longshoremen in the ILA (soon to become the ILWU), renowned for their role in the maritime and general strikes of 1934. The ILA sought to extend the momentum of these actions by forming the Maritime Federation of the Pacific with the other maritime unions. This federation waged a peaceful and successful ninety-nine-day West Coast strike in 1936, consolidating the contracts won in 1934. However, personal and political differences between Harry Bridges and the president of the Sailors Union of the Pacific, Harry Lundeberg, combined explosively with conflicts between the CIO and AFL to dissolve the dream of permanent maritime worker unity within a few years.

Another extension of the ILA's influence came with the "March Inland." Longshore union leaders understood that to protect its wharf jurisdiction they had to organize the warehouses lining the waterfront and in nearby industrial districts. In the Bay Area Local 6 soon boasted nearly nine thousand members. In Los Angeles Local 26 began with a downtown pharmaceutical warehouse and expanded to several more. The local also organized a number of other industrial workplaces. Its most dynamic early leader was Bert Corona.

In 1936 Corona was nineteen years old, attending University of Southern California at night, and "one of a handful of Mexicans" working at Brunswig

Drug Company. He was inspired by the dock strike that year and helped out in "dawn patrols," when ILA members would talk early in the morning in local cafes with truck drivers delivering merchandise, trying to convince them not to cross the picket lines. When ILA organizers asked him to work with them to organize Brunswig, he was eager to do it.

Brunswig workers were underpaid compared to unionized grocery stockers, had a heavier workload, and needed to be familiar with many more items on the shelves. Unlike union grocery stockers, Brunswig workers had no job security. In the fall of 1937, 150 workers held a secret meeting of what became Local 26 in the basement of the Musicians Local 47 hall. Corona was elected recording secretary, since as a college student, he was considered "educated."

The young warehouse worker was taken under the wing of an ex-Wobbly, Loyd Seeliger, who revealed to Corona a cornucopia of one-on-one organizing techniques. From Seeliger, Corona also learned to prefer a simple worker signup over NLRB elections.

> Loyd couldn't understand the idea of holding an election to decide whether or not workers wanted to have a right that, he believed, inherently belonged to them. . . . In his years of organizing, he never participated in an election. He just showed the bosses that he had signed up almost all of their workers and insisted that if they didn't agree now to a contract, the union would strike. The bosses generally agreed.

The method succeeded at Brunswig. The plant manager initially demanded an election. Corona and Seeliger called a meeting for that evening and invited the boss. Recalled Corona, "Out of eight hundred fifty workers, seven hundred ten came out and raised their hands in support of the union." Within six months, in his spare time after work, Corona helped organize two more nearby drug warehouses. By 1941 he was elected president of the local, which now had six thousand members, and expanded its organizing reach to several other industries.

Soon after his election, Brunswig fired Corona, who welcomed the change when Harry Bridges hired him to organize for the CIO. Corona and Seeliger brought thousands of workers first into Local 26, and then into other CIO unions, sometimes in competition with the Teamsters.

Corona was particularly proud of organizing the waste material industry in Los Angeles. The employers deliberately split the workforce between Russian-Jewish and Mexican immigrants, who were paid poorly and worked in hazardous conditions. In a plant that processed used grain bags, "The old machines dispersed a great deal of dust into the plant. Sometimes there was so much dust in the air that it resembled a fog bank. You couldn't see inside, and the workers would be constantly coughing." To help the workers communicate, Corona and Seeliger held meetings with translations from English into Russian, Yiddish, and Spanish.

The CIO, in this way and others, functioned as a bridge between the workplace and organizing in ethnic communities. Many of the Mexican workers' children in the waste material industry were school dropouts and gang members, Corona found. He understood that they had been alienated from school through language difficulties, institutional racism, and poverty. When their parents were on strike, children who were gang members would sometimes come to picket. Corona asked them to enlist their gangs to bolster the picket lines, which often faced physical attacks from the police or employer-hired thugs. In return, the CIO sponsored dances for the gangs, gave them opportunities for a political education, and, when the workers won union-run hiring halls, sent the kids to work.

Corona was able to draw on the California CIO's progressive politics to build community solidarity with union struggles, and to help Los Angeles Mexican Americans work for social justice through the CIO's support for antidiscrimination causes. Local 26, together with the rest of the ILWU, backed the founding of the civil rights-oriented Spanish Speaking People's Congress ("El Congresso") in 1938. The next year the local created the Committee to Aid Mexican Workers, one of several CIO antidiscrimination committees in southern California. It raised funds and sent food and clothing to support Mexican workers and their families on strike, and worked to end the so-called "Mexican wage" that prevailed in most industries. For Corona,

> This is what the CIO was all about. This was particularly important in bringing organization and protection to the unorganized, many of them ethnic workers such as blacks and Mexicans. I had a sense of the historical importance of the CIO, and I viewed the CIO as a movement whose time had come. Nothing could stop it, and—for a time—nothing did.

INDUSTRIAL UNIONISM FOR AGRICULTURAL WORKERS

One group determined to stop the CIO was the Associated Farmers (AF). Growers established the AF in the aftermath of the CAWIU strikes to cooperate against worker organizing, unions, and strikes. It used the criminal syndicalism law whenever possible and worked to pass local antiunion laws. The AF widely disseminated antiunion publicity materials that deliberately blurred unionism and Communism. It created a network of vigilantes ready for (and continuously employing) organized violence against union organizers and strikers. It could instantly activate the machinery of deportation for noncitizen workers whenever the first signs of resistance appeared. It ran the most powerful lobby in Sacramento.

Despite the efforts of the growers, and although the CAWIU had dissolved in 1935, agricultural union organizing did not stop. The lessons—both of the successes and failures of the CAWIU—remained present in the minds of farm labor activists and sympathizers. Mexican and Filipino farmworkers formed temporary unions or went on brief job actions; remnants of CAWIU locals reconstituted themselves into AFL federal unions. The state's labor federation tried to help bring these elements into a single structure for agricultural workers, holding a conference on the topic in Stockton in June 1936. But the effort fell apart as the split within the AFL deepened.

Finally, in Denver, Colorado, in July 1937 activists founded the United Cannery, Agricultural, Packing and Allied Workers of America (UCAPAWA), dedicated to industrial unionism in fields, packinghouses and canneries, and affiliated it with the CIO. Its first convention brought together union men and women of many ethnic and racial backgrounds, reflecting the composition of agricultural labor. The union constitution was a model of activist democracy, setting up an organization concerned with local autonomy and intended to empower rank and file members to act on their own behalf as much as possible.

UCAPAWA got off to a slow start in the fields. By spring 1938 only five hundred workers in the San Joaquin Valley had signed up, partly because another progressive organization seemed to be delivering the goods more quickly.

The Workers Alliance, successor to the Communist-backed unemployed councils, had become active in the valley the year before, organizing farmworkers to pressure the State Relief Administration to raise relief payment rates, which indirectly set agricultural wages by supporting (or not) farm laborers and their families between jobs. The state Agricultural Labor Bureau, controlled by the growers, tried to set "official" wage rates for picking various crops; UCAPAWA and the Workers Alliance worked closely together, especially in Kern County with the assistance of the labor council, to push back and gain a price for labor they could live on.

In 1938 and 1939, with the assistance of a half-dozen UCAPAWA organizers (including former CAWIU organizer Dorothy Ray Healey), workers struck repeatedly for union recognition and higher wages. In October 1939—the same month John Steinbeck's *The Grapes of Wrath* was published—more than a thousand workers struck cotton growers in Madera County. In the face of extreme grower violence fomented by the Associated Farmers, Okie families hung together with Mexican, black, and Filipino workers on the picket lines. Healey recalled,

> All their lives they'd been on a little farm in Oklahoma; probably they had never seen a black or a Mexican. And you'd watch in the process of a strike how those white workers soon saw that those white cops were their enemies and that the black and Chicano workers were their brothers.

With one exception, UCAPAWA could not gain a contract or union recognition during these field strikes; at best they forced growers to raise wages temporarily. The power of the growers, distributed through control over local government and law enforcement, and bolstered by vigilante violence, was too great. As a result the union decided to focus its limited resources on organizing the canning and packing sectors of California agriculture, hoping that those industries, once organized, would serve as a base for reentry into the fields.

The first breakthrough came at California Sanitary Canning Company, known as "Cal San," on Long Beach Boulevard in Los Angeles. Cal San processed seasonal crops, employing four hundred and thirty workers, mostly Mexicano, Russian, and Jewish women. The men in the plant were paid wages, but the women were paid low piece rates. The conveyer belts moved quickly, and many women found themselves dizzy when they started work at Cal San; Julia Luna Mount remembered fainting her first day. They also suffered rashes and allergies from continuous contact with peach fuzz, and cuts from the small, sharp knives that they wielded on the produce as it passed.

Company supervisors only spoke English, and the women reported that they commonly cheated non-English speaking workers on their pay. When Dorothy Ray Healey showed up in summer 1939, she found a receptive audience among the workforce. Mexican family networks ran through the plant, helping to push along the union drive. Many of the workers, both Mexican and Jewish, lived in and around Boyle Heights, a working-class neighborhood just east of downtown.

Cal San's owners, George and Joseph Shapiro, declined the union's request for recognition. On August 31 they found themselves facing a twenty-four-hour picket line when more than four hundred workers left the cannery. For ten weeks the strikers paced the pavements in front of their workplace. They benefited from strong local CIO support. Mexican small businesses, organized through the Spanish Speaking People's Congress, donated food.

What finally broke the stalemate was public humiliation for the Shapiros. Progressive Jews in their synagogue congregation applied pressure to negotiate. At the same time, the strikers' children began picketing in front of the Shapiros' homes, prompting neighbors to feed the kids and urge a settlement.

Following recognition of the union and a contract settlement, including a closed shop, Healey helped to set up UCAPAWA Local 75's committee structure before turning over the local assignment to Luisa Moreno. Moreno, a slender Guatemalan immigrant disowned by her wealthy family, had been a cigar worker in New York. She then worked for an AFL cigar workers union before helping to cofound the Spanish Speaking People's Congress and organize the first UCAPAWA convention. Moreno trained rank and file Cal San workers in contract enforcement. She then moved on to serve as an UCAPAWA national vice president and lead a number of other organizing campaigns.

CHINATOWN NEEDLE TRADES

In early 1934, after Ladies Garment Workers Local 96 in Los Angeles had been placed on solid enough footing to satisfy Rose Pesotta, union president David Dubinsky dispatched her to San Francisco. She arrived in time to offer the support of her union to the maritime unions in their great coast-wide strike in spring and summer. But her actual assignment was to help Cloakmakers Local 8 negotiate a contract, convince employers to recognize newly chartered San Francisco Dressmakers Local 101, and get the bosses to adopt NRA-code wages.

The needle trades in San Francisco were older than those in Los Angeles but employed fewer people. About twenty midtown shops produced women's clothing. The employers were aware of what had transpired in Los Angeles. Pesotta called a meeting of the dress workers, and three hundred showed up, interested in organizing. She let newspaper reporters know that there had been talk of striking during an upcoming fashion show. This got the attention of the employers, who agreed to meet with Pesotta and the local garment-worker leaders. In the meeting, the employers argued that any agreement should cover workers in Chinatown as well as Caucasians in the rest of the city, since their work orders were disappearing into the ghetto sweatshops at a rapid clip.

Not wishing this to be a sticking point, Pesotta arranged for a tour of the garment factories in Chinatown. She was startled at what she found.

> Tourists in Chinatown saw but one side of the picture . . . they never knew that the shadowy adjacent streets and narrow alleys hid factories in which conditions were worse than in the old tenement sweatshops on New York's East Side. . . . Three stories down, where daylight and fresh air never penetrated, we entered long narrow lofts with barely space enough between rows of sewing machines for one person to walk through. . . . We saw entire families of three generations engaged in making garments—husband, wife, grandparents, grandchildren.

Determined to organize these workers, she set up a meeting of several of the larger Chinese employers, the ILGWU's local leadership, and an officer of the San Francisco Labor Council, John O'Connell. During the meeting she received another shock. The employers maintained that if they accepted union conditions, rising costs would force them to lay off some workers, many of whom were kin. When Pesotta sought to reassure them that displaced workers could be taken on in one of the midtown union shops, and turned to O'Connell for support, instead he unleashed a profane anti-Chinese diatribe.

Shaken, Pesotta undertook a crash course in the history of San Francisco labor movement anti-Chinese racism. With her newfound understanding, and the assistance of the San Francisco garment workers, she brought a resolution to the national ILGWU convention asking—and gaining—its support for organizing these workers. But Cloakmakers Local 8, it turned out, was the only union in the city willing to admit Chinese workers, and the labor council was divided even on whether to endorse Local 8's proposed organizing drive.

Pesotta was soon sent by the ILGWU to other parts of the country, and played no further role in San Francisco. Three years later workers employed by the National Dollar Stores took matters into their own hands. Employing 125 mostly women workers—one-eighth of the Chinatown industry—the company was "vertically integrated," owning factory production along with retail outlets that sold its clothing. Employer Joe Shoong paid the best wages, and his factory conditions were superior to others in the Chinatown garment industry.

But management practices were arbitrary and inconsistent, and the women never seemed to get a full paycheck. They felt under pressure to send money home to China, at war with Japan, but couldn't save enough to do so. In November 1937, with assistance from ILGWU organizer Jennie Matyas, eighty workers signed authorization cards and founded Local 341, the Chinese Ladies' Garment Workers' Union. The company refused to recognize the union and demanded an election supervised by the National Labor Relations Board, which the union won in January 1938.

The day after the election National Dollar Stores agreed to a closed shop and a wage increase. Two weeks later Shoong sold the factory to two of his former managers, who, taking the name Golden Gate Manufacturing, declined the union's request that they maintain the agreement with their former boss. They also rejected the workers' wage and hours proposal, and crucially, the demand that Golden Gate guarantee eleven months of work (the company's average over the years) and convince National Dollar Stores to continue to stock its retail stores with the factory's output.

On the morning of February 26 more than one hundred workers walked out and began picketing the factory along with three National Dollar retail shops in the city. It was a hard thing to do. In the tight Chinatown community, the wealthy Shoong was seen as a benefactor who provided work and contributed generously to the Chinese nationalist cause. Striker Sue Ko Lee recalled that mainstream Chinese organizations and businesses were not overtly hostile but "didn't show us any support because we were all called troublemakers." Backing for the strikers by leftist organizations didn't improve the strikers' standing with the more conservative elements in the Chinese community. And in San Francisco Chinatown, unions had traditionally meant one thing above all else: white organizations that discriminated against Chinese.

The National Dollar Stores struggle began to change that history. Although rare, strikes had not been unknown in Chinatown. None, however, had ever been supported before by the official labor movement. The difference this time was huge. The ILGWU gained strike sanction from the San Francisco Labor Council. As a result, the (white) members of the Retail Clerks union who worked in the National Dollar stores honored the factory

FIGURE 29. Garment workers on strike at Golden Gate Manufacturing, producers for the National Dollar Stores, received a breakthrough strike sanction from the San Francisco Labor Council in 1938. Labor Archives and Research Center, San Francisco State University [People's World Collection].

workers' picket lines in front of their workplaces, shutting down the shops. This moment of interracial solidarity on behalf of striking Chinese workers was a first in San Francisco.

The strike lasted fifteen weeks, the lengthiest job action that had ever taken place in Chinatown. It entailed great sacrifices, economic and emotional, for the strikers. The ILGWU supplied the workers strike benefits of five dollars per week, which did not cover living expenses. Jennie Matyas went to the house of Edna Lee, who she had heard was sick and couldn't come to the picket line.

> She was in bed. I asked her how sick she was. "Oh," she said, "I'm not sick at all." I said, "Well, why are you in bed if you're not sick at all?" "Well, you know, it's funny, but if I stay in bed I don't get hungry. And so I often stay in bed because then I don't get hungry."

The workers were closely divided over accepting the negotiated settlement with the companies, which gained them a closed shop, modest wage increase, forty-hour work week with time and a half for overtime, a guaranteed half day of work when the company called, and the continuation of a contract for clothing between National Dollar and Golden Gate for a year. "It wasn't good enough" for some of the more militant members, Sue Ko Lee remembered years later. But she argued for it, saying, "You had to start someplace," and a narrow majority of the union members agreed with her.

One year later, when the contract expired, the factory closed. The ILGWU, true to its promise, found jobs in unionized garment factories outside Chinatown for Local 341 members, who then became members of Local 101. The Chinese Ladies' Garment Workers' Union membership shrank to a handful, which voted to dissolve into the larger and more stable Local 101. Within a few years, after the ILGWU left the CIO and returned to the AFL, the San Francisco Labor Council, historically a bastion of anti-Asian prejudice, accepted the Chinese union members of Local 101, finally ending one of the longest and ugliest stories of exclusion in American labor history.

For the former National Dollar Stores workers, the episode was transformative. Sue Ko Lee and her husband Jow Hing Lee were among the workers provided jobs through the intervention of Local 101. Lee noted that in the uptown shops "You made more money and you had set hours," and her overall assessment was clear: "The strike was the best thing that ever happened. It changed our lives."

IMPACT OF THE CIO IN CALIFORNIA

Due to its inclusive orientation, the CIO essentially functioned as a civil rights movement as well as a union federation, releasing energies in minority communities that had been mostly blocked from participating in the AFL-led labor movement for a half century.

In fall 1937 the national CIO briefly became larger than the AFL, with 3.7 million members. The AFL soon recovered momentum and overtook the CIO, assisted by mass layoffs in basic industry in 1938 when Roosevelt reduced spending on public works programs and precipitated a return to high levels of unemployment. The CIO in California never seriously challenged the AFL's numerical predominance. But it forced the older federation to support organizing, including in industries it had previously ignored or failed to penetrate, and provided a more politically active and socially conscious union alternative for workers.

20

Arsenal of Democracy

INTEGRATING INDUSTRIAL CALIFORNIA
DURING WORLD WAR II

WORLD WAR II LIFTED CALIFORNIA out of the Great Depression. In 1940, the ranks of the jobless were down from their peak in the early 1930s, but still lingered at an unacceptable 12 percent. By 1944, unemployment had fallen to less than 1 percent—effectively nonexistent for anyone who wanted a job, even though the working population of the state had increased by two fifths over prewar levels.

Between 1940 and 1945, the federal government spent over $16 billion on major war production contracts in California. The jobs created by these public expenditures in mostly private defense industries inspired the migration of half a million white workers and their families from the southwest, and a third of a million African Americans. Women, too, were heavily recruited to industrial work, previously a male domain. Re-creating California as an "arsenal of democracy" encouraged workplaces to undergo a rapid conversion to generate different products, transformed social interactions, and channeled Hollywood filmmaking into war propaganda. The war—yet another of the state's periodic "gold rushes"—simultaneously reconstructed the California economy and recomposed its working class.

Manufacturing employment increased from around 300,000 workers before the war to about 900,000 by 1943. A full 80 percent of this industrial workforce growth was in shipbuilding and aircraft production. The shipyards were concentrated around San Francisco Bay, although a few large facilities came online in southern California. The sunny geography stretching from Los Angeles to San Diego became the most important aircraft assembly center in the country. The state developed new infrastructure to feed its factories and set in place the outlines of the postwar economy and labor relations.

To overcome production bottlenecks and reduce transportation costs for the steel necessary to manufacture ships and planes, capitalist Henry Kaiser partnered with New Deal officials to finance the first integrated steel facility on the West Coast capable of competing with eastern and midwestern producers. Kaiser Steel opened in Fontana, previously known for citrus orchards and chicken ranching, sixty miles northeast of Los Angeles, at the end of 1942. At once it increased state steel production by nearly three quarters. The Fontana plant's pride and joy, its twelve-hundred-ton blast furnace, took front stage in a complex of structures occupying a square mile.

Kaiser Steel employed five thousand workers in a thunderous, smoggy enterprise to provide the steel plate to wage war. Henry Kaiser helped redeem the Fordist promise of high wages for industrial workers. His willingness to accept unions as partners in industry was no doubt nurtured by lucrative government contracts, but he stated his support in unusually strong terms: "To break a union is to break yourself."

Next to the war, work and working people were at the center of the public eye. Without maximum productivity on the home front, the armed forces could not be properly supplied. The fierce battles between labor and capital of the previous decade had to be set aside. Other sources of social unrest, such as racial discrimination, had to be overcome in the interests of the unified war effort. Just about everyone—representatives of labor, capital, government, and working people themselves—agreed with the overriding importance of the war. But that surface consensus faced some tests.

KEEPING WORKERS AT WORK

In early 1944, United Automobile Workers-CIO leaders commissioned a group of Hollywood animators to produce a short film for the Roosevelt reelection effort. Gains by the Republicans in the 1942 off-year election resulted in passage the following year of the Smith-Connally Act, which among other antilabor measures forbade direct union political contributions. In response the CIO formed the first political action committee, or PAC, which channeled worker political contributions into a fund one legal arm's length from the methods prohibited by the act.

With this CIO-PAC money the recently formed Industrial Films and Poster Service (later UPA) gathered a talented crew headed by Warner Brothers animation director Chuck Jones. It included songwriter Earl

Robinson, *Wizard of Oz* lyricist Yip Harburg, and some of the most adventurous animators in town. Only a few of these artists actually received a salary. Most held day jobs at unionized cartoon companies and jammed into the cramped animation studio at night to volunteer their unique skills to the labor movement's election effort.

Hell Bent for Election debuted at the UAW convention in August. The CIO-PAC reproduced thousands of sixteen millimeter film copies and dispatched them to union hall screenings across the country.

The thirteen-minute film centers on Joe the Worker. He must make sure he throws the railroad switch at the right moment to allow the Win the War Special to pass while forcing the Defeatist Limited to remain behind on a sidetrack. When the key moment arrives, Joe succeeds, but not before a difficult struggle with a reactionary southern politician, who mouths employer platitudes and seeks to distract Joe from his task. He so enrages Joe with his antiunion diatribes and efforts to derail the Win the War Special that Joe can't help himself: he raises his fist to deliver a well-deserved punch. The narrator's voice calls out urgently, "Wait, Joe! There's a better way." Joe's fist suddenly holds a voting stamp, and he slams it down on a ballot.

No single image better captures the desire of the CIO leadership during the war to keep rank and file anger and attention focused on an electoral solution to their problems and away from direct workplace action.

This took some doing. Pressured by speedups and long hours, and despite no-strike pledges by AFL and CIO, workers sporadically walked off the job throughout the war. From fewer than a million workers on strike in 1942, work stoppages—most of them unofficial, or "wildcat" strikes—increased steadily, involving over three million workers in 1945.

Soon after Pearl Harbor, the Roosevelt administration reconstituted a short-lived National Defense Mediation Board as the National War Labor Board. The president appointed representatives from labor, capital, and the public to oversee industrial conflict resolution. Because of their devotion to winning the war through maximum production, labor leaders had to transform themselves—sometimes to their own surprise—from organizers of workplace resistance to enforcers of workplace discipline.

There were literally thousands of interventions, large and small, by the government to ensure continuous production—typically routine bureaucratic procedures such as administering grievances, holding arbitration hearings, and reclassifying jobs and pay. Other government actions, however, raised serious civil liberties issues, challenging established worker rights as a militarized state attempted to impose discipline over war production.

Most workers pushed hard to produce for the war effort—some out of patriotic feeling, some to make high wages, often due to a combination of these reasons. Many workers nonetheless resisted government and employer efforts to erode traditional work rules and labor rights in the name of the war.

Harry Bridges found this out when he appeared before hundreds of longshoremen in Wilmington at a meeting of ILWU Local 13 in 1942. Like other militant CIO leaders close to the Communist Party, Bridges felt that defense of the Soviet Union, under attack by the Nazi war machine, overrode (temporarily) even the right to strike. When he proposed this view, rank and file members of Local 13 jeered. One told him, "Just because your pal Joe Stalin is in trouble, don't expect us to give up our conditions to help him out."

Union leaders had to perform a delicate and continuous balancing act between promoting war production and defending worker rights. The ILWU learned the navy wished to replace union members with civil service and military personnel in West Coast ports. Supposedly due to military interest in efficient production, the navy's plan also reflected antilabor bias among its officers. The union leadership argued that its members were the most efficient dockworkers around. But the navy turned down ILWU offers to man its facilities at Port Chicago, on the Suisun Bay north of Concord. A tragic, convincing argument came too late when mostly black sailors, with little or no training, were ordered by white officers to load live ammunition onto ships.

The resulting gigantic explosion in July 1944, the greatest home front disaster of the war, killed more than three hundred and injured even more, and led to a mass refusal when the navy ordered loading to begin again a month later. In a civilian workplace this reasonable action by the sailors would be known as a strike against unsafe conditions. In the wartime situation the leaders of the revolt were convicted of mutiny and sent to prison.

Three months after the Port Chicago catastrophe, federal intervention into another Bay Area workplace had a less violent but still ominous and chilling impact on workers.

The Sunnyvale plant of Joshua Hendy Iron Works produced a third of all Liberty Ship engines in the nation. Most of its workers were represented by the International Association of Machinists Local 68, AFL, which boasted a long militant history. Its ten-month walkout with the rest of the Bay Area shipyards' Metal Trades Council during the 1919 strike wave was one of the largest in the country that year. During the open shop period in the 1920s the machinists maintained their wage scales and working conditions through informal negotiations backed up by a tight-knit culture of rank and file shop floor control. That tradition of solidarity continued into World War II in San Francisco and machine shops south of the city where Local 68 represented the workers.

After watching their purchasing power decline between 1942, when they received their last wage increase, and the spring of 1944, the workers were infuriated at the rejection of their requests for a raise to keep up with inflation. Countering the opposition of both the employer and the War Labor Board, the machinists voted to refuse overtime after forty-eight hours per week.

After months of standoff, the navy seized the plant and cancelled the union's collective bargaining agreement. It sent the FBI to interrogate hundreds of workers and informed dozens that their deferment had been terminated, ordering them to report to their draft boards. Eight union activists were fired and blacklisted. After six were reinstated, the remaining two went through lengthy hearings. Despite this level of intimidation, the Machinists' rank and file continued to enforce their missing contract on the shop floor and paid the two fired machinists' wages out of the union treasury until the end of the war.

These events were not unique. As we shall see, there were more spectacular moments of labor conflict that erupted publicly during World War II. But most worker struggles in this period took place, as labor history usually does, below the surface of daily life, tucked away in the crevices of the massive increase of industrial production for war.

BUILDING SHIPS

Before the war, shipbuilding and repair, traditionally part of the Bay Area economy, employed six thousand workers, mostly members of the craft unions belonging to the Metal Trades Council. Within a few years San Francisco, along with nearby communities, became the greatest builder of ships in history. More than 240,000 people, working at union wages around the clock in three shifts, poured hundreds of Liberty Ships, tankers, and other military vessels onto the water from the yards ringing the bay.

This did not represent an expansion of craft labor. To meet the demands of the war, the owners and managers of the four enormous Kaiser shipyards in Richmond innovated assembly line production techniques to turn out ships more quickly. Marinship in Sausalito, built for the war emergency, designed its production process along the same lines. Oakland's Moore Dry Dock and the other traditional yards were forced to rethink and renovate their existing facilities and work methods.

Since the great majority of war workers had never built a ship before and the immediate goal was to build ships faster than German and Japanese submarines could sink them, a four-year apprenticeship was out of the question. Instead, a specialized division of labor, with continuous training for new recruits, replaced the former all-around craft worker with semiskilled industrial laborers, each trained to perform a handful of defined assembly tasks.

The new methods concentrated on prefabrication and preassembly. Of the quarter-million parts that went into the creation of a Liberty Ship, only a few hundred preassembled pieces were actually put together on the "way" next to the water. Some of these parts were three hundred feet long. In Marinship, they were brought to the shipway along an outdoor "assembly line" nearly a mile in length, fed by gigantic cranes on overhead tracks. The yards were laid out like cities, with streets and buildings and machinery dedicated to ship production.

The effect was often overwhelming to the visitor or new worker. Due to wartime labor shortages, Bay Area shipyards had to recruit across the nation, drawing on the booster tactics that had brought waves of new Californians in previous times. One recruiter reported that invoking the magic phrase "just across the Golden Gate Bridge from San Francisco" invariably helped the midwestern or southern worker decide to work at a shipyard. But their new workplace could be a shock to people who had grown up on farms or in small towns.

In Alexander Saxton's novel, *Bright Web in the Darkness,* Joyce Allen hails from a railroad town in Nevada. Her first job in the yard is carpenter's helper. Reacting to her surroundings,

> It seemed to her she had no idea what anybody was doing. The fog was full of an immense clanging and hammering, roaring and hooting. Huge objects, which she could not see, rumbled past high overhead. People scurried through the fog, some carrying tools, some munching sandwiches, some pushing carts, rushing, or sauntering, an endless stream.

About a quarter of the war workers in Bay Area shipyards were women. Around 10 percent were African American. A fifth were Okies, many of whom seized the opportunity to escape their failed dreams of becoming Central Valley farmers.

The reaction to the newcomers by the older, skilled white AFL craftsmen ranged from a resigned acceptance that everyone's help was necessary to win the war, to hostility and fear that their hard-won collective bargaining conditions would be eroded—by the new industrial production methods, the newcomers' ignorance of unionism, or by both. Most of the white workers recruited from the south brought deep racial prejudices with them. Tensions in the workforce, based in clashing cultures, assumptions, and traditions, needed continuous attention if production were to flow smoothly.

This cauldron of differences was observed and recorded firsthand by a University of California, Berkeley graduate student, Katherine Archibald, who took time off from her studies to work as a laborer. Volunteering to serve as a union steward, Archibald came into contact with hundreds of workers. She was saddened at the low level of education achieved by most of them (she estimated it to average about fifth or sixth grade) and appalled by their willingness to display overt racism and prejudice. The subtitle of her book, *Wartime Shipyard: A Study in Social Disunity,* reveals what she found. One example among many she cites: "I remember one old man who drifted through his days, avoiding conflict and choosing self-effacement, but who was decisive on the question of racial equalitarianism: 'Well, a nigger may be as good as you are,' he said, 'but he sure ain't as good as me.'"

And what about the traditional role of unions—helping workers unite? The largest shipbuilding union was the International Brotherhood of Boilermakers, Iron Shipbuilders and Helpers of America. The Boilermakers union was also the dominant force within the AFL Metal Trades Council, which negotiated the closed shop collective bargaining agreement with West Coast shipyard employers that governed wages, hiring, and promotion. Although CIO unions represented workers in many eastern shipyards, their effort to dislodge the entrenched AFL unions on the West Coast had failed before the war, and only a small outpost representing a relative handful of workers, Steelworkers Local 1304, could be found in one Bay Area shipyard, Moore Dry Dock, where Kate Archibald worked.

This made a difference in the newcomers' relationship to their unions. Some AFL unions in the yards were interracial, such as Shipyard Laborers Local 886, which employed Jamaican-born Harry Lumsden as a union staffer.

But the Boilermakers, by far the largest union, refused to admit African Americans. When the employers discriminated, the Boilermakers were not just disinterested in assisting the workers who couldn't get hired or advance to better jobs; the union acted as badly as the employers.

These problems were not unique to Bay Area shipyards. As a result of pervasive employment discrimination in the new war industries, African American union leaders A. Philip Randolph and C. L. Dellums of the Brotherhood of Sleeping Car Porters approached President Roosevelt and requested that he take action. When he declined, they threatened to call a march on Washington to demand fair employment practices. Confronting the potential for an international embarrassment during the war to defend freedom and democracy, Roosevelt agreed to issue Executive Order 8802 in June 1941, which declared that no employer receiving federal funding for defense contracts could discriminate. The executive order established a federal Fair Employment Practices Commission (FEPC) for the duration of the war, with modest enforcement powers and staff, to oversee implementation of its provisions.

Nonetheless, progress was slow, and nowhere slower than in Bay Area shipyards. To obey the letter of the law, the Boilermakers issued employment clearances for black workers while continuing to keep them out of the union. With the assistance of the FEPC, Berkeley native Frances Mary Albrier forced the Boilermakers to clear her for a Kaiser welder's job in 1943 and to accept her dues payment to the union. Instead of being given full membership, she was shunted to a segregated auxiliary local the union set up in Oakland's Moore shipyard.

Soon the Boilermakers created three Bay Area auxiliary locals. More than a thousand black workers fell within the jurisdiction of the Marinship auxiliary, Local A-41. Richmond auxiliary A-36 represented thousands more. The members of these auxiliaries had no right to vote for officers in the "real" locals to which they were affiliated, nor on anything else related to their employment. The Boilermakers national executive board had the power to remove local officers and run locals directly, and faced with dissension, used that power freely. The shipyards' African American workers, most of whom had never been in a union, were rightfully distrustful of the second-class labor organization they found themselves saddled with.

In response to the discriminatory behavior they faced from employers and unions alike, black shipyard workers developed diverse individual and collective strategies. Stubborn persistence combined with legal threats helped

Albrier become the first black female welder at Kaiser Richmond's Yard 2. Workers formed antidiscrimination committees in the East Bay, in San Francisco, and elsewhere on the West Coast, which filed lawsuits against the companies and the Boilermakers, and in some cases organized job actions and community support. The East Bay Shipyard Workers Committee, led by Ray Thompson, a Communist who worked at Moore, at first counseled blacks to join the auxiliaries, pay dues, and fight the Boilermakers' racist practices from within the union. Later it called for a dues boycott.

In this process the auxiliaries played a dual role. They were blunt instruments, unions without many of the weapons workers typically needed and used; they were part of the problem. But with access, albeit sharply limited, to treasuries, and a place to stand, they provided the possibility for communication and organizing among workers, and between workers and the broader community.

This was not completely new. A comparable role had been played by the Brotherhood of Sleeping Car Porters (BSCP) before 1937, the year it finally succeeded in forcing recognition and collective bargaining on the railroad companies after more than a decade of struggle. The Brotherhood founded and supported local chapters of the NAACP, and assisted black communities in struggles for their rights. The difference was the scale and intensity of this situation. The BSCP had dozens or scores of members in most of its locals. The Boilermaker auxiliaries had thousands, in a pressure cooker environment that provided potential leverage for the workers.

In San Francisco, the small but active prewar African American community based in the multiracial Fillmore district swelled with migrants seeking jobs in the shipyards during the war. Some newcomers found places to live in housing recently vacated by several thousand former residents, the incarcerated Japanese Americans who had made the Fillmore area their home for decades. (In the context of wartime anti-Japanese prejudice—not to mention a housing crisis for war workers—few newcomers considered, let alone protested, the incarceration. Nor did many American institutions, including unions, although one exception was the ILWU.)

Despite the crowding and friction between longtime residents and the migrants, shipyard paychecks fueled a vibrant black culture in the Fillmore neighborhood—some called it "Harlem of the West"—and supported hopeful political action.

One recent arrival soon landed at the center of black community aspirations for a better life. Singer Joseph James performed as a member of the cast of the *Swing Mikado,* an all-black production of the WPA's Federal Theater Project, which rewrote the Gilbert and Sullivan light opera as a jazzy musical. After a Broadway run, the show came west to the Golden Gate Exposition on Treasure Island in 1939. When the exposition ended, James moved into the Fillmore. He went to work as a welder at Marinship in 1942, and contributed his vocal talents to ship-launching ceremonies in the yard. He became active in the San Francisco NAACP and served on Marinship's Negro Advisory Board, which helped put out a special issue of the yard's newsletter devoted to racial issues.

Despite his willingness to partner with official Marinship activities, James drew the line at the Boilermakers' exclusionary policies. Along with hundreds of other black Marinship workers, James refused to pay dues to Auxiliary A-41, which he called "a Jim Crow fake union." On November 27, 1943, when the Boilermakers told the company to fire those who were not paying dues, James and most of the eleven hundred black workers, supported by the San Francisco Committee Against Segregation and Discrimination (SFCASD), staged a public demonstration in front of Marinship during a shift change.

James and more than 150 other workers received termination notices. Hundreds of workers stayed off the job in protest, their standoff drawing national attention. Pressures on the company to rehire the workers or reach an understanding that allowed them to stay came from the African American community as well as from state and federal government officials.

The strike, or job boycott, lasted a week. The SFCASD, assisted by C. L. Dellums, filed a federal district court suit on behalf of James and other workers, calling for their reinstatement and monetary fines against the union. A judge issued a temporary restraining order suspending the layoffs, and a week after the trouble began the workers were back at their jobs. But that wasn't the end of it. Soon after the new year, the court agreed with the union's assertion that federal law had no jurisdiction over it.

SFCASD lawyers quickly filed another suit in Marin County Superior Court, this time based on state law. Another restraining order resulted, delaying the terminations once again. While the case slowly moved ahead, skirmishes broke out on other fronts. The FEPC ordered the Boilermakers and shipyard employers to cease discriminating; the union and companies appealed. Welders and Burners Local 681, an East Bay Boilermaker local directly under the national union's control, nonetheless gathered six thousand shipyard worker signatures and submitted them to the Boilermakers union before its national convention in January 1944, calling for it to change its discriminatory practices.

In February 1944 the Marin Court decided *James vs. Marinship* against the Boilermakers union: the union could no longer force workers into auxiliaries, and the company could not fire anyone for refusing to pay dues to the segregated unions. The decision was affirmed a year later, January 2, 1945, on appeal to the California Supreme Court.

The legal victory came too late, however, to have the impact hoped for by the plaintiffs. By 1945, anticipating the end of the war, the government stopped its orders for ships. The shipyards cut back production and laid off workers. Marinship shut its doors for the last time in May 1946. At that point only 600 workers remained from 20,000 at the peak of war production. Joseph James left San Francisco and went back to New York, resuming his former career as a baritone. In 1948 the Boilermakers union in the Bay Area's shipyards was integrated, but that meant jobs for just 150 black workers.

BUILDING AIRCRAFT

Tina Hill began work at North American Aviation in Inglewood in 1943, soon after she arrived from Texas. She was twenty-four years old, with a husband in the army overseas. After a one-month course in riveting, she was placed in Department 17.

> They had fifteen or twenty departments, but all the Negroes went to Department 17 because there was nothing but shooting and bucking rivets. You stood on one side of the panel and your partner stood on this side, and he would shoot the rivets with a gun and you'd buck them with the bar.

The same year, in San Diego, two high school teachers decided to spend their summer vacation working in the main plant at sprawling Consolidated Aircraft. Inspired by a mix of patriotism, curiosity, and the desire to earn some good money, Constance Bowman and Clara Marie Allen made new friends, built B-24 bombers, and found out they could do harder physical work than they had ever done before.

> I had squatted, kneeled, bent, and sat on the floor. I had gritted my teeth, clutched my motor, and pushed as hard as I could push. I had stubbed my toes, cracked my shins, and knocked my head three times on the metal sill

FIGURE 30. Riveters working in southern California aircraft fabrication helped to win the war on the home front. Emannuel Joseph, photo. Labor Archives and Research Center, San Francisco State University [People's World Collection].

about the safety belt holders. I had broken my fingernails, I had cut my fingers, and once I had almost bitten through my tongue.

By 1943, more than 40 percent of aircraft workers in Los Angeles were women, and over a quarter of a million workers were involved in building warplanes in San Diego, Orange County, and Los Angeles. California had become the beneficiary of government production funding because by 1939 it was already the nation's leading airplane assembly center, with the capacity to expand production quickly.

The earliest aircraft companies located in southern California at the same time and for the same reasons the motion picture industry did: good weather and a low level of unionization. In addition the area had a substantial military presence, from the beginning a major supplier of contracts. Although the first companies were established in 1912, the industry did not begin to sink permanent roots until after World War I.

Over the next two decades, the Los Angeles area became home to Douglas Aircraft, Lockheed, Northrup, Vultee, and North American Aviation. Ryan

Aircraft built Charles Lindbergh's *Spirit of St. Louis* in San Diego and established the nation's first daily passenger service. It was joined there by Consolidated Aircraft in 1935, the same year Douglas began production in Santa Monica of the DC-3, which soon dominated passenger travel.

The southern California plants concentrated on production of airplane body parts and assembly, incorporating engines produced in Detroit and the eastern United States. Although competition for contracts from the military and corporations was often fierce, the companies learned to cooperate in their labor relations, forming the Aeronautical Chamber of Commerce (ACC), agreeing on industry wage standards, and keeping a blacklist of union activists.

The companies deliberately recruited young people from the Midwest and eastern cities on the assumption they were ignorant of or immune to unions. According to United Auto Workers organizer Wyndham Mortimer, "The most noticeable thing about the aircraft workers was their youth. Shift change resembled a high school dismissal."

Only one organizing effort reached the stage of an election during the NRA period, at Douglas, and management created a company union that easily won the contest. By the late 1930s, however, as aircraft production began a steady expansion, the employers found themselves facing two strong unions determined to crack the open shop. They came from different corners of the economy and alternative views of unionism: the AFL's International Association of Machinists (IAM), and the CIO's United Automobile Workers (UAW).

In 1937, the UAW tried and failed to organize workers at Lockheed in Burbank. At the same time, at the main Douglas plant in Santa Monica, several hundred workers, out of a workforce of five thousand, supported by the UAW, staged a four-day sit-down strike. Mass arrests ended the sit-down on February 27, but picketing continued outside the plant until March 15, and shop floor strife slowed the assembly lines for months.

Lockheed management understood it was only a matter of time before it had to bargain with a union. Observing the disruptions to production at Douglas, Lockheed's owners decided it would rather sit across the table from the IAM. Within a short time, the IAM was negotiating with Lockheed, but its membership consisted of a few hundred skilled mechanics out of thousands of workers.

The relationship between the IAM local and the company was cooperative. The union did not challenge the industry-standard starting wage set by the Aeronautical Chamber of Commerce, fifty cents an hour, although it did win a wage increase. A more militant Machinists local at Consolidated in San Diego negotiated a stronger contract but did not exceed the ACC's set price for new labor either. The tougher stand taken by the IAM in San Diego was due to its rivalry inside the plant with a nucleus of CIO sympathizers. Although the UAW couldn't win elections in San Diego, its continued presence kept IAM leaders on their toes.

The UAW did win elections elsewhere, and much of the credit goes to Wyndham Mortimer. Mortimer was one of the architects of the Flint, Michigan sit-down strike of 1936–7, which galvanized the organizing drives of the CIO and fired the imagination of workers across the country. In that event General Motors workers occupied their plant for forty-four days in the cold Midwest winter and wrestled union recognition from the powerful and fiercely antilabor corporation. In his mid-fifties at the time, Mortimer was one of the most experienced and successful union organizers in the country. Born into an immigrant family in Pennsylvania coal country, he followed his father into the mines when he was twelve. He worked on the railroad and as a streetcar conductor before settling into the open shop White Motor Company in 1917 in Cleveland, Ohio, running a drill press for thirty-seven cents an hour.

His upbringing and work experiences radicalized him, and he became a fervent believer in industrial unionism and a Socialist. He organized a union at White Motor, and then a midwestern auto workers union council. By the time the Depression rolled around, he had become a Communist. At the founding convention of the United Auto Workers in April 1936 he was elected first vice president. Within a year and a half the union grew from 30,000 to 350,000 workers and affiliated with the CIO.

Despite the phenomenal increase in membership, behind the scenes the UAW leadership was bitterly locked in factional battles. Mortimer lost his officer seat at the second convention but was retained as an organizer. Sent in summer 1939 to see what he could do with the rapidly expanding West Coast aircraft workforce, he wasted no time. He set up a weekly newspaper, *The Aircraft Organizer,* edited by Henry Kraus, and distributed it, with the assistance of the Workers Alliance, throughout the southern California aircraft companies.

Overcoming an anti-Communist campaign conducted by the Machinists union against Mortimer and the UAW-CIO, the autoworkers won a close election at the Vultee plant in Downey, which produced training planes for the military, for the right to represent four thousand workers. As Mortimer put it, the workers understood that "The fifty cent wage was not caused by the Kremlin, and no amount of Red-baiting would raise wages so much as one penny."

Forced to call a strike on November 15, 1940, when Vultee management refused to bargain in good faith, the fledgling local's twelve-day walkout ended with a 25 percent wage increase, bringing the starting rate to sixty-two and a half cents per hour and breaking open the ACC's wage standard. Mortimer attributed this success to the solidarity of the strikers in the face of pressure from the newspapers and an orchestrated campaign by the military to resume production of their planes.

West of Downey, in Inglewood, a larger prize awaited Mortimer and the UAW-CIO in the North American Aviation plant, where nearly ten thousand workers produced fighters. After gaining authorization cards from a third of the workers, Mortimer filed an election petition on behalf of UAW Local 683. Once more the CIO union was faced with a barrage of red-baiting by the IAM, aided by the *Los Angeles Times* and company publicity.

To counter the propaganda campaign, Mortimer came up with creative tactics. The union produced a twenty-page pamphlet, "Facts for Aircrafters," which provided engineering specifications useful to the workers in their daily duties along with union information. When IAM leaflets noted at the bottom that they were handed to workers "by a real 100 percent American," Mortimer responded by hiring Native Americans to pass out flyers for the UAW. Once more, in February 1941, the UAW beat IAM by a narrow margin.

Throughout the spring North American Aviation's management resisted the union's proposal for a seventy-five cent starting hourly wage. The national UAW leadership thought they could sweep the IAM out of southern California aircraft if they were successful in negotiating such a high rate and considered these negotiations so critical that national vice-president Richard Frankensteen, director of the UAW aviation department, came out to lead the bargaining team. When negotiations failed in late May, members, encouraged by Frankensteen, voted to authorize a strike by a margin of 5,829 to 210. On June 5 huge picket lines surrounded the plant and halted production.

However, the political climate had been rapidly shifting in early 1941 toward preparations for United States entry into the war and the primacy of national security. In March 1941 the government created the National Defense Mediation Board, with powers similar to the NLRB, but applying solely to war-related industries. Unions were expected to refrain from striking and to send their complaints instead to this new labor court system. Despite these expectations, a strike wave, including a number of unauthorized, or wildcat strikes, spread across the nation, provoking anger in Roosevelt's administration and calls in an increasingly conservative Congress to restrict labor rights.

Fearful of provoking antiunion legislation in the new situation, Frankensteen and the national UAW leadership reversed course. They ordered Mortimer—who wasn't there when the strike vote took place—to bring the strikers back to work. When he refused he was fired, along with several other UAW organizers who supported Mortimer. Frankensteen, veering rightward, in a radio program denounced "Communist influence" in the strike and tried to do the same at a big rally outside the plant the next day. He was booed until he left the stage under escort.

With the exception of John L. Lewis, the CIO leadership closed ranks behind the UAW's about-face. Through high-level contacts in Roosevelt's administration, they realized that what had worked at Vultee was no longer possible. The CIO brass thus approved the president's action when he sent 2,500 armed United States troops to break up the enormous North American Aviation picket lines by force on June 10 and seize the plant. Sixteen picket captains were arrested. Recognizing the gravity of their situation, the workers voted to return to work, where they endured armed troops posted inside the plant and in their neighborhoods.

President Roosevelt and the military had made their point: no interruption of war production would be tolerated. Yet in the North American Aviation plant, rank and file committees remained in place, stubbornly defiant, slowing production schedules, even after two dozen strike leaders had been fired. The UAW dissolved Local 683 and chartered another in its place. Frankensteen appointed a new group of officers for the local, who were ignored by the workers.

The colonel assigned to oversee a return to normalcy in the factory realized that if the troops were removed under these circumstances the workers would immediately strike again. He conferred with a National Defense Mediation Board official, and they came up with a plan. The company would have to agree to everything the workers had struck for, including the high wage demands and automatic dues deductions from workers' paychecks.

In early July the army left the premises. The workers stayed in place. They were warming up to the new leadership of the local who, as many now saw it,

FIGURE 31. United Auto Workers-CIO Local 683 members taken from their huge picket line to jail by military police during North American Aviation strike. Labor Archives and Research Center, San Francisco State University [People's World Collection].

had delivered the best wages in the aircraft industry. A transformed UAW survived at North American Aviation, rechartered as Local 887, serving as a high-profile example for the rest of the labor movement of the new thinking unions involved in defense industries were expected to embrace.

At war's end there were 29,000 UAW members in the southern California aircraft industry. In addition to North American Aviation and Vultee, the UAW represented workers in Ryan and the Long Beach Douglas plant. The IAM outnumbered the UAW with 56,000 members at Lockheed, the Douglas plants in El Segundo and Santa Monica, and Consolidated. Northrup, mostly nonunion until after the war, nonetheless presented workers with virtually identical conditions and wages as the unionized companies—a textbook case of how a unionized industry forces wages and conditions upward at nonunion shops in order for employers to retain their workforce.

The UAW outperformed the IAM in the important area of rights for women and minorities. Reflecting the political influence of the nearby progressive Los Angeles and California CIO industrial councils, the UAW actively pursued discrimination-related grievances in its plants for African

Americans denied employment and promotion. It also supported "Negro Victory" movements in the surrounding communities, helping build coalitions that fought for admission by blacks into industrial training programs that led to jobs in the war plants.

Thus when Tina Hill came to Los Angeles from Texas, her passage from low-wage domestic to unionized "Rosie the Riveter" industrial worker had been prepared by the CIO/civil rights campaign. She learned how to weld in a downtown training facility run by the Los Angeles School District, which had been the target of a successful campaign to open up to nonwhites. When she got hired at North American Aviation, her starting wage represented a huge advance from her pay as a domestic, and she worked alongside 1,700 other African Americans. The company discriminated in various ways. But unlike in the shipyards, Tina Hill had a union to turn to when she needed it.

21

"We Called It a Work Holiday"

THE OAKLAND GENERAL STRIKE

FOLLOWING NEARLY TWO DECADES of sacrifice due to Depression and war, workers expected that the elusive promise of a "middle class" standard of living would finally be realized.

What the postwar world should look like was spelled out at the end of the UAW-CIO-sponsored 1944 animated film *Hell Bent for Election*. After the Win the War Special had triumphed over the Defeatist Limited, the closing sequences of the cartoon featured a catchy song accompanying images of future postwar prosperity, guaranteed by government social insurance programs and a robust economy: "There'll be a job for everyone, everyone, everyone, there'll be a job for everyone if we get out and vote." The CIO's vision of full employment, high wages, and industrial democracy through collaboration among business, labor, and government—the "People's Program"—seemed like a natural extension of the cooperative successes of the war years.

But something different happened. Rising levels of unemployment due to layoffs in the war industries and veterans flooding into the labor market created a reserve army of labor that allowed businesses to tighten control over their workplaces and labor costs. Employers denied workers wage increases necessary to keep up with galloping inflation and to offset decreased hours of work. In the year following spring 1945 average real earnings fell by 12 percent in San Francisco. By the end of 1946, most Bay Area workers found themselves with less purchasing power than they had had in early 1944. Many of the largest employers and their business organizations, emboldened by their wartime recovery and a politically weakened New Deal, declared that they had only put up with unions during the war because they had to. Now that the war had ended, things should return to "normal": that is, untroubled by unions and the need for collective bargaining with workers' representatives.

Union leaders and activists were mindful of historical parallels with efforts of employers "to break the labor movement and weaken the unions as they did after the close of World War One," as a pamphlet distributed by the Alameda County Central Labor Council put it.

In response, the biggest wave of strikes in United States history washed across the country in 1945 and 1946. Workers struck mass production industries and shut down several cities with general strikes. In the East, these occurred in Hartford and Stamford, Connecticut; Camden, New Jersey; Lancaster, Pennsylvania; and Rochester, New York. Citywide general strikes are rare in the United States: never before (or since) had so many occurred in one year. The cluster in 1946 demonstrated the widespread anger of workers at their unmet expectations and also the high level of organizational competence unions had built over the preceding years.

Across the bay from San Francisco, twenty-eight stores belonged to the antiunion Retail Merchants Association (RMA). During the fall of 1946, the RMA's refusal to recognize a union in two stores set off a chain of events that led to a general strike of more than 100,000 workers from 142 AFL unions throughout Alameda County. In the process Oakland city politics, long dominated by conservative, antiunion forces, began a difficult makeover process, pushed by unions and their allies in minority communities. Although the Oakland General Strike of 1946 did not immediately achieve all of its objectives, its long-term effect was to give Oakland working people a substantial voice in running their municipal affairs for the first time.

KAHN'S AND HASTINGS WORKERS ORGANIZE

Al Kidder came home from the war and got a job selling shoes at Kahn's department store in the downtown Oakland shopping district. He made $28 a week but soon found that at nearby shoe stores, where salesmen had a union, they were making $42 a week. His mother had been working, with many other women, out of the Kahn's "ready room." Under this system, women employees without a regular work assignment would come in at 8 o'clock in the morning and wait, hoping to pick up a few hours of work if a department was shorthanded. Sometimes they waited in the ready room all day. They only received pay for the time they spent working in a department.

Conditions such as these led workers at Kahn's and at Hastings (a men's clothing store), into a months-long effort to gain union recognition beginning in summer 1946. The stores, located across Broadway from one another, refused to negotiate with Retail Clerks Local 1265, even after large majorities of the workers had signed union cards. Management at both stores belonged to the Retail Merchants Association, which demanded that before any store negotiated with the union, all twenty-eight stores in the association had to be organized. Kahn's and Hastings' workers thought the RMA position unfair, and, after one of the women who had signed a union card was fired, the workers at Hastings voted to strike on October 23.

Most of the striking workers were women. A few had picked up jobs in these stores after being laid off at the nearby shipyards when war production wound down. But many of the women had been there for years. The stores also employed some men—nearly all returning veterans. One was Steven Babbit.

Babbit, like Al Kidder, had come home from the war and gone to work at Kahn's. After a few months he had been selected by management to become a supervisor. Despite his promotion, Babbit thought it unreasonable of management to refuse to recognize the union. "When the strike began, the company began to call in all the managers and supervisors one by one and told us that we all had to cross the picket lines. But," said Babbit, "I looked at the line. A lot of them were little old ladies, as well as younger women. I just couldn't cross that line, I couldn't do it." The company then called Babbit and told him if he didn't come in he'd be fired. "Then they sent me a telegram and told me I *was* fired."

Local 1265 set up picket lines in front of Kahn's at the end of October, a week after picket lines were established at Hastings. Al Kidder became a picket captain, helping to keep the strikers scheduled for picket line duty. He recollected that at the outset, "seventy five to eighty percent" of the workers struck. The Alameda County Central Labor Council called on AFL unionists to honor the picket lines. Workers belonging to many other unions came by the picket lines to offer their support. The NAACP also supported the strike. The stores lost a lot of business, but—under heavy pressure from the RMA—refused to negotiate.

Aligned with the RMA were the Oakland City Council and the powerful *Oakland Tribune* newspaper, headed by its wealthy antilabor owner, Joseph Knowland. The publisher, whose son was a U.S. senator, treated Oakland as his personal kingdom, in much the same way that Harrison Gray Otis, owner of the *Los Angeles Times,* had done in that city in the early 1900s. The nine-member Oakland City Council had long been filled with Knowland allies.

His control extended into all levels of Oakland city government. Knowland's *Tribune* provided the RMA with one-sided news coverage of the dispute with its members' employees. Utilizing an antiunion tactic spreading rapidly in the postwar era, Knowland's editorials claimed that "Communists" were behind the strike.

One crucial source of strike support came from Teamster drivers, who refused to bring goods to the struck stores. Despite the RMA's antiunion attitude, Teamsters Local 70, with two thousand members and a militant history, was strong enough to enforce its own closed shop contract with the RMA: only union drivers delivered merchandise to the association stores. The drivers sympathized with the desire of Kahn's and Hastings' workers to unionize and honored the clerks' lines.

As a result, a month into the strike, during peak holiday shopping season, stocks on the stores' shelves dwindled. Alarmed, RMA leaders, Joseph Knowland, the police chief, county sheriff, district attorney, and head of the central bank met secretly and decided to use strikebreakers to move a half-million dollars worth of goods into the stores. It was the consequences of this action that enraged working people and shortly brought the city to a standstill.

THE SPARK

Before daybreak on Sunday, December 1, escorted by hundreds of Oakland policemen, strikebreakers drove twelve truckloads of merchandise through seventy picketers stationed at six entrances to the stores. The drivers worked for the Veterans Trucking company, a Los Angeles firm established by the Merchants and Manufacturers Association for the express purpose of breaking strikes. Its drivers had traveled four hundred miles to Oakland at the invitation of the RMA. To make way for them, the police swept the union picket lines off the street, injuring peaceful picketers.

The composition of that group of picketers proved to be of great significance in the events that followed. Although some were striking Kahn's and Hastings workers, most were officers and staffers of other AFL unions, who came out that Saturday night and Sunday morning in solidarity with the clerks. They had been alerted that Kahn's and Hastings would attempt to move merchandise into the store.

FIGURE 32. Al Brown, an officer in the Amalgamated Transit Union Local 192, refused to take his street-car across a police line, sparking the December 1946 Oakland General Strike. The Oakland Tribune Collection, the Oakland Museum of California, Gift of the Alameda Newspaper Group.

An officer in the typographical union, Joe Chaudet, had been walking the picket line and was outraged by what had happened:

> I was black and blue for months. They all marched over and pushed all the people, shoving you this way, bumping you, hitting you in the throat, pushed all the labor people out the alley, down the street, and set up a cordon around Kahn's and Hastings. The trucks followed right behind them, went on in, and unloaded.

The union activists had received assurance from the Oakland police chief that they could legally park their cars in loading zones near the stores on the weekends and at night. Nevertheless, police towed away the strikers' cars and those of their supporters as soon as the officers had removed the picket lines.

As daylight broke on Sunday morning, December 1, the small crowd of striking clerks and supporters regrouped, facing 250 police posted in front of the stores. The police roped off six square blocks surrounding the stores in the center of downtown and, at 7:30 A.M., herded the twelve trucks to Kahn's and Hastings' loading docks. The union leaders were disgusted that their own tax money was being used to protect strikebreakers. Chaudet later said he believed that the Oakland General Strike was born at that moment, in the bruises and indignant feelings of union leaders who had been lied to, physically assaulted, and found their own tax-supported police force used against them.

When the first Key System streetcar rolled up to the police blockade early Sunday morning, police tried to move it through the gathering crowd. But the driver, Al Brown, an officer in the Amalgamated Transit Union Local 192, learned from the strikers what had happened. He removed the controls from the streetcar and left his vehicle standing in the middle of the street. Next Brown convinced the drivers of the streetcars behind him to do the same. Bus drivers passing through the area also halted their vehicles and joined the picket lines, which by now swelled with union sympathizers. A police three-wheeler ran over one streetcar driver, Newton Selvidge. He had to be taken to the hospital.

After the merchandise had been unloaded and the police left the area, streetcar and bus services resumed. Management at the two stores was jubilant. But Kahn's and Hastings' picketers returned. The battle was just beginning.

THE GENERAL STRIKE

Workers in many unions met all Monday. Sentiment clearly was in favor of a general strike. That evening, at an emergency meeting of five hundred union leaders, the labor council called for a county-wide "work holiday" to protest the police violence, support the Kahn's and Hastings strikers, and demand that police never again escort strikebreakers. The council created a strike steering committee and set up subcommittees to deal with communication among strikers, coordinate food distribution to participants, and keep essential services going in the city.

Union members in 142 AFL unions received notice of the council's decision by telephone, telegram, and radio reports. The word spread far beyond the retail and trade unions at the heart of the dispute. Musician Earl Watkins, working at a popular nightclub in east Oakland, Slim Jenkins' Place, remembered receiving the word there from his union's business agent that no one would be playing until the strike was over.

The next day, Tuesday, December 3, 1946, the city of Oakland came to a stop. Hundreds of buses and streetcars sat empty in their yards, resulting in massive traffic jams on the Bay Bridge. Remembering the furious antiunion propaganda produced by San Francisco newspapers during the 1934 General Strike, Oakland strike leaders made sure to halt the printing presses at Oakland's three daily newspapers, including Knowland's *Tribune.* Most places of businesses closed or were staffed with skeleton management crews. Only vital services, such as hospitals, stayed in operation. Strikers directed traffic.

Contrary to San Francisco newspaper accounts portraying the general strike as "violent" and "Communist-inspired," only minor incidents occurred during three days while up to 130,000 workers took their holiday. There were tense moments when the police attempted to escort strikebreakers into struck businesses. But most of the time the Oakland General Strike remained remarkably peaceful, with union picket captains keeping the more boisterous strikers in line. Teamsters patrolled the streets to make sure that altercations didn't escalate because, as warehouse clerk Dan Breault recalled, "When the police came they only arrested strikers, no matter who might have been at fault."

Harry Lundeberg, president of the Sailors Union of the Pacific (SUP)— part of the Seamen's International Union (SIU)—sent his members, mostly Hawaiians from ships docked in San Francisco, to create "flying squads" of picketers to patrol against strikebreaking activities. They issued large white "SIU-SUP Brotherhood of the Sea" buttons to all seamen or people on the street they knew.

Tuesday evening, December 3, over 10,000 workers attended a mass meeting in the Oakland Auditorium and, outside in the rain, 5,000 more listened by loudspeakers. To a wildly enthusiastic reception, Lundeberg gave a fiery speech denouncing the police-scab escorts. The SUP president reflected the sentiments of the assembly when he told them, "The ordinary finks were the strikebreaking finks. The super finks were in the city hall!"

So high were spirits that evening that Bob Ash, Alameda County Central Labor Council secretary, recalled years later that if he'd asked the crowd to march to city hall with him, "I think they'd have taken that City Hall apart, brick by brick."

Despite the December weather, participants were in a festive mood. According to Stan Weir, a CIO activist and unemployed autoworker at the time of the strike, the atmosphere was joyous, "almost like a carnival in the streets." People played musical instruments, sang labor songs, and danced to the country-swing hit, *Pistol-packin' Mama, Lay That Pistol Down,* blaring from jukeboxes placed on the sidewalks. Belying fearful reports from San

FIGURE 33. Kahn's department store worker and picket captain Gwendolyn Byfield (center) epitomized the exuberant spirit of the "work holiday." The Oakland Tribune Collection, the Oakland Museum of California, Gift of the Alameda Newspaper Group.

Francisco newspapers, the crowds were friendly. People felt a camaraderie; strangers stopped and spoke to one another.

On Wednesday afternoon negotiations took place at the Athens Club between labor leaders and a "citizens committee" consisting of representatives of the RMA, other big business groups, and members of the city government. Tribune owner Knowland attended. The AFL unions, led by labor council secretary Bob Ash, restated their willingness to call off the general strike as soon as they received a promise that the city of Oakland would not in the future use police to escort professional strikebreakers and would "refrain from taking sides in any issues between labor and management."

But even as they were meeting, the seemingly strong position of the unions was being undermined. Despite the solid support given the strike by members and officers of Teamsters Local 70, national Teamster officials were working behind the scenes at cross-purposes with their Oakland members. Relations between International Brotherhood of Teamsters vice president Dave Beck and the East Bay labor movement—including Beck's Teamsters—

had been strained for years. Beck and his ally Charles Real, a high-ranking Teamster official who had emerged from Local 70, had tried to send drivers across labor council-sanctioned picket lines on more than one previous occasion. Now they were threatening to send their members back to work.

Beck, who later went to prison for corruption, publicly called the strike "a lot of foolishness." Bob Ash left the meeting with the citizens committee to talk on the phone with Beck, and extracted a promise from him to hold off on ordering the drivers to end their sympathy strike. But when Ash returned to the meeting room, everyone was reading copies of the *San Francisco Chronicle* featuring a front-page story in which Beck had already issued the back-to-work order!

Balancing the negative effects of Beck's action was a telegram received at the meeting from the Alameda county CIO council, pledging to pull all CIO union members off their jobs by Friday. This would have resulted in the city's water, gas, telephones, and electricity being shut off, since CIO unions represented workers in those services. The CIO's threat caused the city council to vote emergency powers to the mayor.

Whatever might have resulted either from the exercise of those emergency powers or the CIO's entry into the strike will never be known. Late Wednesday night, Oakland city manager J. F. Hassler issued a verbal assurance to union leaders that the police would not in the future escort strikebreakers and would remain impartial in labor disputes. On the strength of that statement, Bob Ash and the other strike committee leaders called an end to the general strike Thursday morning, December 5, at 11 A.M.

Many union members were upset at the decision, figuring that if the CIO unions—representing 30,000 workers at the docks, in heavy industry, in warehouses, and at the public utilities—joined them, they would be invincible. But AFL leaders believed they had achieved the main goal of the general strike. In addition, they feared association with Communists in the CIO leadership and perhaps worried they might lose direction of the general strike to the militant CIO if it became involved. AFL leaders were also concerned at the possible effect of Beck's back-to-work order on the crucial support of the Teamster drivers.

CIO officials, while publicly offering to join the strike, had their own reasons to stay out of the fight. The ILWU's Harry Bridges had overseen a fifty-two-day West Coast longshoremen's strike that had ended just two weeks earlier. He was not enthusiastic about jeopardizing his union's fragile relationship with employers by sending his members out on a general strike—

especially given bitter feelings between the Bay Area-wide ILWU-CIO ware-house local and the AFL Retail Clerks, who had recently battled over juris-dictional rights to organize East Bay warehouse workers.

The Oakland General Strike had ended, but the Kahn's and Hastings workers who started it all were still on strike. The immediate result of more than one hundred thousand workers taking to the streets was simply an agree-ment that the city would no longer allow its police to protect strikebreakers. Yet, almost immediately, police were again escorting strikebreakers through the picket lines at Kahn's and Hastings. Although angry at this violation of the agreement, AFL union leaders were nonetheless not about to call another general strike. What they *did* do was quite effective, however, in its own way.

POLITICAL MOBILIZATION

Out of the Oakland General Strike grew a grassroots political mobilization. Working people had developed a greater sense of solidarity with one another, and these feelings in several cases led to personal and collective action. Elizabeth Mackin, for example, an Oakland grocery store employee and activist in another Retail Clerks local, sent a letter to Kahn's management in February 1947, explaining why she no longer shopped at Kahn's:

> Kahn's has always been my favorite department store and it was a great disap-pointment to me that your executives did not have the foresight or vision to sit down with chosen representatives of your clerks to work out a satisfactory solution to your mutual problems. . . . I wish you to close out my account until you have a happier relationship with those who work for you.

More dramatically, AFL and CIO unions recognized the necessity of united action. Deepening efforts begun during the war, the two labor federa-tions formed a joint political action committee and ran labor candidates for the five open seats (out of nine) in the Oakland City Council elections of May 1947. They helped create a coalition, the Oakland Voters League (OVL), which brought labor together with community and small business groups dedicated to ending conservative control over city government. The OVL, in turn, attracted the United Negro Labor Committee, formed within the shipyards by black trade unionists during their wartime struggle for equality. These activists registered voters and got them out to vote on Election Day in African American neighborhoods.

The OVL's platform, adopted by the five labor-backed candidates, included proposals for public works projects to build parks, playgrounds, swimming pools, and other recreational facilities. It called for rent control and a fair tax structure, enlarged public health services, and more schools. It also specified that the city council would stay out of labor disputes, and promised an investigation of police brutality cases against African Americans.

The spirited 1947 campaign unleashed great energy and political involvement in working-class communities, capped by a mass torchlight parade down Broadway just before the election. Thousands of individuals carried mops and brooms to symbolize the need for political "housecleaning." A float created by the United Negro Labor Committee featured AFL and CIO pallbearers putting a coffin labeled "The Machine" into its grave. A hand-drawn sign next to this tableau showed two fists labeled "Oakland Voters"—one black, one white—pulverizing the *Oakland Tribune* tower, longtime symbol of antiunion politics in the East Bay.

A record number of voters turned out. Working people of Oakland, infused with the memory of their brief control of the city in December, had elected their candidates to four of the five open council seats. The only defeated labor candidate, a former Richmond shipyard worker, lost narrowly. He probably would have won but the confusing election ballot layout made it appear his opponent was the labor candidate. Antisemitism also undoubtedly contributed to his defeat (his name was Goldfarb). As a result, the labor candidates held only four out of nine Council seats. They could not enact their full proworker legislative program, but the formerly invincible Knowland machine had been dealt a blow and workers' voices could no longer be ignored in the halls of city government.

The week after the election, the RMA and Retail Clerks Local 1265 announced that the union would be recognized as the exclusive bargaining agent for workers in the twenty-seven remaining member stores. Although the agreement did not grant a union shop, the RMA agreed not to interfere with union recruitment of salespeople. Hastings had reached a separate pact earlier in the year with the union, one that did include a union shop clause. The store had been forced out of the RMA immediately.

As a result of the unprecedented solidarity of AFL unions and their united political effort with the CIO and community, the RMA was compelled to engage in collective bargaining with Retail Clerks Local 1265 on behalf of thousands of Oakland retail workers. The old Oakland, run by Knowland, the RMA, and their cronies, was no longer intact.

Unfortunately, the Oakland Voters League shortly fell prey to renewed AFL and CIO sectarian infighting. Red-baiting and racism extracted their tolls from the coalition as well; the Oakland Voters League dissolved after a desultory and unsuccessful 1949 city council campaign.

Unlike the San Francisco General Strike a dozen years earlier, the Oakland General Strike did not usher in a new era for working people. Rather, the 1946 strike wave, including what happened in Oakland, might better be understood as a late flower of the mass militancy of the prewar period but without the politicizing environment of an economy in collapse. The differences between the two Bay Area citywide general strikes reflect the moments in which they took place. The events and elements of 1934—massive employer and police violence, the desperate and radicalized workforce, a relative vacuum where labor laws should have been—were not replicated in 1946, which featured a battle fought over different stakes—to maintain recognition for the rights of workers to organize and bargain collectively, and continued respect and status for union leaders—by a larger, more stable labor movement seeking its place in the postwar order. The two strikes were very different bookends for the most dynamic period of growth in working-class consciousness and power in California history.

Hollywood to Bakersfield

POVERTY IN THE VALLEY OF PLENTY

FROM FALL 1947 UNTIL SPRING 1950, near the small town of Arvin, a few miles southeast of Bakersfield, workers employed by the DiGiorgio Fruit Corporation waged a long, bitter strike for union recognition, led by Local 218 of the National Farm Labor Union (NFLU). In several ways this battle foreshadowed efforts of the United Farm Workers two decades later to achieve some measure of justice for the tillers of California's fields. The strike was initially lent a great deal of support by the California State Labor Federation and particularly unions in Hollywood, which made a film called *Poverty in the Valley of Plenty* to assist the farmworkers' public outreach efforts. But as time passed and the corporation, supported by the Associated Farmers, illegally but efficiently brought in strikebreakers, the underfunded NFLU and its suffering members couldn't keep up. Eventually the strike was crushed.

Poverty in the Valley of Plenty played a peculiar and ultimately decisive role in this struggle. Its connection to another labor battle unfolding a few miles but a world away, in Hollywood, revealed the challenges facing unions in the postwar years, as the Depression-launched tide of mass worker militancy receded and Cold War politics and prosperity undermined social justice-oriented unionism.

THE NATIONAL FARM LABOR UNION

The American Federation of Labor granted a charter to the NFLU in 1946. Its leader, H. L. Mitchell, was the visionary founder of the Southern Tenant Farmers Union, which had brought white and black sharecroppers, small farmers, and workers together to oppose Jim Crow racism and economic oppression in the 1930s. Expanding east and west, it carried its civil rights-oriented unionism to California the year after World War II ended and established small but feisty locals in Central Valley farmworker communities. Mitchell sent Hank Hasiwar, a World War II Pacific Theater veteran and New York City union organizer, to staff the NFLU's western front. Given the hostility of the growers, mutual suspicion between Okie and Mexican American workers, and indifference, at best, of government farm agencies, he had his work cut out for him.

Hasiwar was the son of German immigrants, and a former student Socialist Club leader at Columbia University. In 1936 he led a protest against a pro-Nazi dean, for which he was expelled. His student organizing brought him to the attention of Local 94 of the Operating Engineers, which hired him as an organizer. After the war, still in the army, Hasiwar spent a year in Japan, helping to rebuild Japanese unions as democratic, industry-wide organizations. In the process he publicly criticized General Douglas MacArthur, overseer of the American occupation, for siding too closely with Japanese business in the writing of new labor laws. This earned Hasiwar an expedited, although honorable, discharge. A capable and fearless organizer, he arrived in California in February 1947 shortly after the NFLU put him on the payroll.

The giant farm owned by DiGiorgio Fruit Corporation at the southern end of the San Joaquin Valley was not Hasiwar and Mitchell's first choice for a confrontation with the valley's growers. Employing over 1,300 workers at peak season across eleven thousand acres of fruit and vegetables, DiGiorgio's was the largest corporate farm and the pacesetter for California agribusiness.

Bob Whatley, a one-armed, seventy-year-old farmworker who lived in Lamont, sent a letter to AFL president William Green, requesting an organizer for the DiGiorgio workers, while Hasiwar was running a strike of wine grape workers near Fresno. When the strike ended, Hasiwar met with Whatley, who convinced him to talk to the DiGiorgio workers.

After a few months of quiet but persistent organizing, Local 218 had the signatures of 858 of the DiGiorgio workers on union authorization cards and several hundred more from surrounding ranches. The union included Anglos, Mexican Americans, Filipinos, and African Americans (although DiGiorgio hired no black workers).

Some members lived in company-supplied labor camps, segregated by race, on DiGiorgio property. Most resided in slums on the outskirts of Arvin and nearby Lamont and Weedpatch. The sand lots were cheap; even some of the impoverished, transplanted southwestern farm families could afford twenty-five dollars down and ten dollars a month to set up a shack and call it home.

Here—a stone's throw from where John Steinbeck set the events of his 1939 novel, *The Grapes of Wrath*—they slept, cooked their meals, and talked over what California had done to their dreams of reestablishing themselves as farmers. They also talked about Joseph DiGiorgio and as they talked they got angry. One of the first to join Local 218 was Phineas Parks, a preacher who worked in DiGiorgio's packing sheds and who pitched in immediately for the cause. Hasiwar recalled how Parks would start the meetings, telling the workers,

> My God, we need a Union! We got to stand up like men. The bosses are no more men than we are. They get into their pants just like we do, one leg at a time. These guys got so much money they buy Cadillacs so big that when they make a turn they need hinges on them.

By summer the DiGiorgio workers were ready to take on their boss, quicker than Hasiwar would have liked. He and Mitchell had thought they would build a network of supporters throughout the valley first. They had not imagined immediately targeting any one grower, and certainly not the biggest and most powerful. Nonetheless, adapting to changing circumstances, Mitchell and Hasiwar reasoned that if DiGiorgio could be unionized, the rest of the growers would follow.

They recruited a shed foreman, Jimmie Price, to act as lead organizer among the mostly Okie workers. Price, originally from Oklahoma himself, was elected president of the new union local. They also signed up Luis De Anda, who with his wife and four children had migrated from Texas, to organize the Mexicanos. Hasiwar later married De Anda's sister Delphina, who ran an early morning Spanish program on a Bakersfield radio station.

Mitchell hired Ernesto Galarza as the union's education and organizing director and sent him to join the DiGiorgio campaign. Galarza, whose parents came from Mexico when he was a small boy, grew up in Sacramento's poorest neighborhood. He worked his way through college, emerging with a Ph.D. from Columbia University. Before coming to the NFLU he did research for the Pan American Union, predecessor to the Organization of American States.

In September 1947, the new members of Local 218 came up with their contract proposal: a wage increase of ten cents per hour, a grievance procedure, seniority rights, and union recognition. A letter to DiGiorgio informed him that a clear majority of his workers desired a union contract and outlined what they wanted in it. The letter was ignored by DiGiorgio.

On September 30 Jimmie Price led a meeting of several hundred union members in the Weedpatch Grange Hall. He and Hasiwar informed the workers that DiGiorgio had rejected their overtures. The farmworkers voted by a large majority to strike.

On the first day, the company was jolted from its complacency to find nearly nine hundred workers missing. Large picket lines blocked the farm's entrances along the country roads. A majority of field hands, shed workers, tractor drivers, and irrigators had walked off the job. However, the corporation insisted to the press that there was no strike; it was simply a "labor disturbance." It never budged from this word game for the next two and a half years.

Among the strikers were 130 *braceros*—legally imported Mexican workers—whom DiGiorgio had assumed were impervious to union arguments. The Bracero Program, begun as an emergency wartime measure to secure needed crop-pickers, had been manipulated by the powerful Associated Farmers into a means of permanently driving down the wages of domestic farmworkers. Supposedly to be called upon only where domestic farmworkers were unavailable, in practice the *braceros* were often used as strikebreakers and to destroy solidarity and organization in domestic farmworker communities.

On the third day of the strike the *braceros* were convinced by the local sheriff and officials from the state Department of Agriculture to return to work. This provided DiGiorgio with the breathing room needed to keep a minimum level of production going until scabs could arrive several weeks later from Texas. It took the U.S. Department of Labor until mid-November to remove the *braceros,* despite the clear guideline forbidding their use during labor disputes. Meanwhile, several hundred strikebreakers were now working for DiGiorgio. Many had been put up in the former quarters of evicted striking families, whose belongings one day in November had been unceremoniously deposited on a country road in the rain.

By the end of December the strike had settled into a siege. Three-quarters of the strikers, unable to live without steady income, had gone to work in other farms. Some returned to the southwestern United States. DiGiorgio rebuilt its workforce to prestrike levels. The remaining 250 strikers, from their trailer headquarters in a striker's backyard, kept picket lines going and built strong connections with other unions and supportive community and religious groups.

A Bakersfield Central Labor Council committee collected and distributed over one hundred thousand dollars worth of clothes, food, and money to the strikers' families. Much of this support arrived in caravans sent by the Los Angeles and San Francisco labor councils, including one in March 1948, with over three hundred cars and trucks. Victor Van Bourg, a teenaged apprentice painter, rode in a bus chartered by his Communist-controlled Hollywood Painters union local to the DiGiorgio picket lines. It was a formative experience for the young Van Bourg; years later, after he became an attorney, he volunteered his time doing legal work for the farmworker cause.

Teamster drivers and winery workers refused to cross Local 218 picket lines. The Retail Clerks union informed DiGiorgio that they would not handle his produce in Los Angeles, and the California State Labor Federation, AFL, contributed five hundred dollars a month to the strike and called for a consumer boycott of DiGiorgio products. The national AFL, thanks to a personal friendship between AFL president William Green and H.L. Mitchell, also pitched in, covering Hasiwar's expenses.

Despite all its support, the union could never recoup the ground it lost during the first weeks of the strike when the *braceros* were forced back in and strikebreakers recruited. In retrospect, Galarza admitted the union had made a mistake in walking out after the peak of picking, when the corporation would have been more vulnerable.

In February 1948, five picketers were assaulted by thugs, sending three to the hospital. The next morning hundreds of enraged, armed strikers showed up in front of the farm, facing a line of police, prepared for battle. Galarza recalled, "It was one of Hasiwar's worst moments. Himself a man of strong temperament, he nevertheless risked his leadership of the strike to restrain the militant Okies, who had no fear of the law ranged against them with automatic weapons and tear gas." As if anticipating similar moments with the United Farm Workers two decades later, Hasiwar believed that a strike dependent on the good will of the public could not risk violence, however much provoked by the other side.

The union suffered another setback one evening in May 1948 in a meeting held in an Arvin home when Jimmie Price was shot in the head by unknown assailants who fired through the living room window. The DiGiorgio company doctor refused to attend to Price, who almost bled to death on the way to the Bakersfield hospital eighteen miles away. The attackers were never

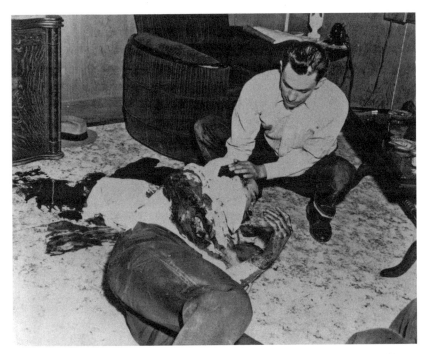

FIGURE 34. National Farm Labor Union leader Jimmie Price was shot in the head by an unknown gunman firing through the window of an Arvin home during the DiGiorgio strike in 1948. Personal collection of the author.

found. Price survived to help keep the strike going, stoically commenting, "Takes more than guns to kill an Oklahoman."

But it was a battle waged still fiercely by just a hundred hard-core union members, drawing on the support of friends whose patience was beginning to wear thin due to the visibly limited potential of the strikers to win.

THE BATTLE FOR PUBLIC OPINION

At this point the battle for public opinion became the union's best hope for success. The strikers could survive, barely, with labor and community support. But to win they needed more than that. The union publicized blatant bias in favor of the corporation by local police and governmental agencies. One example: picketers were arrested, despite no evidence pointing to them, on charges of cutting down plum trees during the night on DiGiorgio property; they were held on $15,000 bail each. Meanwhile the thugs who had rushed and beat pickets with tools and chains from DiGiorgio property were freed on $250 bail. Another: after the Kern County Board of Supervisors passed an ordinance banning the use of P.A. systems on the street, Bob Whatley was arrested for reading the Declaration of Independence through a loudspeaker.

Through meetings, governmental hearings, and newspaper and magazine articles, Local 218 publicized incidents such as these and kept its fight for justice before the eyes of the nation. Delphina De Anda played a crucial role with Spanish language news about the struggle on her Bakersfield radio show—until grower pressure resulted in her firing.

Two factors determined the union's shift to a public relations strategy. The NFLU had begun the strike with a mere twenty-five hundred dollars in its national treasury and could not help the strikers financially except through solicitation of AFL unions and other friendly organizations. More importantly, there were literally no rules to make the corporation play by, since farm labor was excluded from the National Labor Relations Act. (Although California state law did recognize farm labor's right to form unions, it had toothless enforcement mechanisms, which allowed DiGiorgio to stonewall the request to negotiate in the first place.) Organized public pressure, however, could presumably tarnish DiGiorgio's good name and affect profits.

The corporation had its media squad, too, which included sympathetic elected officials such as Jack Tenney and Hugh Burns of the California state senate Committee on Un-American Activities (CUAC). Senator Tenney's history included writing a popular song, "Mexicali Rose," and Communist membership before he turned on the party after it endorsed a political opponent. The senators responded to Joseph DiGiorgio's accusations in the press of "Communist subversion" by subpoenaing union officers.

The hearings found no evidence of Communist participation in Local 218 or the NFLU. This should have been unsurprising, since the leadership and national staff of the NFLU, including Mitchell, Hasiwar, and Galarza, were Socialists, as intense in their opposition to Communism as they were to the growers. Hasiwar later recalled that when members of the Food, Tobacco and Allied Workers-CIO (formerly UCAPAWA) showed up at the DiGiorgio picket line one day, "picketers chased them away."

But the issue of communism in the labor movement did play an important role behind the scenes in the publicity war between the NFLU and DiGiorgio, drawing two men into the fray—one on each side—who later became presidents of the United States.

Richard M. Nixon, then a freshman congressman, accompanied another high-profile team of lawmakers to investigate the strike, eager to ride the rising tide of anticommunism to higher office. A subcommittee of the House Education and Labor Committee arrived in Bakersfield in November 1949 at the invitation of DiGiorgio. Attending the hearing was a twenty-one-year-old farmworker named Cesar Chavez, whose first union card bore the imprint of the NFLU and who had been walking picket lines in a nearby cotton strike.

Nixon's behavior while cross examining witnesses at the hearing so enraged Hank Hasiwar that one night he had to be restrained from punching Nixon in a bar. H. L. Mitchell recalled,

> [Nixon] tried to make each union man or woman who appeared as a witness into a criminal on trial for his or her life. He asked one union witness, "Where were you at seven o'clock on the night of November 31, 1948?" The union man replied, "I guess I was at home, that's about suppertime." Nixon attacked the straightforward Okie with, "Remember, you are under oath! You know perfectly well there is no November 31!"

MEANWHILE, BACK IN HOLLYWOOD

While in Bakersfield Nixon and the other congressional subcommittee members were treated to a film screening. In the spring of 1948 the AFL-affiliated Hollywood Film Council made a short documentary film for the strikers to use in publicizing their cause and raising funds. It ultimately became the decisive element in the strike, although not in a way that either the union or its producers might have imagined.

Poverty in the Valley of Plenty depicted the living and working conditions of DiGiorgio's employees and attacked agribusiness for treating its workers less well than farm machinery. It was shown in union halls and community centers, in churches, and on a TV station in Los Angeles. Narrated by a radio reporter and former war correspondent, Harry Flannery, portions of the twenty-two-minute black and white film resembled Dorothea Lange photographs in motion. The grizzled faces of older farmworkers filled the screen while an urgent voiceover narration condemned the growers, and DiGiorgio in particular.

Flannery had been the second choice to narrate *Poverty in the Valley of Plenty*. Initially Ronald Reagan, then president of the Screen Actors Guild, was considered for Flannery's role in the film. Reagan did help raise funds to produce the film and later worked to distribute it widely.

The Hollywood Film Council consisted of a group of craft unions dominated by the International Alliance of Theatrical Stage Employees (IATSE, or simply "the IA"). The IA had just emerged triumphant from a bloody two-year struggle with progressive unions over job control on Hollywood movie sets. This was a more extreme version of the traditional jurisdictional divisions encouraged by studio producers for decades between AFL building trade unions and the IA. Beginning with the successful Disney studio animators' strike of 1941, painter's union leader Herb Sorrell built a credible democratic union federation, the Conference of Studio Unions (CSU), as an alternative to the corrupt IA, which had been controlled by Chicago mobsters since the early 1930s.

Although the mob's number one enforcer in Hollywood, Willie Bioff, and the IA national president, Richard Walsh, had gone to prison in 1940 along with a producer who had colluded with their money-skimming schemes, most IA Hollywood locals remained in the hands of the old guard. IA activists who had hoped for a revival of union democracy were disappointed; the meetings mostly had no quorums, a legacy of years of intimidation and shakedowns by Bioff's associates. Studio workers interested in improving conditions turned to the Conference of Studio Unions.

The set painters union won a 15 percent raise and the first real collective bargaining agreement in Hollywood in 1937 after a strike. Led by ex-boxer Sorrell, it became the core of the CSU, formed in 1941 with set decorators, screen office workers, animation cartoonists, carpenters, and electricians, along with a breakaway IA lab technician local. Sorrell, a friend of Harry Bridges, flirted with the CIO (which lost a representation election in 1939 to the IA) but kept his group of unions inside the AFL. The unity of these unions, so elusive for decades, threatened the ability of the studios to keep wages low.

In mid-1945, while the war was still underway, the CSU sent its seven thousand members out on strike in support of a small unit of set decorators, whose jurisdiction, with the connivance of studio bosses, was being challenged by the IA. Sorrell's former ally, the Los Angeles branch of the Communist Party, condemned the strike and its leader, due to the party's continued allegiance to the no-strike pledge. This didn't stop Ronald Reagan, the *Los Angeles Times,* and studio publicists from continuously describing the thirty-week labor struggle as a "Communist-inspired strike." Reagan said later that "what the communists wanted to do in terms of the CSU strike was to shut down the industry, and when everybody was angry and dissatisfied with their unions for their failures, the communists would propose one big union for Hollywood with everyone in it from producers to grips."

The CSU strike split the Hollywood labor movement down the middle. On the picket lines in front of Warner Brothers Studio on October 5, 1945, strikers overturned three cars attempting to enter the studio. The crowd of strikers and supporters, numbering in the thousands, was assaulted by gangs of professional thugs, by high-pressure fire hoses, and a nasty rain of nuts and bolts dropped from the studio roof by Warner Brothers executives.

The CSU survived this strike. But there were two more, provoked in rapid succession by the studios, with the IA providing strikebreakers, over the next two years. The ongoing conflict spilled over into the already stormy politics of the Screen Writers Guild and Screen Actors Guild (SAG), climaxed with a bitterly contested meeting of the SAG over whether to cross CSU picket lines.

In that meeting, Frank Sinatra declared that no one could stop him from crossing the CSU lines. Alexander Knox made the mistake of imitating Ronald Reagan during his speech opposing the decision to break with the CSU: "And then we heard this noise, and it was Reagan's 'bodyguards' coming down the aisle slapping bicycle chains against the chairs." The conservative faction of actors in control of the guild ruled Karen Morley's motion not to cross the CSU's lines until after the strike, out of order. The vote went against the CSU while thousands of craft workers stood in silent vigil outside.

By 1947 the CSU dissolved, its members replaced by the IA on the sets. Nearly all its former unions, along with the IA, were brought under the umbrella of a new organization, the AFL-affiliated Hollywood Film Council,

Despite this decisive victory, uneasy rested the crown on the head of the IA's leader, Roy Brewer, who fused a messianic anticommunist political ideology with a flair for publicity. It was Brewer who had convinced Ronald Reagan to abandon his early left-leaning politics in SAG and join the anticommunist bandwagon. And it was Brewer who initiated *Poverty in the Valley of Plenty* as an extension of the Hollywood anticommunist crusade to the Central Valley.

Brewer believed the potential existed for a Communist publicity film in the DiGiorgio strike. The Communist-led CIO farmworker unions of the 1930s had retreated from the fields to packinghouses and canneries, where they narrowly lost a key statewide election against the grower-favored AFL Teamsters in 1946. But they retained enough of a presence that anticommunist forces within the California labor movement feared the Communists might make an effective intervention in the DiGiorgio strike. *Poverty in the Valley of Plenty* was born out of this anxiety, and from the desire of Brewer, Reagan, and other conservative leaders of the Hollywood craft unions to demonstrate that solidarity with farmworkers was not the exclusive property of the left.

NOT A HOLLYWOOD ENDING

More than two years into the strike, in November 1949, the beginning of the end came with the Bakersfield House Education and Labor subcommittee investigation into the dispute. DiGiorgio's lawyers began the hearing by serving a complaint for libel on NFLU officers, suing the union, the Hollywood Film Council, and Harry Flannery for two million dollars damages for *Poverty in the Valley of Plenty.*

In their rush to make *Poverty in the Valley of Plenty,* Brewer and his Hollywood Film Council made a crucial error. The segment of the film focusing on miserable farmworker housing moves rapidly between general conditions for valley laborers and the specific problems associated with DiGiorgio company housing. The narrator, Flannery, identifies the dilapidated housing we see as provided by DiGiorgio for his workers. DiGiorgio's lawyers were able to make much of this implication that the shacks shown were DiGiorgio's, when apparently they were not. The film's overwhelmingly accurate depiction of farmworker conditions and reasoned analysis of the causes of the DiGiorgio strike were undermined by this mistake.

After screening the film, the three members of the subcommittee friendly to agribusiness—including Nixon—signed a report finding that the film was libelous, having been made by "corrupt men deliberately bearing false witness." The DiGiorgio publicity machine rapidly got major daily newspapers to report that congressmen had called the film "a shocking collection of falsehoods." The NFLU was pressured by the California State Labor Federation to end the strike. The union had no money to contest the suit by itself. With its labor support evaporating, the union had run out of options.

In May 1950, the NFLU signed a four-page settlement out of court with DiGiorgio. It agreed that *Poverty in the Valley of Plenty* was libelous, the union would pay one dollar in damages to the corporation, it would recall all copies of the film and destroy them, and it would end the strike. The most significant farm labor challenge to the power of California agribusiness in years—and for years to come—had ended in defeat. None of the strikers ever worked for DiGiorgio again.

Although admitting the bitterness of the loss, in Galarza's view the two-and-a-half-year struggle contained some positive elements. The strikers had proven wrong the prevailing sentiment that farmworkers were incapable of carrying on a fight for more than a few days. They had shown that determination and solidarity could stand up to deep pockets. They had improvised strategies and tactics, turning their underdog status into an asset through astute publicity, and out of David versus Goliath imagery created a support network across the state and country. Their persistence and willingness to sacrifice gave their local struggle national prominence.

Galarza noted that racial and ethnic differences had been overcome to build strong bonds among the union membership. The lesson that skin color or geographic background were less important than shared economic interests with other working people stayed with the Local 218 members long after the strike was over. Many family members of the strikers were "truck drivers, waitresses, service tradesmen, mechanics, and even small merchants. Some of these were members of established unions. The result was a network of connections" throughout their communities which demonstrated to everyone concerned the daily importance of solidarity, from refusing to cross picket lines to extension of credit in local stores to striking families.

From their publicity and fundraising travels with *Poverty in the Valley of Plenty* to the large cities in California and across the country, the strikers returned with knowledge of the prices supermarkets charged for the produce they picked and processed, awareness of how the government's agricultural regulatory bodies were biased in favor of the growers, and a sense of their own importance in the economic food chain.

While these lessons were unable to bring the DiGiorgio strikers victory in the late 1940s, farmworkers carried them to other struggles in other places. Throughout the 1950s growers throughout California were shocked to discover that their employees might organize themselves, however briefly, for better conditions and wages. Often at the center of these local fights for human dignity were people who once worked for Joseph DiGiorgio.

PART V

The Era of Business Unionism

23

Cold War Prosperity

LABOR BECOMES "MIDDLE CLASS"

LIVING THE CALIFORNIA DREAM

Disneyland opened in summer 1955. A million eager visitors streamed in in the first seven weeks. Working families came on their days off from Bethlehem and Kaiser steel mills, from car manufacturing plants in Maywood, South Gate, and Van Nuys, from downtown Los Angeles garment factories, and from the area's largest employer, aerospace. The other employees of "Uncle Walt", who labored in Disney's Burbank studios, came too, alongside the rest of the Hollywood workforce. From near and far, the children of the AFL and CIO made their pilgrimages to the spectacular new Anaheim amusement park, strolling up Main Street USA to Tomorrowland.

Four in ten members of the state's workforce belonged to unions. In the industrial sectors, union density hovered around 50 percent. California, the third-ranking manufacturing state, led the nation in agricultural production and in international shipping. Automobile production in Los Angeles County was second only to Detroit.

Two million of the state's seven million passenger vehicles rolled along the Los Angeles freeways, massive ribbons of concrete, steel, and asphalt raised by union construction labor. Motor vehicle exhaust joined the discharge from smokestack industries concentrated southeast of downtown in a gray curtain of air pollution trapped by the area's basin topography. The industrial Alameda corridor, stretching to the San Pedro harbor through sprawling working-class suburbs and commercial districts alike, was one of the most productive manufacturing centers on earth, even if it helped make the city infamous as the "smog capital of the world."

More working families could afford to own homes than ever before. Blue collar union members in South Gate, a working-class suburb in southeast Los Angeles, owned the nicer houses in the area. Home prices averaged about $10,000, a little over twice the median salary for South Gate's residents. In Lakewood, a development of 17,500 homes built around a shopping center near Long Beach, on what had been sugar beet fields and before that a small part of the Spanish land grant given to Manuel Nieto in 1784, prices were slightly lower for the fourteen models of two- and three-bedroom homes. Twenty-five thousand people waited to examine them when the sales office opened its doors in spring 1950. D.J. Waldie, who grew up in Lakewood, observed, "Every house on my block looked much the same."

But that mattered less to the new homeowners than the proud fact that they lived in their own houses. Between 1940 and 1960, homeownership in California jumped from 43 percent to 58 percent. Two decades of economic depression and war had given way to something different. Waldie noted,

> Some of the men and women in my neighborhood had lived part of their childhood on the outskirts of cotton towns in tents provided by the federal Farm Security Administration. Some had lived in tarpaper shacks among the oil fields outside of Bakersfield. The shacks didn't have indoor plumbing. Some had been the first of their family to graduate from high school.

Richard Carter, a member of United Steelworkers Local 1845, recalled his employment in the Vernon Bethlehem Steel facility just south of downtown:

> For me, having that job there in the plant, it enabled me to buy my home here, it enabled me to buy the car for myself, car for my wife. We took vacations, we accumulated little things together, we worked hard, and it was just the American Dream. . . . You were safe, you had a lifetime job.

Southern California workers could do much of their American Dreaming out of doors, wearing locally made casual clothing suited for the climate. The little tags inside the clothes bore the stamp of the ILGWU. Their cars, on the way to the San Gabriel mountains, the Santa Monica beaches, or drive-in movie theaters, might have been manufactured less than a tank of gas away, by their own passengers, members of UAW Local 216 in South Gate or Local 645 in Van Nuys.

This, finally, was the Fordist utopia: a society of workers able to purchase the products they built. Their purchasing power was buttressed by union wages but also by the last New Deal program, the G. I. Bill, which provided subsidies for mostly working-class military veterans to purchase homes and go to college; and by another New Deal legacy, progressive income tax rates, which redistributed the wealthy's earnings at a top marginal rate of 92 percent to fund government programs.

Within their growing affluence, people were thinking of themselves less as "workers" in the way they understood that term in the Great Depression and more as "consumers" in a successful, middle-class society. To Waldie, whose father was an engineer at a gas company, "There was no obvious way to tell a factory worker from a business owner or a professional man when I grew up."

Unionism, too, came to be understood differently. No longer did most labor organizations face the nagging, persistent threat of extinction. Now, some companies accepted unions as part of the cost of doing business in an American economy dependent on workers' spending. A few forward-looking business leaders even embraced unions wholeheartedly as an advance over the bad old ways of violent class conflict. The Rockefeller Brothers Fund, bankrolled by the capitalist family whose nineteenth-century forebear founded the Standard Oil empire and was notorious for a 1914 massacre of striking miners and their families in Ludlow, Colorado, issued a report in 1958 that would have startled John D. Rockefeller.

> Since labor's role in economic growth is so vital, it is important to establish and maintain an environment which will call for the most honorable, responsible, and imaginative trade union leadership. . . . Cooperation with responsible labor leadership should serve to stimulate the full contribution labor can make to growth and eliminate the forces which might take root in a strained and troubled labor movement.

For workers at Kaiser's enormous Fontana steel facility, with their steelworkers' bowling leagues, and for UAW members at the South Gate General Motors plant, who played on union teams in summer baseball, unions were simply a part of the cultural fabric of their lives, like church, family, PTA, and ethnic organizations. The connection between unions and affluence remained clear in the minds of workers, as well as to most observers of the American economic scene, throughout the post–World War II period.

A few hundred miles to the north, the prosperous Santa Clara Valley bestowed similar rewards in a cooler climate on its occupants. Its worldfamous fruit orchards were giving way before advancing battalions of home

FIGURE 35. After World War II it could seem as if the power of labor stretched into a limitless future, as in this San Francisco Labor Day parade in 1948. Labor Archives and Research Center, San Francisco State University [Labor Herald Collection].

developers, subdividing lands that had been devoted to feeding people since the time of the missions. The earth was disappearing, too, beneath giant new industrial enterprises. But enough agricultural production remained that for a few more years the valley was still the world leader in food processing. Semiskilled employment in the unionized canneries allowed even seasonal workers, mostly immigrant women, to purchase modest homes in east San Jose.

When Lockheed Aircraft began construction in late 1955—a few months after Disneyland opened—on ground near Stanford University, it gave a boost to the rapidly expanding electronics and defense industries. Within a few years 20,000 workers made their living producing missiles at Lockheed. Most paid union dues to the International Association of Machinists (IAM).

Arline Smith, a divorced single mother of two children, was, like Mexican immigrant cannery workers, able to buy a home close by, in Sunnyvale, based on her employment with the military contractor. A steward in her IAM local, she was clear about where her "middle class" life had come from: "Lockheed was one of the best-paying places there was, because of the union."

AEROSPACE AND ANXIETY:
WORKERS AND THE COLD WAR

The aerospace industry, so important to the state's ability to deliver the California Dream to the working class, originated in World War II. But aircraft companies, like the massive Bay Area shipyards, laid off workers and shut down capacity as the war wound down. Aircraft employment hit a wartime peak of 280,000 in southern California; it fell to one-fifth of that within a few years. It is unlikely that what soon became "aerospace" would have continued to expand without the rise of the Cold War.

Following the end of hostilities, the Soviet Union and the United States, formerly allies, found themselves and the economic systems they represented in deadly worldwide competition. The territories they now owned or controlled stretched around the globe. And the Communist Party-run economies of the Soviet bloc presented a direct challenge to the capitalist-run United States. Cooperation fostered by the war disintegrated into mutual mistrust, simmering regional conflicts, and occasionally open warfare, as in Korea by 1950. With both sides possessing nuclear arsenals, every difference of diplomatic opinion carried with it the implicit threat of annihilation.

This ongoing international Cold War provided an opportunity for conservative antiunion forces in the United States to attack militant trade unionism under the banner of "anticommunism." These forces had allies within the labor movement itself.

In the 1930s and 1940s the Communist Party USA (CPUSA) was the largest organization on the political left and became an influential force in a number of unions. It contributed dedicated organizers to the labor movement, and its members were to be found in practically every struggle for social justice. The party appealed to minority workers because it insisted on racial equality on the job and in the community (with some exceptions, as in World War II when production speedup submerged all other concerns).

Controversy always surrounded the party. In part this was due to its radical ideas, which resonated with many working people and middle-class intellectuals disgusted with capitalism through economic depression and war. But the party created its own problems, too. Usually its policies prioritized the needs of the Soviet Union over the needs of American workers. Often the party, especially at the national level, functioned in an undemocratic manner. It didn't help itself by using political jargon derived from the Russian, giving ammunition to critics who portrayed the party as a foreign entity.

Despite these problems, the party grew, because it provided a perspective on what was happening to working people during war and economic depression. Between 1935 and 1955 approximately a million people joined the CPUSA, although the party's membership at any one time never exceeded one hundred thousand. The California section of the Communist Party was its second largest, behind New York. When the political climate grew more conservative, there were plenty of former Communists to investigate.

In 1947 the Taft-Hartley Act passed Congress over President Truman's veto and the bitter opposition of unions. The intent of its authors was to roll back the National Labor Relations Act, and they succeeded. Organizing tactics legal since 1935, and used sporadically for decades, were made illegal, including sympathy strikes, secondary boycotts, and mass picketing.

The most notorious part of the act was Section 9H, which prohibited a union from using the dispute resolution processes of the National Labor Relations Board if any of its officers refused to swear that they were not members of the Communist Party. This section placed progressive union leaders (including noncommunists) in a bind. If they refused to sign anticommunist affidavits, their refusal could hurt the ability of the union to represent its membership. If they capitulated and signed, preserving their union's access to the NLRB, it was at the cost of renouncing their principles and, many of them believed, weakening first amendment protections for everyone.

Roy Brewer of the International Alliance of Theatrical Stage Employees, the top anticommunist in the Hollywood trade unions, held a take-no-prisoners attitude, declaring "It was either them or us. You could not make peace with the Communists." Section 9H of Taft-Hartley wasn't enough for him. He oversaw the insertion of "loyalty oath" clauses into union membership papers and collective bargaining agreements.

"Loyalty oaths," declaring that one was not a member of the Communist Party or an adherent to similar ideas, became the new yellow dog contract, without which people couldn't get work. According to Screen Actors Guild president Richard Masur, who signed the oath when he joined SAG in 1973, "I never stopped to consider what I was signing. It was one in a series of papers I needed to fill out, and I was so eager to join the guild I probably would have signed anything they put in front of me. And I did."

THE WITCH HUNT

The House Committee on Un-American Activities (HUAC) held hearings in the fall of 1947 in Washington D.C., and later in Hollywood, investigating the beliefs of political activists in the movie capital. It attracted national headlines, and made famous the question, "Are you now or have you ever been a member of the Communist Party?"

How someone answered could change the course of his or her life. For ten prominent Hollywood screenwriters and directors, including the former president of the screenwriters' union, their refusal to answer questions they believed violated the First Amendment's free speech protections sent them to prison on contempt of congress charges. It also made them the first official victims of the Hollywood blacklist (although leaders and activists in the Conference of Studio Unions, after losing their jurisdictional battle with the IA, had suffered a similar fate already.)

Brewer and other self-appointed arbitrators of political correctness oversaw the creation of lists—of Communists, suspected Communists, and people who refused to cooperate with HUAC. Continuous hearings and investigations, called "show trials" by their critics, encouraged witnesses to testify against coworkers, friends, and family. Hundreds of people were fired or could no longer find work in the studios, unless they succumbed to the pressure, went through the wrenching process of becoming an informer, and "named names." The effects on their lives ranged from financial difficulties to stress-related illness to death by suicide, or, in the case of actor John Garfield, a descent into alcoholism and fatal heart attack after appearing before HUAC.

A disproportionate number of those named were union activists. Karen Morley starred in dozens of Hollywood films in the 1930s and 1940s. A SAG member who had supported the Conference of Studio Unions during its strikes in the mid-1940s and an enthusiastic volunteer in the production of

Hell Bent for Election, she refused to answer questions in a HUAC hearing. As a result, "It was really murder to find work after being blacklisted, not just for me particularly but for all actors who were prominent, because their faces were well-known." At least blacklisted screenwriters could sometimes find work under assumed names—an impossibility for actors.

The show didn't stop in Hollywood. In San Francisco, the outspoken president of the International Longshoreman's and Warehouseman's Union, Harry Bridges, was put on trial in 1949 for supposedly perjuring himself in an earlier deportation hearing. In all, the government tried to deport Bridges, a naturalized citizen, to Australia four times. It took a U.S. Supreme Court decision to end the travesty. Each time the government failed to prove Bridges was a Communist. Although the government lost the cases, they kept a high-profile left-wing unionist in court through much of the 1950s, spending time and money away from his work.

Joe Springer, born in Warsaw, Poland, the youngest of eleven Jewish children, immigrated to New York in the 1920s. Joining the International Ladies' Garment Workers' Union (ILGWU), he became a sewing machine operator. He moved to Los Angeles, where, by the late 1940s, he rose to become the top leader of the city's ILGWU. He was also an open member of the Communist Party. An effective advocate for his members, he impressed the national ILGWU president, David Dubinsky, who asked Springer to renounce his party membership and accept a union staff position. Springer turned him down. After he refused to testify before HUAC, he narrowly lost his leadership post following a furious election campaign. When he tried to go back to work in the garment shops, he found he had been blacklisted.

His phone was tapped. Springer couldn't find any employment because each employer who hired him would immediately receive a visit from the FBI. The agent would inform the employer that his new worker was a known Communist, and Springer would be looking for a job again. His wife, Preva, would occasionally try to rattle the FBI agents who sat in their car across the street from the Springers' modest two-bedroom, *moderne* home in City Terrace, by walking over and offering them a cup of coffee. Despite such efforts to keep up their spirits, Springer, his wife, and their two sons suffered emotionally as well as financially for years.

Elsewhere in Los Angeles, American Federation of Teachers Local 430, the largest teacher union local in the state, refused to disavow its reputedly Communist leadership, and the national AFT revoked its charter, as it did in New York and Philadelphia.

One reason was Fran Eisenberg. Eisenberg taught journalism in the Los Angeles Unified School District for twenty years. Like many teachers, she put in long hours helping students after school. In addition to serving as advisor to an award-winning student newspaper, she had also edited the Local 430 newsletter. In 1946 she had been investigated by California state senator Jack Tenney's Joint Fact-Finding Committee for Un-American Activities, for "subversive teaching." The charges were ultimately dismissed by the LA school board.

In 1954, however, the school board fired her, along with a dozen other teachers, for refusing to cooperate with another investigative hearing. From then on Eisenberg made her living, at reduced pay, as a private tutor.

Local 430, forcibly separated from its national and state affiliations, reconstructed itself as the independent Los Angeles Teachers Federation. It retained the loyalty of hundreds of teachers and remained larger than its replacement, AFT Local 1021, for several years. But its exile from mainstream labor led to decline, and it gave up the ghost in 1957.

Another leftist union leader, Elinor Glenn, fared better and so did her union, United Public Workers Local 246. The difference in outcomes was due to her extraordinary leadership skills and the pragmatic flexibility of the union that accepted Glenn and her members. Glenn played a key role in California public worker organizing. Born in Brooklyn in 1915 to Jewish immigrants, her mother was a suffragist and her father a socialist. She precociously enrolled in New York University at fifteen. Her effort to become an actress in the Federal Theater Project inspired novelist Herman Wouk's *Marjorie Morningstar*. Glenn moved to Los Angeles in 1944, served as a steward in the National Federation of Federal Employees (NFFE), and was elected president of United Public Workers of America (UPWA) Local 246. She continued to lead Local 246 after it was expelled from the CIO in 1950, along with Sidney Moore, one of the first African American UCLA graduates, who was organizing Los Angeles city and county janitors and sanitation workers in the 1940s while Glenn was organizing in the county hospitals.

Glenn and Moore drew on ties established by the left-led Los Angeles CIO council with the black community to build their organizing campaigns in the 1940s. Glenn recalled, "Public worker unions could not have organized as well as we did if we didn't have the relationship that we had with the black churches, mainly, and with the neighborhood groups."

But between 1950 and 1953 Local 246 led an increasingly isolated and precarious existence. After the hospitals rescinded the union's dues check off,

Glenn collected dues in person, in cash, from the workers on payday. She recalled, "I remember driving out to Rancho Los Amigos Hospital after the union meeting, the members tucking me into my car and seeing to it that it was locked, because I had a few hundred dollars from the dues." This was not a sustainable way to run a union, either for her or Moore. But the two leaders' notoriety as radicals, and Local 246's branding by McCarthyism as "Communist dominated," left them in a difficult box.

Luckily George Hardy didn't worry about that as much as he wanted to organize and represent workers. Hardy had mopped floors as a member of Theater Janitors Local 9, Building Service Employees International Union (BSEIU), in San Francisco before he discovered his calling as an organizer. Hardy had a hand in organizing workers in San Francisco General Hospital and the janitors in San Francisco Unified School District. He founded the state council of BSEIU in 1937 before moving to Los Angeles, where he became West Coast vice president. Hardy also embraced formerly UPWA city and county workers associations in San Francisco and the East Bay.

At Hardy's invitation Glenn brought UPW Local 246 under the protective umbrella of BSEIU Local 347 in 1953. He imposed one condition for Glenn and Moore. Due to their radical pedigrees, he asked that they work under the official leadership of someone else, Al Charleton. Hardy promised that they would actually run things. They agreed to these terms, and the deal worked. Moore brought growing numbers of custodial and sanitation workers into Local 347, and Glenn continued to organize in several public hospitals besides Rancho Los Amigos, including Harbor General, Los Angeles County General, and Olive View.

Despite the political risks involved, Hardy never regretted his decision. He later called Glenn "the greatest organizer we have ever had in our international." She eventually became the first woman elected to the national BSEIU executive board.

IMPACT ON LABOR

During the Cold War, loyalty oaths, Taft-Hartley affidavits for union leaders, and the chill these placed on the expression of controversial opinion greatly diminished the influence of the left in California labor, as in the nation. A thick blanket of conformity fell over not only the labor movement but most social life, from schools to the entertainment industry to daily routine in neighborhoods and workplaces. "That's one of the most frightening legacies of the Blacklist Era," observed SAG president Richard Masur: "the institutionalization of fear and prejudice."

By 1950, eleven national CIO unions—representing over one-fifth of its membership—had been expelled or left the federation, as a result of hearings held by the now firmly anticommunist CIO leadership. In these hearings, according to Paul Jacobs, a CIO staff researcher who helped prepare the anticommunist case against the ILWU in May 1950, "Bridges and everyone else knew the verdict was decided before the trial was held.... there was very little due process."

The Korean War helped provide a rationale for the anticommunist domestic offensive and for massive federal expenditures to develop advanced weapons technology. It underwrote the expansion of the southern California aerospace industry. From just under a hundred thousand workers in 1950, by the mid-1950s nearly a quarter of a million people labored in aircraft, missile, and electronic component production facilities. In five of the six largest companies, workers were represented in collective bargaining either by the International Association of Machinists-AFL or the United Auto Workers-CIO. Loyalty oaths were standard fare at the major companies, but it was considered a nonissue by the two biggest unions in the industry.

The largest Communist-led union, and the third largest union in the CIO, the United Electrical, Radio and Machine Workers of America (UE), boasted close to half a million members at the time of its expulsion. It occupied a strong place within the electrical parts industry, bargaining national contracts with corporate giants GE and Westinghouse. Once outside the CIO it was raided by other CIO and AFL unions alike, which were supported by such institutions as the FBI and the Catholic Church throughout the 1950s in their shared mission of anticommunism.

At a Westinghouse factory in Sunnyvale (the former Joshua Hendy Ironworks), UE Local 1008 lost a unit of several hundred members in 1956. It had been "red-baited," one member said, "to a fare-thee-well." This was typical. As late as 1960 AFL-CIO president George Meany weighed in during another election at the Sunnyvale plant, describing the UE as "an organization expelled from the CIO because it refused to clean up its organization of proven Communist influence." Within ten years after its forced exit from the CIO, the once-mighty electrical union had less than 75,000 members, and the industry's workers, divided among dozens of unions, never again had the same bargaining leverage.

Of all the expelled CIO unions the West Coast-based ILWU fared the best. Blessed with strong leadership, a tradition of rank and file involvement and democracy—the legacy of the 1934 General Strike—and a powerful position in a key industry, the ILWU fended off raids by other unions and attacks by the government and the commercial mass media. Instead of crumbling during the McCarthy era, it became a refuge for radical unionists hounded out of their jobs elsewhere and kept alive the militant, politically progressive traditions of the early CIO.

But the ILWU was the exception that proved the rule. An affluent society was finally delivering on the deferred promise of the American Dream for working people—so long as they didn't mind a few limitations on their civil liberties, accepted the tradeoffs of a rising tide economy based on permanent preparedness for war, and chose not to notice if not everyone was on the boat.

24

Labor and Politics

IN THE YEARS FOLLOWING WORLD WAR II, unions turned increasingly to working within the political system. The rank and file, from representing an independent power capable of settling differences with management by shutting down or sitting down, came to be viewed by labor leaders as citizen-voters who enforced Election Day discipline on public officials. This approach to labor politics seemed to work. It allowed California unions to advance substantial parts of its legislative agenda, such as fair employment practices, and repel some of the most threatening political attacks, like "right-to-work" laws. A shared political and legislative agenda brought the two major state union federations, at war since the mid-1930s, back together by 1958.

Despite these successes, it would pay to remember that the ability of individual workers and their families in the postwar period to become "middle class" and lead "the good life" depended precisely on having acted together, in solidarity, over the previous decades, as a working class. This insight, shared by millions of workers before the 1950s, eroded in collective memory under the dual impact of prosperity and Cold War politics. With the economy booming and unemployment low, militant methods of expressing worker power, like the general strikes in San Francisco and Oakland, came to seem distant and obsolete.

THE STRUGGLE FOR FAIR EMPLOYMENT PRACTICES

If McCarthyism meant the denial of civil liberties for the left, there were broader groups of people who had never enjoyed the full freedoms promised by America in the first place. Earl Watkins grew up in San Francisco. Born in a Fillmore district rooming house into a musical family in 1920, he became a jazz drummer. In a long career he played with Billie Holiday, Earl "Fatha" Hines, and many other musical stars. His talent didn't help, however, when he joined Musicians Local 6 in 1937. He had to join its segregated auxiliary, or he couldn't play in the clubs.

Watkins worked regularly in Oakland after World War II at the famous Slim Jenkins supper club, owned by a local black businessman. Watkins recalled what life was like for African Americans in the East Bay in the 1950s:

> Up and down San Pablo Avenue you couldn't buy a sandwich, or a soda or a cup of coffee. They would have signs up: "We reserve the right to refuse admission." We had job discrimination, discrimination in housing, our unions were segregated, downtown Oakland—you couldn't even get a job in those [white-owned] nightclubs down there.

Franklin Roosevelt's Executive Order 8802, mandating fair employment practices (FEP) in the defense industry, expired at the end of World War II. Federal law no longer protected minority workers from employment discrimination. A coalition of Republicans and conservative Democrats blocked efforts to pass a peacetime federal FEP law, overcoming the support of President Truman and lobbying assistance from civil rights groups and organized labor. Defeated at the national level, the FEP struggle shifted to the states and cities.

Gus Hawkins, an assemblyman from central Los Angeles and a former state CIO political staffer, authored FEP legislation in Sacramento beginning in 1943, and again in 1945. Similar to bills introduced in 1945 in New York, New Jersey, Pennsylvania, and Massachusetts (and adopted into law into those states), Hawkins' bill failed in California.

Undaunted, the California CIO worked with civil rights groups and its network of Popular Front community organizations in 1946 to gather a quarter of a million signatures and place an FEP initiative, Proposition 11, on the statewide ballot. The California AFL endorsed the measure at its convention. Yet in a testament to the prevailing racism of the time, voters defeated Proposition 11 by a greater than two-to-one margin.

But this defeat set in motion a determined campaign for fair employment practices in California that lasted more than a decade. Evolving at the same time as the civil rights struggles of the south, its focus on the workplace distinguished it from efforts such as the Montgomery bus boycott. Before it was over a broad coalition of unions, religious organizations, and minority advocacy groups had stimulated thousands of supporters to volunteer their time on behalf of fair employment.

The FEP effort also survived a bruising, behind-the-scenes transition from reliance on Communist-led civil rights networks, steadily battered and reduced by Cold War politics, to a Socialist- and liberal-directed coalition capable of reaching and changing mainstream political opinion.

The campaign began slowly, with local coalitions attempting to pass municipal laws. The San Francisco Labor Council and NAACP oversaw the formation of the San Francisco Committee for Equal Job Opportunity. San Francisco eventually became the first city in California to adopt a Fair Employment Practices ordinance, although it lacked serious enforcement powers. Meanwhile, in Los Angeles, a series of failed pushes for a law nonetheless created the basis for lasting change. At the center of that story was the Community Services Organization (CSO).

CSO is perhaps best remembered as the training ground for Cesar Chavez. Chavez was the second of five children in a family of extremely poor farmworkers. After the bank foreclosed on his father's farm near Yuma, Arizona in 1938, the family moved to Oxnard and then the San Joaquin Valley, where they followed the crops. After serving in the navy, Chavez moved to east San Jose with his wife, Helen. He was working in a lumberyard when community organizer Fred Ross recruited him to become a CSO staffer in 1952. The CSO helped local communities define goals and achieve them through organizing, voter registration, and direct action. By the late 1950s Chavez had risen through the ranks to become the CSO's national director.

But the Community Services Organization had played a key role in southern California ethnic politics before Chavez. A leading organization within the FEP coalition, the CSO emerged from the unhappiness of Mexican American Angelenos at their lack of representation in municipal government. Activists close to Ed Roybal, who ran for Los Angeles City Council in 1947 and lost, made contact with Chicago-based community organizer Saul Alinsky, who hired Fred Ross to help the group get off the ground.

Ross worked with the CSO to engineer highly successful registration drives of Mexican American voters. The CSO was supported by the Catholic Church and Jewish community organizations, and, crucially, by the Los Angeles garment worker unions, the United Steelworkers, and Laborers Local 300, each of which had large Mexican American memberships. Their financial backing, staff assistance, and volunteer rank and file hours proved a winning combination. The CSO tripled Mexican American voter registration in a few months' time, adding more than 11,000 citizens to the voter rolls in Boyle Heights and neighborhoods east of it. In 1949 these new voters helped Roybal became the first Mexican American elected to the Los Angeles City Council since the nineteenth century.

The Catholic Church figured prominently in the CSO from the outset for two reasons. Most Mexican American workers in Los Angeles were Catholic, so their priests saw the CSO as a vehicle for their congregants' advancement. At the same time Mexican American leaders were emerging in the Los Angeles area's industrial unions, in both the AFL and CIO. Some were Communists, like Frank Lopez, who came out of the Furniture Workers union, but later organized shoe workers and electrical workers at the time CSO was emerging. Others, like Tony Rios of the Steelworkers, a founding board member of the CSO, were anti-Stalinist leftists or liberals. His national union (and the national CIO) was led by Philip Murray, a Catholic who relied heavily on prolabor priests for strategy in his rapidly developing struggle to the death with CIO Communists.

The church preferred the noncommunist variety of Mexican American labor leader. The CSO, unlike a growing number of other liberal community organizations, did not bar Communists. But the new group was clearly seen by the church, steelworkers, garment workers, and others as a viable alternative to Communist-led civil rights organizing.

For these various reasons, CSO leaders, like their counterparts in the NAACP and Jewish Labor Committee (JLC), made the campaign for fair employment an ongoing focus. They worked with Roybal in his determined but unavailing efforts to move an FEP ordinance through the Los Angeles City Council. The JLC, staffed in Los Angeles by Max Mont and in San Francisco by Bill Becker, provided office space and organizing support for the local FEP campaigns.

The Jewish Labor Committee was founded in 1934 by immigrant Jewish trade unionists and Socialists concerned about the rise of fascism in Europe. It sought to be the "voice of the Jewish community within labor and the voice of labor within the Jewish community." It constructed ties with other community organizations in the U.S. that fought prejudice and racism and created networks within the AFL that led to the establishment of the federation's civil rights department. With connections across labor's divide to the liberal, anticommunist leadership of the CIO, the JLC was well placed to play a coordinating role for the FEP effort.

In 1954, Los Angeles unions, led by the garment workers, built a partnership with community and religious groups to form a new Los Angeles Committee for Fair Employment. United Steelworkers staffer Gilbert Anaya served as cochair. Butchers union leader J.J. Rodriguez became treasurer. Both were leading CSO activists.

The FEP coalitions created two things that were new. They presented the opportunity for California AFL and CIO leaders and activists to work together in a sustained set of activities toward a common goal. And in the process, they filled an organizational vacuum opening up in labor-community alliances with the expulsions and decline of the CIO's left-led unions.

The FEP movement began to take on statewide momentum in 1955 with the creation of the California Committee for Fair Employment Practices (CCFEP). The Jewish Labor Committee office in San Francisco served as the organizing center for the state FEP campaign. JLC staffer Bill Becker—a former staffer for the National Farm Labor Union and before that Socialist Party labor secretary—understood the need for unions and civil rights groups to work together on behalf of workers facing discrimination. Drawing on the local FEP coalitions, Becker helped recruit top labor and civil rights leaders to serve on the statewide steering committee, including Ron Weakley of the International Brotherhood of Electrical Workers, California State Labor Federation secretary-treasurer Neil Haggerty, Franklin Williams, leader of the San Francisco NAACP, and John Despol of the state CIO council. The coordinating body elected C. L. Dellums as its chair. Dellums was, as Becker commented, "the logical choice."

Cottrell Laurence Dellums came to Oakland from Texas in 1923, hoping to become a lawyer. The jobs available to a young black man, however, barely paid his rent. He never attended law school. Instead, Dellums landed what was considered a prestigious job in the African American community, as a railroad porter for the Pullman Company.

Dellums helped to organize the Brotherhood of Sleeping Car Porters (BSCP), an all-black AFL union, two years later. It was Dellums who, at the founding convention of the BSCP, coined the union's motto when he told the delegates that all workers must "fight or be slaves." He was elected to local union office the next year and became national vice president in 1929, a position he held for nearly forty years, until he became president in 1968, succeeding his friend A. Philip Randolph. Along the way he served as president for many years of the Alameda County NAACP branch and became chair of the Western States NAACP Region when it was formed in 1944.

Dellums later explained the growing support for a FEP law by pointing to the broad base and steady work of the statewide and local committees. Each year, representatives of the FEP labor-civil rights coalition met in Stockton for several days and then brought hundreds of people to Sacramento to lobby legislators for passage of a law. Forty to fifty organizations were actively represented in these meetings and mobilizations. Dellums and the committee worked closely with assemblyman Gus Hawkins and state senator Byron Rumford, representing the East Bay, who took turns presenting FEP legislation. Each year it inched closer to passage. Commented Dellums years later,

> There's nothing like confrontation . . . go to Sacramento and into the senator's office, the assemblyman's office and have an eyeball-to-eyeball confrontation with him. . . . It is indefensible. Who could stand up and say that he believed in discrimination? Nobody ever believed in discrimination, so you wonder how it lasted so long and is still here.

State legislators who voted against passage of the FEP bills were targeted by the committee in voter registration drives and political campaigns. The committee realized that antilabor politicians, in order to get elected, relied on the political apathy of minority communities in their districts. The committee tapped local connections to raise funds and recruit volunteers from labor and community groups to register minority voters and turn them out on Election Day to elect politicians who would support FEP legislation.

Not all FEP activism focused on legislation or politics. In some industries, unions themselves were the problem, restricting employment for minorities to certain geographic areas or venues, or excluding them entirely. Jazz musician Earl Watkins remembered the time that leaders of American Federation of Musicians (AFM) Local 6 in San Francisco pressured the owner of the Dawn Club to hire white musicians to replace an African American band. The black musicians had a contract with the club; they also belonged to Local 6 but to its segregated subsidiary. The subsidiary sued Local 6, lost the case, and the national AFM revoked the subsidiary's charter, keeping unequal job opportunities for its members in place for years.

Seeking to steer things in the right direction, the California State Federation of Labor at its 1956 convention passed a resolution condemning unions that "give mere lip service and no effective support to our enunciated program in the field of freedom from discrimination." The CSFL itself, however, had no authority to make its affiliates walk the walk. When Jamaica-born maritime union activist Harry Lumsden spoke on the floor of the 1950 federation convention, stirring the delegates to adopt a resolution calling for an end to housing discrimination, his words came to rest on a high stack of fine sounding but unenforceable decrees issued over the years.

Leaders of United Auto Workers (UAW) Local 216, on the other hand, actively agitated for the hiring of black and Mexican American workers in the giant South Gate General Motors plant in the early 1950s. Against company resistance—and uneven attitudes by its own white members toward fair employment practices—the union leadership helped significant numbers of nonwhites to get hired by 1955. Local 216 activist Virgil Collins, who lived in South Gate and worked in the General Motors factory for three decades, remembered the arguments advanced by the UAW officers:

> We said that everybody that worked in this plant had to belong to the union, and was a union brother. Black, white, yellow, red, green—we didn't give a damn what they were, they were union brothers. [The leadership would say] "This guy is a workingman, same as you are. He's got to earn a living, and he's got a right to a job here, same as you have."

Changing hiring practices, however, still left another barrier for workers of color: seniority based on department. Minorities were hired into the hardest and dirtiest departments and then found they couldn't transfer out to pursue promotions and higher pay. Ultimately the union addressed the problem through collective bargaining, replacing department-based progression with plant-wide seniority lists.

A few miles away, alert customers shopping in large retail stores along Florence Avenue, a commercial thoroughfare in south central Los Angeles, might have noticed that the salespeople and clerks serving them were all white. People of color were welcome to spend their money in the stores but couldn't expect to find employment there.

No laws prohibited discrimination in employment. But employers in minority areas were sensitive to the impact that open racism might have on their sales. Employment agencies and employers worked out systems that quietly communicated the qualities they were looking for in potential employees. Hope Mendoza, the first Latina organizer for the Ladies' Garment Workers' Union in Los Angeles, and a key early figure in FEP coalition building, recalled, "They even had a code system. '53' designated the Jews, so it would be, 'No 53s.' African-Americans, their number was '99,' so they would indicate, 'No 99s.'"

According to Alex Alexander, when leaders in his union asked him to get involved in the FEP struggle, "I started participating on weekends in something called the Fair Employment Practices Committee of Florence Avenue." Activists from the Ladies' Garment Workers', UAW Local 216, United Public Workers (UPW), and others joined Alexander in their spare time to pass out leaflets, picket, and discuss the issues with people in the street outside department stores, restaurants, and other large commercial enterprises.

Like Dellums before him, Horace "Alex" Alexander had migrated to California from Texas. The son of sharecroppers, his experiences in World War II had included training in various office skills. But he found on his return to civilian life that white collar work was closed to him. Blessed with a strong back and attracted by a union paycheck, he went to work as a laborer, joining Laborers Local 300. Like workers of color in the nearby steel and auto plants who had been hired only after union pressure but still found themselves relegated to the most difficult and dirty jobs, Alexander's experience of employment discrimination led him to enlist in the FEP cause.

By 1958 the small changes had accumulated beneath the surface. Lobbying and political mobilization organized by the California Committee for Fair Employment Practices, together with demonstrations in front of stores and other commercial establishments and, to a lesser degree, contract language addressing discrimination through the collective bargaining process, had educated union workers and the general population about the need for a FEP law. A few legislators, however—enough to block passage of the bill—needed further instruction. The opportunity to teach them came from an unexpected direction.

THE FIGHT AGAINST "RIGHT TO WORK"

One of the provisions of the Taft-Hartley Act in 1947, the so-called right-to-work section, allowed states to outlaw the union shop—a workplace where all employees receive union representation and all belong to the union as a condition for continued employment. Although given a new name by the Taft-Hartley Act, the basic concept of "right to work" was not new. It first appeared in the early 1900s, when, responding to a surge of union organizing, employers devised the open shop strategy. Proclaiming concern for workers' interests against "union coercion," bosses sought to ban the union shop.

Is a union shop coercion? *Only if democracy is coercion of the minority by the majority.* A union shop comes into existence when a majority of workers votes for it, usually bringing with it higher wages and benefits and a collective voice on the job. This is the real reason some employers prefer nonunion workplaces—not admiration for worker rights. Following World War I, the open shop received a makeover, called "the American Plan," implying that anyone who favored unions was unpatriotic. But it remained, in essence, the open shop program.

And it was still the open shop program in the Taft-Hartley Act in 1947, which contained a provision allowing states to pass what was now called a right-to-work law. The law gave no worker any right to any job. What it did was to expand the open shop concept. Why bar union shops one at a time when it could be accomplished across an entire state? As San Jose plumber Fred Hirsch described it, "The people who wanted to bust the unions gave it a very nice name. It's a hard name to explain. We say, it's a 'right to work for less' law, a right to work without any consideration for the democratic rights of the majority."

Walter Johnson, whose Norwegian immigrant father moved from the Northwest to work in San Francisco's shipyards during World War II, got hired at Sears Roebuck in the early 1950s, selling stoves, televisions, and refrigerators. He soon became active in his union, Local 1100 of the Department Store Employees. In his view, right-to-work laws were unfair because "They would say you don't have to pay dues, but you can still enjoy the rights of the union contract. And it's like me getting on the bus and paying for the bus, and you getting on the bus and riding free."

Across the country, antiunion employers poured money into campaigns to pass right-to-work laws. Unions fought back to defend their right to a union shop. In states where labor was weak (predominantly in the South), the antilabor forces found success: right-to-work laws existed in eighteen states by 1958. This encouraged antiunion groups in California to circulate petitions to make California a right-to-work state. Through paid signature-gatherers, business interests were able to put a right-to-work measure, Proposition 18, on the November 1958 ballot. In April of 1958, public opinion polls showed Proposition 18 leading, 51 percent yes to 44 percent no, with 5 percent undecided.

A boost was given to the Yes on 18 campaign by ongoing hearings held by the McClellan committee of the U.S. Senate, conducting an inquiry into corruption within several unions, including the largest in the country, the International Brotherhood of Teamsters (IBT). Nearly every day newspapers carried revelations about connections between the Mob and leaders of the IBT. In 1957 the AFL-CIO expelled the Teamsters and two other unions for refusing to address the problem. While only a few national unions and their locals were under investigation—and none in California—the timing was unfortunate for the No on 18 campaign. Labor leaders feared that uninformed voters might easily arrive at the simplistic equation "organized labor equals organized crime," which was precisely what the right-to-work proponents were hoping for.

The need for massive mobilization was clear. Unions and their allies formed No on 18 committees throughout the state, setting up offices in every major city. Thousands of volunteers were recruited in the summer to register voters, raise funds, and educate the public. In Oxnard, CSO organizer Cesar Chavez encouraged Mexican-born immigrants to take citizenship classes and more than tripled voter registration in the *colonia*, where many of the area's farm workers lived.

Union members devised creative tactics such as handing out cards while shopping that read "Without the benefit of my union, this purchase would not have been possible. Vote No on Proposition 18."

The campaign gave CIO and AFL unions an opportunity to work together. Although the national AFL and CIO had merged in 1955, in California the divisions were deeper and remained more bitter than elsewhere around the country, and unity negotiations stalled. Statewide AFL and CIO councils had finally agreed in principle by early 1958 to merge, and the joint No on 18 effort helped push the groups closer.

Fred Hirsch lived in the San Fernando Valley at the time. He remembered attending union and community meetings, leafleting shopping centers, driving sound trucks up and down residential neighborhoods, and working with activists from AFL and CIO unions as well as the former CIO—now unaffiliated—ILWU and United Electrical Workers. "We had a coalition," he recalled, "on a local level that was a little bit broader than the AFL and CIO in general."

As working people mobilized, it became clear that the 1958 race for governor would be closely tied to the issue of Proposition 18. The Republican gubernatorial candidate, Senator William Knowland, owner of the *Oakland Tribune* newspaper, was a sponsor of the measure and made its attack on union security a central plank of his platform. The Democratic candidate for governor, California attorney general Pat Brown, came out against Proposition 18.

Knowland and his employer supporters spent close to a million dollars to convince the voting public that the right-to-work proposition would, among other benefits, guarantee minorities fair employment practices. The labor-civil rights coalition overseen by the California Committee for Fair Employment Practices quickly developed literature to counter Proposition 18. The NAACP printed brochures and held meetings against the measure.

Martin Luther King, Jr., lent his support to the No on Proposition 18 campaign, saying that

> The claims that "Right to Work" laws constitute fair employment practices for the protection against discrimination by reason of race, creed, color or national origin are entirely false. . . . It is significant that these "Right to Work" laws are backed by the same reactionary forces which flout the Supreme Court decision on school desegregation.

Organizing efforts reached a feverish pitch as the November 4 election date approached. In San Francisco, Walter Johnson recalled, "We were all out, practically every night. Most of it was done in the streets, and out ringing doorbells, and telephoning." On the last Sunday before the election, the No campaign in Alameda County turned out sixteen hundred volunteers at dawn for an operation that reached virtually every home.

In Oxnard, Cesar Chavez made sure the *colonia* had five precinct organizers, and that each of the neighborhood's fifty blocks had someone appointed to educate the residents and get out the vote. On Election Day, organizers at CSO headquarters, nicknamed "the Hut," served tacos and coffee to the scores of exhausted volunteers and kept track of who had voted and who still needed prodding to get to the polls.

The powerful statewide political mobilization paid off. The right-to-work forces were outgunned at every level: in the precincts, in phone banks, and finally fundraising, as the large corporate donations were overtaken by the small worker contributions bundled by the unions' political action committees. On November 4, Proposition 18 was defeated by over 60 percent of the voters.

Knowland, the only prominent candidate on the ballot who supported Proposition 18, went down to a resounding defeat, as did nearly the entire Republican ticket. California, which hadn't elected a Democratic governor since 1938, put Pat Brown in the governor's office. In the words of George

FIGURE 36. Governor Edmund "Pat" Brown signed the Fair Employment Practices Act on April 16, 1959, as leaders in the FEP coalition celebrate their organizing achievement. Left to right: Bill Becker, Jewish Labor Committee; state senator Richard Richards; Neil Haggerty, California Labor Federation; state senator George Miller; Nathan Colley, NAACP; state assembly member Byron Rumford; C. L. Dellums, Sleeping Car Porters and NAACP; Max Mont, Jewish Labor Committee; state assembly member Augustus Hawkins; and Franklin Williams, NAACP. C.L. Dellums papers, African American Museum and Library at Oakland, Oakland Public Library.

Johns, secretary-treasurer of the San Francisco Labor Council, "The threat of Proposition 18 activated the labor movement. We went to work, defeated Proposition 18, and incidentally Bill Knowland. Pat Brown rode our coattails and became governor."

The California Committee for Fair Employment Practices accomplished its electoral goal, ousting four reactionary state senators with overwhelming margins of victory in minority voter precincts, and replacing them with pro-FEP politicians. It was then up to Governor Brown to keep his campaign promise to sign a FEP bill into law.

The Fair Employment Practices Act was introduced by Rumford in January 1959. At long last, it had the votes, and was signed by Brown on April 16. The law created a permanent Fair Employment Practices Commission, with subpoena power to bring before its hearing panel any person or employer who discriminated against anyone seeking employment for reasons of race, creed, or national origin. It was empowered to assess fines and prison sentences for violators, and given a budget for enforcement staff, overseen by an appointed commission. C. L. Dellums accepted an appointment from Brown to the commission, and later became its chair.

Earl Watkins, who had called on American Federation of Musicians Local 6 to dissolve its segregated auxiliary for years, attended his first integrated meeting in 1960 after the black and white sections merged. "The FEP made a huge difference. The law forced us together, and the employment really opened up after that." Watkins went on to become an officer of the integrated local and made his living playing music for decades afterward, often in clubs, restaurants, and hotels that had previously been off limits.

On December 9, 1958, a few weeks after the election, the California AFL and CIO councils merged, re-creating a united labor movement renamed the California Labor Federation. The foundation for AFL-CIO unity had been put in place years earlier, since political differences between organizations had narrowed; the California AFL no longer objected to industrial organizing, and the California CIO council had jettisoned its left-wing unions.

At the base of the new federation, as unionized workers enjoyed growing economic security, memories of the hard struggles of the pre–World War II years became for many less sharp; the sense of need for social justice, less woven into the fabric of daily life. Most working families stepped up into a new "middle class" defined by unprecedented levels of consumption. California's Tomorrowland seemed, as the Disneyland ride put it, "just a dream away."

25

"Sí Se Puede"

THE UNITED FARM WORKERS

FOR MORE THAN A CENTURY farmworkers had been denied a decent life at work in the fields and in the communities of California's rich agricultural valleys. Essential to the state's biggest industry—but only so long as they remained exploited and submissive—farmworkers and their supporters in the labor movement had tried but failed so many times to organize the giant agribusiness farms that most observers considered it a hopeless task.

But by the early 1960s things were evolving. Within fifteen years close to 100,000 farmworkers were protected by union contracts. The union, the United Farm Workers of America (UFW), was a cross between a labor organization and a social movement. Its leader, Cesar Chavez, had become a nationally revered civil rights crusader. The farmworkers' newfound power was reflected in passage of a state law, the Agricultural Labor Relations Act—first of its type in the nation—that forced the growers to play by the rules of common decency. Wages rose; toxic pesticides were no longer sprayed by growers with impunity on crops and workers alike; workers and their families began to participate in the American Dream and achieve the dignity so long denied them. What had happened?

END OF THE BRACERO PROGRAM

The Bracero Program, an informal arrangement between the United States and Mexican governments, became Public Law 78 in 1951. Started during World War II as a way to provide Mexican agricultural workers to take up the slack for farmworkers who had left for military service and better-paid war industry jobs on the coast, the Bracero Program nonetheless continued after the war ended. It undercut unionization efforts by providing cheap labor and replacements for striking workers.

Recalled Jessie De La Cruz, who later organized farmworkers for the UFW, "When my husband used to go up to Stockton to pick tomatoes, he was getting 25 cents a box for picking tomatoes, those forty-pound boxes, and when the *braceros* came they were paid 12 cents, half of what we were getting." Because of the ever-present threat of deportation, *braceros* were usually afraid to protest employer abuses, of which there were many.

One of the worst consequences of the Bracero Program was that stable, family-based communities of mostly Chicano farmworkers around the edges of major growing areas—fertile ground for union organizing, because they lived in the same place all year round—were broken up. These workers were instead forced to follow crops around the state and even into other states. The Bracero Program brought hundreds of thousands of temporary, disposable Mexican workers to the California fields each year.

Over time, however, farmworkers were able to call upon allies in other unions, and in churches and community groups affiliated with the growing civil rights movement, to put enough pressure on politicians that the Bracero Program was finally phased out of existence by 1964. This occurred despite the loud protests of the growers that their business would fall apart without the *braceros*. Of course no such thing happened. An important obstacle to farmworker unionization had been removed.

CONDITIONS OF FARMWORKERS AND THEIR WORK

But in some respects things hadn't changed much since the Wheatland Hop Affair in 1913. Grape pickers in 1965 were making an average of $1.20 per hour, plus ten cents per "lug" (a 28-pound wooden basket) picked. State laws regarding working standards were loosely enforced, if at all. At one farm the boss made the workers all drink from the same "cup"—a beer can—in the field; at another ranch workers were forced to pay a quarter per cup. Many ranches had no portable field toilets. Jessie De La Cruz described a typical arrangement.

> What they do instead of supplying restrooms and clean water where we can wash our hands, is put posts on the ground with a piece of gunny sack wound around them. That's where we went. And that thing was moved along with

us. It was just four stakes stuck in the ground, and then there was canvas or a piece of gunny sack around it. You would be working, and this restroom would be right there. The canvas didn't come up high enough in front for privacy.

Workers' temporary housing was segregated by race, and they paid two dollars or more per day for unheated metal shacks with no indoor plumbing or cooking facilities. Often the accommodations were infested with mosquitoes. Room and board were deducted from workers' pay. Farm labor contractors played favorites with workers, selecting friends first, sometimes accepting bribes. Child labor was rampant, and many workers were injured or died in easily preventable accidents. The average life expectancy of a farmworker was forty-nine years.

NEW ORGANIZATIONS, NEW POSSIBILITIES

Two organizations were attempting in different ways to represent and organize the farmworkers. One had been formed in 1959 by the AFL-CIO. The Agricultural Workers Organizing Committee (AWOC) was dominated in the beginning by white AFL-CIO staffers, who held the purse strings. But most active AWOC members were older Filipinos, with some Chicano, Anglo, and black workers as well. The Filipino workers in particular had had experience organizing unions and with strikes in the fields.

This core of veteran *manong* (first-generation Filipino immigrants) kept the organization going, even while much attention and funding were directed to various high-profile organizing projects that never got off the ground. Some workers, like Larry Itliong, had participated in leadership roles in other unions, such as the short-lived Filipino Agricultural Laborers Association, which led an impressive one-day strike of several thousand asparagus workers around Stockton in April 1939 to restore wage rates. Itliong and another Filipino, Philip Vera Cruz, had also taken part in a large scale but less successful 1948 asparagus strike.

At fifteen, in 1929, Itliong came to the United States from the Philippines. Like many of the *manong,* he worked as a migrant laborer in West Coast agriculture but also took jobs on the railroad and in canneries. He helped found a salmon cannery workers union, originally chartered as a federal AFL local in 1933 in Seattle and Stockton, which became UCAPAWA, and then Food, Tobacco, Agricultural and Allied Workers (FTA) Local 7. When the

FTA folded in 1950, Local 7's members affiliated with the International Longshoremen and Warehousemen's Union as Local 37. Itliong served as a shop steward and was then elected vice president in Local 37 in Stockton. Due to this resume, he was hired by the Agricultural Workers Organizing Committee (AWOC) as an organizer.

Vera Cruz arrived in the United States three years before Itliong, but he spent seventeen years in Vancouver, Chicago, and other cities outside California before landing in the San Joaquin Valley in 1943 to pick grapes. He was thirty-nine, discharged from the army, and had a cousin in Delano, a farm town north of Bakersfield. He lived for years in labor camps in order to save money and to send some home to his family, who had sacrificed to send their son overseas. Eventually he was able to buy a small house in Richgrove, ten miles east of Delano. Although Vera Cruz served as president of the National Farm Labor Union local in Delano in the 1950s, he had become inactive by 1965, when he joined AWOC.

The other organization was the National Farm Workers Association (NFWA), started by thirty-five-year-old Cesar Chavez in 1962. Chavez was frustrated with the Community Services Organization (CSO) despite having become national director. He believed in the CSO methods of working with communities to solve problems through organizing and direct action, based on the principles of community organizers Saul Alinsky and Fred Ross. But when CSO leaders refused to allow a pilot program to organize farmworkers to move forward, Chavez left to found the NFWA. From his home in Delano, over a period of three years he traveled from town to town in southern San Joaquin Valley, meeting with groups of farmworkers in their living rooms, tirelessly building an organization that he hoped would one day become an effective union. Dolores Huerta, meanwhile, did the same work in the northern valley counties.

They deliberately set dues rates relatively high for the association (Chavez preferred to avoid the term "union" until the organization was on a stable footing). Chavez believed that at $3.50 per month it would be a stretch for most workers, but in the process help the members form a commitment to the NFWA. He was right. Within two years the organization claimed close to a thousand members and was able to pay modest salaries to Chavez and NFWA cofounder Dolores Huerta.

Like Chavez, Huerta had gained organizing skills in CSO after recruitment by Fred Ross. As a small child she had lived in New Mexico while her father worked in the mines, until the mine owners blacklisted him for union activities. After her parents divorced, Huerta and her brothers moved with their mother, who supported the family by running a restaurant and hotel, to Stockton. Self-confident and assertive, Huerta went to college and became an elementary school teacher but also began volunteering for CSO in 1955. She set up the Stockton-based Agricultural Workers Association together with a Catholic labor priest, Thomas McCullough, while raising a growing number of children (eventually eleven). She went to work for AWOC and became its secretary-treasurer. But eventually she left the organization because she disagreed with its approach to organizing.

Huerta thought that organizing meant talking with workers. The AFL-CIO staffers running AWOC took a shortcut; they organized the labor contractors, the middlemen who put together workers and employers for a fee. Their tactics included short strikes when necessary, and gained raises in pay, but resulted in little collective spirit or worker loyalty to an ongoing organization.

This was not AWOC's only mistake. Despite the agreement of May 1950 that ended the three-year DiGiorgio strike, some copies of the ill-fated documentary film *Poverty in the Valley of Plenty* survived. One turned up in the possession of AWOC in 1959. Blissfully unaware of its legal history, or aware but uncaring (former AWOC staffers disagree on this point), the new AFL-CIO union made prints and began screening them in meetings around the San Joaquin valley. DiGiorgio's lawyers hauled the union into a Stockton court on charges of libel. A young labor attorney named Victor Van Bourg, whose experiences on the DiGiorgio picket lines in 1948 as a teenaged painters' union apprentice had steered him in the direction of his future career, attempted to defend AWOC against DiGiorgio's legal department.

Van Bourg, who later became the head of the largest labor law firm on the West Coast, said that he never argued a case better in court. He remained convinced that had the case been tried outside of the San Joaquin Valley the film would not have been found libelous: "In the atmosphere of the times, you couldn't expect a decision in Stockton to go against the growers for something like this." On appeal the $150,000 settlement against the union was reduced to $60,000 in 1961. But the libel decision remained, and the AFL-CIO leadership lost considerable enthusiasm for farmworker organizing. AWOC continued, although with diminished support from the national federation.

Two short strikes occurred in the spring of 1965. Eighty-five farmworkers in a McFarland rose farm asked the NFWA to help them form a union and gain a wage increase. Assisted by Chavez and Huerta, the workers struck. After a few days the growers agreed to the wage increase but not the union. The workers contented themselves with the wage increase and returned to work.

Around the same time AWOC members led a much larger walkout of hundreds of Filipino and Mexican grape pickers in Coachella Valley. Although the Bracero Program had officially ended the year before, a new agreement between the United States and Mexico allowed growers to import Mexican workers if they were paid $1.40 an hour, and never paid more than domestic workers. When Coachella grape growers indeed attempted to pay the domestic workers less than the imported workers, the Filipinos, many of whom were AWOC members, refused to work. Philip Vera Cruz explained why.

> We had a strong labor consciousness. We had been working in this country for over 40 years, and we were aware of prices and profits because we listened to market reports on the radio and then discussed these reports in Ilocano, our dialect. This "workers' consciousness" helped us to be the most organized and united of all the different ethnic groups of farm workers at that time.

Coachella grapes, grown in southern California, ripen first in the state. Getting the grapes picked and to market quickly is crucial to Coachella growers' profits. Ten days later the growers decided to pay everyone, including Chicanos who had joined the Filipinos, $1.40 per hour. Once more, however, no union contract was signed.

IT STARTED IN DELANO

At the end of summer the grapes were ripening in the fields around Delano. Farmworkers from the successful Coachella action had come up to Delano, trailing the grape harvest. Many lived in Delano year round but had traveled south to follow the seasonal work. Expecting to be paid $1.40 per hour, the farmworkers were furious at being offered less once more. On September 8 they struck nine farms. The strike organizer was AWOC's Larry Itliong.

After five days the growers began to bring in Chicano scabs. Itliong approached Chavez and asked the NFWA to join the mostly Filipino strike. At a meeting on September 16, in an old hall in Delano packed with hundreds of workers, the NFWA voted unanimously, to shouts of "Viva la Huelga!" to strike too. Chavez was apprehensive. Asked later when he felt his organization—which had $100 in its bank account—would have been ready to go out on a big strike, he replied, "About 1968."

But the NFWA didn't have until 1968. Events moved quickly, and the NFWA had to march alongside or get left behind. In joining the strike, the NFWA took the lead, for it had many more members than AWOC. It also changed the ethnic makeup of the strike; now the majority of workers involved were Chicano. By September 20 more than thirty farms were struck, with several thousand workers leaving the fields. Despite the large numbers of striking farmworkers, the workers could not muster picket lines at all the ranches simultaneously. For one thing most of the workers couldn't stick around Delano—they had to work and left the area to find crops elsewhere. And as one strike supporter described the situation,

> It's like striking an industrial plant that has a thousand entrance gates and is four hundred square miles large. And if that's not bad enough, you don't know each morning where the plant will be, or where the gates are, or whether it will be open or closed or what wages will be offered that day.

NFWA and AWOC set up a system of roving pickets, with different fields picketed each day. Fifteen or twenty cars full of pickets would go to a field where a grower was attempting to use strikebreakers. Striking workers, often harassed by the growers and police, sometimes violently, would try to get the scabs to leave the fields. Remarkably, their appeals were successful much of the time in emptying the ranches of workers, who were persuaded it was in their interest to strike.

The growers, overconfident, made a mistake almost immediately. They had always been able to end strikes with small wage concessions. Soon after the strike began they raised wages to $1.40 per hour. But this time they were shocked to discover it wasn't enough. The raise merely encouraged the strikers to believe they were being effective. Now there had to be a union contract, too.

A couple months after the strike erupted, Chavez and Huerta, on a suggestion from attorney Stewart Weinberg, initiated a crucial tactic, one that the farmworkers used to remarkable effect: a consumer grape boycott. The union called upon the public to refrain from buying grapes without a union label. Union volunteers were sent out to big cities, where they established boycott centers that organized friendly groups—unions, churches, community organizations—to not buy grapes and to publicize the boycott and pressure stores to remove grapes from their shelves.

This was not a first. The National Farm Labor Union had used the tactic with some success during the DiGiorgio strike. But the grape strike took things to a new level. Combined with the union's public disavowal of violence, this boycott was better funded, more extensive, more organized, and more effective. For one thing, it included a secondary boycott of stores selling grapes, not simply the primary boycott of the product itself. Although part of the difficulty farmworkers faced in organizing stemmed from their exclusion from the National Labor Relations Act, an advantage of being outside the law was their ability to use secondary boycotts, which had been removed from the NLRA by Taft-Hartley in 1947.

The strikers' cause was boosted by other events in the nation at the same time. The civil rights movement had created strong public awareness of the effects of racism, including lowered standards of living for the victims of prejudice in housing, employment, schools, and other areas of daily life. The civil rights movement focused attention on the treatment of African Americans in the south. But once revealed, the situation in the California fields looked similar. The largely Chicano and Filipino farmworkers benefited by the new public understanding of racism.

Sympathetic young people, some of whom participated the year before in the Freedom Summer voter registration drive in Mississippi, or in the University of California at Berkeley's Free Speech Movement, flocked to *la causa*. Many joined in the boycott effort. Others came to Delano to help with strike support. This was the "New Left," idealistic college-educated young people who devoted time and energy to bring about their vision of social justice.

Youthful movement energy fused with solidarity offered by the progressive wing of American labor—at its peak moment of numerical strength and political influence—to give the UFW critical backing. Key leaders like Walter Reuther of the United Auto Workers sent organizers and funding. Politicians like U.S. senator Robert Kennedy enrolled in the cause. Rank and file union members respected picket lines and joined the boycott. ILWU members refused to handle shipments of grapes, leaving them to rot on the San Francisco docks, and ILWU Local 10 formed a "five dollar a month" club so that members could contribute regularly to the farmworkers.

The farmworkers did not forget these acts of solidarity. When the ILWU longshore division went on strike in 1971, Don Watson, a "five dollar a month" club leader, asked the UFW if the farmworkers could help. Recalled Watson, "The next thing I knew they put together this huge food caravan for us. This long grape truck came to the San Francisco waterfront from the Central Valley. There were several trucks from Salinas. They had all this produce. Maybe 150 farmworkers arrived too."

Thousands of volunteers handed out boycott literature in front of stores selling grapes. Enormous publicity was generated for the strikers' cause, and millions of consumers learned about how their table grapes were grown through the exploitation of farmworkers. The boycott stimulated hostile reactions as well. Ronald Reagan, elected governor of California in November 1966, staged high-profile events with growers at which he made a point of eating grapes in front of cameras.

The Catholic Church split badly over the issue, but many priests played important roles building support in their communities and in the church hierarchy for the strike and boycott. Although debates raged as to the precise impact of the boycott on grape sales—and it varied widely from place to place—there can be no doubt it served a crucial function in the strike.

THE BIGGER THEY ARE...

The two biggest growers in the Delano area, Schenley and DiGiorgio, were the most vulnerable to the boycott. Both companies were owned by corporate entities with headquarters far from Delano. For each company grape growing was a relatively minor part of a larger economic empire. And crucially, Schenley and DiGiorgio had union contracts with workers in other parts of their businesses. The boycott had the potential to hurt sales in other product areas and to harm labor relations with their other workers. It didn't help the company's image with the public when soon after the strike began Schenley sprayed striking workers with fertilizer and insecticide.

Schenley was the first to crack. But it took another innovative action to bring the grower to the negotiating table: the NFWA and AWOC organized a march to Sacramento. Seventy strikers left Delano on foot on March 17, 1966, led by Chavez. They walked nearly three hundred miles in twenty-five days. Along the route of *la peregrinacion,* as they called it, they picked up hundreds of friends. They met and talked and rallied with thousands. A Chicano theater group, El Teatro Campesino, staged skits about the struggle from the back of a flatbed truck every night. One of its members, Luis Valdez, wrote a proclamation, "Plan of Delano," updating Emiliano Zapata's manifesto from the Mexican Revolution, which he read at each stop along the way. In the preamble it stated, "Our sweat and our blood have fallen on this land to make other men rich. The pilgrimage is a witness to the suffering we have seen for generations."

The march attracted media attention, public support, and helped generate the strikers' first substantial victory. Arriving in Sacramento on Easter morning, Chavez announced to a cheering demonstration of 10,000 supporters in front of the capital building that Schenley had bowed before the pressure and signed an agreement—negotiated by Dolores Huerta—with the union.

Within weeks, DiGiorgio agreed to hold a representation election. But before the election could be held a complication arose. The International Brotherhood of Teamsters (IBT), an independent union since its expulsion from the AFL-CIO in 1957 and the largest union in the country, offered to be on the ballot too. The IBT represented workers in many agriculture-related industries in California. If field workers were represented by another union and that union decided to strike, Teamster workers might be thrown out of work for the strike's duration. Ignoring the questions of social justice at the core of the farmworkers' campaign for union recognition, the IBT offered itself to DiGiorgio as a conservative alternative to the NFWA/AWOC. The grower eagerly assented. Chavez and the NFWA called for the workers to boycott the election. Heeding the union, more than half the eight hundred workers at DiGiorgio's Sierra Vista ranch refused to vote.

Behind in the polls in a gubernatorial election year and needing union and Chicano votes, Pat Brown yielded to pressure and appointed an arbitrator to decide whether to hold another representation election at Sierra Vista. The arbitrator ordered another election for the end of August. This time the NFWA beat the Teamsters decisively, and the two largest growers in Delano were employers of union labor. Although it took seven months to negotiate a contract with DiGiorgio, the workers ended up with a union shop, a new base rate of $1.65 per hour, a week's paid vacation for workers employed at least forty weeks per year, and reporting and standby pay if no work was available.

LA HUELGA CONTINUES

There were many more growers than Schenley and DiGiorgio, however. The strike dragged on at dozens of grape farms throughout the Delano area. In the past a farmworkers' union would have been unable to survive such a long conflict. But things were different now. More farmworkers joined after the first victories.

Consolidating strength, NFWA and AWOC formally merged during the summer, just before the DiGiorgio election. On August 22, the two organizations became the United Farm Workers Organizing Committee, AFL-CIO (UFWOC). The new union received a steady stream of organizing funds from the AFL-CIO, as well as ever-growing strike support from other unions, consisting of food, cash donations, and equipment for use in the union offices and field operations. UFWOC was able to extend its influence in the fields far beyond the Delano area.

By 1967 the union had over 17,000 members. On the same day in July that year that the UFWOC and IBT announced a jurisdictional agreement giving UFWOC uncontested right to organize fieldworkers, Gallo and Paul Masson, two large growers, announced they were ready to hold elections, realizing they could no longer play off one union against another. Unfortunately, the IBT/UFWOC accord proved to be short-lived. Over the next few years the Teamsters signed dozens of "sweetheart contracts" with growers without any evidence of support from workers.

But over the same period of time UFWOC continued to pick up momentum. Organizing steadily in the fields, the union had contracts covering one-third of all table grape companies, representing 50,000 workers, by mid-1970—by far more than had ever been represented by a union in the history of California agriculture. The most important symbolic moment of victory came in July, when two dozen Delano-area growers signed agreements committing to $1.80 an hour in wages plus a 25 percent increase in the piece rate per lug. Gains included union-run hiring halls to dispatch the workers and a growing set of services: a health clinic and health plan to be paid by an hourly grower contribution. The UFWOC also offered a credit union, community center, and cooperative gas station to members.

The hiring hall meant a serious barrier to discrimination and favoritism by labor contractors, much as the ILWU hiring hall had brought fairness in hiring for longshoremen in San Francisco thirty-five years before. For instance, in March, seventeen black farmworkers were dispatched to the Perelli-Minetti grape ranch from the union hall. It was the first time African American farmworkers had ever been employed there.

The United Farm Workers Organizing Committee (renamed in 1970 the United Farm Workers of America), as Chavez had envisioned, had become both a union and a civil rights movement, and this was the key to its success. The dual character of the farmworkers organization gave it a depth of moral pressure and sense of mission felt by members and supporters alike. It brought the union its victories but also the determined, long-term enmity of the growers, which mobilized all the considerable forces under its influence in the central valleys.

In the late summer and fall of 1970, lettuce and strawberry workers around the Salinas area, who had waited impatiently for the grape strike to be settled, were no longer willing to wait. Emboldened by the victory in grapes, they pushed the UFW to help them gain contracts, as did farmworkers throughout the state.

The UFW leadership told Salinas workers they would help organize after grape contracts were put in place. But before details could be hammered out, the floodgates opened. Besides the workers' impatience, magnifying the urgency of the situation was an unfortunate development: Chavez and the Salinas workers learned that the area's growers had signed secret contracts with the Teamsters covering more than ten thousand workers. Not one worker had been involved in negotiations or even knew about them. The UFW leaders were furious but not as angry as the workers.

Their wrath propelled mobilizations and actions including a mass march, rolling strikes, the threat of a boycott leveled against one of the major growers' corporate parent (United Fruit Corporation), a six-day fast by Chavez, and very effective field organizing by what was now a large, experienced cadre of UFW activists, ultimately ending up with a number of new contracts.

Over the next several years the union sought to consolidate and extend its collective bargaining realm but had to defend every inch of the terrain it had

FIGURE 37. Born in the context of mass social movements and organized labor at its peak, Cesar Chavez's United Farm Workers declined as the political climate shifted right. Dennis Kelly, photo.

won against counterattacks launched by the growers in the fields, the legislature, the courts, and in the media.

Farmworkers and their supporters were injured and killed in acts of violence by growers, their hired goons, law enforcement, and Teamsters, who pitted themselves against the UFW in hundreds of representation elections. When the courts ruled that the union could only use bullhorns to call out the workers in the fields for an hour a day, and limited picketing to one picket every hundred feet, the UFW responded with campaigns of mass civil disobedience. In four months of spring and summer in 1973, more than 3,500 farmworkers and supporters were arrested, clogging the jails of Kern County in a situation reminiscent of the Wobblies' free speech fights in Fresno over a half century before.

Although Chavez and the union leadership consistently preached the gospel of nonviolence to UFW members, the message did not always maintain discipline in the ranks, especially in the face of continuous provocations on picket lines, in labor camps, and on the streets of the small towns dotting the agricultural map.

The violence crested with two farmworker deaths in August. A Yemeni farm laborer, Nagi Daifullah, had served as a UFW picket captain. He was standing in front of a bar in Lamont with friends celebrating UFW members' release from jail. After an argument with a deputy sheriff, the twenty-four-year-old Daifullah was dead—an accident, said the police, but murder, according to UFW witnesses. A few days later, Juan de la Cruz, picketing the Giumarra ranch southeast of Bakersfield, was shot dead by two men passing in a pickup truck.

The deaths triggered wide-ranging discussions within the union and a refocusing of tactics, for a time, from picket lines to the boycott, and ultimately to political action. The UFW helped Jerry Brown win election to the governor's office in 1974, with the expectation that Brown—the son of former governor Pat Brown—would sign a law, the Agricultural Labor Relations Act (ALRA), legalizing collective bargaining for farmworkers. Like many private sector workers before passage of the National Labor Relations Act in 1935, farmworkers were already negotiating contracts with employers. But such bargaining occurred in a tumultuous, unpredictable environment, dependent on power matched against power, with inconsistent rules from one situation to the next, and the constant threat of violence lurking beneath the surface.

Crucial to the act, from the UFW's perspective, was creation of an Agricultural Labor Relations Board to enforce the law. The ideal ALRA should ensure the safety of union activists, protect access by organizers to workers, and see that implementation of farm labor elections was not ignored or delayed, often for years, by growers through the courts.

The growers, for their part, pushed for provisions outlawing strikes during harvest and removing secondary boycotts from the workers' tool kit. Such a law had been signed in Arizona in 1971. It was during the campaign against this legislation that, in refusing admonitions to give up, Dolores Huerta responded, "*Sí se puede*" (Yes, we can). When Governor Brown signed the ALRA in June 1975, it allowed harvest strikes but excluded secondary boycotts.

The governor appointed a proworker majority to the board and provided it with enough funding to open field offices across the state, hire attorneys and staff, and carry out its mission to encourage and oversee collective bargaining. There were scores of elections within the first year. The union's membership, which had sunk below ten thousand, climbed back over twenty thousand. But the growers came up with a new strategy. They filed hundreds of charges against the union and simultaneously persuaded friendly state legislators to withhold funding for the board, which quickly became overwhelmed by its huge case backlog.

The UFW mobilized its volunteer army in the cities to collect signatures and place Proposition 14 on the ballot, which stipulated adequate funding for the board and reiterated the right of the UFW to talk with farmworkers. Proposition 14 lost in November 1976, falling before a heavily bankrolled opposition campaign. But the rights to field access were upheld by a Supreme Court decision. And after the Teamsters signed a pact in 1977 pledging to stay out of the fields, the union won election after election. By 1980 the UFW claimed a hundred thousand members, enrolled under hundreds of contracts.

The forward momentum did not last. The next decade saw a steady reassertion of grower power as the crucial external support for the UFW in labor and public opinion eroded. Born in a context of mass social movements and with the support of organized labor at its peak, the UFW declined as the movements receded and industrial unions were hammered by political attacks and the globalization of the economy. The union struggled to administer contracts and organize in an increasingly hostile political climate. The Agricultural Labor Relations Board turned out to be a two-edged sword after Republican George Deukmejian, elected governor in 1982, appointed a progrower majority to the board.

Matters were not helped by problems inside the UFW. Larry Itliong had left the union in 1971, frustrated over his relegation to the fringes of leadership. In 1977 Philip Vera Cruz resigned in protest when Chavez accepted an award from Philippines dictator Ferdinand Marcos. Chavez's insistence on calling undocumented workers "illegals" and pushing for their deportation split the Chicano community. Internal battles over union democracy and purges of longtime UFW staff and other leaders left the union ill-prepared to cope with the new political environment.

If the UFW ultimately could not live up to the expectations created by its early successes, that doesn't mean it was a failure. In a country where labor history is mostly a history of defeats, and in an industry with such an imbalance of power between workers and owners, the UFW meant something much more.

Prior to the UFW, any advances won by farmworker unions were always brief, eroded by the determination of the solid ranks of growers and by the marginal status of mostly immigrant farmworkers in the economic and political life of the state. Despite herculean efforts, sometimes entailing the sacrifice of lives, workers never managed to build a union in the fields that lasted even a decade.

The United Farm Workers' singular achievement was that it was the first farmworker union that lasted. As a result it had a profound impact on the labor movement and on the public's understanding of where its food came from and how it was produced. A generation of labor activists, leaders, and staff emerged from the crucible of the boycott and farmworker organizing.

The UFW and its struggle provided a central point of reference for the emergence of Chicano identity and culture, not only in California but the United States. The red and black Aztec Thunderbird logo cast a long shadow over Chicano graphic design and visual arts, as did marching farmworkers, grapes, and the iconic faces of Cesar Chavez and Dolores Huerta. The union's successes and stubborn survival provided a foundation for rethinking and rewriting the historic role of people who came from Mexico to California.

The union also made a classroom for consumers out of its struggle. It educated millions of people who, living in urban centers, had lost the ancient, basic human connection with growing the food they ate. Through the strikes, boycotts, and astute publicity efforts, the UFW taught the public about the exploitation of the people who produced what appeared, somewhat mysteriously, in supermarkets and on their tables. They learned about the health problems, for workers and consumers alike, that might be associated with a heavy reliance on pesticides in agriculture. And with the union's struggles, people found that, even against great odds, sometimes these wrongs could be righted. *Sí se puede.*

26

The Rise of Public Sector Unionism

THE 1960S SAW THE RISE of a powerful movement for unionism by workers employed in public service jobs. It was fueled by the example of the civil rights movement, with its courageous moral stand and nonviolent civil disobedience tactics. Like farmworkers, public sector unionists received tangible support from strong private sector unions. But more than anything else, public sector unionism benefited from the prosperity of a society that, through a mature labor movement and voter support for government services, provided the people of the United States with the most equitable distribution of wealth it had achieved, before or since.

The expansion of government programs at all levels in the 1960s was the result of a consensus in place since the New Deal that a strong economy depended on investing in a robust public sector to provide education, safety, health, and security for the general population. It was a society that could afford to be organized and in which living traditions of collective struggle helped make sure that it was.

The first post–World War II generation of teacher unionists benefited from these prevailing social attitudes and the government programs that implemented them. Veterans went to college and became educators themselves, thanks to the G.I. Bill, which paid for their enrollment.

Social workers coming into the workforce a generation later received the same educational benefit, due to growth in state public universities receiving federal subsidies that kept tuition costs modest—or, as in California, free. Like teachers, social workers occupied an employment niche somewhere between working class and professional, but received compensation similar to that of workers, despite training closer to that of professionals. The combination of a college-educated public workforce with compensation levels and workplace rights below unionized private sector standards was a key ingredient in public worker organizing.

Although the upsurge of unionism among public workers was the greatest of any group of workers since the 1930s, the backgrounds and aspirations of public employees were not homogenous. Professionals and semiprofessionals whose work required lengthy, specialized training, including a college education and graduate school, such as teachers, social workers, librarians, and nurses, shared little at first glance with blue collar public employees like police and firefighters, trash collectors, school secretaries, and street maintenance and building construction workers. But what they all wanted—a greater say in how their jobs were run, better pay and benefits, and ultimately the right to bargain collectively to achieve these goals—produced enough glue to help overcome distinctions between "middle class" and "working class" occupations, and propelled a movement.

Due to public employees' service-oriented worldview and relatively high levels of postsecondary education—not to mention large concentrations of women in many job categories—many private sector union leaders thought that they were "unorganizable." A considerable number of public workers themselves agreed with that perspective, which was reinforced by legal barriers and public opinion that frowned on collective action by public employees. No less an authority than Franklin Delano Roosevelt had justified the exclusion of public workers from the National Labor Relations Act because of "the special relationship and obligations of public servants to the public itself and to the government."

Employee associations provided some avenues of representation for public workers without collective bargaining or affiliation with organized labor. The leadership of these associations typically argued, like their bosses, that unionism was inappropriate for the public sector. Their arguments often resonated with members for whom unions symbolized the working-class world their college education was supposed to help them escape.

Nonetheless, the tide ran toward union representation. Private sector union density in the nonfarm workforce topped 35 percent. California workers enjoyed some of the highest pay scales in the country, and public employees—especially those whose family members and neighbors were among the organized workforce—couldn't help but notice. As southern California union leader Elinor Glenn observed, "You couldn't convince a nurse or a teacher that she should get less than a carpenter. But the carpenter had this powerful collective bargaining tool, he was recognized, he had a contract. He deserved it, and they deserved it."

PUBLIC WORKER UNIONS

Public employee union organizing originated in the nineteenth century. But these unions, unsupported by national or state collective bargaining laws, tended to represent workers in one local agency, such as the Los Angeles Department of Water and Power (DWP), where the International Brotherhood of Electrical Workers Local 18 had been in place since before 1900. DWP workers had even gone on strike in 1944. The ability of these unions to advocate for their members depended on relationships with their agency administrators and local elected officials. This meant that collective bargaining remained inherently unstable.

Public sector workers had made several sustained efforts to form unions between World War I and World War II. Veterans reentering the workforce from the battlefield brought with them a no-nonsense attitude; they had sacrificed for their country, were not going to stand for public administrators denying their rights, and felt they deserved to be treated and paid well for their work.

But a cluster of public employee strikes in 1919 created a backlash against unionization. In particular, a well-publicized walkout of Boston police against low pay and unhealthy conditions, which unleashed a brief crime wave, gave antilabor politicians the opportunity to pass laws forbidding public sector organizing and collective bargaining across the country. These laws had a chilling effect on workers and on the AFL, which, for the most part, ignored public sector workers for the next fifteen years.

In 1935 the federation granted a charter to the American Federation of State, County and Municipal Employees (AFSCME). The CIO chartered two public employee unions in 1937, the United Federal Workers of America, and the State, County and Municipal Workers of America. These small left-led unions relied on direct action mobilization and connections with larger CIO unions to advocate for their members but achieved only scattered successes.

Following World War II, public workers attempted to organize again, and many participated in the strike wave of 1945–46. Teachers in St. Paul, Minnesota walked off their jobs protesting low pay and won substantial improvements. Among the half-dozen citywide general strikes in 1946 was one centering on public employees in Rochester, New York, who had invited AFSCME to organize them.

The CIO, hoping to take advantage of the postwar militant mood, merged its two public employee unions into the United Public Workers of America (UPWA), also in 1946. At its peak it claimed a hundred thousand members. Los Angeles was one stronghold of this union, which organized large numbers of minority blue collar workers in public hospitals, sanitation, and the post office. But the CIO expelled the UPWA in 1950 and helped to destroy it with raiding and red-baiting. The national union turned in its charter in 1952. A number of the UPWA's locals survived for a time as stand-alone unions, but more often the remnants were absorbed by other unions and occasionally by public employee associations.

EMPLOYEE ASSOCIATIONS

Public employee associations did not collectively bargain, and their attitudes toward unionism ranged from indifferent to fiercely opposed. They gave members an organizational structure for pressuring state and local governments in other ways. Three of the oldest and largest of the statewide public employee associations were the California Teachers Association (CTA), which descended through predecessor groups back to 1863; the California School Employees Association (CSEA), founded in 1926, to represent the interests of nonteaching or classified school workers; and the California State Employees Association (also CSEA), established in 1931. The associations advocated for their members around personnel policies and retirement issues and provided a number of low-cost services, including group insurance, legal representation, credit unions, and discount purchases.

The California School Employees Association gave its members clout in legislative deliberations on the state's Education Code and persuaded the Public Employment Retirement System to accept classified school employees. The CTA performed similar services for teachers (enrolled in the separate State Teachers Retirement System, which CTA advocacy helped establish in 1913). CSEA worked through its local school district chapters to encourage merit-based personnel policies, and worker representation on civil service-like personnel commissions to determine job classifications. The California State Employees Association brought together diverse groups of state workers for legislative advocacy. Other associations, practicing comparable activities on a local scale, existed for county and municipal employees.

A GROWING SENTIMENT FOR UNIONIZATION

By the 1960s many public employee associations harbored a growing sentiment for unionization. The people who shared these feelings were greatly encouraged by President Kennedy's signature in 1962 on Executive Order 10988, establishing the right of federal workers to engage in collective bargaining.

Firefighters were the first group of California public employees to gain a law, in 1959, officially allowing them to organize, through the efforts of their union, the California Federation of Fire Fighters, affiliated with the International Association of Fire Fighters (IAFF). But the law was silent on collective bargaining, and in line with national IAFF policy, the Fire Fighters Act prohibited strikes.

Minimal organizing and representation rights came with the George Brown Act in 1961, after pro-union forces within the California State Employees Association pushed for the law. The Brown Act did not mandate elections to represent units of workers nor collective bargaining; it was not a "little NLRA," as some public union militants hoped to see.

George Brown had run for state assembly after working as a civil engineer in the Los Angeles Department of Water and Power, where he had been a member of one of the city's oldest employee organizations, the Engineers and Architects Association, and served for a time as its business agent. The International Brotherhood of Electrical Workers Local 18's leadership supported his candidacy on the condition that he carry a bill enabling organizing and collective bargaining for public employees.

Not all unions were on board with this bill. In fact, what kept the Brown Act from creating a California public sector NLRA was not conservative legislative opposition but fierce lobbying from the Building Service Employees International Union, AFL (BSEIU, later Service Employees International Union, SEIU). George Hardy and other BSEIU leaders were not opposed to public employee collective bargaining. They just believed that they were not yet strong enough to win representation elections against the employee associations.

The Brown Act demonstrated a new willingness by legislators to consider broadened rights for public employees and the spectrum of public employees' opinions regarding unions. In some cases, existing associations were resistant to change, and their members formed new organizations to challenge them. In others, pro-union workers were able to take over leadership and begin to transform the old associations into unions from within. These various paths eventually led public employees through direct action and unionization to the creation of collective bargaining laws.

SOCIAL WORKERS OUT FRONT

In August 1963, a dozen social workers in the Los Angeles County Department of Charities formed a Social Workers Action Committee (SWAC). They were members of what was then called BSEIU Local 434, a county employee union that included some social workers, but mostly various other classes of workers employed by Los Angeles County hospitals.

In the wake of public welfare amendments to the Social Security Act signed two years previously by President Kennedy, thousands of social workers—a large number of whom were newly minted college graduates—were hired by social service agencies throughout the country. Together with this influx of federal funding, allocated through the state social welfare department to the counties, there were new standards for hiring (college degrees) and a mandate to provide—not deny—real services to help the poorest working people. The intent was that welfare recipients should not simply scrape by economically but be enabled to get jobs through training. An enormous jump in paperwork accompanied these changes for the new social work hires.

The Social Workers Action Committee's goals included a pay increase and reduction in caseloads, paperwork, and worker-to-supervisor ratios. The committee also had a broader vision: to work together with welfare rights groups, which were emerging from the civil rights movement, to advocate for reform of public assistance agencies. They decided the best way to accomplish these things was to form a separate social workers union. They approached former United Public Workers leader Elinor Glenn, the general manager of BSEIU Local 434.

Glenn supported organizing and appreciated audacity. David Novogrodsky worked with Glenn as a BSEIU researcher in Los Angeles in the early 1960s. He recalled that "She had a reputation as being the "shit house organizer" because she would hold her meetings in the women's bathroom, where the management people, who were all men, they just didn't feel they could walk through that door." Glenn was sympathetic to the social workers' desires but pragmatically wanted some accountability too. So she issued a challenge to the group: organize five hundred workers and she would help them get a charter for their own union local.

There were precedents for this request. Glenn had recently convinced George Hardy to issue a separate charter for Los Angeles County workers—including nurses, social workers, janitors, and others—Local 434, which grew to 7,000 members. She parted paths at this time with Sidney Moore, who stayed with the sanitation workers in Local 347 as it became an all city workers union.

Glenn procured the promised charter in August 1964. In forming the new union, BSEIU Local 535, the Social Workers Action Committee was bolstered by a group that came over from the Los Angeles County Employees Association. Like SWAC, the Social Workers Standards Committee was an island of social workers in a sea of other county employees; it predated the SWAC. Its members were mostly young, and their ideas about how to achieve their professional goals were evolving rapidly. Local 535's activist arguments made sense to them. Novogrodsky facilitated contact between the groups: "We held up the charter that we had worked so hard to get until we could get half the names from the Social Workers Standards Committee and half from the Social Workers Action Committee. We made sure it was a merger rather than a takeover."

Inside a year the membership of 535 reached one thousand. The local hired Novogrodsky as executive director. In early 1966 he demanded that the county bargain with them: "We wanted bona fide collective bargaining, like they had in the automobile industry." They asked for the same raise, $100, for all county social workers. In addition, they told the county representatives that the Bureau of Public Assistance should be "liberated" from the Department of Charities. Initially the county representatives agreed to a 10 percent increase and to bargain, according to a letter from the superintendent of the charities department, on "everything from caseloads to coffee breaks." But at the end of May the county backed away from the agreement, precipitating a strike.

It lasted seventeen days and established a starting salary of $600 per month. A week later, the county authorities once more reneged on the agreement and attempted to punish strike leaders and activists. The workers went back out, this time until July 4. The local union's attorneys filed suit and prevailed, reinstating fired strike leaders and forcing the county to honor its

FIGURE 38. Los Angeles social workers organized and struck for recognition of Service Employees International Union Local 535, the vanguard of California public sector unionism in June 1966. Personal collection of author.

agreement. Within a year and a half the county Department of Charities had been reorganized, with separate departments for county hospitals and public welfare.

Local 535 activists were busy with their own activities but found time to lend their expertise to fellow California workers in need. Soon after the Delano grape strike began, the Kern County welfare department denied benefits to striking farmworker families. Local 535 members, led by Pearl Hazelwood, started up a support committee. It traveled every couple weeks to Delano, where its members steered farmworkers through the claims system, a unique form of solidarity only social workers could offer.

The young union, expanding outside Los Angeles, helped Santa Barbara workers strike for higher salaries and a grievance procedure that same year. The following February Sacramento social workers struck to gain collective bargaining rights and stayed out for the longest public sector strike in U.S. history: two hundred and eighty days. They were led by Bob Anderson, a

Compton social worker who left his agency office during the Santa Barbara strike to help out and never went back.

In late spring 1967, in the midst of the Sacramento strike, social worker union delegates from across California met in the state capital. They were greeted at the airport by strikers and brought to the Sacramento Labor Temple. Here, at a three-day meeting, the social workers established SEIU 535 as a statewide union local and organized themselves into a joint council together with fast-growing SEIU locals representing other public employees.

Marty Morgenstern, a guest speaker at the convention and president of a New York social workers union that had been out on its own strike, made clear the determination of the union to fight for the rights of welfare clients alongside the rights of social workers.

> From coast to coast, the welfare system stinks. The agencies have developed into bureaucracies that only distribute paper; they don't give a damn for the people, but we do. We, unlike the agencies, aren't wedded to the paper work, and we want to work with the people, to be part of the change that has to come.

Morgenstern soon became the national staffer for a new alliance of militant social worker unions, the National Federation of Social Service Employees. It included his own New York Social Service Employees Union, as well as one in upstate New York headed by Kim Moody, Local 535, and others in Chicago and elsewhere. It was committed to close working relationships with welfare rights organizations and to reform of public assistance systems.

The Sacramento strike was difficult (more than 200 picketers were arrested, and 183 lost their jobs) and unsuccessful, but it drew sharp attention to the need for a collective bargaining law for public employees. It also helped convince workers in other northern California counties that this was a union willing to fight for them, and they joined by the hundreds: sometimes as individuals and at other times affiliating entire local employee associations.

Novogrodsky noted, "It shook everything up. Other public workers looked at what happened and said, 'If these social workers could do it, so could we.'" Fired Sacramento strikers scattered around the state and went to work for other local social service agencies. Many of these helped organize their new workplaces.

Even with the loss of such a large number of leaders, the Sacramento social workers voted for representation by Local 535 when challenged by AFSCME. Local 535 soon gained chapters in Santa Clara, Alameda, and elsewhere. SEIU picked up other units of Sacramento county workers, although most opted for AFSCME. This rivalry, and worker militancy, became the pattern across the state as the two unions vied for the allegiance of unaffiliated local associations of public workers.

The relationship between the unions could also be supportive. Twenty-seven-year-old Tom Rankin found that out when he became a social worker in Contra Costa County, across the bay and north from San Francisco. Rankin had just earned his master's degree in history at UC Berkeley. In school he helped organize a graduate student union and was active in the anti–Vietnam War movement, getting arrested in draft protests in Oakland. After graduation in 1967 he fell into county employment as a social worker; the county's social services department needed the workers and Rankin needed work. "It was sort of a professional job, and paid OK; it was actually more appealing as a social movement," Rankin recalled. He hadn't been working long before other Contra Costa County workers, affiliated with AFSCME, struck for higher wages.

Henry Clarke, secretary-treasurer of AFSCME Local 1675, asked for and received strike sanction from the Contra Costa Central Labor Council. Rankin's Local 535 chapter, with about two hundred members, discussed whether to honor the picket lines: "We had our own demands, too, for a salary increase," Rankin remembered years later. But their decision to walk out mostly revolved around support for AFSCME. According to Rankin, "Solidarity was assumed; it took no struggle or debate to convince 535 members to be part of the strike."

The sense of social movement unionism that motivated the social workers' actions during the AFSCME strike extended into their work lives and their interactions with their clients. After work Rankin and others would help organize welfare rights demonstrations or go join United Farm Worker pickets in front of Safeway stores. Following the strike his coworkers elected Rankin president of their Local 535 chapter. Rankin, however, soon ended his brief career as a social worker, going on to work as an organizer and advocate for various public employee unions before hiring on as research staff at the California Labor Federation. He later served as federation president.

LEGAL AT LAST

In 1968 the California legislature passed the Meyers-Milias-Brown Act (MMBA), formally legalizing collective bargaining for local government workers. Much as the National Labor Relations Act had been enacted in 1935 in response to powerful worker movements, the MMBA put into place rules to channel the militant activism of public workers within legal boundaries. It was almost the "little NLRA" public employee unionists had been seeking for years.

However, the MMBA had limitations. It established local bargaining authority but not statewide units; it left the details to local determination and specifically excluded public education and state employees. It also had no enforcement mechanisms, leaving problems to be sorted out with raw power or by the courts. But it did say clearly that public employers had to meet and confer "in good faith" and agreements had to be reduced to writing, or contracts. As such, according to David Novogrodsky, "It was a license to organize."

The Meyers-Milias-Brown Act forced the associations to understand there was now no stopping the union train. They had to win elections and to bargain collectively. The law also helped the already existing unions—especially AFSCME and SEIU—to believe they could win elections against the associations. And they won a lot of them.

27

Creating the Conditions for Teaching and Learning to Happen

From the beginning, we did not say to ourselves, "We're going to get power by going to Sacramento and getting a bill that tells us that we have the right to collective bargaining." We wanted that, but that was not the source of our authority. The source of our authority was in collective action, and watching the peace movement, and the civil rights movement, we could see the strategies one used.

MILES MYERS, OAKLAND TEACHER

KOREAN WAR VETERAN RAOUL TEILHET went to work teaching history at Pasadena High School in the late 1950s. When he was hired the principal handed him, along with his employment papers, membership applications for the Pasadena Education Association, California Teachers Association, and National Education Association. As a former member of "real unions," he surmised these must be company unions, since it was his boss that was signing him up.

Teilhet's suspicions were not far from the mark. The full picture was more complex, since in the public sector there is no "company." But the California Teachers Association (CTA) was not a union. It functioned as a statewide lobbying organization for K-12 public education and offered an array of services for its members, including a credit union, travel assistance, discount purchase arrangements, and insurance programs. Despite its name, and the presence of teacher advocates within the organization, the CTA was dominated by school administrators, school district superintendents, and elected school board officials. It did not support collective bargaining for teachers. In fact, it had opposed collective bargaining bills for teachers and other school employees every time they had appeared before the state legislature beginning in 1953.

The sponsor of those bills was the California Federation of Teachers (CFT), formed during the first wave of public sector union organizing in

1919. But it wasn't until the 1960s that CFT, affiliated with the national American Federation of Teachers (AFT), and with the AFL-CIO, gained the ability to mobilize thousands of teachers over pay, working conditions, and academic freedom issues. Sparked by the success of the national AFT, which had won a number of collective bargaining agreements in large cities in East Coast states through strikes, and backed by organizing grants from the United Auto Workers, the CFT's idea of classroom unionism began to look attainable to the state's teachers. The CFT waged battles on many fronts—legal, legislative, political, and organizing—on behalf of the goal of collective bargaining for "teacher power."

No one was more effective in pursuit of this goal than Raoul Teilhet, a transplanted Ohioan on whose father's living room wall were found the three typical icons of the midcentury coal miner: Jesus Christ, FDR, and John L. Lewis. A gifted public speaker, energetic and fearless organizer, and charismatic union leader, the high school history teacher carried the CFT's message about collective bargaining with messianic fervor to the farthest corners of the state—and not just to K-12 teachers, but community college and university faculty as well.

Teilhet and a growing number of volunteer organizers extended CFT's tradition of social unionism to active support for the United Farm Workers (Cesar Chavez was a regular speaker at CFT conventions) and to the anti–Vietnam War movement. According to Teilhet, no education policy could make sense without fully funding the classroom, freeing teachers from worries about job security, and understanding the broader social context in which public education occurred.

Luisa Ezquerro's experiences were typical of the reasons why Teilhet and other CFT organizers connected to growing numbers of teachers. She became a San Francisco teacher in the footsteps of her immigrant mother and aunt, who had taught in Nicaragua. Ezquerro recalled what happened one afternoon in the early 1960s after her principal developed a dislike for her.

> I got called in by the principal, this old character. There was a phone booth out in the hall. He reaches into his pocket and pulls out some coins and says, "Here, here's some coins, why don't you call around and see where you can get a job." Well excuse me! . . . See, there wasn't a contract. He had no right to do that, but there wasn't anything that prevented him from doing it.

Along with the petty insults came violations of basic rights. There was John Muir High School teacher Paul Finot, placed on leave by the Pasadena

School Board in 1963 because he refused to shave his beard. The school principal worried publicly about the dire impact his appearance would have on Negro students. (Apparently no one noted the irony that the school's famous namesake bore a heavy beard.) When asked at a court hearing, where he was represented by CFT, whether his beard wasn't an "outgrowth of his radicalism," he replied, "No, it was an outgrowth of my six-week fishing trip." The appeals court, ruling that a beard represented a constitutionally protected freedom of individual expression, restored Finot to his classroom.

Teachers resented paternalistic restrictions imposed by administrators, superintendents, or school boards, not only on academic freedom within the classroom to teach as they saw best but also on freedom of speech outside school. Jack Owens was fired in 1959 for "unprofessional conduct" in Shasta for organizing educational forums and writing letters to the editor of the local newspaper critical of school district policy. With union support, he was returned to his job in 1962 through a lawsuit.

Events like these reinforced teacher union activists' belief that the only lasting protection for teacher rights would come with collective bargaining, through contracts that mandated salary schedules based on education and experience instead of administrative whim, grievance procedures to settle individual and group problems peacefully, seniority provisions for fairness and consistency in determining layoffs and transfers, and equitable, transparent rules to evaluate teachers for the purpose of retention and promotion.

A small cadre of AFT members held these values and ideas throughout the post–World War II years, nurturing the seeds of collective bargaining in the minds of colleagues and legislators. Disproportionately veterans, they spent countless volunteer hours after school attending board meetings, representing teachers in informal hearings, writing and distributing mimeographed newsletters, and occasionally finding themselves looking for new jobs as a result. In the face of hostile school administrators, an entrenched, antiunion teacher association, and a mostly indifferent public, they pursued their chimerical vision.

The CTA sponsored a halfway measure toward collective bargaining in 1965. The Winton Act, AB 1474, was in fact intended to stave off collective bargaining. The act established the right of school district negotiating councils to "meet and confer" with administration over employment issues. School boards placed representatives of teacher organizations on the councils in proportion to their membership. These negotiations *could* be used by school boards to inform their decisions, which nonetheless remained final. In his organizing conversations with teachers across the state, Raoul Teilhet provided a metaphor to describe the process: "Meet and confer is what you do with your children. Collective bargaining is what you do with your spouse."

AFT activists like Ezquerro derisively called the practice "meet and defer" or "collective begging." Although the Winton Act was intended to stack the deck in favor of the much larger CTA, CFT members utilized its flaws as an argument for full collective bargaining. In some districts the union boycotted the council and called for elections instead of appointment to the body.

THE MAYOR WHO WENT ON STRIKE

In 1966 local CFT activists used the failure of one district's Winton Council as a catalyst for the first teacher strike in California. This took some doing, since fears of chaos and anarchy during public employee strikes had been stoked by politicians and conservative media every time the possibility arose since the calamitous 1919 Boston police walkout. Of some encouragement were the successful job actions of New York teachers, which in addition to collective bargaining agreements had resulted in a state collective bargaining law. But in California no laws addressed the issue. Strikes also went against the emotional grain carried by most public employees, their sense of public service.

In spring 1966 the Richmond School District found itself with an unexpected tax windfall of $600,000 when local industrial property values were reassessed upwards. Richmond, a few miles north of Berkeley, had a population of 80,000, down from its wartime peak of 100,000. Just a few hundred skilled workers found seasonal employment in the sole remaining ship repair facility, Williamette Iron and Steel Shipyard. Although shipbuilding had come and gone, Richmond remained an industrial town. With 11,000 workers employed in manufacturing—by far the largest job category—it was also a heavily unionized area. The biggest employer was the Standard Oil refinery. Most of the town's 3,500 construction workers were dispatched from local union hiring halls, and the larger retail establishments were likewise organized.

Leaders of the Contra Costa Federation of Teachers, AFT Local 866, told the school board that it wasn't worth the $300 per year per employee to distribute the money in salary increases to the district's 1,700 teachers. Instead, the union suggested the board could do more good by reallocating the money to educational improvements. These included reducing class sizes by hiring more teachers, equalizing the resources and staffing of school libraries, purchasing more textbooks and other curriculum materials, strengthening the remedial reading program, and—in tandem with African American parents threatening a boycott—taking steps to desegregate the district.

The school board responded that it was bound by the Winton Act to negotiate with the Winton Council, not the AFT. Of the nine seats on the council, the board had appointed eight representatives of the Richmond Association of Educators (CTA) and one AFT member. The chair remained vacant, however, since the AFT wanted a vote of all teachers to determine representation on the council; its leaders, confident of better results through an election, refused to take the token seat. The council recommended that the money be distributed as a 3 percent raise for teachers and administrators. This was the same proposal as the superintendent had made, and it left out classified employees, who were not represented on the Winton Council.

Embarrassed by the publicity generated around these discussions, the board asked the council to make a new recommendation, including improvements to instruction. It did, this time including the classified employees (who were threatening to strike) in a blanket 2.25 percent raise, which would have eaten up $537,000 of the $600,000, leaving just $63,000 in proposals for remedial reading, in-service training, and a study of further educational improvements.

AFSCME Local 1675, like AFT, had no official bargaining rights but counted a majority of members among maintenance, cafeteria, and clerical workers in the Richmond district. After taking a vote, its secretary-treasurer, Henry Clarke, offered to reduce the classified employees' salary request if the teachers' educational improvement proposals were agreed to. He also demanded that the board authorize an election among classified employees to recognize the AFSCME local for purposes of collective bargaining.

Clarke was a colorful figure. He had once been suspended as a delegate to the Contra Costa Central Labor Council for a fistfight in the council parking lot with a delegate from another union. Projecting a tough, streetwise image, he was a college graduate and had taught school briefly himself. Serving a stint as AFT staffer in New York City, he was one of the three principal organizers of the first New York teacher strike. After the Richmond School Board refused to budge, Clarke directed Local 1675 members to set up pickets at 45 of the 60 school sites in the district on the first day of school, September 12, 1966.

Perhaps a few hundred teachers refused to cross the picket lines. The teacher unionists were strong in the secondary schools and virtually nonexistent in the elementary sites. Administrators held "classes" in the high schools and middle schools that amounted to babysitting up to one hundred students behind the pickets. Some high school students joined the picket lines. At an evening meeting in the Richmond library, the teachers voted to ask Contra Costa's labor council for strike sanction, which was granted immediately. Teachers and parents—many of whom were members of other unions themselves—began to organize makeshift schools and childcare centers.

On September 19 the teachers joined the classified workers outside the schools once more. But this time, they weren't walking in support of the other school employees; the teachers were themselves on strike. Among the picketers was Milton Spinner, a teacher at Adams Junior High School, and mayor of Richmond.

Spinner had taught social studies for ten years in the district and had been football coach at Roosevelt High School. After serving in the army during World War II, he earned a master's degree in history from Stanford, where he met and married his wife, Helen, who had worked as a welder in the Kaiser shipyards. At the time of the strike the Spinners had four children in the Richmond schools. Spinner and the union's newsletter editor, Howard Mackey, went to talk with the head of Standard Oil to seek his support for the teachers. The oil executive was willing to meet with Mayor Spinner, but was not inclined to support teacher Spinner on strike.

Spinner took out an ad in the local newspaper paid for by Local 866, explaining to the people of Richmond his view that if the school board supported American-style democracy and allowed an election of the teachers they would return to work.

Some local newspapers inaccurately reported the teachers were on strike for higher salaries. The *San Francisco Chronicle*'s coverage landed closer to the mark because its reporter, Dick Meister, was a union activist himself. The local *Richmond Independent* consistently undercounted the numbers of classified employees on the picket lines. The Contra Costa Central Labor Council's weekly newspaper, *Labor Journal*, ran articles on the issues for weeks prior to the strike and provided the most in-depth coverage while events were unfolding.

But after the teachers walked out, events didn't unfold for long. By Monday evening, the school board obtained a restraining order from a judge, and the following day teachers were back in the classroom. Mackey, another World War II vet and math teacher, later ruefully second-guessed his response to a question from a district administrator: "The district asked us if you'd go back if the judge ruled you had to. I said yeah, we don't want to disobey the law. Perhaps that was the wrong answer. Because then they went ahead and got the injunction."

AFSCME Local 1675 defied the injunction for a day and then went back to work. The school board agreed to ask the state attorney general for an opinion as to whether teachers could vote for council representation and to hold an election among classified employees within ninety days.

At the next central labor council meeting, one union leader advised the teachers to go back out. Said Slim Brady, an electrical worker and council vice president, "Can the employer just go down to the court and twist the faucet and out comes a two-bit injunction, all stamped and ready to stop a strike? If I were the teachers, I'd ignore it." Tom Lundy, Local 866's delegate to the council, told Brady that while some teachers agreed with him, the majority had decided to wait for an election before taking to the streets again.

That election never came. It had been within the board's power all along to allow an election instead of appointing teachers to the Winton Council. But pressured on one side by the Richmond Association of Educators, which feared a loss of seats to AFT, and by the antiunion superintendent, the board waffled for months before ruling against an election. The board went ahead and distributed the tax reassessment money as a raise. Despite the lack of apparent results, the strikers felt it had been worth it. According to Mackey, "We knew it was historic. We were really idealistic at that time. We thought we could make a difference."

CFT members across the state applauded the action of the Richmond local. San Francisco teachers sent a donation of a thousand dollars to help defray the loss of a day's salary. Seven years later, the CFT at its convention bestowed a plaque on the local commemorating the first time California teachers collectively walked out of their classrooms on behalf of a principle.

QUALITY EDUCATION

Like the social workers enrolled in Local 535 who felt a responsibility to join with their clients for needed reforms in social services, CFT members thought it was their duty to improve public education itself, starting with listening to the community. As Oakland teacher Miles Myers put it,

> We were trying to create the conditions for teaching to happen, and for learning to happen.... If you think of the African American leaders in the civil rights movement, the young ones, we had them right in Oakland or growing up in Oakland. [Black Panther founder] Bobby Seale's cousin was a teacher in the Oakland system. We had an awareness of that and the students did too. I remember the Black Student Union at Oakland High School proposing that the books ought to be more integrated, and they were.

Through alliance building, direct action, and tenacious defense of teachers' rights, the CFT chartered scores of locals in the late 1960s and early 1970s, picking up thousands of members each year. Its leaders and activists viewed CFT as a movement organization, much as members of the United Farm Workers did their union. And they viewed collective bargaining as one important means to achieve the movement's ends, the most important of which was quality education.

They also received crucial support from their sisters and brothers in manufacturing unions. CFT offices and organizing positions were funded by grants from the United Auto Workers, whose leader, Walter Reuther, understood the importance of extending labor's flanks to the public sector.

As CFT grew at CTA's expense, the association saw the writing on the wall. In 1971 it kicked out its administrator members and embraced collective bargaining. Soon association chapters were going on strike as often as AFT locals. Between 1970 and 1974 CTA chapters and CFT locals engaged in thirty-eight walkouts. San Francisco teachers, led by Jim Ballard, a teacher from a West Virginia miner's union family, struck four times in a dozen years beginning in 1968, in a rivalry pitting CFT and CTA local organizations against one another in a militancy contest for teachers' allegiance.

Los Angeles teachers, following a 1969 walkout, brought CFT and CTA members into the first merged AFT/NEA teacher union local in the country in 1970, creating a much more formidable instrument of the teachers' will. The direct action fever wasn't limited to K-12. A fiery strike at San Francisco State University by students demanding an expansion of curriculum to previously neglected studies of minority cultures and histories was bolstered when United Professors of California-AFT Local 1352, joined the picket lines. The campus, and to a lesser degree the San Jose State University campus, was shut down for months. These activities built pressure on the legislature to pass a

FIGURE 39. Raoul Teilhet, president of the California Federation of Teachers, rallies a crowd of educators in Diablo Valley, as local AFT leader Kaz Mori looks on, during the run-up to a collective bargaining law in 1975. Courtesy of California Federation of Teachers.

collective bargaining bill in 1973, but it was vetoed by Governor Ronald Reagan.

A "REAL NLRA" FOR PUBLIC EMPLOYEES

In 1975, the bill that most public employee unions, associations, and managers wanted was a comprehensive one, a "real NLRA" with enforcement powers, that would fold all types of public employees, and all levels of public education, within its guidelines. Senator Ralph Dills of Los Angeles offered such a bill in SB 275. Newly elected governor Jerry Brown hired former social worker and union leader Marty Morgenstern to run his labor relations office and charged him with getting a bill to his desk that satisfied everyone. Despite Morgenstern's best efforts, the bill fell apart late in the legislative process.

As a consolation prize, Brown fulfilled a campaign promise and signed SB 160, the Educational Employment Relations Act (EERA, also known as the Rodda Act). It was carried by Al Rodda, a former AFT local president and current state senator, and supported by CTA and, reluctantly, CFT. It also received important backing from the California School Boards Association, which belatedly understood collective bargaining as a way to achieve a more peaceful and less disrupted school environment.

The EERA enabled K-12 and community college employees—certificated and classified—to elect exclusive representatives and engage in collective bargaining, district by district, across the state. Unlike Meyers-Milias-Brown, SB 160 created a board with enforcement powers. But it excluded four-year higher education and placed a teacher voice in developing curriculum policies outside the scope of collective bargaining.

Debate within CFT over support of the Rodda Act was fierce. If SB 160 had been law in 1966, the Richmond AFT's demand to negotiate educational improvements would have had no legal basis. The United Professors of California-AFT, with thousands of members in the California State University and the University of California systems, wanted an inclusive bill. Ultimately CFT backed the Rodda Act, because it offered more than it left out, and friendly legislators promised to immediately draft a new collective bargaining bill for higher education. The Rodda Act went into effect January 1, 1976.

The EERA set up local competitions between the CTA and CFT for the next decade for the allegiance of teachers, and among the California School Employees Association, SEIU, AFSCME, and other unions and associations for the various units of classified school employees. Despite its limitations, the Educational Employment Relations Act established basic rights for public education employees: especially the right to resolve workplace disputes as equals with their employers through collective bargaining.

A decisive step forward for public employee unionism, SB 160 put in place the means for public education workers to achieve rough parity with their private sector counterparts. And for teacher unionists like Howard Mackey, it vindicated what had often seemed a quixotic quest in the 1950s and 1960s.

28

Feminist Collective Bargaining
Meets the Civil Service

Now, some things are happening among clerical workers that are
impelling us to unionize, things that are going on in women's
heads. As far as I can tell, there are definitely new feelings of
pride and dignity in being a woman, and outrage at the wages
that we get. I think that the Women's Liberation Movement
overall has had a decided impact on working women, especially
clerical workers.

MAXINE JENKINS, ORGANIZER

THE AMERICAN FEDERATION of State, County and Municipal
Employees (AFSCME) had been one of the beneficiaries of the destruction
of the United Public Workers-CIO, gaining thousands of members on the
East Coast as the left-led union was picked apart in the early 1950s. The West
Coast's AFSCME was less alert to this opportunity, turning down Elinor
Glenn before she approached George Hardy of the Building Service
Employees Union to take in UPW Local 246.

AFSCME may have fallen behind at that moment in California public
worker organizing, but by the mid-1960s it was toiling hard to make up for
lost time, organizing in schools, city and county employment, and in the
University of California system.

In San Jose, the city's civil service workers association, the Municipal
Employees Federation (MEF), affiliated with AFSCME in 1972, forming
AFSCME Local 101. It was here, in the city that Mayor Janet Gray Hayes
never tired of describing as "the feminist capital of the world," that the old
civil service personnel administration methods of adjusting salaries and job
descriptions ran into a three-way pileup with collective bargaining and the
impact of feminism on workplace organizing.

Steering women workers through the collision and out to the other side was
a determined and visionary organizer, Maxine Jenkins. Her vehicle, or weapon:

"comparable worth," which was based on the revolutionary idea that male and female workers should be paid equally for work requiring comparable skill, effort, and responsibility under similar working conditions. (This is different from "equal pay for equal work," which was codified in federal law in 1963, and had its own history of struggle in California dating back to Kate Kennedy, a century earlier.) The battle in San Jose for comparable worth had national reverberations, challenging union tradition, employment law, and gender roles.

PERSONNEL COMMISSIONS

By the late 1970s, Local 101 had grown to eleven chapters, including other cities and school districts within what was about to become known as Silicon Valley and represented a cross-section of San Jose city workers. Local 101 included office workers, librarians, custodians, park and recreation employees, and building trades workers but had long been dominated by male public works employees. The local bargained with city management over wages and working conditions, and advocated on behalf of its members before the city's personnel commission.

A Progressive Era reform, personnel commissions were part of a civil service system intended to remove politics from hiring and promotion in public employment. In the bad old days, newly elected politicians would fire all the previous administration's employees and install their own friends. Personal relationships and politics—and a generous amount of corruption—ruled the process. Instead, as designed in "good government" social engineering, individual job applicants would be screened through a civil service system that fairly hired, promoted, and retained employees through examinations based on merit: ability, experience, and accomplishments, including education. These tests depended on job classification procedures that analyzed the work necessary for the city, county, or other government employers, and grouped similar types of workers in categories for purposes of administration and compensation.

In theory this was a fair way to run a public bureaucracy. In reality, by placing employment decisions in the hands of a personnel commission, real power lay in the hands of managers whose deliberations were often shrouded in mystery. And the supposedly "objective" nature of the standards on which they based their decisions were, as it turned out, shaped by social and cultural biases that were anything but objective.

Women who worked in San Jose's city hall and the public library, some of whom were members of Local 101, had learned about these biases over the previous decade. Most were college graduates, having received their education at a time when the women's movement was having a tremendous impact on campuses—first through political organizing and later in development of curriculum. Although mostly "middle class" in outlook and upbringing, their employment in San Jose city services placed them squarely in the working class—and in a part of the working class that received, on average, 40 percent less compensation than another part, based on one qualification: whether they were women or men.

WOMEN ORGANIZE

Shut out of Local 101's policy discussions by the male public works employees in leadership and unable to influence collective bargaining around their issues, the women formed two independent groups to figure out what to do, City Women for Advancement (CWA) and Coalition of Library Activist Workers (CLAW), which also included men. They criticized the union leadership and the city administration. But their ideas fell on deaf ears until Maxine Jenkins arrived on the scene.

Jenkins had moved to the Bay Area from rural Mississippi, where she was born in 1936 into a family of sharecroppers. She attended the University of Missouri for two years, hoping to become a librarian, before migrating west. Jenkins then enrolled in UC Berkeley in 1964, earning a living as a clerical worker on campus while she attended classes. She soon became involved in helping to organize AFSCME Local 1695, and in addition to working for collective bargaining rights with clerical employees, brought together campus workers, students, and faculty in the widening, overlapping circles of the Free Speech and anti–Vietnam War protests. Captivated by organizing, she never graduated. Instead she worked for several Bay Area unions, including SEIU Local 400, the San Francisco municipal workers union that was heir to the old United Public Workers.

By the time she went to work for AFSCME Local 101 in 1977, Jenkins had been arguing for years that women's wages were suppressed by sexism and that the typical methods used for determining women's wages in the public sector were fundamentally flawed. In a women's conference sponsored by the California Labor Federation in 1973, Jenkins put it bluntly: "In the determination of salaries, we must get out of the bind of depending on surveys which compare salaries with already depressed rates elsewhere. We must make it clear that our unions are not going to accept such surveys any longer as legitimate."

Through her organizing campaigns with various occupational groups of women workers in both the public and private sector, she had learned to reject the standard "market value" comparisons governing public employee pay classification because discrimination in the private sector then translated into discrimination (and low salaries) in the public sector too.

Jenkins helped CLAW and CWA activists to form a new committee within Local 101, the Affirmative Action Committee, which soon came to be known simply as the "Women's Committee." It became the launching pad for much of the next generation of Local 101 leadership.

In 1978 the city administration went to a consulting firm, San Francisco–based Hay Associates, which specialized in analysis of civil service employees' job duties and compensation compared to their counterparts in the private sector. The city asked Hay to examine managerial pay practices to ensure the salary-setting system was consistent and equitable. The Hay investigation found that in predominantly female managerial job classes, pay lagged significantly behind classes with mostly male managers who possessed comparable or lesser education, skills, and job duties. As a result, some managers got whopping pay increases—9.5 percent and pay adjustments for most in these classes, and in the library, and park and recreation departments, up to 20 percent.

The Local 101 Women's Committee produced a paper, "Working Women," that outlined central issues for female San Jose city workers and called for comparable worth. The paper specifically addressed the needs of working mothers, such as childcare and flexible hours, as well as demanding bilingual pay for clerical workers who had to speak Spanish at work. The paper's authors argued that men were being paid much more than women for work of similar difficulty and training requirements. For instance, librarians with college educations were being paid less than road equipment operators. The women called for adjustment of the city's pay scales. The Hay management pay study confirmed their informal analysis. They demanded a similar study for nonmanagerial workers.

The committee also built an alliance with custodians, who, like the women, had been ignored by union leadership. The mostly Latino janitors and mostly white women semiprofessionals together elected their candidate for president of the San Jose city worker chapter of AFSCME Local 101, Mike Ferrero, a librarian.

NOT SO OBJECTIVE

The committee's paper was a revelation for many union members, who had suspected that job classes were not compensated in quite as objective or systematic a manner as the civil service/personnel commission made things seem. Librarian Joan Goddard, for instance, had worked for the library in various capacities and branches since 1971. She only became active in the union when she was asked to run for secretary of Local 101 in 1978 and hadn't paid close attention to the CWA or CLAW. Despite a civil rights and antiwar background (her husband served time in federal prison for refusing to be inducted in the military), her union activities remained separate in her mind from feminist consciousness until she read the paper and became convinced of the importance of comparable worth.

By April 6, 1979, the Women's Committee grew weary of waiting for a response from city management. On that day Jenkins organized a "sick-out"—a strike by another name. Most of the strikers were women, based in their city hall and parks and recreation department strongholds. Roughly one hundred workers participated in the stoppage, the first strike for comparable worth in the United States. In addition to comparable worth, the strikers demanded equal treatment of management and nonmanagement city employees. Before the day was out city management announced it would contract with Hay in a new study of nonmanagement job classes. This represented a substantial commitment of half a million dollars.

A few months later, at a San Jose City Council meeting, Jenkins pushed the city administration one important step further. During his presentation about the upcoming study, the city manager, aware that Jenkins was present, tried to preempt her view of comparable worth by maintaining that the study would be based on labor market wage comparisons. He said that therefore, "some women" might not be satisfied by the outcome.

In response, Jenkins spoke passionately and effectively on behalf of "the women of the city" and against the market standard for wage setting. She demolished the city manager's argument "comparing depressed wages to depressed wages that are artificially depressed not because of the value of the labor but because most of the people doing the work happen to be women."

FIGURE 40. Feminist union organizer Maxine Jenkins argues the case for comparable worth in front of the San Francisco Board of Supervisors. Future U.S. senator Dianne Feinstein is visible behind her. Cathy Cade, photo. Courtesy of the Bancroft Library, University of California, Berkeley.

Her clear analysis and forceful presentation gained a commitment from the city council majority to include market-based wage comparisons as only one factor among others—like internal civil service job comparisons across departments—in the Hay study.

Reinforcing the understanding, Local 101 negotiated a side agreement to the collective bargaining contract stipulating the city would bargain with the union over the eventual results of the study. The findings from the new Hay study were delivered before Christmas 1980 and supported Local 101's position that pay scales associated with job classes filled mostly by women were distorted by sex discrimination.

COMPLICATIONS

Negotiations between AFSCME and the city administration began in the New Year. Several factors complicated bargaining. The impact of Proposition 13, which California voters passed in 1978, lowering property taxes and reducing revenues to local government, was now taking full effect. The force of the blow to public services had been delayed by distribution of a state treasury surplus to city and county governments in the first year of Proposition 13. That money was gone, and across the state painful reductions in public services and the jobs of employees who delivered them were taking place.

In addition, the fall 1980 elections had brought into office a relatively inexperienced city council. Its majority remained committed to the previous administration's promise but struggled to balance it with the budget difficulties they faced. One council member solidly in the union camp was Iola Williams. Maxine Jenkins had convinced Local 101 to back Williams's campaign for an empty council seat. Members went door to door with petitions to get her on the ballot, and she repaid their assistance by remaining a strong ally throughout negotiations. Williams also agreed with Jenkins that the Hay nonmanagement study committees had to include workers, not just managers, from each occupational category.

On the union side of the bargaining table, tensions between groups of city workers had widened over comparable worth. Maxine Jenkins left Local 101 in early 1980 to work with other unions, but her perspective lived on in the AFSCME Women's Committee. The male-dominated blue collar and technical departments took control of the negotiations committee by packing the meeting at which bargaining representatives were elected. They were more interested in a general wage increase than equalizing pay for the job classes affected by gender discrimination. But the upstart women-janitor coalition still held a majority on the union's executive council, and they were able to arrive at a compromise: the bargaining team continued to include the comparable worth demand in negotiations alongside a more traditional position for an across-the-board increase.

They also argued that men were adversely affected by women's pay discrimination. As librarian Joan Goddard, who later served terms as MEF and Local 101 president, said, "We explained that pay equity was a family issue, along with being a women's issue. The rank and file men understood that women's low pay brought down their household income and affected them as well." This was persuasive to many, if not all, of the union's male members.

Recognizing the city's financial difficulties, AFSCME proposed that the pay inequities found in the second Hay study be redressed over four years, instead of the immediate adjustments that the managers had received. The management bargaining team did not respond to this flexibility with any of its own. Instead, it told union negotiators, led by former city gardener Bill Callahan, that management would let them know if it decided to bargain over the second Hay study.

The move infuriated the union leadership, which set a strike deadline of May 5, 1981, if the administration failed to come to terms. A one-day wildcat strike by library and recreation workers in late March—which the union referred to as "Hay fever"—signaled the determination of the workers to follow through with their threat. This drew the attention of the state Public Employment Relations Board, which sent a mediator to assist in negotiations. He got the union to postpone the strike deadline until July 5, when the contract was scheduled to expire.

As bargaining continued, union leadership ramped up organizing efforts among the workers with meetings, leafleting, and rallies, including the transformation of Secretaries Day by a "Raises, not Roses" demonstration in front of city hall. When the city attempted a transparent divide-and-conquer tactic by proposing to fund the comparable worth adjustments from the general wage increase, thereby reducing the size of the across-the-board raise, AFSCME called its members out on strike.

This nine-day work stoppage closed the city's libraries and parks, stacked up paperwork in city hall, and reduced transportation services when Teamsters and union bus drivers honored picket lines. Local 101 business agent Bill Callahan led the walkout. He had worked in the parks and recreation department before his election to union office and subsequent hiring as Maxine Jenkins's replacement on union staff. Callahan was a college-educated father of two daughters. He wanted to make sure his children, when they grew up, could advance economically without being dragged back by sex discrimination. He sported a button that read, "A woman's place is in her union."

Callahan later described this as his "fifteen minutes of fame." He appeared on more radio and television programs than he could count, as the story of the strike for pay equity in the "feminist capital of the world" made national as well as local news. In the end Local 101 gained $1.5 million in a fund to elevate wages in more than sixty job categories, in addition to general wage increases of more than 15 percent over two years. The comparable worth increases for job categories dominated by women brought workers in those classes near to parity. The strikers also attained an agreement that the city would continue to bargain over time on closing the rest of the pay equity gap.

Callahan predicted, "We have lit the fuse in San Jose. I don't think it's going to stop here." He was right. The strike resulted in nationwide discus-

FIGURE 41. Librarians called the first strike over comparable worth in the country in San Jose in June 1981. Walter P. Reuther Library, Archives of Labor and Urban Affairs, Wayne State University.

sion of the comparable worth idea and helped to establish a strong commitment within public sector unions for women's issues in the workplace. The Coalition of Labor Union Women, a national organization founded in 1974, and more radical local women's groups like Union WAGE (Women's Alliance to Gain Equality) in San Francisco also took up the cause.

SEIU Local 535's social workers pushed for and gained comparable worth provisions in contracts across the state. County workers, represented by SEIU locals in Santa Clara, San Mateo, and Contra Costa counties, and AFSCME elsewhere, successfully bargained comparable worth concepts as well.

At the same time unionized women workers were pushing for pay equity through collective bargaining, women not represented by unions elsewhere looked to the courts and government agencies for help. As the San Jose city worker drama unfolded in spring 1979, prison matrons in Oregon, paid less than male prison employees with jobs of similar difficulty, won a Supreme Court case. It found that workers could sue their employers for comparable worth pay differences. As a result women could file complaints through the Equal Employment Opportunity Commission, and Local 101 filed one, hoping to pressure the city managers at another stress point. The union dropped the complaint when the city settled the contract.

THE BIG SQUEEZE BEGINS

The rise of public sector unionism coincided with California organized labor still near its midcentury peak, within a strong diversified economy and tax base. The gains of these workers' movements of the 1960s and 1970s—like those of farmworkers—solidified at a moment when the firm belief in government as the solution for social problems still prevailed in public political discussion. But the ground soon shifted under public workers' feet.

Following passage of the Educational Employment Relations Act, a few more state laws over the next couple of years brought nearly all the major public worker groups the right to organize and bargain collectively. Workers in the California State University and University of California systems were folded into the Higher Education Employment Relations Act (HEERA), and state workers under the State Employer-Employee Relations Act (SEERA), both in 1977.

These laws streamlined various public sector collective bargaining procedures and reconfigured the Educational Employment Relations Board. EERB was expanded from three to five appointees and redesigned to become the Public Employment Relations Board (PERB)—finally the instrument of "a public sector NLRA." PERB was authorized, funded, and staffed to oversee state and local public employment labor issues as well as its original sphere of K-12 and community college public education.

But at the very moment these legislative successes finally brought collective bargaining rights to groups of workers long denied them, the prospects for California's public sector unions to win major economic advances for their members—let alone reform and improve the public services they provided—began to deteriorate in the face of changes in the economic and political landscape.

The inflation rate tripled by the mid-1970s over what it had been a decade earlier. Wages lagged behind cost of living, spurring public worker militancy, which crested in 1975 with 446 public sector strikes in the country, the most ever.

In the midst of another wave of walkouts in 1978, a conservative backlash gained momentum. The most visible sign of the pushback against public sector unionism was the passage of Proposition 13.

This measure, placed on the ballot by the Howard Jarvis Taxpayers Association, an antitax group backed by big business, capped increases in residential property taxes at 1 percent per year. It allowed property tax reassessment to full market value only when the home was sold, providing financial breathing room for older homeowners, especially retirees on fixed incomes.

But in a largely unnoticed coup for big business, the cap on residential property tax increases applied to large corporate properties too. Worse, the law established loopholes for sale of commercial property that allowed businesses to disguise the official transfer of property, keeping the new owners' property taxes at the old rate. This reduced public tax revenues by billions of dollars per year.

Prop 13 also raised the margin necessary to pass a new tax, or even to increase an already existing tax, to two-thirds of the state legislature and the same margin for local municipal tax measures.

With the higher bar to pass a tax, and property taxes no longer keeping pace with inflation and the growth in demand for public services, there was a squeeze on the ability of state revenues to fund adequate services for the public. Over time Prop 13 created a shift in who paid for public services statewide, with a smaller share from big business and the wealthy and a larger share from everyone else.

Such policy changes were accompanied by a hardening of resolve by public administrators to hold the line on union activism in their workforce, starting at the very top. In the early 1970s public administrators had little appetite to permanently replace strikers. By the end of the decade—and before Ronald Reagan redefined the country's labor relations by firing 11,000 air traffic controllers in 1981—other public officials had already ended strikes with mass firings.

The target of the new political mood, and of the social forces that orchestrated it, was not limited to public employees and their unions. That attack was just the opening wedge in a widening battle to restructure economic relationships in California and the country. At stake were the ways capital and labor had divided wealth since World War II.

One more pioneering effect of Prop 13 must be mentioned: its barely concealed racism, which scapegoated poor people and renters, especially people of color, as the most visible recipients of public services, especially welfare. The backers of the ballot measure sent white male workers and homeowners a message that said their hard-earned wages were being reduced by high taxes that funded services for people who would rather receive government checks than work. Prop 13's effectiveness was carefully noted by conservative activists across the country for its ability to divide working people.

As antilabor forces took control of government and the public agenda in the 1980s, public sector unions slowly, almost imperceptibly, began to set aside militant tactics. Instead, they forged coalitions with public administrators where they could to defend public services. They remained champions of civil rights, equal pay, and affirmative action. But strikes and other direct action tactics of the 1960s and 1970s were replaced with political campaigns and legislative advocacy to accomplish similar ends. In this way the public sector unions followed the path taken by private sector unions in the post–World War II period.

The replacement of direct action with political action is a sign of moving from the offensive to a defensive position. Just as the unions after the 1946 strike wave found themselves facing political and public reaction, orchestrated by the employers, which resulted in the passage of the antilabor Taft-Hartley Act of 1947, public sector workers in the late 1970s and 1980s suffered from a right wing-led backlash portraying them as greedy, lazy bureaucrats wasting the public's hard-earned tax dollars. First crystallized in this guise in Proposition 13, antipublic worker sentiment became a potent political idea and an obstacle to funding for adequate public services as well as to the ongoing quest for economic justice for public sector workers.

Comparable worth and affirmative action were casualties within this broader political assault on unions, government, public employees, and taxes. Although no one knew it yet, these events signaled the beginning of the end of the post–World War II economic boom, of the diversified, industrial economy of California, and the social contract between labor and capital that had made the California Dream of upward mobility and "middle class" status a reality for so many working families.

PART VI

Reinventing California Labor

29

The Decline of Manufacturing Unionism

ECONOMIST JOSEPH SCHUMPETER coined a phrase—"creative destruction"—to describe the transformation of society caused by capitalist forces in the transition from one stage to another of the system. Looking at what happened to working-class communities in California as industrial production was sent offshore, at first a slow leak in the 1960s and then broadening into a torrent of lost jobs throughout the 1970s and 1980s, we might ask, Is it more accurate to call what happened to workers, their jobs, their families, and our society's values "creative destruction" or just plain "destruction"?

In 1956 white collar jobs surpassed the number of blue collar jobs for the first time in U.S. history. Production workers began to decline as a proportion of manufacturing employment. But due to advancing automation, worker productivity continued to increase. The country's industrial supremacy remained unchallenged, and California was one of the main reasons why. The state ranked second in manufacturing in the early 1960s, with a diverse industrial sector centered in automobile production, petroleum products, garments, and the cluster of industries known collectively as "aerospace," which included electronics, data processing, and missiles. Without even counting some of its largest industries—agriculture, tourism, and entertainment—California was a prosperous state, based on its manufacturing prowess alone.

A *Business Week* magazine survey in 1963 found that "California is the first choice of executives for new plant sites, and that one of the top criteria in the choice was reasonableness of taxes"; at the time, corporate and banking taxes represented 13 percent of state revenues. A state Economic Development Agency publication aimed at attracting business investment noted,

The California business taxpayer invests among other things in an educational system that is the envy of the nation, in an unexcelled network of toll-free highways, in outstanding law enforcement and other public services, all of which return tangible dividends to him and his company. Experience has shown that businessmen in increasing numbers see the wisdom of making this kind of investment.

Such praise wasn't simply traditional California business boosterism. Thanks to its well-financed public education system, the state boasted the highest rates of high school and college graduation in the country. Even if one didn't graduate high school, manufacturing jobs in the Golden State's robust economy ensured you could work, and the unions in that sector (manufacturing union density hovered around 40 percent into the 1970s) enabled factory workers to earn a decent living.

Then creative destruction set in. It took just over two decades. From six automobile plants employing 25,000 workers in 1978, only one remained in California a few years later. Spinoff manufacturing like tire, glass, and auto parts supply disappeared, along with tens of thousands more jobs. In one industry after another, companies uprooted themselves and set sail for the paradise of super-profits offshore.

In addition to the havoc inflicted on working-class communities due to job losses and erosion of the local tax base, what these changes also severely damaged was collective bargaining as the model for resolution of labor-capital conflict. For fifty years differences between workers and managers in the most important part of the economy had been more or less peacefully settled by rules of the game put in place by the National Labor Relations Act. With industrial unions decimated, employers were emboldened to restore their absolute rule over the workplace. And they didn't stop with manufacturing.

CALIFORNIA LABOR'S GENERATION GAP

Children of the post–World War II period grew up in an affluent society and became the most educated generation in human history. Although this was precisely what their parents wanted for them, their experience differed greatly from parents who had grown up in the Great Depression and fought proudly in World War II. Reflected through the mass media in simplistic caricatures, the clash of viewpoints appeared mostly as opposing choices of clothing and hairstyles, music, and recreational drugs but also surfaced in changing political attitudes toward race relations and U.S. foreign policy. The so-called generation gap played out within the labor movement as well.

Tom Rankin put that generational difference simply: "We were antiwar." The younger leaders coming up—especially within public sector unions—had no difficulty distinguishing the Vietnam War from World War II. The national leaders of most unions either hawkishly supported the Vietnam War, like AFL-CIO president George Meany, or kept their opposition quiet throughout the 1960s, like Autoworkers leader Walter Reuther. UAW West Coast regional director Paul Schrade, however, spoke at an antiwar rally in San Francisco's Kezar stadium in 1967, along with Coretta Scott King. By 1969 the Alameda County Central Labor Council became the first AFL-CIO body to pass a resolution against the war, amid growing antiwar sentiments in the ranks of its affiliated unions.

Opposition to the war was nurtured by the analysis, tactics, and moral fervor developed in the first half of the decade within the civil rights movement, which had a major generational impact on college campuses. Once the idea that a systemic injustice—racial prejudice—was woven throughout American society took hold, upending McCarthy-era patriotic certainties, students and college-educated workers could readily see similar patterns in other areas of society and culture. The war became one of those visible patterns; so did employment practices.

Uneven application of the 1959 Fair Employment Practices Act, employer resistance, and a reservoir of coworker prejudice meant that racist hiring and promotion still ruled many California workplaces. As the movement to integrate America picked up steam in the early 1960s, national attention focused on struggles over access to southern public and commercial spaces and the rights of citizenship. However, large militant protests also disrupted business as usual for northern discriminatory employers who failed to comply with fair employment laws.

In San Francisco in winter and spring 1964 activists launched high-profile civil disobedience actions against racist employers, including the swank Sheraton Palace Hotel and car dealerships along Auto Row. Nonviolent tactics included picketing, massing inside the hotel and car showroom lobbies, and sit-ins resulting in hundreds of arrests.

The problem at the Sheraton Palace was typical: only nineteen African Americans employed, in low-wage jobs, out of a workforce of 550. These protests drew members of civil rights and religious organizations, and unions (although fewer than in the fair employment practices coalition of the 1950s) but were driven and energized by the new student activism, and represented something like a passing of the generational torch. The campaigns resulted in agreements with employers' associations to hire more minority workers.

The convergence of the civil rights and antiwar movements in the radicalism of the New Left mostly failed to translate into a sense of connection or common cause with the industrial workforce. Despite its analysis of "the system," including the proposition that racism and imperialist war were intrinsic aspects of capitalist society, much of the New Left in the 1960s didn't see unionized workers as part of the solution. Instead, neo-Marxist theoreticians like Herbert Marcuse portrayed the industrial working class as privileged, bought-off, and part of the problem.

However, there were some notable exceptions to this perception and the distancing of potential allies it represented; for instance, a number of the protestors arrested during the Auto Row and hotel campaigns were college and university students who happened to be children of ILWU members.

Also, a 1969 strike of the Oil, Chemical and Atomic Workers (OCAW) union at the Standard Oil refinery in Richmond drew hundreds of student supporters from San Francisco State College to their picket lines. OCAW members reciprocated, coming out to demonstrate in solidarity with the students and faculty who shut down the college for nearly five months, starting in November 1968. Bitterly divisive to the surrounding San Francisco community, marked by militant rhetoric and police violence, that campus strike sought to establish ethnic studies departments and broaden academic disciplines to include minority histories and other topics left out of the traditional curriculum. Despite the unity shown by students and unionized faculty, TV news reports seized on images of the university's conservative president, S. I. Hayakawa, in screaming matches with students, reinforcing the simplistic generational-split idea, while ignoring evidence of its opposite.

Nevertheless, in the waning years of the decade, generational differences did play out within industrial unions. As young workers steeped in the civil rights and antiwar movements were hired in steel mills and auto factories, new ideas and tactics percolated in union meetings. Legal challenges and collective bargaining language continued to address the need for fairer hiring and promotion practices. But militancy among younger workers of color and white radicals meant at least a rhetorical shift away from these staples of postwar unionism and traditional nonviolent tactics of the civil rights movement, and sometimes organizing and direct action as well. Such workplace cultural changes left some older progressive trade unionists bemused at the new generation's impatience and posturing, or alienated from it.

As with previous wars, veterans returning from Vietnam contributed to a mood of rank and file militancy in the early and mid 1970s. A strike wave followed the entry of these young, mostly working-class soldiers into the labor force. Many of the job actions were "wildcats" (without the official approval of union leadership). African American and Latino veterans played a large role in the industrial unrest, as they formed or were absorbed into opposition caucuses in unions like the Auto Workers and the Steelworkers, especially when the minority workers learned that despite affirmative laws and contracts, their path to better jobs was blocked by various hidden forms of discrimination.

In Bethlehem Steel in Vernon, workers of color had to file suit to overturn rules that kept seniority, and the ability to bid on better jobs, within departments, concentrating and limiting job opportunities. Those practices ended in 1965 with the creation of plant-wide seniority rules. In the South Gate General Motors plant, similar obstacles to fair promotion were vanquished by UAW Local 216, which bargained for the changes in contract negotiations.

The courage and savvy it took to wage complex battles such as these on multiple fronts at once were often hard won by the 1960s and 1970s generations of industrial workers. It would take all of that experience to deal with what was coming at them next.

THE CAMPAIGN TO KEEP GM VAN NUYS OPEN

When I first was laid off at Southgate I went to the local president and said, "What are we going to do about the plant closing?" and he said there was nothing we could do. So I left with my last paycheck in my hand and tears in my eyes. I wondered, is this a union?

KELLY JENCO, UAW LOCAL 645 ACTIVIST

The cars sold on San Francisco's Auto Row came from all over the country, including half a dozen factories in California. One of these was the General Motors (GM) plant in Van Nuys, which had opened to great fanfare in the San Fernando Valley in 1947. During inauguration ceremonies, the corporation told its enthusiastic audience of autoworkers and their families that the factory had a guaranteed lifespan of fifty years. A half century of prosperity! A half century of progress!

The first president of UAW Local 645 was John "Red" Melton, a World War II veteran. Melton was white, like the overwhelming majority of his members. Employer hiring practices were just part of the reason why. Few minority workers lived in the valley due to racist housing covenants, and few wanted to commute from where they lived in other parts of far-flung Los Angeles County.

But with demand for cars soaring by the early 1950s and a shortage of workers during the Korean War, the company began hiring Mexican Americans. Ten years after the plant opened about a third of the workers were Latino, and 5 percent were black. One Chicano hired in 1958 was Pete Beltran. By 1980 a substantial majority of workers in GM Van Nuys were Latino or African American, and Beltran was president of the local.

Along the way to reaching the local's highest office, Beltran ran for shop chairman, or chief steward, in 1967. It was a symbolic moment.

> I ran against the first president of the local, Red Melton. When I won, Red said, "What did I ever do to you Pete?" I said, "Nothing at all, Red; it's not personal. It's just that things move on sometimes."

Beltran's ascendance tracked the demographic changes in the local, which in this case caused hard feelings. But if the changing of the guard cast a light on differences—generational, racial—the great leveler was that all workers faced the same harsh industrial environment. Isaac Ayala described working conditions inside the sprawling, 2.5 million square foot plant.

> When I first began work at Van Nuys, the line went so fast that at the end of the day even a strong young man just wanted to go home to rest up for the next one. I once called my foreman and asked him if I could go to the bathroom. He told me, "Sure, if you can do it in your shoe while you're working."

Even in the 1980s, autoworker and former civil rights organizer Eric Mann could report that "the place is loud, as in LOUD, with the sound of assembly lines moving, air guns shooting thousands of screws per minute, people yelling and radios blaring. If you don't like noise you don't like working in an auto factory."

Autoworkers put up with the conditions because it allowed them to live the Fordist dream of purchasing the products they made and, thanks to the part of the picture neither foreseen nor desired by Henry Ford—the UAW—

workers could do even more: buy homes and live in a prosperous community. For minority workers especially, employment in unionized industries provided the financial ability to climb up from poor neighborhoods to "middle class" surroundings with single-family homes, better schools, and safe streets.

By the late 1970s all this began to change. Mighty General Motors, the largest corporation in the world, was facing the challenge of increased global competition, particularly from Japan's auto industry. By remaining blind to what the Japanese cars offered American consumers, GM watched its share of the U.S. car market shrink steadily. Its response, when it finally came, included three strategies to increase productivity and profits: stepping up automation; outsourcing production to the Third World; and introducing the team concept of labor-management cooperation, borrowed from Japan, to reduce industrial conflict.

In terms of automation, GM founded a robotics company in 1982, purchased software producer Electronic Data Systems (EDS) in 1984, and bought California-based aerospace corporation Hughes Aircraft for $5 billion in 1985, signaling its recognition that machines were going to play an increasingly central role on the assembly line and computer-related technologies would do the same under the hood. And GM would introduce automation its own way.

AUTOMATION ON THE EDGE OF THE FUTURE

A chapter from California collective bargaining history, circa 1960, could have offered GM and the UAW an alternative approach to greater productivity and profitability via automation. Manufacturers and shipowners pressured Harry Bridges and the ILWU throughout the 1950s to mechanize loading and unloading merchandise from ships onto West Coast docks. The dockworkers, including longshoremen, shipping clerks, and walking bosses, confident of their collective strength, had held back the clock, preserving work rules established following the maritime strikes of the 1930s.

Bridges articulated the members' fear of automation: "Machines when they came appeared as merciless monsters, more deadly by far than slack times, because jobs swallowed never came back, as one could hope would happen when slack times eased." The machines in this case were container cranes, already in operation in ports elsewhere in the world. Their introduction would make West Coast ports more competitive, but at the cost of jobs.

Debate among the members raged across the West Coast for two years before negotiations opened. The question boiled down to, "Do we want to stick with our present policy of guerilla resistance or do we want to attempt a more flexible policy in order to buy specific benefits in return?"

Union negotiators were sent into talks with a comprehensive list of objectives. They would authorize the introduction of new technologies in exchange for the Pacific Maritime Association (PMA) guaranteeing the current workforce continued employment, no compromises on the pace of work or health and safety, and crucially, the transfer of a reasonable share of the cost savings gained through the new machines to the workers, through a special mechanization and modernization fund paid for by the PMA. This savings transfer bought strengthened pensions, lifetime medical benefits, and life insurance policies, as well as a lump-sum payment for early retirement. The members were to be provided with thirty-five hours work per week, or paid a handsome minimum income of $111.65 ($3.19 per hour).

Older workers would be able to retire from the hard physical labor of the docks at an earlier age, due to incentives that made sense to them and to the employer. Higher retirement pensions would initially cost the PMA more but would make room for younger, less expensive workers.

Both parties agreed that the union hiring hall and multiple-employer, coast-wide bargaining remained firm commitments. By 1960, the Mechanization and Modernization Agreement had been submitted to the members, ratified, and signed.

The controversial results were debated for years. Everyone understood that containerization paved the way to a more rapid pace of mechanization and global trade, and to a smaller work force. The president of the employers association, Paul St. Sure, summed up the pragmatic philosophy supporting the deal: "Certainly, the agreement does not solve the overall problems of so-called automation and industrial unemployment. But it does represent an approach to solving the problems of our own industry and the men in the registered work force who look to it for a living." Bridges took a sharper look at some of the implications:

> The rub is that as machines become more efficient they become cheaper than people. Not until we change our own thinking, not until we put people first, or much higher, in our scale of values, and appraise the performance of our society by this measure more than any other, can we guarantee that modern technology will have been a boon to the American nation and not a blight.

To workers and union leaders in 1960, an important key to fulfilling the promise, instead of the threat, of an economy increasingly reliant on machines, was worker power, exercised through collective bargaining. As Bridges put it, "What of the future, then, of this mechanization agreement? Only time will tell; that is, time and the continuance of a strong united union."

GM'S WAY OR THE HIGHWAY

The future of automation had clearly arrived twenty years after the Mechanization and Modernization Agreement. Continuous technological change seemed a given, outside the reach of a labor movement playing defense. Like the ILWU, the UAW boasted militant origins; but the Autoworkers union hadn't sustained the deep traditions of rank and file democracy that the ILWU had. And unlike longshoremen, who occupied a key doorway in the distribution networks of the global economy, autoworkers labored in manufacturing, increasingly vulnerable to shifts in production from one place in the world to another.

Close to 11.5 million American workers were laid off due to plant closings and outsourcing between 1979 and 1984. In the midst of the worst economic downturn since the Great Depression, America's largest corporations saw the opportunity to retool how they did business. At GM, an internal management document leaked to the press in 1984 laid out a plan to further downsize its hourly workforce by 80,000 jobs within six years through a combination of outsourcing and automation.

In the Los Angeles industrial corridor southeast of downtown, 70,000 workers in various industries were removed from their jobs, on top of a regional deindustrialization that had started earlier. By 1982, five of the six California auto plants closed their doors. Along with them went auto parts suppliers, machine shops, steel fabrication facilities, rubber and tire production, and countless small businesses dependent on autoworkers' paychecks.

Profitability wasn't the issue: all but one of the state's car factories were making money. The plants were just not *as profitable* for the corporations as closing them and opening new ones in Mexico, Korea, or the Philippines would be. As GM Van Nuys became the last California auto assembly plant standing, some among its workforce resolved that if the corporation planned to close their workplace they wouldn't go quietly to the unemployment line.

In November 1982, GM Van Nuys management told workers that their plant was on a short list of factories around the country slated for possible closure. On the last day of the month, the entire evening shift was laid off—2,500 people, half the workforce of the plant. While temporary shift layoffs were not unknown, due to model changeovers or slumps in car sales, this one seemed especially ominous.

THE CAMPAIGN BEGINS

A few days later the local's Community Action Program Committee, working with Local 645 president Pete Beltran, called a meeting at the union hall across the street from the plant on Van Nuys Boulevard. The group became central to the fight-back effort that followed. It included former New Left students who had ditched the professional opportunities offered by their college educations for social justice work in the labor movement. One was Eric Mann, who later recorded these events in a book, *Taking on General Motors*.

Two hundred workers came to the meeting. They heard speakers from shuttered car factories and Dick Presto, a leader of a United Electrical Workers local who had helped steer a long but unsuccessful fight against the shutdown of a General Electric plant in nearby Ontario. Presto told them,

> You don't need a union to make concessions. If you want to give things away, just go to the company yourself; they'll be glad to take whatever you offer. But if you want to fight, you have to diversify your tactics—press conferences, church-based initiatives, demonstrations—so that the company is on the defensive.

Out of the day's discussions emerged two central ideas: to threaten GM with a consumer boycott if the company decided to close the factory; and to create a broad, community-based coalition, led by the union, to credibly wage that fight over whatever time it took. It was also clear that with more than 50 percent of the workforce black or Latino, outreach to the major institutions of those communities would be crucial to the campaign's success.

Equally important would be the ability of the union and its coalition partners to convince the public that the main corporate argument for plant closure—its "right" to pursue maximum profits any way it saw fit, at any cost to the surrounding community—was wrong. Instead, the union would have to make the case that corporations have a moral responsibility to their work-

FIGURE 42. Speakers at a May 1983 rally in front of the UAW Hall in Van Nuys included, from left to right: autoworker Eric Mann, coordinator of the Campaign to Keep GM Van Nuys Open; civil rights leader Jesse Jackson; Screen Actors Guild leader Ed Asner; and Pete Beltran, president, UAW Local 645. Courtesy of Eric Mann.

ers and the community, and so long as a plant remains profitable, it must honor its responsibility to stay.

The first major public action by the Campaign to Keep GM Van Nuys Open was a rally on March 1, 1983. Held in the middle of a weeklong down-pour, 700 people—mostly GM Van Nuys workers—showed up nonetheless. In keeping with the campaign's vision of an inclusive alliance, speakers included representatives from the area's African American churches and from a student Chicano group, Movimiento Estudiantil Chicano de Aztlán (MEChA), many of whose parents worked in the GM plant.

In May GM recalled the evening shift to work. Campaign activists worried that the long-term threat of closure and the need to maintain the campaign's momentum might be overshadowed by the relief workers felt at exchanging their unemployment checks for paychecks. But the next rally, held in mid-May, set that fear to rest.

More than a thousand people appeared, the majority this time from the community side of the coalition. The crowd marched once more through the nearby streets, led by Local 645 president Beltran arm in arm with Cesar Chavez, Assemblywoman Maxine Waters, and Los Angeles County Labor Federation leader Bill Robertson. Behind them streamed several hundred plant workers, laid-off steelworkers and autoworkers, UCLA students, San Pedro shipyard workers, ministers from south central Los Angeles, and families whose ability to feed and clothe themselves depended on the plant. All proclaimed their intent to boycott GM in the company's largest regional market in the country should the plant close.

Local 645 activists, encouraged by the support, continued to meet with community representatives to plan and organize. Through changes in union leadership, debates and faction fights within the local, and continuous statements by GM that no union threats would impact any decision it might reach, the campaign and its community coalition kept the issue in front of the public for years.

In early 1984 the campaign succeeded in getting GM president F. James McDonald to a meeting. Assemblywoman Waters, a steadfast ally of the campaign, attended as well. She had tried—and failed—to get a plant closures notice bill through the state legislature. In the meeting campaign activists pushed McDonald hard to commit to keeping the plant open indefinitely, or at least get a clear date out of him. He disclosed that GM Van Nuys would stay open at least two more years.

Following the meeting Waters remarked, "Well, isn't that interesting. When I propose a three-month advance notice bill in the legislature, my colleagues say it's too radical. But by organizing this coalition, we've won a two year advance notice." And beyond: in 1986 the company announced that it would close eleven U.S. plants. GM Van Nuys was not on the list.

With such successes, and the passage of time, some GM Van Nuys workers grew complacent—still supportive but less engaged in campaign activities. Heeding the advice of Dick Presto, the campaign leaders introduced new tactics to keep GM on its heels and to involve the members of Local 645. One was the production of *Tiger by the Tail*, directed by a sympathetic independent video producer, Michal Goldman, and narrated by Ed Asner. The videotape documented the campaign but also advocated on its behalf. The campaign used it in community screenings, union halls, and in the homes of supporters to inform the public and raise funds. While some TV station managers refused to show it, citing fear of losing GM advertising, the tape, which won several awards, proved useful in coalition building and generating hundreds of letters to GM pledging to boycott.

At the same time, a greater challenge to the campaign took shape, proposed by GM but soon embraced by the UAW's national leadership and by factional opponents within Local 645: the team concept. Imported from Japanese corporate management theory and practice, the idea was to "empower" workers by giving them a limited say in decisions on the shop floor in a cooperative approach to production. Highly controversial within union activist circles, the team concept tempted workers tired of working with a sword over their heads. As Eric Mann explained, "At the level of rhetoric, the idea of worker involvement appealed to many of the workers' deepest desires—greater control over their working environment, greater respect for their input into the productive process, and greater job security through higher quality products which facilitate greater competitiveness in the world market."

But there was a problem: by focusing workers on small changes in the work process, the team concept pointed attention away from larger corporate decisions to automate and outsource enormous numbers of jobs. And by emphasizing labor-management cooperation, the type of combativeness necessary for workers to resist these unilateral corporate decisions became stigmatized.

One example of what the team concept looked like was available to GM Van Nuys workers a few hundred miles north. After General Motors closed the Fremont plant in 1982, leaving 7,000 workers jobless, the corporation made a deal with Toyota to reopen the plant as a joint project, called New United Motors, or NUMMI, based on the Japanese management vision. After retooling with the latest assembly line technologies, the factory reopened in 1985—with 2,500 workers. Pete Beltran described what he saw there: "At NUMMI they sped up the line, added work to the jobs, and sped up the line again, to the point it reminds people of the sweatshop conditions that existed before the UAW."

In 1986, with fear of an imminent plant closure playing a large role, the members of Local 645 voted by a narrow margin to support moving toward a team concept. But within a year, new local elections saw the pendulum swing back to a more confrontational approach to management, as in many workers' minds, the team concept came to be seen as synonymous with company unionism.

If success meant keeping the plant running permanently, the Campaign to Keep GM Van Nuys Open failed. However, for ten years, a few thousand workers organized in a single union local held on to their jobs while the biggest corporation in the world tried to take them away. Antiunion presidents occupied the White House during that same period, and antiunion governors sat in Sacramento. The overwhelming majority of plant closings across the country occurred far more quickly than in Van Nuys, often without even a fight.

A decade of struggle gave GM Van Nuys workers ten years more of a decent paycheck and gave the people of California ten years more of corporate tax receipts to support schools and services. Because of the campaign, the members of UAW Local 645, in alliance with community organizations and sympathetic elected officials across Los Angeles, helped the corporation to almost keep a promise—a half century of prosperity!—made in 1947 when the plant opened, which otherwise the company would have broken long before.

SIMILAR STORY

The disappearance of auto manufacturing jobs from California in the late twentieth century was a story that could be told of many other industries that experienced similar catastrophic shrinkage.

Steel production facilities in Vernon, Fontana, and San Francisco downsized dramatically or closed their doors. The aerospace industry, California's largest manufacturing sector, accounted for close to 200,000 workers, or more than a fifth of all manufacturing jobs, in 1987. It celebrated the end of the Cold War in the early 1990s by jettisoning over a third of its employees. Unionized Los Angeles garment factories were dismantled and shipped off to Asia and Latin America—although the industry continued to grow in the city through the reestablishment of low-wage, nonunion sweatshops.

Even agriculture, tied to the geography of the land like no other business, saw large parts of its industrial infrastructure uprooted. In 1994 the Watsonville Green Giant packing plant moved to Mexico. By then, thousands of workers in a dozen plants had lost their jobs in a town that had processed nearly half the frozen foods of the United States only a few years before. A nineteen-month strike by Teamsters Local 912 cannery workers in the late 1980s couldn't stop the industry from doing as it pleased.

In 1980, 21 percent of national income share came from manufacturing. By 2005, it had declined to 12 percent. California's economy was reshaped in twenty-five years as businesses decided to move offshore, seeking higher profits through cheap labor and ineffective or nonexistent labor laws. Left behind were devastated rustbelt communities—not as obvious as in the northeast of the country, due to the sheer size of the Golden State's economy and its economic diversity—but still leaving giant holes where well-paying jobs once were and large numbers of displaced workers. The tax base of cities and counties across the state deteriorated as worker incomes slumped and corporate taxes disappeared, compounding the problem of how to fund local services in the wake of Proposition 13, precisely at the moment when they were most needed.

These transformations in the economic landscape affected all working people but took an especially high toll from women and minority industrial workers. Shifts in capital investment strategies yanked these workers' newfound progress toward the middle class out from under them. For the traditional white male working class, the loss of unionized manufacturing jobs created despair and the conditions for a sharpened sense of resentment toward the perceived gains of other workers, who, ironically, were losing those advances at the same time.

Such were the results of the "creative destruction" of California's unionized manufacturing sectors.

30

Justice for Janitors

ORGANIZING IMMIGRANT WORKERS

One industry, one contract, one union.

JUSTICE FOR JANITORS SLOGAN

AS UNION DENSITY DECLINED throughout the country in the 1980s, a few unions figured out how to move in the other direction. One of these, the Service Employees International Union (SEIU), increased its national membership by 50 percent in the decade, reaching the million-member mark by 1991. Its success came from organizing the unorganized as well as wholesale affiliation of other unions and employee associations.

Under the creative leadership of John Sweeney, elected national SEIU president in 1980, the organization boosted its national staff tenfold. It built on the pragmatic philosophy of earlier president George Hardy, which combined his belief in organizing with ongoing staff training. Sweeney maintained and extended Hardy's practice of hiring college-educated researchers, relying on them to compile employer data and industry analysis before and during campaigns. SEIU benefited from the United Farm Workers' decline at this time, scooping up many of its courageous and tactically seasoned former staff. Reminiscent in some ways of the CIO in its heyday, the SEIU culture was an unusual but successful mix of New Left progressive idealism and modern organizational management practices.

Yet all was not well in SEIU's multiple jurisdictions. A hybrid union of private sector locals concentrated in building services and health care, and various public employee classifications, during the Reagan years it bled members out of its original janitorial division in a number of locations, including Los Angeles.

Here, in the nation's second largest city, SEIU Local 399 represented five thousand janitors in large downtown office buildings in the late 1970s. By 1982 these workers made a respectable twelve dollars an hour, including health insurance and pension contributions, nearly triple the compensation for janitors in nonunion buildings. But from this peak, within just a few years, Local 399 lost more than half its janitors and failed to renegotiate its master agreements with International Service Systems (ISS) and American Building Maintenance (ABM), which controlled a quarter of the Los Angeles office building services labor market between them. Janitorial unionism seemed on the verge of extinction.

DETERIORATING CONDITIONS

Several developments conspired to drive Los Angeles janitors' wages and unionization rates down after 1983. The downtown Los Angeles skyline underwent a radical makeover. As the worst recession since the 1930s forced millions of workers out of their jobs, capital investment poured into a building frenzy. Office construction sent glittering new glass-faced towers soaring upwards forty and fifty floors at a time in the old downtown and along Wilshire Boulevard on the west side. (Construction work remained mostly union on these commercial projects; but construction business leaders took the opportunity offered by the recession to push the city's residential construction industry into the nonunion column). For Local 399 the good news should have been that the new corporate office centers, once built, needed cleaning.

But the union could no longer deal directly with the companies that owned these huge new buildings. The origins of the Building Service Employees International Union (BSEIU) trace back to the 1920s and 1930s in Chicago, New York, and San Francisco, when local capital owned local office buildings, and building owners hired their own workers. Organizing and representing these workers was a relatively straightforward process, especially after passage of the National Labor Relations Act. The union signed up the building's workers, called for a board-supervised election if the company resisted immediate union recognition, and then sat down to negotiate with the employer.

As early as the 1950s, national and even international corporations began to scoop up local commercial real estate companies. These large building owners found it more economical to run things from afar by remote control; they hired building service contractors to assemble and manage custodial and other maintenance functions rather than employ their own workers. By the 1970s this arrangement had become the norm in large office centers.

Local 399 adapted to the new system, and throughout the 1960s and 1970s its thousands of downtown office janitor members were covered by master agreements with the large building service contractors like ISS (international) and ABM (national). Smaller contractors outside these master agreements mostly went with the program.

Until, that is, Ronald Reagan fired 11,000 striking air traffic controllers in 1981. At that moment what had been implicit in deindustrialization became common knowledge: organized labor was no longer a desired partner, either in the public sector with government employers or with capital in the private economy. And antiunion employers had little need to fear government prosecution for labor law violations. As the president declared, "Government is not the solution to our problem; government is the problem." Labor law enforcement shrank. A previously modest-sized union-busting industry employing lawyers and consultants grew like weeds around the president's fertilizer.

In this atmosphere, a number of building service companies rethought past practices. Some offered lower prices to the building owners for their services, thanks to wage and benefit reductions with nonunion labor. Other, unionized contractors pursued an increasingly common practice invented in the construction industry called "double breasting": subsidiary companies, separate from corporate parents in name only, created simply to get out of collective bargaining agreements. The two largest contractors, ABM and ISS, went nonunion in Los Angeles by the late 1980s, despite operating under collective bargaining agreements in other cities. To keep its remaining contracts in downtown L.A., Local 399, now representing just 30 percent of the workforce, and shrinking fast, offered major wage and benefit concessions to the employers. Clearly a crisis was at hand.

The national SEIU couldn't do much, by itself, about the larger, structural problems faced by labor. But the difference between SEIU and other unions dealing with business attacks and declining unionization rates was simple: it analyzed the changes in the industries in which it represented workers and organized on the basis of addressing those changes.

IMMIGRANT WORKERS

One of the most important changes was the flood of immigrant labor from Mexico and Central America into Los Angeles. Although not a new story in

California, immigration from the south had waxed and waned in several cycles since the days of the Californios. In 1960, just 8 percent of southern California was foreign-born. By 1990, more than one-third of Los Angeles's residents came from outside the country. As building service contractors severed their relations with unions, they transformed the composition of their workforce as well.

African Americans comprised a third of southern California janitors, and half of Local 399's membership, in 1970. The big presence of blacks in the custodial workforce reflected historically restricted economic opportunities; but due to the union, the work meant decent compensation for steady employment as industrial job options disappeared. When conditions for building services slid downhill in the 1980s, black janitors made an exodus from downtown janitorial work.

The immigrant labor pool provided replacements and filled thousands more janitorial slots in the new office towers. Los Angeles became a major destination for Central American immigrants in the 1970s. The Central American population of Los Angeles more than tripled, to nearly 150,000. In the following decade refugees fleeing civil war in Guatemala and El Salvador quadrupled this immigrant influx. Most moved into the densely packed "Little Central America" Pico-Union area, a short bus ride from downtown.

The new arrivals went to work alongside Mexican Americans and Mexican immigrants, whose numbers had likewise increased over the years. Famously, more Mexicans called Los Angeles "home" than any place in the world outside Mexico City. By 1990 the number of office cleaning jobs had doubled in a decade; by far the largest proportion—more than 60 percent—belonged to Latino immigrants, with black employment down to one-eighth, and Anglos at 11 percent. The gender composition of the industry changed, too, due to deterioration of wages and conditions. More than half of the Central American janitors were women by 1980, and nearly half of the Mexican immigrant janitors by 1990.

For the building service contractors, their utopian vision for the workforce they offered to the building owners differed little from that of their earliest counterparts in 1850s Los Angeles, when Native American labor was sold and resold each Monday in an auction outside the city jail to local farmers for a dollar, or a bottle of *aguardiente,* for the week. The assumption of the latter-day straw bosses, as in today's Central Valley "factories in the fields," was that a largely undocumented immigrant workforce would put up no resistance to horrible pay and working conditions due to fears of deportation.

But it turned out that this sort of immigrant labor can be a two-edged sword. While some workers lived in fear of the arrival of *la migra,* others saw getting fired, and even deported, for organizing in the United States as a relatively minor problem compared to memories of death squad execution for similar activities in their country of origin. Like Jewish immigrants fleeing the failed 1905 Russian revolution, many Central American workers had experienced class conflict, understood that their own workplace power (or lack of it) rested on a union, and were ready to stand up for themselves given the opportunity.

IT CAME FROM DENVER

The earliest efforts by janitors to employ the militant tactics that came to be known as the Justice for Janitors campaign occurred in Denver, Colorado, in 1986. SEIU president John Sweeney spent three days at the beginning of the campaign talking with Denver janitors and observing the action, and he liked what he saw. SEIU national organizers and local members raised "enough hell in the downtown area that the industry caved." When this organizing model arrived in Los Angeles in 1988, it started by going after the nonunion side of a small, double-breasted company, Century Cleaning, which held a number of building cleaning contracts.

The goal in organizing Century was not a traditional union representation election overseen by the National Labor Relations board. The service contracting system made it too easy for a building owner to switch contractors if one went union. In the view of SEIU organizers, what was needed was a comprehensive campaign, targeting both owners and contractors. Building owners held the real power, since they hired the contractors who hired the building service workers. But NLRA rules shielded the building owners from direct responsibility to bargain with the contract companies' workers (since the contractors were the employers of record) and their union. The union's strategists knew that a stubborn contractor could be persuaded to unionize more easily if the building owners wanted that. The way to make that happen was through placing various forms of pressure on the building owners.

The Century Cleaning campaign allowed Local 399 to try out a variety of tactics that it would soon expand in a larger-scale encounter. These included one-on-one organizing of the workers in the buildings and with house calls;

bringing in California's OSHA (Occupational Safety and Health Administration) and Labor Department inspectors to assess health and safety as well as wage and hour violations in the buildings; and bringing the conflict into the streets with marches and demonstrations. This first effort also staged a moment of guerrilla theater, memorably captured a decade later in British director Ken Loach's film, *Bread and Roses,* when organizers and janitors publicly confronted the company's owner in a fancy restaurant. Some of Century's contracts changed hands to union companies.

In the next battle, the union took on Bradford Building Service, a larger, nonunion, double-breasted company owned by ABM. Janitors and their supporters hit the downtown streets with high-profile actions. Despite its president's hostility to unions, Bradford signed a master agreement with Local 399 in spring of 1989, the first in the city since 1983. This victory provided the launching pad for the effort to re-unionize ISS.

THE BATTLE OF CENTURY CITY

Century City, a cluster of high-rise buildings on the west side of Los Angeles near Beverly Hills, was not really a "city;" no one lived there. But plenty of people worked there at night, including 400 janitors, 250 of whom worked for ISS.

Beginning in the summer, the union mobilized the janitors in street protests outside the buildings, visible to the tenants. Some occupants of the buildings complained to building managers about the events; other expressed support for the janitors. Both responses made ISS uncomfortable, but not uncomfortable enough. The union continued to organize among the janitors but also created a coalition with other unions, community groups, and college students.

In May 1990 the workers voted to strike. Thanks to careful preparations, everyone understood that that meant ratcheting up activities. One organizer reported,

> We had daily actions, every morning we walked along the median strip with human billboards, traffic was really tied up. And on some days we had big actions. On the first big one, we stormed through every single building in Century City, every single one. We had a lot of community people, it was about three or four hundred people. We went marching through the buildings, chanting and banging on drums, saying, "What do we want?

Justice! When do we want it? Now!" Pretty simple, straightforward things. The LAPD called a citywide tactical alert that day. They just completely freaked out.

Not all the actions involved overt militancy, but many had a level of audaciousness that grabbed attention from the public as well as the building tenants. On June 4, National Secretaries Day, janitors passed out thousands of flowers to Century City clerical workers on their way in and out of work—an act of solidarity with other, mostly poorly compensated employees within the buildings.

Eleven days later four hundred janitors and community supporters marched peacefully from Beverly Hills to Century City. At the intersection of Olympic Boulevard and Century Park East, the demonstrators sat down, blocking traffic. More than a hundred Los Angeles police officers in riot gear attacked the protestors with clubs. According to a *Los Angeles Times* report, "several officers ignored calls from supervisors to stop charging the demonstrators."

Dozens of janitors and friends required medical treatment, including children and a pregnant janitor, Ana Veliz, who miscarried shortly afterward. Forty protesters were arrested. A Los Angeles police department spokesperson informed reporters that the police "reacted with quite an amount of restraint." (In 1993 a jury disagreed, awarding the injured demonstrators $2.35 million payable by the Los Angeles City Council, one of the largest settlements of its kind.)

Although SEIU organizers worried that the janitors would be intimidated, the opposite occurred. The members insisted on continuing to press ISS until they had a contract.

The entire police riot played out in front of television news cameras. Lead organizer Jono Shaffer can clearly be seen and heard arguing with the police for restraint before the carnage began. The footage outraged the public and rapidly circulated on videotape cassettes around the country and even internationally. Danish unions pressured homegrown ISS, headquartered in Denmark, to talk with SEIU in Los Angeles.

One viewer in New York was Gus Bevona, president of SEIU Local 32B-J, the largest SEIU local in the country. Bevona summoned the president of ISS, with whom his local had a citywide contract, to a meeting. He told the ISS official it was time to settle in Los Angeles, or else there would be a strike in New York. ISS signed the Los Angeles contract the same day.

FIGURE 43. A Justice for Janitors march on June 15, 1990, in Century City ended in an appalling and expensive display of police violence. Sarah Brown, photo. Courtesy of the Service Employees International Union.

The agreement won wage increases and was scheduled to expire in spring of 1991. But at that time, ISS and ABM's Bradford subsidiary agreed to terms under a new master contract, covering more than five thousand workers in Century City, downtown, and other locations in the sprawling city. It included further wage gains, and dental and prescription drug coverage. However, in recognition that greater competition with nonunion building service firms outside the main office centers drove down the price of labor, the agreement set up lower wage tiers for the non-Century City/downtown areas. Adjustment upward would have to wait until the union had extended its beachhead more broadly throughout the industry.

Despite such shortcomings, the Justice for Janitors campaign had much to show for its efforts. Combining mass mobilization in bold direct-action tactics with the serious investment in planning and staffing necessary for a long-term campaign, SEIU simultaneously demonstrated that *"sí se puede"* organizing was possible in the Reagan-Bush era and that immigrant workers in particular were ready to move.

Equally importantly, Justice for Janitors made a strong case that union-organizing strategies had to think outside the legal box. If the NLRA no longer worked the way it was supposed to, then it was time to go around the NLRA. Rather than focus on dead-end elections, the goal of an organizing campaign should be to create the conditions—legal, political, public opinion—in which a company would see that economic considerations were not the only ones involved in the decision about union representation. There can be more than one way to understand the word "costly," as the Justice for Janitors campaign was about to show high rollers in the computer industry.

JUSTICE FOR JANITORS AND THE NEW ECONOMY

Ground zero of the New Economy, as it was starting to be known in the 1990s, was Silicon (formerly Santa Clara) Valley. Its initial phase included manufacturing that supported computer and other digital products, much of it in aerospace. What made it hum was the convergence of public and private university research, cheap farmland convertible to other uses, vast amounts of venture capital, and a plentiful workforce divided between unskilled and semiskilled immigrant labor, on the one hand, and educated technicians, on the other.

In the valley's transition from industrial to digital, the hype grew fast. In the latest wrinkle on California's chronic gold rush mindset, everyone working in the valley was going to be rich soon—if not through personally inventing a new bit of hardware or software, then by sharing in the bonanza through working for a company that did. But as the New Economy grew, so did economic inequality.

The microelectronics-based workplaces were nearly entirely nonunion. Many of the professional, managerial, and technical occupations required relatively high levels of specialized education. In that higher-paid end of the go-go entrepreneurial culture, few felt the need for union representation, despite often spending ridiculously long hours in the worksites of Apple, Hewlett-Packard, or similar enterprises. This was only part of the workforce, however.

A few unions took stabs at organizing the valley's assembly workers, notably United Electrical Workers in a multiyear effort at game maker Atari. Confronted in supposedly "clean" production facilities with low pay and unseen but toxic chemicals, the effects of which, such as reproductive damage, were becoming obvious over time, workers were receptive to a union message focusing on health and safety. These efforts came to an end when the companies pulled up stakes and found cheaper workers in Asia.

The corporate media paid close attention to digital production and innovation, and celebrated the new desktop computers popping up like electronic mushrooms in workplaces and homes. But uncelebrated and mostly out of view were low-paid services surrounding the glamorous Silicon Valley computer culture. Among these were outsourced janitorial jobs.

APPLE'S SHINE

SEIU Local 1877, based in San Jose, faced similar changes in its industry as had Local 399; the employment structure of the building service industry shifted to contractors, and the workforce transitioned to Latino immigrants, throughout the 1980s. The local also fared poorly, losing members and suffering a series of trustees imposed by SEIU, who negotiated concession contracts for the shrinking membership.

Former United Farm Workers organizer Susan Sachen arrived as the organizing lead in 1987. Fresh from the Denver victory and its newly reestablished master agreement, she hired other UFW alumni who spoke Spanish and in 1988 began a campaign to limit concessions and sign a new contract with employers. Anger among the older members of the local, unhappy at the deterioration of their conditions, helped fuel the organizing. "We got yelled at in ten different languages when we started to organize," recalled Sachen later.

The local benefited from solidifying its ties with the South Bay Labor Council, eventually sharing offices. Through the council, an established political power in the area, Local 1877 built support from other unions, churches, and civil rights groups for the campaign. South Bay Labor Council political director Amy Dean, who later became the council's executive officer, facilitated the contacts.

In 1989 SEIU brought in Mike Garcia, who had followed Sachen through the Denver Justice for Janitors effort. Operating on the principle that industry-wide organizing needed an industry-wide union, Garcia folded the nearby Oakland, Contra Costa, Santa Clara, and San Mateo SEIU janitors locals under the 1877 umbrella. After losing a National Labor Relations Board election among janitors at a small building services contractor, the union decided

FIGURE 44. Apple Computer's public image came under pressure when janitors picketed its MacWorld Expo, gaining some high-profile publicity for the campaign to unionize Silicon Valley's cleaning contractors. Courtesy of the California Labor Federation, AFL-CIO.

its next campaign would bypass the NLRA process. It considered targeting Hewlett-Packard, whose janitors had asked Local 1877 for assistance; but the local decided to go after Apple first, since its cleaners in the company's headquarters in Cupertino all worked for one contractor, Shine Building Maintenance. This meant one less headache for organizing.

Apple's high media profile and "progressive" image, assets in marketing and sales, represented potential vulnerabilities for its defenses against union organizing. This became clear when janitors' protests at the 1991 MacWorld Expo in San Francisco, and at the annual Apple shareholders meeting a month later, drew unwelcome media stories about the company's labor practices.

Local 1877 expanded a community coalition, Cleaning Up Silicon Valley, from groups it had brought together to support its contract campaign a couple years earlier. In June 1991 the coalition held a public accountability session that acquainted local, state, and federal elected officials who attended with the problems faced daily by janitors. They found, through worker testimony and a research report prepared by the union, that low-wage work for a rich corporation fostered the creation of social problems in the broader community. Beyond their poor living and working conditions, the janitors' stories pointed in the direction of the high costs of public assistance programs and social services necessary to supplement their meager salaries.

The logic was clear. A union contract would mean that the highly profitable corporation employing these workers, through fair compensation, would shoulder the costs for them to live—not taxpayers in the surrounding community. More press coverage unfavorable to Apple emerged from the hearing. The message fit with an ongoing political conversation in San Jose, where a slow-growth coalition had taken power in city government precisely due to concerns arising from the consequences of an unregulated New Economy. It didn't help Apple's cause that its CEO, John Sculley, turned down an invitation to attend and present Apple's side of the story.

Feeling some heat, Shine agreed to talk with Local 1877 representatives, but preliminary negotiations went nowhere. So the local and its coalition continued to organize protests, press conferences, a boycott (of Apple computers at local schools by Latino families), and other public events. Apple eventually convinced a court to issue a restraining order against the union for these in-your-face tactics. Community organizing paid off here, however; the protests continued, but under the banner of the Cleaning Up Silicon Valley coalition.

The union upped the stakes in November 1991 as Apple and Shine got ready to renew their janitorial service contract. The coalition put together a "fast for justice" on the property of Apple corporate headquarters in Cupertino. Six janitors, led by Garcia, and joined by Dolores Huerta and other labor leaders for a day or two at a time, fasted for a week. When the union staged an event ending the fast, Cesar Chavez took part; he suggested a full-on boycott of Apple. (Ironically, after Chavez's death, Apple appropriated his image in a photo for an ad campaign for their products.)

No union resulted from the months of media pressure, but in a turn of events reminiscent of agricultural workers organizing in the Santa Clara and San Joaquin valleys in the 1930s, and before the UFW's appearance in the 1960s, Shine offered its janitors increases in pay and, for the first time, health benefits. The workers knew where these improvements had come from and continued to work with Local 1877 to win union recognition.

Over the next few months, the union, once more expanding its tactics, began to put in place a network of supporters to carry out Chavez's ambitious proposal: an international boycott of Apple products. Due to the credibility of this threat, as well as negative publicity arising from janitors bringing charges of sexual harassment against their Shine supervisors, the contractor finally came to the table in March 1992 and signed a collective bargaining agreement.

Later in the year, Hewlett-Packard agreed to a similar contract, not wanting to go through what had happened to Apple; within two years, a majority of Silicon Valley janitors were working under union conditions.

SACRAMENTO: SLOW MOTION REPLAY

Initial expectations in late 1994 were high among Local 1877 leadership that it could quickly replicate its Los Angeles and Silicon Valley victories in Sacramento. But the contractor it went up against, Somers Building Maintenance, employing more than a thousand janitors, proved a tough adversary.

In Los Angeles and San Jose SEIU could rely on solid connections with the local labor movement and progressive politicians to launch and sustain its campaigns. In Sacramento, the union faced a more conservative political context, one in which it had to build its local coalition from scratch. Eventually deploying the same array of tactics as in the earlier efforts, the struggle took four and a half years before ending in a union contract.

At the start, SEIU efforts to interest the Department of Labor, under the control of a conservative Republican administration, in the company's many wage and hour violations—failure to pay overtime, short pay for hours worked, employing children—went nowhere.

After a majority of Somers workers had signed cards and the union asked for recognition, instead Somers hired a notorious antiunion law firm, Littler, Mendelsohn, Fastiff and Tichy, which engaged in various delaying tactics. These included creation of a company union. A blatant violation of the NLRA prohibition, nonetheless it took a year for the NLRB to order the company to disband the "union," invalidate its "contract," and reimburse janitors for dues taken out of their paychecks.

Local 1877 built a coalition with other unions, local churches, and community organizations and began to unleash its now familiar repertoire of tactics: a public accountability hearing; demonstrations in front of buildings owned by clients of Somers that featured Latino community organizations and union members; and civil disobedience in summer 1997, when participants sat down on the K Street light rail tracks, eventuating in thirty arrests, including California Labor Federation secretary-treasurer Art Pulaski, his lobbyist, Bill Camp, and building trades leader Jim Murphy.

These activities drove the Democratic mayor of Sacramento, Joe Serna, who prided himself on his early UFW activism yet had done nothing to aid the campaign so far, to step forward to mediate the dispute. Soon, however, he announced, "The company wasn't ready to negotiate in good faith."

A march of thousands through downtown Sacramento, led by Arturo Rodriguez, who had succeeded Cesar Chavez as president of the UFW, drew upon the farmworker organizing legacy, as did a week-long fast in the newly rechristened Cesar Chavez Park. Finally, the Sacramento Justice for Janitors campaign, now in full flower, marched one hundred and fifty miles along Highway 80 in February 1998 to Hewlett-Packard's headquarters in Cupertino, much of the *peregrinacion* in a torrential rainstorm.

The march solidified support among the janitors' community and labor allies, and provided unwelcome publicity for a Hewlett Packard shareholders meeting occurring at the same time. Following protracted negotiations, Local 1877 and Somers signed a contract in March 1999.

SECRET OF THEIR SUCCESS

Local 1877 faced, in Apple, Hewlett-Packard, Oracle, and the other digital giants, completely nonunion global corporations, companies that had come into existence during the antilabor Reagan era. But what initially seemed an advantage to the companies—a protective layer of hip market culture surrounding the new technologies, their industry and products—hid a vulnerability to image problems soon exploited by the union. Combined with a mobilized and militant immigrant workforce and a supportive coalition of labor, political, and community allies, adverse publicity forced these new economic goliaths to push their building service contractors to the table, where they conceded union recognition and better compensation to their workers.

In the middle of the Sacramento campaign, SEIU consolidated Local 1877 into a statewide structure. The move reflected the traditional union understanding that concentrated power of the employers had to be matched with concentrated worker power. It created an efficient platform, similar to the longshore caucus of the ILWU, capable of mobilizing member support from around the state for local actions and negotiations, with the entire repertoire of research, legal filings, direct action, public embarrassment for bad employers, and political connections.

By the early twenty-first century, the Justice for Janitors campaign had reestablished a solid foothold in an industry difficult to organize. Despite all the obstacles, it had organized twenty thousand janitors, providing them with a collective vehicle for their advancement.

And SEIU and Justice for Janitors were not completely alone in organizing successes with California's immigrant workers. In the 1990s in Los Angeles, Maria Elena Durazo, a former staffer for the International Ladies' Garment Workers' Union, led strong hotel worker organizing drives with Hotel Employees and Restaurant Employees (HERE) Local 11 among the industry's multiethnic workforce. The United Brotherhood of Carpenters, which had lost control of residential drywalling to nonunion contractors in the 1980s, recovered some of that ground by supporting a rank and file-led, southern California-wide strike wave of three thousand Mexican immigrants, *los drywaleros,* in 1992.

Some explosions of militancy hit the newspapers, made a splash, did some good for workers, and receded, like a 1990 wildcat strike of eight hundred mostly Latino workers at American Racing Equipment, a Rancho Dominguez wheel manufacturer, and a port truckers' strike in 1996 of five thousand "independent contractors" at the Port of Los Angeles. The 1990 strike gained a union when the workers voted to affiliate with the International Association of Machinists. The truckers' strike collapsed without one.

Apart from the hostile political atmosphere of the 1980s and 1990s, immigrant workers lacked consistent union support and leadership. This was nothing new; unsteady union assistance has been a hallmark of immigrant worker organizing in California from at least the time of the Oxnard sugar beet workers strike onward. As yet another instance, a multiunion effort to organize the Alameda Corridor—a swath of light industrial enterprises employing hundreds of thousands of mostly immigrant, mostly nonunion workers stretching from downtown to the L.A. harbor—began with hoopla and promise. But within a few years, the Los Angeles Manufacturing Action Project crashed and burned when its sole remaining union, the Teamsters, went through a change in national leadership and abandoned the campaign.

Something closer to that steadying influence was provided by Miguel Contreras, another former Chavista and organizer for HERE sent to Los Angeles in the late 1980s. Elected head of the Los Angeles County Federation of Labor in 1996, Contreras reshaped the political scene in the former "scabbiest city on earth" through union-led registration drives among immigrant voters. Under his leadership, Los Angeles became one of the most successful examples of political power exercised by a strong labor movement, in large part because its workplace organizing insisted on militant direct action at the center of its tactics. Contreras helped steer the national AFL-CIO in its transition toward fully embracing immigrant labor's cause as its own.

As unions shrank in the late twentieth century, imaginative new collective strategies for helping workers emerged. Charting different paths to immigrant organizing, activists utilizing alternative forms of worker resistance were nonetheless aware of and influenced by the ideas and historic successes of Justice for Janitors. And for good reason. When janitorial unionism in California seemed mired in the general decline of labor in the 1980s, immigrant workers somehow turned things around.

The simple equation behind the success of the Justice for Janitors campaign is that SEIU wanted to organize, and the new immigrant workforce, carrying militant labor and other politically progressive traditions from their countries of origin, wanted to be organized. This segment of the new working poor—a growing portion of the population as economic inequality increased following the Reagan years—comprised people who labored as hard and as well as they could but saw no ladder up from poverty to the receding horizon of the California Dream. In that way they resembled native-born workers facing the same forces.

The precise difference between the janitors of Local 1877 and other low-wage workers is that they organized. As a result, instead of pulling down the low end of the economic structure in a race to the bottom of the global economy, they tugged it, even if only slightly, upwards.

31

Teachers, Nurses, and Firefighters

THE ALLIANCE FOR A BETTER CALIFORNIA

CALIFORNIA TURNED 150 YEARS OLD as it entered the twenty-first century. The legendary land of golden opportunity continued to beckon hopeful workers and entrepreneurs to its sunny shores. Its boosters projected the same images—sparkling beaches, towering redwoods, agricultural cornucopia, Hollywood—that had always dazzled people dwelling in less favored realms. The rise of Silicon Valley contributed the latest gold rush to the list. But disrupting the traditional California celebration narrative were unhappy new developments in the state's educational system, legislature, and once-spectacular job-creation machine.

Formerly the pride of California, public education had struggled for decades with defunding, due to Proposition 13's limits on property taxes and the supermajority two-thirds vote straitjacket it imposed on raising taxes through the legislature and in local ballot measures. Despite the stated intent of Prop 13 to protect homeowners, their overall share of property taxes within state revenues increased, as large commercial property owners, kept by the law at below-market tax rates, paid a smaller proportion, essentially robbing the state of revenue.

Five years into the new century, California had fallen to forty-eighth among the states in per-student funding. It ranked dead last in teacher-student ratios, and in librarians, nurses, and counselors per student. The once free public higher education system, serving nearly three million Californians, and the crown jewel of the state's economic mobility escalator, filled the gap between its expenses and reduced state revenues by increasing fees on students and hiring cheaper, part-time faculty without benefits to replace full-time professors.

Other state-funded services—public safety, parks and recreation, transportation, public health—likewise suffered budget cuts. The fabric of daily life for millions of low-income Californians frayed and grew more difficult.

New jobs generated in the private sector were split between well-paid professional-managerial work requiring (harder to get) college degrees—many demanding postgraduate education—and a far larger array of jobs in service occupations, increasingly part-time, that paid poorly. Employment supporting a home-owning working class was increasingly held by older workers, and evaporating as they retired.

By 2005, California's top 1 percent of income earners pulled in 23 percent of the state's total income, doubling its take from a decade before, and nearly triple its share a quarter century earlier. At 9.3 percent, the state's highest marginal income tax rate was far below its World War II peak of 15 percent. Any proposals that the new plutocracy might help solve the state's growing budget and employment problems with a return to higher tax rates were swiftly squelched by its representatives in the state legislature.

That year movie star-turned-governor Arnold Schwarzenegger called a special state election, setting in motion, with three ballot measures, an assault on public sector unions. Schwarzenegger's action provided a clear answer to the central financial question facing California's elected officials, Does the state pay for education and services by asking those with the most wealth to contribute a larger portion of their income, or does it downsize the public sector and thereby shrink the California Dream for everyone else?

To defend against Schwarzenegger's ballot measures, California labor produced a grassroots mobilization of union members and community supporters, welded to a positive public image campaign centering on a secular holy trinity of admired public servants: teachers, nurses, and firefighters. In the process, unions shone a light on Schwarzenegger and his wealthy base, revealing them not simply as the antagonists of the trinity but of the public interest as well. The battle, and this stark depiction of contending forces, had been brewing for years.

THE CHRONIC FISCAL CRISIS OF CALIFORNIA

Jack Henning stepped up to the microphone in front of the capitol on April 3, 1991, after his introduction by Willie Brown, speaker of the state assembly, who was serving as emcee of the rally. The crowd of ten thousand greeted him with polite applause. Although Henning had led the California Labor Federation for more than twenty years, other speakers that day were better known to the teachers, students, parents, and trade union members standing before him.

But by the time he finished his short speech, calling on the Republican governor and Democratic legislature to solve the state budget crisis caused by the economic recession (a staggering $14 billion deficit out of a $56 billion total budget) by raising taxes on the rich and corporations, the cheers were as loud as they had been for Cesar Chavez and Jesse Jackson.

When Henning had been elected by the state's unions for the first time to lead the federation, in 1970, taxes didn't have to be raised to support schools and services; the federal top marginal rate was more than 70 percent on high-income earners and the state corporate tax rate, while officially just 7 percent, was real, as yet unriddled by massive loopholes that later brought its effective rate down below 5 percent. And the state's strong industrial base provided a large proportion of the public budget through local property taxes on corporations and their unionized workers' homes.

Henning's leadership of the state's labor movement spanned a quarter century. He helped organize triumphs for working people such as the establishment of the state's Occupational Safety and Health Administration and passage of collective bargaining laws for farmworkers and public employees. He served as a University of California regent, leading the charge to divest UC's financial holdings from the apartheid regime in South Africa, and never swerved from his work building strong connections between labor and civil rights organizations.

But Henning also watched helplessly as the California and world economies changed. His federation failed to persuade the state legislature to pass laws with teeth addressing plant closures. As industrial corporations shifted investments overseas, the auto, steel, rubber, and similar jobs—once occupations well-represented at state AFL-CIO conventions—disappeared.

Outsourcing industrial jobs served a dual purpose for the corporations and their rich shareholders. It created greater profits through cheap overseas labor, and it weakened the unions at the center of the industrial sector of the economy. Those unions not only defended their members' workplace rights and share of the profits from what they produced. In the political arena, they stood watch over the government programs that redistributed excess private wealth to working people and the poor. In these ways, unions, between

World War II and 1980, barred the return of severe economic inequality that the country had seen before the rise of the industrial unions in the 1930s.

By the beginning of the twenty-first century, the percentage of union members in the state's workforce had shrunk from more than 40 percent at its peak before 1960 to just over 17 percent. With weakened unions, lower property tax rates, reduced revenues from corporations, and the resulting squeeze on the ability of state government to fund public education and services, a chronic fiscal crisis gripped California. Working people were hammered from two directions: by deteriorating job quality and prospects and by an inability to address social problems through government intervention.

Government itself seemed to be stuck in permanent gridlock, due to the legislature's two-thirds vote requirement to pass any tax as well as to pass the annual state budget—a double-jeopardy situation unique to California among the states. The Republican legislative caucus hovered just over one-third, refusing to move any legislative agenda except to say no to solutions to any problems that involved increased taxes.

ARNOLD AND THE "GRAY DAVIS CAR TAX"

Into this picture rode movie star Arnold Schwarzenegger in 2003. His campaign for governor, playing out in parallel to a recall of the Democratic governor Gray Davis, cobbled together a generic populist anger, a pose of nonpartisan moderation, a vague call for state budget reform, and a no-new-taxes pledge, all without articulating—for good reason—any policies reflecting this unworkable mix beyond one: repeal of what Schwarzenegger, echoing a Republican mantra, called the "Gray Davis car tax" (vehicle license fee, or VLF).

In 2002, tax receipts had fallen precipitously as the economy went into recession. The burst of the dot-com bubble, decline of the stock market, rate gouging by energy corporations (later found to be illegal), and reductions in state tax rates all combined to bring drastically lower revenues and a massive budget deficit to California.

The Democratic governor, Gray Davis, proved unable to clearly lay this problem out for the public. When his Republican predecessor Pete Wilson faced a similar deficit he had combined program cuts with temporary revenue increases—including the original version of the vehicle license fee (VLF) jump plus bumps in upper-bracket income and sales taxes—to solve the problem. Jack Henning's call to tax the rich at the 1991 rally on the state capitol steps (or at least the idea) had actually been heeded by Wilson—the last time a major California Republican politician took such an approach to address the state's problems.

Davis reinstated Wilson's regressive VLF, which had expired (technically not a tax because it only required a simple majority vote), but he couldn't bring himself to retax the rich and generate enough revenue to narrow the budget deficit. Nonetheless, he faced a concerted right-wing media assault. Day in and day out, the Republicans, sniffing blood in the water, were on message: the state's citizens were suffering because a tax-and-spend Democratic governor had imposed the horrific Gray Davis car tax on their already overburdened shoulders.

Davis inexplicably failed to communicate that this was a Republican governor's car tax. Without a progressive tax on the rich or corporations to provide political counterweight, the Gray Davis car tax became the lightning rod of the 2003 recall campaign. And it meant that Schwarzenegger, in keeping his campaign promise, blew an additional four billion dollar hole in the already ragged body of the state budget (total budget: $80 billion; budget deficit before rescinding the VLF: $10 billion) the day he took office.

The numbers didn't add up, and couldn't. The state's education unions agreed to help out in 2004 by taking an IOU from the governor for $2 billion transferred from the public education portion of the budget to other obligations, on the promise of repayment the following year. But this promise the governor didn't keep. Worse, despite public evidence to the contrary, he claimed he never promised to repay the money he borrowed from education.

Then, dropping all pretense to moderate, independent politics, Schwarzenegger embraced a hard-line conservative agenda, calling a costly special election in an off year with ballot measures attacking public employee pensions, union political spending, and teacher employment rights, along with another one giving the governor the power to sideline the legislature with unilateral budget decisions.

Schwarzenegger accompanied his ballot strategy with harsh polemical attacks on teachers, nurses, and other public employees. He asserted that once past probation, "Teachers can never be fired" and "then all they have to do is just show up." This led, he said, to a "dance of the lemons," with school administrators forced to shuffle bad teachers from one school to another instead of firing them. When confronted with a small group of California Nurses Association (CNA) members picketing at a meeting of ten thousand women in Long Beach, he called them "special interests" and boasted they were angry at him because "I am always kicking their butts in Sacramento." He said, "I love firefighters—it's their unions that cause the problems."

For union activists, his intentions were clear: divert public attention from his budgetary incompetence by scapegoating public employees and unions; reshape the budget by shrinking government programs, including reneging on pension obligations; and destroy the ability of worker advocates to stand in his way or in the way of business interests. The question facing the unions boiled down to this: how to communicate to the electorate that a recently elected and still-popular governor was promoting policies on behalf of the real "special interests"—big business and the rich—while twisting words and their customary meanings into their opposites.

BAD BOSS

There's a saying in the labor movement: the best organizer is a bad boss. The governor's assault with Propositions 74, 75, and 76 and his inflammatory rhetoric unified the often fractious ranks of the California labor movement, in much the same way that William Knowland managed to in 1958 with Proposition 18, the "right-to-work" initiative. As in 1958, at the outset of the campaign things looked grim, with polling showing labor's side trailing. But both times, hubris and overreach led a wealthy conservative politician to underestimate his opponent; and both times, the attack on basic union rights provided the motivation for a united response, and ultimately a successful fight.

At the outset of this effort, union leaders were worried. If Proposition 74— "Put the Kids First"—passed, new teachers would have to serve a five-year probationary period rather than two years, during which time they would enjoy no employment rights, including the right to simply have a fair hearing on the cause of their dismissal.

Proposition 75 was framed by its backers as "paycheck protection." It would have required public employees to sign a written form every year if they wanted any of their dues to be used for union political activities. Its corporate and right-wing sponsors' motive was to place time-consuming bureaucratic burdens on public employees to deter their involvement in politics. A similar measure affecting all union members had been defeated in 1998.

Under Proposition 76, the "California Live Within Our Means" act, the governor could have declared a "fiscal emergency" and unilaterally cut funding for public services like education, health care, fire, and police without getting the approval of the legislature or anyone else.

One more initiative, which would have forced public employees into risky 401K plans instead of the more secure public employee pension systems, didn't make it out of the signature-gathering phase. Sloppily drafted, the measure was withdrawn when the widows of firefighters and police officers who had lost their lives in the line of duty began publicly testifying, to great effect in the media, that the measure would cut them off from their deceased husbands' pensions.

Perhaps at this point Schwarzenegger might have reassessed what he was getting into and saved some trouble for everyone. But he didn't.

THE ABCS: TEACHERS, NURSES, AND FIREFIGHTERS

To defend themselves the public sector unions formed the Alliance for a Better California (ABC). Its leading players were the California Teachers Association (CTA), the California Professional Firefighters (IATF), and the California Nurses Association (CNA). But the coalition included every major public employee union in the state.

The CNA in particular played a key role. Although the nurses' organization brought funding to the table, just as important for its role in the ABC was its militant "street heat" orientation. As soon as Schwarzenegger announced he would side with hospital corporations to roll back legislation signed by Gray Davis that had set hospital staffing ratios at what the nurses considered a safe level for patients—five patients to one registered nurse— nurses began to picket his public events. This was the issue over which the governor let loose his crude "kick their butts" remark.

The CNA had spent most of the twentieth century since its founding in 1903 as a professional association, but like the CTA made itself over as a union in the hothouse atmosphere of the 1960s and 1970s, supporting the right to strike beginning in 1966. In the 1980s and 1990s it fought through collective bargaining against the deskilling and automation of its members' work as nonprofit hospitals were taken over by health care corporations and the managed-care model. It became a strong advocate for quality patient care and a broader vision of what a health care system should look like, including supporting a badly outspent state ballot measure for a single payer health care system, Proposition 186, in 1994. By 2005, the CNA had gained its legislative

FIGURE 45. After attacking safe nurse-patient staffing ratios at the behest of hospital corporations, Governor Arnold Schwarzenegger couldn't appear in public without nurses picketing. Jaclyn Higgs, photo. Courtesy of the California Nurses Association.

goal of a safe nurse-patient staffing ratio law and was not about to give up the achievement easily when Schwarzenegger and hospital management groups put it in their crosshairs.

The ABC, although initially organized by public sector unions, nonetheless worked closely with their private sector counterparts through the California Labor Federation. Led since the retirement of Jack Henning by Art Pulaski, a former community organizer and officer of the San Mateo Labor Council, the federation provided state unions with political and legislative planning and coordination, and oversaw the same work locally through its network of two dozen central labor councils. Its participation signaled recognition by the private sector unions that although the principal target of the governor's initiatives was public employees and their unions, no union member would be safe if these measures passed.

The alliance's strategy had two basic components: a paid media "air war," with large television, radio, and billboard ad purchases featuring real teachers, nurses, and firefighters; and a grassroots mobilization fueling a complementary "ground war," which simultaneously activated union membership and educated the public about the issues through news coverage. The campaign provided images directly contradicting Schwarzenegger's dogged contention that his opponents were privileged "special interests."

Beginning in spring 2005, commuters along the heavily traveled Highway 80 corridor next to the Oakland Coliseum stadium could easily absorb the message on a giant CNA-sponsored billboard. The top half featured a photo of Patricia Gonzalez, a nurse at Children's Hospital, with the caption, "She heals." Below, an angry looking Schwarzenegger loomed over "He wheels and deals." The billboard stayed up for months, reaching hundreds of thousands of drivers.

But that billboard's impact was modest compared with the television ad featuring CTA member and 2004 Contra Costa County Teacher of the Year Liane Cismowski. A soft-spoken Concord high school teacher, registered Republican, and regular churchgoer, her straightforward lines resonated with millions of primetime viewers immediately: "Keeping your word. It's a cherished principle we teach our students. So how can Governor Schwarzenegger break his promise?"

Pushing these ideas up from below, and bolstering the paid advertising with documentary evidence, was a swelling number of protestors outside the governor's public events. The opportunities were many. Alongside the usual high-profile ribbon-cutting and policy announcement press conferences conducted by a governor, Schwarzenegger, disregarding his original campaign promise that he would never have to raise funds while in office because he was independently wealthy, presided over a series of big-ticket $5,000 a plate appearances, attended by conservative rich people, movie stars, and corporate executives.

These events at fancy clubs and hotels were attended by growing numbers of union members, too. Initially dozens, then hundreds, and ultimately thousands, alerted by phone and email trees, came out to demonstrate over a period of months. The publicity-loving former movie star began his residency in the governor's office with massive and uncritical media coverage, and seized every opportunity to appear in public in front of the cameras. Now he was arriving at his fundraisers through a back door, whisked through quickly before anyone could notice, and his ribbon-cutting ceremonies were not preceded by so much as a press release.

A PRICE FOR PRINCIPLE

A moment caught on news cameras captured the anger among members of the unions under attack by the governor, and also highlighted the price an individual can pay for acting on principle. Firefighter Bob D'Ausilio served as (unpaid) president of the International Association of Fire Fighters (IAFF) Local 1578 in Alhambra, in the San Gabriel Valley. Two weeks before the election D'Ausilio, a Republican, stood picketing with three other off-duty firefighters outside the governor's appearance at a town hall meeting in nearby Arcadia. He was furious that a few days previous, following a fire in Ventura County, exhausted firefighters in the base camp had been ordered to line up for the TV cameras as Schwarzenegger swooped in and shook their hands. Listening outside the town hall, D'Ausilio recalled, "I never in my life heard a politician trash cops and firefighters like that." Then Schwarzenegger emerged and walked toward them.

Amid the scrum of cameras, the governor attempted to shake D'Ausilio's hand. The firefighter put his hand behind his back and told Schwarzenegger to do something anatomically impossible. The photo appeared on the front page of the *Los Angeles Times* the next day. Retaliation was swift, the punishment severe. D'Ausilio soon found himself placed on paid administrative leave, and then out of a job. A string of lawsuits followed, but at fifty, his firefighting career was over.

The results night after night on the evening news were not good for Schwarzenegger. Asked about the demonstrators, the governor said, "They're all union officials and staff people." This was unconvincing when the comment was paired with images of and interviews with the demonstrators. Some, like D'Ausilio, were certainly union officers; the overwhelming majority—nurses, teachers, and firefighters out front—obviously were not. Schwarzenegger's harsh rhetoric looked increasingly inept as he attempted to paint his working-class opponents as "special interests" with one hand while accepting millions in corporate contributions with the other.

On November 8, Schwarzenegger's campaign to demonize public employees and their unions went down to solid defeat. The Alliance for a Better

FIGURE 46. Alhambra firefighter and International Association of Fire Fighters Local 1578 president Bob D'Ausilio refused to shake the hand of the governor who tried to replace firefighter pensions with a 401K. Kevork Djansezian, photo. Copyright Associated Press.

California had placed the human beings who put their lives on the line defending neighborhoods against crime and fires, teaching the state's children, and providing care for the ill, into the streets and onto the television screens of the electorate and sharply contrasted their interpretation of reality with the caricature produced by someone who had been revealed as a bully, liar, and hypocrite.

LESSONS OF ABC

The ABC campaign was a defensive victory, as most labor campaigns in the twenty-first century have been. But it opened up the possibility for going on offense, because with teachers, nurses, and firefighters at the front of the march, it reminded the public in a powerful, iconic way how important education, public health, and public safety programs are. It refreshed collective memory about the common good public employees support and gave public sector unions a platform to ask for restoring funding to programs everyone needs.

But if the 2005 election strategy suggested an emerging outline for a new working-class agenda, the opportunity quickly slipped away. Union activists were worn out and the unions' treasuries depleted after the ABC campaign. Schwarzenegger, contrite, tacked back to the center for reelection the following year. Union-led political change had to wait for another season.

32

Labor and the Community

RECLAIMING CALIFORNIA'S FUTURE

CALIFORNIA IS FAMOUSLY EARTHQUAKE COUNTRY. But the hidden stresses originating in tectonic plates, radiating upward to the surface of the Golden State, are not its only ones. Social and economic pressures—especially growing income and wealth inequality and changes in population demographics—resulted in significant shifts in the political landscape for working people at the beginning of the twenty-first century.

After the 2005 special election, labor began to reshape the statewide political conversation about government and taxes, long dominated by the conservative view embodied in Proposition 13. Unions worked with community coalitions to make the state budget process more democratic; beat an antilabor billionaire running for governor; engineered the defeat of yet another antiunion ballot measure, Proposition 32; and secured passage of a progressive "tax the rich" initiative, Proposition 30, to fund schools and services.

These successes depended on connecting the organizing experiences and resources of public sector workers with those of immigrant rights advocates, who had founded worker centers to meet immigrant community needs, and with other grassroots activist groups, all sharing a common set of political goals.

It also took an historic window of opportunity for the statewide efforts to pan out. The Great Recession sharply accelerated trends in economic inequality underway for thirty years. After Wall Street banks crashed the economy in 2008 with their speculative housing bubble, California housing prices declined by 45 percent, and the state lost more than a million jobs—nearly one in ten in the private sector. Three California cities—Stockton, Modesto, and Riverside—were among the ten hardest hit in the country, with massive numbers of homes "under water" (owing more to the bank than the house is worth). By 2011 a quarter of California's population was living below the official federal poverty level.

Under such circumstances the traditionally optimistic California Dream narrative struggled to maintain its hold against popular anxieties about the future. The Occupy Wall Street movement, although short-lived, nonetheless played an important role in helping people who experienced the full force of the disaster to understand its origins and reorient themselves to the new normal.

These elements came together to create a community of interests in 2012 electoral coalitions. Such a community may not be as stable or long lasting as one in a neighborhood, workplace, or religion, and no doubt has less cohesion than a union itself does. But it offered proof that labor and its natural allies could find one another, shape something that registers on the political Richter scale, and might result in longer lasting collaborative efforts.

COALITIONS PUSH LOCAL WORKER ORDINANCES

Even before the Great Recession, the uneven impact of surging inequality could easily be seen across the landscape of the Golden State. On one hand, an emerging new gilded age in the late twentieth and early twenty-first centuries featured skyrocketing salaries and stock options for northern California billionaire titans of the tech industry such as Apple's Steve Jobs, Oracle's Larry Ellison, and Google founders Larry Page and Sergey Brin. Their mansions and privilege recalled the conspicuous consumption of the Big Four and the silver kings in pre-1906 quake San Francisco.

Trailing in their wake, the affluence of a throng of lesser software millionaires transformed formerly affordable neighborhoods in San Jose, San Francisco, and Oakland, jacking up house and apartment costs and pricing out workers and their families.

On the other hand, over the same period the average real income of the poorest fifth of California families fell by more than 5 percent. "Creative destruction" in the job market created an hourglass economy with growth concentrated in high-paying and low-wage jobs, and relatively few jobs generated in the middle. The predominance of poorly paying jobs in service and retail sectors resulted in a new subclass of full-time workers who made so little money they qualified for public assistance. More than half the families of fast food workers working forty hours a week received food stamps or qualified for MediCal or the earned-income tax credit.

With the state government blocked by supermajority rules from raising taxes to increase services to the working poor and the federal government reducing its budgets for local assistance, labor activists and community allies turned to local government for piecemeal action on behalf of low-wage workers and their families.

Across the state local coalition efforts led by unions established new floors for the lowest paid workers. In San Francisco, San Jose, Oakland, Los Angeles, San Diego, and in smaller municipalities, city councils and boards of supervisors agreed to help workers who, through no fault of their own, had lost the ability to provide for themselves and their families.

The most successful string of local efforts, beginning in the mid-1990s and sustained over time, achieved strong gains for workers in San Francisco, where inequalities were growing faster than in the rest of the state, which in turn were greater than in the nation as a whole.

San Francisco labor traditions, while diminished from their heyday, still provided a firm social justice perspective in the debates over how to address the problems of poverty amidst affluence. Low-wage workers and their advocates forged coalitions with an array of community allies and passed pioneering ordinances by exerting direct pressure on government officials and placing ballot measures before the voters.

As a result of the establishment of several new local labor laws over a dozen years, tens of thousands of San Francisco's workers benefited from protections against discrimination in employment (Equal Benefits for Domestic Partners, 1996), the ability to unionize hotels and restaurants on city properties without coercive employer resistance (1997), access to prevailing wages in various service occupations (1999), a citywide minimum wage indexed to inflation (2003), health benefits (2006), paid sick leave (2007), and better labor standards enforcement through a new city department—making the city practically a little Sweden in America.

Employer representatives, following in the footsteps of their predecessors in predicting calamity if such measures were to be adopted, instead found decreased employee turnover and greater productivity among such diverse occupations as food servers, airport security workers, and home health care providers. Dire forecasts of plunging employment due to these supposed "job killer" policies have likewise proven untrue; employment growth in the city is virtually identical with that of surrounding counties.

At the San Francisco Airport, before implementation of another new policy, the Quality Standards Program (QSP) in January 2000, educational and training requirements for the workers were left up to the employers. The turnover rate for screeners was high, and morale and customer service were poor. The QSP put in place living-wage provisions for screeners and baggage handlers and allowed for union organization.

In order to receive permits to do business in the airport, private contractors were required to hire applicants possessing at least a high school diploma and to maintain minimum worker-training standards. They also had to pay their workers a rate substantially above the minimum wage ($12.93 an hour by 2013) and provide them with twelve paid days off a year. Close to a third of the airport's 30,000 workers benefited from these new standards. Employer surveys found improvements in worker performance and retention, reduced absenteeism, and fewer disciplinary actions. According to airport director John Martin, "Airport safety is not well served when exhausted employees have to work two jobs just to make ends meet." The QSP, he said, "has been an overwhelming success."

Similar agreements raised wages and enforced higher workplace standards in the Oakland, San Jose, and Los Angeles airports, with substantial gains for workers and for the businesses where they spend their increased earnings.

In order to secure passage of these new laws, unions had to find allies in the community and come to agreement with their partners about their goals and how to achieve them. The coalitions were not the same each time. Although the San Francisco Labor Council was an important partner in nearly all of its city's efforts (and the San Mateo Labor Council in the airport QSP), a rotating cast of unions and community groups stepped forward to advocate for each new law. Once in place, enforcement of the laws required the continuing involvement of many organizations, as well as the creation of the Office of Labor Standards Enforcement in 2001.

This municipal department beefed up the local workplace watchdog role that federal and state labor agencies could no longer provide due to inadequate staffing levels. The California workforce grew by almost 50 percent between 1980 and 2000; over the same period the state's Department of Labor Standards Enforcement staff was actually *reduced* by 7 percent. Especially in immigrant communities, enforcement of the laws depended on ongoing education and outreach programs to inform low-wage workers of their rights and on the willingness of workers to report violations. This is where worker centers came into the picture.

In the 1980s, official labor organizations began to establish closer relationships with immigrant workers. These connections developed through workplace organizing and collective bargaining-related activities, like the Justice for Janitors campaign, but also in political campaigns and community activism. In 1989, after the U.S. Congress passed the Immigration Control and Reform Act, the Los Angeles County Federation of Labor set up the California Immigrant Workers Association (CIWA), with four regional centers, to provide undocumented workers assistance in applying for legal status under the law. The CIWA also funneled labor support to immigrant-led strikes.

Considering the rapidly growing numbers of immigrants in the low-wage workforce in southern California, such assistance made good sense for unions. But as organized labor's density and power declined, especially in private sector employment, where most immigrant workers were concentrated, unions had less ability to provide resources. CIWA closed its doors after four years.

Nonetheless, Los Angeles union leaders and members marched with the immigrant community, one hundred thousand strong, against Proposition 187, a xenophobic state ballot measure passed by voters during the recession of 1994 that would have denied public services to undocumented immigrants. It was later found illegal by the courts.

The anti-immigrant groundswell was not limited to political attacks. Conservative politicians at the national and state levels slashed workplace oversight programs, and emboldened employers took advantage of the enforcement vacuum in low-wage industries employing large numbers of undocumented immigrants with wage theft, an epidemic of health and safety violations, and threats to deport workers if they spoke up. One response by immigrant workers and their allies was the creation of "worker centers."

Worker centers serve many purposes. They provide organizing, legal assistance, and worker education to assist struggling immigrant workers who have nowhere else to turn. The centers fill the gap where unions should be, and have sometimes been in the past, for low-wage immigrant workers. They play various roles in support of worker rights, and are involved in a wide range of relationships (or not) with unions. Some are union-funded or housed in union halls. Others are foundation-funded or receive financial assistance from a combination of unions, foundations, and public budgets.

The Los Angeles Garment Worker Center was founded in 2001 independently of UNITE HERE (a union formed through a consolidation of shrinking garment unions and their merger with the hotel and restaurant union). The union had tried and failed to reorganize the local garment industry in the 1990s. Among other activities, the center, through a boycott of retail clothing store chain Forever 21 and publicity around it, forced the company to stop subjecting its workers to substandard working conditions and wage theft.

The Korean Immigrant Workers Association and the Pilipino Workers Center each started off in one community but over time embraced workers of other ethnic origins who labored alongside them. In all, as of 2013, there were some two hundred worker centers in the United States, most but not all in urban areas, with a large percentage in California.

Worker centers played a major role in organizing a national day of action for immigrant worker rights. On May 1, 2006, in cities throughout the country, immigrants, their families, and supporters in the community and labor movement came out to march against pending anti-immigrant legislation in Congress and for amnesty. Several hundred thousand people marched in San Francisco, and nearly a million in Los Angeles, an all-day human tidal wave, the largest demonstration among more than five million marchers across the country.

Out of this inspirational moment, surprising many with its enormous numbers, grew stronger connections between unions and worker centers. The National Day Laborer Organizing Network, with dozens of member worker centers across the country, emerged from groups originally independent of unions and at times hostile to unions; some unions, too, were antagonistic toward worker centers. But in summer 2006 these groups reached an agreement with the national AFL-CIO to work together.

Similarly, the CLEAN Carwash Campaign (Community Labor Environmental Action Network) was formed in a joint effort of worker centers and the United Steelworkers to represent immigrant workers in a largely unorganized industry in Los Angeles. It started with a focus on legal defense of worker rights, winning some important wage, health, and safety violation settlements. It evolved to embrace union organizing and collective bargaining. In 2011 CLEAN organized three carwashes and bargained first contracts with them, achieving raises, a guarantee of meal breaks, critical health and safety protections, and grievance procedures. Soon more than a dozen carwashes were brought under contract. In 2014, a state law proposed by CLEAN came into effect, ensuring that carwash owners are bonded.

FIGURE 47. Nearly a million people marched in Los Angeles on May 1, 2006 on behalf of immigrant rights, the largest of similar demonstrations across the country. David Bacon, photo.

In San Francisco, the Office of Labor Standards Enforcement collaborated with and provided modest amounts of funding to worker centers to reach into immigrant communities with education and training programs. These included the Chinese Progressive Association, La Raza Centro Legal, and the Filipino Community Center. An alliance of San Francisco worker centers toiled steadily to help raise public awareness about wage theft. The Chinese Progressive Association, with the Asian Law Caucus, won a $4 million settlement for workers at Yank Sing restaurants in 2014.

Worker centers have also been involved in raising political consciousness and increasing electoral activism. Mobilize the Immigrant Vote, a statewide coalition of worker centers and other community groups, concentrated from its founding in 2004 on voter education, voter registration, and Election Day turnout of immigrant voters.

UNIONS FIX THE BUDGET PROCESS

This organizing dynamism within the immigrant communities of California overlapped with the goals of the progressive unions that had forged the

Alliance for a Better California in 2005. Two of them, the California Federation of Teachers and United Domestic Workers/AFSCME, organized a march in spring 2010 through the Central Valley from Bakersfield to Sacramento in order to promote three ideas: restore the promise of public education, build a state and economy that work for all Californians, and levy fair taxes to fund California's future. Just six marchers walked every step (parole officer Irene Gonzalez; educators Jim Miller, David Lyle, Jenn Laskin, and Gavin Riley; and student Manny Ballesteros), but they were joined each day by anywhere from a handful to hundreds of friends.

Consciously modeled on the United Farm Workers' *peregrinaciones,* over forty-eight days the march gave its participants opportunities to talk up the ideas, meet with local labor and community activists, hold demonstrations (the last day, in Sacramento, with 10,000 supporters), and collect signatures for the Majority Vote Budget Act.

The act became Proposition 25, a ballot measure backed by the same public employee groups that had formed the Alliance for a Better California. It was designed to replace the two-thirds supermajority rule in the state legislature for passing a budget with a simple majority rule and thus help break the logjam in the capitol. It passed in November, which was also when former California governor Jerry Brown defeated a billionaire Republican candidate and returned to the top elected office in California. His opponent, Meg Whitman, a Silicon Valley business executive, ran on the same antilabor, antipublic employee platform that Schwarzenegger had promoted in 2005. During the campaign unions, led by the California Labor Federation, crafted a populist economic theme to support Brown, foreshadowing what was to occur in the state's general election two years later.

This populism was fueled by the Wall Street-induced crash of the economy in 2008. Although it took a couple of years, the November 2010 gubernatorial election served as an early indicator of the public's dawning awareness of the new economic inequality—an awareness that would soon take form as the "Occupy Wall Street" movement. The CNA, foreshadowing the guerilla theater tactics of Occupy, sent a nurse in a tiara-topped "Queen Meg" costume to rallies, and labor's campaign effectively tied Whitman to Wall Street greed.

It was not a difficult case to get across. Whitman spent more of her own money—$140 million—than any candidate for political office in the history of the United States. Her standing wasn't helped with Latino voters when she fired her children's nanny during the campaign after learning of her undocumented immigration status. In 2010 nearly one in five voters in California was Latino, and 70 percent of them voted for Jerry Brown.

This represented just the tip of the potential immigrant vote bloc. More than one-quarter of the state's population was now foreign-born. Nearly five million were naturalized citizens and eligible to vote.

LABOR AND THE OCCUPY MOVEMENT

The growth of economic inequality took on enormous momentum between the mid-1980s and 2010. Over three-quarters of the total income increase in California went into the pockets of the top 10 percent of taxpayers in this period. During the three years of "economic recovery" from the Great Recession, 2009 to 2012, the top 1 percent raked in 95 percent of the gains.

According to conservative free market economic theory, this should have "trickled down" into employment opportunities for workers as the "job creators" invested their new wealth. Instead, one out of twelve working Californians, or 1.3 million individuals, wanted to work full time, but could only find part-time jobs. Unemployment in late 2011 topped 12 percent, the second highest rate in the nation, and the highest in state history since the Great Depression.

The populace's consciousness of these problems, even if they were unaware of the precise numbers involved, rose throughout 2011, until the launch of the Occupy Wall Street movement over the summer sharply posed the disparities between the 1 percent and the 99 percent. At the same time, and equally important, the movement proposed a solution to economic inequality: take it back with direct action. (The Occupy movement was preceded in this insight by the response of workers in Midwestern states to escalating political attacks on union rights. The Tea Party wave of conservative statehouse victories in November 2010 and its consequent antiworker policies precipitated mass sit-ins and occupations of state capitols, beginning in Wisconsin in February 2011.)

One of the most spectacular instances of mass action arising out of the new awareness of inequality came on November 2, 2011. Occupy Oakland featured a huge encampment of tents in front of city hall, a block away from the downtown epicenter of the Oakland General Strike sixty-five years before. The tent city's occupants included homeless people, college students facing heavy debts, displaced and unemployed construction workers, and progressive activists of many stripes.

In its diversity, radicalism, large presence of contingent workers, and distrust of fixed leadership, Occupy Oakland probably more resembled the IWW, a hundred years later, than any movement that had come along in between. Extraordinary conversations between people who don't normally find themselves in the same discussion went on for days, weeks, and months. When the discussions turned to action, the Occupy movement took on the classic character of a "festival of the oppressed." The largest Occupy demonstrations in the country outside New York occurred in Oakland following a severe head injury dealt to an Iraq War vet by a police-lobbed tear gas canister during a protest.

This incident sparked a vote during the nightly Occupy meetings for a "general strike," to be held on November 2. Although the precise meaning of this term seemed to vary for different groups and individuals, leaders of the Alameda County Labor Council understood the historical implications and were especially aware of legal ramifications to their unions (fines and jail sentences) if they violated their contracts with employers to take a work holiday. One controversial aspect of the planning was set to occur toward the end of the day: a clause in the International Longshore and Warehouse Union's West Coast contract with shipping employers allowed members to leave the job if they believe their safety is threatened. If enough people showed up to demonstrate, the workers could invoke this contractual clause and thus shut down the port.

The labor council and the ILWU issued statements in the days leading up to November 2 supporting a "day of action" while distancing themselves from the port idea; the council called on unions to encourage members to participate (without using the word "strike") and to donate time and funding for a huge dinner in the square in front of city hall to feed the crowd. Signs in support of the 99 percent and condemning the 1 percent went up in the windows of businesses and residences. Behind the scenes, and each night in the plaza, planning moved forward with the participation of hundreds of students, retirees, and people who had lost their jobs and homes—in other words, workers left behind by the broken promise of the California Dream.

On November 2 the crowd began gathering before 8 A.M. in the plaza. By noon on a cloudless and unseasonably warm day, thousands were on hand, splitting into groups that fanned out and shut down banks in protest of their predatory housing lending practices, which had led to the 2008 crash and

Great Recession. Pedestrian 99 percenters took over the streets of downtown Oakland. As with the 1946 Oakland General Strike, few automobiles could move on the blockaded avenues between Lake Merritt and city hall.

The day stayed largely peaceful, although the corporate news media focused on small groups of anarchists causing some property damage. The big story should have been the sheer size of the crowds and their radical consciousness. Everywhere people held aloft "tax the rich" placards and union banners, chanted anticorporate slogans, and soapboxed speeches condemning Wall Street. Music and costumes abounded.

Adult-school educator Ana Turetsky summed up the wonder and optimism that many felt as the day unfolded: "I think people are getting really energized at the idea that we have power. I haven't seen that before. I haven't seen people coming up to strangers, talking to them, sharing ideas, and saying, 'We can do it, we can organize this, and we don't need a leader.'" It may not have been a general strike by traditional labor history standards, but "work holiday" described the scene well.

As the shadows grew long in the brilliant late autumn afternoon, the crowds swelled with people leaving work early to join the festivities. Over twenty thousand made their way across the overpass spanning the train yards to the docks and shut down the Port of Oakland. After walking the three miles back from the port to the plaza, they were greeted with a hot meal, courtesy of the labor council and its volunteer union members (firefighters the most prominent among them) staffing the impromptu but efficient outdoor "restaurant for the masses."

RECLAIMING CALIFORNIA'S FUTURE

When Jerry Brown took office in January 2011, he inherited from Arnold Schwarzenegger the largest state budget deficit ever to afflict California: $25 billion, or one-quarter of the entire budget. He proposed to solve the problem with what he called a "balanced" solution of deep program reductions and temporary, regressive tax increases. He believed he could convince the handful of Republicans necessary to get over the legislative two-thirds hurdle to pass such a budget. (Proposition 25 allowed him to pass a budget without Republican legislators' votes, but he still needed two-thirds for a tax increase.) He failed, leaving a cuts-only budget, and (to everyone but the shrinking

FIGURE 48. Occupy Oakland mobilized tens of thousands of people in November 2011 for a "day of action" to shut down the Port of Oakland on behalf of the 99 percent. Fred Glass, photo.

minority of Republicans in the legislature) the obvious need to raise some revenue.

Anticipating this, the California Federation of Teachers commissioned an opinion poll to test the waters on a state ballot measure. It found enormous support for a tax on the rich. It also discovered that large majorities now understood how unequal the economy had grown and accepted the idea that rich people and large corporations needed to pay a bigger share of taxes to shore up public education and services.

On the basis of the research, a group of unions began preparing a ballot measure. Unfortunately, although he had been shown the polling numbers, Governor Brown had his own idea about how to increase revenues, as did wealthy liberal lawyer Molly Munger and a group of Silicon Valley entrepreneurs, each of whom fielded their own proposals. Brown refused to join with CFT in a joint progressive tax effort; instead, exerting the behind-the-scenes power of his office, he peeled away the other unions, leaving CFT as the only labor organization within a coalition of community groups, called Reclaiming California's Future (RCF), to push for a "Millionaires Tax." A purely progressive permanent tax, the proposal calculated raising $6 billion by increasing the top marginal income tax brackets from 9.3 percent to 12.3 percent (on an income of $1 million per year) and to 14.3 percent (on $2 million per year).

Brown, attending to the polling numbers, redesigned his original regressive tax measure. It remained a temporary, five-year tax. But he reduced his sales tax proposal from a one cent bump to a more palatable half cent and converted his across-the-board income tax increase proposal to a progressive tax on individuals making $250,000 or more. Nonetheless the Millionaires Tax consistently outpolled Brown's measure and left the others in the dust.

A classic labor-community coalition, Reclaiming California's Future included, in addition to the CFT, the Alliance of Californians for Community Empowerment, a grassroots network pushing for banks to pay for the damage their lending policies had created in the housing bubble and Wall Street collapse; California Calls, a coalition of organizations in a dozen cities dedicated to engaging occasional voters, particularly immigrants and low-income people of color, more deeply in the political process; and the Courage Campaign, an online community that had formed to combat Proposition 8, an antigay marriage measure eventually overturned by the courts as unconstitutional.

As 2011 drew to a close, California's Occupy encampments faced harsh pressure from increasingly impatient city authorities, and winter weather made tent living less attractive. The physical Occupy presence faded away. But its activists, seeking a cause that related to its central idea of redressing inequality, latched onto the Millionaires Tax campaign. Their somewhat amorphous but highly visible presence, and their recent organizing experiences, injected the campaign with the trappings and spirit of their movement.

From December into March 2012, a high-stakes competition unfolded as the dueling ballot measure campaigns gathered signatures. The governor's allies told the media that if on Election Day the voters faced multiple tax measures, all would go down to defeat. The Millionaires Tax coalition, meanwhile, held at arm's length from its natural allies in the labor movement, built an impressive list of other endorsers (school boards, city councils, immigrant rights groups, college and university student organizations, progressive politicians) and kept collecting signatures. It also came out on top in five straight opinion polls sampling voter views on the dueling initiatives.

The game came to a head on Monday, March 5. Thousands of college students protesting fee hikes, skyrocketing student debt, and cuts to higher education paraded outside the governor's office. Their ranks stretched solidly for several blocks. It seemed like every other marcher carried a Millionaires Tax sign. The day was capped with an occupation by hundreds of students, and a sprinkling of workers, of the capitol rotunda for several hours.

Two days later the Millionaires Tax coalition held a Sacramento press conference, announcing that it had tested the idea that competing measures would result in their common ruin. A new statewide poll had found that the governor's and Molly Munger's ideas both sank well below 50 percent, while the Millionaires Tax remained above 60 percent.

At this point the governor sued for peace. Calling in CFT president Joshua Pechthalt, a Los Angeles high school history teacher, the governor offered a merger of the two initiatives. Negotiations dropped the sales tax to a quarter cent and boosted the additional tax on upper-income earners to three tiers of 1 percent, 2 percent, and 3 percent, which would bring more than $6 billion per year to the state. The governor, while refusing to make the tax on the wealthy permanent, agreed to extend it to seven years and reduce the sales tax to four years. The compromise—slightly less progressive than the Millionaires Tax due to the residual sales tax but more progressive than Brown's original measure—became Proposition 30.

LABOR'S CAMPAIGN

It immediately joined Proposition 32, an antiunion measure, as the marquee priority of the labor movement in the November election. As in 2005 (and 1998, and 1958), the plausible sounding but deceptive arguments of the antilabor forces initially led the public to support Proposition 32. It proposed that unions, as well as corporations, be prohibited from using payroll deductions to raise political action funds. Sounds even-handed. The catch? Virtually all unions utilize that method, and virtually no corporations do.

The California Labor Federation oversaw the labor movement's political operation, coordinating the activities of its member unions in the all-out effort to defeat Prop 32. After polling found the electorate had caught on to the ruse of Prop 32 by mid-October, unions switched most of their remaining funds and campaigning to support of Prop 30.

On Election Day, California's supposedly bulletproof antitax electorate passed the largest tax on the wealthy—both in terms of the percentage of the tax increase and the amount of revenue it would bring in—since World War II. Proposition 32 went down to defeat.

One key to the victories was strong, targeted outreach by labor and the RCF coalition to immigrant voters. Just one of the coalition's partners, Mobilize the Immigrant Vote, educated 50,000 immigrant voters about Prop 30 and Prop 32 and brought them to the polls. In all, the RCF coalition talked with two-thirds of a million voters, a large chunk of which were immigrants.

The synergy between the two ballot campaigns meant class themes emerged during the election battle more openly than usual. Considerable overlap existed between the opponents of Prop 30 and supporters of Prop 32, mostly wealthy business interests and right-wing antitax organizations. Governor Brown had worked hard to keep the Chamber of Commerce out of the Prop 30 opposition column; the business lobby demanded as their price for neutrality that Brown not "demonize the rich" with his tax campaign. The governor's insistence on maintaining a small sales tax as part of the revenue package—so that "everyone paying their fair share" literally meant *everyone,* not just the implied wealthy shirkers—originated in that agreement.

Spending tens of millions of dollars didn't work for the antitax rich this time. In fact, it backfired. By simultaneously promoting what became publicly understood as a deceitful campaign to prevent unions from engaging in politics, while opposing a progressive tax increase that would help the vast majority of Californians by stopping cuts to schools and services, wealthy conservatives did more to demonize themselves than anything the labor movement might have come up with.

LIMITED TOOLS

The electoral victories of 2012 for labor in California reflected a successful labor-community coalition effort based in the state's demographic changes, a post–Occupy Wall Street recognition in the electorate of the dire impact of growing economic inequality, and the focused unity of unions themselves due to the need to respond to the attack represented by Proposition 32.

Proposition 30 provided a lift to public education and services battered by years of underfunding and recession-fueled revenue losses. But the victories only partially stemmed the tide running against unions and the working class in California.

That's because the California labor movement doesn't exist in a national vacuum. Ultimately the lasting success of workers' organizations in the Golden State will depend on how much unions and allies in other states pay attention to and understand the factors that went into the 2012 California election results as a way out of austerity, and become inspired to launch similar efforts.

The tentative nature of the advances in 2012 on the left coast demonstrates the fragility of a workers' movement that relies mostly on political mobilization to wage its battles. Roots sunk in an electoral community naturally grow and recede with electoral seasons. They are no substitute for deep and lasting workplace organization. With just over 16 percent of California workers enrolled in unions, the state ranks among the highest densities (sixth) remaining in an era of decline, and its workplace foundation makes the electoral work possible.

Whether that foundation will erode to the levels common in other parts of the country, or provide a solid base from which to organize more broadly, remains to be seen.

AFTERWORD: A PLACE IN THE SUN

The last two surviving workers who built the Golden Gate Bridge in the 1930s passed away within a week of one another in spring 2012. Edward Ashoff, 97, hauled rivets in the towers as a nineteen-year-old. He became a toll collector after the bridge opened and rose to captain, the highest position in the Bridge District, overseeing road and toll operations, before retiring in 1976. Jack Balestreri, 95, a bridge cement worker at age seventeen, later played minor league baseball before joining one of the oldest unions in the Bay Area, Sheet Metal Workers Local 104, working in that trade for many years. Their deaths came a few weeks before the seventy-fifth anniversary of the bridge's opening.

Their work is likely to outlive them for a long time.

The bridge, symbolic doorway to the western United States, extends nearly two miles across the entrance to San Francisco Bay. Its road surface sits 220 feet above the swift-moving tidal waters of the Pacific Ocean where they meet the freshwater outflow of the Sacramento Delta. Twin Art Deco towers soar 75 stories toward the sky.

Every day, more than one hundred thousand people drive, walk, and bike across the Golden Gate Bridge. Each motor vehicle pays a toll to the Bridge District, a portion of which goes for maintenance of the structure, the rest subsidizing ferry and bus services between San Francisco and counties north of the bridge. The tolls bring in some $100 million per year.

A plaque on the south tower provides the opportunity for visitors to find out that until February 17, 1937, four years after construction of the bridge began, just one worker had been killed on the job, a remarkable safety record in an era when every million dollars worth of bridge building was accompanied by a death. The reader also learns that on that day ten workers fell to their death in one horrendous accident.

Today about two hundred people—mainly ironworkers and painters, together with smaller numbers of operating engineers, mechanics, electricians, and road

FIGURE 49. Electrician Fred Brusati helped build the Golden Gate Bridge. Leonard Muller, photo. Labor Archives and Research Center, San Francisco State University.

repair crews—maintain the bridge. They stem the forces of corrosion borne every moment on wind and fog from the saltwater below, eating away at the paint and the steel, and repair the roadbed from the pounding it takes from millions of vehicles.

A few miles from the bridge in San Francisco Bay, easily visible to traffic, is Angel Island, known as the "Ellis Island of the West." Before the bridge was completed in May 1937, hundreds of thousands of Asian immigrants had been detained in the island's immigration facility: processed, interrogated, and either allowed into the country or turned back to where they came from, starting in 1910. It was closed in 1940.

It was only during the final years of operation of the immigration center that its temporary inhabitants might have looked westward and beheld the graceful, deep orange structure sweeping dramatically from San Francisco to the landmass of northern California. By then the promise offered by the Golden Gate was already a century old.

Indeed, it didn't take building the bridge for this entrance to California to be understood as "golden." U.S. Army captain John C. Fremont named the strait between the San Francisco and Marin shorelines in 1846 when he observed presciently, "It is a golden gate to trade with the Orient." Three years later the Gold Rush indelibly reinforced his idea when, as one writer put it, "the world rushed in."

It is still rushing in. Today California is home to over ten million foreign-born residents, more than one-quarter of its population, the highest such figure in the country. Nearly 30 percent of the electorate are either naturalized citizens or children of immigrants, and more than a third of the state's workforce is immigrant labor. How is the California Dream working out for these millions of people?

For one thing, the actual site of immigration into California today does not closely resemble the Golden Gate Bridge or even Angel Island. Instead, it is 125 miles of borderland with Mexico, much of it fenced—and, especially for approximately two million undocumented Californians, considerably less picturesque.

More to the point, the answer is a moving target. For immigrants in the state less than a decade, poverty numbers are higher than in the general population, but that reality changes fairly quickly: immigrants in California for thirty years or more have lower levels of poverty than the rest of the state and a higher rate of homeownership.

Part of the picture has to do with whether the immigrant held a union card for at least a portion of those thirty years. Naturalized immigrants in the California workforce in 2013 were represented by unions at a higher rate than in the general population (18.7 percent vs. 16.9 percent). Since unionized workers' wage advantage over nonunion workers in comparable occupations averaged better than one-fifth higher, union membership clearly contributed to the overall economic advancement of first-generation immigrants.

These realities are not new. Western European immigrants to California in the nineteenth and early twentieth centuries provided the backbone for union organizing in the construction trades. Southern and eastern European as well as Mexican newcomers helped forge the great CIO manufacturing unions in the 1930s and 1940s. Mexicans, Filipinos, and southwestern U.S. migrants strived mightily to plant the flag of agricultural unionism in the fields during the same period and on into the 1970s. Today Central American and Asian immigrants fuel service sector organizing and staff worker centers devoted to various projects to improve the lives of newly arrived workers.

Arguably the most active labor council in the country fighting on behalf of immigrant workers in recent times has been the Los Angeles County Federation of Labor. The national AFL-CIO elevated its leader, Maria Elena Durazo, to a new national position, heading the federation's efforts to secure a full place for immigrant workers within American society. Said Durazo,

> We cannot have a prosperous nation and recreate the middle class as long as there is an underclass of 11 million people who do not have rights. By fixing this and getting them all on the road to citizenship, we address a huge issue that is the cause of enormous exploitation—of wage theft and other massive violations of labor laws.

Despite their best efforts, and some real successes, organizers have their work cut out for them. A clever animated graphic in *Inequality for All,* a 2013 documentary film starring economist Robert Reich, superimposes a graph showing the income share of the top 1 percent across the past one hundred years over the profile of the Golden Gate Bridge: the peaks of its two towers map the moments of greatest concentration of income in the hands of the wealthy, in 1928 and 2007—or just before the two worst stock market crashes and brutal economic recessions the country has experienced.

It is likely, although the full numbers are not yet in, that the income concentration of the 1 percent has now (2014) climbed back even higher than during the last peak, to more than 20 percent. That's because policies that enabled the most recent crash and recession essentially remain in place, reflecting the power imbalance between workers and capital.

West of the Golden Gate sprawls the world economy, emissaries of which pass in steady procession beneath the bridge: enormous container ships, whose cargoes are offloaded in Oakland. When Balestreri and Ashoff began working on the bridge, cargo ships came into San Francisco, and workers wrestled their loads down to the dock with cargo hooks and winches. Now ILWU members sit far above East Bay wharves in the cabs of giant white cranes resembling mechanical horses or drive front loaders that move containers around the docks, and right here we have the convergence of factors revealing the underlying dynamic for California workers today and for the foreseeable future: outsourcing and automation against skilled labor leveraging, to the best advantage possible, its position within the global economy.

FIGURE 50. Automation and the globalization of the economy are pitted against the legacy of the International Longshore and Warehouse Union's direct action and collective bargaining protections on West Coast docks. David Bacon, photo.

A longshore member of the ILWU can make well over $100,000 a year with overtime, with excellent retirement and health benefits—a far cry from the 95 cents per hour with which longshoremen emerged from the 1934 General Strike. The coast-wide longshore collective bargaining agreement remains a pacesetter for workers in the private sector in a time of general labor decline, with strong protections against health and safety violations and the potentially dangerous conditions always lurking in an industrial setting.

Such "middle class" industrial employment was far more common forty years ago, when the state had a half-dozen auto plants, several large steel mills, and a huge aerospace industry. Today these jobs are the exception, a testament to the ILWU's tenacious history and the critical spot it occupies in the country's economic supply chain.

By way of comparison, the state's median household income in 2013 was $57,000. The average single-earner salary was $35,000. But worse than these numbers is their context: wage stagnation festering over the last several decades. The trends do not indicate improving prospects in the near future for most working-class families.

Recoveries from recessions since the 1980s show a steady decline in the job growth that followed each one, from 4 percent in the mid 1980s, to 3 percent in the mid 1990s, 2 percent following the dot-com crash of 2000, and less than that after the Great Recession that began in December 2007. A long-term slower growth regime has set in, both in California and the United States.

Then there is the quality of employment. More than a quarter of the jobs created since 1979 have been low-wage jobs, concentrated especially in services like food preparation. This trend too will likely continue. California's Employment Development Department thinks that the largest category of jobs created by 2020 in the private sector will be in educational services, with large cohorts in hospitality and food services, construction, and health care.

Professional and semiprofessional jobs requiring at least a four-year degree will grow alongside the low-end employment, and it's a good bet that organizing will take place in all of these areas. What leverage could workers in these sectors expect to generate if they seek union representation?

The advancement of skilled and unskilled workers alike will be challenged by technological displacement, contingent employment, and ongoing legal, political, and legislative assaults by employers on job security and due process rights, probably requiring increasingly militant collective action to maintain a simple equilibrium. Public sector unions still provide a bulwark against the efforts of the employing class to roll back rights and economic traction for public employees, but even union strongholds like the Golden Gate Bridge are not immune to the logic of automation; the last thirty human toll takers were replaced by digital cash reception in 2013.

Professionals without unions will need to figure out how to act collectively or find their work evaporating all the more quickly.

Private sector unions, with just under 7 percent of employment, exercise power within but a few niches of a generally hostile economic environment, in collective bargaining oases such as large-scale construction projects (building trades unions), utilities (electrical workers), telecommunications (communications workers) and transportation (Amalgamated Transit Union, Transport Workers Union, the railroad brotherhoods, airline unions, teamsters).

For low-wage workers in the service and food sectors, as well as in the state's giant agribusiness economy, organizing has increasingly required innovative hybrid activities involving direct action, effective communications with the public, and persistent pressure on employers inside and outside the workplace. The unions that will succeed in the future will bring together sufficient forces in labor and the community to support political and legislative initiatives alongside workplace organizing. They will need to bolster public authorities that oversee private sector employment and require reluctant employers to pay above a poverty wage floor and observe laws maintaining humane conditions at work. Unions such as SEIU and UFCW are organizing efforts like these.

If new organizing occurs, we should not be surprised. Workers have always sought and found the possibilities for mutual aid in the economic structures of their time. In the 1880s brewery workers in San Francisco were roused from long hours and enormous quantities of beer to organize strike actions and boycott activities until their employers paid them a living wage.

Fifty years later, maritime unions in California's port cities devised tactics that included direct action at the point of production, escalation to a general strike, and expansion of legislative activities to consolidate the gains made on the streets. Workers in privately owned businesses dared to occupy the premises until a modest share of job ownership, through collective bargaining, was ceded by the employer to the people who generated the company's profits.

In the 1960s and 1970s, California's most exploited workers—agricultural laborers—utilized all the above weapons and more, fashioning economic action, a massive boycott, legislative lobbying, and solidarity from a still vibrant private sector labor movement into the greatest assault on the owners of the factories in the field yet mounted. Unfolding alongside their struggle, public sector unionism drew on the militancy of the civil rights movement and the same support from strong private sector unions that undergirded the UFW's victories to achieve collective bargaining laws and the protections they afforded to public servants.

Within the last few years the Occupy Wall Street movement generated a more tenuous and ephemeral alliance among contingent workers, students, and formerly full-time workers dumped out of the economy by the Great Recession. Despite its limitations—both those that were self-imposed and its harsh dispersal through militarized police actions—the Occupy movement punched through some persistent illusions of the past half-century, like the notion that unbridled, unregulated profit-making by Wall Street and the financial sector equaled prosperity for all, and that the rising tide that lifted all boats in the early 1960s for John Kennedy was going to continue indefinitely. It also restored militant direct action against the incursions of private capital and its contempt for public good to a valued place among mass movement protest tactics. It renewed the understanding—sporadically nurtured by assorted people's struggles against social injustice—that rebellion against abusive private ownership is a right, just like the right to contest unjust governmental power.

In California today, the role of unions, much like the job of maintenance workers on the Golden Gate Bridge, is to push back against often unseen but enormously strong forces ceaselessly working to corrode what they are protecting—in this case the modest dreams of economic security and social advancement carefully nurtured by working people and their families.

Contrary to the conservative ideologists who endlessly repeat the myth that unions were once necessary but are now no longer needed, the labor movement still protects workers' earning power, as well as their rights on the job and in their communities, through collective bargaining, politics, legislation, organizing, and direct action—all needed today no less than before.

Unions still form a barrier between workers and employers whose desire for profits exceeds their concern for their workers' wellbeing. The two million members of unions in California understand this. Their picture of the Golden State and its promise includes a living role for collective worker action, no matter whether the workers are relatively well off, or vulnerable and in dire need.

Immigrants and native-born workers wash against each other all the time in the California economy, like the tides moving in and out of the bay beneath the Golden Gate Bridge, coming together only to be pushed apart by powerful forces.

The difference between metaphor and reality is that water and tides are not sentient. Workers are conscious and capable of changing direction together if the current in which they find themselves is not to their benefit or liking. California labor history offers examples of such decisive moments, when working people, overcoming the obstacles they usually contend with, draw some relevant lessons and move toward a warmer spot in the state's famous sunshine.

LABOR ORGANIZATIONS AND ACRONYMS

Agricultural Workers Organizing Committee (AWOC)

Alameda County Central Labor Council

Amalgamated Association of Street and Electric Railway Employees of America

Amalgamated Transit Union (ATU)

American Federation of Labor (AFL)

American Federation of Labor-Congress of Industrial Organizations (AFL-CIO)

American Federation of Musicians (AFM)

American Federation of State, County and Municipal Employees (AFSCME)

American Federation of Teachers (AFT)

American Railway Union (ARU)

Bakersfield Central Labor Council

Brotherhood of Locomotive Firemen (BLF)

Brotherhood of Sleeping Car Porters (BSCP)

Building Trades Council (BTC) (San Francisco, Los Angeles)

California Federation of Teachers (CFT), previously California State
     Federation of Teachers

California Immigrant Workers Association (CIWA)

California Labor Federation, AFL-CIO (CLF), *previously* California State
     Federation of Labor (CSFL) *or* California State Labor Federation

California Nurses Association (CNA)

California Professional Firefighters, *previously* California Federation of Firefighters

California School Employees Association (CSEA)

California State Employees Association (*also* CSEA)

California Teachers Association (CTA)

Cannery and Agricultural Workers Industrial Union (CAWIU)

City Front Federation

Coalition of Labor Union Women (CLUW)

Communications Workers of America (CWA)

Community Labor Environmental Action Network (CLEAN Carwash Campaign)

Conference of Studio Unions (CSU)

Congress of Industrial Organizations (CIO), *previously* Committee for Industrial Organization

Contra Costa County Central Labor Council

Federated Trades Council

Food, Tobacco and Allied Workers-CIO (FTA), *previously* United Cannery, Agricultural, Packing and Allied Workers of America (UCAPAWA)

Hotel Employees and Restaurant Employees (HERE)

Industrial Workers of the World (IWW)

International Alliance of Theatrical Stage Employees (IATSE, *or* IA)

International Association of Bridge, Structural and Ornamental and Reinforcing Iron Workers, *formerly* International Association of Bridge and Structural Iron Workers

International Association of Fire Fighters (IAFF)

International Association of Machinists (IAM)

International Brotherhood of Boilermakers, Iron Shipbuilders and Helpers of America

International Brotherhood of Electrical Workers (IBEW)

International Brotherhood of Teamsters (IBT)

International Ladies' Garment Workers' Union (ILGWU, *or* ILG)

International Longshoremen's Association (ILA)

International Longshore and Warehouse Union (ILWU), *previously* International Longshoremen's and Warehousemen's Union (ILWU)

International Typographical Union (ITU), *previously* National Typographical Union

International Union of Operating Engineers (IUOE)

Iron Molders Union of North America

Jewish Labor Committee (JLC)

Kern County Labor Council

Laborers International Union of North America (LIUNA)

Los Angeles County Federation of Labor, *previously* Los Angeles Council of Labor

Marine Transport Workers Industrial Union

Marine Workers Industrial Union (MWIU)

Maritime Federation of the Pacific

Municipal Employees Federation (MEF)

National Day Labor Organizing Network

National Education Association (NEA)

National Federation of Federal Employees (NFFE)

National Federation of Social Service Employees

National Farm Labor Union (NFLU)

National Farm Workers Association (NFWA)

Needle Trades Workers Industrial Union (NTWIU)

Noble Order of the Knights of Labor

Oil, Chemical and Atomic Workers (OCAW), *previously* Oil Workers International Union-CIO, *previously* International Association of Oil Field, Gas Well and Refinery Workers of America

Retail Clerks International Union

Sailors' Union of the Pacific (SUP), *previously* Coast Seaman's Union

San Francisco Labor Council

San Mateo Central Labor Council

Screen Actors Guild (SAG)

Screen Writers Guild (SWG)

Service Employees International Union, *previously* Building Service Employees International Union (BSEIU)

South Bay Labor Council

State Building and Construction Trades Council of California

State, County and Municipal Workers of America-CIO

Sugar Beet and Farm Laborers' Union (SBFLU), *previously* Japanese-Mexican Labor Alliance (JMLA)

Union Labor Party (ULP)

Union of Needletrades, Industrial and Textile Employees/Hotel Employees and Restaurant Employees (UNITE HERE)

Union Women's Alliance to Gain Equality (Union WAGE)

United Automobile Workers (UAW-CIO)

United Brotherhood of Carpenters and Joiners (UBC)

United Cannery, Agricultural, Packinghouse and Allied Workers of America (UCPAWA)

United Domestic Workers/AFSCME (UDW)

United Electrical, Radio and Machine Workers of America (UE), *or* United
Electrical Workers

United Farm Workers of America (UFW)

United Food and Commercial Workers International Union (UFCW)

United Public Workers of America (UPWA, *or* UPW)

United Steelworkers (USW)

Wage Earners' Suffrage League (WESL)

BIBLIOGRAPHIC NOTE

Necessity made me write this book. When I began teaching labor history at City College of San Francisco I found many good books, articles, and films on topics in California labor history, but no reader or video that gave my students an overview. I set out to pull together a book and a video series. The ten-part video series, *Golden Lands, Working Hands,* saw the light of day in 1999. The book took longer. What follows is a selective description of the literature I found to guide my writing. I am grateful to my predecessors and the work they left me to draw from and build on.

GENERAL OVERVIEWS

Ira Cross's *A History of the Labor Movement in California* (1935) provides the bedrock through World War I; his monumental, meticulous research remains the place to start. The work of a professional economist sympathetic to labor, it is a classic example of institutional labor history focused on unions and their leaders.

David Selvin, longtime labor journalist and author of a number of slim but valuable union histories, wrote *Sky Full of Storm: A Brief History of California Labor* in 1966 (revised in 1975), bringing the story into the early era of the United Farm Workers and public employee unionism. Its compact, readable one hundred pages were written before the "new labor history" in the 1970s; consequently it doesn't venture much into how race, gender, or the sharper edges of class relate to the trajectory of labor.

Dan Cornford's anthology *Working People of California* (1995) remedied that problem with a collection of essays by labor historians providing advanced scholarship on key issues. A superb tool for graduate-level courses, it is not as accessible to the undergraduate or to the worker interested in finding out where her rights came from.

Cornford also served as the lead writer for the *California Labor History Map* project, a joint effort by unions and the State Library, which eventuated in 2003 in a circulating exhibit of photo/text panels, a wall map with 250 entries in a timeline, and longer essays on an interactive website (http://calpedia.sfsu.edu/calabor/).

A Selective Bibliography of California Labor History (1964), by Mitchell Slobodek, surveys the field up to that moment. *At Work: The Art of California Labor,* edited by Mark Dean Johnson (2003), is a beautifully produced coffee table book with historical essays on the art and culture arising from labor sympathies among professional artists and workers who also made art.

Former California state librarian Kevin Starr's epic history of California, *Americans and the California Dream,* pauses to catch up with labor history in *Endangered Dreams: The Great Depression in California* (1996), taking a flashback approach with several chapters in the fourth volume of his series.

Although at first glance simply a history of the anti-Chinese movement, Alexander Saxton's *The Indispensable Enemy: Labor and the Anti-Chinese Movement in California* (1971) is also a well-written and sharply political overview of nineteenth-century labor history.

A number of statewide unions have produced house histories, some quite good, usually on the occasion of a significant anniversary, looking at the arc of California's history from the perspective of their industry and membership. There are likewise many useful unpublished scholarly papers and dissertations, which tend to be more local in focus.

REGIONAL STUDIES

Los Angeles labor history received an overdue full-length treatment with John Laslett's *Sunshine Was Never Enough: Los Angeles Workers, 1880–2010* (2012), although Ruth Milkman's *L.A. Story: Immigrant Workers and the Future of the U.S. Labor Movement* (2006) had already made a good start.

In San Diego, Mike Davis, Kelly Mayhew, and Jim Miller picked up where Frederick Ryan's *The Labor Movement in San Diego: Problems and Development from 1887–1957* (1959) left off, with their *Under the Perfect Sun: The San Diego Tourists Never See* (2003).

San Francisco, where once "labor [held] undisputed sway," has no substantial narrative of its labor history except in relatively short slices of a few decades at a time. Important elements of the Bay Area's labor history are covered in William Issel and Robert Cherny's *San Francisco 1865–1932: Politics, Power, and Urban Development* (1986) and across the bay, *No There There: Race, Class, and Political Community in Oakland,* by Chris Rhomberg (2004). See also Albert Lannon's *Fight or Be Slaves: The History of the Oakland-East Bay Labor Movement* (2000).

The social history of Silicon (formerly Santa Clara) Valley is ably conjured in Glenna Matthews's *Silicon Valley, Women, and the California Dream: Gender, Class and Opportunity in the Twentieth Century* and Stephen J. Pitti's *The Devil in Silicon Valley: Northern California, Race, and Mexican Americans* (both 2003). Both feature a strong emphasis on workers and their organizations.

Many more histories of California, not labor histories per se, nonetheless deal meaningfully with workers and the labor movement. The mother ship of California social history emerged from the work of Carey McWilliams, author of *California: The Great Exception* (1949) and *Southern California Country: An Island on the Land* (1946). Michael Kazin's essay reflecting on the work of McWilliams and its relationship to California labor history, "The Great Exception Revisited," *Pacific Historical Review*, v. 55, No. 3 (1986), celebrates and critiques his legacy, making the deceptively simple point that there are really three distinct albeit related California labor histories: north, south, and central valley.

Mike Davis's *City of Quartz: Excavating the Future in Los Angeles* (1990, 1992) renewed the McWilliams tradition of integrating labor history within broader critical themes and helped jumpstart a now abundant literature on the city's various ethnic histories, many of which pay close attention to labor issues. These are too numerous to list here; for relevant social histories of cities and regions in the state, see the bibliography.

KEY INDUSTRIES

For farm labor, still useful today is Carey McWilliams's *Factories in the Field,* which came out the same year as John Steinbeck's *The Grapes of Wrath* (1939); also useful is Ernesto Galarza's *Farm Workers and Agri-business in California, 1947–1960* (1977). The initial successes of the United Farm Workers inspired a generation of scholars and journalists, and eventually a host of UFW alumni, to join in documenting its rise and fall, and stimulated interest in the struggles that came before. We need to single out Richard Steven Street's essential *Beasts of the Field: A Narrative History of California Farmworkers, 1769–1913* (2004) for its depth of research, synthesis of historical strands, and grace of presentation, and also his *Everyone Had Cameras: Photography and Farmworkers in California, 1850–2000* (2008). A good place to start for the UFW is *The Fight in the Fields: Cesar Chavez and the Farmworkers Movement,* by Susan Ferriss and Ricardo Sandoval (1997), which accompanied the two-hour PBS documentary of the same name. But as the best-documented labor struggle in the country's history, there are plenty of other books on every aspect of the topic.

Maritime unionism receives attention in Bruce Nelson's *Workers on the Waterfront: Seamen, Longshoremen, and Unionism in the 1930s* (1990), Harvey Schwartz's *Solidarity Stories: An Oral History of the ILWU* (2009), and the earlier

Andrew Furuseth: Emancipator of the Seamen, by Hyman Weintraub (1959), which shares the era and concerns of institutional labor histories but stands above the genre with its clarity and breadth.

Two books to note on the construction trades are Paul Bullock et al.'s *Building California: The Story of the Carpenters' Union* (1982), spanning the history from the Gold Rush on, and Michael Kazin's *Barons of Labor: The San Francisco Building Trades and Union Power in the Progressive Era* (1986), dealing in fascinating detail with the moment of greatest union power in one American city.

Books on moviemaking's labor history include *Hollywood's Other Blacklist: Union Struggles in the Studio System,* by Mike Nielsen and Gene Mailes (1995); *The Hollywood Writers' Wars,* by Nancy Lynn Schwartz (1982); and Tom Sito's *Drawing the Line: The Untold Story of the Animation Unions from Bosko to Bart Simpson* (2006). Steven J. Ross's *Working-Class Hollywood: Silent Film and the Shaping of Class in America* (1998) illuminates how the commercial motion picture industry eliminated its once-sizeable class-conscious competition. A cottage industry of books exposes the anticommunist Hollywood blacklist, with significant labor history embedded.

California public sector unionism needs a good comprehensive contemporary overview. *Organized Civil Servants: Public Employer-Employee Relations in California,* by Winston W. Crouch, is a relatively late (1978) entry following the institutional approach. *Success While Others Fail: Social Movement Unionism and the Public Workplace* (1994), by Paul Johnston, looks at several mostly public sector case studies involving nurses, municipal workers, custodians, and others in northern California. *Strength Through Solidarity: A 75-Year History of California Professional Firefighters,* by Carroll Wills (2014), is a detailed and handsome house history.

WORLD WAR II

A watershed moment for the country and the labor movement, World War II put in place new rules for labor-capital conflict. *American Labor in the Era of World War II* (1995), edited by Sally Miller and Dan Cornford, is an excellent anthology focusing on home front California. Charles Wollenberg's *Marinship at War: Shipbuilding and Social Change in Wartime Sausalito* (1990), Shirley Ann Wilson Moore's *To Place Our Deeds: The African American Community in Richmond, California, 1910–1963* (2000), and Marilynn S. Johnson's *The Second Gold Rush: Oakland and the East Bay in World War II* (1993) unearth the stories of African American and women workers. *Slacks and Calluses: Our Summer in a Bomber Factory,* by Constance Bowman and Clara Marie Allen (1944, 1999) engagingly presents the experiences of two San Diego teachers who became Rosie the Riveters.

Michael Reich, Ken Jacobs, and Miranda Dietz's *When Mandates Work: Raising Labor Standards at the Local Level (2014)* and Ruth Milkman, Joshua Bloom, and Victor Narro's *Working for Justice: The L.A. Model of Organizing and Advocacy* (2010) bring the stories of local and regional labor mobilizations up to the moment, providing case studies of the impact creative tactics combined with grassroots collective action can have on regulatory and legislative bodies as well as employers.

FINALLY, FICTION

A few personal favorites drawn from the well of California labor fiction, beyond Steinbeck, include Upton Sinclair's *Oil,* the two stellar Chester Himes novels of the World War II home front workplace, *If He Hollers Let Him Go* and *Lonely Crusade,* Tillie Olsen's incandescent *Tell Me A Riddle,* Gordon DeMarco's *Frisco Blues* and *October Heat,* Jack London's two short stories "South of the Slot" and "The General Strike," along with the first half of his novel *Valley of the Moon,* Budd Schulberg's *What Makes Sammy Run,* Alejandro Morales's *The Brick People,* and Jim Miller's *Flash.*

SOURCES

Abate, Tom. "History Likely to Repeat Itself at NUMMI Site." *San Francisco Chronicle* 28 Feb. 2010. Print.

Adamic, Louis, *Dynamite: A Century of Class Violence in America, 1830–1930*. London: Rebel Press, 1984. Print.

Adler, Patrick, Chris Tilly, and Ben Zipperer. "The State of the Unions in 2013: A Profile of Union Membership in Los Angeles, California, and the Nation." *UCLA Institute for Research on Labor and Employment* 2013. Web. www.irle.ucla .edu/publications/documents/StateoftheUnions2013Final.pdf

Ah Wah. "Testimonies." Clippings from *Riots in San Francisco. San Francisco Chronicle* and *The Mail* 26 July 1877. Print.

Alexander, Horace "Alex." Personal interview. 2 April 1998.

Alexander, William. *Film on the Left: American Documentary Film from 1931 to 1942*. Princeton: Princeton University Press, 1981. Print.

Allegretto, Sylvia, and Luke Reidenbach. "Shrunken Public Sector Stunts California's Recovery." *CPER Online Journal* 208 (2012). Web.

Allegretto, Sylvia, et al. "Fast Food, Poverty Wages: The Public Cost of Low Wage Jobs in the Fast-food Industry." *University of Illinois at Urbana-Champaign and U.C. Berkeley Labor Center*. Labor Center, Berkeley, 15 Oct. 2013. Web. http:// laborcenter.berkeley.edu/fast-food-poverty-wages-the-public-cost-of-low-wage-jobs-in-the-fast-food-industry

Allen, Arthur P., and Betty V. H. Schneider. *Industrial Relations in the California Aircraft Industry: West Coast Collective Bargaining Systems*. Berkeley: University of California, Berkeley, Institute for Research on Labor and Employment, 1956. Print.

Almaguer, Tomas. "Racial Domination and Class Conflict in Capitalist Agriculture: The Oxnard Beet Workers' Strike of 1903." *Working People of California*. Ed. Daniel Cornford. Berkeley: University of California Press, 1995. Print.

Archibald, Katherine. *Wartime Shipyard: A Study in Social Disunity*. Urbana: University of Illinois Press, 2006. Print.

Aronowitz, Stanley. *From the Ashes of the Old: American Labor and America's Future.* New York: Houghton Mifflin, 1998. Print.

Ash, Robert. "Alameda County Central Labor Council during the Warren Years." *UC Berkeley Oral History Project.* By Miriam Stein and Amelia Fry. Berkeley: Bancroft Library, University of California, 1976. Audio.

Bacon, David. "West Coast Janitors Get Ready to Fight." *Unions* 28 Feb. 1997. Web. http://dbacon.igc.org/Unions/01L1877.htm

———. "Sacramento Janitors' 11-day March for Justice." *Unions* 21 Feb. 1998. Web. http://dbacon.igc.org/Unions/06janitr.htm

Baker, Bob. "Largest Non-Union Janitorial Service Agrees to Labor Pact." *Los Angeles Times* 27 Feb. 1991. Print.

Barabak, Mark Z. "Reluctant Warrior Bests Gov." *Los Angeles Times* 10 Nov. 2005. Print.

Bardacke, Frank. *Trampling Out the Vintage: Cesar Chavez and the Two Souls of the United Farm Workers.* London: Verso, 2011. Print.

Bean, Walton, and James J. Rawls. *California: An Interpretive History.* New York: McGraw-Hill, 1988. Print.

Becker, William. Personal interview. 2 April 1998.

Beebe, Rose Marie, and Robert M. Senkewicz, eds. *Lands of Promise and Despair: Chronicles of Early California, 1535–1840.* Berkeley: Heyday Books, 2001. Print.

Bell, Florence. *At the Works: A Study of a Manufacturing Town.* London: Thomas Nelson and Sons, 1911. Print.

Bergan, Mary. "30 Years Looking Back: Memoir of a Union Lobbyist." *CPER Journal* 137 (1999). Print.

Bethlehem Steel Company, Shipbuilding Division. *A Century of Progress, 1849–1949, San Francisco Yard, Bethlehem Steel Company, Shipbuilding Division.* General Offices, Bethlehem Steel Company, 1949. Print.

Beyette, Beverly. "Dispute in San Jose: Equal Pay for Comparable Worth." *Los Angeles Times* 13 July 1981. Print.

"Beyond Recovery: Making the State's Economy Work Better for Low and Mid-Wage Californians." *Economy Brief. CalBudgetCenter.org.* California Budget Project, Aug. 2014. Web. http://calbudgetcenter.org/wp-content/uploads/140831_Beyond_Recovery_EB.pdf

Bionaz, Robert Emery. "Death of a Union: The 1907 San Francisco Streetcar Strike." *Ex Post Facto: Journal of History Students at San Francisco State University* V (1996). Ed. Karen Christianson and Patricia O'Flinn. 17 June 2007. Web.

Bohn, Sarah. "California's Future: Economy." *Public Policy Institute of California* Jan. 2014. Web. http://www.ppic.org/main/publication.asp?i = 898

Bonacich, Edna, and Richard P. Appelbaum. *Behind the Label: Inequality in the Los Angeles Apparel Industry.* Los Angeles: University of California Press, 2000. Print.

Bonnet, Theodore. *The Regenerators: A Study of the Graft Prosecution of San Francisco.* San Francisco: Pacific Printing Company, 1911. Print.

Bonnett, Wayne. *A Pacific Legacy: A Century of Maritime Photography 1850–1950.* San Francisco: Chronicle Books, 1991. Print.

Bowman, Constance, and Clara Marie Allen. *Slacks and Calluses: Our Summer in a Bomber Factory*. Washington, D.C.: Smithsonian Institution Press, 1999. Print.

Boyden, Richard P. "The San Francisco Machinists and the War Labor Board." *American Labor in the Era of World War II*. Eds. Sally M. Miller and Daniel A. Cornford. Westport: Praeger, 1995. Print.

Brewer, Roy. Personal conversation. 3 May 1994.

Brody, David. *Labor Embattled: History, Power, Rights*. Urbana: University of Illinois Press, 2005. Print.

Brommel, Bernard J. *Eugene V. Debs: Spokesman for Labor and Socialism*. Chicago: Charles H. Kerr, 1978. Print.

Broussard, Albert S. *Black San Francisco: The Struggle for Racial Equality in the West, 1900–1954*. Lawrence: University Press of Kansas, 1993. Print.

Bruns, Roger A. *Knights of the Road: A Hobo History*. New York: Methuen, 1980. Print.

Bullock, Paul, with Cara Anderson, Jack Blackburn, Edna Bonacich, and Richard Steele. *Building California: The Story of the Carpenters' Union*. Los Angeles: Institute of Industrial Relations Publications, UCLA, 1982. Print.

Burke, Robert E. *Olson's New Deal for California*. Berkeley: University of California Press, 1953. Print.

Burt, Kenneth. *The Search for a Civic Voice: California Latino Politics*. Claremont: Regina Books, 2007. Print.

———. "The Fight for Fair Employment and the Shifting Alliances among Latinos and Labor in Cold War Los Angeles." *Labor's Cold War: Local Politics in a Global Context*. Ed. Sheldon Stromquist. Chicago: University of Illinois Press, 2008. Print.

Burt, Kenneth, and Fred Glass. "When Job Discrimination Was Legal." *San Francisco Examiner* 16 April 1999. Print.

Busman, Gloria. Personal conversations and correspondence with author. 1994–1995. Manuscript.

Callahan, Bill. Personal interview. 10 September 1995.

Camarillo, Albert. *Chicanos in a Changing Society: From Mexican Pueblos to American Barrios in Santa Barbara and Southern California, 1848–1930*. Cambridge: Harvard University Press, 1979. Print.

Cantarow, Ellen. *Moving the Mountain: Women Working for Social Change*. New York: The Feminist Press, 1980. Print.

Carter, Richard. Personal interview. 6 April 1999.

Cary, Lorin Lee. "Spare Nothing: The AFL-CIO Joint Organizing Campaign in Los Angeles and Orange Counties, 1963–64." 11th Annual Southwest Labor Studies Conference, 30 March 1985. Typescript.

Casey, Conor, "A Union Divided: The Role of the American Federation of Teachers Local 1352 in the San Francisco State College Strike of 1968–1969." Unpublished student paper, Labor Archives and Research Center, San Francisco State University, n.d. Typescript.

Chan, Sucheng. *This Bitter-Sweet Soil: The Chinese in California Agriculture, 1860–1910*. Berkeley: University of California Press, 1986. Print.

Chan, Sucheng, and Spencer Olin, ed. *Major Problems in California History.* Boston: Houghton Mifflin, 1997. Print.

Chavez, Cesar. *An Organizer's Tale: Speeches.* New York: Penguin Books, 2008. Print.

Chorneau, Tom. "Dogged by Protesters, Schwarzenegger Opts for Less Public Venues." *San Francisco Chronicle* 3 June 2005. Print.

————."Weakened Schwarzenegger Faces Re-Election." *Los Angeles Times* 4 Jan. 2006. Print.

Chown, Paul. *The War Against Labor: Memoir of a Union Organizer.* Berkeley, 1992. Typescript.

Choy, Philip P., Lorraine Dong, and Marlon K. Hom. *Coming Man: 19th Century American Perceptions of the Chinese.* Seattle: University of Washington Press, 1994. Print.

Cleland, Robert Glass. *The Cattle on a Thousand Hills: Southern California, 1850–80.* San Marino: Huntington Library, 1991. Print.

Cobble, Dorothy Sue. *Dishing it Out: Waitresses and Their Unions in the Twentieth Century.* Urbana: University of Illinois Press, 1991. Print.

Cochrane, Bert. *Labor and Communism: The Conflict that Shaped American Unions.* Princeton: Princeton University Press, 1977. Print.

Coolidge, Calvin. "The Press Under a Free Government." American Society of Newspaper Editors. Washington, D.C., 17 Jan. 1925. Address.

Cooper, Muriel H. "Green Giant Dumps Workers in Former Valley." *AFL-CIO News* 17 Jan. 1994. Print.

Cornford, Dan. "'We all live more like brutes than humans': Labor and Capital in the Gold Rush." *California History* 77.4 (1998). Print.

Crippen, David. "First Statewide President Outlines Brief History of BSE Social Workers, Local 535." *Service Union Reporter* July 1967. Print.

Cross, Ira B. *A History of the Labor Movement in California.* Berkeley: University of California Press, 1935. Print.

Cross, Ira B., ed. *Frank Roney: Irish Rebel and California Labor Leader: An Autobiography.* Berkeley: University of California Press, 1931. Print.

Crouch, Winston W. *Organized Civil Servants: Public Employer-Employee Relations in California.* Berkeley: University of California Press, 1978. Print.

Daily and Weekly Call. *California As It Is: Being a Concise Description of the State by Counties, with Memoranda of the Progress of Each in Agricultural, Horticultural, Mining and Other Industries, Up to the Year 1887–'88.* 5th ed. San Francisco: San Francisco Call Company, 1888. Print.

Dana, Richard Henry, Jr. *Two Years Before the Mast.* New York: Penguin Books, 1981. Print.

Daniel, Cletus E. *Bitter Harvest: A History of California Farmworkers, 1870–1941.* Berkeley: University of California Press, 1982. Print.

D'Ausilio, Bob. Personal interview. 2 Feb. 2014.

Davey, Monica. "Unions Suffer Latest Defeat in Midwest with Signing of Wisconsin Measure." *New York Times* 9 March 2015. Print.

Davis, Mike. *Prisoners of the American Dream: Politics and Economy in the History of the US Working Class.* London: Verso, 1986. Print.

———. *City of Quartz: Excavating the Future in Los Angeles.* New York: Vintage Books, 1992. Print.

Davis, Mike, Kelly Mayhew, and Jim Miller. *Under the Perfect Sun: The San Diego Tourists Never See.* New York: The New Press, 2003. Print.

Delgado, James P. *To California by Sea: A Maritime History of the California Gold Rush.* Columbia: University of South Carolina Press, 1990. Print.

Dellums, Cottrell Laurence. *Oral History.* Berkeley: Bancroft Library, University of California. Transcript. Print.

DeMarco, Gordon. *A Short History of Los Angeles.* San Francisco: Lexicos, 1988. Print.

De Roussailh, Albert Benard. *Last Adventure: San Francisco in 1851.* Trans. Clarkson Crane. San Francisco: Westgate Press, 1931. Print.

Deverell, William. *Railroad Crossing: Californians and the Railroad, 1850–1890.* Berkeley: University of California Press, 1994. Print.

———. *Whitewashed Adobe: The Rise of Los Angeles and the Remaking of its Mexican Past.* Berkeley: University of California Press, 2005. Print.

Dicker, Laverne Mau. *The Chinese in San Francisco: A Pictorial History.* New York: Dover, 1979. Print.

Donahoe, Myrna Cherkoss. *Resolving Discriminatory Practices against Minorities and Women in Steel and Auto, Los Angeles, California: 1936–1982.* Los Angeles: Institute of Industrial Relations Publications Center, UCLA, 1991. Print.

Douma, Frank Hartzell. "The Oakland General Strike." MA thesis. University of California, Berkeley, 1948. Print.

Drew, Jesse. "San Francisco Labor in the 1970s." *Ten Years that Shook the City: San Francisco 1968–1978.* Ed. Chris Carlsson. San Francisco: City Lights Books, 2011. Print.

Dubofsky, Melvyn. *We Shall Be All: A History of the Industrial Workers of the World.* Urbana: University of Illinois Press, 2000. Print.

Dumke, Glenn. *The Boom of the Eighties in Southern California.* San Marino: Huntington Library, 1944. Print.

Dunn, Geoffrey. "Reflexivity and Conflict: Watsonville on Strike." *Jump Cut* 35 (1990). Print.

Dunne, John Gregory. *Delano: The Story of the California Grape Strike.* New York: Farrar, Straus & Giroux, 1967. Print.

Durbin, Martina. *Lima Beans and City Chicken: A Memoir of the Open Hearth.* New York: E. P. Dutton, 1989. Print.

Eargle, Dolan H., Jr. *The Earth Is Our Mother: A Guide to the Indians of California, Their Locales and Historic Sites.* San Francisco: Tree Company Press, 1986. Print.

Eaves, Lucile. *A History of California Labor Legislation.* Berkeley: The University Press, 1910. Print.

"Elinor Glenn: Henry Fiering Union Advocacy Award." Program Booklet. Jewish Labor Committee annual awards banquet, n.d. Print.

Ellsworth, Ted. Personal conversations. May–June 1996.

Englander, Susan. *Class Coalition and Class Conflict in the California Woman Suffrage Movement, 1907–1912: The San Francisco Wage Earners' Suffrage League.* Lewiston: Mellen Research University Press, 1992. Print.

Erickson, Christopher L., Catherine L. Fisk, Ruth Milkman, Daniel J. B. Mitchell, and Kent Wong. "Justice for Janitors in Los Angeles: Lessons from Three Rounds of Negotiations." *British Journal of Industrial Relations* 40.3 (2002). Print.

Ezquerro, Luisa. Personal interview. 10 June 1998.

Fabry, Joseph. *Swing Shift: Building the Liberty Ships.* San Francisco: Strawberry Hill Press, 1982. Print.

Farris, George W. *Diaries.* Berkeley: Bancroft Library, University of California, Berkeley. 1878–1880, 1902–1910. Print.

Ferriss, Susan, and Ricardo Sandoval. *The Fight in the Fields: Cesar Chavez and the Farmworkers Movement.* New York: Harcourt Brace, 1997. Print.

Fink, Leon. *Workingmen's Democracy: The Knights of Labor and American Politics.* Urbana: University of Illinois Press, 1983. Print.

Flamming, Douglas. *Bound for Freedom: Black Los Angeles in Jim Crow America.* Berkeley: University of California Press, 2005. Print.

Foner, Philip S. *The History of the Labor Movement in the United States, Volume 3: The Policies and Practices of the American Federation of Labor 1900–1909.* New York: International Publishers, 1964. Print.

———. *U.S. Labor and the Viet-Nam War.* New York: International Publishers, 1989. Print.

Franks, Kenny A., and Paul F. Lambert. *Early California Oil: A Photographic History, 1865–1940.* College Station: Texas A&M University Press, 1985. Print.

Fraser, Steve, and Gary Gerstle, eds. *The Rise and Fall of the New Deal Order, 1930–1980.* Princeton: Princeton University Press, 1989. Print.

Freeman, Jo. "From Freedom Now! to Free Speech: How the 1963–64 Bay Area Civil Rights Demonstrations Paved the Way to Campus Protest." Panel Commemorating Mario Savio, Annual Meeting of the Organization of American Historians. San Francisco, 19 April 1997. Web. www.uic.edu/orgs/cwluherstory/jofreeman/sixtiesprotest/baycivil.htm

Fukuyama, Yoshio. "The Japanese in Oxnard, California, 1898–1945," *Ventura County Historical Society Quarterly* 39.4 (1994); 40.1 (1994). Print.

Furillo, Andy. "Voters talked to Union Members on Prop. 75." *Sacramento Bee* 10 Nov. 2005. Print.

Galarza, Ernesto. *Merchants of Labor: The Mexican Bracero Story.* Santa Barbara: McNally Loftin, 1964. Print.

———. *Spiders in the House and Workers in the Field.* Notre Dame: University of Notre Dame Press, 1970. Print.

———. *Farm Workers and Agri-business in California, 1947–1960.* Notre Dame: University of Notre Dame Press, 1977. Print.

Gall, Gilbert. "The CIO and the Hatch Act: The Roosevelt Court and the Divided New Deal Legacy of the 1940s." *Labor's Heritage* 7.1 (1995). Print.

Gallagher, Tom. "Everybody Loved It, But . . ." *Z Magazine* (1998). Print.

Galloway, J. H. "II.F.2.—Sugar." *The Cambridge World History of Food*. Eds. Kenneth F. and Kriemhild Conee Ornelas. n.d. Web. http://www.cambridge.org/us/books/kiple/sugar.htm

Garcia, Mario T. *Memories of Chicano History: The Life and Narrative of Burt Corona*. Berkeley: University of California Press, 1994. Print.

Garlock, Jon. "The 1946 General Strike of Rochester, New York." n.d. Web. http://www.rochesterlabor.org/strike/index.html

Garnel, Donald. *The Rise of Teamster Power in the West*. Berkeley: University of California Press, 1972. Print.

Geissinger, Steve. "Arnold's Foes Are Growing Louder: Protesters in S.F. Hope to Drown Out Governor's Special Election Pitch." *Oakland Tribune* 5 April 2005. Print.

Glass, Fred, ed. *70 Years: A History of the California Federation of Teachers, 1919–1989*. Oakland: California Federation of Teachers, 1989. Print.

———. "California Labor History, Part IX: *Poverty in the Valley of Plenty*," *California Classified Exposition* 10.3 (1994). Print.

———. "We Called It a 'Work Holiday': The 1946 Oakland General Strike." *Labor's Heritage* 8.2 (1996). Print.

———. "Winning the Battle but Losing the War: Inadvertent Labor Media Politics at Work." *ILCA Reporter* Dec. 2005. Print.

———. *Occupy Oakland: The 99% Take the Streets for a Day*. 2011. Video. https://www.youtube.com/watch?v = mghTi_wkNuE

———. "We're Taxing the Rich . . . and So Can You." *Labor Notes* 412 (2013). Print.

———. "Work, Money and Power: Unions in the 21st Century" Berkeley: U.C. Berkeley Labor Center, 2013. Print.

Glenn, Elinor. Personal interview. 25 June 1998.

Goddard, Joan. Personal interview. 15 Nov. 2010.

Goldblatt, Louis. *Men and Machines: A Story about Longshoring on the West Coast Waterfront*. Photos by Otto Hagel. San Francisco: West Coast Waterfront Publishers, 1963. Print.

———. "Working Class Leader in the ILWU, 1935–1977." *Oral History*. Berkeley: Bancroft Library, University of California, 1978–1979. Transcript.

Gomez-Quinones, Juan. *Mexican American Labor, 1790–1990*. Albuquerque: University of New Mexico Press, 1994. Print.

Goodman, Jeff, and Michael Tompane. "Hollywood Local: The Hollywood Craft Unions 1927–1947." North Hollywood: The Harman Press, 1983. Broadsheet Photographic Exhibit Notes. Print.

Greenstein, Paul, Nigey Lennon, and Lionel Rolfe. *Bread and Hyacinths: The Rise and Fall of Utopian Los Angeles*. Los Angeles: California Classics Books, 1992. Print.

Gregory, Linda. "Transcription of November 2008 Interview with David Novogrodsky." *For California Labor History, Labor and Community Studies 88*. San Francisco: City College of San Francisco, 2008. Transcript. Print.

Gribble, Richard E., Jr. "Peter Yorke and the 1907 San Francisco Carmen's Strike." *Southern California Quarterly* 73.1 (1991). Print.

Grossman, Jonathan P. *William Sylvis, Pioneer of American Labor: A Study of the Labor Movement During the Era of the Civil War.* New York: Columbia University Press, 1945. Print.

Hackel, Steven W. "Land, Labor and Production: The Colonial Economy of Spanish and Mexican California." *California History* 76.3 (1997). Print.

Harp Week Cartoons. "Street Car Salad." *Harpers Weekly* 23 March 1867. Print.

"Harry Lumsden: Labor and Rights Leader." *California Labor News* 21 June 1996. Print.

Healey, Dorothy Ray, and Maurice Isserman. *California Red: A Life in the American Communist Party.* Urbana: University of Illinois Press, 1993. Print.

Heizer, R. F., and M. A. Whipple, eds. *The California Indians: A Source Book.* Berkeley: University of California Press, 1971. Print.

Heizer, Robert F., and Alan J. Almquist. *The Other Californians: Prejudice and Discrimination under Spain, Mexico and the United States to 1920.* Berkeley: University of California Press, 1971. Print.

Hendrick, Irving G. "From Indifference to Imperative Duty: Educating Children in Early California." *California History* 79.2 (2000). Print.

Herndon, James. *The Way It Spozed to Be.* New York: Simon and Schuster, 1968. Print.

———. *Notes from a School-Teacher.* New York: Simon and Schuster, 1985. Print.

Himes, Chester. *If He Hollers Let Him Go.* New York: Thunder's Mouth Press, 1986. Print.

———. *Lonely Crusade.* New York: Thunder's Mouth Press, 1986. Print.

Hirsch, Fred. Personal interview. 1998.

History Video Parts 1—3. California Nurses Association, 2009. Video. http://www .youtube.com/watch?v = 5GhJ1NIeS2Q

Hoene, Chris, and Luke Reidenbach. "Growing Economic Divide Threatens California Dream." *San Francisco Chronicle* 20 Dec. 2013. Print.

Hofstadter, Richard. *The American Political Tradition and the Men Who Made It.* New York: Alfred A. Knopf, 1948. Print.

Huerta, Dolores. Personal conversations. 1994–1995, 2015.

Huie Kin. *Reminiscences.* Beijing, China: San Yu Press, 1932. Print.

Hurtado, Albert L. "California Indians and the Workaday West: Labor, Assimilation, and Survival." *California History* 69.1 (1990). Print.

Ichioka, Yuji. *The Issei: The World of the First Generation Japanese Immigrants, 1885–1924.* New York: The Free Press, 1988. Print.

Immigration Policy Center, American Immigration Council. "New Americans in California: The Economic Power of Immigrants, Latinos, and Asians in the Golden State." *ImmigrationPolicy.org.* Immigration Policy Center, May 2013. Web. http://www.immigrationpolicy.org/just-facts/new-americans-california

Information Department, International Longshoremen's and Warehousemen's Union. *The ILWU Story: Two Decades of Militant Unionism.* San Francisco: International Longshoremen's and Warehousemen's Union, 1955. Print.

"Is Negotiation Council Acting in Best Interest of Students." *Contra Costa County Labor Journal* 9 Sept. 1966. Print.

Issel, William, and Robert W. Cherny. *San Francisco 1865–1932: Politics, Power, and Urban Development.* Berkeley: University of California Press, 1986. Print.

Jackson, Helen Hunt. *Ramona: A Story.* New York: Penguin Putnam, 2002. Print.

Jackson, Robert H. *From Savages to Subjects: Missions in the History of the American Southwest.* Armonk: M. E. Sharpe, 2000. Print.

Jackson, Robert H., and Edward Castillo. *Indians, Franciscans, and Spanish Colonization: The Impact of the Mission System on California Indians.* Albuquerque: University of New Mexico Press, 1995. Print.

Jensen, Joan M., and Gloria Ricci Lothrop. *California Women: A History.* San Francisco: Boyd and Fraser, 1987. Print.

Johnson, Marilynn S. *The Second Gold Rush: Oakland and the East Bay in World War II.* Berkeley: University of California Press, 1993. Print.

Johnson, Walter. Personal interview. 22 April 1998.

Johnston, Paul. *Success While Others Fail: Social Movement Unionism and the Public Workplace.* New York: ILR Press, 1994. Print.

Jones, William P. "The Infrastructure of South-Central Los Angeles: Unions, Public Service and the New Black Middle Class." Unpublished paper, presented at the Center for the Study of Work, Labor, and Democracy, University of California, Santa Barbara, 23 Jan. 2009. Typescript.

Jung, Maureen. "Capitalism Comes to the Diggings: From Gold-Rush Adventure to Corporate Enterprise." *California History* 77.4 (1998–99). Print.

Katz, Sherry. "Frances Nacke Noel and 'Sister Movements': Socialism, Feminism and Trade Unionism in Los Angeles, 1910–1916." *California History* 67.3 (1988). Print.

———. "Dual Commitments: Feminism, Socialism, and Women's Political Activism in California, 1890–1920." Diss. UCLA, 1991. Print.

———. "Kate Kennedy." *European Immigrant Women in the United States: A Biographical Dictionary.* Ed. Judy Barrett Litoff. New York: Garland Publishing, 1994. Print.

Katzman, David and William Tuttle, eds. "The Biography of a Chinaman: Lee Chew." *Plain Folk: The Life Stories of Undistinguished Americans.* Urbana: University of Illinois, 1982. Print.

Kazin, Michael. "Prelude to Kearneyism: The 'July Days' in San Francisco, 1877." *New Labor Review* 3 (1980). Print.

———. "The Great Exception Revisited." *Pacific Historical Review* 55.3 (1986). Print.

———. *Barons of Labor: The San Francisco Building Trades and Union Power in the Progressive Era.* Urbana: University of Illinois Press, 1989. Print.

Keeran, Roger. *The Communist Party and the Auto Workers' Unions.* Bloomington: Indiana University Press, 1980. Print.

Kemble, John Haskell. *San Francisco Bay: A Pictorial Maritime History.* New York: Bonanza Books, 1957. Print.

Kimeldorf, Howard. *Reds or Rackets? The Making of Radical and Conservative Unions on the Waterfront.* Berkeley: University of California Press, 1988. Print.

Klein, Jennifer. *For All These Rights: Business, Labor, and the Shaping of America's Public-Private Welfare State.* Princeton: Princeton University Press, 1993. Print.

Knight, Robert. *Industrial Relations in the San Francisco Bay Area, 1900–1918.* Berkeley: University of California Press, 1960. Print.

Kransdorf, Martha. *A Matter of Loyalty: The Los Angeles School Board vs. Frances Eisenberg.* San Francisco: Caddo Press, 1994. Print.

Kurashige, Scott. *The Shifting Grounds of Race: Black and Japanese Americans in the Making of Multiethnic Los Angeles.* Princeton: Princeton University Press, 2008. Print.

Kushner, Sam. *Long Road to Delano: A Century of Farmworkers' Struggle.* New York: International Publishers, 1975. Print.

"Labor Council Acts to Help Teachers." *Contra Costa County Labor Journal* 23 Sept. 1966. Print.

Lannon, Albert Vetere. *Fight or Be Slaves: The History of the Oakland-East Bay Labor Movement.* Lanham: University Press of America, 2000. Print.

Larrowe, Charles. *Harry Bridges: The Rise and Fall of Radical Labor in the United States.* Westport: Lawrence Hill, 1977. Print.

Laslett, John, and Mary Tyler. *The ILGWU in Los Angeles, 1907–1988.* Inglewood: Ten Star Press, 1989. Print.

Laurie, Bruce. *Artisans into Workers: Labor in Nineteenth-Century America.* New York: Hill and Wang, 1989. Print.

Leahy, Margaret. "On Strike! We're Gonna Shut it Down: The 1968–69 San Francisco State Strike." *Ten Years that Shook the City: San Francisco 1968–1978.* Ed. Chris Carlsson. San Francisco: City Lights Books, 2011. Print.

Lemke-Santangelo, Gretchen. *Abiding Courage: African American Migrant Women and the East Bay Community.* Chapel Hill: University of North Carolina Press, 1996. Print.

Levy, Jacques. *Cesar Chavez: Autobiography of La Causa.* New York: W. W. Norton, 1975. Print.

Lewis, Oscar. *The Big Four: The Story of Huntington, Stanford, Hopkins, and Crocker, and of the Building of the Central Pacific.* New York: Alfred E. Knopf, 1938. Print.

Lichtenstein, Alex. "Engine of Injustice: African American Labor and Technological Change at the Sloss Furnaces." *Industrial Archeology* 7.2 (1994). Print.

Lichtenstein, Nelson. *Labor's War at Home: The CIO in World War II.* Philadelphia: Temple University, 2003. Print.

Lingenfelter, Richard E. *The Hardrock Miners: A History of the Mining Labor Movement in the American West, 1863–1893.* Berkeley: University of California Press, 1974. Print.

Lipsitz, George. *Rainbow at Midnight: Labor and Culture in the 1940s.* Urbana: University of Illinois Press, 1981. Print.

Lockwood, Charles. *Suddenly San Francisco: The Early Years of an Instant City.* San Francisco: San Francisco Examiner Division of the Hearst Corporation, 1978. Print.

London, Jack. "South of the Slot." *The Social Writings of Jack London.* Ed. Philip Foner. Secaucus: Citadel Press, 1964. Print.

London, Joan, and Henry Anderson. *So Shall Ye Reap: The Story of Cesar Chavez and the Farm Workers' Movement.* New York: Thomas Y. Crowell, 1970. Print.

Lotchin, Roger W. *San Francisco 1846–1856: From Hamlet to City.* Urbana: University of Illinois Press, 1997. Print.

Luck, Mary Gorringe. *Wartime and Postwar Earnings, San Francisco, 1944–1946.* Berkeley: University of California Press, 1948. Print.

Mabalon, Dawn B., and Rico Reyes. *Filipinos in Stockton.* Charleston: Arcadia Publishing, 2008. Print.

Mackey, Howard. *Federation Newsletter* 11 May 1959. Print.

———. Personal interview. 2011.

Mackin, Elizabeth. Letter to Kahn's Department Store. 6 March 1947. MS, courtesy of Ed Mackin.

Manheim, Jarol B. "The Emerging Role of Worker Centers in Union Organization: A Strategic Assessment." Working Paper for U.S. Chamber of Commerce, Nov. 2013. Web.

Mann, Eric. *Taking on General Motors: A Case Study of the UAW Campaign to Keep GM Van Nuys Open.* Los Angeles: Center for Labor Research and Education, Institute of Industrial Relations, UCLA, 1987. Print.

Marelius, John. "Initiative on Unions May Start Rush." *San Diego Union Tribune* 4 May 2005. Print.

Margolin, Malcolm. "Introduction and Commentary." *Life in a California Mission: Monterey in 1786: The Journals of Jean Francois de La Perouse.* Berkeley: Heyday Books, 1989. Print.

Markham, Edwin. *California the Wonderful.* New York: Hearst's International Library Company, 1914. Print.

Martin, John. "Raising Wages at Airports." *New York Times* 13 Nov. 2013. Print.

Mason, Mary Anne. "Neither Friends nor Foes." *California Progressivism Revisited.* Eds. William Deverell and Tom Sitton. Berkeley: University of California Press, Berkeley, 1994. Print.

Matthews, Glenna. *Silicon Valley, Women, and the California Dream: Gender, Class and Opportunity in the Twentieth Century.* Stanford: Stanford University Press, 2003. Print.

Matthews, Lillian Ruth. "Women in Trade Unions in San Francisco," *University of California Publications in Economics,* vol. 3, no. 1 (1913). Print.

Matthiessen, Peter. *Sal Si Puedes (Escape if You Can): Cesar Chavez and the New American Revolution.* Berkeley: University of California Press, 1969. Print.

"Maxine Jenkins: Labor Organizer, Activist." *San Francisco Examiner* 20 Oct. 1994. Print.

"May 9, 1950 Agreement." *Ernesto Galarza Papers.* Stanford: Department of Special Collections, Stanford University Libraries. Print.

McGilligan, Patrick, and Paul Buhle, eds. *Tender Comrades: A Backstory of the Hollywood Blacklist.* New York: St. Martin's Press, 1997. Print.

McGuire, Mike. "A New Way to Equal Pay." *Dollars and Sense* April 1982. Print.

———. "Feminist Strike in San Jose." *Workshop in Nonviolence* 18.9 (1982). Print.

McWilliams, Carey. *Southern California Country: An Island on the Land.* New York: Duell, Sloan and Pearce, 1946. Print.

———. *California: The Great Exception.* Santa Barbara: Peregrine Smith, 1979. Print.

Medina, Jennifer. "Hardship Makes a New Home in the Suburbs. " *New York Times* 9 May 2014. Print.

Mendel, Ed. "In Unions, Governor Finds Nest of Hornets." *San Diego Union Tribune* 7 Nov. 2005. Print.

Mendoza-Schechter, Hope. Personal interview. 4 March 1998.

Metzgar, Jack. *Striking Steel: Solidarity Remembered.* Philadelphia: Temple University Press, 2000. Print.

Migration Policy Institute. "MPI Data Hub: Migration Facts, Stats, and Maps." MigrationPolicy.org. Migration Policy Institute, 2001–2015. Web. http://www.migrationpolicy.org/programs/data-hub

Milkman, Ruth. *L.A. Story: Immigrant Workers and the Future of the U.S. Labor Movement.* New York: Russell Sage Foundation, 2006. Print.

Milkman, Ruth, and Rachel E. Dwyer. "Growing Apart: The 'New Economy' and Job Polarization in California, 1992–2000." *The State of California Labor.* Berkeley: Institute of Industrial Relations, UC Berkeley and UCLA, 2002. Print.

Milkman, Ruth, and Daisy Rooks. "California Union Membership: A Turn of the Century Portrait." *The State of California Labor.* Berkeley: Institute of Industrial Relations, UC Berkeley and UCLA, 2003. Print.

Milkman, Ruth, Joshua Bloom, and Victor Narro, eds. *Working for Justice: The L.A. Model of Organizing and Advocacy.* Ithaca: Cornell University Press, 2010. Print.

Miller, Bruce W. *Chumash: A Picture of Their World.* Los Osos: Sand River Press, 1988. Print.

Miller, Paul T. *The Postwar Struggle for Civil Rights: African Americans in San Francisco, 1945–1975.* New York: Routledge, 2014. Print.

Miller, Sally M., and Daniel A. Cornford. *American Labor in the Era of World War II.* Westport: Praeger, 1995. Print.

Mitchell, H. L. *Mean Things Happening in this Land: The Life and Times of H. L. Mitchell, Cofounder of the Southern Tenant Farmers Union.* Montclair: Allenheld and Osmun, 1979. Print.

———. *Roll the Union On: A Pictorial History of the Southern Tenant Farmers Union.* Chicago: Charles H. Kerr, 1987. Print.

Monroy, Douglas. *Thrown Among Strangers: The Making of Mexican Culture in Frontier California.* Berkeley: University of California Press, 1990. Print.

———. *Rebirth: Mexican Los Angeles from the Great Migration to the Great Depression.* Berkeley: University of California Press, 1999. Print.

Montgomery, David. *Citizen Worker: The Experience of Workers in the United States with Democracy and the Free Market during the Nineteenth Century.* Cambridge: Cambridge University Press, 1993. Print.

Moore, Shirley Ann Wilson. *To Place Our Deeds: The African American Community in Richmond, California, 1910–1963.* Berkeley: University of California Press, 2000. Print.

Morgenstern, Marty. "30 Years Looking Back: A Random History of Collective Bargaining." *CPER Journal* 134 (1999). Print.

———. Personal interview. 26 July 2010.

Morrissey, F. W. "The Oakland General Strike." Unpublished Economics 298 paper, University of California, Berkeley, 1947. Typescript.

Mortimer, Wyndham. *Organize! My Life as a Union Man.* Boston: Beacon Press, 1972. Print.

Mowrey, George E. *The California Progressives.* New York: Quadrangle/New York Times Book Company, 1976. Print.

Munoz, Michael S. *"Pilebutt": Stories and Photographs about Pile Driving.* San Leandro: Pilebutt Press, 1986. Print.

Murray, John. "A Foretaste of the Orient." *International Socialist Review* 4 (1903). Print.

Murphy, Marjorie. *Blackboard Unions: The AFT and the NEA, 1900—1980.* New York: Cornell University Press, 1990. Print.

Musser, Charles. "Work, Ideology, and Chaplin's Tramp." *Resisting Images: Essays on Cinema and History.* Eds. Robert Sklar and Charles Musser. Philadelphia: Temple University Press, 1990. Print.

———. *The Emergence of Cinema: The American Screen to 1907.* Berkeley: University of California Press, 1994. Print.

Myers, Miles. Personal interview. May 1998.

Narro, Victor. "Impacting Next Wave Organizing: Creative Campaign Strategies of the Los Angeles Worker Centers." *New York Law School Law Review* 50 (2005): 465. Print.

———. "Si Se Puede! Immigrant Workers and the Transformation of the Los Angeles Labor and Worker Center Movements." *Los Angeles Public Interest Law Journal* 1 (2009): 65–106. Print.

Nazario, Sonia. "Janitors' Suit Settled: Council to Pay $2.35 Million for Union Members Beaten by Police." *Los Angeles Times* 4 Sept. 1993. Print.

Nelson, Bruce. *Workers on the Waterfront: Seamen, Longshoremen, and Unionism in the 1930s.* Urbana: University of Illinois, 1988. Print.

Nicolaides, Becky M. *My Blue Heaven: Life and Politics in the Working Class Suburbs of Los Angeles, 1920–1965.* Chicago: University of Chicago Press, 2002. Print.

Nielsen, Mike, and Gene Mailes. *Hollywood's Other Blacklist: Union Struggles in the Studio System.* London: British Film Institute, 1995. Print.

Nolte, Carl. "Jack Balestreri, Golden Gate Bridge Builder, Dies." *San Francisco Chronicle* 27 April 2012. Print.

Nordhoff, Charles. *California for Travellers and Settlers.* Berkeley: Ten Speed Press, 1973. Print.

Norris, Frank. *The Octopus: A Story of California.* Toronto: Doubleday/Bantam, 1971. Print.

Norwood, Stephen. *Labor's Flaming Youth: Telephone Operators and Worker Militancy 1878–1923*. Urbana: University of Illinois Press, 1991. Print.

———. *Strikebreaking and Intimidation: Mercenaries and Masculinity in Twentieth Century America*. Chapel Hill: University of North Carolina Press, 2002. Print.

Novogrodsky, David. Personal interview. 25 July 2010.

"The Oakland General Strike of 1946." *Bay City Blues*. Prod. Craig Gordon, Tim Reagan, et al. Pacifica Radio Network. KPFA-FM, Berkeley, 29 Nov. 1976. Radio.

O'Connor, Harvey. *History of Oil Workers International Union-CIO*. Denver: Oil Workers Intl. Union (CIO), 1950. Print.

O'Farrell, Brigid, and Joyce L. Kornbluh. *Rocking the Boat: Union Women's Voices, 1915–1975*. New Brunswick: Rutgers University Press, 1996. Print.

Olmsted, Roger R. "The Chinese Must Go!" *California Historical Quarterly* 50.3 (1971). Print.

———. *Scow Schooners of San Francisco Bay*. Cupertino: California History Center, 1988. Print.

Olmsted, Roger R., ed. *Scenes of Wonder and Curiosity from Hutchings California Magazine, 1856–1861*. Berkeley: Howell-North, 1962. Print.

Olsen, Tillie [Lerner]. "The Strike." *Partisan Review* Sept.–Oct. 1934. Web. http://newdeal.feri.org/voices/voce05.htm

"Our Candidates: Fearless Champions of the Rights of the People." *The Los Angeles Citizen* 7 July 1911. Print.

Ovnick, Merry. *Los Angeles: The End of the Rainbow*. Los Angeles: Balcony Press, 1994. Print.

Parker, Carleton. *The Casual Laborer and Other Essays*. New York: Harcourt, Brace and Howe, 1920. Print.

Paul, Rodman W. *California Gold: The Beginning of Mining in the Far West*. Lincoln: University of Nebraska Press, 1947. Print.

Pawel, Miriam. *The Union of Their Dreams: Power, Hope and Struggle in Cesar Chavez's Farm Worker Movement*. New York: Bloomsbury Press, 2010. Print.

Peradotto, Louis B., ed. *California Profit Opportunities*. Sacramento: Printing Division, Documents Section, Economic Development Agency, State of California, 1964. Print.

Perry, Jim, "In Memoriam: John B. 'Red' Melton, 1916–1988, A Personal Tribute," n.d. Print.

Perry, Louis B., and Richard S. Perry. *A History of the Los Angeles Labor Movement, 1911—1941*. Berkeley: University of California Press, 1963. Print.

Pesotta, Rose. *Bread Upon the Waters*. Ithaca: ILR Press, 1987. Print.

Pickelhaupt, Bill. *Shanghaiied in San Francisco*. San Francisco: Flyblister Press, 1996. Print.

Piketty, Thomas. *Capital in the Twenty-First Century*. Trans. Arthur Goldhammer. Cambridge: Belknap Press of Harvard University Press, 2014. Print.

Pintar, Laurie. "Behind the Scenes: Bronco Billy and the Realities of Work in Open Shop Hollywood." *Metropolis in the Making: Los Angeles in the 1920s*. Eds. Tom

Sitton and William Deverell. Berkeley: University of California Press, 2001. Print.

Pitt, Leonard. *The Decline of the Californios: A Social History of the Spanish-Speaking Californians, 1846–1890.* Berkeley: University of California Press, 1966. Print.

Pitti, Stephen J. *The Devil in Silicon Valley: Northern California, Race, and Mexican Americans.* Princeton: Princeton University Press, 2003. Print.

Phillips, George Harwood. *Chiefs and Challengers: Indian Resistance and Cooperation in Southern California.* Berkeley: University of California Press, 1975. Print.

Preis, Art. *Labor's' Giant Step: The First Twenty Years of the CIO.* New York: Pathfinder Press, 1964. Print.

Quam-Wickham, Nancy. "Who Controls the Hiring Hall? The Struggle for Job Control in the ILWU during World War II." *The CIO's Left-Led Unions.* Ed. Steve Rosswurm. New Brunswick: Rutgers University Press, 1992. Print.

———. "Another World: Work, Home and Autonomy in Blue-Collar Suburbs." *California Progressivism Revisited.* Eds. William Deverell and Tom Sitton. Berkeley: University of California Press, 1994. Print.

Quin, Mike. *The Big Strike.* Olema: Olema Publishing Company, 1949. Print.

Quinnell, Kenneth. "Major Milestones in AFL-CIO's Campaign for Immigration Reform." 21 Nov. 2014. Web. http://www.aflcio.org/Blog/Political-Action-Legislation/Major-Milestones-in-AFL-CIO-s-Campaign-for-Immigration-Reform

Quivik, Fredric L. *Kaiser's Richmond Shipyards, with Special Emphasis on Richmond Shipyard No. 3, a Historical Report Prepared for National Park Service, Rosie the Riveter/World War II Home Front National Historical Park.* Richmond, CA: Historic American Engineering Record, 2004. Print.

Rankin, Tom. Personal interview. 20 Dec. 2010.

Rawls, James J. *Indians of California: The Changing Image.* Norman: University of Oklahoma Press, 1984. Print.

Register, Cheri. *Packinghouse Daughter: A Memoir.* Minnesota: HarperCollins, 2001. Print.

Reich, Michael, Ken Jacobs, and Miranda Dietz, eds. *When Mandates Work: Raising Labor Standards at the Local Level.* Berkeley: University of California Press, 2014. Print.

Reinhold, Robert. "California Stalemate Ends in a Budget." *New York Times* 18 July 1991. Print.

"Restraining Orders End School Strike." *Contra Costa County Labor Journal* 23 Sept. 1966. Print.

Rhomberg, Chris. "Collective Actors and Urban Regimes: Class Formation and the 1946 Oakland General Strike." *Theory and Society* 24.4 (1995). Print.

———. *No There There: Race, Class, and Political Community in Oakland.* Berkeley: University of California Press, 2004. Print.

Rice, Richard B., William A. Bullough, and Richard J. Orsi. *The Elusive Eden: A New History of California.* New York: McGraw-Hill, 1996. Print.

"Richmond School Teachers Move Near Strike." *Contra Costa County Labor Journal* 9 Sept. 1966. Print.

"Richmond Students Learn Key Lesson." *Contra Costa County Labor Journal* 16 Sept. 1966. Print.

Rintoul, William. *Spudding In: Recollections of Pioneer Days in the California Oil Fields.* San Francisco: California Historical Society, 1976. Print.

———. *Oildorado: Boom Times on the West Side.* Fresno: Valley Publishers, 1978. Print.

Robinson, W. W. *Land in California: The Story of Mission Lands, Ranchos, Squatters, Mining Claims, Railroad Grants, Land Scrip, Homesteads.* Berkeley: University of California Press, 1979. Print.

Rogin, Michael P., and John L. Shover. *Political Change in California: Critical Elections and Social Movements, 1890–1966.* Westport: Greenwood Publishing, 1970. Print.

Rosenzweig, Roy. *Eight Hours for What We Will: Workers and Leisure in an Industrial City, 1870–1920.* New York: Cambridge University Press, 1983. Print.

Rosenburg, Mike. "Golden Gate Bridge Toll Takers Share Stories, Secrets on Way Out." *San Jose Mercury News.* 17 March 2013. Print.

Rosier, Sharon A. "Janitors Set a Single-Minded Goal." *AFL-CIO News* 22 April 1996. Print.

Ross, Fred. *Conquering Goliath: Cesar Chavez at the Beginning.* Keene: El Taller Grafico, 1989. Print.

Ross, Steven J. "How Hollywood Became Hollywood: Money, Politics, and Movies." *California Progressivism Revisited.* Eds. William Deverell and Tom Sitton. Berkeley: University of California Press, 1994. Print.

Rosswurm, Steve, ed. *The CIO's Left-Led Unions.* New Brunswick: Rutgers University Press, 1992. Print.

Rudy, Preston. "'Justice for Janitors,' Not 'Compensation for Custodians': The Political Context and Organizing in San Jose and Sacramento." *Rebuilding Labor: Organizing and Organizers in the New Union Movement.* Eds. Ruth Milkman and Kim Voss. Ithaca: Cornell University Press, 2004. Print.

Ruiz, Vicki L. *Cannery Women, Cannery Lives: Mexican Women, Unionization, and the California Food Processing Industry, 1930–1950.* Albuquerque: University of New Mexico Press, 1987. Print.

Ryan, Frederick L. *Industrial Relations in the San Francisco Building Trades.* Norman: University of Oklahoma Press, 1936. Print.

Ryder, David Warren. *Men of Rope: Being the History of Tubbs Cordage Company; Together with an Account of Some of the Collateral Activities in Which Its Pioneer Founders Engaged.* San Francisco: Historical Publications, 1954. Print.

St. Clair, David J. "The Gold Rush and the Beginnings of California Industry." *California History* 77.4 (1998–99). Print.

Sachen, Susan. Personal conversation. 18 Jan. 2014.

Salladay, Robert, and Carla Marinucci. "Schwarzenegger's Vow: 'Miracle of Sacramento.'" *San Francisco Chronicle* 18 Nov. 2003. Print.

Salvatore, Nick. *Eugene V. Debs: Citizen and Socialist.* Urbana: University of Illinois Press, 1982. Print.

Sanchez, George J. *Becoming Mexican-American: Ethnicity, Culture and Identity in Chicano Los Angeles, 1900–1945*. New York: Oxford University Press, 1993. Print.

Saul, Eric, and Don Denevi. *The Great San Francisco Earthquake and Fire, 1906.* Millbrae: Celestial Arts, 1981. Print.

Saxton, Alexander. *The Indispensable Enemy: Labor and the Anti-Chinese Movement in California*. Berkeley: University of California Press, 1971. Print.

Schaaf, Evelyn. Personal interview. 31 May 1995.

Schaaf, Valmar. Personal interview. 31 May 1995.

Scharlin, Craig, and Lilia Villanueva. *Philip Vera Cruz: A Personal History of Filipino Immigrants and the Farmworkers Movement*. Los Angeles: UCLA Labor Center, Institute of Industrial Relations, and UCLA Asian American Studies Center, 1992. Print.

Schiesl, Martin, and Mark M. Dodge, eds. *City of Promise: Race and Historical Change in Los Angeles*. Claremont: Regina Books, 2006. Print.

Schlipf, Paul. Interview by Ben Visnick. 1980. Audio.

Schnapper, M. B. *American Labor: A Pictorial Social History*. Washington D.C.: Public Affairs Press, 1972. Print.

Schoeni, Robert F., et al. *Life After Cutbacks: Tracking California's Aerospace Workers*. Santa Monica: Rand, 1996. Print.

"School Strike Seems Certain in Richmond." *Contra Costa County Labor Journal* 9 Sept. 1966. Print.

Schwartz, Harvey. *The March Inland: Origins of the ILWU Warehouse Division, 1934–1938*. Los Angeles: Institute of Industrial Relations, UCLA, 1978. Print.

———. *Solidarity Stories: An Oral History of the ILWU*. Seattle: University of Washington, 2009. Print.

Schwartz, Nancy Lynn. *The Hollywood Writers' Wars*. New York: McGraw Hill, 1982. Print.

Schwartz, Stephen. *SUP, Brotherhood of the Sea: A History of the Sailors' Union of the Pacific, 1885–1985*. New Brunswick: Transaction Books, 1986. Print.

———. "Maxine Jenkins." *San Francisco Chronicle* 20 Oct. 1994. Print.

Selden, David. *The Teacher Rebellion*. Washington, D.C.: Howard University Press, 1985. Print.

Selvin, David. "The Way It Was in San Francisco." Adapted from *A Century of Democratic Unionism*. San Francisco: International Typographical Union, 1972. Print.

———. *Sky Full of Storm: A Brief History of California Labor*. San Francisco: California Historical Society, 1975. Print.

———. *A Terrible Anger: The 1934 Waterfront and General Strikes in San Francisco*. Detroit: Wayne State University Press, 1996. Print.

Service Employees International Union Local 22, AFL-CIO. "Comparable Worth Study Sacramento City Unified School District: A Proposal." 25 Aug. 1981. Print.

Sexton, Patricia Cayo. *The New Nightingales: Hospital Workers, Unions, New Women's Issues*. New York: Enquiry Press, 1982. Print.

Shaw, Randy. *Beyond the Fields: Cesar Chavez, the UFW, and the Struggle for Justice in the 21st Century*. Berkeley: University of California Press, 2008. Print.

Shumsky, Neil L. *The Evolution of Political Protest and the Workingmen's Party of California*. Columbus: Ohio State University Press, 1991. Print.

Sides, Josh. *L.A. City Limits: African American Los Angeles from the Great Depression to the Present*. Berkeley: University of California Press, 2003. Print.

Sinclair, Upton. *Oil!: A Novel*. New York: A & C Boni, 1927. Print.

Sito, Tom. *Drawing the Line: The Untold Story of the Animation Unions from Bosko to Bart Simpson*. Lexington: University Press of Kentucky, 2006. Print.

Smith, Duane A. "Mother Lode for the West: California Mining Men and Methods." *California History* 77.4 (1998–99). Print.

Smith, Grant H. "The History of the Comstock Lode, 1850–1920." *Geology and Mining Series. University of Nevada Bulletin* 37.3 (1943), July 1943. Print.

Smorra, Allan G. "The Last Two Surviving Golden Gate Bridge Builders Have Passed Away." *Ohm Sweet Ohm: Adventures in Life from the Sunshine State to the Golden Gate*. 29 April 2012. Web. http://ohmsweetohm.me

Snyder, Nancy. "Local History: SEIU 790." *Labor Archives and Research Center Newsletter, No. 3* (Winter 2003). San Francisco: San Francisco State University. Print.

Soto, Gary. *Jessie de la Cruz: A Profile of a United Farm Worker*. New York: Persea Books, 2000. Print.

"Speeches and Resolutions." *Women in the Labor Movement. California State Federation of Labor Women's Conference, May 19–20, 1973*. San Francisco. Print.

Stanley, Jerry. *Digger: The Tragic Fate of the California Indians from the Missions to the Gold Rush*. New York: Crown Publishers, 1997. Print.

Starr, Kevin. *Endangered Dreams: The Great Depression in California*. New York: Oxford University Press, 1996. Print.

———. *Golden Gate: The Life and Times of America's Greatest Bridge*. New York: Bloomsbury Press, 2010. Print.

Stegner, Wallace. *Joe Hill: A Biographical Novel*. Garden City: Doubleday, 1969. Print.

Stillman, Don. *Stronger Together: The Story of SEIU*. White River Junction: Chelsea Green Publishing, 2010. Print.

Stimson, Grace. *Rise of the Labor Movement in Los Angeles*. Berkeley: University of California Press, 1955. Print.

Stone, Irving. *Clarence Darrow for the Defense*. New York: Signet, 1969. Print.

Street, Richard Steven. "First Farmworkers, First Braceros: Baja California Field Hands and the Origins of Farm Labor Importation in California Agriculture." *California History* 75.4 (1996–97). Print.

———. *Beasts of the Field: A Narrative History of California Farmworkers, 1769–1913*. Stanford: Stanford University Press, 2004. Print.

———. *Everyone Had Cameras: Photography and Farmworkers in California, 1850–2000*. Minneapolis: University of Minnesota Press, 2008. Print.

Swados, Harvey. *Standing Fast*. New York: Doubleday, 1970. Print.

Taft, Philip. *Labor Politics American Style: The California State Federation of Labor*. Cambridge: Harvard University Press, 1968. Print.

Takaki, Ronald. *Strangers From a Distant Shore: A History of Asian Americans*. Boston: Little, Brown, 1989. Print.

Taylor, Ronald B. *Chavez and the Farm Workers: A Study in the Acquisition and Use of Power*. Boston: Beacon Press, 1975. Print.

"Teachers Get CLC Strike Sanction." *Contra Costa County Labor Journal* 16 Sept. 16, 1966. Print.

Teilhet, Raoul. "Oral History." *AFT Oral History Project*. 1986. Audio.

"Terminating the Deficit: Does the Governor's Proposed 2004–05 Budget Restore California's Fiscal Health While Protecting Public Services?" *CalBudgetCenter. org*. California Budget Project, Jan. 2004. Web. http://calbudgetcenter.org /wp-content/uploads/2004chartbook.pdf

Thomas, Keith. *The Oxford Book of Work*. London: Oxford University Press, 1999. Print.

Tong, David. "The Man behind the Sex Bias Strike." *Oakland Tribune* 7 July 1981. Print.

Topakian, Greg, and Laura Henze. "Proposition 13: Fighting Cutbacks in Alameda County." *Crisis in the Public Sector: A Reader*. Ed. Martha Cameron. New York: Monthly Review Press, 1981. Print.

Trimble, Peter. "Shelley Gets No-Bias Pact on Hotel Jobs." *San Francisco Examiner* 8 March 1964. Print.

Tucker, Floyd. "Janitors Fight for Master Contract." *California AFL-CIO News* 3 May 1996. Print.

Tygiel, Jules. "Introduction." *Oil!: A Novel*. Upton Sinclair. Berkeley: University of California Press, 1997. Print.

"UC Davis Study: California's Latino Vote Increases but Still Lags." *Sacramento Bee* 31 May 2013. Print.

United States. Bureau of Labor Statistics, Department of Labor. *Union Members—2014*. Washington: GPO, 2015. Web. http://www.bls.gov/news.release /union2.nro.htm

———. *History of Wages in the United States from Colonial Times to 1928: Bulletin of the United States Bureau of Labor Statistics, No. 499*. Washington: GPO, 1929. Print.

———. Commission on Civil Rights. "Comparable Worth: Issue for the 80s." *V2: Proceedings*. Washington: GPO, 1984. Print.

———. U.S. Congress, Joint Special Committee to Investigate Chinese Immigration. *Senate Report 689*. Washington: GPO, 1877. Reprint. New York: Arno, 1978. Print.

United Steelworkers of America. *The 1959 Steel Strike: A Triumph of Unity and Democracy: Pamphlet No. PR-112*. Pittsburgh: United Steelworkers of America, n.d. Print.

Van Bourg, Victor. Correspondence with author. 1994. Manuscript.

———. Personal conversations. 1994.

Voss, Kim. *The Making of American Exceptionalism: The Knights of Labor and Class Formation in the Nineteenth Century*. Ithaca: Cornell University Press, 1993. Print.

Waldie, D. J. *Holy Land: A Suburban Memoir*. New York: St. Martin's Press, 1996. Print.

Waldinger, Roger, Chris Erickson, Ruth Milkman, Daniel J. B. Mitchell, Abel Valenzuela, Kent Wong, and Maurice Zeitlin. "Helots No More: A Case Study of the Justice for Janitors Campaign in Los Angeles." *Organizing to Win*. Eds. Kate Bronfenbrenner et al. Ithaca: Cornell University Press, 1998. Print.

Walker, Richard A. *The Conquest of Bread: 150 Years of Agriculture in California*. New York: The New Press, 2004. Print.

Watkins, Earl. Personal interview. 2 April 1998.

Weber, Devra Anne. "Mexican Women on Strike: Memory, History and Oral Narratives." *Between Borders: Essays on Mexicana/Chicana History*. Ed. Adelaida R. Del Castillo. Encino: Floricanto Press, 1990. Print.

———. *Dark Sweat, White Gold: California Farm Workers, Cotton, and the New Deal*. Berkeley: University of California Press, 1994. Print.

Weinberg, Stewart. "30 Years Looking Back: Ruminations of a Public Employee Union Lawyer." *CPER Journal* 136 (1999). Print.

———. "The Winton Act: A History Lesson About Special Interest Legislation." *CPER Journal* 177 (2006). Print.

Weinstein, James. *The Decline of Socialism in America 1912–1925*. New Brunswick: Rutgers University Press, 1984. Print.

Weintraub, Hyman. "The IWW in California, 1905–1932." MA thesis. UCLA, 1947. Print.

———. *Andrew Furuseth: Emancipator of the Seamen*. Berkeley: University of California Press, 1959. Print.

Weir, Stan. "American Labor on the Defensive: A 1940s Odyssey." *Radical America* 9.4–5 (1975). Print.

Wilentz, Sean. *Chants Democratic: New York City and the Rise of the American Working Class, 1788–1850*. New York: Oxford University Press, 1984. Print.

Woirol, Gregory R. *In the Floating Army: F. C. Mills on Itinerant Life in California*. Urbana: University of Illinois Press, 1992. Print.

Wollenberg, Charles. *Marinship at War: Shipbuilding and Social Change in Wartime Sausalito*. Berkeley: Western Heritage Press, 1990. Print.

———. *Photographing the Gold Rush: Dorothea Lange and the Bay Area at War, 1941–1945*. Berkeley: Heyday Books, 1995. Print.

Wolman, Philip J. "The Oakland General Strike of 1946." *Southern California Quarterly* 57.2 (1975). Print.

Wood, R. Coke, and Leon Bush. *California History and Government*. San Francisco: Fearon Publishers, 1962. Print.

Workers of the Writers' Program of the Work Projects Administration in Northern California. *San Francisco: The Bay and its Cities*. New York: American Guide Series, Hastings House, 1947. Print.

Wyman, Mark. *Hard Rock Epic: Western Miners and the Industrial Revolution, 1860–1910*. Berkeley: University of California Press, 1979. Print.

Yung, Judy. *Unbound Feet: A Social History of Chinese Women in San Francisco*. Berkeley: University of California Press, 1995. Print.

Zavella, Patricia. *Women's Work and Chicano Families: Cannery Workers of the Santa Clara Valley*. Ithaca: Cornell University Press, 1987. Print.

Zieger, Robert H. *The CIO, 1935–1955*. Chapel Hill: University of North Carolina Press, 1995. Print.

Ziegler, Wilbur Gleason. *Story of the Earthquake and Fire*. San Francisco: Murdock Press, 1906. Print.

INDEX

Page numbers in *italics* indicate illustrations.

Agricultural Labor Relations Act (ALRA, CA, 1975), 332, 345–46

Agricultural Labor Relations Board, 345–46

agricultural products: California's rank in food processing, 310; Chinese pioneers in, 81; Indian production of surplus, 17; packing plant outsourced, 396; Pullman strike's impact on, 97. *See also* agriculture

—SPECIFIC CROPS: asparagus, 334; cantaloupe, 218; cotton, 217–18; fruits and vegetables, 102–3; grapes, 103, 333–34, 337–42, 343; hops, 106, 194–96, 202, 333; lettuce, 218, 343; roses, 337; strawberries, 343; sugar beets, 40, 106 (*see also* sugar beet production); wheat, 21, 48, 102, 103, 104–5, 112

agricultural workers. *See* farm labor and farm labor migrants

Agricultural Workers Association, 336

Agricultural Workers Industrial League (AWIL), 218

Agricultural Workers Organizing Committee (AWOC), 334, 335, 336–38, 341, 342

agriculture: California's ranking in, 307; DiGiorgio's influence in, 293; harvesting wheat, 21; industrialization and mechanization of, 103–4; land drained for, 108–9; land ownership and scale of, 102–5; Native Americans and, 11; real estate development vs., 309–10. *See also* agricultural products; farm labor and farm labor migrants; rancheros/ranchos and ranching

The Aircraft Organizer (newspaper), 275

aircraft production: expansion in WWII, 262, 273; layoffs, 311; union organizing in, 274–79; women workers in, 272–73, *273*, 279. *See also* aerospace industry

airports, QSP for, 429

air traffic controllers, 379, 400

Alameda County: General Strike support in, 242. *See also* Oakland

Alameda County Central Labor Council: anti–Vietnam War resolution of, 385; on employers after WWI, 281; Occupy movement and, 435; strikes supported

by, 250, 282; "work holiday" called by, 285–89

Alameda industrial corridor, organizing of, 412

Alameda Industrial Union Council, 250

Albrier, Frances Mary, 269, 270

alcohol use: of brewery workers, 136; in hardrock mining, 29; of Indians on early ranches, 21, 26; recruitment of maritime workers and, 35–36; by workers in idle periods, 41. *See also* temperance movement

Alexander, George, 179–80, 187, 188

Alexander, Horace "Alex," 5, 326

Alinsky, Saul, 321, 335

Allen, Clara Marie, 272–73

Alliance for a Better California (ABC): constituents of, 420–23; immigrant organizing and, 432–33; lessons of, 424–25; two-part strategy of, 422–24. *See also* California Nurses Association; California Teachers Association; International Association of Fire Fighters

Alliance of Californians for Community Empowerment, 438

ALRA (Agricultural Labor Relations Act, CA, 1975), 332, 345–46

Alta California: first mission in, 10; Indians as workforce in, 13–17, *16*; missions' vs. rancheros' needs for workers in, 18–19; U.S. acquisition of, 20, 25

Alta California (newspaper), 41, 43–44

Amalgamated Association of Street and Electric Railway Employees Local 205: demise, 160; female supporters of, 160–61; founding, 132; strike by, 150, 155–59, *156*

Amalgamated Streetcar Workers, 242

Amalgamated Transit Union Local 192, *284*, 285

American Beet Sugar Company: development of, 116–17; labor contracting and, 118–19, 125; spokesman for, 120, 123

American Building Maintenance (ABM), 399, 400, 403, 405

American Dream, Chinese workers' hopes for, 66–67, 75. *See also* California Dream

American Federation of Labor (AFL): ARU compared with, 95; CIO's united front with, 289–90, 328–31; CIO vs., 249–51, 291; civil rights department of, 322; collective bargaining in Cold War, 317; craft unionism philosophy of, 147, 161; division in, 248; exclusionary policies of, 125–26; federal unions chartered by, 174, 197; general strike against rules of, 242; goals of, 87–88; IA disputes with, 205–6; IWW's view of, 192; labor organizers funded by, 173; Los Angeles Council of Labor and, 101; national convention (1911), 186; no-strike pledge in WWII, 264; political stance changes, 149; post-WWI challenges for, 199; "Preparedness Day" parade boycotted by, 202; public sector charters of, 350; San Diego free speech fight and, 193; strikes supported by, 179, 283–85, 287, 296; on teacher rights, 361. *See also* AFL-CIO; California AFL; California Labor Federation

American Federation of Musicians (AFM), 149, *156*
—LOCAL 6, 149, 320, 324, 331
—LOCAL 47, 252

American Federation of State, County and Municipal Employees (AFSCME): charter, 350; classified school employees in, 368; growth of, 369; MMBA used by, 358; SEIU challenged by, 356–57; strikes and, 351
—LOCAL 101: comparable worth complaint of, 378; gender discrimination in, 370, 371–72; origins of, 369; strike by, 373, 376–77, *377*; Women's Committee, 372–75, *374*
—LOCAL 535, 357
—LOCAL 1675, 363–65
—LOCAL 1695, 371

American Federation of Teachers (AFT), 360, 366–67
—LOCAL 430, 314, 315
—LOCAL 866, 362–63
—LOCAL 1021, 315

"American Plan," 199, 203, 204. *See also* open shop agreements

American Racing Equipment, 412

American Railway Union (ARU), 94–95, 96–97, 98–101. *See also* Pullman boycott and strike
—LOCAL 80, 94

American River sawmill, 25

amusements. *See* leisure and entertainment

anarchism, 222

Anaya, Gilbert, 323

Anderson, Bob, 355–56

Angel Island ("Ellis Island of the West"), 445

anti-Chinese movement: growers' conundrum in, 109–11; Pesotta's encounter with, 257; unions linked to, 86, 258; violence in, *71*, 71–72; "white worker labels" on commodities, 69; of WPC, 73–75, 78. *See also* boycotts

anticommunism: in Hollywood, 300–301; of IAM, 275–76; legacy for unionization, 316–18; motivations underlying, 311–13; red-baiting tactic, 198–99, 276, 291, 317, 351; strike leaders accused of being Communists, 235, 236, 237, 238, 243, 283, 286, 298–99. *See also* blacklists; Cold War; House Un-American Activities Committee; loyalty oaths

antimonopolist efforts, 78

antipicketing ordinance (LA): call for and passage of, 170, 175–76, 179–80; promise to undo, 185; stepped-up arrests for, 182. *See also* picket lines

antiwar movements: in 1934, 235–36; CFT's support for, 360; opposition to Vietnam War, 357, 360, 371; retaliation against, 191; younger unionists in, 371, 385–87

Apple (corp.), 406, *408*, 408–10, 427

Arbuckle, Fatty, 196

Archibald, Katherine, 268

Argonauts, 27–28

Arizona, strikes outlawed in, 345–46

Arnold, Charles, 124

ARU. *See* American Railway Union

Arvin: farmworker housing in, 293–94; picketers arrested in, 297–98; strikers' confrontation with growers in, 220; Teamsters support for strikers, 296. *See also* DiGiorgio Fruit Corp.

431; GM threatened with, 392, 394, 395; of grapes, 339–42; of lettuce and strawberries, 343; of *Los Angeles Times*, 89, 90, 91–93; of Montgomery buses, 320; of "Preparedness Day" parade, 202; secondary type of, 92–93; of specific beer brands, 136, 179, 180; of URR streetcars, 155–59, 165. *See also* Pullman boycott and strike

Bracero Program, 295, 332–33

Bradford Building Service, 403, 405. *See also* International Service Systems

Brady, Slim, 365

Brannan, Sam, 26

Bread and Roses (film), 403

Bread Upon the Waters (Pesotta), 223

Breault, Dan, 286

Brewer, Roy, 301–2, 312–13

breweries, 135–36, 144, 179, 180, 182

Brewers and Maltsters Union of the West Coast, 136

Bridges, Harry: agitation for union, 231–32; on automation and modernization, 389–91; CIO role of, 249, 252; circle of, 300; in Embarcadero march, *235*; in funeral march, 240; ILA leadership of, 233–34, 237, 244, 288–89; ILWU case and, 317; Lundeberg's conflict with, 251; perjury trial of, 314; Soviet Union support from, 265; unemployment's impact on family, 212. *See also* International Longshoremen's and Warehousemen's Union

Bright Web in the Darkness (Saxton), 267

Brin, Sergey, 427

Brotherhood of Locomotive Firemen, 94

Brotherhood of Railway Conductors, 91

Brotherhood of Sleeping Car Porters (BSCP), 269, 270, 323

Brown, Al, *284*, 285

Brown, Edmund "Pat": anti–racial discrimination initiative of, 5; FEP act signed by, *330*; response to grape strike, 341–42; "right-to-work" laws opposed by, 329–30; son of, 345

Brown, George, 352–53

Brown, Jerry: ALRA signed by, 345, 346; budget crisis faced by, 436–40; collec-

tive bargaining law efforts of, 368; reelection of, 433–34

Brown, Willie, 415–16

Brown Act (CA, 1961), 352–53

Brunswig Drug Company, 251–52

Brusati, Fred, *444*

BSCP (Brotherhood of Sleeping Car Porters), 269, 270, 323

BSEIU. *See* Building Service Employees International Union

BTC. *See* San Francisco Building Trades Council

Buckingham, Hecht and Company, 68–69

Builders Exchange, 203

building service contractors: emergence of, 399–400; organizing workers of, 402–6, 407–11, *408*; workforce envisioned by, 401–2. *See also* janitorial, custodial, and sanitation workers; Shine Building Maintenance

Building Service Employees International Union (BSEIU), 316, 352, 399–400. *See also* janitorial, custodial, and sanitation workers; Service Employees International Union

—LOCAL 347, 316, 354

—LOCAL 434, 353–54

—LOCAL 535, 354–55

building trades workers: film studio work of, 204–5; organizing of, 51, 86, 133–34, 137–38; planing mill owned and operated by, 142; strikes for eight-hour day, 140–42; teamsters and, 144–45; unemployment in Depression, 212. *See also* carpenters; construction industry; electricians

Burns, Hugh, 298

Burns, Williams, 182, 187–89

buses, 320, 376

Busick, Bill, 224

Business Week, 383–84

Byfield, Gwendolyn, *287*

Calhoun, Patrick: antiunion retaliation by, 156–57; bribes from, 152, 156; guns and police intervention requested by, 150, 155–56; investigation and indictment of, 154, 157–58; justice eluded by, 160. *See also* United Railroads

California Supreme Court: on segregated unions and auxiliaries, 272; UFW rights to field access upheld, 346

California Teachers Association (CTA): as ABC ally, 420, 422; bills sponsored by, 361–62; EERA supported by, 368; function of, 351, 359; merger of, 366–67; in Richmond district, 363

California Wireworks Company, 40

Californios, 19, 20, 21, 82, 102. *See also* Mexican workers

Callahan, Bill, 376

Cal San (California Sanitary Canning Company), 255–56

Camp, Bill, 411

Campaign to Keep GM Van Nuys Open. *See* Van Nuys GM plant

Cannery and Agricultural Workers Industrial Union (CAWIU), 211, 218–19, 221, 248, 253–54. *See also* United Cannery, Agricultural, Packing and Allied Workers

cannery workers, 254–56, 310, 396

canoe building, 12, 15

capitalism: communists' and workers' opposition to, 312; "creative destruction" in transitions of, 383–84, 396–97, 427–28; Depression-era attacks on, 214–15; emergence of, 83; IWW's vision of demise of, 192; "trickle down" theory and, 434

carmen and streetcar workers: cars disabled in general strike, 285; demands of, 242; female supporters of, 160–61; IWW organizing among, 193; organizing and strikes by, 150, 155–60; police presence in cars, 175

carpenters: coalitional council support from, 137; "earthquake shacks" built by, 153; in eight-hour day movement, 54; Farris as exemplar of, 138–39; film studio work of, 204–5; industry decline in WWI, 201–2; organizing of, 84, 85–86, 121, 133–34; strikes by, 41, 140–42, 203–4; unemployment in Depression, 212. *See also* building trades workers

Carpenters (union)
—LOCAL 22, 133–34, 139–40, 201–2
—LOCAL 56, 84
—LOCAL 158, 171

Carter, Richard, 308

carwashes, organizing workers of, 431

Casey, Mike, *145*; circle of, 157; in City Front strike, 147, 242; in General Strike negotiations, 236–37; response to ULP and Schmitz's corruption, 158; strike called by, 145–46

casual labor force: garment workers viewed as, 223; hops harvest wages and conditions for, 194–96; Wobblies drawn from, 193–94. *See also* farm labor and farm labor migrants

Catholic Church: anticommunism of, 317; baptism in, 14; CSO supported by, 321, 322; priest's support for strike, 157, 159; split over grape boycott, 340. *See also* mission period

CAWIU. *See* Cannery and Agricultural Workers Industrial Union

CCFEP (California Committee for Fair Employment Practices), 323, 326, 329–30

Central Pacific Railroad: construction of, 3, 55–58, *57*, 61, 70, 108; political corruption linked to, 73; under Southern Pacific Railroad, 98; wage reduction reversed by, 70

Central Valley, oil workers in, 196–97

Century City area (LA), Justice for Janitors campaign in, 403–5, *405*

Century Cleaning, 402–3

Cesar, Julio, 15–16

Cesar Chavez Park (Sacramento), 411

CFT. *See* California Federation of Teachers

Chambers, Pat, 218, 219, 220, 221

Chambers of Commerce: anticommunism of, 238; City Front strike and, 148; functions of, 91–92; neutrality on Prop 30, 440; "Preparedness Day" parade supported by, 202; *Ramona* used to promote Los Angeles, 79; unionists called "Bolsheviks" by, 198; wages set and blacklist kept, 274, 275, 276

Chaplin, Charlie, 194, 204

Charleton, Al, 316

Charlie ("Foghorn Charlie"), 231–32

Chaudet, Joe, 284–85

Chavez, Cesar, *344*; depicted in *Golden Dreams*, 4; fast of, 343, 409; first union membership of, 299; frustrations of, 335; grape strike and boycott organizing by, 337–40, 341; iconic face of, 347; mentioned, 416; on nonviolence, 345; organizers' objections to actions of, 346; other unions' support for, 360; "right-to-work" laws opposed by, 328, 329; support for campaign to keep GM plant open, 394; voter registration campaigns of, 321, 328

Chavez, Helen, 321

Chicano community, 346, 347, 392–93

Chicano workers, 334, 337–38, 339, 388. *See also* Latino workers; Mexican American workers

child labor: grape picking, 334; hops harvest, 195; hours limited for, 189; Indian minors "apprenticed," 80; newspaper boys' refusal to distribute *Times*, 98; railroad construction, 56

children: Halloween parade of, 225; on picket lines, 256; segregated schools, 49, 329, 363. *See also* public education

China: granite imported from, 39; political turmoil in, 67

Chinatowns: Little Tokyos next to, 112; Methodist minister in, 109; needle trades in, 256–60, *259*; populations of, 81–82

Chinese community: immigrant population of, 67–68, 77; labor contracting systems of, 107; segregated neighborhoods of, 82; segregated schools for, 49. *See also* anti-Chinese movement

Chinese Exclusion Act (U.S., 1882), 75–76, 82, 83, 163

Chinese Ladies' Garment Workers' Union, 258–60, *259*

Chinese Progressive Association, 432

Chinese workers: abandoned ships dismantled by, 38; blamed for reduced wages and unemployment, 67–68, 69–70, 71–72; economic niches in Los Angeles, 78; excluded from immigration, 75–76; excluded from Knights of Labor, 87; as

farm laborers, 61, 105–6, 108–11, *110*; as Forty-Niners, 28; as garment workers, 257–59; as laborers in early Los Angeles, 80, 81–82, 83; motivation of, 66–67, 75; railroad brotherhoods' antagonism toward, 91; railroad construction, *57*, 57–58, 61, 81, 108; as stonemasons, 39; as strikebreakers, 68–69, 75; strikes by, 58, 75; as sugar beet labor, 121; WPC's riots and attacks on, *71*, 71–72, 73–75, 76

Chino, sugar refinery in, 116, 120

Chumash tribe, 12, 14–15

cigar makers, 69

CIO. *See* Congress of Industrial Organizations

Circo Azteca (troupe), 219

Cismowski, Liane, 422

The Citizen (newspaper), 184

Citizens' Alliance groups, 151, 169, 170

City Front Federation, 146–50, 157

city ordinances: coalitions push for local worker ordinances, 427–29; FEP, 321; free speech and freedom of assembly limited, 170; soapboxing ban, 193, *193*. *See also* antipicketing ordinance

City Women for Advancement (CWA), 371, 372

civil rights movement: grape boycott in context of, 339–40, 343; longshoremen's defense of, 238, 253; Montgomery bus boycott in, 320; public sector unionism fueled by, 348; systemic injustice evidenced in, 385–87; unions' support for, 260–61, 278–79, 322

civil service workers: context of organizing, 369–70; differences among, 348–49; eight-hour day law for, 54; personnel commission and, 370–71; reductions in force and, 374–75; women's organizing of, 371–74. *See also* public sector unionism

Civil War (1861–65), 48, 68

CIWA (California Immigrant Workers Association), 430

Clare Dress Company, 223–24

Clarke, Henry, 357, 363–64

class divisions: carmen's strike and, 158–59; in mayoral elections, 149–50; post-

WWI revival of, 198; railroad cars as reflection of, 60–61, 64; unions as advance over, 309. *See also* economic conditions; middle class; upper class; working class

CLAW (Coalition of Library Activist Workers), 371, 372

CLEAN Carwash Campaign (Community Labor Environmental Action Network), 431

Cleaning Up Silicon Valley (coalition), 408–9

Clerks' Association, 53

Cleveland, Grover, 101

climate: agriculture linked to, 102; attractions of southern California, 79, 83–84; clothing and activities suited to, 308; drought, 62, 82

Cloakmakers Local 8, 256, 257

closed shop agreements: BTC's success in, 142–43; craft (trade) unions' use of, 87; first in California, 51; printers in Los Angeles, 90; San Francisco as heart of, 175. *See also* open shop agreements; union shop

clothing, locally union made, 308

CNA (California Nurses Association), 418–19, 420, 422, 433

Coachella Valley, grape picker strike in, 337

Coalinga, oil workers' local in, 197

Coalition of Labor Union Women, 377

Coalition of Library Activist Workers (CLAW), 371, 372

coalitions: local worker ordinances passed, 427–29; national context of, 440–41; in Occupy movement, 427, 433, 434–36, 438, 449; state budget crisis solutions of, 436–40; of unionists and immigrant rights advocates, 426–27, 430–32

Coast Seamen's Union, 136, 147. *See also* Sailors' Union of the Pacific

Cold War: anxieties in, 311–13, 317; left wing impacted in, 316–18; witch hunt in, 313–16. *See also* anticommunism

collective action: of African American workers, 269–70; in Depression era, 248–49; erosion of memory of, 319; missing in *Golden Dreams*, 3–4; neces-

sity of, 51; of public employees, 349. *See also* unionization; *and specific strategies*

collective bargaining: backlash against, 384; Brown Act and, 352–53; building service contractors' agreement, 403, 405, 410; CIO/AFL division's impact on, 250–51; expansion of, 378; for farmworkers, 345–46; federal employees' right to, 352; minority hiring included in, 325; passage of laws for, 416; as path to quality education, 366–67; public employees' demand for, 354, 356; for public sector employees, 357–58; push for state law on, 367–68; teachers' need for, 359–64. *See also* feminist collective bargaining

Colley, Nathan, *330*

Collins, Virgil, 325

Coloma, gold discovery in, 26

Colver, Frank, 87, 89–90

Commission on Immigration and Housing (CA), 190, 196

Commission on Industrial Relations (U.S.), 190, 196

Committee for Industrial Organization. *See* Congress of Industrial Organizations

Committee on Un-American Activities (CUAC), 298, 315

The Communist Manifesto (Marx and Engels), 33

Communist Party (LA), 300, 312

Communist Party USA (CPUSA): appeal to minority workers, 311–12; CAWIU support from, 218–19; growth of, 213–15, 312; oaths repudiating, 312–13; witch hunt for members of, 313–16

Communists: AFL fears of associating with, 288; CIO leaders accused of being, 250; farm labor organizing by, 211, 218; garment worker organizing of, 222; increased number in Depression, 213–15; not barred from CSO, 322; strike leaders accused of being, 235, 236, 237, 238, 243, 283, 286, 298–99; Youth group demonstrations, 235–36. *See also* Workers Alliance

Community Action Program Committee, 392

Community Labor Environmental Action Network (CLEAN), 431

Community Services Organization (CSO), 321–22, 329, 335

company towns: Oxnard, 116–17, 122–23, 124; Pullman (IL), 95–96; Salinas, 117; Spreckels, 116

company unions: aircraft industry, 274; Depression-era impetus for, 216; film studio workers, 206; "fink books" burned by strikers, 243–44; fink halls of, 229–30, 233, 237; NIRA's support for, 216, 247; NLRA prohibition of, 410; team concept akin to, 395

comparable worth: in AFSCME–San Jose city negotiations, 375–76; backlash against, 380; city council discussions of, 373–74, *374*; concept, 370; first strike over, *377*; national attention to, 376–77; women's gains of, 377–78

Comstock Lode (Nevada silver mines), 40, 56, 63–64, 65

Conference of Studio Unions (CSU), 300–301, 313

Congress of Industrial Organizations (CIO): AFL's united front with, 289–90, 328–31; AFL vs., 249–51, 291; anti-communism in Cold War era, 317–18, 322; electoral focus of, 263–64; farm labor union in, 254–55; FDR reelection PAC of, 263–64; founding and growth, 248–49; impact in California, 260–61; "People's Program" of, 280; public sector charters of, 350, 351; strikes supported by, 256, 288–89; UPWA expelled by, 315; WWII no-strike pledge of, 264. *See also* AFL-CIO; California CIO Council

Connelly, Slim, 250

Consolidated Aircraft, 272–73, 275, 278

construction industry: building supplies for, 203; carpenters' failed strike in, 203–4; decline in WWI, 201–2; dry-wallers' strike in, 412; labor shortage and higher wages in, 38–39; seasonal work in, 41; technologies and manual labor in early, 37–38; union attacks on sites, 171; union losses in LA construc-

tion frenzy, 399. *See also* building trades workers; carpenters; electricians

consumerism: Fordist ethos of, 191–92, 263, 308–9, 388–89; industrial unionism in relation to, 249; overproduction and inadequate demand, 212

containerization: longshoremen impacted by, 389–91; as world economy symbol, 446–47, *447*

Contra Costa AFT Local 866, 362–65

Contra Costa Central Labor Council, 250, 357, 363, 364–65

Contra Costa County, social workers' strike in, 357

Contreras, Miguel, 412–13

convict labor, 51, 81, 401

Cooks' and Waiters' Alliance Local 30, 161

Coolidge, Calvin, 192

"coolies," 67

Corcoran, strikers' encampment at, 219, 221

Cornelius, Richard, 157, 158, 160

Corona, Bert, 251–53

Cortage, Edward, 70

cotton workers: conditions for, 217–18; strikes by, 218–21, *220*, 255

Coulter, James, 200, 201

Coulter, John, 200, 201

Courage Campaign, 438

Coxey's Army, 4

crime, 43, 77–78. *See also* police; violence

Criminal Syndicalism Act (CA, 1919), 198

"criminal syndicalism" prosecutions, 218, 221

"crimps," role of, 133, 148

Crocker, Charles: Chinese workers imported by, 57–58, 75, 97, 108; labor shortage of, 56; legacy of, 55; Nob Hill mansion of, 64

Cross, Ira, 46

CSEA (California School Employees Association), 351, 368

CSEA (California State Employees Association), 351–52

CSFL. *See* California Labor Federation

CSO (Community Services Organization), 321–22, 329, 335

CSU (Conference of Studio Unions), 300–301, 313

CTA. *See* California Teachers Association

CUAC (Committee on Un-American Activities), 298, 315

custodians. *See* janitorial, custodial, and sanitation workers

CWA (City Women for Advancement), 371, 372

Daifullah, Nagi, 345

Daily Alta (newspaper), 35

Daily Call (newspaper), 33

Dana, Richard Henry, 19, 36

Darcy, Sam, 240

Darrow, Clarence: as McNamara brothers' defense lawyer, 182–83, 185, 187, *188*, 189; on "open shops," 170; suspicions about case, 188

D'Ausilio, Bob, 423, *424*

Davis, Gray, 417–18, 420–21

Dawn Club (San Francisco), 324

Dean, Amy, 407

De Anda, Delphina, 294, 298

De Anda, Luis, 294

Debs, Eugene, *100*; ARU role of, 94–95; conspiracy charges against, 100; Darrow as lawyer of, 183; imprisonment and pardon of, 198; on industrial violence, 190; IWW role of, 192; presidential campaign of, 176, 198; Pullman strike and, 96–97, 98; Red Special train of, 202

Decker, Caroline, 218–19, 221

defense industry: competition in, 274; expansion in Cold War, 311–13, 317; fair employment practices mandated in, 269, 320. *See also* aerospace industry; aircraft production; shipbuilding

De La Cruz, Jessie, 213, 333–34

de la Cruz, Juan, 345

Delano: grape fields of, 337–38; grape pickers' strike and boycott in, 338–40; growers targeted in strike, 340–42

Dellums, C. L. (Cottrell Laurence): as chair of FEP commission, 331; federal suit filed by, 271; FEP efforts of, 269, 323–24, 326, *330*

Democratic Party, 44, 74. *See also* elections; *and specific candidates and governors*

demonstrations, marches, and parades: for amnesty for immigrants, 431, *432*; of Communist Youth group, 235–36; for eight-hour day, 54; explosion at, 202; on fiscal crisis and antiunionism, 415–16; for fixing California government, 433; for grape pickers, 341–42; Halloween, 225; in ILA strike, 234–36, *235*, 240–41; of janitors, 403–5, *405*, *408*, 408–9, 410–11; to keep GM plant open, *393*, 393–94; Labor Day, 139, 140, 166–67, *167*, 186, *310*; parade float for, 290; "Raises, not Roses," 376. *See also* picket lines

Denver (CO), Justice for Janitors campaign in, 402–3

Department Store Employees Local 1100, 327

department store workers, 281–82, 325–26. *See also* Oakland General Strike; Retail Clerks

deportation: Bridges's hearing for, 314; Chavez's support for, 346; of "subversives" and Communists, 198, 218, 243; of union leaders, 221; workers' fear of, 224, 254, 333, 401–2, 430

Despol, John, 323

Detroit (Mich.): airplane engines produced in, 274; auto production in, 307

Deukmejian, George, 346

Deveney, Dominic, 105

Diaz, John, 221

Diaz, Porfirio, 177

DiGiorgio, Joseph, 294, 295, 298, 303

DiGiorgio Fruit Corp.: *braceros* hired by, 295, 296; contract proposal for, 294–95; lawsuit of, 302–3; number of workers and size of, 293; public opinion of strike against, 296, 297–99; strikes and boycott of, 292, 295–97, *297*, 301–2, 339, 340–42; worker housing of, 293–94

Dills, Ralph, 367–68

direct action: IWW's focus on, 192; shift to political action from, 281, 289–91, 345–46, 380. *See also* boycotts; demonstrations, marches, and parades; mass mobilization; picket lines; strikes disease: cholera, 34; dysentery, 109, 195; Indians' resistance to, 18; malaria, 109, 195; tuberculosis, 160, 176; typhoid, 195. *See also* worker conditions

Disneyland, 307, 310–11, 331

Disney Studios, 3–4, 5, 7, 300, 307

Dollar Steamship Company, 230

domestic services: Chinese laundries burnt, 71–72; of Irish immigrants, 66; of Native Californian women, 21; union for, 433; wages of welders vs., 278–79; of white women, 49. *See also* service industry

"double breasted" companies, 400, 402, 403

Douglas Aircraft, 273, 274, 278

Draft Law and Riots (1863), 66

Draymen's Association, 146

Driffill, J. A., 120, 123

drought, 62, 82

drywallers' strike, 412

Dubinsky, David, 223, 248, 256, 314

Durazo, Maria Elena, 412, 446

Durst, Ralph, 194–96

Dust Bowl migrants (including Okies): as cotton workers, 217, 219, 255; as farm laborers, 293, 296; motive for migrating, 213; shipyards work of, 268

DWP (Los Angeles Department of Water and Power), 350, 352

earthquakes: as metaphor, 426; occurrences in 1850s, 33; San Francisco (1906), 144, 152–54, 157, 160–61, 175

East Bay Shipyard Workers Committee, 270

Eaves, Lucille, 42–43

economic conditions: agriculture's role in, 102; cost of living in Gold Rush, 39; end of California's isolation, 62–63; idle workers in downturns, 41; layoffs and deindustrialization, 391–92, 396–97; prosperity prompts union revival, 51–52, 137–38; WWII's impact on, 262–63. *See also* employment; financial and banking industry; income and wealth inequality; outsourcing and offshore production; unemployment; wages

Economic Development Agency, 383–84

economy: boom collapse, 88, 89; depressions (19th c.), 65, 96, 103, 105, 109, 135; dot-com bubble collapse, 417, 447–48; Great Recession in, 426–27, 433, 434, 446, 448–49; inflation, 266, 378–79; New Economy, 406–7, 409; prosperity in, 47–48, 51–52, 137–38; recessions and recoveries, 399, 447–48. *See also* capitalism; Great Depression

Edison Company, 123–24

education. *See* public education; universities

Educational Employment Relations Act (EERA, Rodda Act, CA, 1975), 368, 378

Educational Employment Relations Board (EERB), 378

eight-hour day: demise in 1870s, 62–63, 69; employers' opposition to, 53, 54, 55, 62; for oil workers, 197; strikes for, 58, 140–42, 155–57, 178–79; struggle for, 52–54, 59; for women, 166. *See also* hours and workweek

Eisenberg, Fran, 315

elections: gubernatorial, 5, 226–27, 417–18, 433–34; labor coalitions in, 427–29; labor-community coalitions in, 439–41; Los Angeles, 183–90; national, 176, 214; San Francisco mayoral, 149–50, 158, 159, 160; San Jose city council, 375; suffrage for women, 167–68, 187; workers as citizen-voters in, 319. *See also* labor politics; *and specific candidates*

—PROPOSITIONS: ALRA funding and UFW rights to field access (Prop 14), 346; antigay marriage (Prop 8), 438; budget process fix (Prop 25), 433–34, 436; FEP measure (Prop 11), 320; payroll deductions for unions (Prop 32), xiii–xiv, *xiv*, 426, 439–40; public services for undocumented immigrants (Prop 187), 430; "right-to-work" measure (Prop 18), 327–30, 419; Schwarzenegger's ballot measures (Props 74, 75, 76), 415, 419–20; single payer health care (Prop 186), 420; tax changes (Prop 13), xiv, 374–75, 379–80, 414–15; tax revenues for schools (Prop 30), xiii–xiv, *xiv*, 426, 437–40

Gold Rush *(continued)*
economic developments due to, 25,
30–31; labor shortages due to, 38–39, 56;
maritime workers central to, 34–35;
people of, 27–28; San Francisco
impacted by, 32–34; technologies used,
37, 40; weather's impact on, 41; workers'
wages in relation to, 39, 43
Gompers, Sam: Darrow hired by, 182–83;
Harriman endorsed by, 185, *186*; labor
politics dismissed by, 101; racist attitudes of, 125–26; suffrage support
from, 167
Gonzalez, Irene, 433
Gonzalez, Patricia, 422
"good government" ideas, 157–58
Google, 427
Grant, James, 42
grapes, 103, 333–34, 337–42, 343
The Grapes of Wrath (Steinbeck), 255, 294
Gray, Jim, 205
"Gray Davis car tax," 417–18
"greaser" (racial epithet), 21
Great Cotton Strike (1933), 217–21,
220, 255
Great Depression (1929–30s): cotton work-
ers' conditions and strike in, 217–21,
220, 255; duration and severity of, 211–13;
garment worker organizing in, 221–26;
labor unrest and response to, 216; plan
to end poverty, 226–28; political
responses to, 213–15; public works
spending in, 215, 261; social change and
collective action in, 248–49. *See also*
New Deal
Great Northern Railroad, 95
Great Recession, 426–27, 433, 434, 446,
448–49
The Great Train Robbery (film), 123–24
Green, A. M., 93–94
Green, William, 249–50, 293, 296
Green Giant, 396
Griffiths, D. W., 172
grocery stockers, 252
Guatemala. *See* Latino workers
guerrilla theater, 403, 433
guild traditions, 44–45. *See also* handicraft
production

Guyana (West Indies), contract laborers
in, 115

Haggerty, Neil, 323, *330*
Haiti (earlier, St. Dominique), revolution
in, 115
Hammett, "Big Bill," 219
Hampton, Benjamin, 204
handicraft production, 12, 14. *See also* guild
traditions
Haraszthy, Agoston, 108
Harbor General Hospital, 316
Harburg, Yip, 264
Hardy, George, 316, 352, 354, 369, 398
Harriman, Job: illness and death, 190, 191;
labor-socialist fusion of, 176–78, 185–
86; legal defense work of, 178, 182, 183,
188; mayoral campaign of, 183, 185–87,
189; metal workers' strike activities of,
179; on proposed picketing ban, 180
Harriman, Theo, 176
Hasiwar, Hank, 293, 294, 295, 296, 298, 299
Hassler, J. F., 288
Hastings's department store, 281–82, 283–
85, 289. *See also* Oakland General Strike
Hawkins, Augustus (Gus), 227, 320, 324,
330
Hayakawa, S. I., 386
Hay Associates, 372, 373–74, 375, 376
Hayes, Janet Gray, 369
"Hay Fever," 376
Haymarket affair (Chicago, 1886), 135
Haywood, William "Big Bill," 182
Hazelwood, Pearl, 355
Healey, Dorothy Ray, 254–55
Hearst, George, 64
Hearst, William Randolph, 64
Hell Bent for Election (film), 264, 280, 314
Henning, Jack, 415–16, 417–18, 421
HERE (Hotel Employees and Restaurant
Employees) Local 11, 412
Hewlett-Packard, 406, 408, 410, 411
Higher Education Employment Relations
Act (HEERA, CA, 1977), 378
Hill, Joe, 195
Hill, Tina, 272, 279
Hillman, Sidney, 248
Hines, Earl "Fatha," 320

hiring: Builders Exchange, 203; employer-run halls, 119, 206, 216; employers' code system for, 325–26; federal arbitrators' decision on, 245; fink halls for, 229–30, 233, 237, 243–44. *See also* building service contractors; company unions; labor contractors

hiring halls (union-run): construction trade, 85–86, 362; farm laborers, 342–43; longshoremen's demands for, 232, 233, 237; maritime workers, 5, 133, 244, 390; waste material industry, 253. *See also* worker centers

Hirsch, Fred, 327, 328

A History of the Labor Movement in California (Cross), 46

Hittel, John, 30

HLL (Humane Legislation League), 168

H. M. S. Pinafore (musical), 139

Hockin, Herbert, 188

Holiday, Billie, 320

Hollywood Film Council, 299–303

Hollywood Painters union local, 296

Hollywood studio film workers: animators' strike, 300; blacklist of, 7, 313–14; company union for, 206, 216; conditions for, 205; divisions in, 301; memorandum of understanding for, 206, 207; organizing of, 5, 204–6; set painters union contract, 300. *See also* film and movies

Hollywood studios, 7, 262, 313–14. *See also* film and movies

Holman, Lee, 233

homeownership, working-class, 191, 212, 308–11, 388–89. *See also* housing

"honey buckets," 29

Hopkins, Mark, 55, 56, 64, 73

hospital staffing legislation, 420–21

hospital workers, 315–16, 420–21. *See also* nurses; United Public Workers of America

Hotel Employees and Restaurant Employees (HERE) Local 11, 412

hotel workers, 86, 385–86, 412, 428, 431. *See also* restaurant workers

hours and workweek: in 1850s San Francisco, 40; brewery workers, 136; child and women's labor, 189; iron worker's notes on (1870s), 46–47; law limiting hours per day, 42; ten-hour day law and, 53. *See also* eight-hour day

House Education and Labor Committee, 299, 303

House Un-American Activities Committee (HUAC), 5, 7, 313–16

housing: boardinghouses, 35, 118, 133; construction in San Francisco (1850s), 38–39; decline of values, 426–27; Depression-era foreclosures, 212; earthquake and fire's destruction of, 152–53; farm labor migrants, 106–7; farmworkers, 293–94, 299–300, 302, 334; Mexican neighborhoods, 171–72; of technology and software millionaires, 427; tenements in San Francisco (1906), 144; workers evicted from company-owned, 295; for workers in sugar beet company towns, 117, 119; workers' vs. Nob Hill, 73. *See also* company towns; homeownership

Howard Jarvis Taxpayers Association, 379

HUAC (House Un-American Activities Committee), 5, 7, 313–16

Huerta, Dolores: background, 335–36; fast of, 409; grape strike and boycott organizing by, 337–40, 341; iconic face of, 347; organizing against outlawing strikes, 345–46; rose farm strike and, 337

Hughes Aircraft, 389

Humane Legislation League (HLL), 168

Huntington, Collis, 55, 56, 97, 174. *See also* Central Pacific Railroad

Huntington, Henry: African American strikebreakers of, 174–75; antiunionism of, 179; Citizens' Alliance support from, 169, 170; railroad construction by, 171–72

Huntington Beach, oil field beneath, 197

I, Governor of California . . . (Sinclair), 227

IA. *See* International Alliance of Theatrical Stage Employees

IAFF. *See* International Association of Fire Fighters

IBT. *See* International Brotherhood of Teamsters

Idaho, governor's assassination in, 182

ILA. *See* International Longshoremen's Association

ILGWU. *See* International Ladies' Garment Workers' Union

ILWU. *See* International Longshoremen's and Warehousemen's Union

Immigrant Aid Association, 61–62

immigrant rights, 426–27, 430–32, *432*

immigrant workers: California unions' embrace of, xv, *xv*; Chinese excluded as, 75–76; context of organizing, 398–400; encouraged to move to California, 61–62; influx of, 400–402; IWW support from, 192; miners' tax on, 28; organizing backgrounds of, 43, 44–45; travel from China, 67; unionism of, 7; as union organizers, 249; union's benefits for, 445–46; votes and voter registration drives of, 413, 432, 433–34, 439–40; worker centers for, 430–32. *See also* Service Employees International Union; *specific locals*; *and specific immigrant groups*

Immigration Act (1924), 191

Immigration Control and Reform Act (1989), 430

Imperial Valley Workers Union (La Union de Trabajadores del Valle Imperial), 218

income and wealth inequality: call to fix, 433; film on, 446; increase of, 414–15, 426–28, 434; Occupy movement in response to, 427, 433, 434–36, 438, 449

Indians. *See* Native Americans

In Dubious Battle (Steinbeck), 221

Industrial Accident Commission (CA), 189, 201

Industrial Association (San Francisco): newspaper friends of, 235, 236, 238–39, 243; police antiriot gear supplied by, 234, 237; strikebreakers used by, 234, 237, 238, 239

Industrial Films and Poster Service (later UPA), 263–64

industrial unionism: concept and principles, 94–95, 219, 232, 248; for farm workers, 253–56; generational differences in, 386–87; keeping idea alive,

229, 233; leaders noted, 275, 322; need for, 201, 248–49; political attacks on, 346–47, 384. *See also specific unions*

Industrial Workers of the World (IWW): campaigns of, 193, 194–96; on contracts, 138; demise in maritime trades, 233; industrial unionism of, 248; leadership imprisoned, 198; oil strikers' rejection of, 200; organizing techniques of, 252; political stance of, 192–93, 222; "Preparedness Day" parade boycotted by, 202; red membership card of, 194; slogan of, 236; vision of, 192–94, 231

industries. *See* manufacturing industries

Inequality for All (film), 446

injunctions, 94, 98, 101, 179. *See also* restraining orders

International Alliance of Theatrical Stage Employees (IA or IATSE): AFL disputes with, 205–6; corruption in, 300; founding, 204–5; loyalty oaths demanded in, 312–13; strikebreakers provided by, 301

International Association of Bridge and Structural Iron Workers, 171, 188

International Association of Fire Fighters (IAFF), 352

—LOCAL 1578, 423, *424*

International Association of Machinists (IAM): aircraft employers' relationship to, 274–75; anticommunism campaign of, 275–76; collective bargaining in Cold War, 317; membership of, 278, 311, 412

—LOCAL 68, 265–66

International Brotherhood of Boilermakers, Iron Shipbuilders, and Helpers of America, 268–72

International Brotherhood of Electrical Workers, 162, 204, 323

—LOCAL 18, 350, 352

International Brotherhood of Teamsters (IBT): agreements of, 144–45, 150; City Front strike in support of, 147–49; competition for, 252; farm laborers undermined by, 342, 343; General Strike negotiations and, 236–37; grape strikers and union election offer of,

Jackson, Jesse, *393*, 416
Jacobs, Paul, 317
James, Joseph, 270–72
James v. Marinship (1944), 271–72
janitorial, custodial, and sanitation workers: alliance with librarians, 372–73; deteriorating conditions for, 399–400; immigrant origins of, 401–2; organizing of, 315, 316, 354, 402–6, 407–11, *408*; police attack on, 404–5, *405*; strike of, 403–4; success of, 411–13; union vs. nonunion wages, 398–99. *See also* building service contractors; Justice for Janitors campaign
Japan: auto industry in, 389; rural turmoil in, 111; team concept in, 395; union organizing in, 293
Japanese American community, 270
Japanese-Mexican Labor Alliance (JMLA): AFL's rejection of charter, 125–26; organizing of, 119–22, *122*; significance of, 126–27; strike by, 122–24
Japanese workers: in beet sugar production, 117, 118, 119–20; as farm laborers, 111–13, 119; isolation of, 120; as labor contractors (*keiyaku-nin*), 107, 111, 112–13, 116, 118, 119–20; Mexican workers allied with, 119–27, *122*; militancy and organizing by, 112–13; railroad construction by, 174; union formed by, 119–20. *See also* Japanese-Mexican Labor Alliance
Japan Towns (Little Tokyos), 111–12
Jazz Age, 191–92
Jenco, Kelly, 387
Jenkins, Maxine: AFSCME–San Jose city negotiations and, 375; background, 372; comparable worth arguments of, 373–74, *374*; on flawed wage system, 371–72; organizing MEF into AFSCME local, 369–70; replacement of, 376
Jerome agency, 200, 203
Jewish community organizations, 321, 322
Jewish Labor Committee (JLC), 322–23
Jewish workers, 211, 252–53, 255–56, 402
JMLA. *See* Japanese-Mexican Labor Alliance
Job Harriman clubs, 185
Jobs, Steve, 427

Johns, George, 329–30
Johnson, Hiram, 189, 196
Johnson, Hugh, 243
Johnson, Walter, 327, 329
Joint Marine Strike Committee, 237
Jones, Chuck, 263–64
Jones, "Mother" Mary, 190
Joshua Hendy Iron Works, Sunnyvale plant, 265–66, 317
Journal of Trades and Workingmen (newspaper), 52
Journeymen Bakers' Union Local 45, 86
Journeymen Boilermakers' Protective Union, 52
Journeymen Painters Union, 51
The Jungle (Sinclair), 197, 226
Justice for Janitors campaign: achievements of, 405–6, 411–12, 413; in Century City, 403–5, *405*; in Denver, 402–3; in Sacramento, 410–11; in Silicon Valley, 406–10, *408*

Kahn's department store, 281–82, 283–85, *287*, 289. *See also* Oakland General Strike
Kaiser, Henry, 263
Kaiser shipyards, 267, 269, 270, 364
Kaiser Steel (Fontana), 263, 309
Kearney, Denis, 73–75, 76, 138–39
Kenaday, Alexander, 51–53
Kennedy, John F., 352, 353, 449
Kennedy, Kate, 49–51, *50*, 66, 87, 370
Kennedy, Robert, 340
Kern County: farm laborers in, 254, 355; strikers arrested and killed in, 344–45. *See also* Bakersfield
Kern County Board of Supervisors, 298
Kern County Labor Council, 251
Kidder, Al, 281, 282
Kimura, Sakuko, 116, 118
King, Coretta Scott, 385
King, Martin Luther, Jr., 329
Knights of Labor: industrial unionism of, 248; Los Angeles assemblies of, 84, 86; organizing structure and vision of, 87–88; printers' strike supported by, 90
—ASSEMBLY 5855, 87
—DISTRICT ASSEMBLY 140, 86

laws (federal): Chinese Exclusion Act, 75–76, 82, 83, 163; Draft Law, 66; eight-hour day, 53; equal pay for equal work, 50, 370; Espionage Act, 198; Glass-Steagall Act, 215; Immigration Act, 191; Immigration Control and Reform Act, 430; National Industrial Recovery Act, 216, 232, 247; Securities Act, 215; Securities Exchange Act, 215; Sedition Act, 198; Sherman Anti-Trust Act, 101; Smith Connally Act, 263; Social Security Act, 227, 353; Taft-Hartley Act, 312, 326–27, 339, 380. *See also* National Labor Relations Act

Lee, Edna, 260

Lee, Jow Hing, 260

Lee, Sue Ko, 258, 260

left wing politics: Cold War's impact on, 316–18; FEP efforts of, 321–23. *See also* Communists; New Left; Popular Front; Socialists

leisure and entertainment: choices in 1906, 144; in company towns, 117; for cotton strikers, 219; East Bay boating and recreation, 48; of labor migrants, 107, 112; open air speeches, 71; railroad excursions, 47, 48; theater, 139, 144; women's money spent on, 164–65; Woodward's Gardens, 47. *See also* Disneyland; film and movies; theater

Lewis, John L., 248–49, 277

Libertad (ship), 67

Liberty Ships, 265, 266, 267. *See also* shipbuilding

Librado, Fernando, 14–15

librarians, 372–73, 376–77, *377*

"Lie Factory," 227

Lindbergh, Charles, 274

Lindsay, Estelle Lawton, 189

Ling, Ah, 57

literacy, 44–45

Littler, Mendelson, Fastiff and Tichy (firm), 410

Lizarras, J. M., 121–22, 123, 124, 125–26

Llano del Rio (communal experiment), 190

Llewelyn Iron Works, 182, 187

Loach, Ken, 403

Local 16 (brewery workers), 136

Lockheed Aircraft, 273, 274, 278, 310–11

London, Jack, 144, 176

Long Beach, oil field beneath, 197

Long Beach Local 128, 201

longshoremen: automation debates of, 389–91, *447*; company-run vs. workers' unions of, 231–32; leisure of, 144; murdered on Bloody Thursday, 239–40, *241*, 246; strikes by, 202, 229–30, 233–34; unions for, 45, 216; work of, 56, 230

Longshoremen's Association of San Francisco and the Bay Area, 231–32

Looking Backward (Bellamy), 88

Lopez, Frank, 322

Los Angeles: aircraft companies in, 273; Chinese neighborhoods in, 81–82; conditions for workers in (1900s), 170–73; conservative culture of, 79–80; Depression-era unemployment and hunger in, 212–13; downtown construction frenzy in, 399; early land speculation in, 84–85, 103; Garment Center Building explosion in, 222; Harriman trials in, 176–80; home prices and ownership in, 308; immigrants in (1970s–90s), 401; Japanese neighborhoods in, 112; labor as radical force in, 89, 93–94; labor-socialist fusion politics in, 183–89; lawlessness in, 77–78; layoffs and deindustrialization in, 391–92; "Little Central America" Pico-Union area, 401; police actions in, 175, 226, 404–5, *405*; population, 78, 83, 173; printers' unionization in, 51, 86, 89–90; skilled workers' choices in, 83–84; teachers' strike in, 366; union organizing in (mid-19th cen.), 85–88; union organizing in (1880s–1900s), 173–76; union setbacks in 1920s, 191–92; white working class's emergence and majority in, 80–85; worker centers in, 431; WPC's rise and fall in, 78–79. *See also* Hollywood studio film workers

Los Angeles Board of Fire Commissioners, 181

Los Angeles Building Trades Council, 204–5

Los Angeles Chamber of Commerce, 91–92

Marcuse, Herbert, 386
Maricopa, oil workers' local in, 197
Marine Transport Workers Industrial
    Union, 231
Marine Workers Industrial Union
    (MWIU), 233, 243
Marinship (company), 267, 269, 271, 272
Maritime Federation of the Pacific, 251
maritime unionism: City Front Federation
    strike and, 147–49; Communist back-
    ing in, 233; organizing in, 216; solidarity
    in, 229–30, 234–35, 236, 244–45; strike
    for eight-hour day, 53; success of, 245–
    46. See also International Longshore-
    men's Association; Sailors' Union
    of the Pacific; San Francisco General
    Strike
maritime workers: central to port city
    transformation, 34–35; conditions for,
    36; "crimps" for, 133; hours of work in
    1870s, 46–47; number at San Francisco
    port, 132–33; recruitment of, 35–36; shift
    to gold mining, 27, 35. See also long-
    shoremen; sailors; shipping industry
Marjorie Morningstar (Wouk), 315
Market Street Railroad, 155. See also United
    Railroads
Markham, Edwin, 102
Marshall, James, 25, 33, 45
Martin, John, 429
Marx, Karl, 33
Massachusetts: Boston police strike, 350,
    362; FEP bill passed in, 320; IWW-led
    strike in, 192
mass mobilization: ABC's deployment of,
    422–23; in Justice for Janitors cam-
    paign, 403–5; Occupy movement, 427,
    433, 434–36, 438, 449; against
    Schwarzenegger's ballot measures,
    415–17. See also demonstrations,
    marches, and parades; strikes
Masur, Richard, 313, 317
Matyas, Jennie, 258, 260
Maulhaupt ranch workers, 106
McCarthy, Patrick Henry: as BTC leader,
    140, 141, 141, 142–43, 146; decline of
    influence by, 201–2; Los Angeles organ-
    izing and, 175; mayoral hopes of, 158,

159, 160, 166; resignation of, 203;
    Schmitz support from, 151
McCarthyism. See Committee on Un-
    American Activities; House Un-Ameri-
    can Activities Committee; red-baiting
    tactic
McClellan committee, 327–28
McCullough, Thomas, 336
McDonald, F. James, 394
McElroy, Bob, 234
McGlynn, Michael, 92
McKittrick, oil workers' local in, 197
McManigal, Emma, 188
McManigal, Ortie, 182, 188
McMartin, Edmund, 121, 124
McNamara, James, 182, 186, 186, 187–88,
    189, 191
McNamara, John: arrested for Times
    bombing, 182, 186; confession of, 187–
    88, 191; on employers' antiunion tactics,
    171; Gompers and, 186; Harriman
    endorsed by, 183; sentence of, 189; trial
    of, 186
Meany, George, 317, 385
MEChA (Movimiento Estudiantil Chi-
    cano de Aztlán), 392
mechanics: in aircraft industry, 274; defini-
    tion of, 54; expenses of, 153; imported
    from Germany, 117; mentioned, 303,
    443; NY vs. CA wages, 204; skill of,
    134, 147; unionization in early Los
    Angeles, 84
Mechanics' Eight-Hour League, 79
Mechanics' League, 51
Mechanics State Council, 54
Mechanization and Modernization Agree-
    ment, 390–91
media: ABC's deployment of, 422–24; on
    Apple's labor practices, 408–10; global
    companies' vulnerability to, 411; police
    attack on janitors captured, 404–5, 405;
    radio, 191–92, 224, 225, 294, 298. See
    also newspapers
Medina, Francisco, 221
MEF (Municipal Employees Federation),
    369
Meister, Dick, 364
Melton, John "Red," 388

Melville, Herman, 36

Mendoza, Hope, 325–26

Merchants and Manufacturers Association (M&MA): antiunionism of, 101, 169–70, 178–79; assistance for companies with "labor troubles," 170, 179; attitude toward dressmakers, 225; bombing of *Times* building and, 182, 188; garment workers accused of violence by, 222; open shop goal of, 93; picketing ban proposed by, 179–80; police and judicial cooperation with, 94; response to maritime strike, 234; strikebreakers used by, 206; success of, 175; trucking firm of, 283; victims of, 176

Merriam, Frank, 227

metal trades and industry, 39–40, 48, 62, 266

Metal Trades Council, 178–79, 265–66, 268

metal trades workers: conditions and hours for, 40, 46–47, 169–71; craft workers replaced with semiskilled, 267; Golden Gate work of, 443, 445; iron molders as, 52, 63; ironworkers as, 169–71; strikes by, 146, 170, 178–79, 182, 187, 265–66. *See also* steel workers

"Mexicali Rose" (song), 298

Mexican-American War (1846–48), 20, 25, 51, 82

Mexican American workers: as autoworkers, 388; as cotton workers, 217–18, 219; as farm laborers, 105–6, 293–94; as janitors and custodial staff, 401; organizing of, 321–22. *See also* Chicano workers; Latino workers

Mexican Revolution, 223, 341

Mexican workers: backgrounds of, 82; as *braceros*, 295, 332–33; as cannery labor, 255–56, 311; CIO's support for, 253; citizenship for and voting of, 328; as cotton workers, 217–18, 219; drywallers' strike by, 412; as farm laborers, 111, 117, 118, 119–20; farm labor organizing by, 254–55, 295; as garment workers, 211, 223–26; home buying by, 311; as janitors and custodial staff, 401; as laborers in early Los Angeles, 80, 82–83; for missions, 21; post-Bracero Program import of, 337; railroad construction by, 83, 171–72, 174, *174*; segregated barrios in Los Angeles, 83, 117, 121, 171–72; as waste material workers, 252–53. *See also* Californios; Japanese-Mexican Labor Alliance; Latino workers

Mexico: Alta California taken from, 20, 25; Green Giant packing plant moved to, 396; land grants from, 19. *See also* Mexican Revolution

Meyers-Milias-Brown Act (MMBA, CA, 1968), 357–58, 368

microelectronics-based workplaces, 406–10, *408*, 411, 427. *See also* Silicon Valley

middle class: cross-class suffrage work of women in, 163–68, *167*, 184–85; Fordist vision of ascent into, 191–92; industrial employment limited in, 446–47; as streetcar riders, 159; working class move into, 4, 280, 307–18, 319, 331

Midway-Sunset oil fields, 196

militancy, 112–13, 356, 385–87

Miller, George, *330*

Miller, Jim, 433

Millionaires Tax campaign, 437–39

mills, 40, 48, 49, 140–42

miners: conditions and number of, 29–33; as Forty-Niners, 27, 28, 33, 34, 44, 131; icons of, 360; Native Americans as, 26, 28; strike of, 75; technology and types of mining, 28–29, *30*, 64. *See also* Gold Rush; silver mining

minority workers: communism's appeal to, 311–12; conditions and wages for, 223, 324–25; federal unions and, 174; loss of manufacturing impact on, 397; unionization's benefits for, 260–61, 278–79, 389; votes of, 324, 330. *See also* fair employment practices; racism and racial discrimination; *and specific groups*

Misner, E. H., 183

"Mission Days," 22, 79

Mission Indians, 10, 14, 20–21, 80–81

mission period: Indians as workforce in, 13–18, *16*; institutional model in, 18–19; legal protection for Indians in, 80; nostalgia for culture of, 9–10, 22, 79; secularization of missions, 19, 20

"Mister Block" (song), 195
Mitchell, H. L., 292–93, 294, 296, 298, 299
Miwok tribe, 12
MMBA (Meyers-Milias-Brown Act, CA, 1968), 357–58, 368
Mobilize the Immigrant Vote, 432
Modesto, "under water" homes in, 426–27
Mont, Max, 322, *330*
Moody, Kim, 356
Mooney, Tom, 202, 240
Moore, Sidney, 315, 316, 354
Moore Dry Dock (Oakland), 267, 268, 269, 270
Moreno, Luisa, 249, 256
Morgenstern, Marty, 356, 368
Mori, Kaz, *367*
Morley, Karen, 301, 313–14
Morning Call (newspaper), 53
Mortimer, Wyndham, 274, 275–76, 277
Motion Picture Producers Association (MPPA), 205–6
Mount, Julia Luna, 255
Movimiento Estudiantil Chicano de Aztlán (MEChA), 392
Munger, Molly, 437, 439
Municipal Employees Federation (MEF), 369
municipal workers, eight-hour day law for, 54. *See also* civil service workers; public sector unionism
Murphy, Jim, 411
Murray, John, 114, 121, 124, 125–26
Murray, Philip, 322
music. *See* songs and music
musicians union. *See* American Federation of Musicians
mutual aid societies, 161, 216, 218
Mutual Alliance of Studio Employees, 206, 216
Mutual Organization League, 184
MWIU (Marine Workers Industrial Union), 233, 243
Myers, Miles, 359, 366

NAACP: FEP efforts of, 321, 322; local leaders of, 323–24; predecessor to, 183–84; "right-to-work" laws opposed by, 329; strike support from, 282; support for, 270, 271

National Association of Manufacturers, 169
National Day Laborer Organizing Network, 431
National Defense Mediation Board, 264, 276–78. *See also* National War Labor Board
National Dollar Stores, 257–60
National Education Association, 359
National Erectors' Association, 169–70, 171, 187–89
National Farm Labor Union (NFLU), 292
—LOCAL 218: contract proposal of, 294–95; DiGiorgio's suit against, 302–3; diversity of members, 293–94; strike of, 292, 295–99, *297*, 302, 339
National Farm Workers Association (NFWA), 335–38, 341, 342
National Federation of Federal Employees (NFFE), 315
National Federation of Social Service Employees, 356
National Guard (CA), 72, 240, 243
National Industrial Recovery Act (NIRA, 1933), 216, 232, 247
Nationalism (philosophy), 88
nationalism (WWI), 191
National Labor Relations Act (NLRA, 1935): building owners shielded in, 402; groups of workers excluded from, 298, 339, 349; impetus for, 5; janitorial, custodial, and sanitation workers under, 399; labor strategies outside box of, 406, 407–8; provisions summarized, 247–48; Taft-Hartley's impact on, 312; undermining of, 384; violation of, 410
National Labor Relations Board (NLRB), 247, 252, 258
National Longshoremen's Board, 244
National Recovery Administration (NRA): general strike condemned by, 243; lack of enforcement by, 226; NIRA overseen by, 216; response to cotton strike, 220–21; union organizing and, 222, 223; wages code of, 256
National Secretaries Day, 404
National Typographical Union, 45, 78
National War Labor Board, 264, 266. *See also* National Defense Mediation Board

"Put Kids First" (Prop 74), 419

Quality Standards Program (QSP, San Francisco, 2000), 429
quartz mining, 29–30, *30*
Quin, Mike, 235–36, 239, 241

racial segregation: housing and neighborhoods, 16, 82–83, 106, 172, 293, 334; schools, 49, 329, 363; unions, 3, 49, 269, 272, 320, 324, 331
racism and racial discrimination: in ARU eligibility requirements, 95; by Boilermakers, 268–72; in employers' code system, 325–26; FEP legislation and overcoming, 269, 319–26; in Prop 13, 379–80; of shipyard workers, 268–72; systemic nature of, 339, 385–87; by WPC, 73–75. *See also* anti-Chinese movement; racial segregation
radio, 191–92, 224, 225, 294, 298
Railroad Commission, 75
railroad owners ("robber barons"): blamed for political corruption, 73–75; as parasitic class, 88; union recognition by, 270; use of term, 55; wage declines and strike against, 70–72
railroads and railroad development: consolidation of, 171; early locomotives in California, 39–40, 47; fare war between rail lines, 80; labor espionage tactics of, 155; leisure excursions on, 47, 48; national competition in locomotive production, 62; Pullman and Silver Palace cars described, 60, 64; San Francisco–Los Angeles link, 79, 83; transcontinental completed, 60–61. *See also* General Managers Association (GMA); *and specific railroads*
railroad workers: "beneficial associations" of, 90; company town for, 95–96; construction of railroads, 55–56, 58, 83, 171–72; organizing among, 91, 94–95; strikes by, 58, 70–72, 94, 95, 96–98, 173–76; unemployment of, 61–62
Ramona (H. H. Jackson), 10, 79
rancheros/ranchos and ranching: breakup of, 80, 82, 102; Indian laborers for,

14–15, 19, 20–22, 80–81; origins and growth of, 19, 20–22; shift from skilled to unskilled labor on, 82–83
Rancho Los Amigos Hospital, 316
Randolph, A. Philip, 269, 323
Rankin, Tom, 357, 385
Ray, Dorothy (later Healey), 214–15, 255
La Raza Centro Legal, 432
Reading Railroad, 155
Reagan, Ronald: air traffic controllers fired by, 379, 400; anticommunism of, 300–302; antiunionism of, 398; collective bargaining vetoed by, 367; elected to presidency, xiv; grape eating by, 340; role in *Poverty in the Valley of Plenty*, 299–300
Real, Charles, 288
real estate development: affluence and, 309–10; city railroad construction linked to, 172; construction frenzy in downtown LA, 399–400; oil discovery and, 197; speculation in, 84–85, 103. *See also* land development
Reclaiming California's Future (RCF), 437–38, 440
recreation workers, 376–77, *377*
red-baiting tactic: AFL/CIO infighting and, 291; in CSU strike, 300–301; employers' use of, 198–99; solidarity against, 276; strike leaders accused of being Communists, 235, 236, 237, 238, 243, 283, 286, 298–99; union losses due to, 317, 351
Red Scare (post-WWI), 191, 198–99, 243
Refregier, Anton, *42*
Reich, Robert, 446
Reid, Hugo, 14
"Report on the Conditions and Needs of the Mission Indians of California" (H. H. Jackson), 10
Republican Party, 166, 227. *See also* elections
restaurant workers: mentioned, 49, 83; organizing of, 86, 151, 412, 428, 431; strike by, 146; wage theft case of, 432
restraining orders, 271, 364–65, 409. *See also* injunctions
Retail Clerks (union), 93, 258–59, 289, 296. *See also* department store workers
—Local 1265, 282–83, 290, 296

Retail Merchants Association (RMA), 281–83, 287

Reuther, Walter, 340, 366, 385

Richards, Richard, *330*

Richmond, Standard Oil Refinery in, 362, 364, 386

Richmond Association of Educators (CTA), 363, 365

Richmond Independent (newspaper), 364

Richmond School District (CA), 362–64

Riggers and Stevedores union, 230, 231

"right-to-work" laws: as election issue, 5; fight against, 319, 326–31; states' passage of, xiii, 327. *See also* open shop agreements

Riley, Gavin, 433

Rios, Tony, 322

riots, anti-Chinese, *71*, 71–72. *See also* demonstrations, marches, and parades; violence

Riverside, "under water" homes in, 426–27

RMA (Retail Merchants Association), 281–83, 287

"robber barons." *See* railroad owners

Roberts, George, 108

Roberts, Mrs. Thomas, 99

Robertson, Bill, 394

Robinson, Ben, 181

Robinson, Earl, 263–64

Rochester (NY), public workers' strike in, 351

Rockefeller, John D., 190, 309

Rockefeller Brothers Fund, 309

Rodda, Al, 368

Rodda Act (Educational Employment Relations Act, CA, 1975), 368, 378

Rodriguez, Arturo, 411

Rodriguez, J. J., 323

Rogers, Earl, 170

Rolph, James, 220–21

Roney, Frank: on Chinese workers, 73, 76; diary of, 46–47, 65, 138, 139; Federal Trades Council founded by, 135; hard times faced by, 65–66; jobs of, 48, 63, 65, *65*; opposed to 1878 state constitution, 75; trade-union concerns of, 74

Roosevelt, Franklin D.: economic conditions facing, 211–12, 215; FEP mandated by, 269, 320; NLRA signed by, 247, 349; public spending reduced by, 261; reelection campaign film, 263; response to labor unrest, 216, 229, 277; Sinclair not endorsed by, 228. *See also* New Deal

"Rosie the Riveter," 279

Ross, Fred, 321, 335

Rossi, Angelo (mayor), 236, 243

Roush, Joseph, 237–38

Roybal, Ed, 321–22

Ruef, Abe, 150–51, 152, 154, 156

Rumford, Byron, 324, *330*

Russailh, Albert Benard de, 33–34, 38

Russian Jewish workers, 211, 252–53, 255–56, 402

Russian Revolution (1917), 198–99, 402

Rutter, Bill, 244

Ryan, Frank, 171

Ryan, Joe, 233, 236–37

Ryan Aircraft, 273–74

Sacco, Nicola, 222

Sachen, Susan, 407

Sacramento: printers' unionization in, 51; public employees' strike in, 355–56; Pullman strike confrontation in, 99–100; SEIU Local 1877 organizing in, 410–11; wage scale reductions in 1860s–70s, 63. *See also* California State legislature

Sacramento Labor Temple, 356

SAG (Screen Actors Guild), 299, 301, 313

sailors: conditions for, 36, 232–33; law on, 35, 80, 189; shanghaied, 35, 133

Sailors International Union, 199

Sailors' Union of the Pacific (SUP): extent and activities of, 133; federal arbitration on strike demands of, 245; "fink books" burned by, 244; Oakland streets patrolled by, 286; predecessor of, 136, 147; racial exclusion of, 126; strike and decline of, 199, 231, 232–34

Salinas County: farm laborers' mobilization in, 343; sugar beet production in, 116–17

Salvation Army, 193

San Buenaventura mission, 15

Sances, Jos, *16*

San Diego: aircraft companies in, 272–73; free speech battle in, 192–93, *193*

San Francisco: anti-Chinese riots in, *71*, 71–72; antiunionism in, 144–46, 203–4; Bloody Tuesday in, 158, 160; bombing of parade in, 202; cable and streetcar systems in, 40, 131–32, 152; Chinatown in, 67–68, 71–72; civil disobedience against racist employers in, 385–86; construction and growth of, 32–39; corruption in mayor's office, 150–52, 154; Depression-era foreclosures in, 212; earthquake/fire (1906) and rebuilding in, 144, 152–54, 157, 160–61, 175; economic prosperity in 1860s, 47–48; eight-hour day law for city and county workers, 54; Fillmore neighborhood of, 270–71; labor movement in early, 40–45; labor shortage in, 38–39, 43; maritime workers central to, 34–36; metal industry in, 39–40, 48; Municipal Railway of, 160; mural project in, *42*; needle trades in, 256–60, *259*; new labor protections in, 428–29; Nob Hill mansions in, 64, 73, 153; parades and rallies in, 202, 235, *235, 310*, 385; population (1900), 131; schools in, 49–51, *50*, 316; stock exchange and speculation in, 64; support for strike of 1877 in, 70–71; teachers' strikes in, 366–67; unionization and support in, 51–52, 134–36, 137–38, 175; union setbacks in 1920s, 191–92; women's union organizing in, 160–68; worker centers in, 432. *See also* Gold Rush; San Francisco General Strike; San Francisco Police

San Francisco Airport, 429

San Francisco Athletic Club, 147

San Francisco Board of Supervisors, 54

San Francisco Building Trades Council (BTC): daily lives' impacted by, 138–39; founding, 135; McCarthy's leadership of, 140; rank and file vs. officers in, 146; role in 1906 earthquake recovery, 153; strikes supported by, 159, 179; tactics and power of, 140–43; ULP aligned with, 151; women's strike and, 162; working card of, 137–38, 142; WWI and

demise of, 201–4. *See also* San Francisco General Strike

San Francisco Bulletin (newspaper), 51, 151

San Francisco Chamber of Commerce, 148, 202, 238

San Francisco Chronicle: anticommunism of, 238

—TOPICS DISCUSSED: anti-Chinese riots, 72; Pullman strike, 99; teachers' strike, 364; Teamsters back-to-work order, 288; women and strikes, 162, 165

San Francisco Committee Against Segregation and Discrimination (SFCASD), 271–72

San Francisco Committee for Equal Job Opportunity, 321

San Francisco Dressmakers Local 101, 256–57

San Francisco General Hospital, 316

San Francisco General Strike (1934): beginnings of, 233–34, 242–43; depiction of, *6*; federal arbitration of, 245; ILA strike precipitating, 234–42, *235, 241*; Oakland General Strike compared with, 291; significance of, 5, 215; strikebreakers in, 234, 237, 238, 239; success of, 244–46

San Francisco Industrial Association, 202, 203

San Francisco Labor Council: Chinese garment workers and, 257, 260; FEP efforts of, 321; founding, 135; garment worker organizing and, 257, 258–59; local worker ordinances passed, 429; San Francisco General Strike decisions of, 242–43; strikes supported by, 158–59, 179, 296; suffrage supported by, 165–66; teamsters' strike and, 146; women's strike and, 162–64

San Francisco Labor Temple, 166

San Francisco Police: antiunion raids by, 243; strikebreakers protected by, 203–4, 239; strikers' confrontations with, 148, 233–34; strikers wounded and killed by, 234, 235, 240–42, *241*; students beaten by, 236; withheld in labor disputes, 150, 151, 155–56, *156*, 157

San Francisco Port, 38, 132–33, 147–49, 153

San Francisco State University, 366–67, 386

San Francisco Trades' Union, 51–53

San Francisco Typographical Society, 41, 45, 51

San Francisco Unified School District, 316

sanitation workers. *See* janitorial, custodial, and sanitation workers

San Joaquin Valley: cotton growing in, 217; Depression-era unemployment in, 213; organizing NFWA in, 335. *See also* DiGiorgio Fruit Corp.; farm labor and farm labor migrants; Great Cotton Strike; oil workers

San Jose: AFSCME negotiations with, 374–78; female city workers in, 371–74; organizing in, 369–71; slow-growth coalition in, 409

San Jose City Council, 373–74

San Jose State University, 366–67

San Luis Rey mission, 14

San Mateo Labor Council, 421, 429

San Pedro, maritime striker killed in, 234

Santa Barbara, public employees' strike in, 355

Santa Clara mission, 20

Santa Clara Valley: developers and affluence in, 309–10; transition from industrial to digital, 406–7. *See also* Silicon Valley

Santa Fe Railroad, 80, 91, 97–98

Santa Fe Springs, oil field beneath, 197

Santa Monica, aircraft company in, 274

Santa Ynez mission, 17

Savage Silver Mining Works (Washoe, NV), 29, *30*

Saxton, Alexander, 267

SBA (Studio Basic Agreement), 206, 207

SBFLU. *See* Sugar Beet and Farm Laborers' Union

scabs. *See* strikebreakers

Scammon, C. M., 36

Schenley (grower), 340–42

Schmidt, Henry, 238

Schmitz, Eugene: corruption of, 150–51, 152; earthquake and fire response of, 153; elected mayor, 149–50, 151; indictment and conviction, 154, 156, 158; refusal to involve police, 150, 151, 155–56, *156*, 157

schools. *See* public education; teachers

Schrade, Paul, 385

Schumpeter, Joseph, 383

Schwarzenegger, Arnold: ballot measures of, 415, 419–20; budget crisis under, 415–16, 436; gubernatorial campaign of, 417–18; picketing and demonstrations against, 420, *421*, 421–24, *424*; polemical attacks by, 418–19

Screen Actors Guild (SAG), 299, 301, 313

Screen Writers Guild, 301

Sculley, John, 409

Seale, Bobby, 366

Seamen's International Union (SIU), 286. *See also* Sailors' Union of the Pacific

Sears Roebuck, 327

secretaries, 349, 376, 404

Securities Act (U.S., 1933), 215

Securities Exchange Act (U.S., 1934), 215

Sedition Act (U.S., 1918), 198

Seelinger, Loyd, 252–53

SEERA (State-Employer-Employee Relations Act, CA, 1977), 378

Selvidge, Newton, 285

Serna, Joe, 411

Serra, Junipero, 13, 17

Service Employees International Union (SEIU): as ABC ally, 420; approach to declining unionization, 400; classified school employees in, 368; growth of, 398–99; merger of locals in, 407–8; MMBA used by, 358; origins of, 352. *See also* Building Service Employees International Union; Justice for Janitors campaign

—LOCAL 32B-J, 404

—LOCAL 399: actions of, 402–5, *405*; origins of workers in, 401; success and decline of, 398–99, 413. *See also* Justice for Janitors campaign

—LOCAL 400, 371

—LOCAL 535: comparable worth gains of, 377–78; goals, 365; growth of, 356–57; strike for union recognition, *355*

—LOCAL 1877, 407–11, *408*, 413

service industry, 86, 146, 161, 427–28, 448. *See also* domestic services; janitorial, custodial, and sanitation workers; restaurant workers

songs and music *(continued)*
IWW, 193, 195; jazz, 191–92, 271; labor
migrants, 107; postwar prosperity
hopes, 280
Sonoma County, Chinese farm laborers
in, 108
Sonoratown, use of term, 83, 117, 121,
171–72
Sorrell, Herb, 300
South Bay Labor Council, 407
Southern Pacific Railroad, 79, 80, 81, 97, 98
Southern Tenant Farmers Union, 292–93
South Gate (LA): GM plant, 249, 307, 309,
325, 387; housing and lifestyle in, 212, 308
Soviet Union: CPUSA influenced by, 312;
establishment of, 198–99; U.S. labor
support for, 265. *See also* Cold War;
Russian Jewish workers
Spanish colonialism, 13, 16–19. *See also*
mission period
Spanish Speaking People's Congress ("El
Congresso"), 253, 256
"special interests," use of term, 418–19, 423
Sperry, Howard, 240, 241, *241*, 246
spies of antiunion companies, 95–96, 155,
170, 179, 182
Spinner, Helen, 364
Spinner, Milton, 364
Spirit of St. Louis (plane), 274
Spreckels (sugar beet company town), 116
Spreckels, Claus, 106, 116–17
Spreckels, John D., 193
Spreckels, Rudolph, 152, 157–58
Springer, Joe, 314
Springer, Preva, 314
Stagehands Local 33, 205
Standard Oil, 196, 197, 200, 362, 364, 386
Stanford, Leland, 55, 56, 61
State, County and Municipal Workers of
America, 350
State-Employer-Employee Relations Act
(SEERA, CA, 1977), 378
State Teachers Retirement System, 351
Steam Laundry Workers Local 26, 161
"steam paddies," 37
steam power, 40, 48
steel workers: attempts to unionize, 169–
70, 199; number in WWII period, 263;

organizing of, 268, 322; production
decline and, 396; wages and home
buying of, 308. *See also* metal trades
workers
Steinbeck, John, 221, 255, 294
Stephens, Uriah, 52–53
St. Louis, general strike of 1877 in, 70
Stockton: printers' unionization in, 51;
"under water" homes in, 426–27; wage
scale reductions in 1860s–70s, 63
St. Paul (MN), teachers' strike in, 350–51
streetcar workers. *See* carmen and streetcar
workers
strikebreakers (scabs): African Americans
as, 75, 97, 174–75, 184; *braceros* as, 295,
296, 333; Chicano workers as, 338;
Chinese as, 68–69, 75; employers' vs.
union members' appeals to, 52; in
farmworkers' strike, 292; in film studios
strike, 206; general strike due to, 283–
85; guns carried by, 158; oil workers'
response to, 200; Oxnard strike and,
123, 124; police protection for, 90, 148,
203–4, 239, 283–85, 289; in San Francisco General Strike, 234, 237, 238, 239;
union losses due to, 63, 135; union
printers as, 92; women's support for,
165; workers' refusal to work with,
244–45
strikes: assistance for workers during,
51–52; benefits for, 259–60; early (1850s),
43; federal troops used in, 94, 98,
99–100; first recorded in California, 41;
for pay equal to white workers (1868), 3;
postwar waves of, 199, 281; sit-down
type, 274, 404, 410–11; wages and hours
issues in, 52, 140–42; "wildcat," 264,
277, 376, 387, 412. *See also* demonstrations, marches, and parades; general
strikes; Great Cotton Strike; injunctions; International Longshoremen's
Association strike; Oxnard sugar beet
workers strike; police; Pullman boycott
and strike; restraining orders; San
Francisco General Strike; *and specific
occupations*
St. Sure, Paul, 390
student movements, 385–87, 392, 438–39

Tveitmoe, Olaf, 138, 202
Twain, Mark, 33, 48, 51
Twitchell Island, drainage of, 108–9
Two Years Before the Mast (Dana), 19, 36
typographers (typos). *See* printers
Typographical Union Local 44, 78, 181. *See also* International Typographical Union

UAW. *See* United Automobile Workers
UCAPAWA. *See* United Cannery, Agricultural, Packing and Allied Workers of America
UE. *See* United Electrical, Radio and Machine Workers of America
UFW. *See* United Farm Workers of America
UFWOC. *See* United Farm Workers of America
ULP. *See* Union Labor Party
undocumented immigrant workforce: assumed as unorganizable, 401; backgrounds of, 402; electoral candidates and, 433–34; as "illegal" (Chavez), 346; worker centers for, 430–32
Unemployed Commission (CA), 213
unemployment: in 1870s, 62–63, 69; business cycles' impact on, 41; in depressions, 65–66, 212–14; in Great Recession "recovery," 434; from plant closings, outsourcing, and offshore moves, 383, 384, 391; postwar, 280–81; of railroad workers, 61–62; of women, 74; WWII's impact on, 262–63
La Union de Trabajadores del Valle Imperial (Imperial Valley Workers Union), 218
Union Iron Works, 40, 47, 48, 62, 135, 136
unionization: Chinese excluded from, 69; Cold War's impact on, 316–18; Depression-era impetus for, 214–15; in economic prosperity, 51–52; Japanese-Mexican alliance in, 119–27, *122*; limitations on, 84; "March Inland" in, 251–53; peak in 1950s, 4; reflections on past and future of, 445–50; setbacks in 1870s, 62–63, 69; Taft-Hartley's impact on, 312–13; thinking outside the box in, 406. *See also* closed shop agreements; direct action; eight-hour day; unions

union labels, 308, 339–40
Union Labor Party (ULP): candidates of, 166; disgrace of, 154, 156, 157, 158; founding and leadership of, 149–50; political stance and successes of, 150–52; women campaigning for, 163
Union Labor Political Club, 180, 183
union locals: employment bureaus (hiring halls) of, 85–86; first on West Coast, 41, *42*, 44–45; gender segregation of, 69; increased number in Los Angeles (1900s), 175; number and size of, 4; strike losses' effect on, 63
Union Pacific Railroad, 56
unions: accepted as part of business, 309; automation debated in, 383, 389–91; auxiliary type of, 269–70, 271, 272; avoidance of term, 335; blamed for *Times* bombing, 181–83, 187; coalition of immigrant rights advocates with, 426–27, 430–32; conspiracy charges against, 98, 100, 101; cross-union solidarity among, 5, 44, 85–86, 125, 135, 137–38, 174, 234–36, 237, 283–84, 289, 339–40, 355, 386, 404; deteriorating conditions for, 399–400; fusion politics of, 183–89; institutional power in San Francisco, 134–36; investigation of mafia ties with, 327–28; limits of, 448; number/percentage of workers in, xvi, 251, 261, 278, 307, 349–50, 398, 417, 441; pro- vs. antiwar leaders in, 385; roles of, 416–17; Schwarzenegger's polemical attacks on, 418–19; single craft (trade) unions vs. cross-trade central unions, 87–88; Socialists' cooperation with, 93–94, 176–78; state budget crisis response of, 433, 437–38; working women's appeal on suffrage to, 165–66. *See also* direct action; industrial unionism; unionization; *and specific unions*
union shop, definition of, 327. *See also* closed shop agreements
Union WAGE (Women's Alliance to Gain Equality), 377
United Automobile Workers (UAW): in aircraft industry, 274, 275–79; animated film by, 264, 280, 314; automation

debated in, 389–91; campaign to keep
Van Nuys plant open, 393–96; CFT
supported by, 360, 366; collective bargain-
ing in Cold War, 317; FDR supported by,
263–64; grape pickers' strike supported
by, 340; strike by, 274, 276–77; team
concept accepted by some in, 395
—LOCAL 216, 249, 308, 325, 326, 387
—LOCAL 645, 308, 392–96
—LOCAL 683, 277, *278*
—LOCAL 887, 278
—LOCAL 683, 276
United Brotherhood of Carpenters, 412
United Brotherhood of Carpenters and
Joiners Local 56, 85–86
United Cannery, Agricultural, Packing and
Allied Workers of America (UCA-
PAWA), 254–56, 334. *See also* Food,
Tobacco and Allied Workers-CIO
—LOCAL 75, 256
United Domestic Workers/AFSCME, 433
United Electrical, Radio and Machine
Workers of America (UE), 317, 322, 328,
392, 406–7
—LOCAL 1008, 317
United Farm Workers of America (UFW;
earlier United Farm Workers Organ-
izing Committee, UFWOC): achieve-
ments of, 4, 332, 343, 347, 366; begin-
ning of, 337–38, 342–43; big growers
targeted, 340–42; CFT's support for,
360; collective bargaining issues and,
343–44; context of, 332–37; decline of,
346, 398; grape boycott and, 339–40;
precursors to, 292; shift to political
action, 345–46
United Federal Workers of America, 350
United Fruit Corp., 343
United Mine Workers, 248
United Negro Labor Commission, 289–90
United Professors of California-AFT, 368
—LOCAL 1352, 366–67
United Public Workers of America
(UPWA), 326, 351, 369
—LOCAL 246, 315–16
United Railroads (URR): bribes paid by,
152; carmen's strike against, 150, 151,
155–59, *156*; railroad purchased by, 155;

San Francisco streetcar system owned
by, 131; service reinstated by, 159–60;
service restored after 1906 earthquake,
153; women's attacks on, 160–61. *See also*
Calhoun, Patrick
United States Steel Corporation, 169–70
United Steelworkers, 268, 322, 431
—LOCAL 1304, 268
—LOCAL 1845, 308, 321
UNITE HERE (union), 431
universities: declining funds for, 414;
divesting South Africa holdings, 416;
fee hikes protested, 438–39; free access
to public, 348–49; graduate student
union at, 357; legislation on workers in,
378; organizing in, 369; students' strike
at, 366–67; student support for union
strikes, 386
University of California, 148, 369, 378, 416
University of California, Berkeley, 357
upper class, consumer purchases of, 212. *See
also* employers; railroad owners
UPWA. *See* United Public Workers of
America
URR. *See* United Railroads
U.S. Congress: anti-immigrant legislation
in, 431; Chinese immigration investigation committee of, 69–70; European
sugar tariffs imposed by, 116; industrial
relations hearings and commission of,
190, 196; railroad barons' influence on,
55. *See also* House committees; laws
(federal)
U.S. Constitution, 312, 313, 361
U.S. Department of Labor, 295
U.S. House of Representatives. *See* House
committees
U.S. mail, 97, 98
U.S. military, 277, *278. See also* defense
industry
U.S. Navy, 265, 266
U.S. Senate, 327–28
U.S. Supreme Court: ARU leaders' appeal
to, 100; Bridges case, 314; comparable
worth case, 377–78; on NIRA, 247

Valdez, Luis, 341
Valdez, Rosaura, 217

Vallejo, Mariano, 19
Van Bourg, Victor, 296, 336
Vandeleur, Ed, 242, 250
Van Nuys GM plant: layoffs, 392; opening of, 387–88; on possible closure list, 391–92; recalls of workers, 393; robotics of, 389; workers' campaign to keep plant open, 393–96
Vanzetti, Bartolomeo, 222
Vasquez, Luis, 124
vehicle license fee (VLF), 417–18
Veliz, Ana, 404
Venice: Luna Park in, 186; plans for, 172
Ventura County: labor contracting in, 118–19; sugar beet production in, 115, 116–17. *See also* Oxnard sugar beet workers strike
Ventura Daily Democrat, 122
Vera Cruz, Philip, 334, 335, 337, 346
veterans: G. I. Bill for, 309, 348; killed during strike, 240; as "law and order" patrols, 199–200; militancy of, 387–88; in Occupy movement, 435; organizing by, 293, 350, 359, 364, 365; reentering workforce, 282, 350; unemployed, 69, 280; widow's protest, 4
Veterans Trucking company, 283
Viader, Jose, 18
Vietnam War, 357, 360, 371, 385, 387
vigilante mobs: anti-Chinese violence of, 71–72, 109; cotton strikers attacked, 219–20, 254, 255; parade bombing trial and, 202; in Red Scare, 198; Wobblies attacked, 193. *See also* xenophobia
Vinette, Arthur, 84, 85, *85*, 87
vineyards and wineries, 103, 108, 293, 342
violence: boycott and disavowal of, 339–40; in carpenters' strike (1926), 203–4; against cotton strikers, 219–20; depicted in Westerns, 123–24; in DiGiorgio strike, 296–97, *297*; against farm laborers, 344–45; in gold country, 28; hops harvest wages and conditions as context of, 194–96, 202, 333; industrial sabotage advocated, 193; against janitors, 404–5, *405*; Oakland General Strike and, 283–85, 286; retaliation against employers' antiunion tactics,

171; strikers accused of, 43–44, 222; in Warner Brothers picketing, 301. *See also* International Longshoremen's Association strike; police; San Francisco General Strike; strikebreakers
VLF (vehicle license fee), 417–18
voting and voter registration: attempts to defeat capitalism via, 190, 192; CSO role in voter registration, 321–22; FEP efforts related to, 324; immigrant workers and, xv, 413, 432, 433–34, 439–40; machines used for, 151; suffrage for women, 163–68, *167*, 184–85, 187; workers as citizen-voters, 319
Vulcan Iron Works, 39
Vultee (Downey), 273, 275–76, 277, 278

WACC. *See* Western Agricultural Contracting Company
Wage Earners' Suffrage League (WESL), 166–68
wages: declines of, 28, 63, 67–68, 69, 70–72, 92, 280–81; dictated by employers' association, 203; East vs. West Coast, 41, 43; gender discrimination in, 371–74, 375–76; increased without union recognition, 337; labor shortage linked to higher, 38–39; market standard rejected, 373; minimum wage, 223, 428; pay scales (1960s), 349–50; piece rate vs. daily wage, 41; skilled craftsmen vs. first gold miners, 26; stagnation (2000s), 447–48; unionized workers' advantage in, 445–46
wage theft, 7, 430–32, 446
Wagner Act. *See* National Labor Relations Act
Wah, Ah, 72
Waitresses Local 48, 161, 164, 165, 166–67, *167*
Waldie, D. J., 308, 309
Walsh, Richard, 300
Warner Brothers Studio, 301
Wartime Shipyard (Archibald), 268
waste material industry, 252–53
Waterfront Worker (newsletter), 232, 233, 240
water issues, 34, 62, 82

worker centers, 430–32. *See also* hiring halls

worker conditions (health and safety): agriculture's mechanization and, 104–5; conditions generally (1900s), 170–73; dangers of (1850s), 40–45; deadliness of swamp drainage, 108–9; hours and workweek, 40, 42, 46–47, 53, 136; in Los Angeles (1900s), 170–73; oversight programs slashed, 430; sanitation issues in hardrock mining, 29; state commission on, 189. *See also* disease; eight-hour day; wages; *and specific occupations*

workers: as citizen-voters, 319; current and future challenges for, 447–48; disabled, 69; diverse strategies used by, 4; generation gap of, xv–xvi, 384–87, 388; grassroots political mobilization of, 289–91; growing affluence of, 307–11; right to organize and bargain collectively, 216; rural-to-urban movement of, 60–61; westward movement of, 61–62. *See also* pensions and retirement; unions; wages; worker conditions; *and specific occupations*

Workers Alliance, 254–55, 275

Workers Film and Photo League, 220

working class: BTC as institutional power of, 137–38; Depression-era struggles of, 211–15; economic squeeze on (2000s), 414–15, 426–27; emergence and majority in Los Angeles, 80–85; historical perspective of, 7–8; homeownership of, 191, 212, 308–11, 388–89; immigration's role in recomposing, xv–xvi; move into middle class, 4, 280, 307–18, 319, 331; neo-Marxist depiction of, 386; role model for, 50–51; unionism and identity of, 163. *See also* collective action; women workers

Workingmen's Party of California (WPC): anti-Chinese push in, 73–75; decline of, 75–76; founding and goals of, 44–45, 72–73; leaders of, 4, 46; rise and fall in Los Angeles, 78–79

Workingmen's Party of the United States, 70–71, 101

"Working Women" (AFSCME Local 101), 372, 373

work slowdowns and stops: after San Francisco General Strike, 244–45; aircraft industry, 274; WWII-era, 264, 265–66. *See also* strikes

Works Progress Administration (WPA), 215, 271

World War I: labor strike during, 231; Red Scare in aftermath of, 191, 198–200

World War II: aircraft production in, 272–79; employers' opposition to unions in aftermath of, 282–83; G. I. Bill for veterans of, 309, 348; interventions for production in, 263–66; manufacturing employment during, 262–63; migrants as labor in war production, 262–63; shipbuilding in, 266–72; Vietnam War compared with, 385; workers' political and legislative actions during, 5. *See also* Bracero Program

Wouk, Herman, 315

WPA (Works Progress Administration), 215, 271

WPC. *See* Workingmen's Party of California

xenophobia, 68–70, 191, 198, 317, 430. *See also* vigilante mobs

Yamaguchi, Y., 118, 119–20, 121–22, 126

Yank Sing restaurants, 432

Yarrow, Walter, 197, 200

Yellow Peril, 81

Yerba Buena area, 32, 36

Yokut tribe, 12

Yorke, Peter, 157, 159

Younger, Maud, 161, 163–64, 165–66, 184

youth: demonstrations in General Strike, 235–36; generation gap and, xv–xvi, 384–87, 388; in grape strike and boycott, 339–40. *See also* antiwar movements

Zapata, Emiliano, 341

Zeehandelaar, Felix, 169, 170

Zorro (movies and television series), 9